ARCIMBOLDO
BASSANO
BRUEGEL

ARCIMBOLDO BASSANO BRUEGEL

Edited by
Francesca Del Torre Scheuch

An exhibition of the Kunsthistorisches Museum
11 March to 29 June 2025

Nature's Time

HANNIBAL

Contents

CATALOGUE

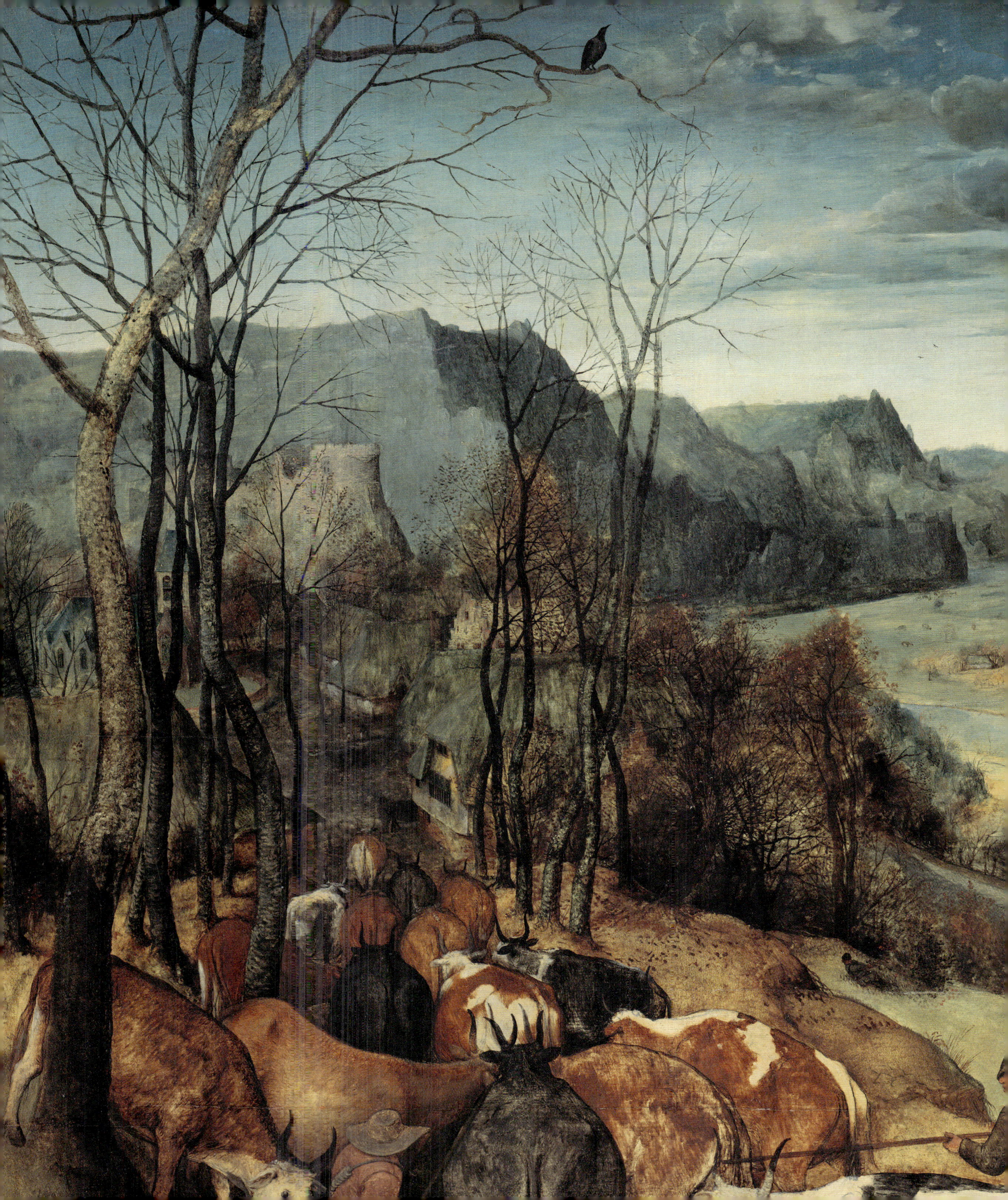

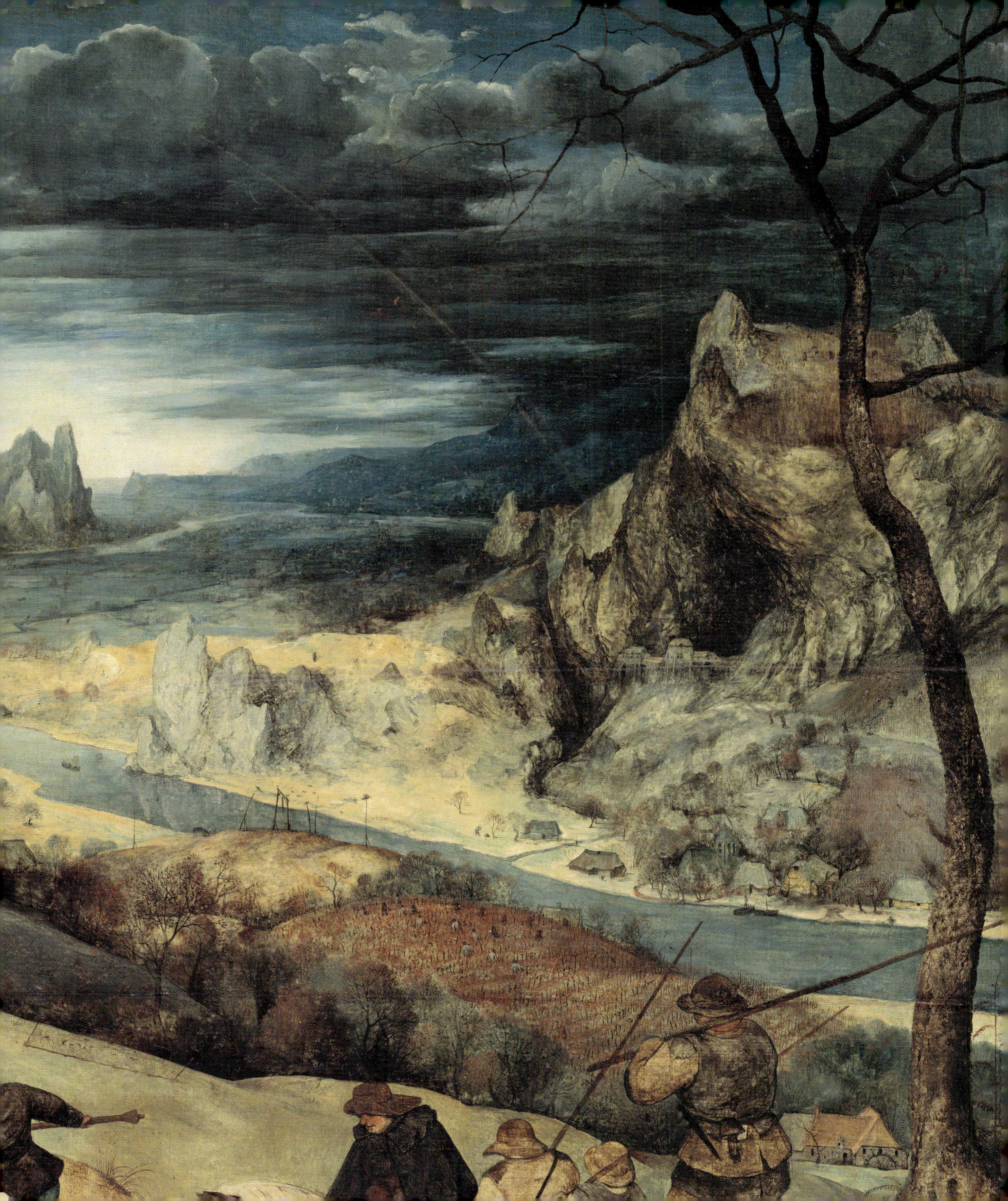

Foreword

The title of this publication, and of the exhibition it accompanies, focuses on two themes that play a central role in human life: the nature of time and the times of nature.

There have always been differing perceptions of time. Early on, humans realized that certain natural events repeated themselves frequently: animal migrations, seasonal and astronomical conjunctures, the alternating cycle of day and night. This knowledge helped them better understand (and master) their environment.

Time, however, can also be understood as a linear sequence of events. Greek philosophers such as Heraclitus and Aristotle associated time with change, moving forward inexorably in a predetermined direction, almost as if on a track. The Christian conception of time is also linear and proceeds from the creation of the world to the Last Judgement, when history and time will end. Today too we construct time as a linear progression over which we have no influence.

But linear perceptions of time did not replace cyclical ones. In the Middle Ages, for instance, they coexisted with a cyclical understanding of time made tangible in the repeating liturgical year. The church year traditionally starts on the first Sunday of Advent and is organized around recurring Sundays and holy days. For people living in the Middle Ages, the year and their lives followed this pattern. People anchored and reckoned large and small events in their lives in relation to this annual cycle, which is reflected in the annual cycle of horticultural life.

The Renaissance's growing interest in observing nature led to new scientific conceptions of time and to the development and refinement of clocks and calendars in Europe. The latter allow us to 'position (ourselves) in the sequence of generations', as Norbert Elias wrote in his analysis of temporality *Time: An Essay*. The perception of time was and remains a complex subject of study in human history.

The second major theme explored in this publication is the relationship between people and nature, which played a crucial role in public awareness long before the climate crisis. In the Renaissance, people began to explore nature in new ways, to observe the differences in the changing (of the) seasons, and to enjoy the abundance of the flora and fauna the seasons brought forth.

In 1336, Petrarch climbed Mont Ventoux purely out of curiosity and to enjoy the view from the summit. He no longer regarded the 'windy mountain' as an obstacle, as something that blocked his way and forced him to take a detour. His famous description of his ascent documents a new understanding of nature. In contrast to medieval people, who were more likely to view nature as hostile and threatening, something to be feared, in the Renaissance the natural world became a source of recreation and enjoyment.

That this was done in conscious imitation of much-admired antiquity is, of course, no coincidence. The new, positive view of nature was partially informed by literary works produced during the early Roman Empire, which celebrated bucolic life in a villa surrounded by magnificent gardens located far from the hectic metropolis, where one could indulge in creative leisure (*otium*) and enjoy the beauty of nature tamed.

The Renaissance's new interest in nature was, of course, not limited to climbing mountains and laying out gardens. Natural phenomena, fauna and flora were now examined with scientific intentions. All this was, of course, also reflected in the arts, in scientific studies and in paintings, numerous examples of which are brought together in this volume.

Giuseppe Arcimboldo is the first of the three great artists featured in this publication. As court painter to three Habsburg emperors, his work celebrates the diversity and abundance of nature in a unique idiom. Unlike his more conventional (and numerous) portraits, now all but forgotten, his few fantastic composite heads composed of a wealth of natural objects depicted with unrivalled verisimilitude are unforgettable (cats. 28–30, 33, 90). Many of these paintings were conceived as part of different series depicting the seasons or the elements. They illustrate the abundance of Creation. I am particularly pleased that in addition to the four celebrated works by Arcimboldo held by the Kunsthistorisches Museum, we can show seven more paintings by him in the exhibition.

Pieter Bruegel the Elder painted his magnificent series depicting the seasons in 1565. Today, three of the (probably originally) six paintings are held by the Kunsthistorisches Museum (cat. 15). Bruegel dispensed with biblical scenes and concentrated on nature and the role of humanity during the progression of the seasons. Although the pictures with their elevated viewpoint recall Patinier's 'world landscapes', their realism and immediacy appear modern and timeless. Here, nature plays the leading role in the composition. Bruegel's *Hunters in the Snow* is simultaneously proof of the so-called Little Ice Age and perfectly captures the hues and the mood of a freezing winter's day (cat. 15.3).

A major focus is on cycles of the months and the seasons, which were immensely popular, especially in sixteenth-century Italy. The workshop founded by Jacopo Bassano and successfully carried on by his sons specialised in such subjects. This publication presents a particularly impressive series that was extensively restored for the accompanying exhibition. In it, biblical motifs are combined with scenes from everyday rural life (cat. 62). The paintings document Bassano's successful attempt to merge different conceptions of time – linear time, the liturgical year, and the seasons – in his compositions. The Venetian patricians, who commissioned Palladio and other architects to design their splendid new villas in the Veneto, presumably enjoyed the pastoral genre motifs that fill the foreground of his compositions, while appreciating his references to biblical events (cats. 62, 66).

For the exhibition, Francesca Del Torre Scheuch, curator of Italian Renaissance painting, combined many important loans from major museums with selected masterpieces from the endlessly rich collections of the Kunsthistorisches Museum for a narrative that explores these topics in fascinating ways and provides food for thought. My special thanks go out to her. She and the entire team of the KHM-Museumsverband have done a superb job.

I also wish to thank our lenders, whose generosity with their works made this exhibition possible.

And, last but not least, I want to express my deep gratitude to UNIQA, a long-standing partner of the Kunst historisches Museum, which has once again provided generous support.

Jonathan Fine
Director General

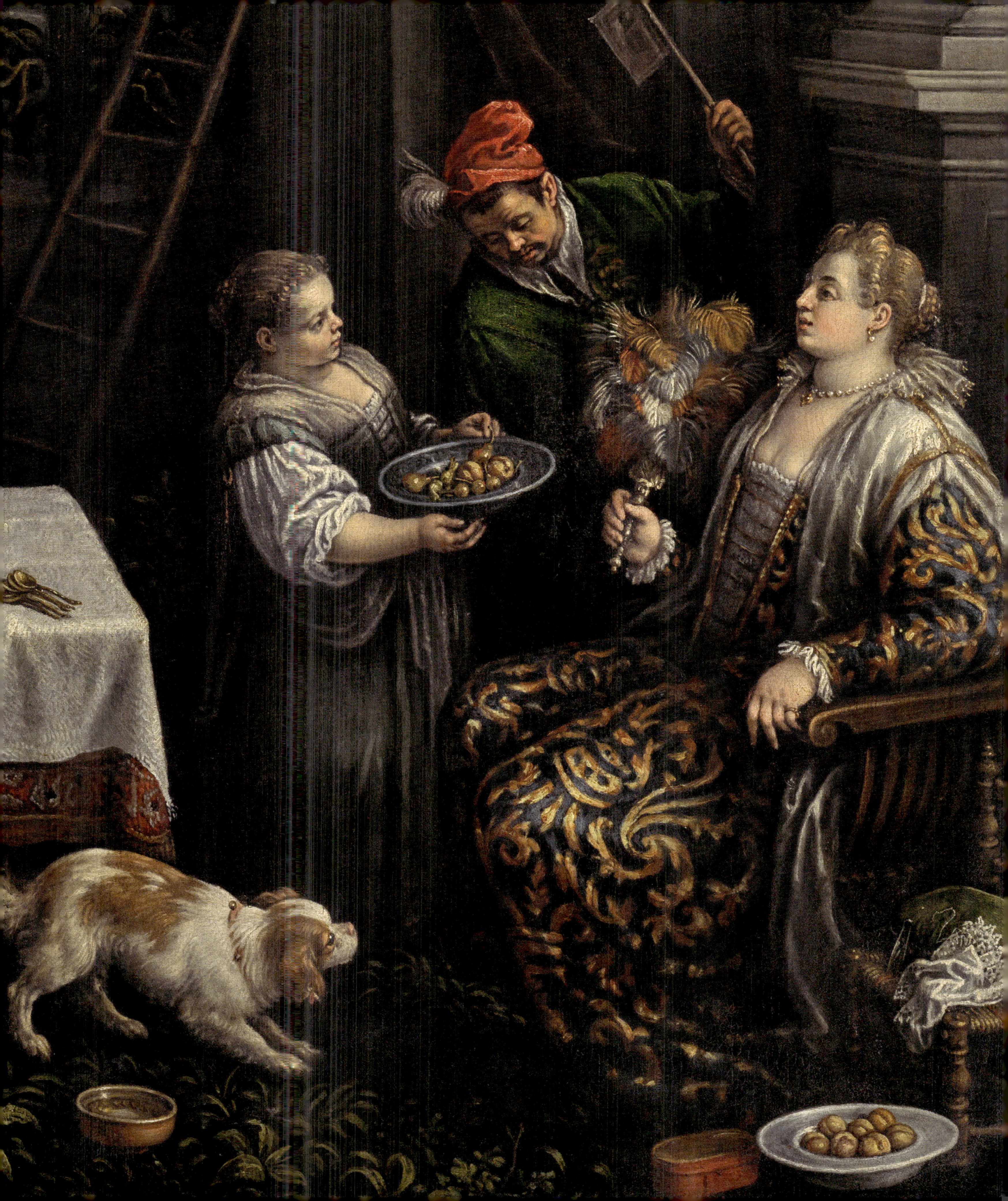

FRANCESCA DEL TORRE SCHEUCH

Nature's Time

A Ridolfo Imperadore mandò i dodeci mesi.
Carlo Ridolfi, *Maraviglie dell'Arte*

In his *Maraviglie dell'Arte*, published in 1648, the Veronese painter and art connoisseur Carlo Ridolfi reported that Jacopo Bassano, an artist active in the region between Bassano del Grappa and Venice until the end of the sixteenth century, sent Emperor Rudolf II twelve paintings depicting the months of the year.

Examined and re-evaluated as part of a project researching the Kunsthistorisches Museum's Bassano Collection, this impressive late Renaissance cycle offers numerous art historical findings, suggestions, and insights into various cultural contexts suited to visual presentation in an exhibition.

These magnificent paintings were intended for an aristocratic residence and, with their imposing format, continue to impress today. Their lively narrative is enriched by a multitude of precisely depicted objects and utensils – genuine parts of a still life – and illuminated with lively colours. These pictures are unique in Venetian painting and provide a point of reference for labours of the months in following years.

All of the paintings are signed by Leandro, Jacopo Bassano's third son, and yet are to be regarded as the product of the family workshop. To understand the significance of these creations, the personality of the father – the ingenious artist and founder of the workshop – needs to be examined more closely. He is less well known to the general public today than his famous fellow artists, Tiziano Vecellio, Jacopo Tintoretto, and Paolo Veronese. But he was very well known and highly appreciated in the sixteenth and seventeenth centuries. Every collection of note had to have 'Bassano' paintings. The Medici, Emperor Rudolf II, Archduke Leopold Wilhelm, the rulers of France and Spain, as well as the English aristocracy collected pictures by this family of painters until well into the seventeenth century. The rise of a new genre contributed to this success, the biblical pastoral, in which episodes from the Bible were depicted in rural settings.

The exhibition sets out to trace the reasons for the development of this old-but-new theme by reconstructing the cultural context from which it emerged and situating its roots in the new view of nature that was becoming established throughout Europe at the start of the sixteenth century. This approach reveals a highly interconnected cultural world that exchanged ideas and knowledge constantly thanks to the development of publishing and, subsequently, illustrated books.

Thanks to the wealth of the Kunsthistorisches Museum's interwoven collections, the core of which was assembled in the sixteenth century, the exhibition is able to draw on an extremely wide-ranging and high-quality selection of paintings, sculptures, and objects that, in their many fascinating combinations, bear witness to the history of Habsburg collecting.

Supplemented by select, first-class loans, the objects from the museum's own collections have been organised into eleven thematic sections. The exhibition opens with Jacopo Bassano's *Pastorale*, which takes up the main themes of the exhibition – nature and humanity – in a striking manner. Taken together with it, the moving scene on the *Ara Grimani* with its depiction of a sheep with a lamb in a bucolic landscape testifies to Augustan culture's love of nature.

A new view of nature

Since the end of the fourteenth century, a new awareness of nature had developed at the courts of the Po Valley and Lombardy, where the International Gothic style had gained a foothold.

Giovannino de' Grassi, a painter at several courts in northern Italy, collected depictions of animals in the *Taccuino* (notebook) – which is leaving Italy for the first time since 1948 – for his atelier. The pictures are sophisticated and at the same time extraordinarily modern because they are depicted from life.

Around the same time, knowledge about the animal and plant world and its therapeutic properties was spreading throughout Europe and was collected and systematised in the medieval *Tacuina sanitatis*. These are encyclopaedic works of a medical nature in which the characteristics and effects of plants are described in word and picture, and presented in relation to their use by humans. The focus of the depictions of the four seasons and the twelve months of the year was agricultural work, animal husbandry, and the use of livestock.

In addition to the practical knowledge in the *Tacuina*, the systematisation of botanical knowledge can be observed in the magnificently illustrated herbaria of the Po Valley. The text and its accompanying illustrations, although still schematic, is a harbinger of what would be perfected in the following century with the advent of scientific illustration.

At the beginning of the sixteenth century, nature was given a new significance in the works of two outstanding artists. Leonardo da Vinci had devoted himself to the depiction of flowers, animals, and natural phenomena since his youth, and the making of these pictures was the result of close observation. His extraordinary creative powers, which blossomed under the influence of the International Gothic, developed further during his stay in Milan, where he found fertile surroundings and a pronounced sensitivity for nature. The two magnificent sheets from the Royal Library in Windsor – preparatory studies for flowers and plants in *Leda and the Swan* painted in Milan – show how the precise reproduction of natural elements is accompanied by a deep understanding of atmospheric values, expressed in delicate chiaroscuro and resulting in pure poetry. Leonardo left behind not only paintings and drawings, but also a depiction of magnificent, ingeniously interwoven vegetation that seems to replace parts of the architectural elements in the Sala delle Asse in the Castello Sforzesco.

Contemporaneous with Leonardo, Albrecht Dürer captured the wonders of nature in his drawings with meticulous precision, creating enchanting depictions of particular appeal which he often developed further in his paintings and engravings. The *Bouquet of Violets* and the brilliant plumage of the *Dead European Roller* are evidence not only of the painter's outstanding artistic mastery but also of his specific interest in nature and its exploration. The precise draughtsmanship of his lifelike depictions made Dürer a role model for his numerous successors, who reproduced his studies and provided material for scientific illustrations.

The commentaries on Dioscorides' *Materia medica* were published first in Latin and later in Italian by the Sienese physician Pietro Andrea Mattioli, who also worked in the service of the Habsburgs. These commentaries were supplemented with more than 500 illustrations in the 1554 edition. Conrad Gessner added illustrations to his five-volume encyclopaedia *Historia animalium* (1551–1558), which in turn was used as a source by artists looking to depict animals in their paintings.

That completed an essential process. Illustrations became an indispensable supplement to the texts, clearly illustrating the characteristic diversity of plants and animal forms. The world with all its phenomena and inhabitants had become the subject of research and study, and art a useful instrument for the dissemination of knowledge. Numerous artists, including Giorgio Liberale, Giuseppe Arcimboldo, and Jacopo Ligozzi, made their art available to scholars, naturalists, and collectors of curiosities, such as Ulisse Aldrovandi of Bologna, a diligent scientist who maintained contact with colleagues throughout Europe, with whom he exchanged information, discoveries, curiosities, and illustrations.

Venice

As a city strategic for trade in the Mediterranean and with the Orient, Venice was for centuries a place where cultures met, a place of development and the dissemination of knowledge through publishing and cartography, a place of exchange and distribution, not only of valuable goods but also of curiosities, animals, plants, and essences that arrived in the harbour. Giorgione's *Three Philosophers* bears witness to this cultural encounter and to the pronounced interest in science of the Venetian aristocracy, as confirmed by the recent documentary discovery of Giulia Zaccariotto.

This leads to the subjects of astronomy and cartography, together with extraordinary objects such as Albrecht Dürer's magnificent *Maps of the Sky* (1515), which served as the basis for print versions of Gerhard Mercator's three-dimensional celestial globes.

Towards the end of the fifteenth century, a particular sensitivity to the landscape had developed in both literature and art in the territories of the Republic of Venice. Jacopo Sannazaro's literary work *Arcadia* (1504) inspired not only poetry but also painting. It celebrated the rural landscape in images that testified to the harmony of man and nature that we are familiar with from the verse of Virgil. The gentle Venetian landscape is echoed in the paintings of Giovanni Bellini, Giorgione, and Titian. Titian's subtle drawings, which were disseminated in iconic woodcuts and engravings such as the *Landscape with a Milkmaid*, were crucial for the development of landscape painting in Venice in the sixteenth century.

Nature and science at court

At the turn of the fifteenth and sixteenth centuries, interest blossomed in the depiction of the four seasons as personifications that were based on the iconography of classical antiquity. Until then, depictions of the twelve months had been predominant. They were better suited to the decorative needs of monumental settings. Closely linked to the Christian tradition, these images adorned the portals of cathedrals as well as courtly spaces in the form of tapestries and frescoes, such as the magnificent cycle in Palazzo Schifanoia in Ferrara.

Around the middle of the century, the three main protagonists of this story, Giuseppe Arcimboldo, Pieter Breugel, and Jacopo Bassano, explored, almost simultaneously, man's relationship with nature in depictions on the theme of the seasons. As interpreters of a new zeitgeist, they brought the seasons to the walls of intimate spaces intended for conversation and intellectual exchange.

The *Seasons* by Pieter Bruegel, painted for the country estate of the businessman and collector Nicolaes Jongelinck, assign a central role to the landscape and thus to nature. The landscape, imbued with light and atmosphere, is the real protagonist of his depictions of the seasons. Humans there seem to lose themselves in their seasonal activities and merge into it.

Giuseppe Arcimboldo, on the other hand, chose the traditional courtly iconography of personification, designing his composite heads as allegories composed of the elements that characterise each season. In his Viennese works, Arcimboldo celebrates the Habsburg dynasty and its rulers as a factor of equilibrium and continuity, which is reflected in the cyclical nature of the seasons.

Johann Neefe, Augustus of Saxony's physician, confirmed the convivial settings in which Arcimboldo's works were enjoyed. He recorded in his diary how Emperor Ferdinand I entertained his educated guests by showing them the Milanese painter's works and expounding on their peculiarities and curiosities.

The following section is introduced by Chronos – the Greek deity who rules over time – and the scene in which the Sphinx poses her fateful question. They provide a brief glimpse into the topic of the transience of human existence and the influence of time on humans over the centuries.

The Etruscan terracotta head of the god Janus, the protector of spatial and temporal transition, leads us to reflections on the iconography of the seasons, closely linked to the classical tradition of Ovid, and here placed in relation to the elements and planets. These depictions form the basis of a definition of the relationship between man and nature at the start of the sixteenth century and, in particular, for the question of how humans find their place in creation and how they orient themselves in the cosmos.

The third artist at the centre of the exhibition is Jacopo Bassano, whose *Seasons* were created in a particular political and cultural context. Like Pieter Bruegel, Bassano also chose to depict the seasons in the iconographic tradition of agricultural activities. He establishes a connection to the religious dimension, expressed in biblical scenes that allude to the story of redemption by Christ.

They also owed their success to the special circumstance of a growing interest on the part of the Venetian nobility in land investment on the mainland. This was encouraged by the development and dissemination of agronomic knowledge in a lively programme of publications. The expansion of agricultural activities and the construction of villas on the Venetian mainland are important elements that also included painting and architecture. The kitchen and market scenes of contemporaries, such as Pieter Aertsen, Joachim Beuckelaer, and Vincenzo Campi, serve as a link to the cycles of the seasons by Francesco and Leandro Bassano.

They free themselves of the religious dimension in their *Seasons* by replacing biblical scenes with signs of the zodiac. Leandro's *Months* introduce important iconographic innovations to the urban scenes that characterise the months of February and March. The dictates of the Counter-Reformation played an important role in this. The monumental scenes are interwoven with descriptive elements of documentary value and still lifes, some modelled in part on life, others on illustrations from Gessner's and Mattioli's treatises.

The astrological theme, in conjunction with the epochal depiction of farm labour, yields images of an 'ennobled' rural life that confirm its place in the context of the aristocracy. Francesco and Leandro Bassano's relationships with medical and botanical scholars as well as scientists of the calibre of Giovan Francesco Sagredo and Galileo Galilei shed light on the group of personalities depicted by the Bassano brothers, who were active at the University of Padua and in the adjoining botanical garden.

As meeting places for European scholars, botanical institutions collected, processed, and disseminated knowledge about plants from all over the known world, as evidenced in the work of Pietro Antonio Michiel and his *Erbario*. The Botanical Garden of Pisa is represented in the exhibition by magnificent illuminated works by Jacopo Ligozzi and Daniel Fröschl, artists who testify to the vitality of the network of European scientists. The court in Prague was a centre of cultural exchange for all the arts and sciences. Interest in nature in all its varied forms was fuelled by the scientific revolution, which, as we have seen, made use of art to illustrate texts and treatises.

The development of the relationship between art and science, expressed in the depictions of the seasons and months, favoured the genre of still life and the emergence of a new taste. In the final gallery of the exhibition, the courtly iconography of the tapestry from the *Grotesque Months* series meets the bourgeois dimension of Jan Baptist Saive's *Seasons*, which paved the way for the still life.

The exhibition's epilogue is left to the genius of Arcimboldo, who unites the natural cycle of the four seasons in a single head. With this melancholic portrait (self-portrait?) of a person immersed in meditation, the artist summarises the passage of time in an iconic work.

The exhibition catalogue's seven in-depth essays, along with the entries on the individual objects in the exhibition, offer a detailed look at all of these topics.

Taking Ovid's *Metamorphoses* as a basis, Mino Gabriele examines the structure of philosophical thought between ancient and modern times, in which the cyclical character of the four seasons, the doctrine of the elements, the temperaments, and the ages of man are anchored. The earthly and heavenly worlds are closely connected and in constant motion, and every natural phenomenon has its explanation and raison d'être.

Sylvia Ferino-Pagden's essay pursues this structure of thought in Giuseppe Arcimboldo's work. The artist drew on the classical iconography of personification, albeit in his own personal and original manner. Arcimboldo transforms the charm and quirkiness of the composite head from the popular tradition of Lombardy into allegories of imperial dignity. He composed his heads from components characteristic of the seasons and elements, thus achieving an identification of the sitter with nature itself.

Sabine Pénot analyses Pieter Bruegel's monumental cycle of the *Seasons*, which illuminates the relationship between man and nature. Fascinated by sub-alpine landscapes, Bruegel gives them a dominant role to humanity, over which he seems to pass moral judgement. Animals and nature are described with compassion and interest, while the human figures seem to be of secondary importance. The author points out the interesting correspondence between Arcimboldo's and Bruegel's depictions, which appear to be so far apart, but approach each other in their reification of man, who is shown through his activities rather than his individuality.

My chapter on the Bassanos traces the evolution of the *Seasons* and *Months* inside the workshop, from the solemn humanist vision of the dignity of rural life to the trivialisation of the iconography by the sons Francesco and Leandro, who, following their predilection for narrative, transformed their father's creations into sumptuous images full of naturalistic detail. The step to the autonomy of the still life, freed of narrative pretexts, is a very short one.

Giuseppe Olmi and Lucia Tongiorgi Tomasi shed light on the complexity and richness of the cultural environment in Venice as it pertains to the natural sciences, which were closely linked to the European courts. From a very broad perspective, the authors illustrate the Venetian scholars' predilection for the study of the animal and plant world, which was supported by the Aristotelian tradition at the University of Padua. The focus is on the role of the Serenissima as a privileged locus for the exchange and dissemination of knowledge, the result of Venice's numerous printing houses, which made the city the centre of European publishing.

Mario Infelise and Sabrina Minuzzi analyse the success of agricultural publishing in Venice. They trace the stages of the agronomic publishing boom and underscore the abundance of published material. In the course of the sixteenth century, treatises were written in the vernacular that moved beyond the tradition of the Latin classics on the subject and were characterised by originality and innovation. Accompanied by illustrations, they developed into important reference works for landowners who wanted to expand their knowledge in order to increase the productivity of their estates.

An analysis of the economic structures of Veneto in the sixteenth century contributes to an understanding of the close links between the Viennese labours of the months and the region around Vicenza and Bassano. Based on extensive documentary material, Edoardo Demo's essay illustrates the geographical features as well as the social and economic structures that facilitated the development of manufacturing industries, in particular wool and silk processing.

To conclude this brief overview, let me express my sincere thanks to my colleagues at the lending institutions who have generously made works of extraordinary importance available.

My personal thanks go to Sylvia Ferino-Pagden for her many years of support for the project. Peter Kerber has promoted its development. Sabine Haag and Jonathan Fine enthusiastically accepted the proposal for this project.

Katja Schmitz-von Ledebur, Georg Plattner and Veronika Sandbichler made objects entrusted to their care available for the exhibition.

This exhibition and the accompanying catalogue are the result of intense cooperation with colleagues who make up the scientific committee and colleagues at the Kunsthistorisches Museum who have promptly supported this project from the very first discussions.

The exhibition would not have come to fruition without the intelligent, attentive, and flexible scientific and organisational support of Alexandra Sattler. Nikolaus Keusch and Julia Neudorfer mastered the complexity of the many valuable loans. Special thanks go to Elke Oberthaler, who supported the project with an extensive restoration campaign of the Bassano paintings in our collections and made it possible to present some of the works in new frames. Gerhard Veigel designed exhibition architecture that does justice to the complexity of the themes and the diversity of the objects exhibited.

My thanks also go to Franz Pichorner and the publications department for their work on the catalogue: Benjamin Mayr and Rafael Kopper for catalogue management, Catherine Phillips, Annette Van der Vyver, and Karin Zeleny for their copy editing. We thank Tim Bisschop for the catalogue's graphic design, Stefan Zeisler, Michael Eder, Jakob Gsollpointner, Thomas Ritter, and Daniel Sostaric for the image editing.

Our exhibition is an invitation to reflect critically on the development of the relationship between man and nature over the course of the sixteenth century as seen through the eyes of the three Renaissance artists.

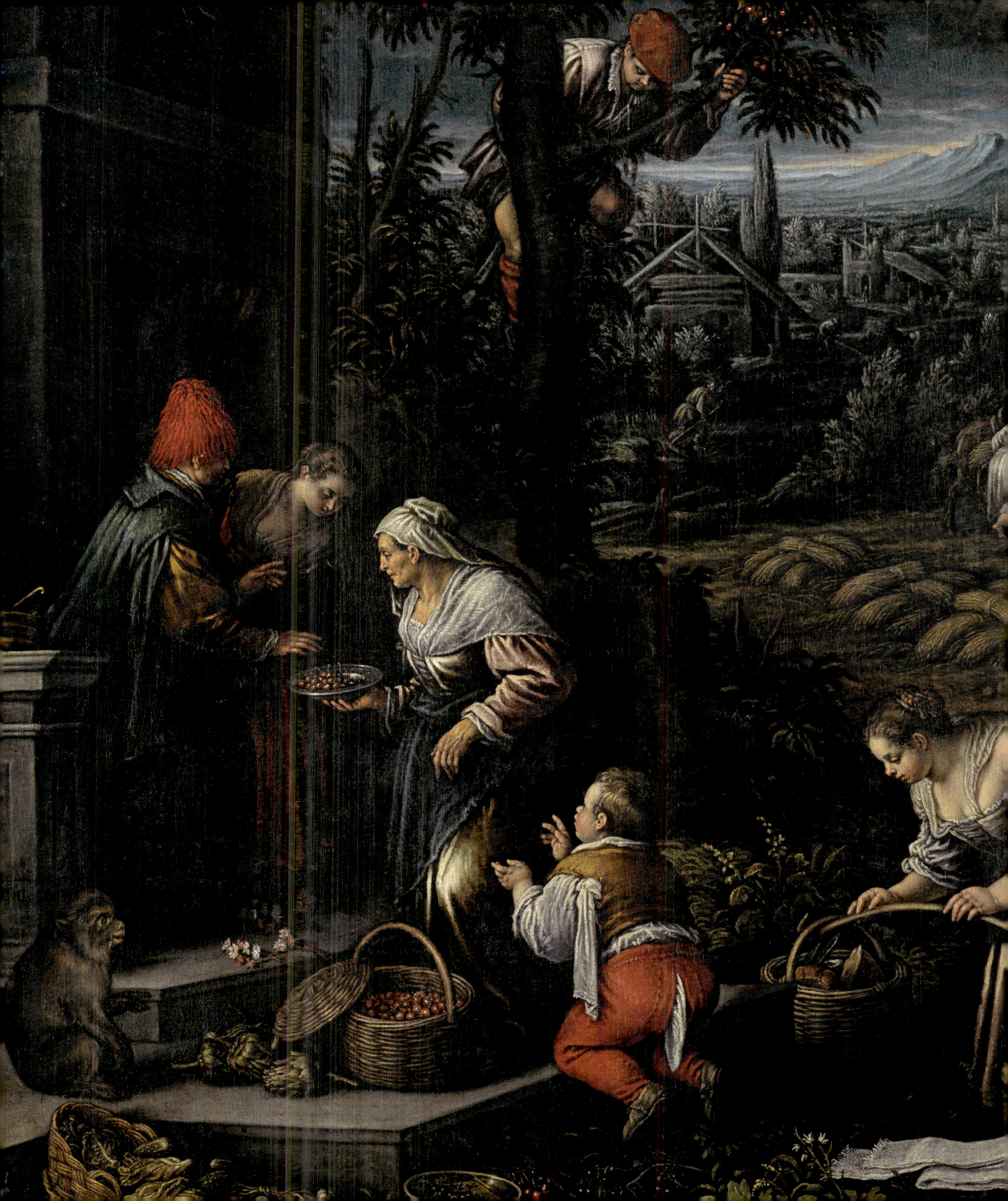

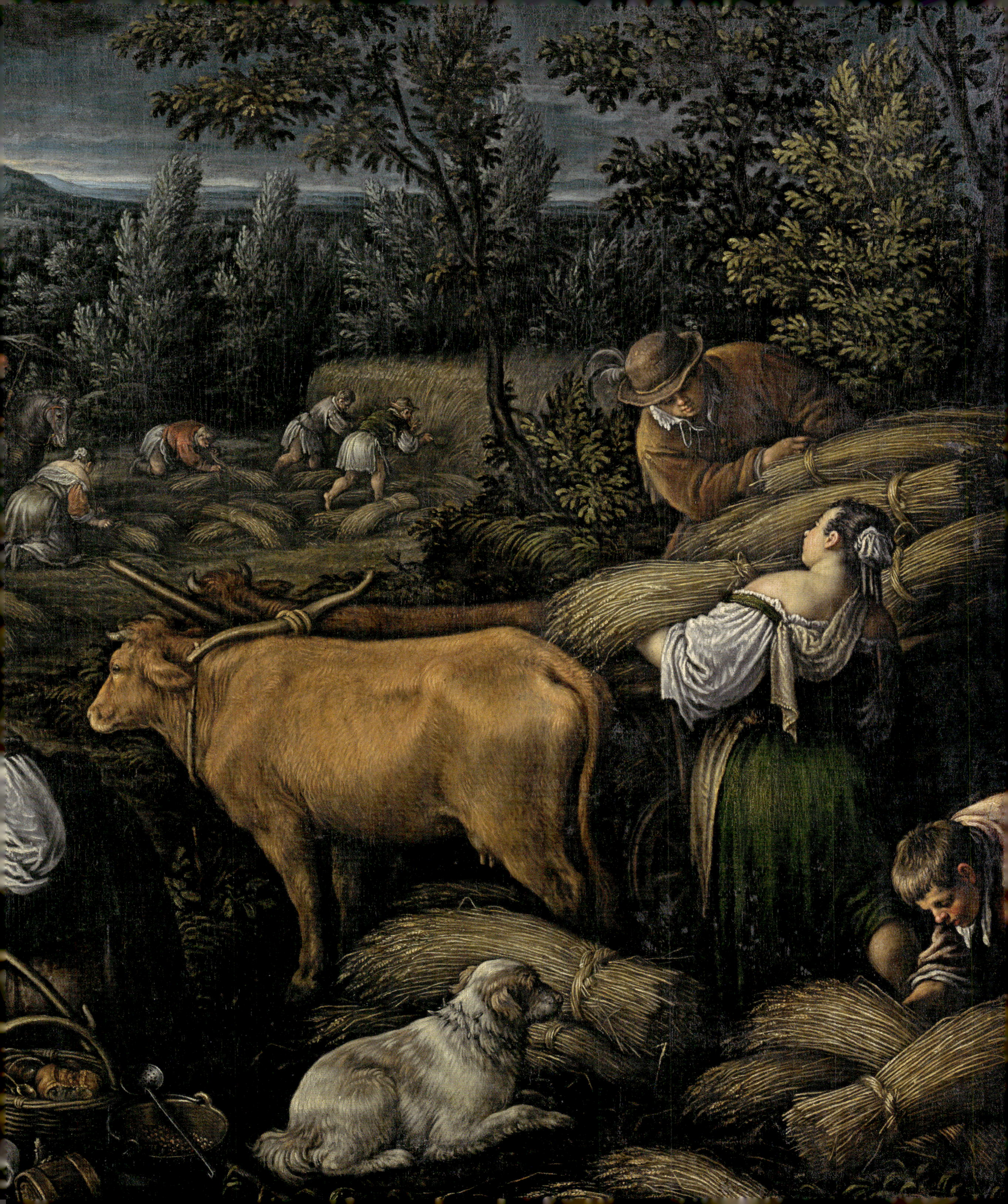

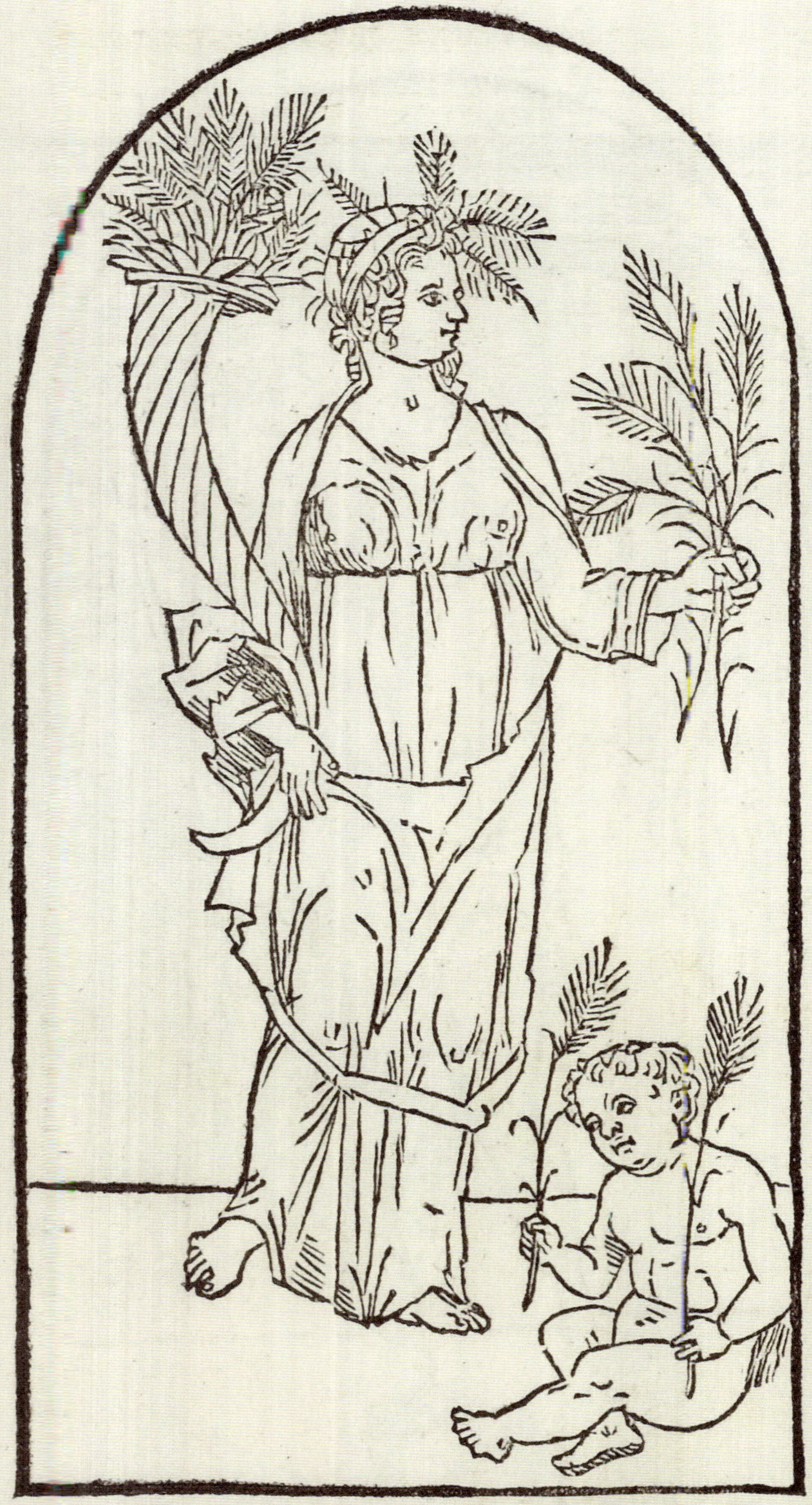

FLAVAE MESSI.S.

MINO GABRIELE

The Seasons of Man

All things change, but nothing dies: the spirit wanders hither and thither, taking possession of what limbs it pleases ... but never at any time does it perish. Like pliant wax which, stamped with new designs, does not remain as it was, or keep the same shape, but yet is still itself, so I tell you that the soul is always the same, but incorporates itself in different forms. ... So the moments of time at once flee and follow, and are ever new. What was before is left behind, that which was not comes to be, and every minute gives place to another. You see the nights, completed, pass into day, the shining rays of morning succeed the darkness of the night. ... Or again, don't you see the year passing through a succession of four seasons, thus imitating our own life? [1]
Ovid, *Metamorphoses*

These famous lines of Ovid, set within his poetic explanation of the doctrine of Pythagoras,[2] express a view of the world in which all things are but the transitory expression of a larger cosmic transformation; that is, of a nature that constantly dies and renews itself, whose rhythm is dictated by the order of time, whose rhythms ensure perennial, stable impermanence. It is a conception that in different philosophical and religious inflections has permeated Western thought and beyond. The last two lines, still topical, compare the unfolding of human life to the seasons, following a relationship formulated by an ancient medical/cosmological tradition[3] – codified in Isidore of Seville,[4] who was able to draw on earlier sources – which juxtaposes and thus sets out the following pairs: spring/childhood, summer/youth, autumn/maturity, winter/old age, but which the same tradition correlates to a broader micro-macrocosmic network[5] of subjects, as summarized in the following table:

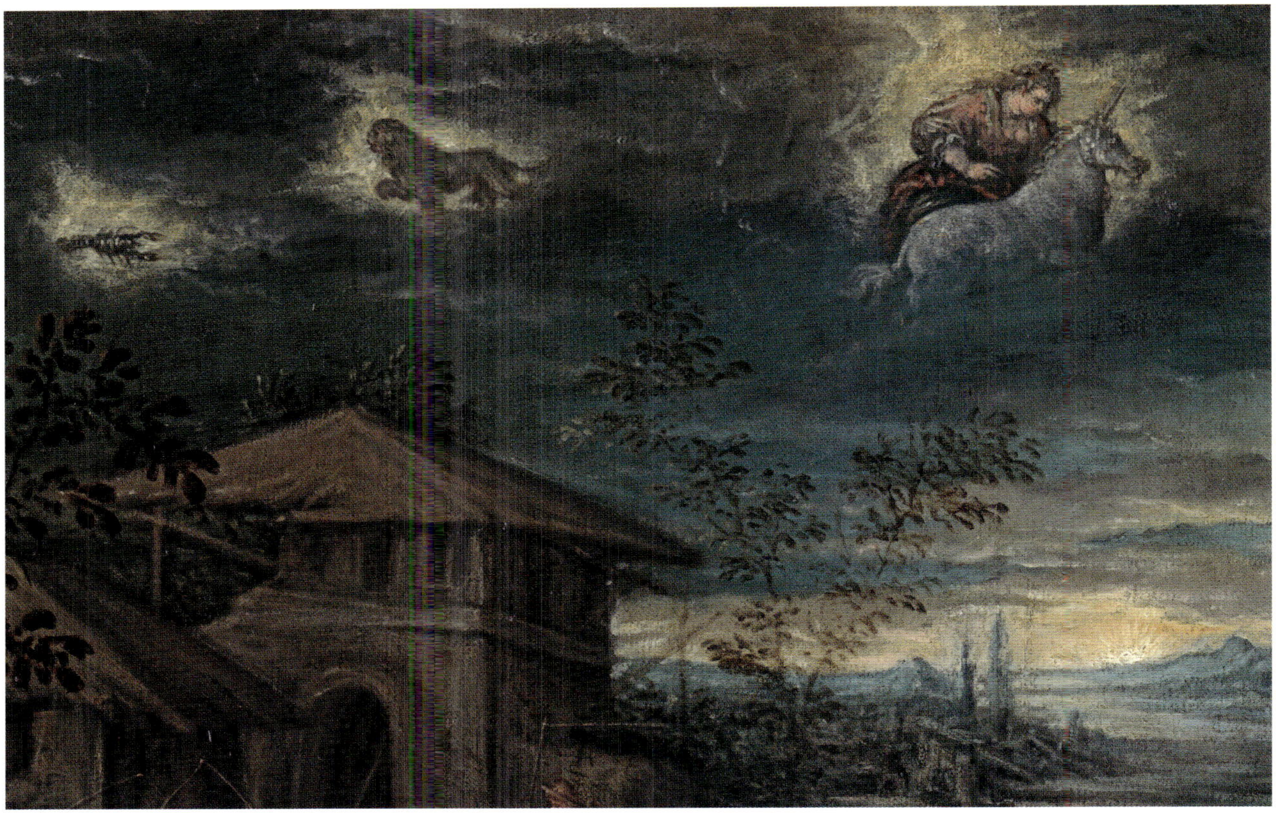

Fig. 1

Francesco dal Ponte, called Bassano, *Summer (June, July, August)*, detail, 1585/90. Vienna, Kunsthistorisches Museum, Picture Gallery, inv. 4289

world	**year**	**sky**	**man**
East, air, hot-wet	spring	Jupiter	blood, sanguine, childhood
South, fire, dry-hot	summer	Mars	yellow bile, choleric, youth
West, earth, cold-dry	autumn	Saturn	black bile, melancholic, maturity
North, water, wet-cold	winter	Moon	phlegm, phlegmatic, old age

If we associate the signs of the zodiac with the ages of man[6] and the respective four seasons (childhood/spring: Aries, Taurus, Gemini; youth/summer: Cancer, Leo, Virgo (fig. 1); maturity/autumn: Libra, Scorpio, Sagittarius; old age/winter: Capricorn, Aquarius, Pisces), we then have a complete space-time picture of the conjugation between man and the cosmos, and vice versa.

These are ancient, vital themes, that, precisely because of their pre-eminence, have been given endless testimony in art and science. Here we look at some of the principles behind those themes and their connection with the images and artistic language that have expressed them, substantiating them, in different forms and ways, in signs, colours, metals and more.

In the network and circulation of numerous elements, as in the table to the left, it is the sphericity of the cosmos that conflates everything and gives unity: the world is spherical[7] because, in containing the totality of creatures and elements, it can only have the figure that includes all other possible figures, namely the sphere.[8] Because the circle is perfect, with all parts of it proportional to each other, its form is a sign of eternal divine completeness. In Aristotle's geocentric theory, later perfected by Ptolemy, such a cosmic sphere has the Earth at its centre with the region of the four elements through to the Moon, followed by the other planets (Mercury, Venus, Sun, Mars, Jupiter, Saturn), then the firmament or fixed stars with the zodiac.[9] This complex *machina mundi* was the predominant model from antiquity to the Renaissance, then gradually gave way to the Copernican heliocentric view. The part of this *machina* that has not altered, though, in the long historical process that characterizes it, is essentially its astronomical and geographical coordinates: the north–south axis and the east–west solar transit, the ecliptic, the poles, the zodiacal belt, the celestial tropics, equinoxes, and solstices, the solar and lunar cycles; in short, all the data that make up the celestial revolution and that have a corresponding order in the equator and the terrestrial tropics, in the wind-rose,[10] in the systems for orienting and founding cities and temples. Exemplary testimony of this is given by Hyginus Gromaticus,[11] when he observes that the ritual origin for establishing boundaries is celestial and that such a procedure is unchangeable. Indeed, he continues, boundaries are always established according to the cosmic order, in that the *decumani* are parallel to the course of the Sun and the *cardines* follow the direction of the celestial axis. Similarly, churches were established starting from the rising of the Sun on a given day and point in space, and from this the horizontal east–west line was drawn along which the sacred building was raised.

It is an earthly world that reflects the ways and times of the celestial one, hence the objective relevance of the seasons, months, days and atmospheric phenomena to life and human activities. The dynamics of the various correspondences cited and the numerous effects they relate and produce manifest none other than the clock of creation to which everything is subject. The hegemony of the number four emerges here (seasons, ages, elements, cardinal points etc., of which there are various excellent artistic portrayals in the exhibition), resulting from the orthogonal meeting of the north–south cosmic axis with the east–west heliacal transit in the apparent movement of the Sun, giving the quadripartition of the cosmos. This number is the child of two, the primary spatial, temporal, and linguistic distinction:[12] right/left, before/after. Such partitions are necessary for determining the individual's place in the world so as to rationally relate him to it and its parts. Indeed, the path from right to left, in the boreal regions, follows the course of the Sun, shining from east to west: it is the measure of the celestial vault and the Earth, which, with respect to the north–south axis, places the east/dawn on the right and the west/sunset on the left. Hence light and dark, the basic pair with which to distinguish and separate space and time, with the inevitable supremacy of vital brightness over darkness.

'And it is a universal law,' writes Aristotle,[13] 'that, as regards above and below, front and back, right and left, the nobler and more honourable part invariably is placed uppermost, in front, and on the right, rather than in the opposite positions, unless some more important object stands in the way.' The anthropometric and cosmological logic of the observation seems evident: above is the firmament, the divine, and man's head;[14] in front is that which is seen and known; on the right the gods and Nature give favourable signs. The right is the propitious, benevolent, and augural direction par excellence, in both its mantic and religious, and its moral and eschatological connotations;[15] indeed, this is a way to walk solemnly in the otherworldly and soteriological places. It is a sacred and ritual orientation system (Greek, Etruscan, and Latin) that captures in the right–left opposition the sense of an order concerning every action. The case of the soothsayer Manto in Seneca's *Oedipus* is exemplary, in which drawing omens from the innards of sacrificed animals she notices that none of these occupy their natural place in the victim's body, so the principle is overturned and the response becomes a fatal premonition:

> Everything is wrong!
> The organs lie where none of them belong.
> On the right-hand side a lung lies bleeding,
> unable to expand enough for breathing;
> on the left side no heart, a gaping hole,
> no soft-stretched membrane covering it all.
> Anarchic creature, lawless in the womb![16]

If right/left are the directions of space, Janus (in the exhibition with a splendid second-century head; cat. 45) is that of time, the before and after: 'The Mythographers say that, when Janus was king, every man's house was sacred and inviolable.... Moreover, some think that he has received the epithet "two-faced" because of his knowledge of the past and foreknowledge of the future.... Some are of the opinion that Janus represents the Sun and that his two faces (*geminus*) suggest his lordship over each of the two heavenly gates, since the Sun's rising opens and his setting closes the day.'[17]

Going back to the number four, it is inevitable, following the table shown above, to mention specifically the four elements: earth, water, air, and fire. They constitute the first principle of bodies. The theory concerning them, already present in pre-Socratic and Pythagorean philosophy,[18] handed down mainly by the works of Aristotle,[19] was to dominate scientific thinking until the seventeenth century. The theory, in brief, considers that all the substances existing in the sublunary world are the result of proportionally different combinations of the four elements. These, in turn, are 'mixtures' produced by the combination of four qualities (hot, cold, dry, wet) that unite two by two exclusively on the basis of the active–passive relation, two of them being active (hot and cold) and the other two passive (dry and wet). There are six possible combinations of the four qualities: hot + wet, wet + cold, cold + dry, dry + hot, hot – cold, dry + wet. However, these last two must be discarded because, being made up of two qualities that are both active or passive, they cannot be united. So only the first four remain that thus generate the four elements, also agreeing with their number: cold + dry = earth; wet + cold = water; wet + hot = air; hot + dry = fire (see fig. 2):

Such relations allow one element to be transformed into another, provided that the dynamics of the change do not alter each element's own active and passive constitution. So fire can turn into air by the change of only one of its two qualities; that is, dry into wet, in that fire is hot and dry, while air is hot and wet: so it is sufficient that dry becomes wet for air to be generated, and from air, in turn, water is generated when its cold is replaced by the hot of the other, as can be seen by the relations in the diagram. The most common portrayal of the four elements is the geometrical one, rendered with equilateral triangles:[20] fire △, earth 🜃, air 🜁, water ▽. It cannot be ruled out that this association of the elements with the corresponding triangular *signa* derives from Platonic tradition,[21] according to which triangles are the primary elements of the physical world, because the triangle is the first spatial form, the beginning of every surface. All the other geometrical figures and the Platonic regular solids themselves are derived from it: tetrahedron = fire, octahedron = air, icosahedron = water, cube = earth. There is then no lack of original allegories, such as Arcimboldo's extraordinary anthropomorphic representations and the refined personifications on gilt-silver cups attributed to Paul Hübner (cat. 50).

(active)	hot	→	AIR	←	wet	(passive)
	↓		↑		↓	
	FIRE	←	opposites	→	WATER	
	↑		↓		↑	
(passive)	dry	→	EARTH	←	cold	(active)

Fig. 2

The six possible combinations of the four qualities of the four elements (hot, cold, dry, and wet)

Fig. 3

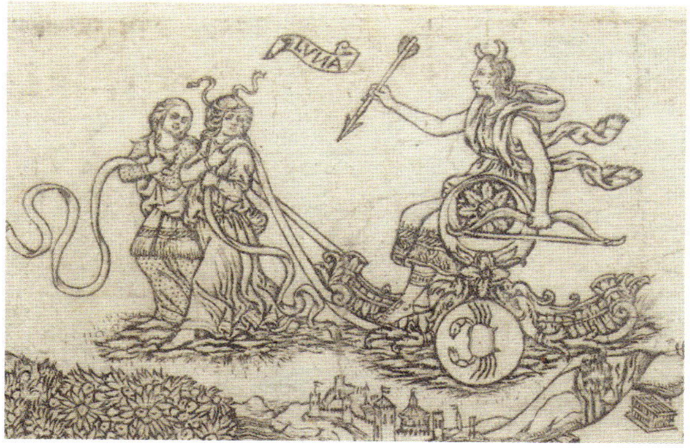

Attributed to Baccio Baldini, *The Planet Luna*, detail, c.1460. Pavia, Musei Civici, Castello Visconteo, inv. St. Mal. 1588

Fig. 4

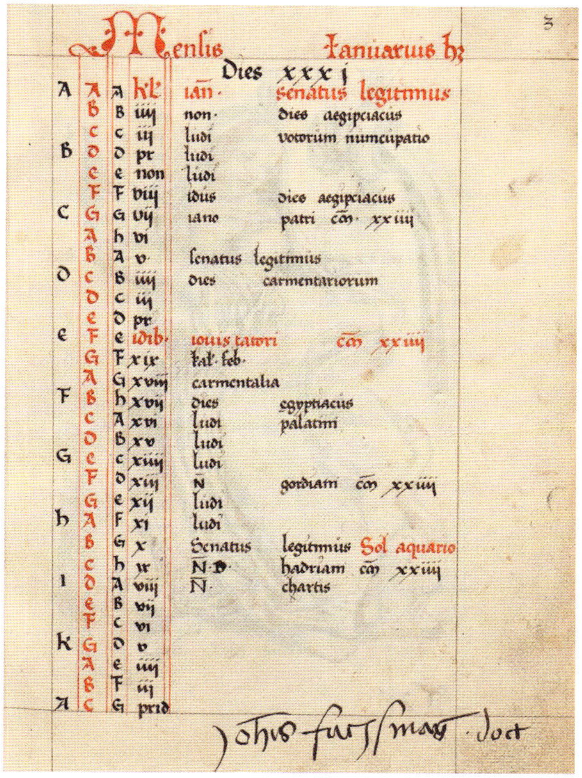

Mensis Ianuarius, in *Wiener Filocalus* (copy of the *Chronograph of 354*), c.1510. Vienna, Austrian National Library, Department of Manuscripts and Rare Books, Cod. 3416, 3r

It may now be understood how the various representations of the seasons and months present in the exhibition (cats. 15, 16, 27–30, 33, 35, 46, 48, 49, 62, 66, 67, 73, 88, 89, 90) inevitably imply, though without manifesting them, the mechanics of the four elements on which they depend for the rhythms of the four qualities, as in the diagram above. Similarly, the images of planets (fig. 3) and signs of the zodiac do not merely express specific celestial movements or periods of the year, but concern, according to more or less implicit iconographies, astral virtues and influences[22] on the cycles of Nature, the benefits that descend from them to the Earth and to man's work. So in the paintings of the seasons by Francesco Bassano (cat. 66) or the months by Leandro (cat. 67), in which the signs of the zodiac appear, but also in Jacopo's seasons (cat. 62) without such references, one cannot fail to grasp the continuity of an astrological tradition, in this case familial, which considers the Earth with its fruits and its times as mirrors of the celestial motors. The engravings of Baccio Baldini (cat. 47) are particularly noteworthy, in which, following a medieval iconic type already consolidated in the mid-fifteenth century, the triumphant planet on a chariot with the appropriate attributes appears in the upper part of the composition, and below the 'sons', i.e., those who, born under the influences of that god, perform activities or express tendencies favoured or inspired by him. For example, the festive dancing lovers, followers of the planet Venus, and armed men with standards and the spoils of war, followers of Mars. No less interesting, for the variety of attributes and iconological specificity that qualify the figures, are those of the *Chronograph of 354* by Furius Dionysius Philocalus (fig. 4),[23] an excellent example of such calendarial tradition. Indeed, along with images of cities and emperors, the illustrations in this document also feature the planets, the signs of the zodiac and the months: of the latter, March, August, October, and December may be admired in the exhibition,[24] personified and qualified according to their respective seasonal attributes.

The tradition of visualizing natural phenomena was thus perpetuated, albeit in different circumstances, giving substance to a visual vocabulary that would memorize the cosmic transits, to which artistic production could not fail to look: from Pieter Bruegel's *Hunters in the Snow (Winter)* (cat. 15.3) to the *Tacuinum sanitatis* (cat. 16), from the *Allegory of Astronomy* by Giambologna (cat. 10) to Ligozzi's *Parrots* (cat. 84) and on to the brilliant contrivances – works of art in their own right, like the *Planetary Clock* (cat. 36), the drawing of a nocturnal held by the old man in Giorgione's *Three Philosophers* or *Magi Kings* (fig. 5; cat. 6), and the *Geographical-Astronomical Compendium* of Erasmus Habermel (cat. 7.2).

But all this, it is perhaps worth remembering, is nothing more than the result of synergies between scientific and philosophical knowledge (various and differing over the centuries), which with logic and mathematics have endeavoured to give rational form to the incessant impermanence of the world and its natural and artistic manifestations.

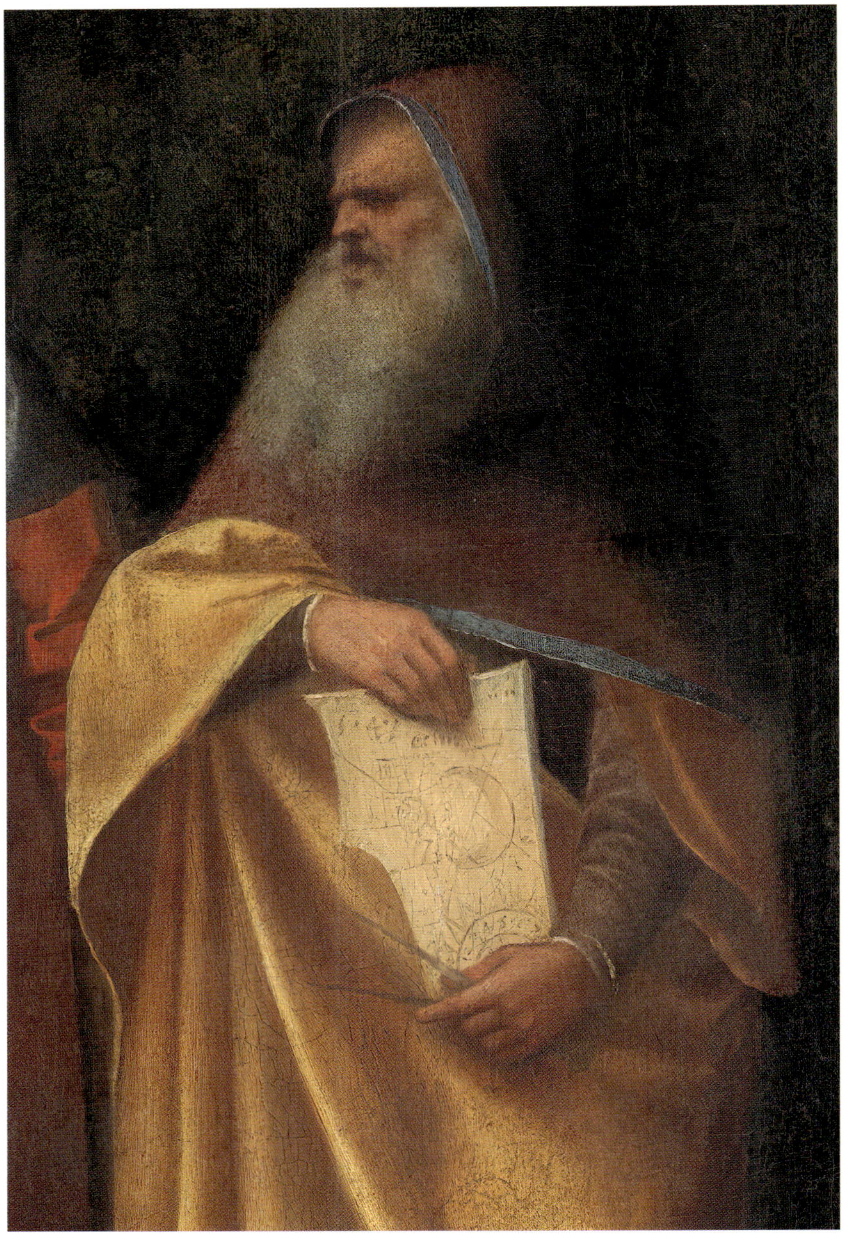

Fig. 5
Giorgio da Castelfranco, called Giorgione, *The Three Philosophers*, detail, 1508/09. Vienna, Kunsthistorisches Museum, Picture Gallery, inv. 111

* This essay discusses, albeit briefly, the conceptual tradition that inspired the works shown in the current exhibition: cosmological and cosmographical speculations that since antiquity have influenced European iconographic and iconological culture in different times and ways.

1 'Omnia mutantur, nihil interit. Errat, et illinc / huc venit, hinc illuc, et quoslibet occupat artus / spiritus... / ...nec tempore deperit ullo. / utque novis facilis signatur cera figuris, / ... / sed tamen ipsa eadem est, animam sic semper eandem / esse, sed in varias doceo migrare figuras. / ... / ipsa quoque assiduo labuntur tempora motu, / non secus ac flumen.... / Tempora sic fugiunt pariter pariterque sequuntur / et nova sunt semper, nam quod fuit ante relictum est / fitque quod haud fuerat momentaque cuncta novantur. / Cernis et emensas in lucem tendere noctes, / et iubar hoc nitidum nigrae succedere nocti. / ... / Quid? non in species succedere quattuor annum / aspicis, aetatis peragentem imitamina nostrae?'; Ovid, *Metamorphoses* 15, 165–200.

2 Ovid 1955, 339–40.

3 Schöner 1964; Klibansky, Panofsky, and Saxl 1964.

4 Isidore of Seville, *De natura rerum*, IV–XVIII Becker.

5 The specular relation between man and universe, or microcosm (μικρὸς κόσμος = small world) and macrocosm (μέγας κόσμος = big world) refers in its terminology to Plato and Aristotle, and constantly returned in subsequent centuries (essential reading: Conger 1922; Allers 1944; Des Places 1964). This relation has its foundations both in the celestial origin of the soul and in the analogy between the 'rationality' of man and of the divine, which regulates the normative function of the cosmos. It not secondarily concerns the human body and its health, such as in the medical theory and practice of melothesia, iatromathematics, and the associated astral influences: Gundel 1992, 33, 44, 132–5, 322–8; for the sources see Le Boeuffle 1987, 61–2; Saxl 1985, 47–146, 280ff.

6 Sears 1986; Chew 1962, 144–73.

7 See the armillary sphere (cat. 8), the painting by Bramante with the terraqueous globe in the centre (cat. 11), Dürer's skies (cat. 12), and Gerhard Mercator's terrestrial and celestial globes (cat. 14).

8 Plato, *Timaios*, 33b–34b; Aristotle, *De caelo*, 269a; Cicero, *De natura deorum*, 2, 47 Pease; Macrobius, *Commentarii in somnium Scipionis*, 1, 6, 46–8; 1,14, 22–6; Ficino, *Theologia Platonica*, 18, 3; cf. Obrist 2004, 55–76, 91–110; Bertoldini 2006.

9 On the different orders of the celestial spheres, on the ninth heaven, the Primum Mobile or Crystalline Heaven: Heninger 1977, 18–20, 34–8, 134–41; Gizzi 1974, vol. I, 45–77, 197–205; Grant 1994, 38, 308–14; Obrist 2004, 72–6; Eastwood 2007, 31–8.

10 The equilibrium of the heliacal motions and the seasons is aided by the winds, periodically fluttering and emanating from the four regions of the world, which are distinguished according to their origin: a subject of considerable importance for any cosmographic argument (see cat. 50.3). The four principal winds are represented in antiquity by two bearded men and two beardless youths, contrasted because they blow from opposite directions and thus indicate the two aspects of their nature: violence and stormy force on one side and beneficial tenderness on the other, according to the different seasonal periods in which the airs blow. The dual aspect recurs in a widespread iconography, in Greek and Latin monuments (sufficient to mention the famous octagonal Tower of the Winds in Athens, described by Vitruvius, 1, 6, 4–55, with the eight winds depicted winged, half of them bearded and half beardless: among them Boreas and Euros with beards, Notus and Zephyrus without). The four winds have indicated, since Homeric tradition, the cardinal points (Boreas blows from the north, Notus or Auster from the south, Euros from the east, Zephyrus from the west), the seasons, and the celestial zones of the world; Nielsen 1945; Obrist 1997; Eastwood 2007, 158–70.

11 *Constitutio limitum*, 131 Thulin; Gottarelli 2013.

12 Benveniste 1971, 51: 'In language everything must be defined in dual terms; everything carries the imprint and seal of oppositive duality'; on the subject: Cuillandre 1944; Curletto 1990, 57–63; Aretini 1998; Gottarelli 2013, 30–42, 67–74, 155–6; see note 16 below.

13 *De partibus animalium* 665a, 22–25 (trans. William David Ross and John Alexander Smith, Oxford 1912, vol. V, p. 110).

14 Plato, *Timaios* 44d; cf. *Timaios* 70a and *De Republica* 8, 13, 560b: the head 'rules' the body like the acropolis the city. To Plato, the head, the highest part of the body, is the seat of the *noûs* and its elevated position implies that man must be guided by his own divine nature.

15 Virgil, *Aeneid* 8, 302 'tua dexter adi pede sacra secundo'; Servius, *ad l.*, 'Dexter adi id est propitius. Pede secundo omine prospero'; Ovid, *Fasti* 1, 69; Persius, 5, 114; Statius, *Silvae* 3, 4, 63–4; Paulus-Festus, *s.v.*; cf. Lobeck 1829, vol. II, 914ff.; Bouché-Leclercq 1882, vol. I, 136–45; Cuillandre 1944, 185–279, 325–60; see note 13 above.

16 'Mutatus ordo est, sede nil propria iacet, / sed acta retro cuncta: non animae capax / in parte dextra pulmo sanguineus iacet, / non laeva cordi regio, non molli ambitu / omenta pingues viscerum obtendunt sinus: / natura versa est, nulla lex utero manet.' Seneca, *Oedipus*, 366–71 (trans. Seneca 1995).

17 Macrobius, *Saturnalia* 1, 9, 2–9 (trans. Macrobius 1969, 66ff.); Ovid, *Fasti* 1, 121, 139, 171; Pliny, *Naturalis historia*, 34, 33; Plutarch, *Quaestiones Romanae*, 22; Servius, *Commentary on Vergil's Aeneid* 7, 607; *Mythographus Vaticanus III*, 4, 9 Bode.

18 Heidel 1906 is still fundamental; cf. Cerri 1998.

19 Aristotle, *De generatione et corruptione* 329a–336a; *Meteorologica* 378b–390b: cf. Düring 1944, 9–25; Baffioni 1981, 205–28.

20 Gettings 1981, 108–9.

21 *Timaios* 31a–33a, 53a–63e.

22 Hauber 1916; Saxl 1985; Bezza 1995, vol. I, 95–107, vol. II, 600–4, 681–2, 744–52, 820–1; Blume 2000, in particular 139–200; Venturi 2010, 49–105.

23 Stern 1953, 203–98; Burgess 2012; Burgess 2017.

24 Each image is accompanied by tetrastichs that define the qualities and activities of the month.

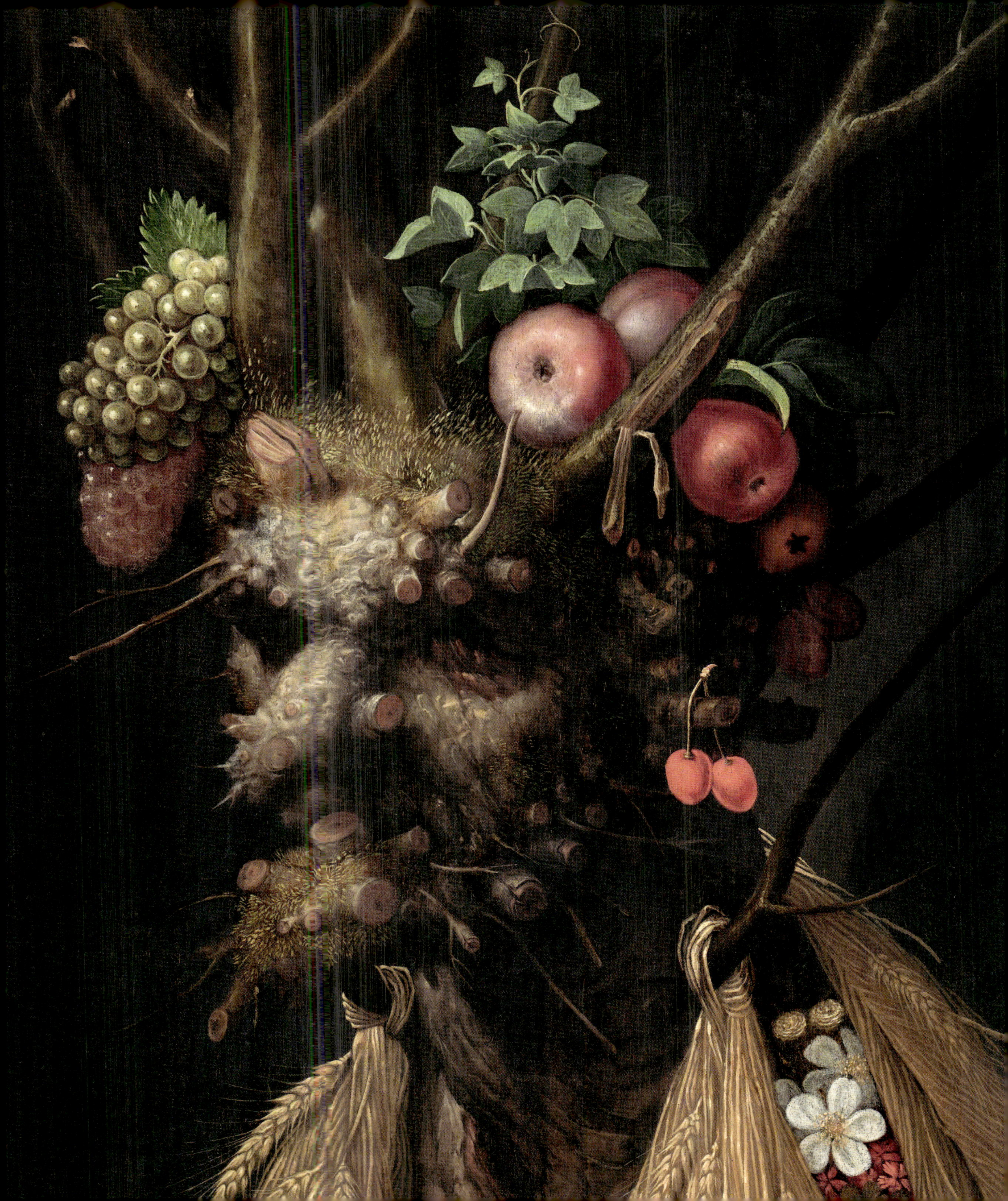

SYLVIA FERINO-PAGDEN

Reflections on Arcimboldo's *Four Seasons*

Giuseppe Arcimboldo's depictions of the *Four Seasons* (cats. 28, 29, 90) are renowned for their exceptional composite structure – a method of artistic expression that made the painter famous during his lifetime and, thanks to the Surrealist movement, led to a resurgence in his reputation during the twentieth century. At the time, this had less to do with the artist's chosen theme of the changing seasons. The current exhibition focuses on nature in the context of cosmogony and cosmology, as well as on the annual metamorphoses that occur from spring through to winter, which are structured by the passage of time and can be compared to the cycle of human life from birth to death. Ovid and other ancient writers composed wonderfully evocative descriptions of these phenomena, and philosophers have been attempting to explain them since antiquity. Planets, astrological signs, and smaller units of time such as months, but also the elements that make up earth's matter play key roles in these fascinating processes, as illustrated by the exhibited artworks and discussed in the contributions to this catalogue.

All three painters who feature in the current exhibition – Arcimboldo, Bassano, and Bruegel – created artworks on the theme of the four seasons. In contrast to the paintings made by the Bassano family (cats. 62, 66, 67) and by Pieter Bruegel the Elder (cat. 15), which represented the seasons as landscapes with human subjects performing corresponding activities, sometimes in combination with astrological signs or other elements, Arcimboldo's depictions drew on the ancient tradition of personification. Adopting a unique and highly distinctive approach that will be examined in greater detail in this essay, he created composite heads that incorporated the characteristic attributes of the different seasons.

Pictorial representations of the four seasons can be traced back to antiquity. Derived from Greek predecessors – the Horae – the dancing 'Pompeian' maidens who adorned chamber walls in private houses in Rome conferred seasonal blessings upon the inhabitants, as is conveyed in Roman prayers.[1] The propitious influence of these personified seasons was later incorporated into

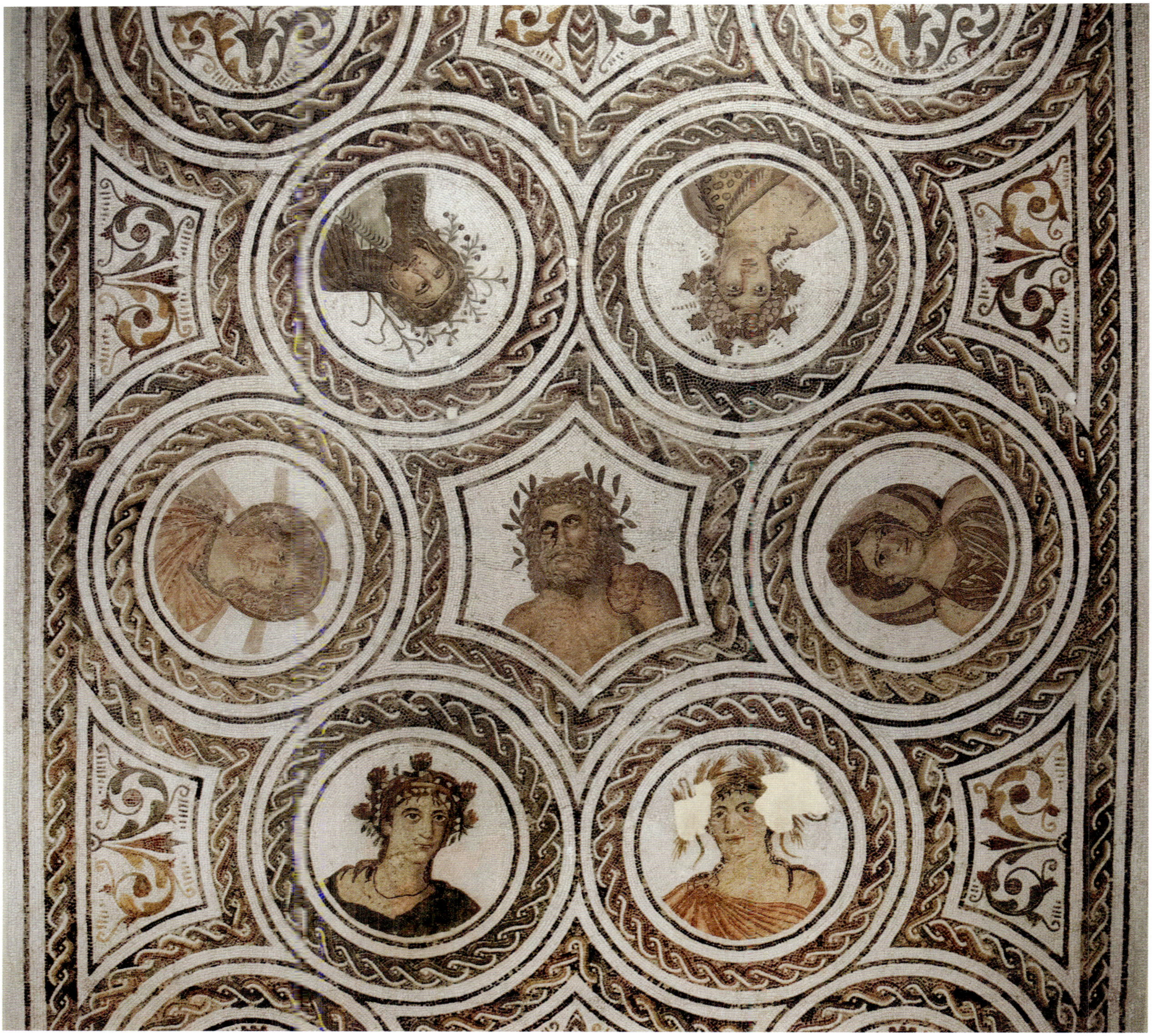

Fig. 1

Floor mosaic from the Casa del Sileno di Thysdrus, El Jem, *Aion, Helios, Selene, and the Four Seasons*, 3rd cent CE, Musée Archéologique d'El Jem

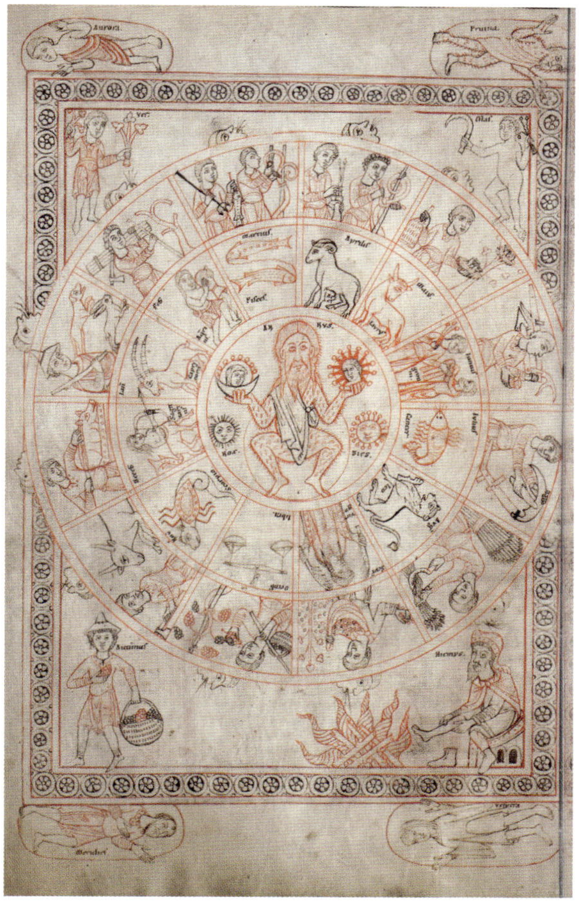

Fig. 2

Cosmological Depiction of the Seasonal Cycle (Annusbild), in *Annales*, c.1162. Stuttgart, Württembergische Landesbibliothek, Cod. hist. 2° 415, fol. 17v

Christian art. Another type of seasonal depiction developed in the Roman imperial period: the *tempora anni* – male genii with attributes that reference the seasons – which were above all found in sarcophagus art.[2]

The dominant mode of seasonal depiction in the Middle Ages, on the other hand, was developed from ceilings and floors of late Roman buildings, mostly in the form of mosaics. Here, the personifications of the seasons, usually inscribed as busts in geometric fields, were placed in the corners of the design around a central deity – sometimes Aion (fig. 1).[3] A similar arrangement also appears in illustrations to medieval religious books and in fresco decorations, such as in the famous cosmology of the *Zwiefaltener Kalender*, which is now held in the Württembergische Landesbibliothek in Stuttgart (fig. 2).[4] In these images, the focus is on Christ rather than on an ancient deity. In the Middle Ages and early Renaissance, allegorical depictions of the calendar months were often preferred to the seasons – as can be seen, for example, in the Palazzo Schifanoia in Ferrara – or they were jointly represented, as in the frescoes in the Torre Aquila in Trento. (see essay Del Torre Scheuch, p. 57, fig. 6)

The ancient personifications of the four seasons reappear sporadically in Italy towards the end of the fifteenth century, among others as full-figure depictions in niches – in the illustrations to the *Hypnerotomachia Poliphili* (cat. 48), for example – and resurface in a similar form in frescoes in Venetian villas during the sixteenth century. Further examples include a relief attributed to Bertoldo di Giovanni on the gable of the villa of Lorenzo de' Medici at Poggio a Caiano, and a series of panel paintings by the workshop of Sandro Botticelli. From the sixteenth century onwards, the four seasons increasingly featured in painted depictions on wood panels and canvas.

Perhaps for the first time since late antiquity, the seasons were depicted in the four vaulted areas of the Sala delle Stagioni in Palazzo Corboli in Asciano, near Siena, which dates from the last quarter of the Trecento (fig. 3). Here, the seasons appear as portrait busts in tondi,[5] and comparable room designs on this theme may have existed throughout Italy. For Arcimboldo, the number four and the manifold possibilities of spatial representation it offered may have been particularly significant.[6]

Diary entries made by Dr Johann Neefe, a personal physician to Augustus, Elector of Saxony, during his stay in Vienna in 1563/64, include a description of a lunch during which Emperor Ferdinand I presented and elucidated four paintings by a 'foreign' (*welsch*) artist.[7] These paintings hung on the four walls of one room and the depicted faces symbolized the four seasons. In the company of humanists, botanists, and above all doctors whose task was to safeguard his increasingly fragile health – including Johannes Crato von Krafftheim, Stefan Laureus, Giulio Alessandrini, Giovanni Besozzi, Giovanni Odorico Melchiori, and, for a time, Pietro Andrea Mattioli – Ferdinand also used these paintings to discuss issues related to health, flora, fauna, the microcosm, and the macrocosm. Even if these diary entries were not published until 100 years later, translated from Latin as part of the *Tafelreden Kaiser Ferdinand I* (The *Tafel-Reden* of Emperor Ferdinand I), they are extremely important sources of information in this context.

The vibrancy and abundance of the magnificently ripened, opulently arranged, and carefully orchestrated fruits that surround a smiling, almost aggressively cheerful profile in *Summer* (cat. 29.1) provide a clear indication of the artist's origins. Arcimboldo has playfully inscribed his name on the collar of the figure's straw cloak and placed the year 1563 next to the shoulder seam. Only an Italian could create such a convincing depiction of these diverse and wonderfully ripe fruits and vegetables, due to his familiarity with such opulence from his homeland. To this day, Italian markets offer a wealth and variety of fruits and vegetables that do not thrive so well in the central European climate, even under the influence of global warming.

The 'foreign' painter who created this impressive work served three generations of Habsburg rulers and, when he returned to his homeland after 25 years at court, received the highest honour of being made a count palatine.

Emperor Ferdinand I was very familiar with lush vegetation that flourished in sunny and warm climates, with fruit and vegetables, citruses, figs, and other produce that represented Mediterranean abundance and beauty. He spent his childhood and youth in Spain where, in the company of his grandfather, King Ferdinand II of Aragon (called Ferdinand the Catholic), he could admire and enjoy the new gardens that had been laid out in Valencia and Seville.[8] Surprisingly, however, it was not Ferdinand but his older brother Charles, who knew little about the country, that became King of Spain. Ferdinand was entrusted with the government of the Austrian hereditary lands. Having relocated to central Europe, he wanted to continue eating Mediterranean fruit, so he had new gardens laid out in all of his residences, most notably in Vienna, Prague, and Linz.[9] Gardeners from all over Europe, above all from Italy and Spain, were brought in to keep these summer fruit trees alive during the cold winters. Everything we know about these gardens is derived from historical reports that describe, for example, how gardeners learned to construct heatable spaces in which bitter orange and fig trees could withstand the winter chill.[10]

Officials were tasked with buying seeds and plants from all over Europe and sending them back to the imperial court. Grapevines, fig and pomegranate trees, and peach and almond kernels arrived from Trieste, for example, and Ferdinand received seeds from abroad from his relatives at the Spanish court. Today we can at best draw inspiration from the artworks that depict such gardens, such as Pannemaker's tapestries of the Granvelle Gardens (cat. 26).[11] Ferdinand particularly loved eating fresh fruit and was not prepared to forego this pleasure even while travelling. He even had particular types of sour cherries and melons sent to him from Prague. Walking around the gardens every morning and evening gave him the contemplation and relaxation he needed in order to cope with the daily strains of government.

It was also Ferdinand I who brought the famous doctor and botanist Pietro Andrea Mattioli to his court in Prague.[12] Mattioli's studies found their way into

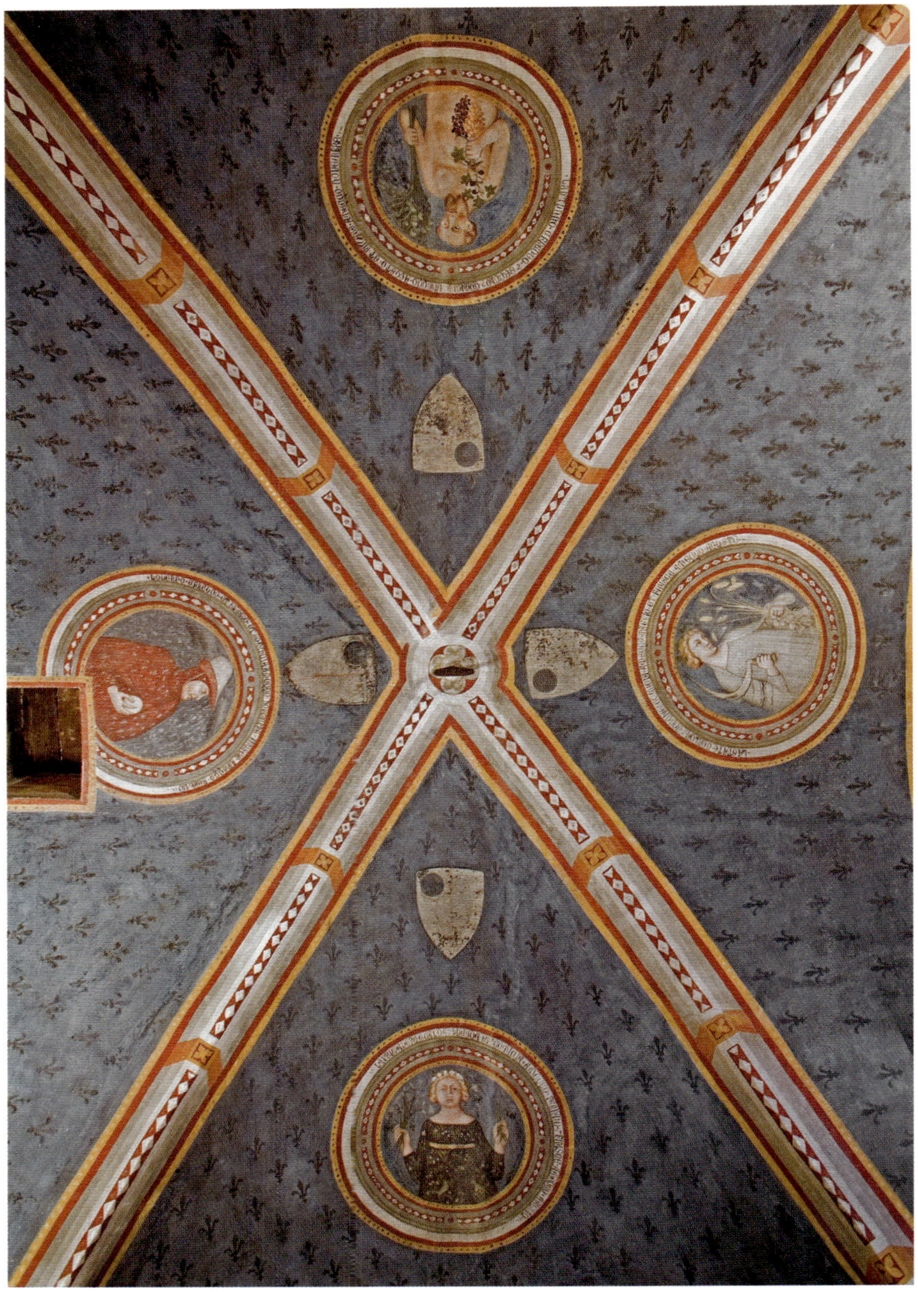

numerous illustrated publications, including the lavishly illustrated *De Materia Medica* (cat. 20) by Dioscorides; his commentary was among the best-known publications of its kind and appeared in several international editions. Ferdinand's ambassador at the court of Suleiman the Magnificent, Ogier Ghiselin de Busbecq, travelled to Asia Minor on the emperor's behalf. Busbecq was always on the lookout for new plants, which were captured in drawings by the artist Melchior Lorck. In this way, Busbecq brought tulips to Vienna and successfully planted lilac.[13] He also identified a famous late antique manuscript by

Fig. 3
Cristoforo di Bindoccio and Meo di Pero, ceiling fresco of the Sala delle Stagioni, Asciano (Siena), Museo Civico Archeologico e d'Arte Sacra – Palazzo Corboli

Dioscorides in 1569 and recommended that the emperor acquire this work for his collection.[14]

Emperor Ferdinand I's sons, Maximilian and Ferdinand, inherited their father's passion for art and the natural world. Even as children, they had been encouraged to work in the court gardens in Innsbruck, equipped with the appropriate tools.[15] Following his return from Spain, where he had been impressed by Mediterranean garden design, Maximilian had a new garden complex laid out in Hirschbrunn. A *Lusthaus* (summer house) was built in the Prater and a *Fasangarten* (pheasantry) was founded on land leading towards Ebersdorf, where the castle-like palace was reconstructed under his direction between 1558 and 1562. A menagerie had already been installed in the gardens at Ebersdorf; this was also where the elephant that had been brought to Vienna in 1552 was kept.[16]

After Ferdinand died, Maximilian II sought to realize his visionary ambitions; these included the creation of a *palazzo di natura*, as Johann Jakob Fugger described it. Following the devastating defeat by the Turks in 1566, Maximilian increasingly devoted himself to the pleasures of art and nature, gathering together distinguished humanists and scientists, including Crato, Clusius, Dondaeus, Fabrizius, and even Lipsius, to assist him in these pursuits.[17] Maximilian's aim was to build a grand, spacious *villa suburbana* that would be based on the Italian model and include extensive gardens.[18] The project probably began by laying out very ambitious *Lustgärten* (pleasure gardens), which were exceptionally large by contemporary Austrian Habsburg standards. These gardens were surrounded by walls and corner towers and given structure by arcaded courtyards. Numerous fountains, some of which may have been based on designs by Arcimboldo – such as the drawing of a fountain (fig. 4) that has been recognized as a work of Arcimboldo by myself – served as decorative elements in the gardens.[19] Later, what had previously been a kind of gallery building was developed into the impressive Neugebäude Palace; its overall concept and architectural forms were modelled on villas designed by Raphael and Giulio Romano, which were in turn based on ancient models.[20]

The growing importance of nature and the pursuit of increasingly intensive scientific studies can be traced through the three generations of Habsburg rulers for whom Arcimboldo worked – first at the imperial court in Vienna, then in Prague. To put it simply, Ferdinand I's primary interest was plants: he placed great emphasis on their medicinal properties, as well as on the nutritional value of fruit and vegetables. Maximilian, on the other hand, became increasingly interested in studying animals, with a particular focus on rare species from the New World. In this respect, he competed with other European princes, especially his Spanish relatives.[21] Maximilian and, above all, his younger brother, Ferdinand II of Tyrol, was also fascinated by the diversity of marine creatures; this led to the creation of some outstanding artistic depictions, among others by the miniaturist Giorgio Liberale da Udine, who had previously worked for Mattioli in Gorizia and followed him to Prague.[22] Rudolf II went one step further with his scientific interests and, aided by astronomers such as Tycho Brahe and Johannes Kepler, explored the depths of the universe. Their spectacular achievements included discovering new stars and recalculating the orbits of planets around the sun.[23] Rudolf also surpassed his predecessors with his insatiable passion for collecting high-quality and famous artworks, as well as with his patronage of first-rate artists. Newly acquired knowledge about nature, mythology, philosophy, and the natural sciences was brought together and magnificently reflected in their works.

Returning to the subject of Arcimboldo's *Four Seasons*, it is interesting to note that, according to Neefe, Emperor Ferdinand was already drawing attention to the dichotomy that surprises viewers when they first encounter one of Arcimboldo's composite heads: from a distance, the image resembles a monster, but closer inspection reveals a wealth of individual details.[24] This successive effect is, of course, largely lost when the image is viewed as a photographic reproduction on the internet.

The underlying artistic principle of the composite head was by no means new, and early examples of such depictions were doubtless already familiar to those in learned circles. This compositional method is found in various geographical regions and historical periods, ranging from ancient art to Persian miniatures, from India under the Mughal Empire to Japan under Utagawa and his successors. Deconstructing the human face and replacing facial features with other objects was also a literary device; it was employed in the Old Testament, for example in the *Song of Songs* (*Canticum Canticorum*), as well as in ancient poetry.[25] In Arcimboldo's time – the sixteenth century – this device was very popular in Lombardy, as reflected in the burlesque poetry of writers influenced by Francesco Berni.[26] The creation of such 'monsters' was based on different premises and motivations, depending on the cultural context. But even if all of these works employ similar principles of accumulation, one should not make the mistake of attributing the same meaning to them.[27]

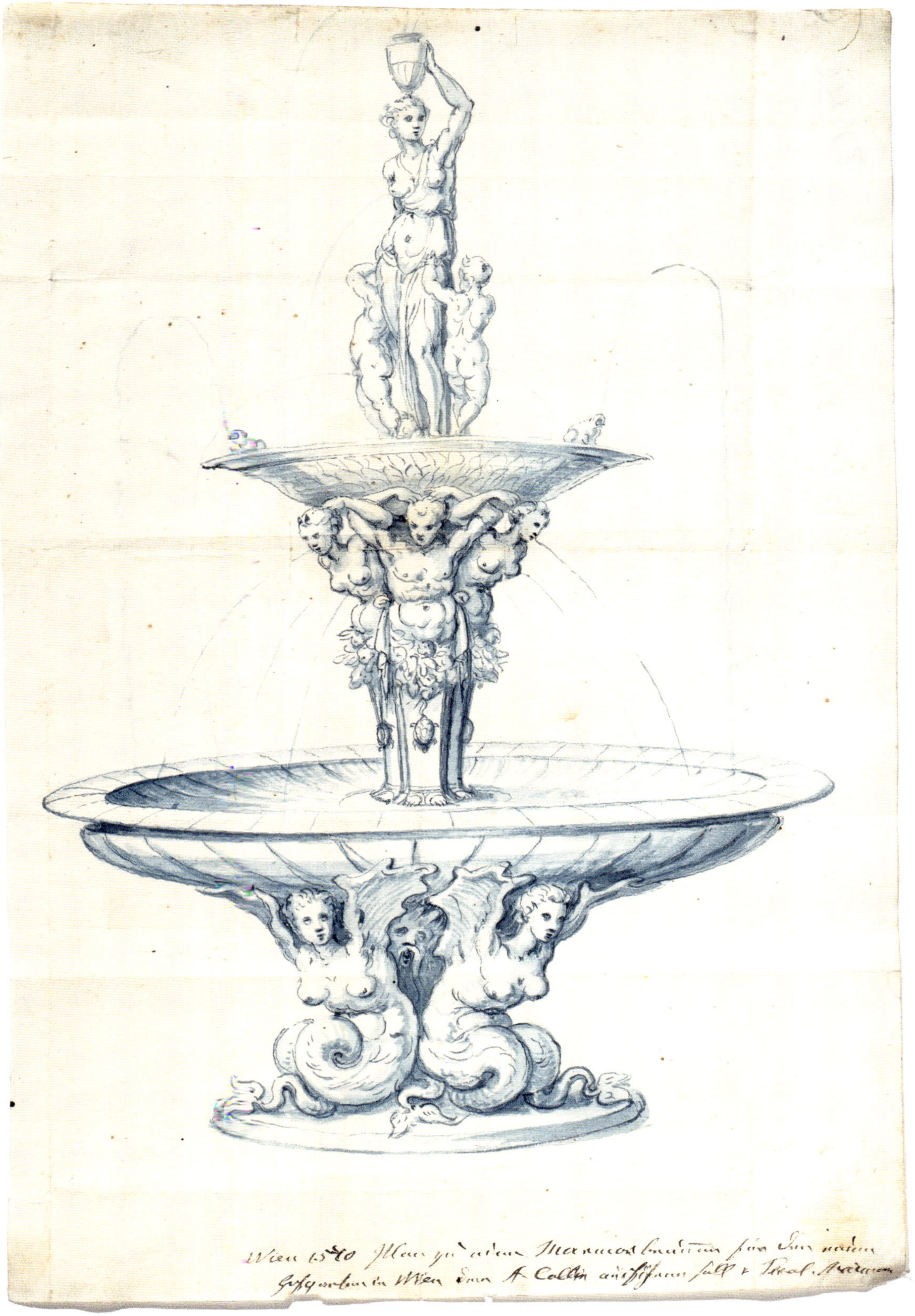

Fig. 4

Giuseppe Arcimboldo, *Design for a Fountain*. Innsbruck, Tiroler Landesmuseen, Ferdinandeum, Grafische Sammlung, inv. DM/ 62

When the Dadaists and Surrealists rediscovered Arcimboldo in the 1930s, they regarded him as a forerunner of their own art. In an excursus in the first modern monograph on Arcimboldo, the renowned Expressionist painter Oskar Kokoschka describes him as the 'patriarch of Surrealism' and suggests that Arcimboldo's portraits 'consist of a confusion of things' that could have been brought together by a 'meaningless coincidence'.[28] This is, however, precisely where Arcimboldo's art differs from that of the Surrealists. Arcimboldo very deliberately selected objects in order to convey the specific meaning of each composite head. He thus created specific levels of meaning for the individual heads – not only in his series of *Seasons* and *Elements*, but also in his other works – that were based on the detailed and accurate observation of nature, but were sometimes also densely allegorical and consolidated by ancient ideas.

By comparing the images in the different series of paintings – considering, for example, the Munich depiction of *Summer* (cat. 28.2) – in relation to the Viennese *Summer* (cat. 29.1), it is possible to trace the increasing integration of individual components into an anthropomorphic whole; this is less successful in the Munich series than it is in the Viennese works.[29] The engravings of *Spring* and *Summer*, or *Autumn* and *Winter* – which show portrait busts facing each other in profile – were reprinted in several editions until around 1700, always with slight modifications (cat. 27).[30] These engravings may predate the rather rigid, less fluid compilations of individual objects into anthropomorphic faces in the Munich series and could reflect an early form of the development that was later also sought after in Italy, independent of Arcimboldo's series that mainly circulated at courts outside Italy.[31]

It therefore seems quite likely that the Milanese historian Morigia was referring to this early form of '*bizzarie*', as reflected in the Munich series, which carried Arcimboldo's fame to Vienna and may also explain why he was invited to the Viennese court, where he arrived in autumn 1562 at the age of 36.[32] Here, he continued to develop the seasonal images, adding references to the Habsburgs as rulers and to himself as the executor of the works through his signature and the year, which are skilfully woven into the straw cloak worn by the figure of *Summer*.[33]

Arcimboldo also took pleasure in depicting *Winter* as an ancient, gnarled tree trunk with lips formed by a tree fungus and hair made of tangled, ivy-covered branches, while two citrus fruits dangle from a twig that protrudes from the figure's chest. It is not until the Viennese version (cat. 29.2) that we find – woven into the straw cloak – fire irons, symbolizing the chivalric Order of the Golden Fleece that was under Habsburg leadership. The large 'M' that is partially visible on the back of the cloak also alludes to Maximilian II, in whose tomb a cloak with a similar woven 'M' was found.[34]

After Emperor Ferdinand's death, Arcimboldo created a series of depictions of the *Four Elements* (cat. 30). According to ancient writers, the elements with their characteristic properties on the one hand constituted the seasons,[35] and on the other they represented human dispositions. In his series of works on this theme, Arcimboldo strengthened the iconographic link to the House of Habsburg by increasing the number of visual references to the imperial dynasty.[36] This is exemplified by the Viennese version of *Fire*, which consists not of natural objects but of man-made, fire-generating instruments such as fire irons and the chain of the Order of the Golden Fleece, along with the ram's fur and the double-headed eagle. The depiction of the element *Earth* (fig. 5) consists of a large number of intertwined mammals that Arcimboldo had for the most part studied at first hand, such as the wild boar, moose, red deer, fallow deer, and blackbuck (figs. 6a–f).[37] Here, too, however, several details make unambiguous reference to the House of Habsburg, such as the crown-forming antlers, the lion skin of Hercules, and the ram's fur that symbolizes the Order of the Golden Fleece.

Arcimboldo presented the *Seasons* and *Elements* to mark the beginning of the new year in 1569, together with a poem by the humanist Giovanni Battista Fonteo (or Fontana), who may have accompanied him back to the imperial court when he returned from his stay in Milan in 1566/67. In the poem, the seasons and elements are interpreted as fundamental components of the course of the world that determines the micro- and macrocosm, and as a metaphor for the good government of the Habsburg dynasty.[38] Since antiquity, the seasons have been associated with good government in mosaics and frescoes.[39]

The fact that these composite heads date from the period when Arcimboldo was already in Vienna led to the development of a theory that they could only have been created at the imperial court, in the circle of elite European intellectuals who gathered there. The sole purpose of these images would accordingly have been panegyric: a perfect visualization of Habsburg imperial iconography.[40] Researchers into Lombard art in sixteenth-century Italy, on the other hand, had for a long time regarded Arcimboldo's pictorial inventions as typical products of the fertile soil of Lombard art that had been enriched by Leonardo's

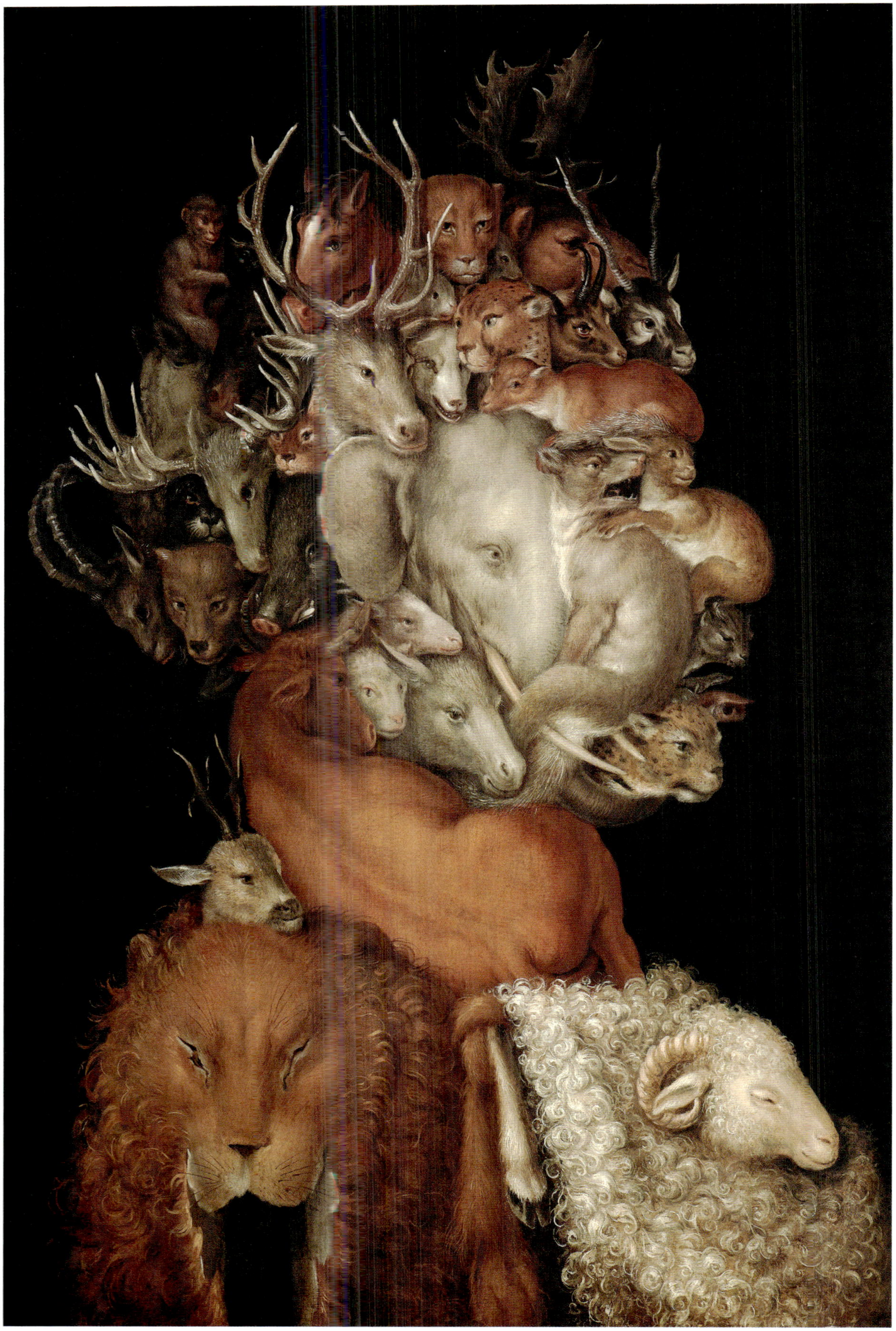

Fig. 5

Giuseppe Arcimboldo, Earth, c.1566. Liechtenstein, The Princely Collections, Vaduz – Vienna, inv. GE 2508

Figs. 6a–f

Giuseppe Arcimboldo, *Nature Studies*, 16th cent. Selected folios: *Red Deer and Chamois*, fol. 20r (top left); *Chamois and Ibex*, fol. 22r (top centre); *Sketches of Antlers*, fol. 11r (top right); *Wild Boar* (detail), fol. 6r (bottom left); *Blackbuck* (detail), fol. 21r (bottom centre); *Moose and Plants* (detail), fol. 8r (bottom right). Vienna, Austrian National Library, Department of Manuscripts and Rare Books, Cod. min. 42

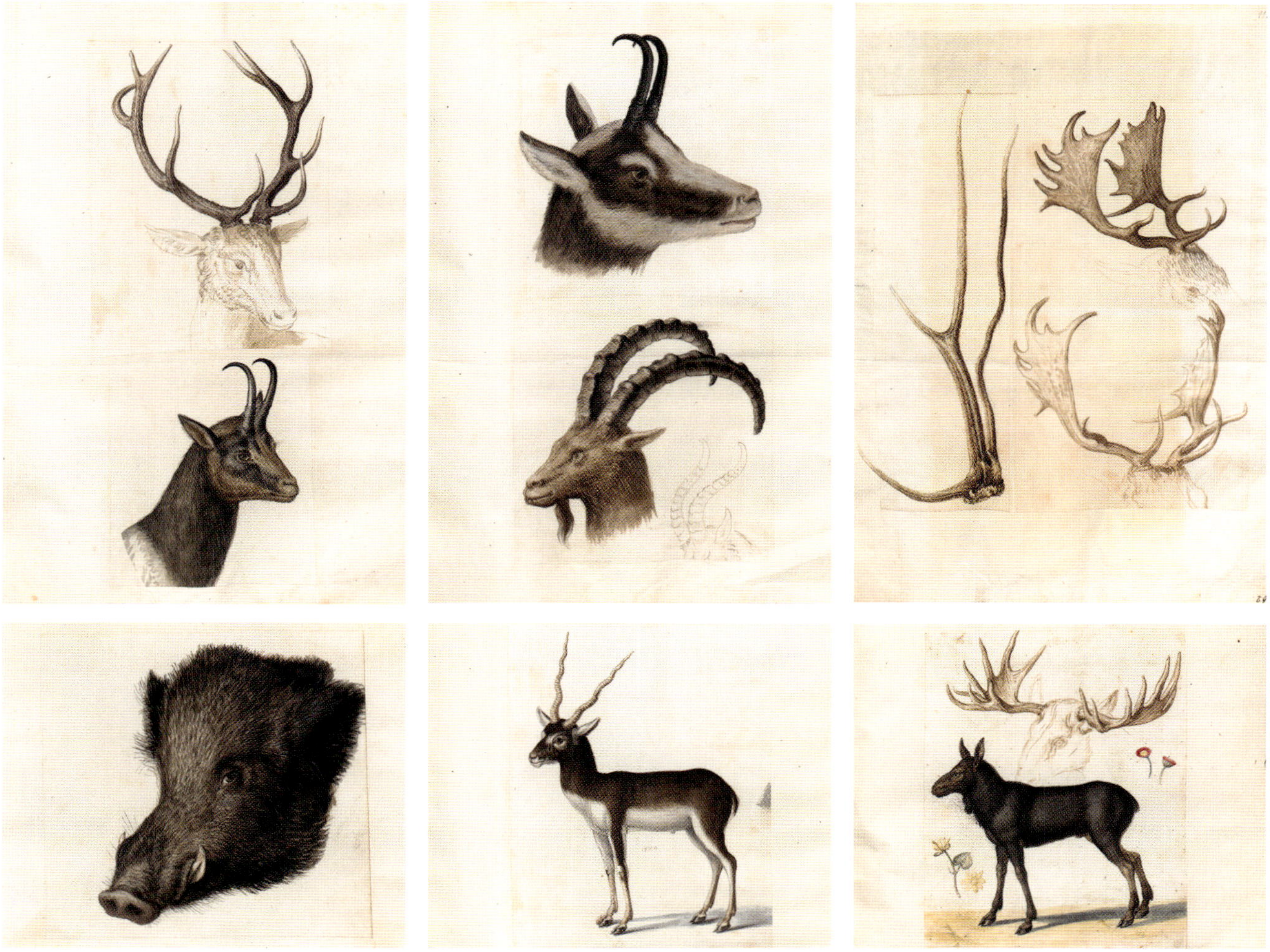

extended stay in the region.[41] With its incredibly rich culture, which always integrated northern influences into both its visual art and its literature, Lombardy was predestined to be open to new ideas and practices. By that time, the city of Milan had already become the place where the finest luxury goods were produced for the various courts of Europe; these included magnificently decorated rock crystal vessels (cat. 49), lapis lazuli works, objects made of other precious materials that attested to the highest level of goldsmithing expertise, bronzes, armour, and much more besides.[42] This extensive mutual exchange between north and south is also the reason why the taste for so-called 'low-genre' imagery developed earlier in Lombardy than in other Italian centres. Scenes from everyday life began to appear in paintings – perhaps initially as *pitture ridicole* (comic depictions), but certainly to the great delight of artists and their patrons, who mainly belonged to the humanistically educated elite. The influence of the burlesque tradition in the realm of literature, examples of which range from Francesco Berni to the Accademia dei Facchini della Val di Blenio, as well as in art, from Leonardo's *teste caricate* to illustrations of edible headdresses worn during carnival celebrations and burlesque jokes in genre scenes, has been a topic of discussion in art historical literature since the late 1970s.[43]

But to return to Ferdinand I's *Tafel-Reden*: one of the subjects that was discussed around the emperor's table was the significance of the sense of sight – the eye – whereby Ferdinand implicitly gave precedence to images over texts. He dismissed his physician Alessandrini's observation that philosophers deprived themselves of sight in order to be able to meditate more intensely, branding them 'fools'. The ability of the eye to see both in the distance and close up was another subject of intense debate and is relevant in the context of the dichotomous view of Arcimboldo's inventions.[44] In this circle of carefully selected guests, who were mainly doctors and humanists, *objets d'art* and items from *Wunderkammern* (cabinets of curiosities) were also presented and discussed; these included 'monsters' of nature and artworks made of particular natural materials; while they cannot be elucidated here, they make it easier to understand how Arcimboldo's reputation became established at the Viennese court. As the emperor was already in fragile health – he died a few months after these entries were made – he had probably instructed his son Maximilian, then king of Bohemia, to invite Arcimboldo and look after him, as is substantiated by the surviving documents.[45] Maximilian's foreseeable succession as emperor may have led Arcimboldo to integrate a greater number of panegyric references to the House of Habsburg into his composite heads.

In this specific context, however, it should also be considered whether it must have been the famous Viennese series of *Seasons* – of which now only *Summer* and *Winter* survive – that hung on the walls. Every guest, above all Dr Neefe, would surely have recognised the name of the artist and the date, at least in the depiction of *Summer*, and noted these in his diary. Is it not possible, or indeed more likely, that this was the series that had been in Munich from 1598 onwards, which had been created without any visual references to the imperial dynasty while Arcimboldo was still in Milan, and which the artist had brought with him or even sent ahead?[46] Maximilian would then have commissioned another set of *Seasons* for himself, perhaps also in relation to the *Elements*. Both series would subsequently have been dedicated to the emperor by the artist and the humanist Giovanni Battista Fonteo, and presented to him along with the panegyric poem on New Year's Day 1569.

This is the only way in which the theory put forward by Kaufmann and defended since 1978 – that the heads were created mainly to serve a panegyric purpose – could be at least partly saved; based on the elucidations in the *Tafel-Reden*, Rudolf maintains, Kaufmann's theory is no longer tenable.[47]

Arcimboldo's homage to Emperor Rudolf II as *Vertumnus* (cat. 33), in which everything is simultaneously blossoming and bearing fruit, symbolizes the return of a golden age as a result of the emperor's good government.[48] In the accompanying booklet, which contains numerous poetic texts related to the work, two of these texts bear the initials G.A.; this is generally understood to be Arcimboldo's signature. His humorous self-portrait as a 'paper head' thus raises the question: do the rolls of blank paper allude to his intellectual capacities as a poet, author, or even philosopher, or was he inviting the writers of Milan to fill these blank pages with descriptions of his fame?[49] A *scherzo* entitled 'delle Quattro Stagioni dell'anno', which Arcimboldo gifted to Gregorio Comanini, is described in detail and with gratitude by the latter in his treatise *Il Figino* (cat. 90):[50]

> Have Comanini show you Arcimboldo's playful treatment of the Four Seasons; you will see a lovely work. A knotty tree trunk forms the chest and the head in which certain cavities serve as mouth and eyes and a protruding knob as the nose. Knots covered with moss form the beard, and some branches in front form the horns. This stump, stripped of its own leaves and fruit, represents Winter, which produces nothing but enjoys what is produced by other seasons. Some flowers placed on the breast and over the shoulder signify Spring. Summer is represented by bundles of wheat and a few attached twigs, a straw cloak that covers the shoulders, two cherries hanging from a branch that forms the ear, and two plums arranged behind the head. Autumn is represented by two bunches of grapes, one white and one red, hanging from a branch, and by some apples showing among green ivy branches that spring from the top of the head. One of the branches of the head has been peeled slightly from around the middle, and the little scraps of bark curl back from the white part which is inscribed ARCIMBOLDUS P. All in all, the work will please you wonderfully when you see it.[51]

A stark contrast can be seen, however, between Arcimboldo's image of *Four Seasons in One Head* and the monstrous figure of *Vertumnus* he dedicated to Rudolf, which is characterized by its all-encompassing energy and fertility. The season of winter provides the main structure for the depiction of *Four Seasons in One Head*, but to whose winter does it refer? The winter of Comanini, the recipient of the gift, or that of Arcimboldo, who was a quarter of a century older? Does this unification of the four seasons in a single image perhaps constitute a kind of summary of all of Arcimboldo's previous naturalistic and artistic experiences, a quintessence of the pursuits to which he devoted his life? Did he not dedicate himself to the micro- and macrocosm, transforming his precise nature studies into a highly individual world view? Was the artist, as he approached the end of his life – the winter of his days – brooding melancholically over his bygone *stagioni*? In this work, the signature ARCIMBOLDUS P. is scratched into the substance of a branch. Even if one is not convinced by the association with Michelangelo's curious signature in the *Last Judgement*, where the artist has tattooed his face on to the skin of St Bartholomew, one can still appreciate this melancholically jocular self-reference.[52]

1 Paruzzo 2021, 79–94, 80.
2 Boschung 2013, 179–200.
3 Rigon Forte 2021, 138ff., figs. 15 a, b, 16, 17, 18, 19.
4 Rigon Forte 2021, 220, figs. 31 a, b.
5 Paruzzo 2021, 80–1; Rigon Forte 2021, 255, fig. 37.
6 It would be taking it too far, of course, to view Lomazzo's mention of the *teste composte* in his *Trattato della pittura* from 1584 in the context of mercurial places – i.e. taverns – as possible illustrations of the seasons on the four walls of such an establishment. See, most recently, Ferino-Pagden in exh. cat. Rome 2017/18, 22.
7 Rudolf 2015, 133–65.
8 Santamaria and Salvador Palomo 1996, 141.
9 Lietzmann 2003, 259–63; Lietzmann 2007, 37–65; Schütz 2007/08, 73–9.
10 Lietzmann 2007, 56–8 describes the many attempts that were made to keep citrus trees alive during the winter. Heating rooms for this purpose even led to a fire breaking out in the castle in 1567.
11 Lietzmann 2003, 258, 378, cat. IV.26.
12 Schütz 2007/08, 75; Olmi and Tongiorgi Tomasi 2011, 115, 118, and cats. 158, 183, 184.
13 Schütz 2007/08, 76; Busbecq 1554–1562 (2005).
14 Österreichische Nationalbibliothek, Cod. med. gr. 1.
15 Lietzmann 2003, 262.
16 Lietzmann 1987, 30–3.
17 Schütz 2007/08, 75–7.
18 Lietzmann 1987, 36–7.; Schütz 2007/08, 77–8.
19 Ferino-Pagden 2011, 198–201, fig. 10.
20 The mediating role played by Jacopo Strada, who worked as an antiquarian and an architect, cannot be discussed in greater detail here. See, most recently, Jansen 2019, 430–519, and Hassmann 2024, 37, 44, 67, 83, 96.
21 Staudinger in exh. cat. Paris and Vienna 2007/08, 160, fol. 28r: Aplomadofalke (Aplomado falcon), 163, IV 24, fol. 28; Kaufmann 2009, 129, 270, note 62.
22 Staudinger in exh. cat. Paris and Vienna 2007/08, 156–7, cat. IV. 23; exh. cat. Milan 2011, 115.
23 Rainer 2015, 79–105. See also DaCosta Kaufmann 1993, 137–50.
24 Rudolf 2015, 133–65.
25 Porzio 2011, 230, esp. 230 and 252, note 4.
26 Porzio 2011, 221–53.
27 Beyer 2017, [140]–5.
28 In Geiger 1960. This excursus is not included in the Italian edition that was published in 1954, *I dipinti ghiribizzosi di Giuseppe Arcimboldi, pittore illusionista del Cinquecento* (1527–1593), Florence 1954.
29 Porzio 2011, 221–30.
30 Porzio 2011, 228, 230.
31 Further versions have most recently been reproduced in exh. cat. Rome 2017/18, 44–5, cats. I. 28, 29, 147, cats. V. 4, 5.
32 Morigia 1592, 566.
33 Perhaps in reference to the painter Zeuxis, who is mentioned by Pliny the Elder. Zeuxis demonstrated his wealth by having his name woven into his outer garments in golden letters. See Wied in exh. cat. Paris and Vienna 2007/08, 127–8, cat. IV. 3. One might be tempted to consider this a frivolous *scherzo* by Arcimboldo, an allusion to more generous patrons of the past, if we were not all so conditioned by the constant demand to see only 'serious' – in other words, elevated – 'jokes' in his depictions. Most recently, DaCosta Kaufmann 2018, 368–75; DaCosta Kaufmann 1990, 59–80.
34 DaCosta Kaufmann 1993, 123–4. Winter marked the beginning of the new year in ancient Rome, and we also know that Maximilian once took part in a pageant wearing a 'winter' costume. At this point, it is important to remember that almost all of the other series refer back to either the Viennese *Seasons* or the set (now held in Paris, Louvre) that was painted for the Saxon Elector, with the result that the straw cloak of *Winter* contains either the fire irons or the crossed swords, but not just simple triangles, as in Munich.
35 See essay Gabriele, p. 19.
36 Wied in exh. cat. Paris and Vienna 2007/08, 148, cat. IV.18.
37 Ferino-Pagden in exh. cat. Paris and Vienna 2007/08, 103–111, above all fig. 3.
38 DaCosta Kaufmann 1978; DaCosta Kaufmann 2009, 50ff.
39 On antiquity, see Rigon Forte 2021, 53–4, figs. 4a, 4b and pl. I. On Lorenzetti's frescoes on the theme of *Buono Governo* (Good Government) in Siena's Palazzo Publico, see, most recently, Paruzzo 2021.
40 DaCosta Kaufmann 1978; DaCosta Kaufmann 2009, 50ff.
41 Porzio 1979; Porzio 1987; Porzio 1993 (1994), 2/4, 37–42; Porzio in exh. cat. Lugano 1998; Porzio in exh. cat. Milan 2011, 221–53.
42 Distelberger 2002; Ferino-Pagden 2015, 39–76.
43 Porzio 1979, Porzio 1987; Porzio and Kahn Rossi 1998; most recently, Porzio in exh. cat. Milan 2011, 230–1.
44 Rudolf 2015, 141.
45 Schütz in exh. cat. Paris and Vienna 2007/08, 81–4.
46 As Porzio has already proposed, the series that was documented in Munich in 1598, of which only *Autumn* survives in a rudimentary state, could have entered the Munich collection on the occasion of the marriage between Maria Anna, daughter of Albrecht V (a keen patron of the arts), and Maximilian's son Charles in 1571.
47 Rudolf 2015, 155, note 4, rejects DaCosta Kaufmann's theory on the grounds that the *Seasons* were already hanging in Ferdinand's *camera* in 1564.
48 Berra 1988, 11–39.
49 Most recently, Beyer 2012, 287–9.
50 Ferino-Pagden in exh. cat. Paris and Vienna 2007/08, 144–6, cat. IV.15. Comanini 1591 (1962), vol. 3, 268ff. The 1656 inventory of the extensive and famous collection of Giovan Pietro Cortoni in Verona lists the painting 'Le quattro Stagioni che formano una testa', whose dimensions compare to this work. From this one may conclude that it was created after Arcimboldo's return to Italy and was still recorded there in the seventeenth century.
51 Comanini 2001, 27–8.
52 Parts of this essay were published in 2023 in the journal *Finestre sull'Arte* V, 17, in an article titled 'Giuseppe Arcimboldo e l'imperatore Ferdinando I'.

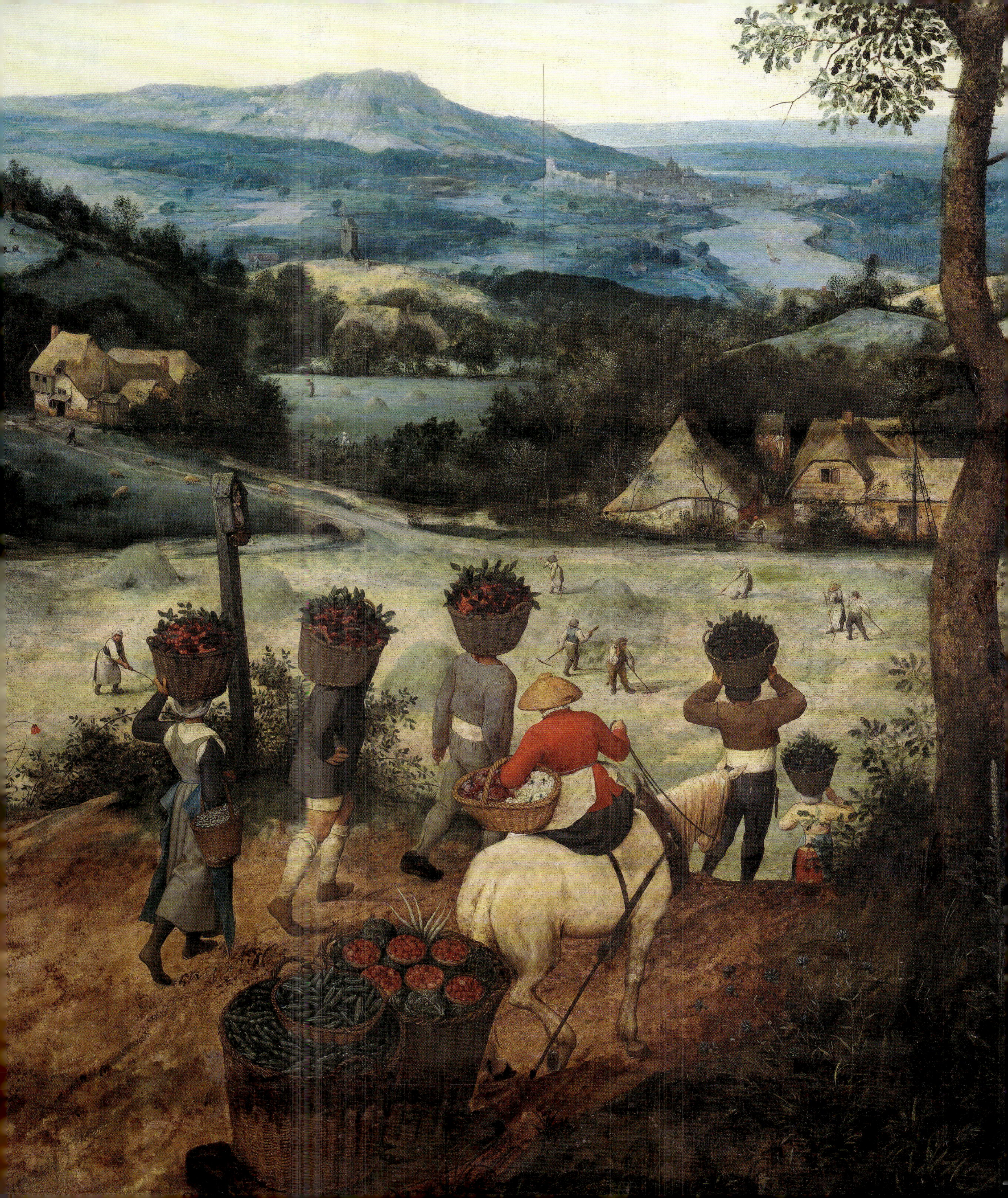

SABINE PÉNOT

The Cycle of the *Seasons* by Pieter Bruegel

A Milestone in the Development of European Landscape Painting

> According to reports, when the painter Eupompus was asked who he took as models, he pointed at a group of people and said it was nature itself that one should imitate and not an artist. This was also true for our Breugel, whose works I speak of not as works of art, but much more as works of nature. And I do not call him the best painter, but truly the nature of painters.
>
> Abraham Ortelius, *Album amicorum*

The *Cycle of the Seasons* (cat. 15) is the only verified series of paintings by Pieter Breugel the Elder. It is the high point of his oeuvre and also a milestone in the development of European landscape painting. Since the beginning of the twentieth century, the paintings have been traditionally known as *The Gloomy Day* (early spring; the painting of spring is lost), *Haymaking* (early summer; fig. 1), *The Harvesters* (late summer; fig. 2), *The Return of the Herd* (autumn), and *Hunters in the Snow* (winter). The division of the year into six pictures – which seems odd from today's point of view – was a common way of breaking up the annual cycle in the Netherlands since, at the time, early spring and spring were distinguished from one another, as were early summer and high summer.

Breugel's seasons were painted in 1565[1] when the painter (then probably almost 40 years old, in any case over 35)[2] was already established in Brussels. The monumental series of pictures represents the culmination of Breugel's career as a landscape painter. The genre had always been considered one of his primary focuses, first as draughtsman during his travels in Italy, later as a painter. According to Karel van Mander, it was, above all, the drawings that Bruegel made during his trip to Italy (1552–54) and the prints which followed that were decisive for his accurate depiction of nature. The critic describes those depictions in glowing terms: 'He drew many vedute from nature during his journeys, so that it was said that when he was in the Alps, he swallowed all the rocks and

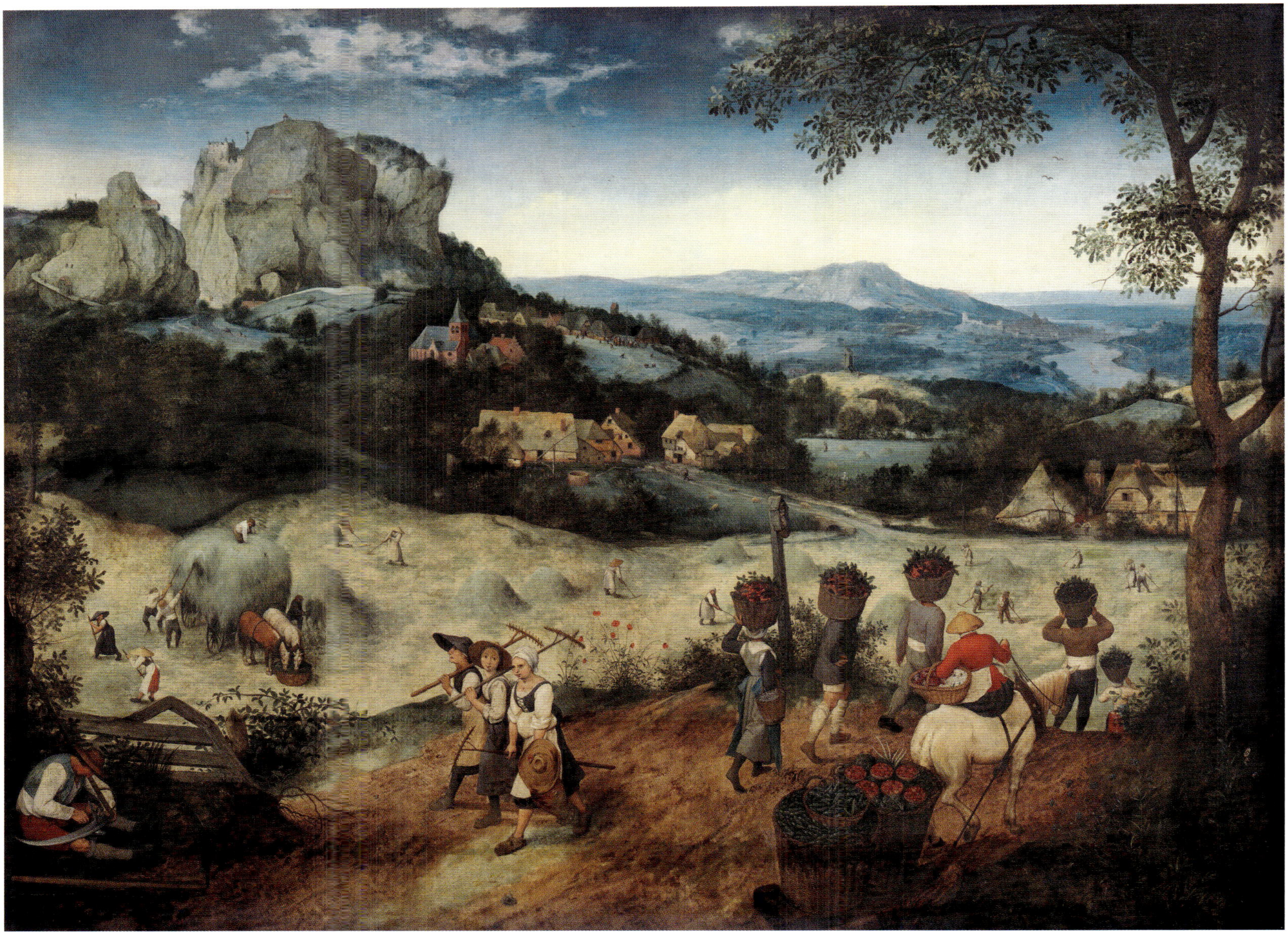

Fig. 1
Pieter Bruegel the Elder, *Haymaking*, 1565. Prague, Palais Lobkowicz, Prague Castle

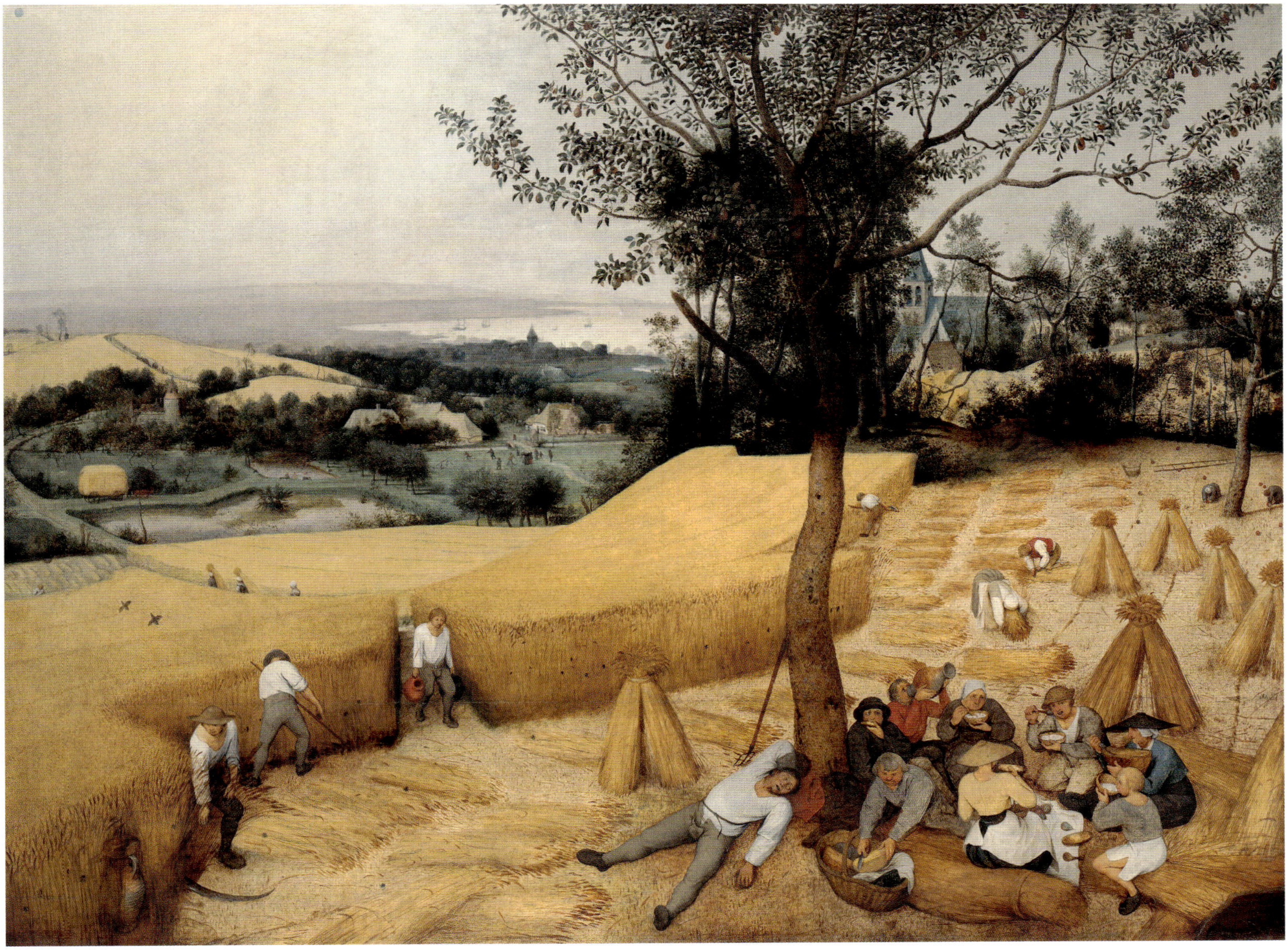

Fig. 2
Pieter Bruegel the Elder, *The Harvesters*, 1565. New York, The Metropolitan Museum of Art, inv. 19.164; Rogers Fund, 1919

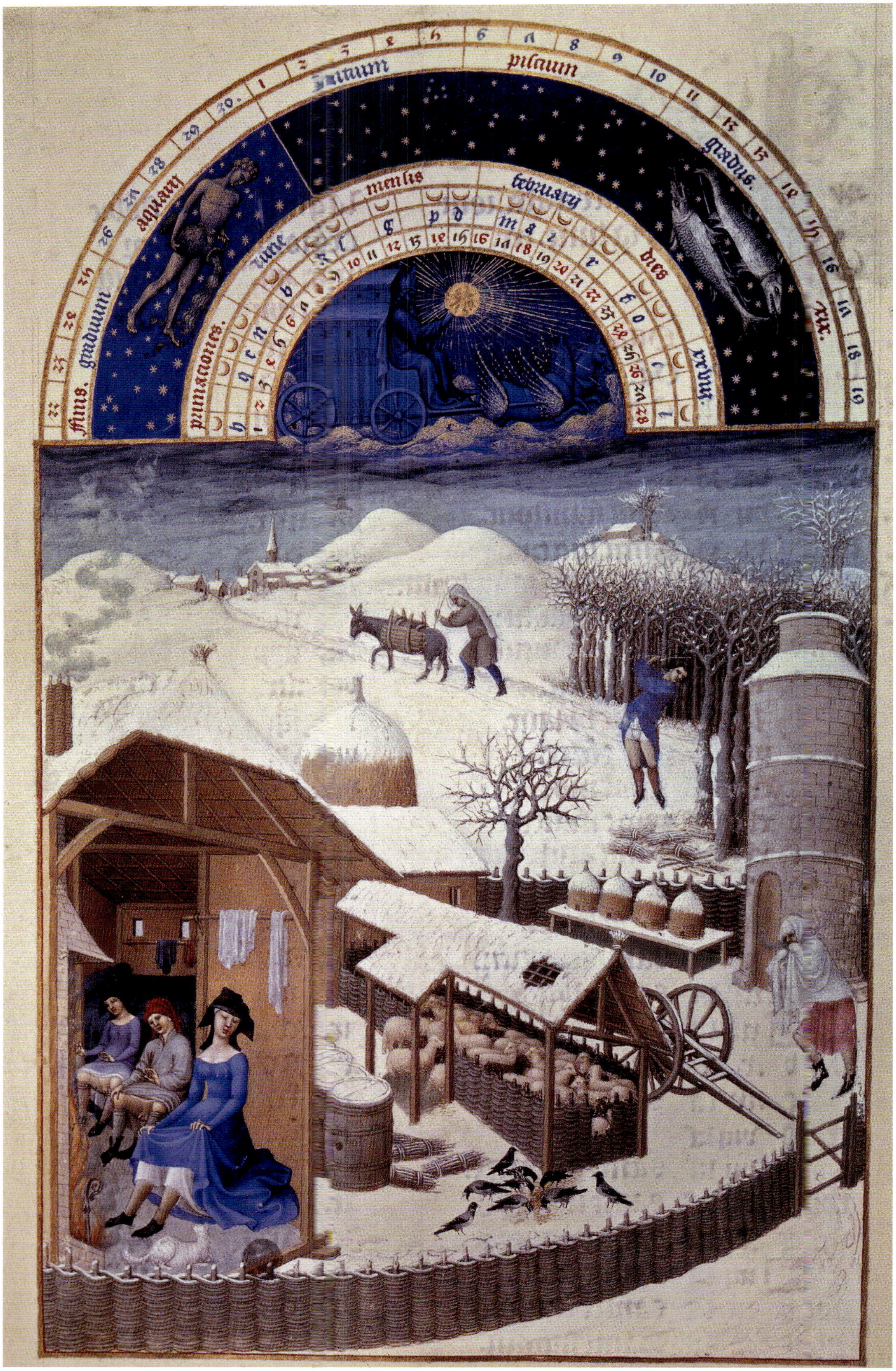

Fig. 3

Winter, from: Limbourg brothers, *Très Riches Heures du Duc de Berry,* c.1416. Chantilly, fonds principal, 0065 (1284), fol. 2v

Fig. 4

December, from: Simon Bening (workshop), *Calendar Cycles,* 15th cent. Munich, Bayerische Staatsbibliothek, Clm 23637, fol. 6v

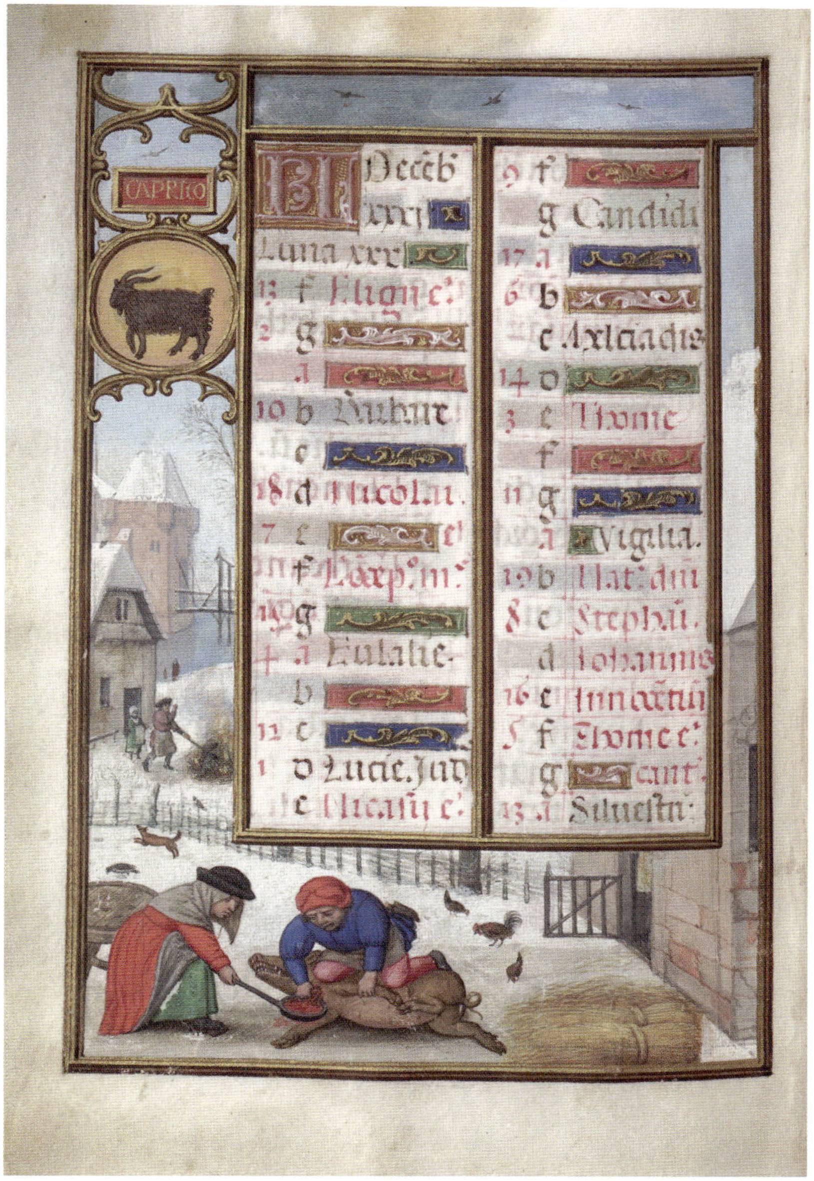

mountains and disgorged them again on to canvases and painting boards when he was home again, so close was he able to come to nature in this and other respects.'[3] The humanist and cartographer Abraham Ortelius, a friend of Breugel's, also gave the highest praise to these depictions of nature. In his *Album amicorum* he pays tribute to the artist in a two-page entry: 'No one who is not led astray by envy, rivalry, or ignorance will deny that the painter Pieter Breugel was the best of his time. But he was taken from us in the full blossom of his years. Should this be attributed to Death, who might have decided that he had [already] done enough given the mastery of his art? Or should nature be blamed, which feared it would be despised because he had imitated it so artfully and ingeniously?' Referring to a passage in *Naturalis Historia* by the Roman author Pliny the Elder (XXXIV, 19), Ortelius also elevates Breugel's art to the rank of a second nature (see the quotation at the beginning of this essay).

In his *Seasons* cycle, Breugel gives nature a then-unprecedented importance. Here, the months are depicted for the first time in large-format paintings. The series testifies to the general secularisation of landscape painting and can be seen as a milestone in secularising depictions of the seasons. Reproducing the typical ambience of nature is sufficient, in and of itself, to characterise each season. A harmony of distinctive colours, alternating from deep brown to green, yellow, golden ochre, and – apparently – white characterises the sequence of typical seasonal weather. *Hunters in the Snow*, the earliest example of a large-format winter landscape in Western painting, has even become *the* winter picture par excellence.

Breugel's sequence represents the pinnacle of a tradition of artistic exploration of the cyclical course of the year that extends back to antiquity, but there are no direct precursors to his cycle of seasons. Breugel took his inspiration for his series mainly from Netherlandish miniature painting of the fifteenth and the first half of the sixteenth centuries, and especially from calendar illustrations in books of hours. The Limbourg brothers, Simon Bening, and Gerard Horenbout are among the most important artists to mention here. If one considers, in particular, the development of winter landscapes before Breugel's groundbreaking imagery, a few works stand out. The earliest winter landscape enlivened by human figures is the month of January (see essay Del Torre Scheuch, p. 57, fig. 6) from the fresco cycle of the twelve months of the year in the Torre Aquila of the Castello del Buonconsiglio in Trento. Shortly afterwards, north of the Alps, *Très Riches Heures* (fig. 3) was created for the Duc de Berry by the Limbourg brothers; for the first time, labours of the months were integrated into naturalistically depicted landscapes. The full-page miniatures in this masterpiece of book illumination also break with the medieval tradition of restricting calendar illuminations to the margins of books of hours and prayer books. The calendar cycles of Simon Bening's workshop in Bruges date from about a century later (fig. 4). They continue this tradition of full-page landscape miniatures, their iconography being particularly revealing with regard to Bruegel's choice of motifs.[4] The activities depicted as the main themes in these paintings of months tend to appear as secondary scenes in Bruegel's cycle of seasons. The artist, who was trained as a miniaturist by his mother-in-law Mayken Verhulst, was a friend of the most famous miniaturist of his time, Giulio Clovio. The extent to which Bruegel's cycle either fits into an existing tradition or strikes out on a path of its own is shown by Buchanan's comparative study of 1990 and others. In any case, Bruegel's seasons go far beyond the Netherlandish tradition of calendar illustration.

Just as miniatures inspired Bruegel on a small scale, his conception of landscape was also shaped by large-format cartoon designs for tapestries and tapestry series. His *Seasons* cycle was made in Brussels, then the most important centre of tapestry art, whose key players moved in the same circles as Bruegel. The preparatory cartoons for the *Hunts of Maximilian*, created in Bernard van Orley's studio, were just as famous as the Raphael cartoons that were the basis for the tapestries woven in the Brussels workshop of Pieter van Aelst (also known as Pierre d'Enghien) between 1516 and 1521. But even if most of the motifs in the *Seasons* cycle can be traced back to miniature painting, landscape painting, and tapestries, nevertheless the spirit of Breugel's cycle fundamentally differed from them all.

'We find at the basis of grotesque imagery a special concept of the body as a whole and of the limits of this whole.'[5]

The depiction of the animals in Bruegel's *Seasons* cycle is a great deal more nuanced than that of the humans, who very rarely possess any personal characteristics (it is often just a matter of differentiating features that indicate a different status, as in the case of the rider in *The Return of the Herd*). The differentiation of classes is one of the aspects that later play an important role in Jacopo Bassano's seasonal paintings. In Bruegel's winter landscape (cat. 15.3), the differences between various kinds of dogs are depicted in great detail[6] (see also the technical infrared image, which provides evidence of the creative process). In contrast, the hunters are only seen from behind in silhouette. In addition, in some compositions animals make eye contact with the viewer (cows in *The Return of the Herd* and dogs in *Hunters in the Snow*, for example), while the people often remain 'faceless'. Some of the farm workers even blend into the natural scenery itself (the shepherds in *The Return of the Herd*) or with the fruits of their labour, where they play an essential role in the rhythm of the sequence of images.

The pictorial phenomenon of the reification of humans in the seasonal cycle appears particularly interesting in the context of Arcimboldo's *Four Seasons* (cats. 28, 29, 90). In Breugel's *Haymaking*, for example, the female figure going to market in the foreground with her back to the viewer is clearly balancing a full basket on her head; the baskets of the other bearers gradually block their heads, in such a way that 'basket heads' lead the way into the valley. In *The Harvesters*, Bruegel breaks down the individual activities of the summer harvest into small snapshots, which together visualize for the viewer the steps involved: scything, raking, drying the grain, bundling the sheaves, setting up and carrying the corn dolls. Here too, the line between human and object gradually blurs. Bent over the sheaves of grain, the workers, their silhouettes reduced to geometric shapes, almost look like bundles themselves; loaded up to their heads with sheaves, they seem to sink into the gaps between the rows of corn.

Bakhtin identifies fluid transitions and the associated fusion with nature among other things as a characteristic of grotesque bodies: 'The grotesque body, as we have often stressed, is a body in the act of becoming. It is never finished, never completed; it is continually built, created, and builds and creates another body. Moreover, the body swallows the world and is itself swallowed by the world.'[7] Breugel's drawing of the so-called *Beekeepers* (mid-sixteenth century; fig. 5) and Pieter van Heyden's engraving after Breugel, *The Battle of the Moneybags and the Strongboxes* (after 1570), are exemplary of this spirit in which the active human is equated with the attributes of his activity.

If one looks for a possible common source of this reification, one thinks of inspirations from Italy, Leonardo da Vinci's grotesque heads, Carnival culture, and the ingenious thought experiments at the court in Milan.[8]

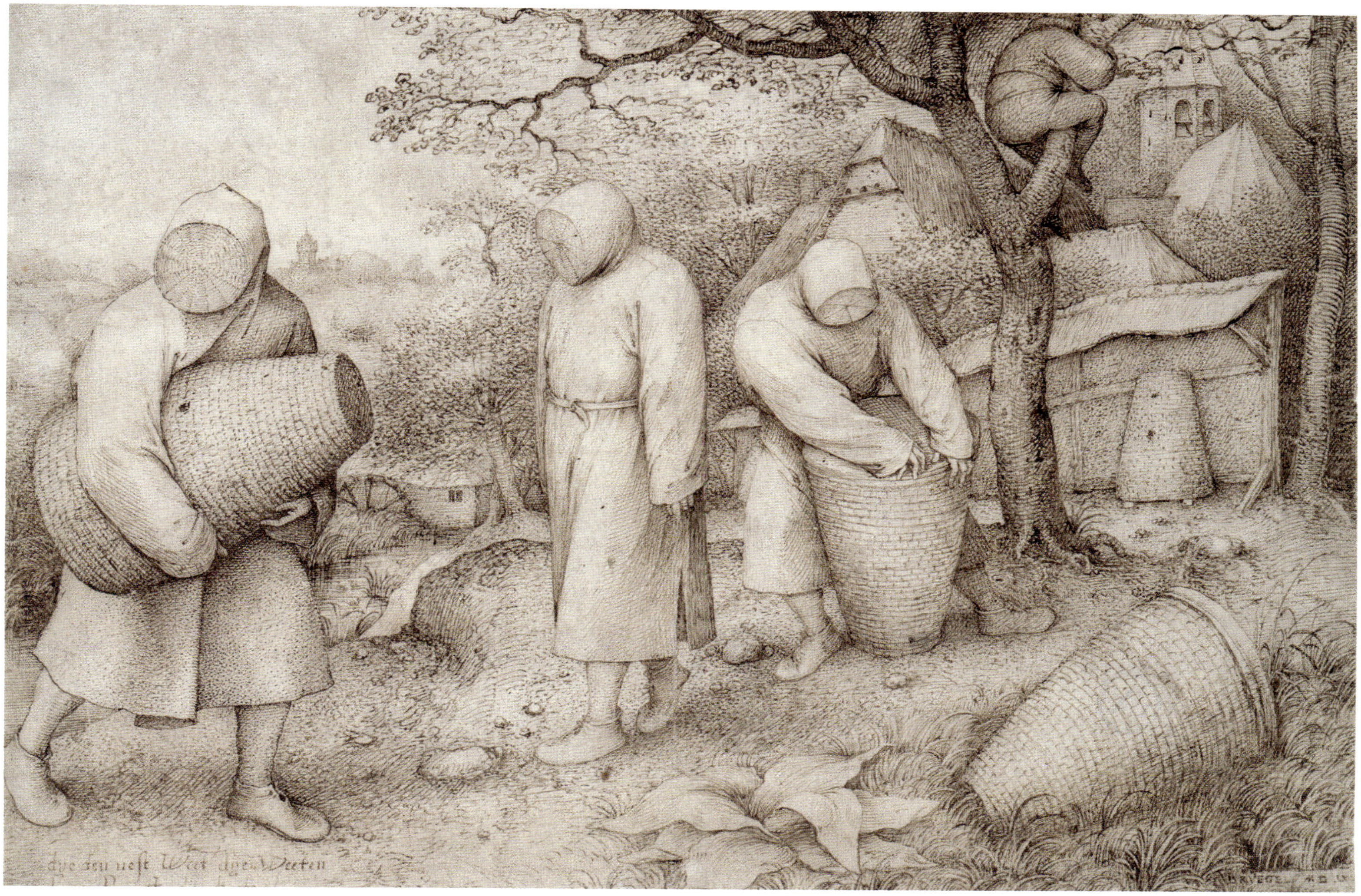

Fig. 5
Pieter Bruegel the Elder, *The Beekeepers,* 2nd third 16th cent. Staatliche Museen zu Berlin, Kupferstichkabinett, inv. KdZ 713

The *Seasons* cycle as conversation piece

Pieter Breugel designed the *Seasons* series for the country house 't'goed ter Beke' in present-day Markgravelei near Antwerp, which belonged to businessman and art collector Nicolaes Jongelinck. The cycle of paintings was probably part of the interior decoration of the dining hall. The impression made on Jongelinck's guests upon entering the room must have been overwhelming. A three-dimensional 'world landscape' of unsurpassed size occupying all four walls, a harmony of finely coordinated colours of extraordinary effect, a panoramic landscape painted with a view of nature itself against which Breugel is ultimately measuring himself. This perpetual wall calendar was supplemented by the actual cycle of nature, which could be seen from the windows of the dining room. In addition, the memories of Italy that were part of Bruegel's compositions conjured distant landscapes in the Netherlandish interior, for example, through the depiction of mountains in the midst of local nature.

The cycle's original target audience around Jongelinck consisted of high-ranking, educated, well-to-do individuals who, from the manor's distinguished interior, observed the everyday life of farmers, who in turn looked out from the pictures at the higher classes. The perception of the peasantry in the sixteenth century was habitually characterised by satire, a rather crude attitude that Bruegel does not seem to have shared. Rather, the painter brought to bear a humorous touch, appreciated by the viewers, in the play of the implied exchange of glances between two mutually alien worlds. The messengers of death in the landscape (gallows and torture wheels) and the fusion of mankind with nature seem to allude to the fate of peasants, and humans in general, in those politically turbulent and climatically challenging times and bring to mind more explicit depictions such as Bruegel's *The Big Fish Eat the Little Fish* (1556). The winter of 1564/65 was notoriously horrible and it was followed by a major famine.[9]

Bruegel places his major work in a tradition of artistic engagement with the cyclical course of the year that extends back to antiquity. He consciously confronts the challenge of depicting nature, which ancient authors had deemed to be the highest goal of an artist. In terms of composition and painterly technique, Bruegel establishes a position by building on the landscape tradition – a particularly rich one in the Netherlands – and then surpassing it. The agricultural activities he shows are integrated into naturalistically depicted panoramic landscapes whose tradition goes back to Patinir. However, these are not topographically accurate landscapes, but compositions created in the studio; in these 'mixed' landscapes, memories of the Alps are combined with typically Flemish motifs. The viewer's approach to the various scenes in the cycle is staged in a similar fashion. In each painting, from a slightly elevated position the view opens out on to a wide, panoramic landscape. Typical Bruegel repoussoir figures (humans and animals) and elements (trees), intensify the spatial depth of the compositions. The viewer's involvement contributes significantly to the direct effect of the panel paintings.

The coexistence of periods of work and rest, or often pastimes depicted small-scale, runs through the cycle under the conditions set by nature. Parallel to the narrative thread carried out by the main figures, Bruegel stages a wealth of outdoor activities on a micro-scale, testifying to the diversity of life in all its ups and downs, joys and sorrows. What is interesting is the perception on different levels, or the non-perception of threats and suffering. The details can only be perceived by taking one's time, ideally when viewed alongside and in dialogue with others.

In addition to the most important feature of man's rivalry with nature itself, Bruegel demonstrates in his animated landscapes how painting – in the sense of 'Paragone' – competes with poetry and offers an almost unlimited *varietas*, while at the same time adding humorous notes and using the rhythm of the scenes as a resource – all marks of quality in landscape painting (which Pliny the Elder had described in his *Naturalis Historia,* XXXV: Colours, Painting, Sculpture), and a welcome opportunity to incorporate witty allusions based on them, which gave pleasure to his circle of clients. Bruegel thinks and acts as a painter in a humanistic environment.[10] His virtuoso masterpiece of landscape art perfectly fulfils the expectations of a humanist audience interested in understanding the world on both a large and small scale as well as the laws of nature. It does so by depicting a wide range of natural phenomena that testify not only to great powers of observation, but also to a precise knowledge of visual perception and art theory, which were then being debated in the circles around Ortelius. But it is above all the work of a superb painter who demonstrates his skill and inventiveness – in the sense of *aemulatio* (emulation). Bruegel's landscape art was disseminated extensively in both northern and southern Europe, especially through prints, while the paintings of the *Seasons* cycle, of which there are no copies, were initially only accessible to a limited group in Nicolaes Jongelinck's circle. The most important landscape cycle in the history of Western art was only on display in Jongelinck's house for a short time. Buchanan's assumption that it was presented there in combination with a series of statues of the planets as part of a larger programme is appealing, as these would place the cycle of seasons in the tradition of antique country house decorations, which were strongly influential in the Netherlandish sixteenth century, as they are also reconstructed in the exhibition. 'In the sixteenth century, a significant segment of urban social life shifted to the *villa suburbana* and *villa rustica*. Here, city dwellers could freely converse, garden, walk, hunt, fish, play *kaats* (a special type of rounders), and enjoy themselves. The *hof van plaisantie* thus formed an island of urban culture, scholarship and sophistication in the countryside.'[11] Illustrations of sixteenth-century interiors, although they cannot be regarded in the same way as photographs, demonstrate a design that included paintings and sculptures. Perhaps Karel van Mander does not mention the *Seasons* in his *vita* of Bruegel because the cycle was presented together with other works?

Like Arcimboldo's compositions, Brugel's *Seasons* cycle was not primarily created for a courtly setting.[12] The six panels probably remained together at their original location for no more than half a decade. On 1 July 1594, the series was purchased by the city of Antwerp from Hane van Wijk and later bequeathed to Archduke Ernest; the cycle is listed in his estate in 1595.[13] Whether the gift to Archduke Ernst can be interpreted as the cycle of the seasons having a symbolic meaning as an expression of *buon governo* (good government) remains to be seen.

* This text is based on the following publication: Pénot and Oberthaler 2018/19.

1 The panels of *The Gloomy Day*, *The Harvesters*, and *Hunters in the Snow* bear the date 1565. The other panels no longer have a legible date.

2 Pieter Bruegel the Elder's date of birth is not known. It is assumed that he was born around 1526/30.

3 Van Mander 1604, fol. 133r.

4 Borchert 2019.

5 Bachtin 1965, 315.

6 'This shows again that no standard breeds existed in the 16th century. It is a pack of hunting dogs, or rather hounds, which are sometimes so slim that they could also be classified as greyhounds. Colour, coat, and ears are simply not yet defined. Many things occur side by side.' My thanks to Erich Pucher (Natural History Museum Vienna) for his verbal communication.

7 Bachtin 1965, 317.

8 See essay Ferino-Pagden, p. 27

9 See among others De Rock and Limberger 2018, 226.

10 Despite the *Seasons*' obvious painterly virtuosity and groundbreaking artistic invention, the Bruegelian imagery of the series has been interpreted in art historical literature, especially since the end of the 1970s, against the background of humanist discourse. The Christian form of the Stoic view of the world is now generally regarded as the interpretive horizon of the picture cycle. In recent years, valuable information has been produced on Bruegel's humanist environment. Research projects continue to devote themselves to these topics. They enlighten us about the master's background and educational horizon and help us to better understand the socio-cultural context of the creation of the *Seasons*.

11 De Rock and Limberger 2018, 166.

12 In her interpretation, Sylvia Ferino-Pagden points out that Arcimboldo's *Heads* were only ennobled during his time at the Habsburg court; they were not originally created for a courtly setting.

13 In Archduke Leopold Wilhelm's inventory of 1659, the cycle had already been reduced to five paintings.

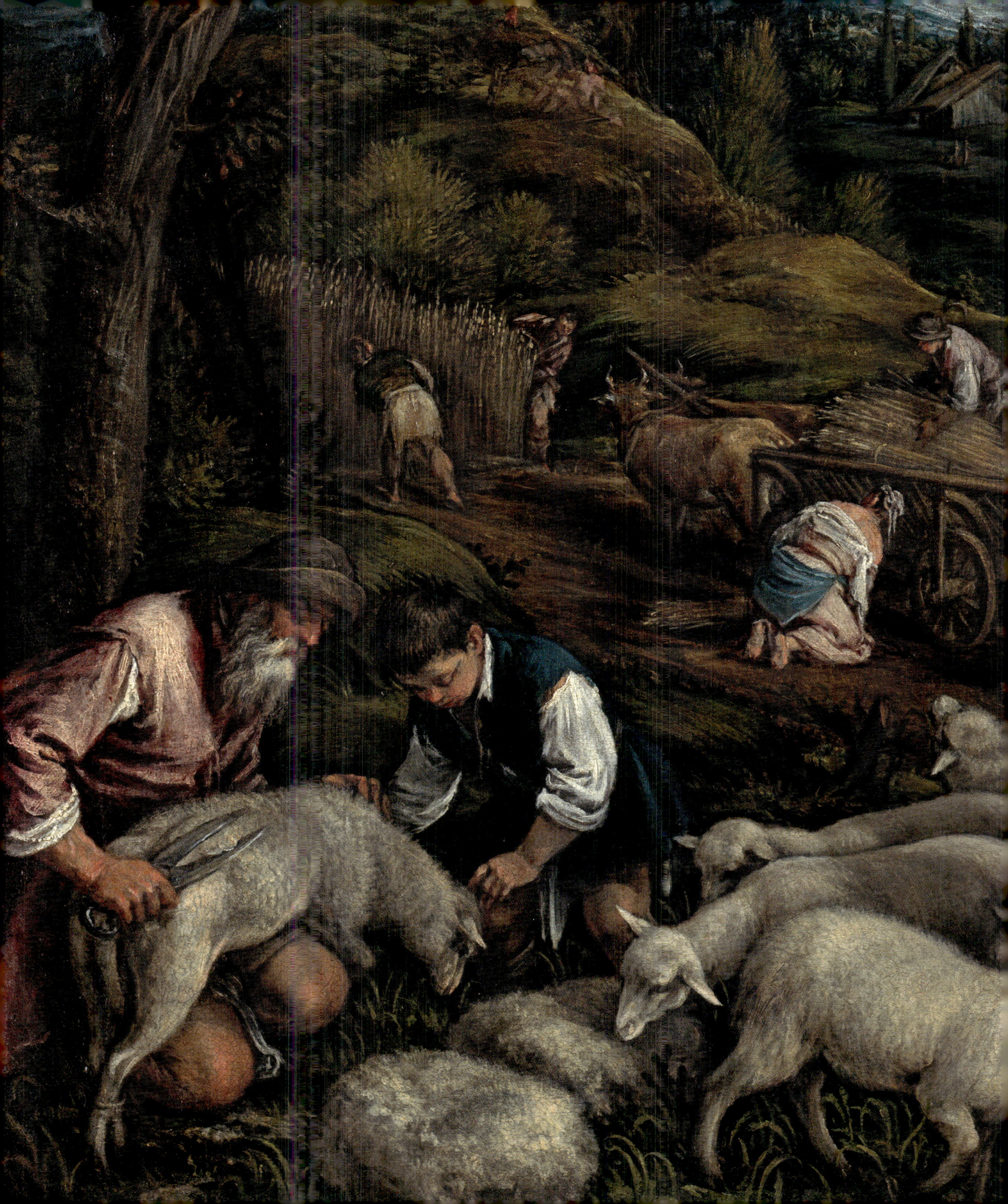

FRANCESCA DEL TORRE SCHEUCH

The Bassanos and the Invention of the Seasons

The Bassanese miraculous at painting pastoral things.[1]
Rocco Benedetti, *Ragguaglio delle Allegrezze*

Around the mid-sixteenth century, Giuseppe Arcimboldo (1526–1593), Pieter Bruegel the Elder (1525/30–1569), and Jacopo Bassano (1510/12–1592), three great artists of different lineage and provenance, staged allegories of the seasons in their paintings. Each of them gave the age-old subject of the relationship between man and nature an entirely personal interpretation that symptomatically reflects the culture of the society to which they belonged. Less well known than the other two painters, Jacopo dal Ponte, called Bassano after his city of origin, must nonetheless be numbered among the great artists of sixteenth-century painting, alongside Titian, Jacopo Tintoretto, and Paolo Veronese. Although he lived a 'secluded' life and worked on the margins of Venice's artistic centre, his paintings show that the capital and its artists were a constant point of reference throughout his career and that he always kept himself updated and informed.[2]

He was born into a family of provincial painters in whose activity he soon became involved. The Dal Ponte family, aided by a tight network of local commissions, met the needs of a clientele requesting not only religious paintings but also less skilled, craft-like works, thus placing themselves in the tradition of the late medieval workshop. Jacopo was first educated in art in Bassano by his father Francesco, who then sent him to Venice in around 1530 to complete his training with the Veronese artist Bonifacio de' Pitati. The latter managed his workshop, one of the most important in Venice after Titian's, in a more open and flexible way than most 'family-run' artistic workshops. Bonifacio had set up his studio in an open structure in which he welcomed passing artists or those still training, mostly from the mainland.[3] The time Jacopo spent in Bonifacio's studio must have been a very profitable arrangement for both and cannot easily be pinpointed to a specific period. In the 1530s, thanks to the flexibility offered by his work with Bonifacio, Jacopo was perhaps fairly mobile between Venice and Bassano,

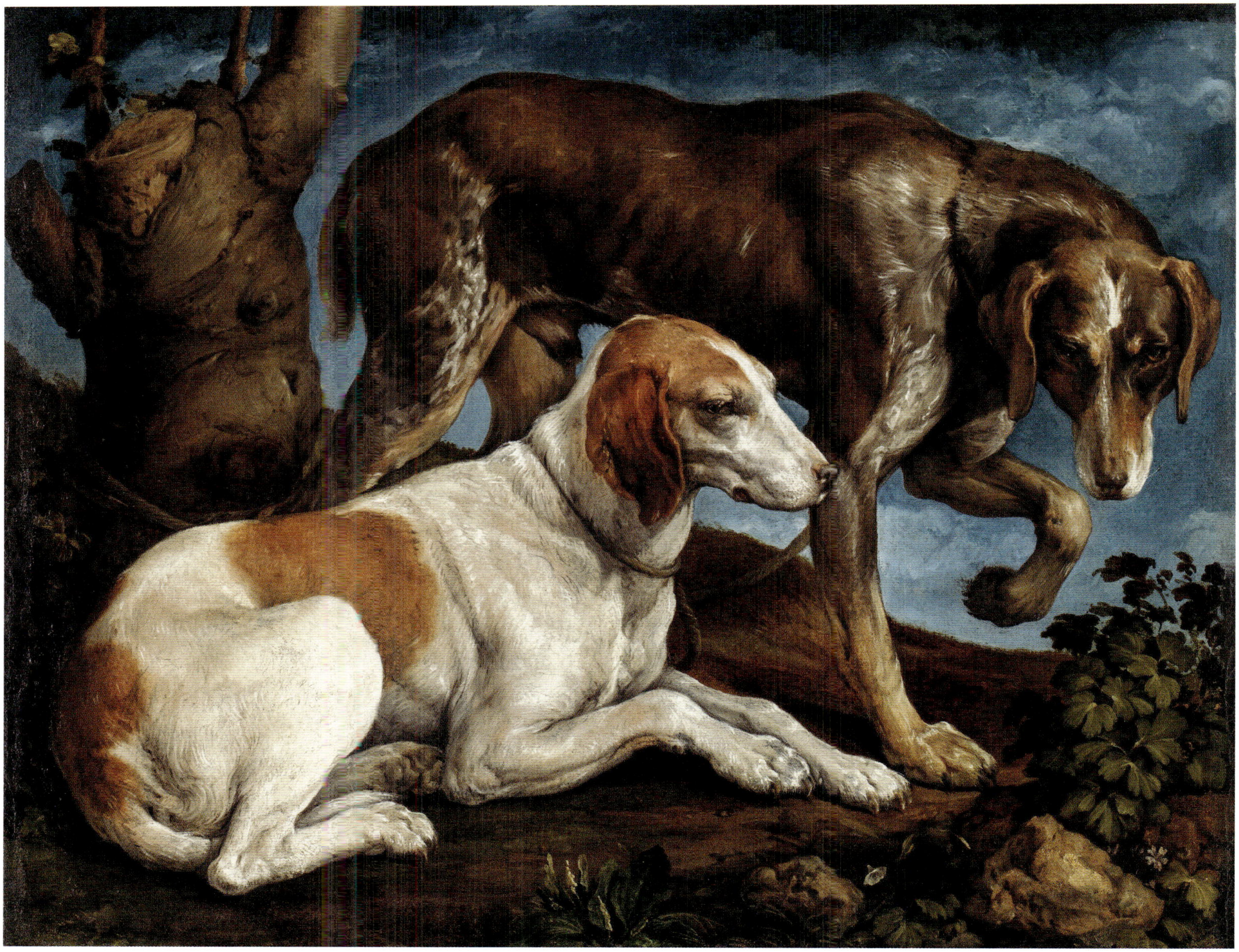

Fig. 1
Jacopo dal Ponte, called Bassano, *Two Hunting Dogs Tied to a Tree Stump*, 1548–50. Paris, Musée du Louvre, Département des peintures, inv. RF 199423

where his father's workshop was particularly active, also in fresco decorations.

Jacopo's association with Bonifacio's workshop was very important to him; by keeping in contact with the Venetian art world he could update his provincial style according to the different trends present in the capital. He was – like Jacopo Tintoretto – an artist of Mannerist training who took an inquisitive and experimental approach to the artistic stimuli of Venice, reformulating them in a completely original manner. Jacopo also kept up to date through constant study of the prints that circulated in Venice; the city was a very lively publishing centre supplying all of Europe, where engravers worked closely with the publishers of illustrated books. He knew, and probably collected, engravings by artists of various schools, such as Albrecht Dürer, Marcantonio Raimondi, Raphael, Titian, Lukas von Leyden, Martin Schongauer and many others.[4] From this very rich stock of images he drew ideas and compositional cues, which he reworked in a confident and original manner. In this way, he discovered the art of Raphael and Francesco Salviati's central Italian Mannerism[5] and later, possibly, Parmigianino, mainly through Andrea Schiavone, who also frequented Bonifacio's workshop.[6] Paying very close attention to Titian, Jacopo's point of reference to the end of his career, he enthusiastically adhered to the 'Michelangelesque' ideas received through Pordenone. References to Lorenzo Lotto and Girolamo Romanino, whose frescoes in Buonconsiglio castle in Trento he probably knew, emerge in his first two decades of activity.

Jacopo's situation as a provincial painter far from the commissioning and market dynamics of the Venetian art world allowed him to adopt ideas of style and subject from outside the lagoon city. This situation was the basis for Jacopo's stylistic and thematic choices and particularly the invention of the 'biblical-pastoral' genre.

The eclectic experimentalism and complex make-up of Jacopo's figurative culture, as mentioned above, are reflected in the different stages that distinguish his artistic output. These elements were identified by seventeenth-century art writers, who saw in their analysis of Jacopo's different manners and stylistic exegesis the key to understanding his personality. Carlo Ridolfi was the first to analyse Bassano's style, identifying its cultural coordinates and describing it in three stages: the first, after Bonifacio, influenced by Titian; the second in which he imitated Parmigianino's drawings; and finally the last manner 'made in strokes and bold patches'.[7] Marco Boschini, a great admirer of Jacopo, described (while using a new critical language) the refinement of his painting technique enlivened by remarkable colouring, elegant highlights and mastery of foreshortening.[8] At the end of the eighteenth century, Giambattista Verci relied on the profound technical knowledge of Giambattista Volpato (available in manuscript)[9] to further specify Jacopo's styles, identifying four in total. Today, five are counted, thanks to Ballarin's studies, which identified the works of Jacopo's very late period when, leaning towards late Titian, light prevails over colour in nocturnal pictures of great dramatic power.[10]

The Bassanos' workshop accounts book (*Libro dei conti*) relating to the period from 1520 to 1550 provides information on local clients and also documents the commissions entrusted to Jacopo by Venetian clients. These were mainly members of the nobility at the start of their career as executives in the Bassano area, who requested portraits, religious paintings, and works for decorating public buildings at affordable prices.[11] At the end of their appointment they often took Jacopo's paintings with them, thus circulating knowledge of his works in the capital. Venetians who owned property in the Bassano area were also particularly important, acting as a bridge for the circulation of Jacopo's paintings in Venice. The case of Antonio Zentani is particularly interesting. In 1548, this nobleman and owner of rural land in the area commissioned *Two Hunting Dogs Tied to a Tree Stump* (fig. 1) from Jacopo, which denotes a capacity for expression and transposition of the immediate and natural reality into a painting of extraordinarily refined design and chromatic splendour.[12]

A profound understanding of nature and its inhabitants is one of the most poignant aspects of Jacopo's personality, which is manifested, in embryo, from his very first works (fig. 2) and emerges even at the time of his closest adherence to extreme Parmigianinesque Mannerism. Such understanding is also documented by the fact that Jacopo cultivated a garden of simples at his home, to which he devoted himself 'for recreation' and which provided models for the plants and flowers he added to his paintings.[13] Although the 1550s were characterized by close and constant study in which Jacopo explored all the possibilities of the Parmigianino-inspired language, culminating in his *Adoration of the Magi* (fig. 3), he never lost his grip on the reality he came from and lived in, which emerges in his focus on nature and its inhabitants – be they peasants or the animals that accompanied them in their daily work. This was the driving force that impelled him to elaborate and surpass the Mannerist phase, resulting in his invention, at the start of the 1560s, of the new biblical-pastoral genre in which the Veneto landscape is the setting for episodes from the Old and New Testaments – a genre that brought him fame and success. His pastorals, attentive to the rural world, attracted the interest of patricians and citizens involved in transforming the Veneto lands. In line with a process under way in northern Italy between the fifteenth and sixteenth centuries, crops were also being intensified and refined in the Veneto countryside to meet the high demographic growth at the turn of the century. The gradual process of Venetian interests and investments moving from maritime trade to the mainland, already begun during the fifteenth century, was also nearing completion. Triggered by the imperious establishment of new Atlantic trade routes, replacing the traditional Mediterranean ones led by Venice, this was reflected in the attention paid to farming and was accompanied, on a cultural level, by the rediscovery of ancient agronomic texts, published in both Latin and vernacular editions. The impulse to structure the knowledge of the ancients and the need to formulate new knowledge and techniques culminated in the publication of a variety of

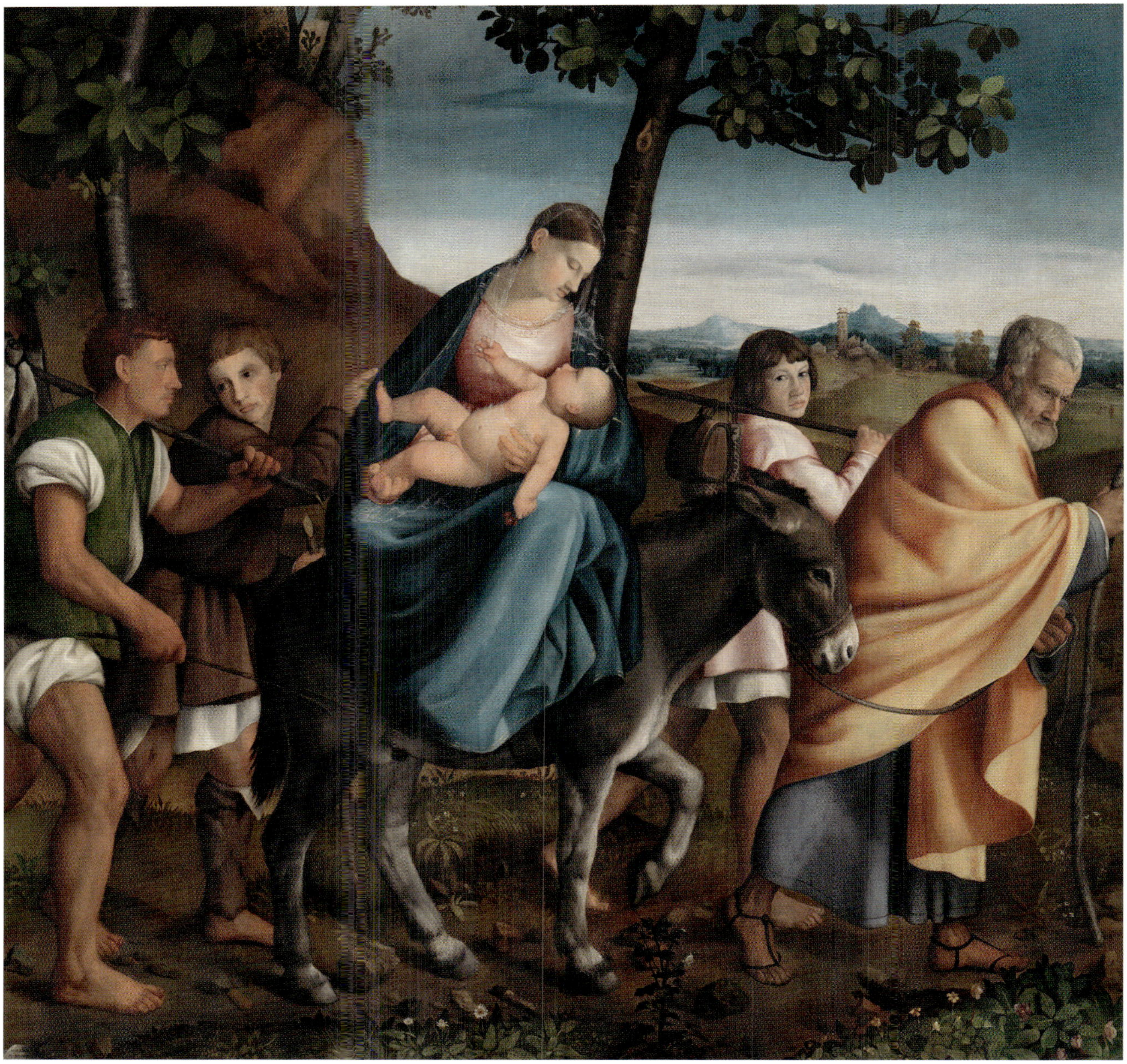

Fig. 2

Jacopo dal Ponte, called Bassano, *The Flight to Egypt*, 1534. Museo Civico Bassano del Grappa, inv. 6

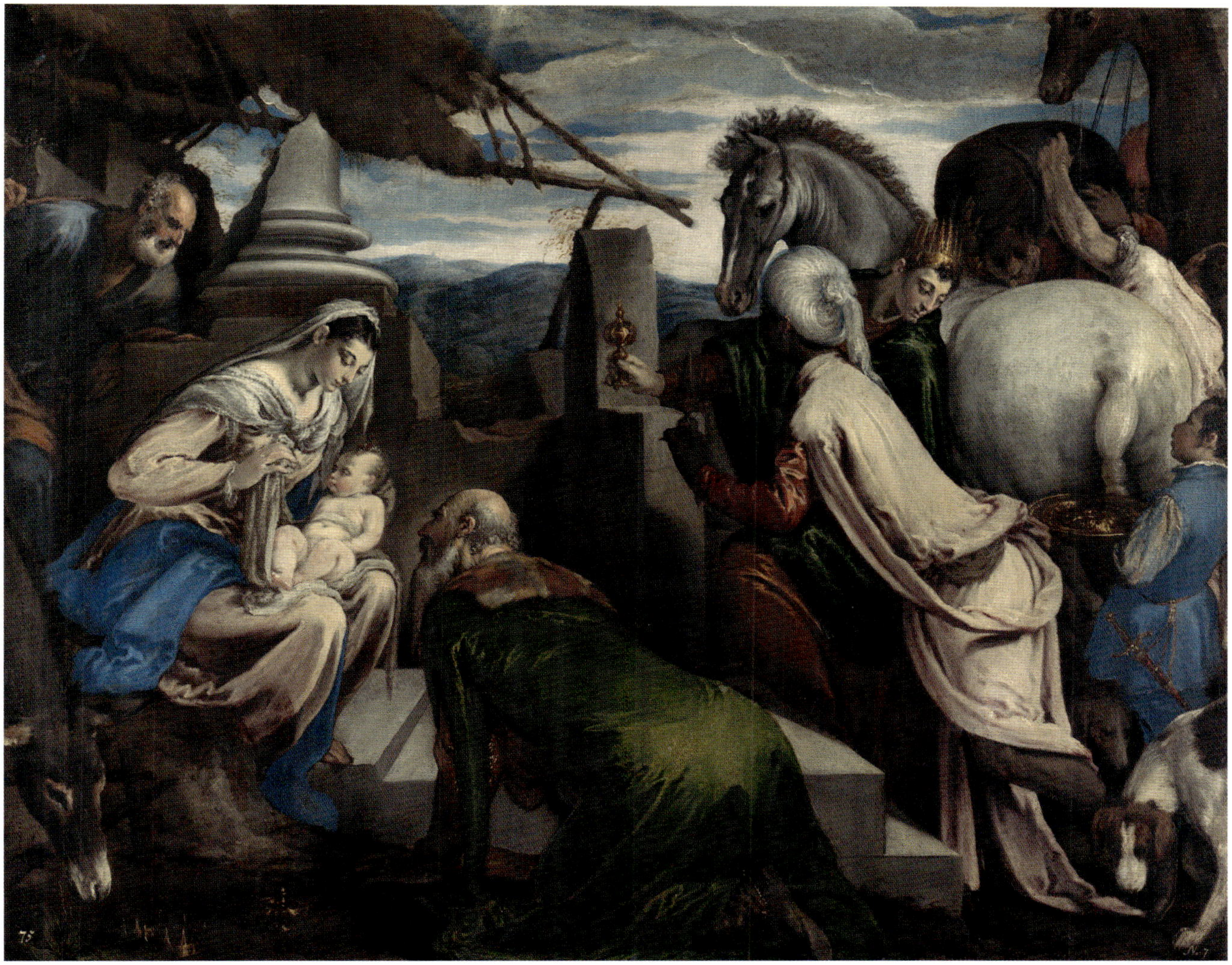

Fig. 3

Jacopo dal Ponte, called Bassano, *Adoration of the Magi*, c.1555. Vienna, Kunsthistorisches Museum, Picture Gallery, inv. 361

agronomic treatises,[14] and in a new approach to scientifically structured botanical knowledge. The development of settlements on the mainland led to the construction of residences on agricultural estates; these perfectly set villas were genuine farm management centres, but also places of intellectual exchange and humanist meditation.[15] The importance of exploiting the land sparked the development of manufacturing, and the transformation and marketing of products, which in turn stimulated strengthening of the road network.[16]

At the end of the 1560s, Jacopo let natural lighting and warm colours flow into his paintings, reconsidering Titian and opening up also to Veronese's innovations. There are numerous masterpieces from these years in which Jacopo relied on the power of a unifying lighting to soften the occasionally dissonant chromatic passages that still reveal their Mannerist origin. Jacopo used refined compositional layouts, marking the space with vivid colours, but infusing it with a completely new naturalness, as shown by *Jacob's Journey* in Hampton Court, an absolute masterpiece of the early 1560s and perhaps his first pastoral painting (fig. 4). By the end of the 1560s, Jacopo's fame as a painter of pastoral subjects had crossed the Italian borders. A list of paintings included in the correspondence of Jacopo Strada concerning antiquities and works of art to be sent to the duke of Bavaria, probably dates from around 1570.[17] Five paintings by 'Jacopo dal Ponte' are named in the list of paintings 'of delightful subjects' representing *Noah's Ark*, *Moses and the Burning Bush*, *Moses Striking the Rock* and two *Nativities*. Ferdinando de' Medici bought a series of four scenes of the *Flood* for Villa Medici in Rome, which are documented in the inventory of 1578, along with other classic Bassanesque subjects that confirm the Medici interest in Venetian painting.[18] The development

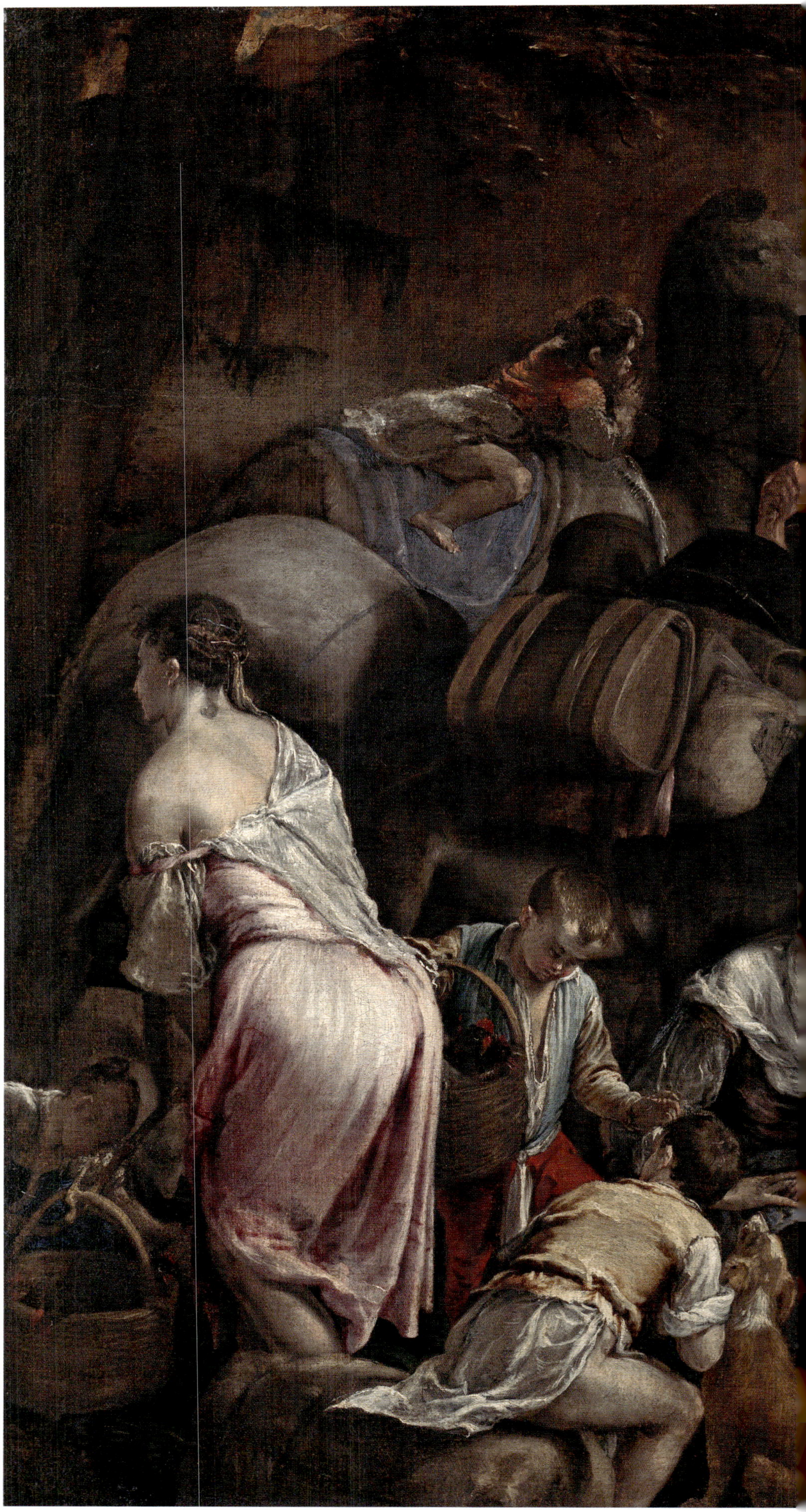

Fig. 4
Jacopo dal Ponte, called Bassano, *Jacob's Journey*, c. 1561. Royal Collection Trust, inv. RCIN 402928

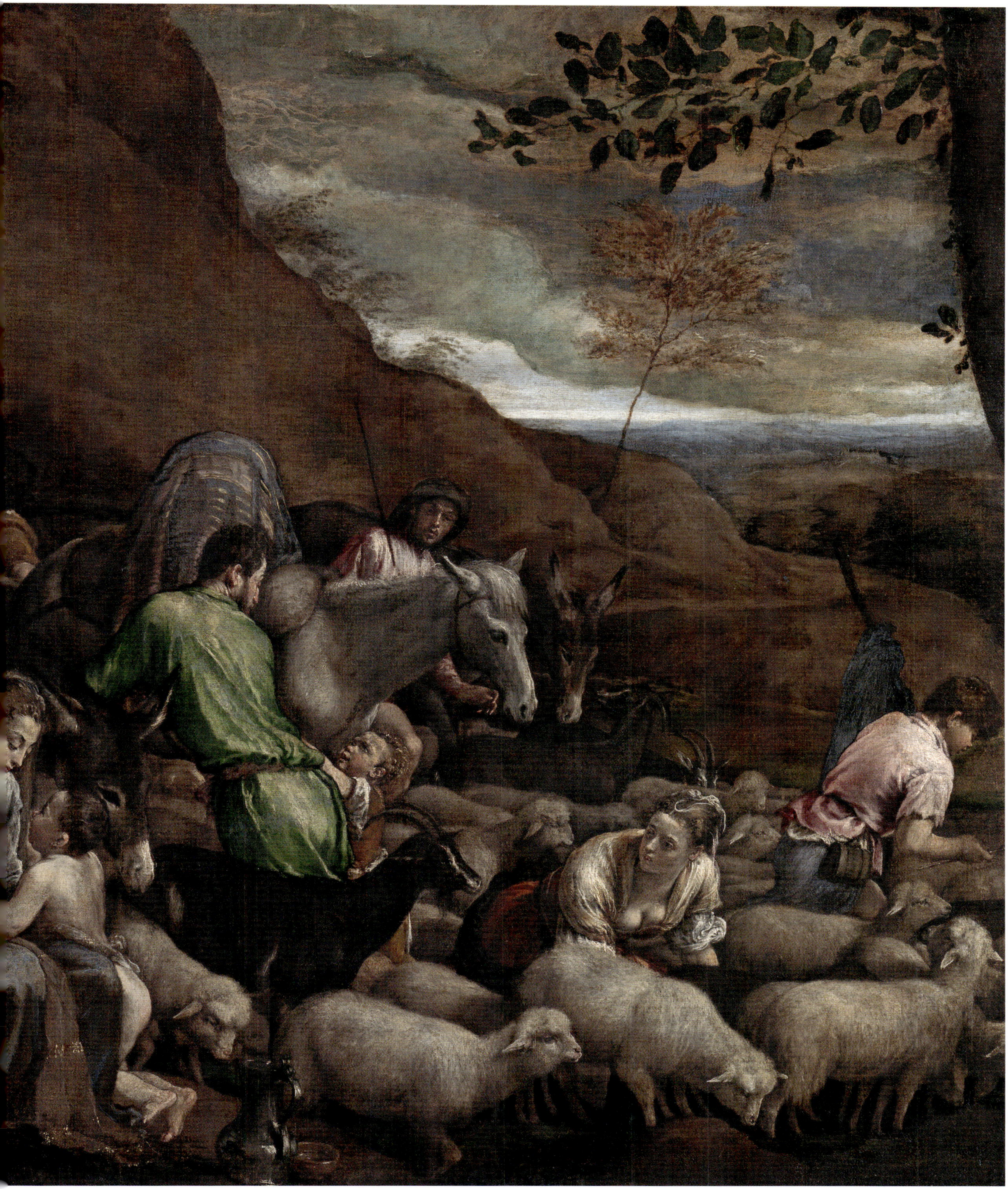

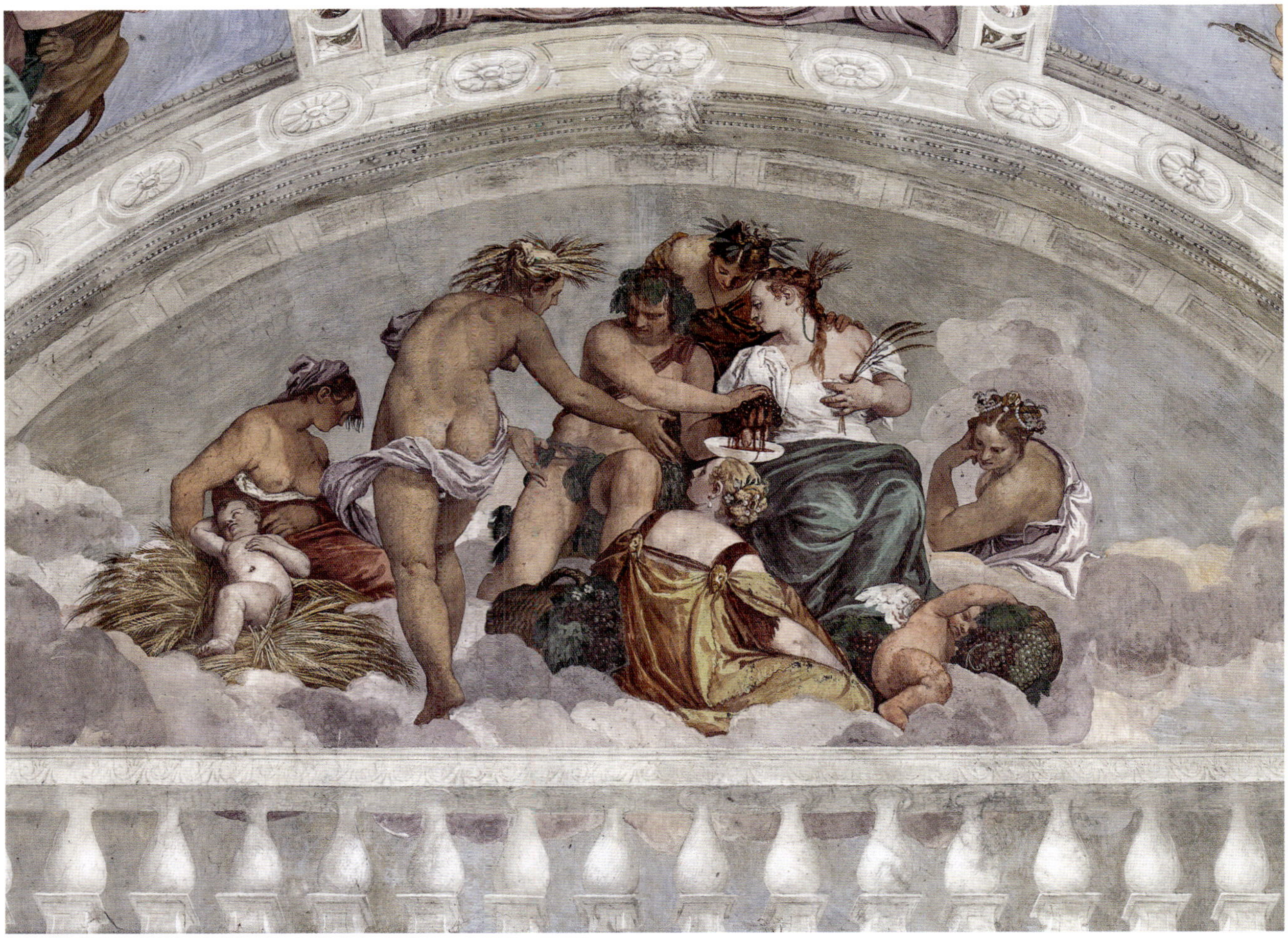

of biblical subjects, to which the elements were added, was now well under way and such works were known and requested beyond the borders of the Republic.[19] Jacopo could already count on the indispensable assistance of his eldest son, Francesco, born in 1549, who was by then in his twenties and had ably mastered the brushes. He was subsequently joined by Giambattista, Leandro, and Girolamo.[20] Jacopo organized the workshop's production on a vast scale to meet the high public demand. He formulated various compositional layouts and perfected his repertoire of biblical-pastoral scenes. At the start of the 1570s, he added representations of the seasons to his 'catalogue' of pastoral subjects. Up to that point, Jacopo Tintoretto in 1546/48 and Paolo Veronese in 1560/61 had painted the seasons in the Veneto region, on canvas and fresco, respectively.[21] The iconographic choice of both artists was tied to the aristocratic context for which their pictures were intended. Tintoretto's seasons, focused on the human figure and set in bold foreshortened landscapes, decorated the ceiling and walls of two Venetian palaces; those of Paolo Veronese were part of the decorative fresco complex at Villa Barbaro in Maser and portray groups of figures harmoniously conversing, posed in an elegant monumentality (fig. 5). Both artists opted for allegorical figures accompanied by attributes, an iconography that originated in classical antiquity (cat. 48).[22]

In contrast, Bassano chose to represent the seasons in small, almost easel-size paintings, intended to decorate secluded rooms such as a *studiolo* or a space suited to conversation. He chose, like Pieter Bruegel the Elder,[23] the late ancient and medieval iconography depicting man's works in relation to the rhythm imposed by nature (cat. 15). He would have found fine examples of these in the frescoes of Torre Aquila in Trento (fig. 6), easily reached from Bassano, or in the miniatures contained in the *Breviario Grimani*, part of the collection of the patrician Grimani family in Venice (fig. 7). Thus, he made these subjects – which until then were restricted to

Fig. 5

Paolo Veronese, *Summer and Autumn (Bacchus and Ceres),* in the Hall of Olympus, 1560/61, Maser (TV), Villa Barbaro

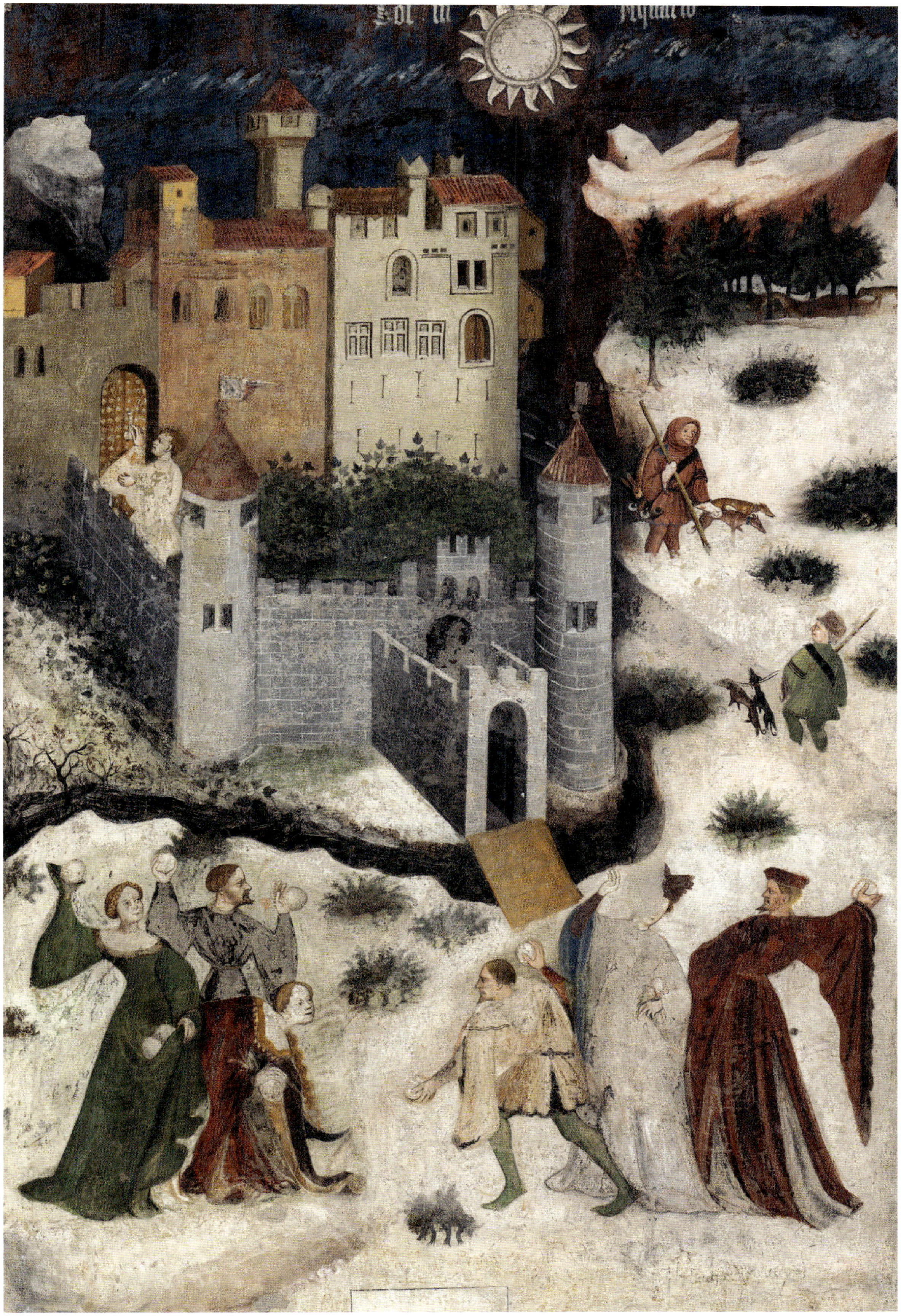

Fig. 6

January, part of the *Cycle of the Months* at Torre Aquila, c.1400. Trento, Castello del Buonconsiglio

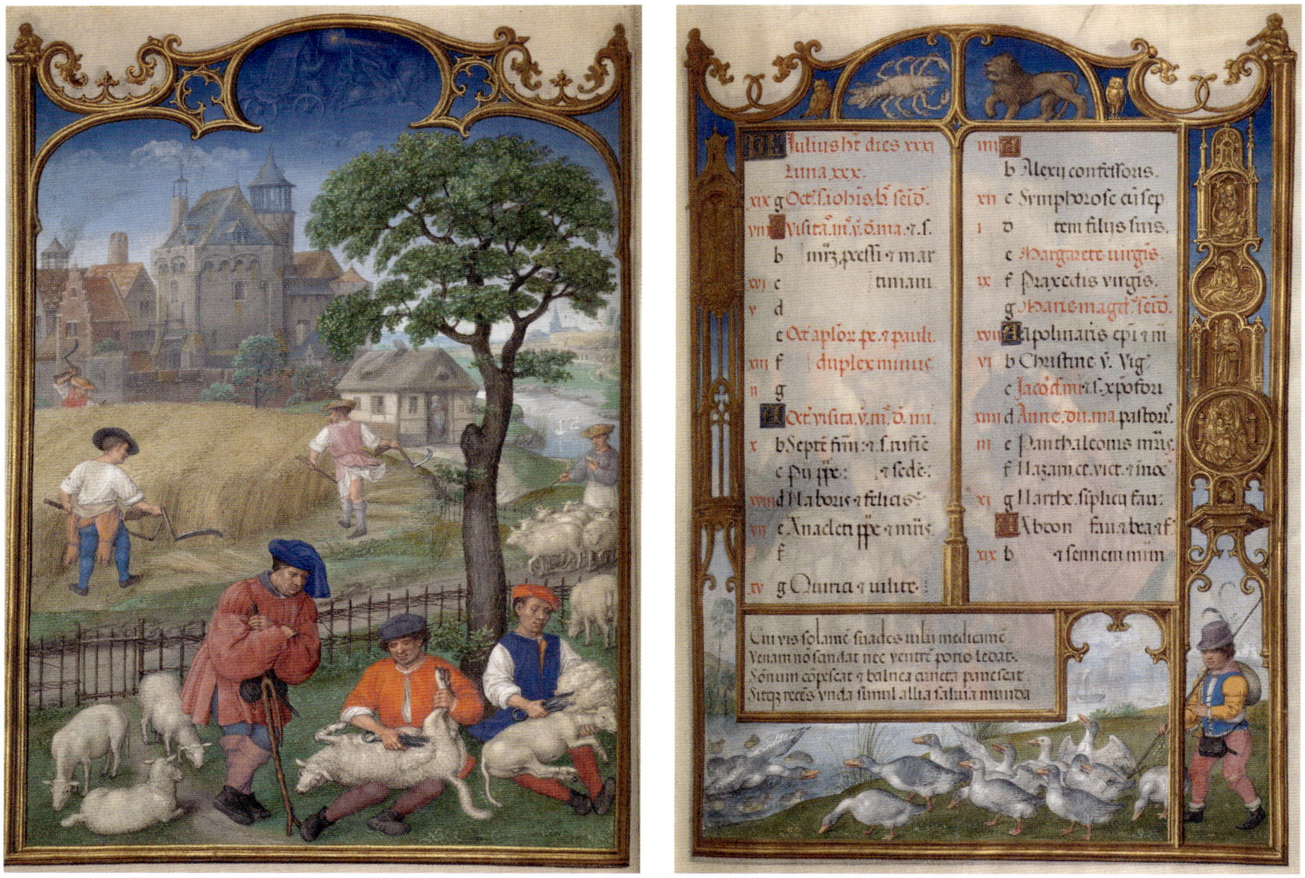

Fig. 7
Summer, in *Breviarium secundum consuetudinem Romanae curiae (Breviario Grimani)*, 1510–20. Venice, Biblioteca Nazionale Marciana, cod. Lat. I, 99 (=2138), fol. 7v, 8r

frescoed decorative programmes or tapestries – accessible to a wider public.[24]Although Jacopo could not have known Bruegel's paintings directly for reasons of geographical distance and the fact that his *Seasons* were was never copied,[25] he could have turned to the prints of *Spring* and *Summer* made by Pieter van der Heyden for the publisher Hieronymus Cock in 1570, a year after Bruegel's death.[26] In fact, Jacopo's *Seasons* were inspired by the compositional structure of Bruegel's works, organized on parallel planes (cat. 59). They depict gentle landscapes sloping down towards the horizon with animals and peasants engaged in work in the foreground. Smaller figures in the middle distance and background populate the countryside and emphasize the perspective structure. Each season can be distinguished by its typical agricultural activities and by the small biblical scene added in the middle distance, almost a vignette painted with a few, quick brushstrokes (fig. 8). In a similar way to Pieter Bruegel, each season is distinguished by precise lighting: auroral in spring, warm and golden in summer, afternoon-like and intense in autumn, nocturnal and cold in winter.[27] Such differentiation has its origin in the cosmological tradition that links the four seasons to the ages of man and thus to the four-part division of the day,[28] and which Bruegel and Bassano interpreted with sensitivity to the charm of nature and its rhythms. In the former, nature and animals predominate over the human figures, which seem to blend into them and identify with their occupation,[29] while in Bassano the humanist tradition prevails (based on the rediscovery of Arcadia and the idealization of nature, inaugurated in painting by Giorgione's works, the central place of man, his dignity and his destiny within the divine project).

The presence of biblical stories is an original and distinctive element in Jacopo's *Seasons*: the close relationship between the cycles of nature that determine human activities and the story of salvation through the sacrifice of Christ.[30] Closer studies of the season iconography have been made by Eskelinen, connecting it to the festivities of the Quatuor Tempora, whose precepts defined by the Council of Trento gave new importance to the annual liturgical cycle.[31]

Ridolfi had already noted Jacopo's religiosity and his knowledge of holy scripture, from which he drew inspiration for the biblical-pastorals.[32] These reflect the artist's profound religious sentiment, perceptible also in the representation of New Testament stories by an 'exegetic' intelligence that transferred the divine word to pictures comprehensible to the public, in keeping with the precepts of the Council of Trento.[33] This highly personal religious tension is the key to interpreting Jacopo's artistic pathway and relevant to understanding how his sons developed such representations. Only three *Seasons* series and a few other odd pictures show biblical scenes in the background (fig. 9).[34] The others (currently known) are devoid of any religious element and show how the Bassano workshop adapted to the demand for new iconographies detached from a sacred context and aligned to the new trends widespread in Europe at the time. These are documented by engravings by 'northern artists', which also acted as a model for the applied arts (cats. 50, 73).[35] The series was repeated by Jacopo and his workshop in numerous variants of format and figure combinations, which the prints by the Sadeler family circulated throughout Europe in the seventeenth century.[36]

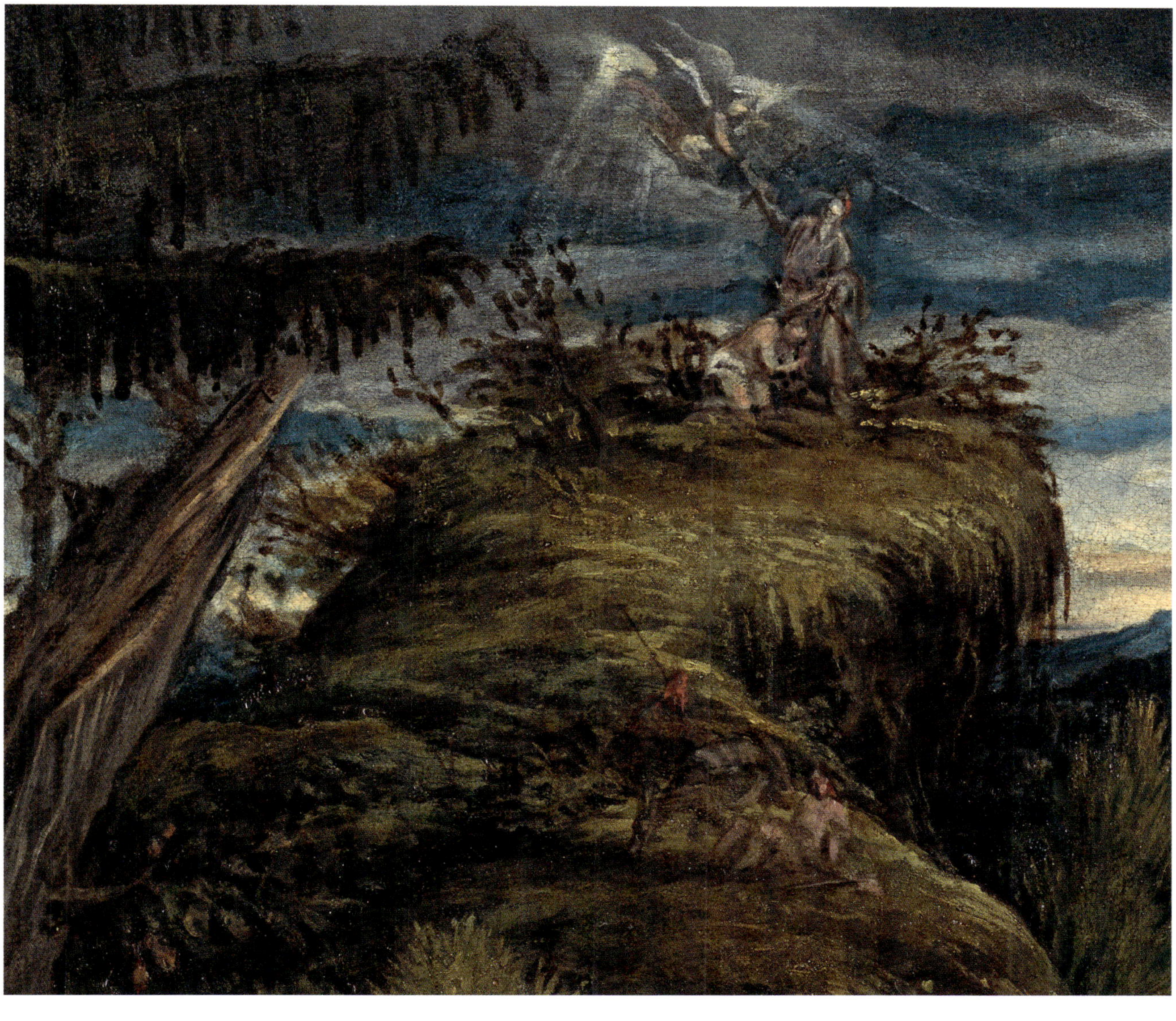

Fig. 8

Jacopo dal Ponte, called Bassano, *Summer (Sacrifice of Isaac)*, detail, c.1576. Vienna, Kunsthistorisches Museum, Picture Gallery, inv. 4302

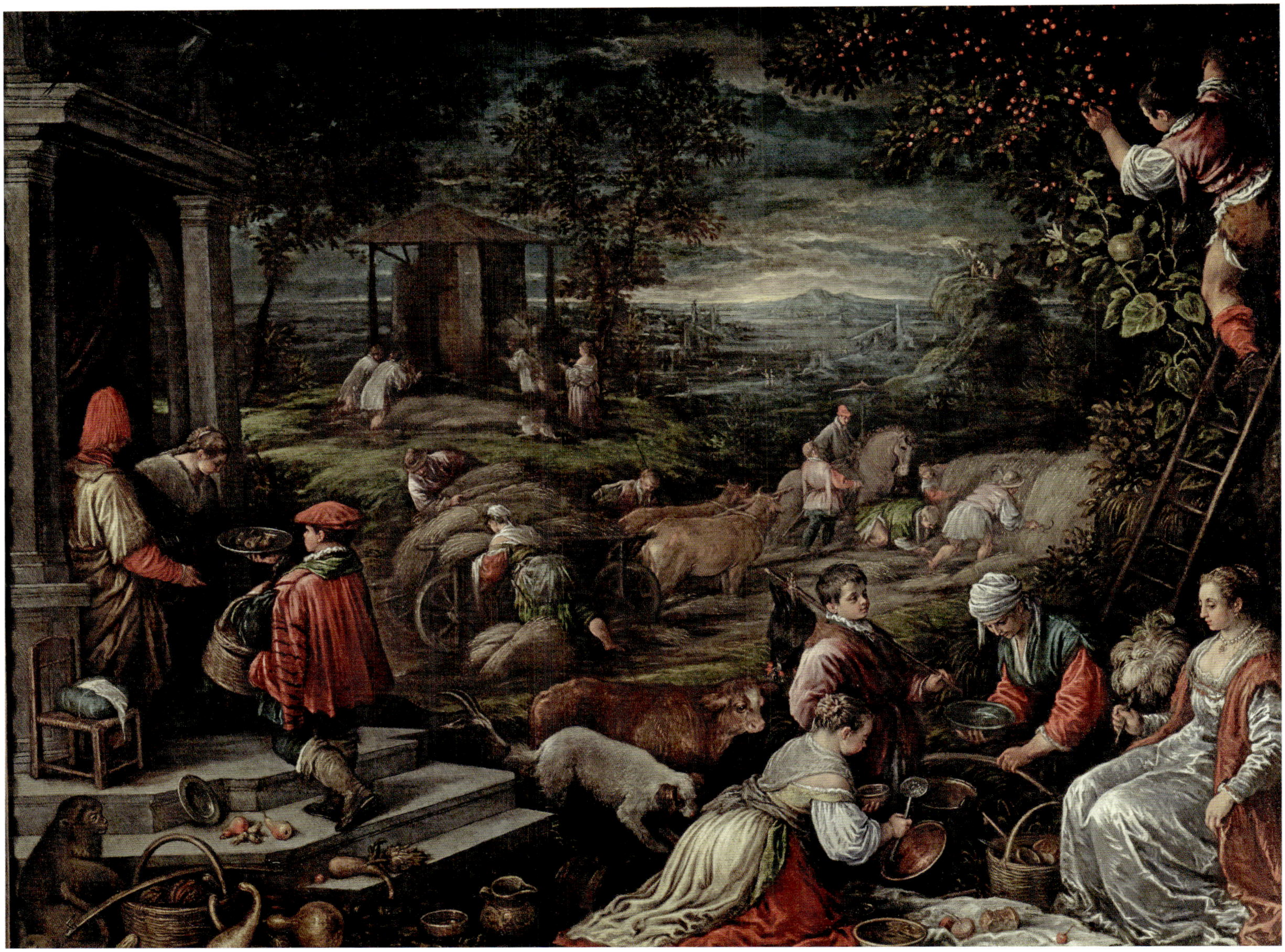

Fig. 9
Jacopo dal Ponte, called Bassano, *Summer*, 1575/80. London, Spier Collection

Francesco and Leandro Bassano's Seasons and Months

In 1578, Francesco Bassano settled in Venice where he opened a workshop and became involved in the prestigious decorative project in the Palazzo Ducale's Sala del Maggior Consiglio, destroyed by fire in 1577. With the opening of this new studio, Francesco came into direct contact with clients, dealers, agents, and connoisseurs who lived in or visited the capital in constant search of works of art. Over the course of the works in the Palazzo Ducale, Francesco also found himself immersed in a lively exchange with artists such as Jacopo Tintoretto and Paolo Veronese, who accompanied one another and often vied for commissions.[37] Exchanges of ideas and meetings with other artists were the order of the day, as was the possibility of gaining access to rich private collections. The Venice workshop met the demands of a cosmopolitan clientele. Jacopo, who often came to the capital, supported and advised his son on the conception of new compositions.[38]

The popularity of depictions of the seasons remained constant, as shown by Venetian collection inventories drawn up between 1580 and 1600. The large number of *Seasons* in various stages of completion, recorded in the workshop inventories of Jacopo in Bassano (1592) and of Gerolamo in Venice (1621), confirm the continuing interest in these subjects well into the seventeenth century.[39]

In May 1581, Francesco Bassano wrote a letter to Nicolò Gaddi, Florentine connoisseur and art consultant to the Medici, with whom he had already been in contact for some time. The letter was sent with some drawings by his father and himself. Gaddi had previously informed him that there were important clients (possibly the Medici themselves?) who wanted large paintings for their palace, so Francesco took the opportunity to propose a cycle of months and saw the request for large formats as a chance to be able to paint (large) figures to 'show art in my own way'. The letter provides key clarification about the planning of the large-format cycle of the months that Francesco painted with his brother Leandro (cat. 67).[40]

Francesco's letter to Gaddi also provides information on the relationship between the Bassano workshop and Florence. Arslan and Rearick mentioned contacts with the Medici and the Florentine art world.[41] As mentioned above, by 1578 Cardinal Ferdinando had already bought a Bassano *Flood* cycle for Villa Medici in Rome, and over the years he bought several others by the Bassanos, often sent as diplomatic gifts.[42] The painting now in Kassel's Gemäldegalerie that depicts (according to some scholars) Francesco I de' Medici, grand duke of Tuscany, could have been painted during one of Francesco Bassano's visits to Florence and could have been mediated by the Venetian noblewoman Bianca Cappello, grand duchess from 1579.[43]

The cultural climate of Florence was determined by the scientific and naturalist interests of Francesco I. Moreover, the grand duke shared interests then widespread in the courts and seigniories of Europe, which all supported research into the natural sciences, medicine, and astronomy and the development of scientific thinking in general. They acted as centres and very potent accelerators of the frenzied exchange of knowledge and, through their support for universities, consolidated the dominance of modern science.

The works of Jan van der Straet, called Stradano (cat. 72), known also through engravings, and of Paolo Fiammingo, who was initially active in Florence and then moved to Venice, were an important influence on the Bassanos, who were formulating the themes of seasons, markets, and months, and enriching them with naturalist elements.[44]

The works of Pieter Aertsen and Joachim Beuckelaer (cats. 63, 64) had already appeared in Flanders around the mid-sixteenth century. Their paintings staged episodes of everyday life in kitchens or town squares, accompanied by scenes from the Bible that were relegated to the background. Although the works of these artists were engraved only towards the end of the century, the fame of the market scene or kitchen interior, closely linked to the Fleming socio-cultural context of the 1540s–60s, was widely known by artists, collectors. and agents. The market scenes painted by Jacopo and Francesco Bassano (fig. 10), also taken up in Francesco and Leandro's *Months*, are certainly indebted to these works.[45]

Francesco Bassano's *Seasons* (cat. 66) are directly derived from Jacopo's works and were formulated in the Bassano workshop. The decision to use large canvases allowed him to indulge his narrative vein and add a number of everyday objects that are given an almost classificatory attention, in line with the dominant taste that required paintings to have a descriptive naturalism. The large figures in turn draw attention to the activities conducted, which are more appreciable at a large scale. The addition of the three signs of the zodiac relating to their respective seasons confirms the end of the brief digression of religious references in Jacopo's *Seasons*, and a renewed reference to the traditional astrological context.

The imposing *Months* cycle signed by Leandro – shown in the exhibition – is the culmination of the development of the seasons theme within the Bassano workshop. Although there is no precise information as to who commissioned these paintings, firm indicators to their chronology can be established.[46] As mentioned above, Francesco was already working on this project in 1581. In 1590, a complete *Months* cycle, later identified as that signed by Francesco and now held (incomplete) in Madrid, was sent by Ferdinando I de' Medici as a diplomatic gift to the Medici embassy in Spain.[47] It is known that in 1587 a series of months was being worked on in the Bassano workshop, under the guidance of Jacopo.[48] Still clearly visible signs of the squaring grid in twelve water-coloured drawings portraying the months confirm that the workshop was able to replicate the scenes in different sizes according to demand.[49] The dating of the cycles by Francesco and Leandro can thus be placed between 1581 and 1587, or 1590 at the latest. Despite the lack of information, apart from the previous mention by Carlo Ridolfi, it is likely that the Viennese cycle, sent to Rudolph II in Prague, was commissioned by the emperor's agents, who probably frequented both Bassano workshops and may have seen the series painted by Francesco for the Florentine noblemen. The grandiose conception of the *Months* series is certainly a response to the request of noble patrons who intended decorating a large space.

The presence of different social classes in the paintings, or rather of aristocratic figures interacting with peasants or merchants, confirms that the paintings were intended for those who wished to see representations of the rural activities over the course of the year, just as they saw them practised on their own estates. The rural world, reassessed and ennobled also by the church, was no longer the object of mockery, but rather awakened the interest of landowners now mindful of the countryside and of those who worked there, in harmony with the dictates of the Council of Trento, which consolidated the practice of noble and sacred agriculture.[50]

The representations of February and March, months when farming activities were paused, are particularly interesting because they are innovatively set in an urban context. The two paintings take up the popular theme of the contrast between Carnival and Lent, against the background of the post-Tridentine spiritual climate, representing in March the triumph of the sacred over rural activities.[51] The identification of the new *Missale Romanum* of 1576 as the model for the iconography chosen by the Bassanos is very interesting. The influence of the Roman

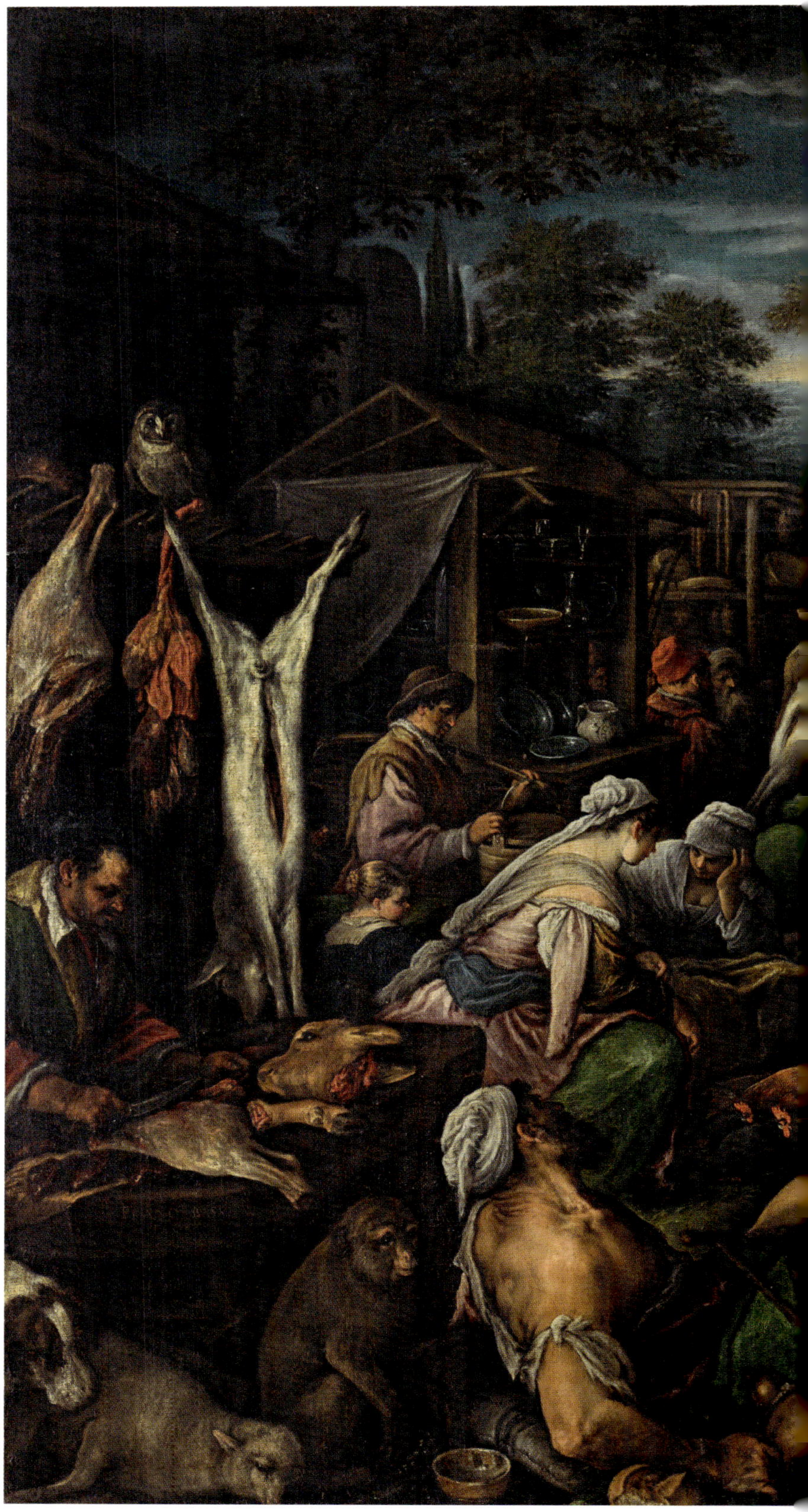

Fig. 10
Francesco dal Ponte, called Bassano, *Market Scenes*, 1580/85. Vienna, Kunsthistorisches Museum, Picture Gallery, inv. 4319

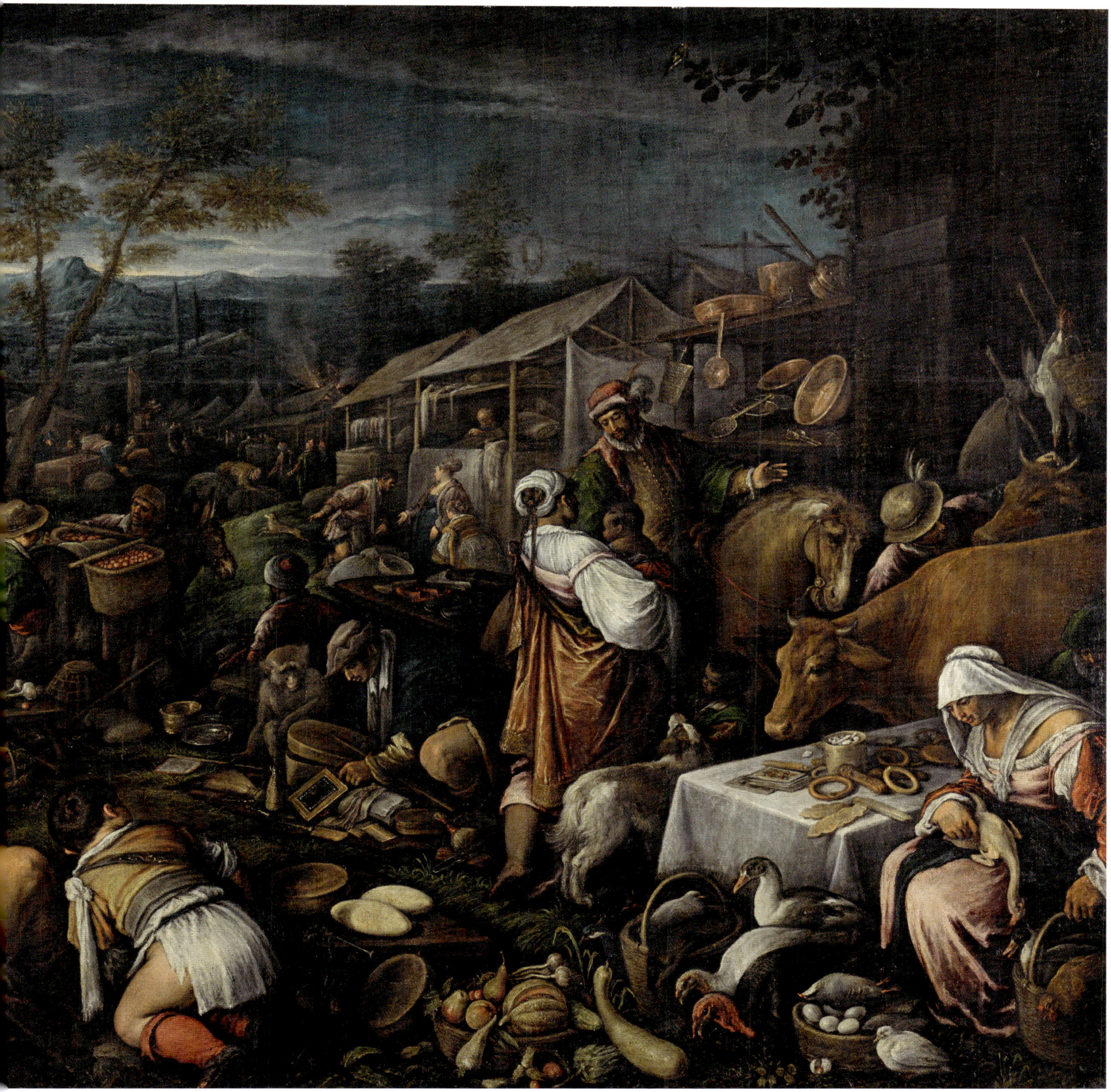

Missal developed in two directions: the thematization of the contrast between Carnival and Lent in an urban context, in which the religious fervour for atonement is portrayed in the figures proceeding to vigils and sermons in various parts of the city; and the inspiration taken by the Bassanos from the illustrations in the 1576 edition, which for February shows a Carnival scene with the mask of Pantalone.[52]

This cycle of paintings highlights the great inventiveness of the Bassano workshop and especially its ability to adapt the subjects to the wishes of its clients, making use of a well-tried 'modular' system that allowed always new and extremely pleasant and decorative scenes with infinite variants to be composed at will.[53] The focus on the natural world, which had its origin in Jacopo Bassano's artistic research, was further developed in Francesco and Leandro's creations towards the description of animal and vegetable species in a kind of illustrated catalogue. The Bassanos' friendly and professional involvement in the intellectual and scientific circles of the University of Padua, which were in touch with scholars from all over Europe, reinforced the naturalist vocation of these painters, who were almost predestined to respond to the demands of the cultural climate at the end of the sixteenth century. Physicians, botanists, and astronomers were also their clients, who in turn, generating a fertile network of mutual stimuli, encouraged artists to represent the wonders of nature and paved the way for the still life genre and seventeenth-century naturalism.[54] When the *Months* entered the collection of Rudolf II in Prague, possibly towards the end of the 1580s, these 'fashionable' representations captured the emperor's attention, because they were highly naturalistic, narrative in concept, and imbued with Venetian charm. However, appreciation of the series has much deeper roots in the self-image promoted by the dynasty from the mid-sixteenth century. In their cyclical rotation, the months and the seasons represent continuity and the role of the Habsburgs as guarantors of moderation and political stability in Europe, as brilliantly expressed in Giuseppe Arcimboldo's *Allegories*. The importance of the Bassanos' work in Europe is thus confirmed; having ascended to 'imperial' status as interpreters of a specific cultural moment.

1 'Il Bassanese miracoloso nel pingere cose pastorali'; Benedetti 1571, 6v.
2 The bibliography on Jacopo Bassano is enormous. In addition to Arslan 1960 see the essays by Marini, Rearick and Ballarin in exh. cat. Bassano and Fort Worth 1992. Ballarin's fundamental studies reprinted in 1995; Nichols 2018, Brücher 2019, Nichols 2023 and the recent bibliographic update in exh. cat. Helsinki 2024 are fundamental.
3 Rearick 1992/93, 48, and broadly Cottrell 2009, 50–7; Cottrell and Humfrey 2021, 100–17.
4 Rearick 1992/93, 59.
5 Ballarin 1967, 77–101.
6 Vinco 2021, 54.
7 'fatta a colpi e di fierissima macchia'; Ridolfi 1648 (1914/24), Part I 386, 389, 394, 396.
8 Bassano's art is discussed in Boschini 1660 (1960), 297–405.
9 Verci 1775. Giovanni Battista Volpato's manuscript is conserved in the Biblioteca del Museo Civico di Bassano. See also the monograph by Bordignon Favero 1994. For a survey of the sources of Bassano's technique, see Avagnina 1992, 233–44 and Cerasuolo 2016, 787–801.
10 Ballarin 1966, 112–36, esp. 116; reprinted in Ballarin 1995b, Scritti, vol. 1, 71–95, esp. 75.
11 Marini 1992, 22–6; Rearick 1996/97, 53–82; Ballarin 2010, 41–55.
12 Paris, Musée du Louvre, inv. RF 1994 23; see Brown 2021 with previous bibliography.
13 Ridolfi 1648 (1914/24), Part 1, 401.
14 See essay Infelise and Minuzzi, p. 89.
15 See a recent overview by Svalduz 2019, 133–50.
16 See essay Demo, p. 103.
17 Stockbauer 1874, 43; Jansen 2019, 615–19, dates the list to the early 1570s.
18 Cecchi 1999, 60, 64 note 11.
19 On the circulation of works by the Bassanos in Spain see Falomir 2001, 19–20 who cites a despatch of 21 January 1574 to Philip II from Diego Guzmán de Silva, ambassador to Venice between 1569 and 1578. On the circulation in France, see Caramanna 2013; Jimenez Diaz 2001, 101 and Aikema 2011, 121–3 for the knowledge of the Bassanos in Rudolf's circle. See also Caramanna 2024.
20 Arslan 1960, 183–226 (Francesco), 233–75 (Leandro); Alberton Vinco da Sesso 1986, 173–7 (Francesco); 188–92 (Leandro).
21 Jacopo Tintoretto for the Palazzo Barbo at San Pantalon, Venice, 1546–48: *Spring*, Chrysler Museum of Art, Norfolk, Virginia, inv. 71.1301, and *Summer*, National Gallery of Art, Washington, Samuel Kress Coll., inv. 1961.9.90. Later on he painted *Autumn and Winter* and *Spring and Summer* (1575–85) for an unidentified palace, now at Carnegie Institute, Pittsburgh, invs. 62.13 and 63.6. Paolo Veronese: *Seasons*, Sala dell'Olimpo, Villa Barbaro Maser, 1560/61.
22 Paruzzo 2021, 87–9.
23 See essay, Pénot p. 39.
24 Bruegel's seasons were intended for a similar audience.
25 See essay Pénot, p. 39.
26 The series was completed with *Autumn* and *Winter* by Hans Bol.
27 Ballarin 2004, 91; Eskelinen 2024, 103.
28 See essay Gabriele, p. 19.
29 See essay Pénot, p. 39.
30 Rearick 1992/93, 145–6; Ballarin 1968, 240–1; Aikema 1996, 131–7: Mason 1999, 558–9; Eskelinen 2024, 97–109.
31 Eskelinen 2024, 105–8.
32 Ridolfi 1648, 395.
33 Berdini 1997, 60–80.
34 Musei Civici di Milano, Raccolte Artistiche (Pinacoteca and Museo d'Arte Antica), invs. 69–72, see also Bianchi in Mmus. cat. Milan 1998, 38–44; Galleria Borghese in large format. invs. 3, 5, 11, see Della Pergola 1959, 101–2 and Herrmann Fiore 2006, 9; entries by Antonio Jommelli in the online catalogue https://www.collezionegalleriaborghese.it/; Estate, coll. Spier.
35 See the wide circulation of engravings portraying the elements and planets by Maarten de Vos after Adriaen Collaert who illustrated the elements accompanied by zodiac signs, still combined with biblical episodes. For the prints by Etienne Delaune, see cat. 73.
36 Corsato 2010.
37 Paolo Veronese wanted his son Carletto to be trained in Francesco's workshop.
38 Ridolfi 1648, 406.
39 Mason 1999, 559: the owners of five *Seasons* cycles belong to the class of citizens that also included merchants and secretaries to the offices of the state administration. The works' success increased in the years after 1600 when a good sixteen series are recorded in inventories. For the inventory of Gerolamo Bassano, see Mason 2009.
40 Bottari and Ticozzi 1822, 265–6.
41 Borghini 1584, 564; Arslan 1936, 111–12; Rearick 1992/93, 166 note 376.
42 Cecchi 1999, 60, 61, 63.
43 Rearick 1992/93, 166 note 376. Moreover, Francesco Bassano painted altarpieces for churches in Florence and Rome; Kassel, Schloss Wilhelmshöhe, Gemäldegalerie Alte Meister, inv. GK 515.
44 Mason 1999, 559; Ballarin 1995b, vol. 1, 34–6.
45 For the markets see the *Big Market* painted before 1582 for Charles Emmanuel of Savoy signed by Jacopo, Bava 1995, 212–19; Bava 2016, 505–17 and that signed by Francesco, Vienna, Kunsthistorisches Museum, Picture Gallery, inv. 4319, Del Torre Scheuch 2019, 38–40.
46 Ridolfi 1648, 399; Del Torre Scheuch 2009, 115.
47 Goldberg 1996, 535–6 note 47; Falomir 2001, 22–5, 125–33.
48 See Van Buchell in Lanciani 1900, 13 recently recalled by Caramanna 2024, 44.
49 The drawings, which faithfully reproduce the Viennese *Months*, are published in Schleier 1981, 15–29.
50 Berdini 1997, 19; Nichols 2023, 93. Both scholars refer to Agostino Valier's *De Rhetorica Ecclesiastica ad clericos libri tre* (Verona 1574); see also essay Infelise and Minuzzi, p. 89.
51 Moldovan 2021, 123–7.
52 Moldovan 2021, 137–8.
53 Del Torre Scheuch 2021, 159.
54 See essay Olmi and Tongiorgi Tomasi, p. 67.

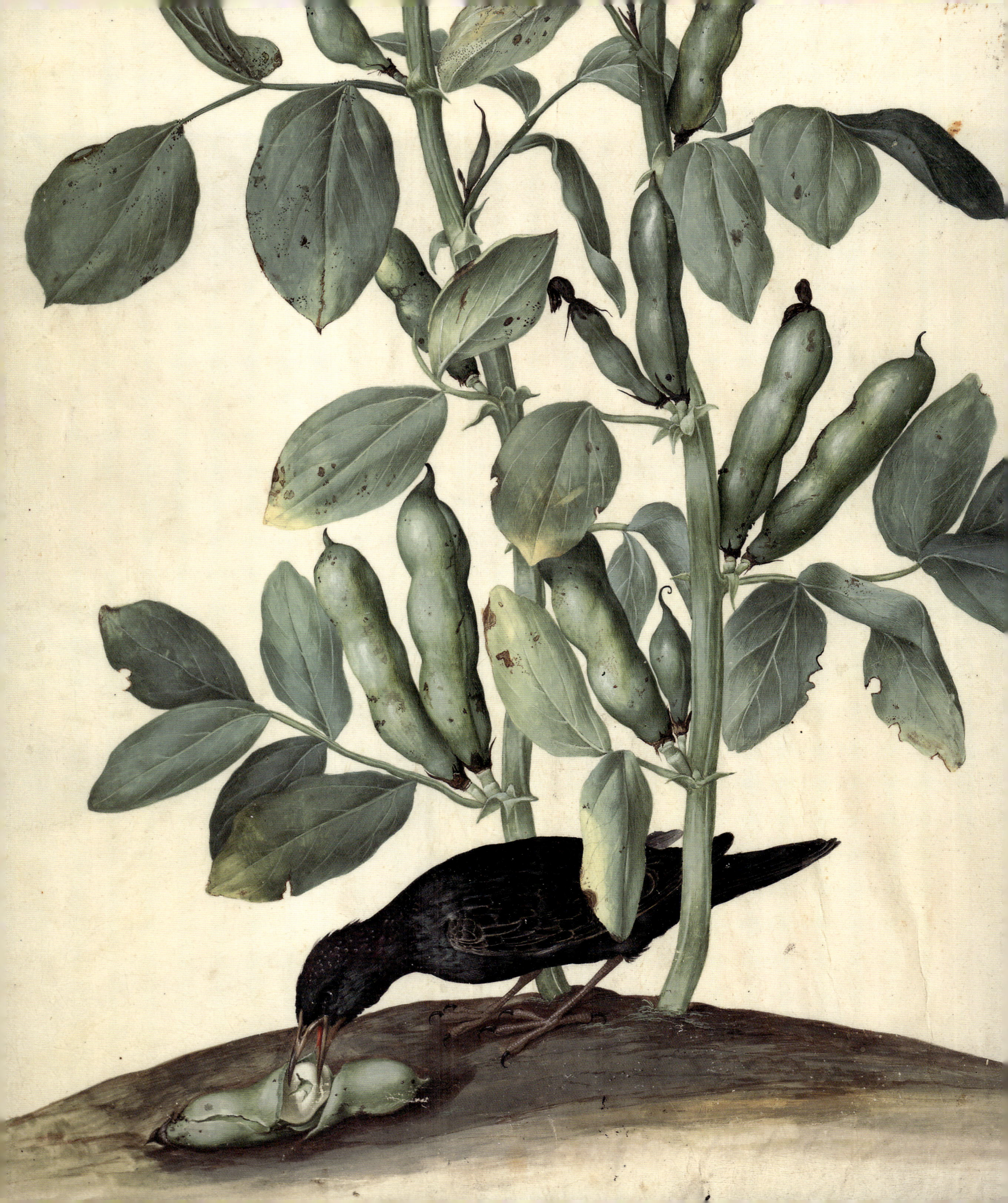

GIUSEPPE OLMI, LUCIA TONGIORGI TOMASI

Warehouse of Wonders

Art and Nature in the Territories of the Serenissima in the Early Modern Age

In sketching the surroundings of the city of Verona in his *Descrittione di tutta Italia* (1550), Leandro Alberti wrote: 'Medicinal herbs are found for the health of mortals, and especially on the very high Monte Baldo, which is above the City. Where from every part of Europe herbalists converge to gather roots and herbs very profitable for every great infirmity'.[1] Sixteen years later, the Veronese apothecary Francesco Calzolari, who had a shop known as the Campana d'Oro in Piazza Erbe, published a small work entitled *Il viaggio di Monte Baldo, della magnifica città di Verona*, arising out of his experience as a herbalist and conceived as a guide for those intending to go to the same mountain to collect primarily those plant essences that were 'necessary in the apothecary's shop'. In it, he did not hesitate to praise the 'place' as one where 'such a variety of warm and cold by nature, and sylvan and domestic, aquatic and mountain plants, as in no other in Italy' were to be found.[2] The extraordinary and intense interest in nature that developed in the Veneto area and more generally in the dominions of the Serenissima, which started in the late Middle Ages and continued for centuries after, was not due to the large variety of botanical species that could be found on Monte Baldo – or, at least, not only. It was marked by a fruitful intertwining of art and science involving not only physicians, apothecaries, 'the curious', university teachers, noble owners of gardens, diplomats, and even the makers of fake monstrous creatures, but also painters and sculptors. Among the reasons for such a vast interest in the natural world, the presence in the region of Padua University, dating from the early thirteenth century, is crucial. Over the years, the university became known as a centre of Aristotelianism that did not conflict with 'the rigour of rational methods combined with recourse to experience'.[3] It gained particular prestige for its medical studies, alongside which the botanical garden was established in 1545. Venice's trading network with the East and the city's possessions in the Mediterranean were equally important. Pre-eminent among the latter was the island of Crete, which had always been regarded as a special place for studying and collecting plants.

There was also a close and traditional relationship between the Venetian lands (and Venice, in particular) and northern European areas, especially Germany. This was initially established through trade,[4] but quickly extended to cultural exchanges (the German brothers Johann and Wendelin of Speyer were the first to introduce printing with moveable type to Venice). This relationship intensified during the early modern age, when both countries were deeply impacted by the cultural 'humus' of Humanism, albeit with very different outcomes, inspiring travels and sojourns by scholars, students, physicians, philosophers, and artists, who followed the route that led from the north to the shores of the Adriatic, and vice versa. An emblematic example is that of Erasmus of Rotterdam, who in his youth had stayed in Venice (feeling himself to be 'at home') at Aldus Manutius's printing house and who used to assert that Padua University was 'the richest emporium of knowledge'.

It is worth noting that in the first decades of the fifteenth century there was already a marked interest in the world of nature in Italy (and subsequently in Germany and the Netherlands), inspired partly by the increasing circulation of classical texts. The treatises of the *Scriptores rei rusticae*, alongside Aristotle's *De partibus animalium*, the botanical works of Theophrastus and Dioscorides, and, especially, Pliny the Elder's *Naturalis Historia* (then critically analyzed in search of the 'errors' scattered through it),[5] were all carefully studied and popularized, as were the works of the great Arab physicians.

Starting in northern Italy in the first decades of the fifteenth century, a new way of perceiving plants and animals, now considered in their individual specificity and placed in a more rational context, was more precisely defined and circulated. This led to a rejection of the passive reproposal of the symbolic and allegorical concepts and the unrealistic and schematic illustrations that had marked the manuscripts and first incunabula of medieval tradition.

During this process, the image took on a fundamental role and, alongside the physician and the herbalist, the figure of the artist became increasingly significant in the experimental work of his own workshop, whether assisting the specialists in reproducing the finds under examination, or independently approaching the natural world, impelled by curiosity and imagination, but also by the didactic need to confront the 'real'. The image, which carefully examines surrounding reality, ended up being far more eloquent than the written word, because it is able to direct the gaze and make visually explicit

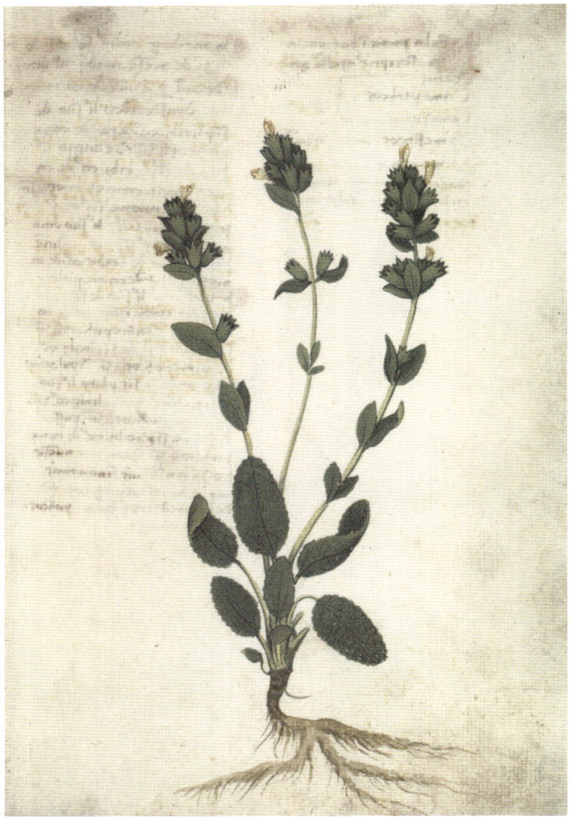

Fig. 1

Nicolò Roccabonella, *Liber de simplicibus Benedicti Rinii,* 1st half 15th cent. Venice, Biblioteca Nazionale Marciana, Cod. Lat. VI, 59=2548, fol. 28r

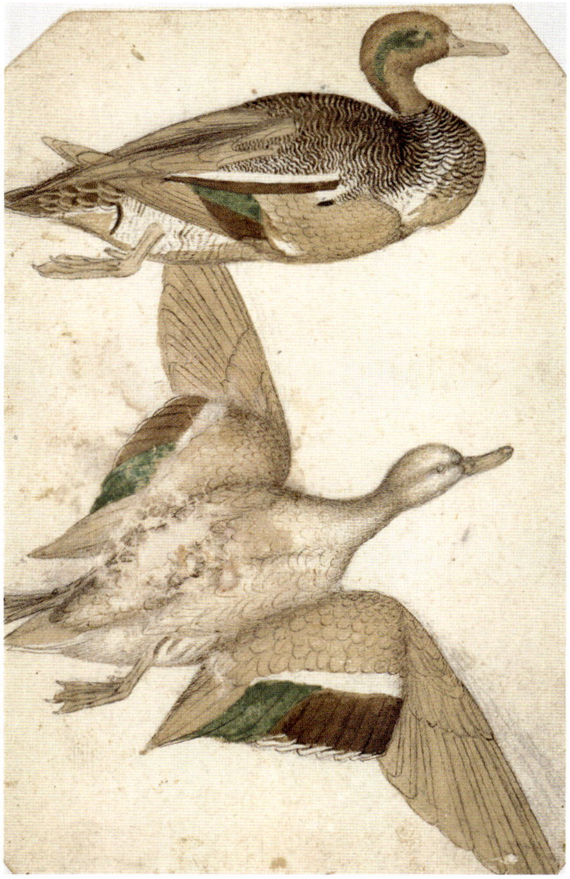

Fig. 2

Antonio di Puccio, called Pisanello, *Male Eurasian Teal, Swimming, and Female Eurasian Teal, Flying,* 1430/40. Paris, Musée du Louvre, Département des Arts graphiques, inv. 2463r

problems and phenomena that men of science had not yet recorded. This propensity to naturalism is confirmed by some fifteenth-century herbals: from what is known as the *Erbario Carrarese*[6] to the *Liber de simplicibus Benedicti Rinii medici et philosophi veneti*, now in the Biblioteca Nazionale Marciana, Venice (fig. 1).[7] Compiled in the 1440s and owned from 1534 by a certain Benedetto Rinio, the manuscript was actually written by the Conegliano physician Nicolò Roccabonella; it features some previously unpublished information on plants, their virtues and the methods of collecting them – many illustrated for the first time and accompanied by their names in various languages. The full-page botanical plates, almost 500 in total, were painted by the little-known Venetian miniaturist Andrea Amadio, defined in the introduction as 'Venus pictor',[8] who managed to imbue the plant varieties with a new vitality of movement. In bequeathing the work to his son, Rinio warmly urged him to safeguard it because it was 'painted from life'.[9]

An entirely new interest in secular subjects and a new sensibility towards the world of nature were asserted in the context of International Gothic, that complex cultural phenomenon that swept through many European courts (first and foremost those of the Po Valley–Veneto area) from the last decades of the fourteenth century. Even the cherished manorial pursuit of hunting encouraged artists to investigate zoological subjects, which were thus placed alongside 'herbs' endowed with therapeutic virtues and featured in the various editions of the *Tacuina sanitatis*, one of which was drawn up in Padua in the mid-fifteenth century (cat. 16).

The Viennese art historian Otto Pächt spoke in the 1950s of 'late-Gothic naturalism', identifying some 'early Italian studies on nature', documented not only by the *Tacuina* but also by Giovannino de' Grassi, the Lombard miniaturist working under the aegis of the Viscontis.[10] 'Interrupting the medieval custom of abstract invention,' asserts Pächt, 'Giovannino now finds his models in nature itself, but at the same time transforms the recently discovered material into motifs, models and workshop formulas' that become precious reserves of ideas.[11]

The eclectic graphic repertoire of the artist included numerous exercises carried out in various techniques (from silverpoint to watercolour) depicting birds, deer, dogs, monkeys, hares, and cheetahs, some of which are static and were made from dead or stuffed examples, or 'from memory' (see, for example, some of the birds), accompanied by other more spontaneous examples painted 'from life', perhaps modelled on the examples that populated the court menageries and thus the result of close observation (cat. 2).[12]

In the dominion of the Serenissima, in Verona (which was also a crucible-city of interesting cultural and visual experiences, especially in the sphere of the miniaturist schools), another artist was active from 1405: Antonio di Puccio, known as Pisanello. He produced a series of animal drawings – horses, dogs, donkeys, monkeys, and birds, but also a bear and an ostrich – captured in a range of behaviours and in precise anatomical detail (fig. 2).

A place of absolute pre-eminence in the practice of naturalist illustration belongs, however, to Leonardo di Vinci. When he arrived in Milan from Florence in 1483, the artist brought with him a wealth of ideas, observations, and experiences on the world of nature to which he had felt particularly attracted since his early childhood, spent in the countryside of Anghiari and Vinci. He had given youthful proof of this in the plants depicted in the field of the lost cartoon of Adam and Eve, noted with admiration by Giorgio Vasari and the Anonymous Magliabechiano. This precocious 'discovery' was followed by a more considered awareness in his Milan years, the result of concrete experience with the most diverse physical phenomena, as shown by Leonardo's reflections on the law of phyllotaxis and the problem of the circulation of sap in plants. Not coincidentally, Leonardo, who was fascinated by the secret of life that throbs in all organisms, stated that 'experience' was the 'mother of all certainty'. Alongside the depictions of plants, flowers, and animals in his paintings (such as the *Virgin of the Rocks*) and the myriad manuscript citations and reflections (indeed, to him the relationship between 'describing' and 'figuring' was indissoluble), Leonardo's extensive graphic corpus must also be considered, offering a visual interpretation of the artist's botanical and zoological world, simultaneously both 'scientific' and 'imaginary'.[13]

His nature studies, made with the most varied, experimentally mixed, graphic media, should be seen as theoretical reflections intended to investigate a world in constant change, a *natura naturans* in which 'over time everything changes'.[14] A long way from the static visual codes expressed in the contemporary herbals, Leonardo's images of plants are always portrayed with great accuracy, immersed and floating in an atmospheric mist that makes them seem 'realistic' and 'imaginary' at the same time. Emblematic examples are offered by the sheet with an oak branch with acorns emerging from the shadow, next to a finely sketched branch of dyer's greenweed (cat. 3.1), and two aquatic plants on the front and back of the same

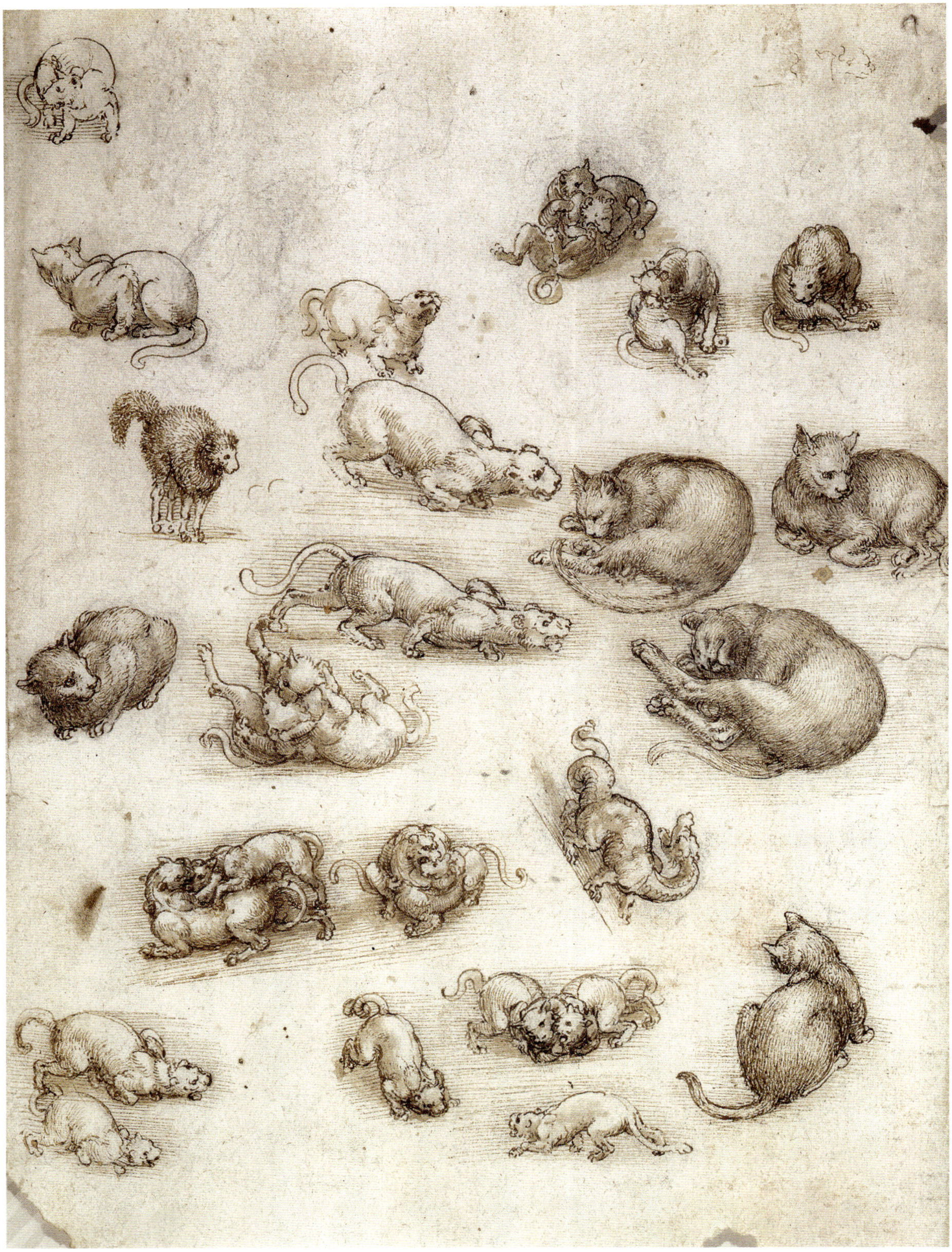

Fig. 3

Leonardo da Vinci, *Cats, Lions, and a Dragon*, 1517/18. Royal Collection Trust, inv. RCIN 912363

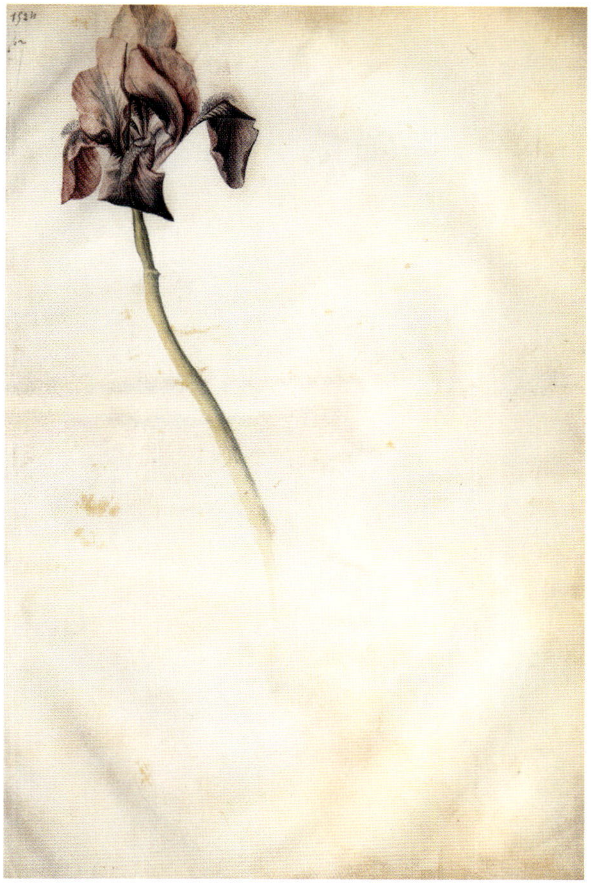

Fig. 4

Jacopo Bellini, *Bearded Iris*, c.1450. Paris, Musée du Louvre, Département des Arts graphiques, inv. RF 1524, 70

sheet (cat. 3.2), which can be attributed to the preparatory studies for the lost painting of Leda. The richness and variety of his animal drawings and sketches are also astonishing; alongside the many devoted to horses and intended for the Sforza and Trivulzio monuments, and those on the flight of birds, note the sheet where several cats appear caught in lively, domestic behaviours (fig. 3).

Leonardo, undoubtedly worried by the ominous winds of war blowing over the Milan duchy, arrived in Venice in March 1500, stopping briefly before continuing on to Friuli for engineering consultancies.[15] Although none of his works is documented in the lagoon city, the artist's presence must not have gone unnoticed in the painters' workshops and the more informed Venetian circles. Much later, the strange events that dictate the movements of works of art led to one of his most famous works, the so-called *Vitruvian Man*, ending up in Venice's Gallerie dell'Accademia.

Between the last years of the fifteenth century and the first years of the sixteenth, the Serenissima and its hinterland were thus teeming with new ideas that innovatively embraced the complexity and variety of the surrounding world, and which were also stimulated by the presence of numerous foreign artists. Antonello of Messina's sojourn in Venice, from 1474 to 1476, for example, was rich in technical teachings and luminist ideas, and he also had a decisive influence on the interpretation of the landscape, which became a constant and privileged subject of meditation and experimentation among artists.

Numerous northern European paintings and illuminated manuscripts (particularly Flemish) had also begun circulating on the market and gaining considerable acclaim for their unusual style and the highest accuracy in rendering of naturalist subjects and landscapes.

A focus on the natural world passed through the Venetian and Veneto art world, albeit with different stylistic interpretations, in a close connection of interactions and commissions. It was common practice in the multifaceted 'workshop-school' of Francesco Squarcione in Padua, for example, to include fruit and flowers in paintings. Carlo Crivelli, Cosmé Tura, and the young Andrea Mantegna all served their apprenticeships with him. The latter was a lover of classical antiquity, but also a keen observer of nature: in his *Camera Picta* he took delight in attributing the wings of jays and butterflies to the putti holding dedicatory tablet above the entrance, portraying them with a new realism.[16]

The Bellini family, who were related to Mantegna, dominated Venice at the time. The father, Jacopo, included a watercolour in one of his drawing books that captures with extraordinary sensitivity the form and colours of a fragile branch of flowering iris (fig. 4).[17]

The narrative descriptivism that typifies the production of Venetian *teleri* (large canvases) also inspired one of Vittore Carpaccio's late masterpieces: *Young Knight in a Landscape* (fig. 5). He overlooks the microcosm of a luxuriant background of botanical examples populated with animals (along with the usual horse, there is a dog, a falcon, a heron, rabbits, and a small frog among the vegetation) and plants (including a periwinkle, two irises, a cuckoo pint, and a columbine), all rigorously, scientifically identifiable.[18]

Giorgione, who has been unanimously credited with the 'invention' of the modern landscape immersed in natural light – as in the background of the *Three Philosophers*, a painting with a story very closely linked to scientific tradition (cat. 6) – also introduced some naturalist inserts, such as the luxuriant festoons of fruits and flowers in the damaged frescoes on the Fondaco dei Tedeschi, subsequently recovered and reworked in the Rome of Leo X by Giovanni da Udine.

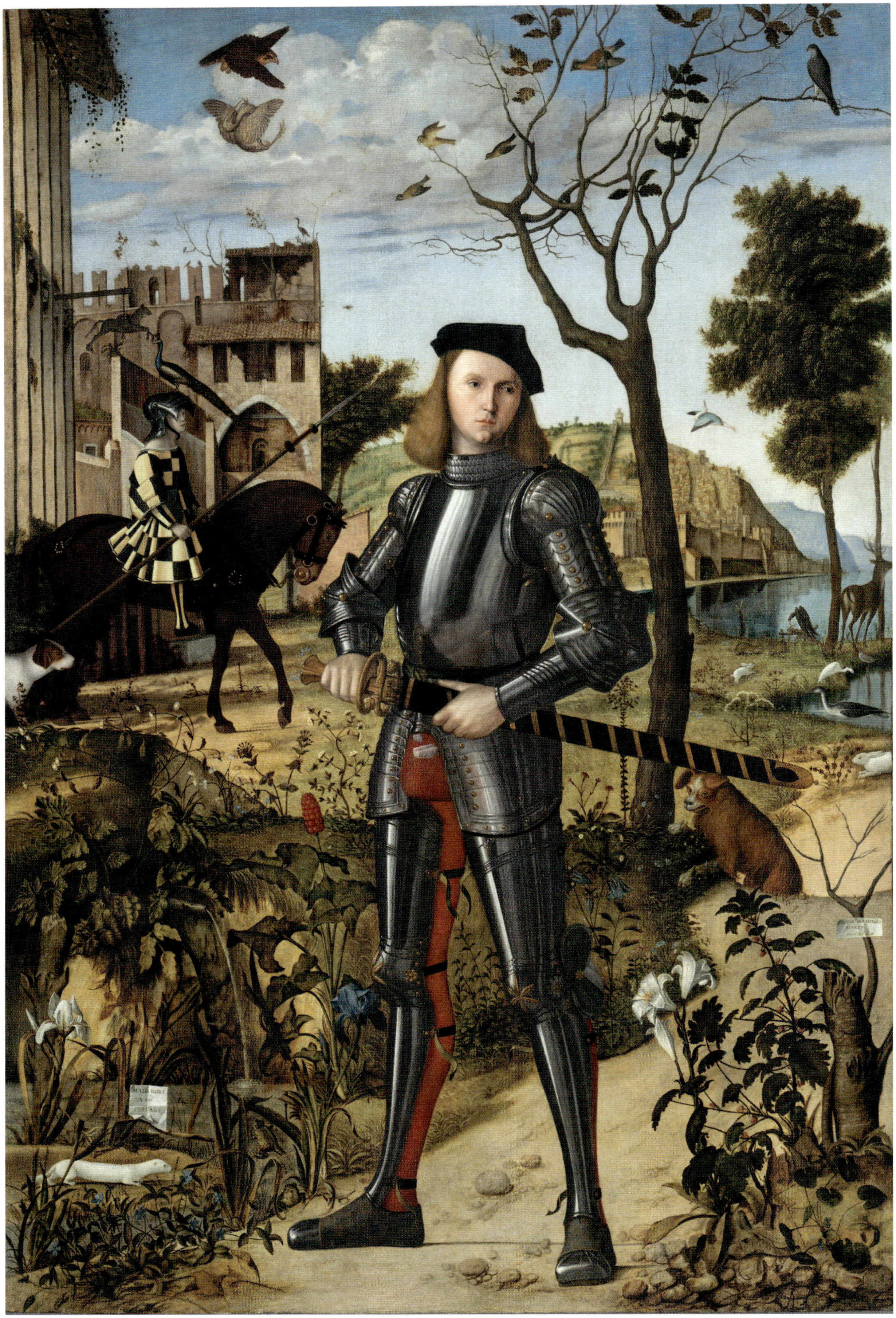

Fig. 5

Vittore Carpaccio, *Young Knight in a Landscape*, c.1505. Madrid, Museo Nacional Thyssen-Bornemisza, inv. 82 (1935.3)

Fig. 6

Albrecht Dürer, *Great Piece of Turf*, 1503. Vienna, Albertina, inv. 3075

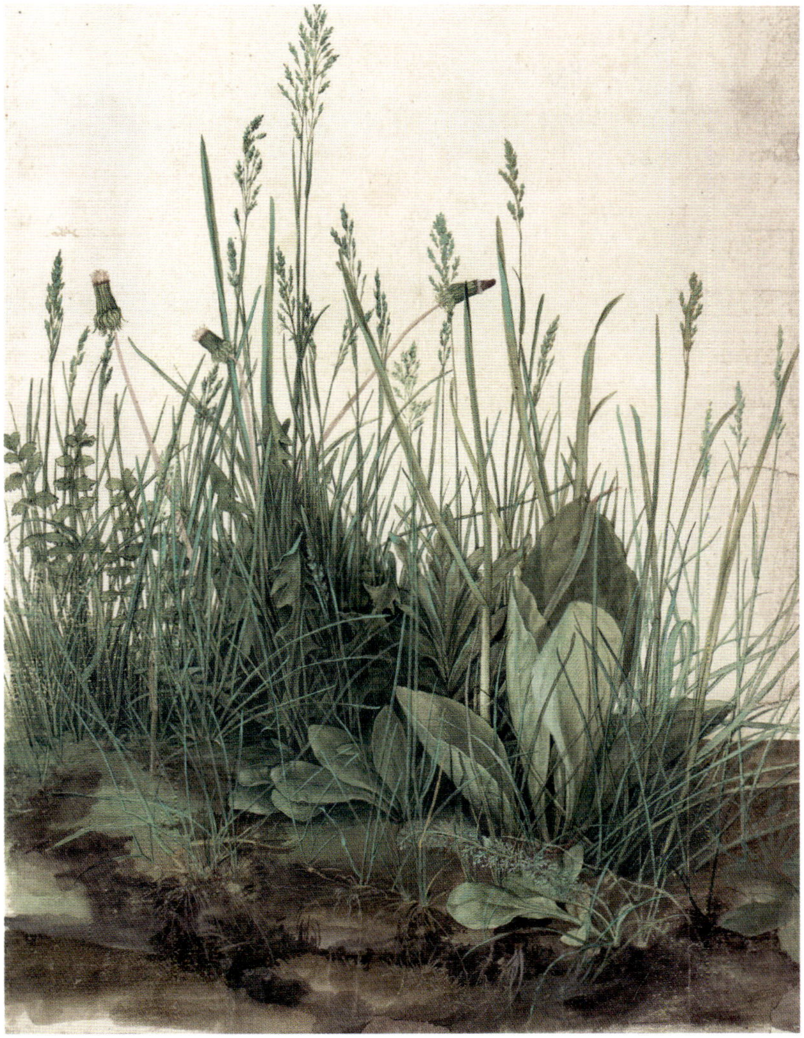

Another artist, whose paintings and graphic studies of animals, plants, and landscapes made a decisive contribution to depictions of the world of nature, spent even more time (and more often) in Venice than Leonardo. This was the German Albrecht Dürer, who, fascinated by classical antiquity and the natural world, and already familiar with humanist culture in his native Nuremberg, wished to explore this further in the lands of its origins, in particular studying the problems from a practical-theoretical perspective. After travelling through the Rhine Valley, which was full of successful printing workshops where the young 23-year-old occasionally lent a hand, he arrived in the lively city of Venice in autumn 1494. Here, Dürer came into contact with contemporary artists including the then elderly Giovanni Bellini, whom he described as 'the best in the art of painting', and Mantegna, and with a technique he deepened and soon mastered.[19] Several years later, from 1505 to about 1507, the German painter – now an acclaimed master – also returned to Italy (to depict Alpine landscapes), sparking a period of mutual creativity with his Italian colleagues.[20] His relationship, with the Venetian painter and engraver Jacopo dei Barbari (possibly already established in Germany) is of particular significance, with their shared passion for engraving and the subject of game and dead birds hanging up.[21]

However, unlike Leonardo (whom he never seems to have met), Dürer used mainly watercolours and temperas in his nature studies. Using the ancient technique of the miniature, he applied the pigments within the carefully defined outlines of the figures, which, in contrast with the atmospheric rendering favoured by Leonardo, stand out sharply and almost in trompe l'oeil, as in the *Great Piece of Turf* (fig. 6) – an extraordinary homage to a seemingly unremarkable part of nature – the *Stag Beetle* and the very lively *Young Hare*.[22] Among the depictions of animals, the tempera of a *Dead European Roller* (cat. 4.1) stands out (though the monogram and the date '1512' have resulted in a dating problem). The bird, portrayed naturally in the rigidity of death with its powerful, half-open beak and stiffened legs, adopts a figurative topos that began with the fresco of game in Pompeii and continued to the partridge in a famous still life by Jacopo de Barbari (1504, Munich, Alte Pinakothek). The subject, taken up again by Lucas Cranach and often reproduced, as in Hans Hoffmann's copy of Dürer's *Jay*, became common in European naturalist iconography. Compared to other ornithological temperas by Dürer, the miniature technique he used to paint this passerine with its unmistakeable blue livery is distinguished by the intensive use of the pen.[23]

The attribution to the German master of the small *Bouquet of Violets* (cat. 4.2) is more controversial because of the probable chromatic retouching, apparently made later, identified by some scholars in the petals of the flowers that thicken at the centre of the crown of leaves. The result of the same detailed, meticulous observation of botanical reality as the *Great Piece of Turf*, the work stands out thanks to the absolute originality of the subject, which made it into a successful 'icon' that prefigured the invention of the still life.[24]

The success of Dürer's work (Emperor Rudolf II, for example, was an avid collector) resulted in the immediate development of a school and the making of numerous copies – even of forgeries that impudently reproduced the master's famous monogram.[25] Alongside the phenomenon of forgeries (primarily of Dürer's botanical and zoological works), it is worth noting that, in the field of naturalist illustration, copies should be seen not only as the result of a refined technical practice, but as affirmation of the existence of a given individual or species, the knowledge of which it was appropriate to circulate among naturalists, who were accustomed to exchanging images to keep in their collections and use for educational purposes.

Among Dürer's followers, his younger Nuremberg compatriot Hans Hoffmann stands out. Hoffmann was later taken on by Rudolf II as court painter in Prague. As well as reworking some of Dürer's subjects, he also copied several of them, such as the *Stag Beetle* (cat. 5), whose gigantic lower jaw and stout wing case he reproduced with particular accuracy.[26] Nature inspired in him more expressive compositions, such as the small painting of the *Expulsion from Paradise* (cat. 38) in which numerous tiny animals are hidden on the ground between a plantain, a lily of the valley and possibly an exotic sunflower, almost as if the artist amused himself by challenging the observer to decipher them.[27] The *Earthly Paradise* theme actually allowed artists to test themselves with the depiction of animals and plants, as in the works of Daniel Froeschl (cat. 37) and Roelant Savery (cat. 39).

As already shown by the composition of the *Carrarese* and *Rinio* herbals, signs were evident in the various Veneto centres, even before the full expansion of Venetian rule on the mainland, of an entirely 'natural' scientific culture that, including the study of the body and the three natural kingdoms, became more and more widespread over the course of the modern age. This was certainly very evident in Padua, thanks mainly, as mentioned, to the presence of the university. Several scholars from the thirteenth to fourteenth centuries ought to be remembered,

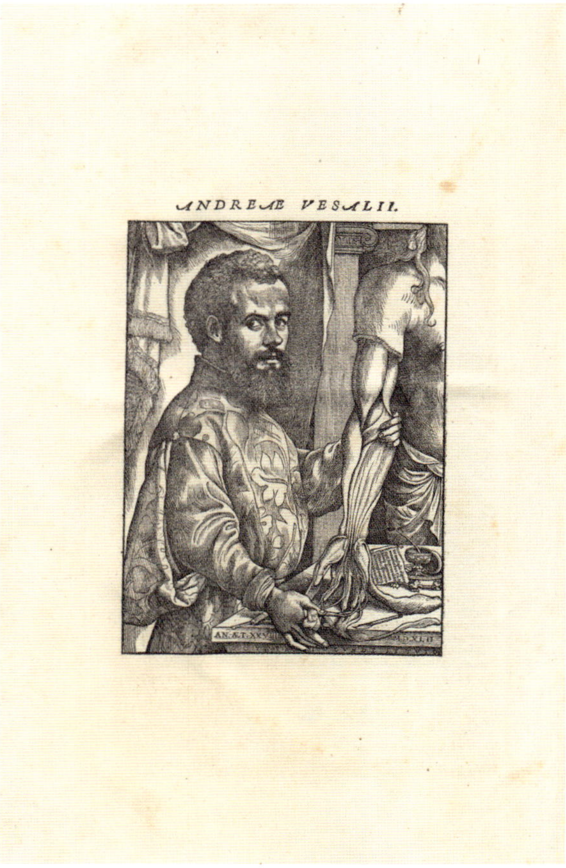

Fig. 7

Andrea Vesalius, *De Humani corporis fabrica*, Basel 1543. Vienna, Austrian National Library, Department of Manuscripts and Rare Books, *69.B.55 ALT PRUNK, 22

Fig. 8
Girolamo Fabrizi d'Acquapendente, *Scimmia, bertuccia*, in: *Theatrum totius animalis fabricae, De anatomia animalium*, 1575–1625. Venice, Biblioteca Nazionale Marciana, Rari 113.1, fol. 0:248884

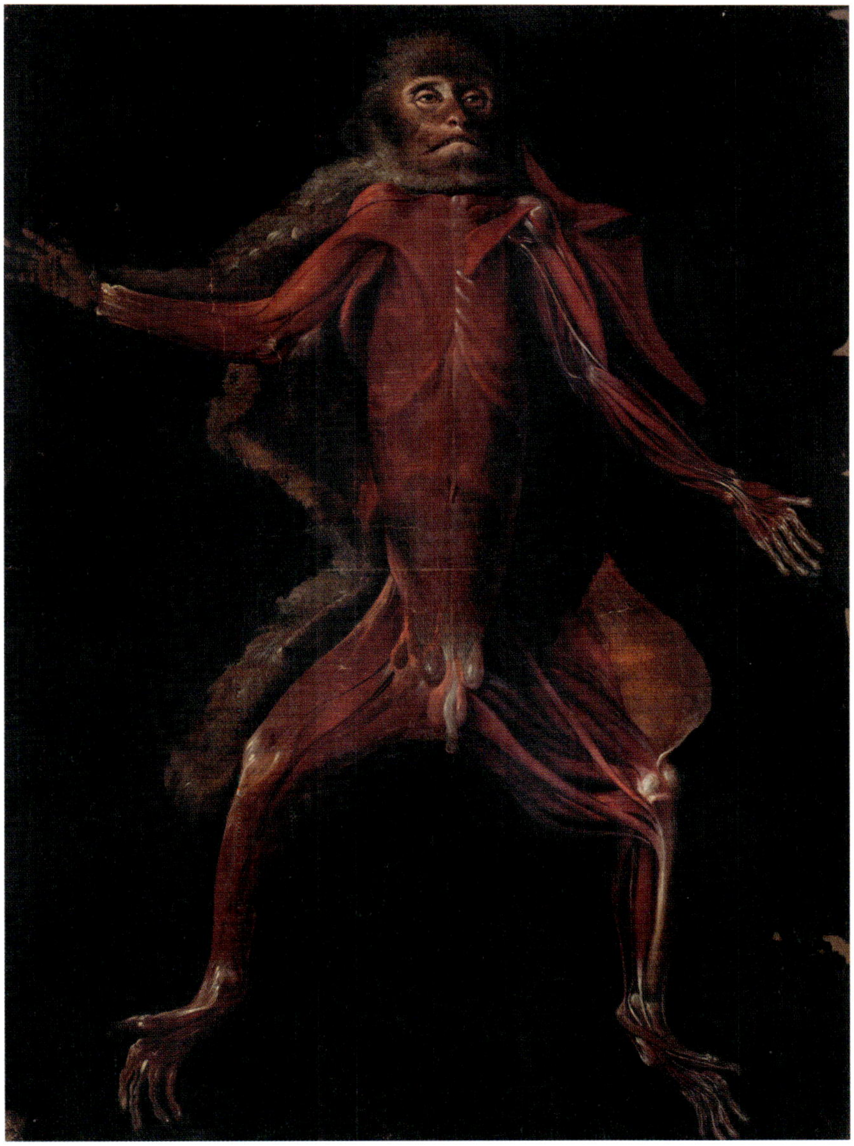

including Pietro d'Abano, who travelled all the way to Constantinople to learn Greek so that he could read the classical medical texts without the mediation of Arabic and Latin translations; Petrarch's friend Giovanni Dondi dall'Orologio, who was renowned for having built the *Astrarium*, a complicated astronomical clock, 'one of the most important machines of all time';[28] the physician Bartolomeo Montagnana; and Alessandro Benedetti, inventor of a moveable amphitheatre for public anatomical demonstrations.

The Padua school of anatomy, both human and comparative, led the field in Europe in the sixteenth century, thanks mainly to the anatomists Andrea Vesalio, Realdo Colombo, Gabriele Falloppia, and Girolamo Fabrici d'Acquapendente. Although Colombo and Falloppia did not manage to enrich their works with an iconographic apparatus, despite their wishes, it is known that those of Vesalio and Fabrici attained an extraordinary and spectacular unity between art and science; their works were among the most successful of the visual culture that, also associated with anatomy, was coming to the fore in the first decades of the sixteenth century.[29] The woodcuts illustrating Vesalio's *De humani corporis fabrica* – probably by one or more artists working in Titian's Venice workshop, among whom was the Fleming Jan Stephan van Calcar – were not only intended to make the description in the text clearer, i.e. 'visible', but undoubtedly favoured 'an aesthetic reception of knowledge of the human body' and thus aimed to circulate anatomical knowledge beyond specialist readers (fig. 7).[30] Fabrici d'Acquapendente – physician to Galileo, who claimed to have 'received health several times' from him,[31] and teacher of William Harvey[32] – had his works illustrated not with woodcuts but copperplates, and of a significant quality. Apart from believing that images were indispensable, he realized that their didactic and more generally communicative value would be much greater if they were in colour. To this end, he launched a grandiose project that aimed to produce a coloured, illustrated atlas of human and animal anatomy, the *Theatrum totius animalis fabricae*. Ultimately, this was not published, apart from some prototypes, but he managed to amass 300 plates in oil on paper (fig. 8), which he described as 'coloured pictures of anatomy'.[33] Some of these have been attributed to the workshop of Jacopo Bassano and his sons.

In 1545, a rather important innovation was made to the course of studies at Padua University. At the insistence of Francesco Bonafede, who had already started teaching a new course on herbal medicine, a botanical garden was set up so that theoretical lessons could be profitably followed by direct observation of the plant essences. One of the first institutions of its kind in Europe, along with those in Pisa and Florence, the garden certainly helped increase Padua's prestige as an international centre of medical-anatomical and naturalist studies.[34] The Venetian nobleman Daniele Barbaro, amateur architect, and translator of and commentator on Vitruvius's *De architectura*, took a leading role in designing the layout of the garden.[35] A scholar from an early age of philosophy, mathematics, astronomy, and optics, he was also interested in the natural world. Between 1542 and around 1550 he amassed a collection of drawings of fish from the Adriatic, the Mediterranean, the Atlantic and various Italian rivers and lakes (more than 300, according to the French naturalist and traveller Pierre Belon, who saw them in London and copied some of them). Many were executed by a certain Maestro Plinio, recently identified as Plinio Scarpelli, to whom Barbaro paid a salary for eight years. Ulisse Aldrovandi and Ippolito Salviani, author of the *Aquatilium animalium historia*, and probably other scholars, took various images from this *Libro dei pesci* for their own printed works.[36]

Shortly before the founding of Padua's botanical garden, two major publishing ventures in Germany had significant impact on the field of botany and nature studies more generally. The *Herbarum vivae eicones* by Otto Brunfels appeared in 1530, followed in 1542 by the *De historia stirpium commentarii* by Leonhart Fuchs (cat. 19). The key innovation in both books was the presence of illustrations (more than 500 woodcuts in Fuchs's book, which were immediately watercoloured in many copies); as has been pointed out, this reflected the new concept of the relationship between the artist and nature, inaugurated a few years earlier in Italy and Germany by Leonardo and Dürer.[37] The response was immediate in Italy, especially in the Venetian Republic. In 1544, the physician Pietro Andrea Mattioli – who had graduated from Padua University and, after a stay in Trento in the service of Cardinal Bernardo Clesio,[38] was working in Gorizia – published the work of the ancient Greek author Dioscorides, translated, integrated and commented on by himself.[39] This was the first of various editions without illustrations, as initially Mattioli did not want them, but it was followed by versions illustrated with small and large woodcuts based on drawings by Giorgio Liberale of Udine. Mattioli's *Commentari* (cat. 20) was an extraordinary publishing success. Its numerous editions in Latin and Italian, and translations in various other languages, rapidly became and long remained a key reference work for physicians, apothecaries, and botanists, and those simply curious about nature.[40]

Venice with its port, a point of arrival for novelties and oddities from the East (including naturalist ones), and Padua, with its reputation for medical learning, attracted many scholars and students who would become scholars.[41] In 1543 or (according to some authors) 1544, the Swiss Conrad Gessner was in the lagoon city, where he came into possession of some pictures of fish. Later, he had these engraved into his impressive zoological work (cat. 23), which for a long time influenced scholars and provided models for artists.

But it was in the second half of the sixteenth century that the passion for studying nature exploded in the Veneto area, involving several social classes and moving well beyond the circle around Padua's botanical garden. This had immediately established itself as an important research centre, including at a European level; the garden's layout, along with a list of the plant varieties cultivated there, was published in 1591 by Giacomo Antonio Cortuso (cat. 79). Venetian publishers certainly helped to sustain this passion, as they were keen to publish travel reports and works of 'medicinal material', also concerning the New World and other distant lands, from which information on animals, plants, and minerals was avidly gathered. Between 1550 and 1559, Giovanni Battista Ramusio published three large volumes of *Navigationi et viaggi*, the last of which included a translation of the works of the Spanish traveller and naturalist Gonzalo Fernandez de Oviedo.[42]

Among the physicians and apothecaries who devoted themselves to studying nature, including for professional reasons, we mention a few, starting with Agostino Alpago of Belluno. He was not the author of any publication, but a respected expert on flora and in contact with the first director of Padua's botanical garden, Luigi Squalermo (known as Anguillara) as well as Aldrovandi, Mattioli and Pietro Antonio Michiel.[43] Alpago took part in a scientific expedition on Monte Baldo with Anguillara, Aldrovandi, and others. The group was led by the Francesco Calzolari (mentioned above), who worked closely with the most important Italian and European naturalists in the second half of the century. He set up a museum of 'things of nature' and curiosities above his apothecary's shop in Verona, which soon became famous and was described as 'a universal theatre, of all the most exquisite and singular things in the world'.[44] A few decades later, another Veronese apothecary, Giovanni Pona, following

Calzolari's footsteps, set up his own museum;[45] in 1617, he published a guide to Monte Baldo that included illustrations of endemic plants.

The interest in the natural world was widespread at all levels of society and throughout the territory of the Venice Republic, and not only for therapeutic purposes. In Padua, Vincenzo Pinelli was at the centre of a European network of scholars, whom he managed to put in contact with one another and many of whom he welcomed to his home. He owned not only a very rich library, but also scientific instruments, maps, fossils, seeds, and a garden with many rare plants. Naturalist finds and curiosities were to be found in Venice, in the collections of (to cite only a few cases) the merchant Andrea Odoni ('crabs, fish, petrified snakes, a dried chameleon, small and rare sea snails, crocodiles, bizarre fish'),[46] though he preferred to have himself portrayed by Lorenzo Lotto among antiquities and medals, which were more suited to his social advancement; Gabriele and then Andrea Vendramin; and Federico Contarini, in whose home Aldrovandi recorded the presence 'among the other beautiful things' of 'an earth with very rubicund, petrified drops of blood'. Giacomo Contarini, a man of encyclopaedic culture and 'special protector' of one of Jacopo Bassano's sons, Francesco,[47] possessed some items from the natural world, though his collection consisted mainly of paintings and mechanical and scientific instruments.[48] He also owned two gardens, one 'very beautiful and abundant'[49] at his villa in Dolo, the other at his palazzo in Venice. The presence of private gardens among the Veneto nobility is further testimony to the widespread interest in nature. In Padua, for example, there was the garden of Cardinal Pietro Bembo, later enriched by his son Torquato,[50] and in Venice, at San Trovaso, that of the aforementioned Pietro Antonio Michiel, 'extremely learned, and especially in the identification of plants',[51] which its owner was fairly reluctant to show to visitors. In any case, the whole of Venice and its mainland territories were teeming with gardens, vegetable plots and kitchen gardens, some arranged on terraces or buildings, others consisting simply of plants grown in pots.[52]

The academic studies, or naturalist interests more generally, were also supported by the results (printed reports, letters, and collections of finds) of the travels that numerous scholars made in the East, especially in Venice's Mediterranean possessions. From Crete, Onorio Belli of Vicenza sent plants and pictures of plants, often drawn by himself, to other naturalists.[53] Prospero Alpini (see cats. 75, 76) visited Egypt from 1580 to 1584; Anguillara visited the Greek islands, Aleppo, Tunisia and probably Egypt; and Melchior Guilandino, Anguillara's successor as director of the Padua botanical garden, went to Palestine and Egypt, after earlier botanical expeditions in the East.[54] Venice was the ideal departure point for every scholar embarking on a scientific expedition because of the ease of boarding ships sailing to many parts of the Mediterranean; it was from there that Giuseppe Casabona, a 'herbalist' in the service of the Grand Duchy of Tuscany, left to go and botanize in Crete,[55] from where he brought back a rich corpus of pictures of island plants (cat. 85).

Venice was also, of course, the perfect place for purchasing all types of natural finds. Aldrovandi visited the lagoon city twice as well as other Veneto cities, where he not only 'saw infinite natural marine and terrestrial things', but also 'collected many rare things'.[56] Aldrovandi was a client of Leone Tartaglini, one of the most renowned sellers of *cose di natura,* including 'artificial' monsters, along with medicinal secrets. He was one of the many charlatans who thronged the squares of Venice and the rest of Italy, but he was not without knowledge of natural history and had set up his own museum – though he was more than happy to sell its contents.[57] Apart from seeking finds for his collection, Aldrovandi wished mainly to procure illustrations of animals, plants, and minerals;[58] by the end of his life, he had managed to collect about 8,000 colour plates (cf. cats. 31, 32).[59] Venice with its large number of artists, including many from the north, could certainly satisfy him in this respect. As the cases of Daniele Barbaro and Conrad Gessner show, illustrations of fish were particularly easy to find in the lagoon city, as the abundant fish stalls could easily provide models. The large parchments on which Giorgio Liberale depicted the fauna of the Adriatic for Archduke Ferdinand of Tyrol are still extant – and still awe-inspiring (fig. 9). Tintoretto might also have visited these fish stalls to make sketches, given the fairly realistic portrayal of fish, birds, and other animals in his *Creation of the Animals.*[60] At the beginning of his research work, Aldrovandi had already turned to Michiel to obtain pictures of fish; the latter had commissioned illustrations of more than a thousand plants, mainly by the painter-engraver Domenico Dalle Greche.[61] The outcome of this request is not known, but the fact that for Aldrovandi the Veneto area was, like the Medici in Florence, a place to obtain pictures of 'things of nature', is amply documented in his manuscripts. Furthermore, the artist who worked in Aldrovandi's employ the longest, about thirty years, was Giovanni Neri, from Verona.

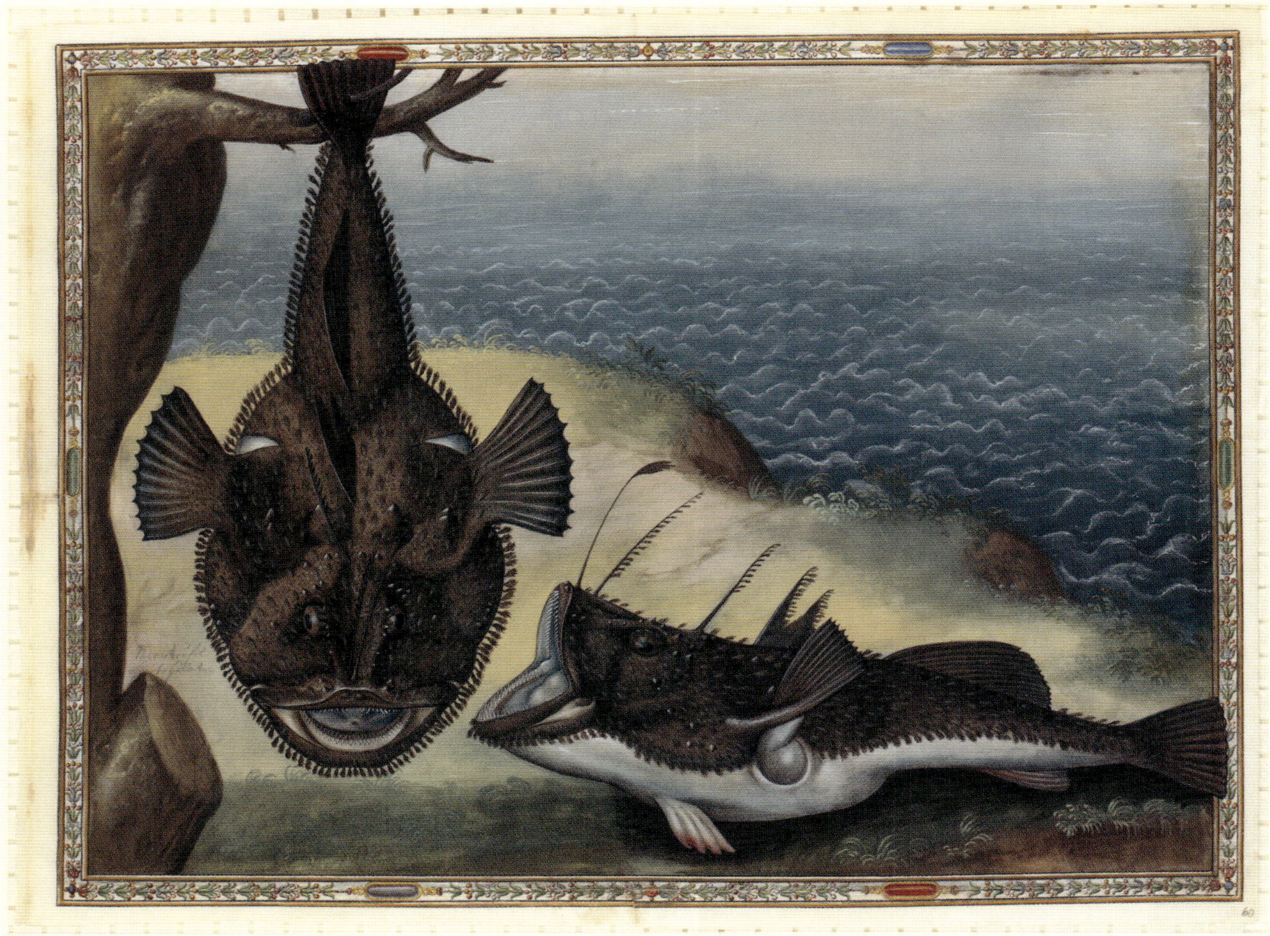

Fig. 9

Giorgio Liberale, *Album with Animal Illustrations (Marine Fauna of the Adriatic Sea)*, 1562–before 1580. Vienna, Austrian National Library, Department of Manuscripts and Rare Books, Cod. Ser. n. 2669, fol. 60r

A painter, particularly of birds, he alternated his artistic work with astrology, predictions, and prognostications.

One of the greatest nature illustrators of the late sixteenth century was also active in Veneto, before moving to Florence: Jacopo Ligozzi, born in Verona, the home of distinguished naturalists and artists sensitive to nature. When Aldrovandi was in Florence in 1577 as a guest of Francesco I de' Medici, this inquisitive nature lover was astonished by the sight of the 'pictures painted from life by Signor Jacomo Ligozzi, which lack nothing if not spirit'.[62] Aspects of Ligozzi's time in Veneto remain obscure and the few traces we have still need to be fully verified. If the 'Giacomo painter from Verona' mentioned by Leone Tartaglini in his will is Ligozzi, it is evident that Tartaglini owned fifteen pictures of 'very rare fruit' by the artist, and possibly a book of fish and one of 'birds and plants', all on parchment.[63] These illustrations attracted the attention of Aldrovandi and other naturalists because they were unanimously regarded as being of an extraordinary descriptive quality. The aforementioned apothecary Francesco Calzolari, who owned 'numerous books' with 'various and rare plants depicted from life', also used the same painter as Tartaglini.[64] After Calzolari's death, his nephew, also called Francesco, printed a new catalogue for the museum he had inherited, furnishing it with a fine view (cat. 80) in which 'many books' ('molti libri') containing pictures of plants portrayed *ex vivo* are mentioned. It is particularly interesting that it also lists the names of the painters, all born in Verona, who had been in the service of his uncle: there are quite a number, confirming how many artists in the Veneto area were willing to work with scientists in various ways. Along with Felice Brusasorzi and Paolo Farinati, a Ligozzi is mentioned and then Marcoleone and Caroto.[65] Little is known of Francesco Marcoleone (or Marcoleoni), but if, as it seems, he was a painter of still lifes, this would be in keeping with work as an illustrator of nature. Aldrovandi described him as a 'pupil of Ligozzi, a rare painter'.[66] As for Caroto, it is likely, for reasons of age, that this was not Giovan Francesco but his younger brother, Giovanni, 'highly skilled in the art of drawing'.[67] In this case too, it is plausible that one of the two artists had worked for Calzolari, since their father (and then also Giovan Francesco and his son Bernardino) had opened an apothecary's shop in the same square as that of the author of *Il viaggio di Monte Baldo*.[68] Regarding 'Ligozzi', it is natural and tempting to think once again of Jacopo, to whose activity in Veneto the parchments with figures of birds have been referred, and especially those with illustrations of fish cited in the inventory of Rudolf II's collections, which are possibly to be identified as those previously owned by Tartaglini.[69] Nevertheless, in the light of later, signed temperas of plants, birds, fish, and mammals produced in Florence for the Medici grand dukes by the eclectic Veronese artist, who continued to also paint devotional subjects, *vanitates*, anatomies, and portraits, it is fairly difficult to attribute both collections unconditionally to the same hand.

In any case, the images in Rudolf's ornithological manuscript certainly show not only an assured talent in the miniature technique, but also a 'specialist' attention focused on the examples. We could conjecture that this iconographic corpus was drawn by Jacopo's brother Francesco, who worked in Venice and specialized primarily in the depiction of bird life.[70] It is more likely that Jacopo put his hand to the ichthyological images of the second codex, drawing at least some of these in Venice.[71]

What is certain is that when Jacopo arrived in Florence at the age of thirty he must have fully mastered naturalist painting.[72] The learned and inquisitive Grand Duke Francesco de' Medici immediately availed himself of this talent to create a large collection of plates (now held in the Gallerie degli Uffizi, along with some loose sheets and copies), some of which were generously sent by the sovereign to Aldrovandi.[73] Many of the copies were probably by one of Jacopo's relatives, perhaps his brother Francesco or his cousin, also called Francesco, son of his uncle Mercurio Ligozzi. One significant example of the technical skill and vitality that Jacopo brought to the subjects he portrayed is the large picture of an Angelica plant (cat. 81). The bean plant (cat. 82), again from the Rudolf collections, is also of undoubted prominence; although of high quality, it seems to include a partial contribution by one of Jacopo's relatives.

It is clear that in the early modern age a close relationship linked naturalist imagery to a new way of perceiving the landscape, an awareness that plants and animals are inseparable from their natural environment. This phenomenon spread throughout Europe from the mid-sixteenth century when the increasingly deeper thinking on the natural world was endorsed by scientific knowledge.

A fundamental element of this process was made by the painting and graphic work of Pieter Bruegel the Elder. In the wake of fifteenth-century Flemish tradition and surpassing the age-old custom of the landscape being interpreted as 'background', Bruegel painted landscapes capable of illustrating the changing appearance of vegetation from luxuriant to bare, the atmospheric variations

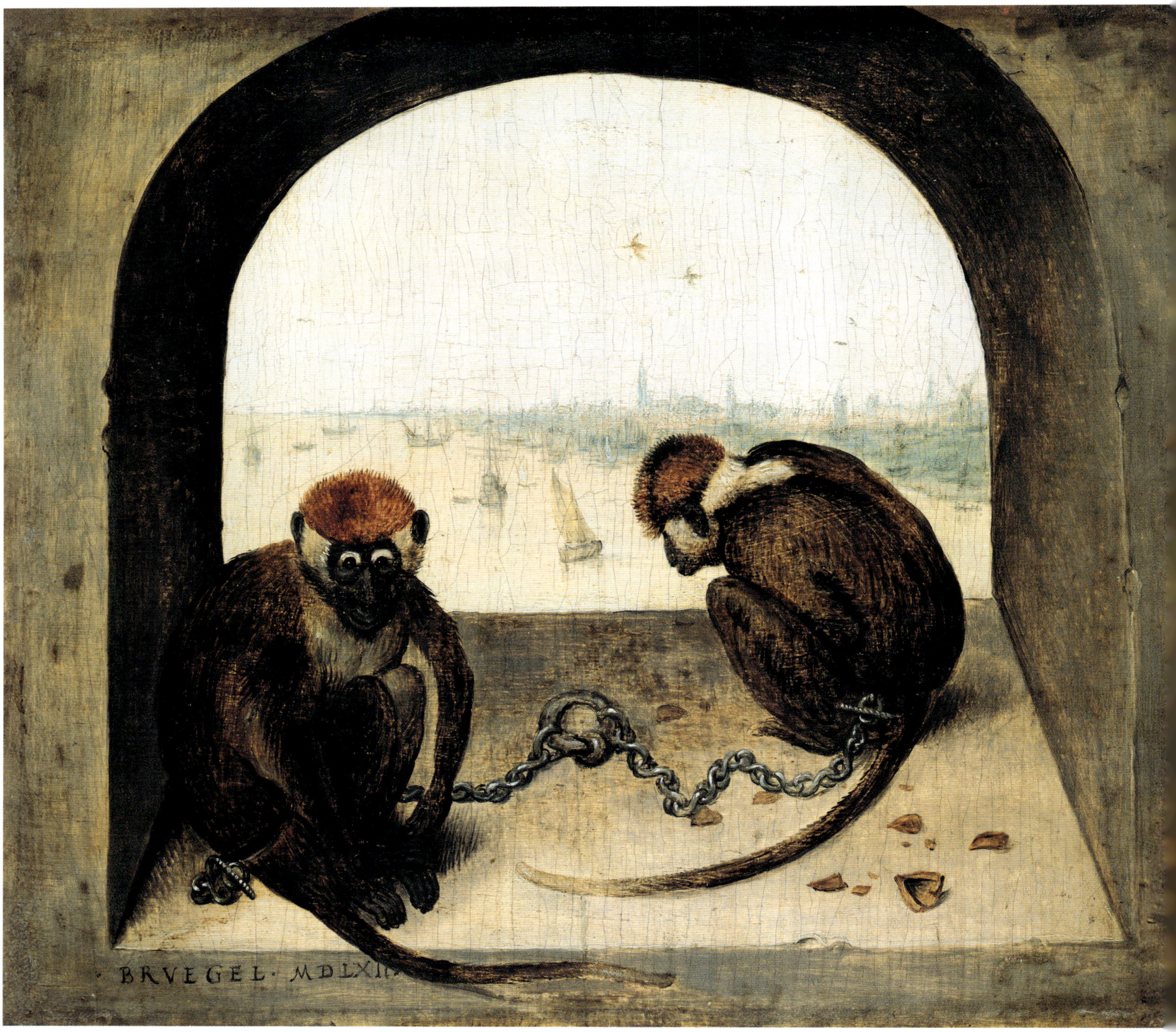

Fig. 10
Pieter Bruegel the Elder, *Two Chained Monkeys*, 1562. Staatliche Museen zu Berlin, Gemäldegalerie, inv. 2077

of light at different hours of the day, the alternation of the seasons, various human activities (such as *The Harvesters* and the beautiful drawing depicting *The Beekepers;* see essay Pénot, p. 39, figs. 1, 5) and the constant presence of animals. Bruegel also painted a small picture marked by extraordinary scientific precision: *Two Chained Monkeys* (fig. 10),[74] in which, regardless of the symbolic and allegorical meanings applied to them, the primates are portrayed from life and in great detail. Red-capped mangabeys, they might have come from Africa to the port of Antwerp, which is depicted in the background.

An interesting phenomenon occurred in the last decades of the sixteenth century thanks to the increasingly extensive circulation and knowledge of miniated naturalist plates and monographic works dedicated to the vegetable and animal worlds (which emerged with greater frequency from European printing houses), arousing the interest and imagination of the artists.

The most singular use of this material were the bizarre and disorienting 'inventions' of Giuseppe Arcimboldo, who, already attracted by the natural world in his youthful Milanese period, found plenty to inspire him at the Habsburg courts of Vienna and Prague. Ulisse Aldrovandi had received from Prague drawings painted by Arcimboldo of unusual animals, such as a desert rat, a Central American bird of the *Cracidae* family, and a coati.[75] The artist was inspired by Conrad Gessner's full-bodied treatises to paint the numerous mammals that make up the face of *Earth* (cat. 30.3) and the birds in the lost painting dedicated to *Air*. The ichthyological works of Guillaume Rondelet, Pierre Belon, and Ippolito Salviani also prompted him to create that extraordinary assemblage of marine organisms that make up the head of *Water* (cat. 30.2). The painter also looked to the vegetable world; see, for example, the corn and aubergine in the head of *Summer* (cat. 28.2) and the peony, iris, and tulip in that of *Spring* (cat. 28.1). It should be noted that the ideas offered by these did not restrict or attenuate the liveliness of the organisms depicted, which, under Arcimboldo's brush – using a more condensed technique than that of the 'naturalist miniature' – veritably pulsate with life.

An opposite phenomenon took place from the middle of the sixteenth century. Men of science now took an interest in figurative works that interpreted aspects of the natural world according to completely new criteria. These were the result of profound economic changes, of new systems of agricultural cultivation, production, and trade that improved the living conditions of the peasants and led, eventually, to the spread of richer, more varied diets.

New genre scenes including markets, kitchens, and butcheries spread from the flourishing lands of Germany and Flanders, where the privileged social classes appreciated paintings with 'low culture' subjects. The initial cue still came from biblical stories, but these, relegated to the painting's background and small in scale, were actually now quite irrelevant. The accentuated naturalism and tactile presence of nature's bounty in the foreground, offered by cheeky saleswomen and staunch salesmen and almost invading the viewer's space, ended up clouding the polysemic allusions suggested by the critics, be they allegorical, satirical, or lascivious. Pieter Aertsen from Flanders and his nephew Joachim Beuckelaer specialized in portraying market stalls with opulent displays of vegetables in baskets and trays, numerous kinds of fish, slices of meat, live and plucked birds, and lambs' heads, all portrayed with bright colours and meticulous detail taken from real life. Jan Baptist Saive (cat. 89) was later to adapt the subject to the 'seasons of the year'.

In Italy, the butchery genre was practised by Bartolomeo Passarotti (who was in contact with Aldrovandi) and Annibale Carracci, both from Bologna. Vincenzo Campi of Cremona (cat. 65) painted five market pictures commissioned by the influential German banker Hans Fugger.[76]

Highly skilled in portraying everyday and rural subjects, these artists probably paid little attention to the modern zoological and botanical monographs drawn up by men of science, who, conversely, ended up appreciating and collecting an ever-increasing number of fruit and vegetable paintings. Stimulated by anatomical curiosity, they also collected temperas depicting plucked chickens and beefsteaks, as shown by that plates that seem out of place but were an entirely valid part of the collection of the ancient Giardino dei Semplici in Pisa (fig. 11; cat. 70).

A profound change in the perception of landscape and the environment also occurred in Venice and Veneto in the second half of the sixteenth century. This was a result of the increasing interest that the nobility, traditionally linked to the sea, took in the mainland and in agricultural management. These areas were now dominated by the villa, which had become a place of delight, but also a centre for land cultivation (see essay Demo, p. 103). Such sensitivity towards a more extensive physical space was taken up and personally expressed by three geniuses who marked the figurative culture of Venice, Italy, and Europe in the second half of the century: Titian, Veronese, and Tintoretto.

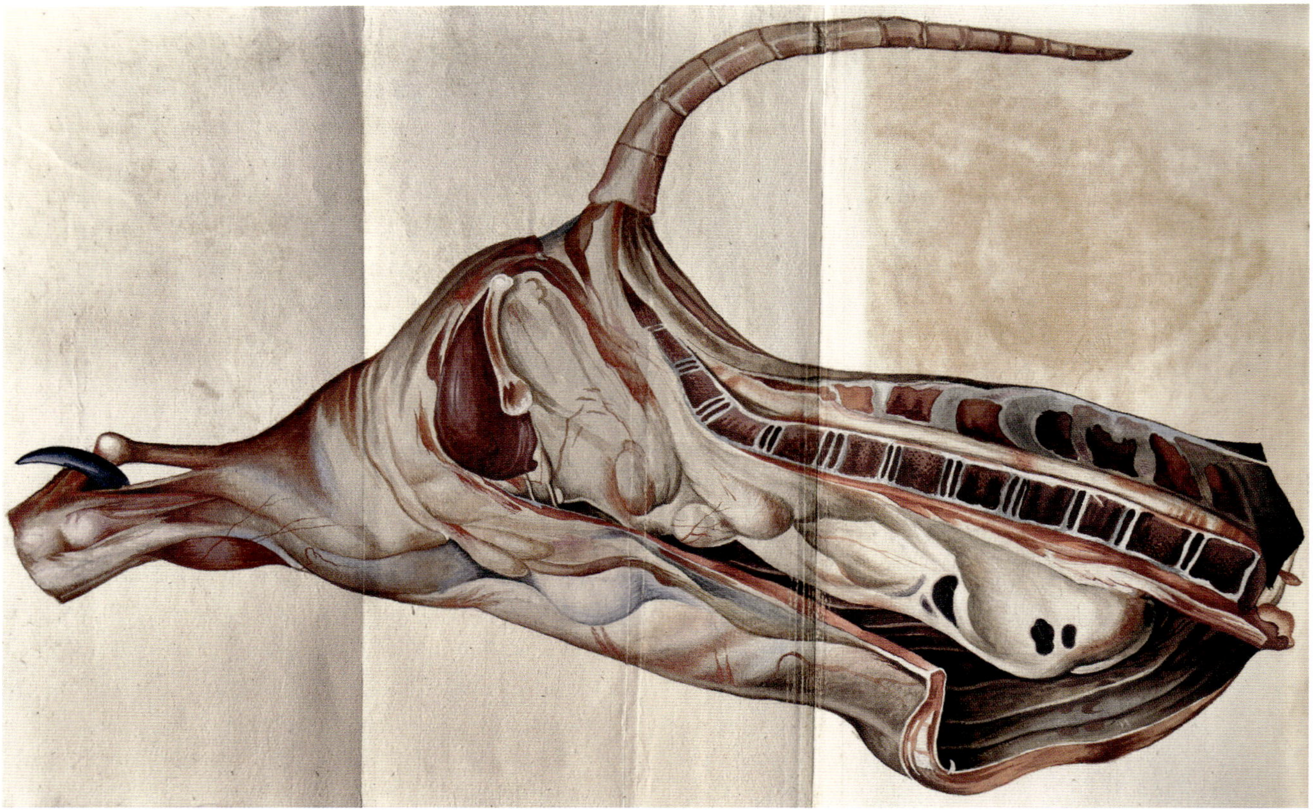

Fig. 11

Attributed to Daniel Fröschl, *A Piece of Meat*, in: *Disegni di animali*, late 16th cent./early 17th cent. Pisa, Biblioteca Universitaria, Ms. 514, fol. 368r

Titian – of whom Carlo Ridolfi recalled 'some shepherds and animals' in woodcut[77] – was one of the first artists to elaborate rural and pastoral subjects, as shown by *Landscape with a Milkmaid,*[78] a drawing attributed to him that was probably inspired by an engraving of the same name by Lucas van Leyden (cat. 57). Whatever the case, the subject (already present in Mattioli's botanical work) was adopted, reworked, and enriched with scenes of agricultural work such as ploughing and minding herds by numerous contemporary engravers. These included Domenico Campagnola and Niccolò Boldrini (cat. 58), who are linked to Titian's multifaceted workshop, where (as mentioned above) the woodcuts for Vesalio's great anatomical project were also made.

It was this landscape, crowded with animals and events of rural life, that was to provide the background for many paintings that came from the Dal Ponte workshop in Bassano. The family – later known as the 'Bassano' – was headed by Jacopo (much admired by Titian), who, apart from amusing himself with poetry and playing the lute, as once again Ridolfi recalls, 'was pleased... to live in his homeland, benefiting from its native air, enjoying the comfort of his home, sometimes for recreation cultivating a certain little garden, full of herbs (*semplici*) that were given to him by Alfonso, Duke of Ferrara, and other Lords, among which he placed snakes and other animals painted on cards, which at first sight gave cause for apprehension'.[79]

Jacopo's sons, all also variously active in Venice, collaborated in a well-organized workshop that was capable of satisfying the demands of the Venetian nobility, Italian lords, and European sovereigns. Francesco, the eldest son, was followed by Giovanbattista, Gerolamo, and Leandro, the latter specializing in portraiture (following Titian, Veronese, and Tintoretto), but who – again in the words of Ridolfi – conceived 'many notions, where animals, fish, and household effects, and other things went in, which he also... drew with much application from the natural'.[80] The workshop ended with Jacopo Apollonio, who had trained under his uncle, Leandro.

Subjects such as the *Seasons*, the *Months*, the *Elements*, and *Noah's Ark* – perhaps with a fleeting allusion to biblical stories in the background and with subtle symbolic meanings – presented in structured theatrical sceneries, became an authentic genre that studied rural life, analyzing it with a lucid yet benevolent eye. Although the social context may seem idealized by the variety of the represented elements, by the compositional exuberance and by the expert colouring, we do see an essentially realistic recording of certain aspects of rural life and related crafts, alongside a plethora of animals.[81]

These were not the wild, exotic, or unusual creatures that populated the pages of the zoological treatises, but common domestic examples: placid herds of cattle, cows, calves, donkeys, flocks of sheep and goats, often being shorn (an image that Mattioli again made use of and is represented by Jacopo in his *Summer*; cat. 62.2), poultry, the odd peacock, cats and especially dogs, which must have been dearly loved by Jacopo Bassano and his sons. Jacopo himself painted a genuine 'portrait' of 'two hounds, i.e. only dogs' for a Venetian nobleman (see essay Del Torre Scheuch, p. 49, fig. 1), while in another small picture owned in 1633 by Cardinal Scipione Borghese, he had painted a sheep suckling a lamb.[82] The *Portrait of a Greyhound* (in a private collection) is of an extraordinary quality. It has been noted, rightly, that an impulse of vitality and dynamism is apparent in the 'seemingly so motionless' image of the dog, thanks to the tension of the veins, arteries, and muscles, to the 'minute bristle vibration' expressed by Jacopo: essentially, this painting is another example of the artist's great ability 'to mimic life, to recreate nature with painting'.[83]

A monkey is the only occasional exotic presence among the mainly farmyard animals that populate the paintings by Jacopo, his sons, and the workshop. Among Leandro's paintings, a monkey appears in *The Feast of Anthony and Cleopatra*, *The Rich Glutton and Poor Lazarus*, and the month *June* (cat. 67.6) in the *Cycle of the Months*. It was probably inserted to illustrate the *ars simia naturae* concept –that is, to proclaim the mimetic capacity of painting, or to indicate the mastery over instincts and lower passions.[84] It is often the same monkey, depicted in the same pose, suggesting that the various artists reworked as needed sketches that we know were abundant in the workshop. It is not unlikely that the original models were living examples; monkeys must have been fairly common in Venice (they also appear, for example, in paintings by Giovanni Bellini and Vittore Carpaccio), but it cannot be ruled out that the Bassano relied on previous prints.

Far from having a scientific purpose, the animals portrayed by the Bassano, singularly or as 'actors' in more structured compositions, are thus the result of rigorous attention focused on the peculiar behaviour of each species. It is not perhaps incidental to recall that the Bassano family aspired to cultural ascent: Leandro was nominated 'knight', while the young Gerolamo was sent to study medicine at Padua University, but soon called home to help meet the pressing demands of the workshop.

The Bassano and, in particular, Leandro, who 'knew how to live among the powerful and intellectuals',[85] seem to have had more than sporadic relations with the world of scientific research, which between the sixteenth and seventeenth centuries was marked by profound renewal. After his return from Egypt, whose natural reality and the therapeutic practices of the local physicians he illustrated in various works, Prospero Alpini practised as a doctor for some years in Bassano, where he also took a wife.[86] It was certainly during this period that he came into contact with the Bassano, as he treated some members of the family.[87] Moreover, it seems clear from a passage in his book that he was well aware of the 'savage melancholy' that had impelled one of Jacopo's sons, Francesco, to commit suicide.[88] Alpini had a house in Bassano where he used to go during the summer months to study in peace and enjoy the healthier air, even after he had become director of Padua's botanical garden and a professor at the university.[89] Leandro painted a portrait of Alpini aged 31 (cat. 75) in 1586, probably as a sign of gratitude for the medical treatments administered to his family: in the affectionate dedication on the back the painter states that the gift was made 'with grateful spirit' and as an expression of 'warm friendship'.[90] A second portrait of Alpini in old age was once thought to be the work of Leandro, but has more recently been attributed to the Bassano workshop.[91]

The practice of portraiture was very much alive in this busy workshop, especially with Leandro. He painted the likeness of an anonymous person whom we assume, due to the austere clothing, is a botanist or physician, captured in the act of presenting in a vase a large branch of hollyhock or *Alcea*, a plant endowed with well-known pharmaceutical virtues in addition to its horticultural value (cat. 77).[92] This latter portrait – like that of Alpini (to which one of an anonymous person held by the Philadelphia Museum of Art may be compared)[93] and that, unfortunately lost, of the public anatomist in Venice, Leone Bonzio or Leo Bontius (fig. 12), intent on dissecting a forearm and hand, in a pose resembling that of Vesalio in

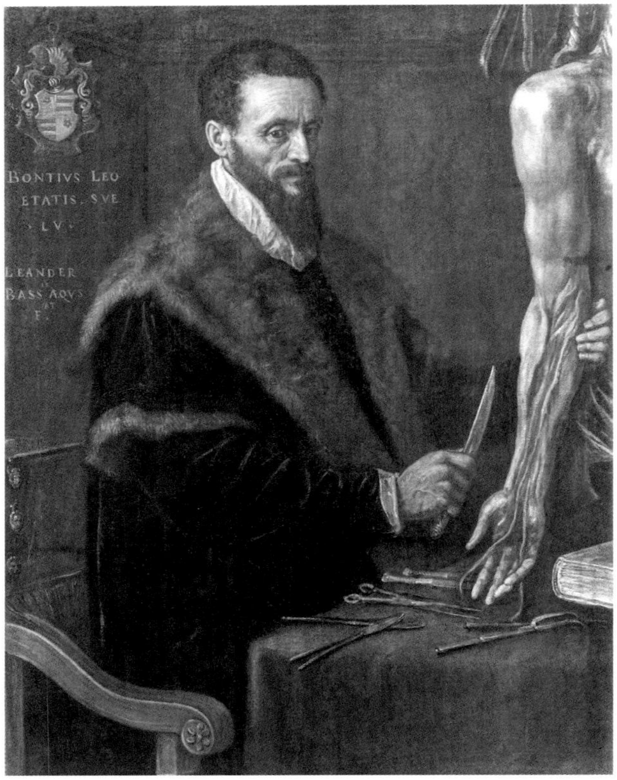

the woodcut contained in the *De humani corporis fabrica*[94] – confirm Leandro's predilection for painting 'people of middle-class extraction: physicians, merchants, jurists, Dominican friars, musicians and artists'.[95]

Leandro (or Gerolamo?) Bassano also painted another fine portrait for his friend Giovanni Francesco Sagredo (fig. 13), a member of a noble Venetian family, a dabbler in physics problems and a collector of paintings and scientific instruments – whom Galileo Galilei was to insert in his *Dialogo sui massimi sistemi* as the personification of the modern, enlightened man of science.[96] The friendly relations between Leandro and Sagredo are apparent from the correspondence that the Venetian exchanged with the Tuscan scientist,[97] from which not only a diatribe emerges on a series of the *Four Seasons* sent to the Grand Duke of Tuscany attributed by Gerolamo to 'Bassan Vecchio', which did not convince the buyers, but also other artistic matters. They discuss the respective portraits that the two friends intended exchanging (that of Sagredo by Leandro or Gerolamo), on 'two very beautiful nocturnes on touchstone' painted by the same Bassano, on a possible commission for a family portrait, along with the singular experiment that was made in Venice with 'some little spyglasses' that were used 'to see [the] paintings close up'.[98]

The story told to Galileo of a trip into the country in October 1618 is also fairly amusing, led by Sagredo in the company of 'Sir Bassano ... and a whore and her buffoon and a wench of mine', on the occasion of which Leandro 'wanted to portray the house, the barns, the cellar, the stalls, the lanes, all the fruits and animals he saw, but finally with difficulty I had him sketch the wench and my head, a plate of truffles, another of peaches'. These observations confirm the growing fortunes of the painting of everyday objects and of that apparent *sermo humilis* that the Bassano liberally inserted in their paintings.[99]

Giovanni Francesco Sagredo died in 1619 and Leandro followed him in 1622. Two years later, Galileo officially made known to the members of the Accademia dei Lincei about the '*cannoncino*' – that is, 'a beautiful little eye-glass that makes things appear that until now you didn't know had ever been created'.[100] A new science of nature was born with the microscope, which was also to have a great influence on the visual arts.[101]

Fig. 12

Leandro Bassano, *Portrait of Leo Bontius*, 1596. Present whereabouts unknown, formerly Ivenack Castle

Fig. 13

Attributed to Gerolamo Bassano, previously attributed to Leandro Bassano, *Portrait of Giovanni Francesco Sagredo*, 1619. Oxford, Ashmolean Museum, inv. WA1935.97

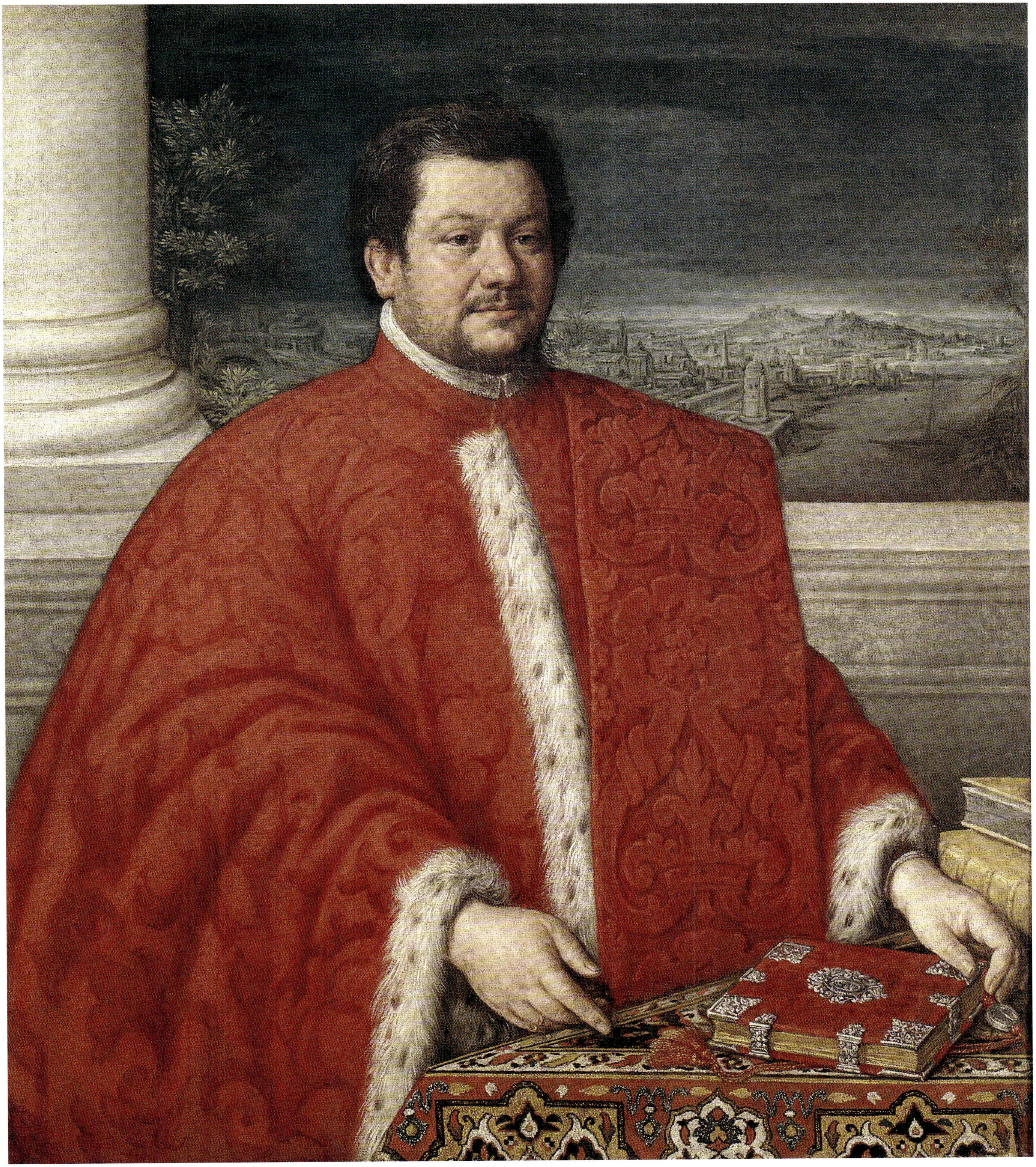

1 'Ritrovansi medicinevole herbette per sanità dei mortali, & massimamente nell'altissimo Monte Baldo, ch'è sopra la Città. Ove da ogni parte di Europa concorrono Herbolati a raccogliere Radici, & Herbette molto profittevole ad ogni grande infirmità', Alberti 1550, 417r–417v.
2 'Nelle spetierie necessarie'; 'luogho'; 'tanta varietà di piante e di natura calde e fredde, e silvestre e domestiche, acquatiche e montane, quanta in nissun'altra della Italia', Calzolari 1566, 4, 7.
3 Garin 1983, 17. Cf. Berti 1986, 19–25.
4 Simonsfeld 1887; Roeck 1999; Wirtz 2006.
5 The Pliny treatise came to light in Venice in 1469. On Pliny's 'errors', cf. Barbaro 1534.
6 London, British Museum, Cod. Egerton 2020.
7 Cod. Lat.VI, 59 =1565. Cf. Blunt and Raphael 1990, 73–7.
8 Pitacco 2002, 11–23.
9 Blunt and Raphael 1990, 77; Mariani Canova 1988, 25–6.
10 Pächt 1950.
11 Pächt 1950.
12 Bergamo, Biblioteca Civica. Cf. Rossi 2002; Recanati 1998, 17–43. The *Historia Plantarum* codex, Rome, Biblioteca Casanatense, has been attributed to Giovannino and his school.
13 Cf. exh. cat. London 1981; Emboden 1987; Taglialagamba 2010; exh. cat. London and Edinburgh 2019/20.
14 'Col tempo ogni cosa va variando', London, British Library, Codice Arundel 263, fol. 57r.
15 Mantua, Archivio di Stato, Archivio Gonzaga, serie E, busta 1439, f. 55r. Cf. Vecce 2024, 321–8. Cf. exh. cat. Venice 1992.
16 Tongiorgi Tomasi 2000, 133–52.
17 Paris, Louvre Museum.
18 The work, which presents some animals exemplified on Pisanello's drawings, is held in Madrid at the Thyssen-Bornemisza National Museum. Cf. Tongiorgi Tomasi 2000, 138; exh. cat. Washington and Venice 2022/23, 224–7.
19 Panofsky 1967. Cf. exh. cat. Rome 2007; exh. cat. Rome 2011.
20 Koreny 1985.
21 See Jacopo de Barbari, *Still-Life with Partridge and Gauntlets,* 1504, Alte Pinakothek München, inv. 5066.
22 Cfr. Tongiorgi Tomasi 2000, 133–4.
23 Koreny 1985, 54–5.
24 Koreny 1985, 218–19.
25 Koreny 1985.
26 Koreny 1985, 122–3.
27 Cf. Olmi and Tongiorgi Tomasi 2011, 117.
28 Pesenti 1992, 97.
29 Carlino 2004, 76.
30 Carlino 2004, 85–6. Cf. also Carlino 1994.
31 Favaro 1890–1907, vol. IV, 49–50; cf. Arslan 1966, 123–8.
32 Cunningham 2006, 129–49.
33 'Pitture colorate d'anatomia'. Rippa Bonati and Pardo Tomás 2004; Fabrici d'Acquapendente 2021. Although the plates do not constitute a homogeneous corpus, as they were undoubtedly produced by various artists, they present 'a pictorial quality quite incomparable to any other medical illustration of the time' precisely 'due to the unusual use of oil for anatomical images': Kemp 2000, 99.
34 Cf. Azzi Visentini 1984; Azzi Visentini 1986; Minelli 1995.
35 Tafuri 1985, *passim*; Angelini 1999; Marcon and Moretti 2015; Lemerle et al. 2017.
36 For the identification of Maestro Plinio and on his activity, see the fine article by Hochmann 2010, 42–53 (with previous bibliography on the *Libro dei pesci*).
37 Tongiorgi Tomasi and Willis 2009, 32.
38 Ciancio 2015.
39 Dioskurides 1544.
40 Pesenti 1985.
41 On the dense network of nature scholars in Venice and its mainland territories, cf. Pugliano 2011.
42 Donattini 1980; Romanini 2007; Donattini 2019.
43 Alpago-Novello 1937; Alpago-Novello 1940.
44 'Un Theatro universale, di tutte le più esquisite, e più singolar cose del mondo'. Cf. Olmi 2007, 347. The following are excellent works giving a general outline of naturalist collecting in the Venice Republic: Pomian 1989; Pomian 2004; Findlen 2005.
45 Pona 1601.
46 'Granchi, pesci, bisse pietrificati, un camaleonte secco, caragoli piccoli e rari, crocodilli, pesci bizzarri'; Michiel 2000, 52.
47 'Fra l'altre belle cose'; 'una terra con gozze di sangue impetrito rubicondissimo'; 'particolar protettore'. Ridolfi 1648, Part I, 398.
48 Cf., also for the previous bibliography, Hochmann 1997.
49 'Vaghissimo et copiosissimo'. Anguillara 1561, 152. Alpini 1591, 138r described Contarini as 'senator clarissimus, plantarumque materiae doctissimus, atque studiosissimus'.
50 Benedetto Varchi, in the funeral address for Pietro Bembo, recalled that the cardinal, as well as being a great collector of statues, paintings, 'medals, vases, stones, gems, and various other very precious things' ('medaglie, vasi, pietre, gioie, & altre varie cose pretiosissime'), had a notable 'knowledge of simples' ('cognitione de' semplici') and that in his 'beautiful garden' ('bellissimo giardino') in Padua 'numerous herbs, domestic and foreign, could be seen by anyony wishing to' ('si potevano vedere da chiunque voleva, infinite herbe così nostrali, come straniere'): Sansovino 1561, 53v. Bembo also owned astrolabes, globes, and naturalist finds, such as the stones received from Ramusio. Cf. Gasparotto 2013 and Nalezyty 2017, *passim*.
51 'dottissimo, & spetialmente nella cognitione delle piante'. Anguillara 1561, 129.
52 Cf. Sansovino 1663, 369–70; Marsili 1840; De Visiani 1840, 3–4; Bussadori 1988; Azzi Visentini 1988; Minuzzi 2016, 91–106.
53 Cf. Baldacci and Saccardo 1900; Belli 2000.
54 Olmi 2009.
55 Tongiorgi Tomasi 1984; Olmi 1991; Tongiorgi Tomasi and Garbari 1995. Alpini 1656, 'Prosper Alpinus Ad Lectorem', recalling that Casabona had been able to go to Crete thanks to the 'bountiful' ('ex munificentia') generosity of Cappello, states that he had received from the latter rare plants both from Crete and Constantinople and celebrates him as 'a man very learned in all disciplines and especially adept in the knowledge of plants' ('uomo assai erudito in tutte le discipline e soprattutto abile nella conoscenza delle piante'). This work by Alpini was published posthumously and dedicated by his son Alpino to another noble botany scholar, Nicolò Contarini, described as being 'second to none in his knowledge of plants' ('a nessuno secondo nella conoscenza delle piante'), who owned a garden near Padua, rich in 'very rare, and foreign' ('rarissime, & peregrine') plants. Giovanni Pona also dedicated his *Monte Baldo* to him.
56 'Vide cose naturali marine infinite e terrestri'; 'raccolse molte cose rare'. *La vita* 1907, 12, 17. The number of people in the Venice Republic

with whom Aldrovandi was in contact and from whom he received assistance for his research is astonishing: from the nobles Daniele Barbaro, his brother Marcantonio and G. Cappello to the pharmacists Calzolari and Pona, from the directors of the Padua botanical garden to university teachers such as Falloppia and on to a 'Vicenzo di Forti, Venetian boatman or helmsman' ('Vicenzo di Forti Venetiano barcharolo o nochero'), who had promised to give the Bolognese naturalist 'various things from the sea' ('varie cose dal mare').

57 Findlen 2002; Findlen 2005, 61–2; Minuzzi 2016, *passim*; Pugliano 2023.

58 Olmi 1992, *passim*; Olmi and Tongiorgi Tomasi 1993.

59 Tongiorgi Tomasi 1988.

60 Venice, Gallerie dell'Accademia.

61 Michiel 1940. Cf. Pardo Tomás 2006; Mason and Pardo Tomás 2020.

62 'Tutte le pitture dipinte al vivo dal signor Jacomo Ligozzi a' quali non mancha se non il spirito'; exh. cat. Florence 2014, 32.

63 'Giacomo dipentore da Verona'; 'frutti rarissimi'; 'uccelli et erbe'. The will is published in Tartaglini 1996, 41–51.

64 'Numerosi volumi'; 'piante varie e rare ritratte dal naturale'. Biblioteca Universitaria Bologna, Ms Aldrovandi 38[2], vol. III, c. 61v. (but see also the passage in another letter, c. 63r). Cf. Cermenati 1908, 48, 50.

65 Ceruti and Chiocco 1622, 721. It has been suggested that 'un libro... di miniature in carta pecora di Girolamo da i Libri, e di Gio: Francesco Carotto' may have belonged to Calzolari; it is listed in the encyclopaedic collection of Lodovico Moscardo da Dal Pozzo 1718, 289.

66 'Allievo del Ligozzi raro pittore'. Biblioteca Universitaria Bologna, MS. Aldrovandi 137, vol. I, c. 113r.

67 'Peritissimo nell'arte del disegnare'. The painter is described thus by Saraina 1540, 8r.

68 Rossi, Peretti, and Rossetti 2020.

69 Conigliello 1991; Conigliello 2014, 13. The Ligozzi family's relations with the Habsburg imperial court and a stay by Jacopo himself in Vienna seem to be documented.

70 Cf. Olmi 1992, 83.

71 MS. 83 is composed of 20 plates on parchment, consisting of 19 marine organisms and an iguana. Cf. Conigliello 1991. On the problem, cf. also exh. cat. Vienna 1988/89, 138–43 and Tongiorgi Tomasi 2014, 32. Ligozzi also painted another 'Pesce San Pietro', now in the Galleria degli Uffizi (2015 Orn.); cf. exh. cat. Florence 1961, 32.

72 Tosi 1989.

73 Tongiorgi Tomasi 1993; exh. cat. Florence 2014; exh. cat. Florence 2014a.

74 Staatliche Museen zu Berlin, Gemäldegalerie. Apart from the symbolic meanings on which various scholars have dwelt (H.W. Janson, E. Panofsky, P. Tomkins, etc.), the precision with which the monkeys are portrayed has been rightly pointed out by Sullivan 2014. The Polish poet and winner of the Nobel Prize for Literature, Wislawa Szymborska, has dedicated a poem to this very famous work.

75 Cf. DaCosta Kaufmann 2009, 122–9 and *passim*; Olmi and Tongiorgi Tomasi 2011, 127–8.

76 Paliaga 1997.

77 'alcuni pastorelli, & animali'. Ridolfi 1648, Part I, 183.

78 Paris, Louvre Museum, Cabinet des Desseins, inv. 5573. Cf. exh. cat. Washington 1976/77, 144. On the problem, cf. exh. cat. Milan 2012.

79 'Si compiacque... di habitare nella Patria sua, conferendole l'aria nativa, godendosi della commoda sua Casa, coltivando tal'hora per ricreratione certo suo giardinetto, ripieno di semplici de' quali veniva regalato da Alfonso Duca di Ferrara, e da altri Signori, tra i quali fraponeva biscie & altri animali dipinti sopra cartoni, che a prima vista davano materia di timore', Ridolfi 1648, Part I, 389. Information taken up by Verci 1775, 43. Cf. Ballarin 1995.

80 'Molti pensieri, ove entravano animali, pesci, e massaritie, & altre cose, che pur anche... traheva con molta applicatione dal naturale', Ridolfi 1648, Part II, 169

81 Rigon 1983.

82 'ritratto'; 'du cani brachi, cioè cani solo'. Paris, Louvre. The painting of dogs, commissioned by the Venetian nobleman Antonio Zantani, was enhanced many years ago by Alessandro Ballarin: cf. exh. cat. Bassano del Grappa 2010, 86–9. The painting of the sheep with the lamb is in the Galleria Borghese, Rome.

83 Ballarin 1995b.

84 Bortolami 2009/10, 179.

85 Mazzucco 2022, 73.

86 The best biography of Alpini is still Ongaro 1961/62–1962/63.

87 Alpini 1591, 82r–82v.

88 'malinconia ferina'. Alpini 1719, 610. On the sad event, cf. Ridolfi 1648, Part I, 399.

89 Alpini repeatedly mentions his summer stays in Bassano in his letters to Gaspard Bauhin and to Joachim Camerario, published in Ongaro 2011, 333–44 and Ongaro 2016, 365–91.

90 'con anima grata'; 'calda amicizia'. Verci 1775, 188 states that Leandro 'declared a special friendship' ('professava singolar amicizia') towards Alpini.

91 Cf. Ongaro and Gamba 1994/95.

92 The portrait is in the Castello Sforzesco, Milan. The plant is called 'Malva maggiore' by Mattioli 1568, 483 who asserts it to be 'una delle più volgari, & più conosciute herbe, che si ritrovino tra le piante in tutti gli horti d'Italia'. Cf. Mattioli 1568, 485.

93 Ericani 2011/12, 486.

94 Dondi 1960; Wolf-Heidegger and Cetto 1967, 298. Leo Ponzio (*sic*) according to Arslan 1960, vol. I, 269. In Venice Bonzio was also prior of the medical-surgical college.

95 Sclosa 2009/10, 131.

96 The portrait of Sagredo in consular dress with the city of Alexandria in the background is in the Ashmolean Museum, Oxford. On the problem of the relations between Leandro, Sagredo, and Galilei, cf. Tongiorgi Tomasi 2009, 33–5. Another portrait of Sagredo attributed to Leandro, previously in the Palazzo Doria Pamphili, Rome, has been lost, while yet another portrait is held in Zhytomyr, Ukraine. Cf. Wilding 2014, 14, 138.

97 Gabrieli 1989, 963–9.

98 'Due Not[t]i in paragone assai belle'; 'alcuni cannoncini'; 'per vedere [le] pitture da vicino'. Favaro 1890–1907, vol. XII, 400–1.

99 'Cavalier Bassano... e una sgualdrinotta e un suo bufone e una mia putella'; 'voleva ritrare la casa, le teze, la cantina, la stala, i calli, tutti i frutti et animali che vedeva, ma infine a fatica ho fatto abbozzare la putta et fare la mia testa, un piato di tartufi, un altro di persici'.

100 'Un bellissimo occhialino che fa apparire cose che finhora non si sapeva fossero state create'. Letter from Giovanni Faber to Federico Cesi in Gabrieli 1989, 875.

101 Olmi and Tongiorgi Tomasi 2024.

MARCI CATONIS PRISCI DE RE RVSTICA LIBER.

EST INTERDVM PRAESTARE MERcaturis rem quærere: ni tam periculosum sit: et item fœnerari: si tam honestum sit. Maiores .n. nostri hoc sic habuere: et ita ī legibus posuere: furē dupli cōdemnari: fœneratorē q̄drupli. Quāto peiorē ciuē existimarint fœneratorem q̄ furem: hic licet existimare. Et uirū bonū quom laudabant: ita laudabāt: Bonum agricolam bonumq; colonum. Amplissime laudari existimabatur: qui ita laudabat. Mercatorem autem strenuum studiosumq; rei quærendæ existimo: uerum (ut supra dixi) periculosum & calamitosum. At ex agricolis & uiri fortissimi & milites strenuissimi gignuntur: maximeq; pius quæstus stabilissimusq; cōsequitur: minimeq; inuidiosus. Minimeq; male cogitantes sunt: qui in eo studio occupati sunt. Nunc (ut ad rē redeam) quod promisi institutum primum hoc erit.

Quomodo agrū emi parariq; oporteat. Caput. i.

PRædiū cū comparare cogitabis: sic in animo habeto: uti ne cupide emas: neue opera tua parcas uisere: & ne satis habeas circumire. Quotiēs ibis: totiens magis placebit quod bonū erit. Vicini quo pacto niteant: id animaduertito. In bona regione bene nitere oportebit: et uti cum introeas et circūspicias: uti inde exire possis: uti bonum cælum habeat: ne calamitosum siet. solum bonum sua uirtute ualeat. Si poteris sub radice mōtis siet: in meridiem spectet: loco salubri: operariorū copia siet bonum: in quem aquarium oppidum ualidum prope siet. Si autē mare aut amnis quo naues ambulant: aut uia bona celebris quæ siet. In his agris qui non sæpe dominos mutant: qui in his agris prædia uēdiderit: quos pigeat uēdidisse uti bene ædificatum siet. Caueto ne alienam disciplinam temere contemnas. De domino bono colono bonoq; ædificatore melius emetur. Ad uillam cum uenies: uideto uasa torcula et dolia multa ne sient. Vbi non erunt: scito pro ratione fructum esse. Instrumenti magni ne siet: bono loco siet. Videto q̄ minimi instrumenti. Sumptuosus ager ne siet. Scito idem agrum quod hominem quāuis quæstuosus siet: si sumptuosus erit: relinquere non multum. Prædium quod primum siet: si me rogabis: sic dicam de omnibus agris. Optimo loco emito iugera centū agri. Vinea est prima: si uino multo est: secūdo loco hortus irriguus: tertio salictum: quarto oletum: quīto pratum: sexto campus frumentarius: septimo silua cædua: octauo arbustum: nono glandaria silua.

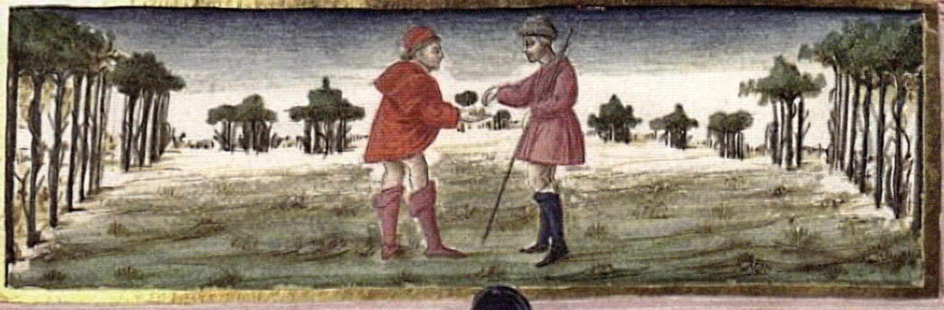

MARIO INFELISE, SABRINA MINUZZI*

Early Modern Agronomic Literature

The Birth of a Publishing Genre

Introduction

The history of agronomic literature has its roots in classical antiquity, from which, along with its early contents, it inherits the monthly and seasonal rhythms in the organization of the subject matter. Since the Middle Ages, it has shared some features with the related herbal genre – which investigated the knowledge relating to the medicinal virtues of the vegetal 'simples', the *materia medica* – and with the *Tacuina sanitatis* (cat. 16), which in the synthetic form of the *taqwīm* (illustrative plates with text-caption at the foot of the page) offered their noble buyers the first visual representations of rural work and of the food and drink resulting from man's efforts, marked by the stars and the seasons. All these subjects are also found in the contemporary books of hours and in some painted cycles.[1] Although still stylized and reflecting the visual angle of contemporary court society, the *Tacuina sanitatis* nourished the imagination and were almost an illustrated counterpart to the agronomy publications, in which the word always prevailed over the image. The everyday aspect of the man–nature relationship burst forth for the first time in the medieval *Tacuina*, and over the course of the fifteenth and sixteenth centuries attained a maturity that fed art on one hand and various textual genres on the other.[2] As this exhibition shows, it was precisely in this period that the forms and material substance of nature in itself and in relation to the human being began to be studied. Drawing and painting explored the forms; from being a generic backdrop for different subjects, nature increasingly emerged in the foreground of paintings and pictorial compositions until it became an independent subject, triumphant in the naturalistic transfiguration of the personification of the seasons by Arcimboldo (cats. 28, 29, 90). At the same time, nature was studied in its materiality by enthusiastic investigators (professionals and amateurs alike), both for its still little-known medicinal properties (*materia medica*) and for the usefulness that could also be derived from it – the 'economic' benefits in the etymological sense of the term (*oikos nomos*), the result of regulated management of the three natural kingdoms. All this fuelled a production of texts that, after an initial amalgam, gradually became specialized and distinguished into two branches: herbals and *Horti sanitatis* on one hand and agronomic literature on the other.[3]

At the turn of the fifteenth century, the growing interest of the urban ruling classes in land investments transformed the rural landscape of northern Italy. More or less sumptuous villas and homes arose in their hundreds in the Veneto and Lombard countryside, becoming one of the distinguishing features of the land, notably overlapping the areas where the *Tacuina sanitatis* had flourished a couple of centuries earlier, often circulating bound together with copies of agronomy books.[4]

Although not always easily identifiable, despite the rich surviving fiscal documentation, numerous signs remain of these 'villa-farms', places of both work and residence, endowed with appurtenances such as granaries, hay barns, dovecotes, vegetable plots, orchards, and gardens.[5] The existence of a large urban landowning class aroused intense interest in agronomic knowledge, which the printing revolution helped to disseminate. Manuscript production continued uninterrupted, while a vibrant publishing line grew up around some writers who, for several decades, were the focus of booksellers and their clients, contributing to a change in Europeans' perception and sensibility of the countryside, the activities engaged therein and the natural environment as a whole. Some estimate this European phenomenon at 710 reprints of ancient and medieval authors and 622 editions of contemporary authors.[6] Those who read them were seeking a very broad range of information: soil characteristics, building methods, necessary equipment, the alimentary and medicinal qualities of plants and herbs, and sowing calendars.[7]

The agronomic Renaissance: Ancient and medieval authors

At the height of humanism, prior to the recovery of the ancient classics, barely known in the late Middle Ages, the European agronomic renaissance stemmed from a medieval text that, after widespread circulation in manuscript, became the object of publishing attention from 1471. This was the work of Pietro Crescenzi (c.1233–c.1320), a very learned Bolognese judge and official. At the end of a career that had enabled him to acquire good first-hand knowledge of rural management in the Po Valley area, he retired to his own property at Villa dell'Olmo, near Bologna. Here, between 1304 and 1309, he wrote the *Opus ruralium commodorum*, or *Ruralia commoda*, the most important treatise on medieval agronomy, which was very widely circulated across Europe until the late sixteenth century.[8] Only partly based on classical authors, the *Ruralia commoda* was the result of close observation of agricultural customs in northern Italy, and conceived as a kind of practical encyclopaedia intended to offer the necessary skills to those urban classes, not necessarily aristocrats, who were buying significant estates in the countryside. The text is divided into twelve chapters (*Libri*) that systematically present the entire subject. In order: siting and arrangement of farm buildings; cultivation of plants; field work and fruits of the land; viticulture and wine; arboriculture and properties of trees; the virtues of cultivated herbs; pastures; woods; gardens; animal husbandry; hunting and fishing. The *Ruralia commoda* ends with a chapter in the form of a calendar, in which the subjects already looked at are taken up again, month by month, on the basis of the priorities dictated by the seasons.

Crescenzi's work was an extraordinary publishing success.[9] The first edition, issued in Augsburg in 1471, was followed by twelve others through to the end of the fifteenth century – in Leuven (three), Strasbourg, Florence, Vicenza, Venice, Paris (two), and Speyer (three). These also included the first translations into the vernacular, in French (*Le livre des ruraulx prouffitz*, Paris 1486), Italian (*Il libro della agricultura*, Florence 1478), and German (*Petrus de Crescentijs zu teutsch mit figuren*, Speyer 1495). Its success continued for much of the first half of the sixteenth century, with an estimated 12,500 copies circulating between 1471 and 1564.[10] Alongside the vernacular editions of Crescenzi's treatise were illustrated ones, which also played an important part in its dissemination. The first appeared in central Europe in the early 1490s and showed a marked similarity to the many folio *Horti sanitatis* published in the same areas, embellished with woodcuts depicting herbs, trees, and scenes of life in naturalist settings, with the text in Gothic type arranged in two columns.[11] The first illustrated edition of Crescenzi's work in Italian dates from 1495, in a smaller format (4°), and marked by a more original appearance than the herbals then in circulation. This is the *De Agricoltura* printed by Matteo Capcasa (Codecà) and illustrated with 36 woodcuts, increased to 47 in the subsequent edition of 1504, the *De Agricultura. Istoriato.*[12] Plants are not portrayed as

Fig. 1

Pietro Crescenzi, frontispiece for *De Agricultura. Istoriato*, Venice 1504. Vienna, Austrian National Library

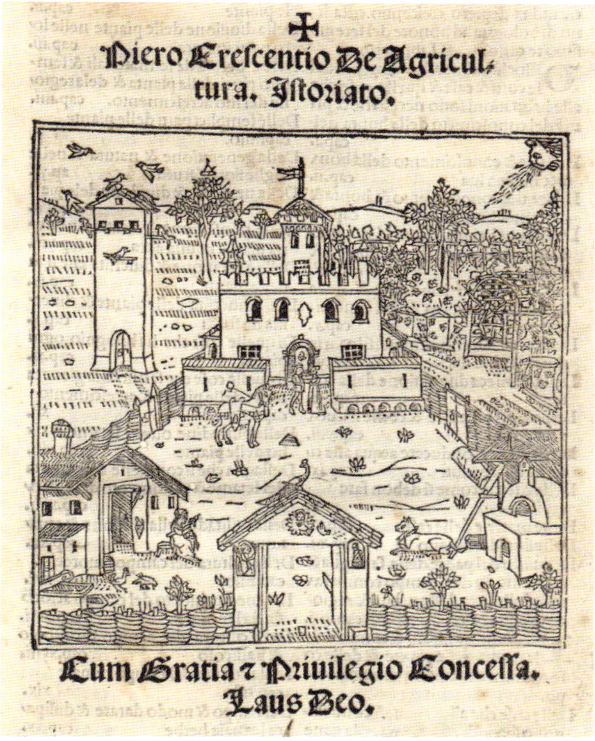

in the herbals and the first editions of Crescenzi, but small scenes of rural work punctuate the text with an elegant simplicity; sometimes repeated, they are, however, always related to the content and highlight the rural residence as a place of production and work, but also of meetings and delights. The frontispiece features a full-page woodcut of a Veneto villa – the first such documented testimony – with all the said characteristics, on the model of the villa-enterprise (fig. 1). The building in the centre of the scene is crowned by a tower. At the entrance a just dismounted rider is greeted by a lady. The farmyard surrounds all with various domestic animals, tools, and an oven, while a peasant woman seated on the threshold of a cottage among the adjoining buildings is intent on household work. A dovecote is set in the field in the background, along with a garden and fruit trees, vines, and vegetation expertly arranged on pergolas and supports.[13] The readership must have been much more varied and extensive than that of the weighty Latin editions – even Leonardo da Vinci owned a copy.[14] The 1511 edition was retypeset line by line by Alessandro Bindoni that same year, applying an expedient he used to reduce printing times when there was a very high demand for copies, and again in 1519.[15] But the *De Agricultura* illustrations soon gave way to text alone, or embellished solely by some woodcut initials. Although the public success of Crescenzi's work is undeniable, it is clear that for agronomy readers it was more important to have a low-cost handbook than to leaf through ornate pages: the illustrations were not as essential as in the herbals, where they acted as a means of identifying less well-known or entirely unknown plants. The agronomy texts also dealt with plants, but only those cereals, pulses, herbs, and flowers required for the proper running of a rural estate. They were easily recognizable to anyone, but not everyone knew how to correctly cultivate them. Only some rare editions of Crescenzi's *De Agricultura* published outside Italy, in Latin and in elegant folio, continued to be illustrated with exemplifying scenes of work in the fields.[16]

Alongside the printing and success of Crescenzi's work, the burgeoning publishing industry immediately offered anthologies of the Latin classics on the subject. In 1472, Nicolas Jenson had the first edition of the writings of Cato, Varro, Columella, and Rutilius Palladius printed in Venice under the title *Scriptores rei rusticae*, thus establishing the line for the subsequent fifteenth-century editions; all in large format (folio) and of about 300 pages, these too without printed illustrations.[17] An important stage in the printing tradition of the agronomy classics collection was the Aldine edition of 1514 (cat. 53.1), in 4°.

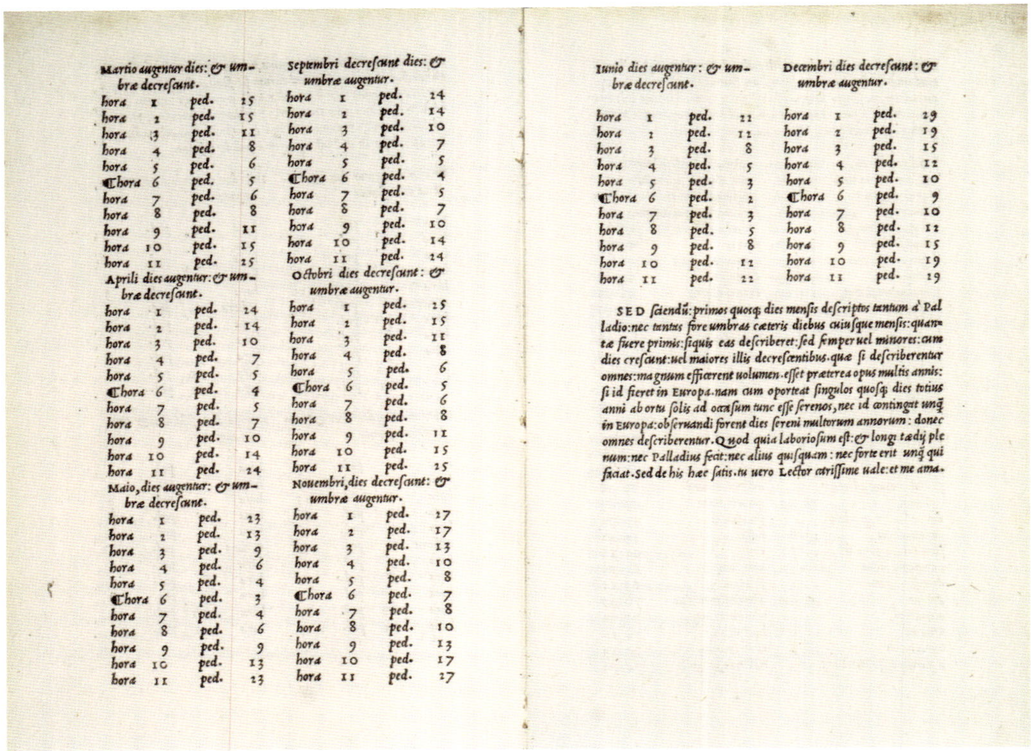

Martio augentur dies: & umbræ decrescunt.

hora	1	ped.	25
hora	2	ped.	15
hora	3	ped.	11
hora	4	ped.	8
hora	5	ped.	6
¶ hora	6	ped.	5
hora	7	ped.	6
hora	8	ped.	8
hora	9	ped.	11
hora	10	ped.	15
hora	11	ped.	25

Aprili dies augentur: & umbræ decrescunt.

hora	1	ped.	24
hora	2	ped.	14
hora	3	ped.	10
hora	4	ped.	7
hora	5	ped.	5
¶ hora	6	ped.	4
hora	7	ped.	5
hora	8	ped.	7
hora	9	ped.	10
hora	10	ped.	14
hora	11	ped.	24

Maio, dies augentur: & umbræ decrescunt.

hora	1	ped.	23
hora	2	ped.	13
hora	3	ped.	9
hora	4	ped.	6
hora	5	ped.	4
¶ hora	6	ped.	3
hora	7	ped.	4
hora	8	ped.	6
hora	9	ped.	9
hora	10	ped.	13
hora	11	ped.	23

Septembri decrescunt dies: & umbræ augentur.

hora	1	ped.	24
hora	2	ped.	14
hora	3	ped.	10
hora	4	ped.	7
hora	5	ped.	5
¶ hora	6	ped.	4
hora	7	ped.	5
hora	8	ped.	7
hora	9	ped.	10
hora	10	ped.	14
hora	11	ped.	24

Octobri dies decrescunt: & umbræ augentur.

hora	1	ped.	25
hora	2	ped.	15
hora	3	ped.	11
hora	4	ped.	8
hora	5	ped.	6
¶ hora	6	ped.	5
hora	7	ped.	6
hora	8	ped.	8
hora	9	ped.	11
hora	10	ped.	15
hora	11	ped.	25

Nouembri, dies decrescunt: & umbræ augentur.

hora	1	ped.	27
hora	2	ped.	17
hora	3	ped.	13
hora	4	ped.	10
hora	5	ped.	8
¶ hora	6	ped.	7
hora	7	ped.	8
hora	8	ped.	10
hora	9	ped.	13
hora	10	ped.	17
hora	11	ped.	27

Iunio dies augentur: & umbræ decrescunt.

hora	1	ped.	22
hora	2	ped.	12
hora	3	ped.	8
hora	4	ped.	5
hora	5	ped.	3
¶ hora	6	ped.	2
hora	7	ped.	3
hora	8	ped.	5
hora	9	ped.	8
hora	10	ped.	12
hora	11	ped.	22

Decembri dies decrescunt: & umbræ augentur.

hora	1	ped.	29
hora	2	ped.	19
hora	3	ped.	15
hora	4	ped.	12
hora	5	ped.	10
¶ hora	6	ped.	9
hora	7	ped.	10
hora	8	ped.	12
hora	9	ped.	15
hora	10	ped.	19
hora	11	ped.	29

SED sciendū: primos quosq; dies mensis descriptos tantum a' Palladio: nec tantas fore umbras cæteris diebus cuiusque mensis: quantæ fuere primis: siquis eas describeret: sed semper uel minores: cum dies crescunt: uel maiores illis decrescentibus. quæ si describerentur omnes: magnum efficerent uolumen. esset præterea opus multis annis: si id fieret in Europa. nam cum oporteat singulos quosq; dies totius anni ab ortu solis ad occasum tunc esse serenos, nec id contingat unq̃ in Europa: obseruandi forent dies sereni multorum annorum: donec omnes describerentur. Quod quia laboriosum est: & longi tædij plenum: nec Palladius fecit: nec alius quisquam: nec forte erit unq̃ qui faciat. Sed de his hæc satis. tu uero Lector carissime uale: et me ama.

Fig. 2

Libri de re rustica, Venice (Aldo Manuzio) 1514. Venice, Biblioteca Nazionale Marciana

The *Libri de re rustica* – its new title – was perfected thanks to the philological contribution of the great humanist and architecture theorist Fra' Giovanni Giocondo (1443–1515), with an extensive discussion by Aldus Manutius himself on the cycles of time, the division of the day into 24 hours and the differences between the summer and winter solstices, accompanied by a series of charts recording the monthly lengthening and shortening of the days (fig. 2).[18] Although distinguished by European success in Venice, Paris, and Strasbourg, the classics anthology remained an elitist publication intended for learned readers who had a good mastery of Latin and nourished an interest in the historical roots of agronomy.[19]

The works of individual classical authors were much more widely distributed, having been translated into the vernacular since the fourteenth century (and, in the process, reduced compared to the original text), with an extraordinary circulation first in manuscript form and later in print. Among these, the *Opus agriculturae* by Rutilius Taurus Palladius (fifth century) was the most quoted and reprinted in the early modern age, and was incorporated into his *Ruralia commoda* by Pietro Crescenzi himself – unsurprisingly, Palladius is considered the intermediary par excellence between ancient knowledge and medieval authors.[20] His treatise, covering about 80 pages in the simple form of a monthly calendar of agricultural works, was well suited to purely practical use and ended up providing a secular model for the instruments of this kind and ways of portraying agricultural work. When it first appeared in an Italian translation, in Siena in 1526, the title chosen by the Sienese bookseller and printer Simone Nardi emphasized the need to also circulate such a text among the less learned, 'so that those who do not know Latin may draw usefulness and delight from its brief and ordered precepts'. Nardi endorsed the intention of the Umbrian popularizer, Pietro Marino, who had translated it 'so that those who have no knowledge of Latin language and culture (who are much more numerous than the learned) may also put into practice the necessary and pleasing principles collected in this small and magnificent book, and draw from them inconceivable and sought-after benefits'.[21]

Only a few years later (1528) the vernacular version of Palladius was added to the catalogues of Venetian booksellers, ensuring its greatest independent circulation and sanctioning the organization of the material by months, as in the *Tacuina*. The first of these booksellers was Niccolò Zoppino, one of the most interesting Venetian printers of the time, devoted in particular to popular editions and Italian translations – he published the first Italian version of a writing by Luther (1525).[22] And in just a few years the *Palladius... de la agricultura* took on the typical layout of the low-cost popular editions, published in 1538 by Bernardino Viani in an even smaller format (8°) and with a full-page woodcut on the frontispiece (cat. 53.2).[23] These were not illustrated nor philologically impeccable publications, but the accessibility of the vernacular, along with the airy and spaced arrangement of the contents in less than 100 pages, with printed marginal references, made them extremely easy to use for a wide range of readers even of limited literacy.

The early modern authors. The *materia medica* fades, economics triumphs in the villa

Publishing tended to diversify from the mid-sixteenth century. Crescenzi began to decline as the reference agronomic text throughout Europe, albeit very slowly, while the different national areas began to produce original treatises: Gabriel Alonso de Herrera in Spain, Konrad Heresbach in Germany, Charles Estienne in France, Agostino Gallo and others in Italy. Venetian publishing, in those decades the most efficient and productive in Europe alongside that of Paris, held a substantial monopoly in Italy and offered a wide range of books, reprinted with a certain frequency to satisfy the growing demand due to the increasing investments in rural holdings. From 1557 to the end of the century, and through to the first decades of the seventeenth century for authors of a subsequent generation, the following were published: nine editions of Gabriel Alonso de Herrera, five of the French publisher and writer Charles Estienne, twenty of the Brescian Agostino Gallo, a dozen-odd of Giuseppe Falcone of Piacenza, seven of Camillo Tarello of Lonato, Brescia, six of Marco Bussato da Ravenna and ten of Giuseppe Falcone of Piacenza – many of which were protected by privileges issued by Venice, the pope or other Italian sovereigns.

In 1557, Michele Tramezzino, one of the most active and influential printers in those years, with a printing house in Venice and also a bookshop in Rome, printed a translation of the *Libro di agricoltura* by Gabriel Alonso de Herrera, which had been released in Castilian in 1513, without illustrations.[24] Herrera drew on classical models, but also added the precious experience of the Arab-Andalusian farmers with which he was familiar, devoting five chapters to: the quality of the soils and the crops suited to each place (I), the cultivation of vines (II) and trees (III), gardens, water, vegetable gardens, and herbs (IV), animal husbandry and veterinary treatments (V). The book ends with the usual month-by-month division of the works to be carried out. Forty-six small woodcuts that had already been in circulation for almost ten years – and which will be discussed in more detail in the following section – also made their entrance into Tramezzino's edition, illustrating a fair number of plants.[25]

New agronomy authors soon also appeared in Italy, many from the Po Valley area – more or less coinciding with the area of origin and/or patronage of the *Tacuina* a couple of centuries earlier – along with frescoed and painted cycles of the months.

Agostino Gallo (1499–1570), a small landowner in the Brescia region, gained particular prominence. In 1564 he published his *Le dieci giornate dell'agricoltura e de' piaceri della villa*, a treatise in which every day is given over to the treatment of a specific subject. It was a very successful work and thus rapidly expanded by the author, increasing the number of days to thirteen and then twenty in 1569.[26] Gallo's aim was to illustrate the 'real' agriculture in the villa, intended both as farming enterprise and place of delights and pleasures unavailable in urban areas. Presenting the definitive edition, he explained in the *Proemio* that he wished to show 'the great advantage and pleasure to be gained from cultivating the earth, which, like a benign Mother, not only offers us its fruits in abundance, but also makes us aware that the Lord God especially loves and favours those engaged in virtuously cultivating it and with noble spirit'.[27] The treatise, in the form of a dialogue between several gentlemen, was intended to illustrate the advantages of well-managed, rationally and wisely organized agriculture, open to innovation, a 'divine art' capable, in the author's words, of providing much greater profits than those of trading:

> ...there is no income more honest, abundant, certain, and stable, and at the same time more worthy of a noble and free person than that which is perceived through this divine art... How blind are those merchants who laboriously go to sea, the land, and

> forests, risking their lives and their own substance, to pursue a profit of 20 or 30%. Why do they not abandon that sorrowful profession to embrace this, which almost always returns more than triple the amount invested?[28]

The villa was at the same time also a place of socializing, able to provide pleasures that could not be found in urban spheres.[29] Indeed, a whole day, the eighteenth, develops the reasoning 'that it is better to live in the villa than the city'. Gallo devotes plenty of space to 'villa life', to the advantages over the city, to 'glorification [of the] pleasures of the villa' and of those 'noble Brescians who exercise it with good intelligence'.[30] Villa life began to take on a previously unknown socio-cultural importance: it provided economic income in a setting of soothing delights, the result of man's activity related to nature. The remaining subjects are the usual ones with something extra: care of vegetables and garden, alfalfa, vines, hemp, animal husbandry and veterinary treatments, beekeeping, hunting and fishing, and even the breeding of silkworms; it is impossible not to think, leafing through Gallo's pages, of man's activity in Leandro Bassano's cycle of months. And it may be assumed that the Bassanos were also familiar with treatises such as *Le vinti giornate*. Constantly reprinted from 1569 to 1628, then less frequently until 1674, in regular and unauthorized editions – the latter being a clear indication of its success – there were seventeen in all (one in Brescia, thirteen in Venice and three in Turin), along with French translations (1571 and two reprints in 1572 and 1576).[31] The type of illustrations in *Le vinti giornate* (cat. 54) is interesting, concentrated in the last pages, where nineteen full-page woodcuts portray the equipment needed for properly carrying out agricultural work: ploughs, harrows, shovels, vats for winemaking and every other possible implement. Plants – repositories of both medicinal and nutritional properties that had made the first printed agronomy treatises so similar to the *Horti sanitatis* – are not provided with any illustrations, just as the medicinal component of herb and plant descriptions tends to disappear.

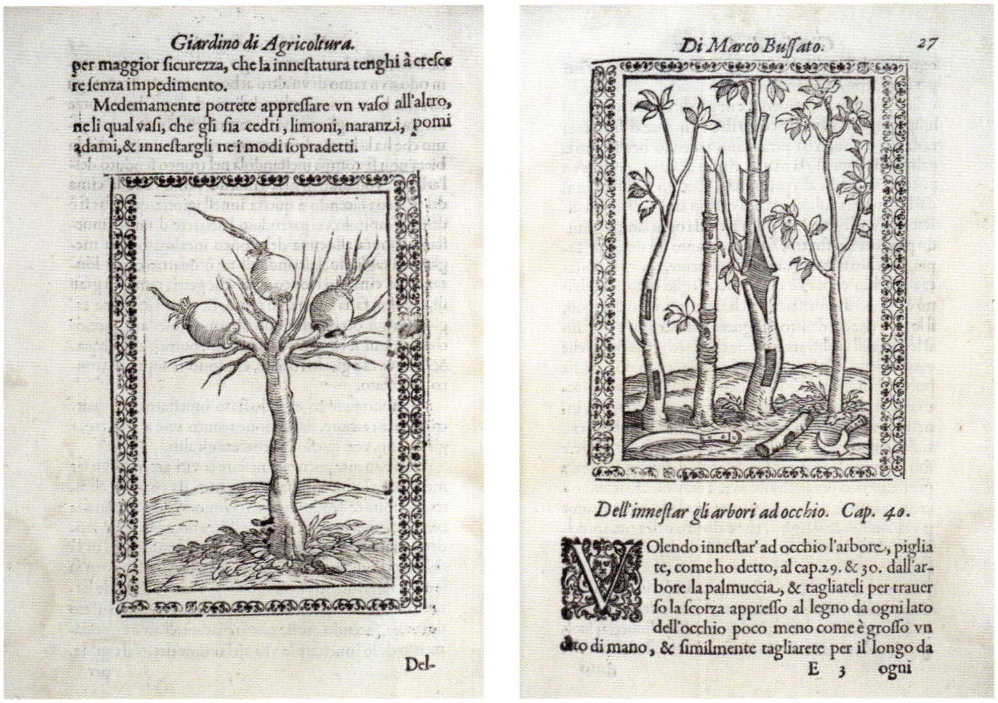

Giardino di Agricoltura.

per maggior sicurezza, che la innestatura tenghi à cresce re senza impedimento.

Medemamente potrete appressare vn vaso all'altro, neli qual vasi, che gli sia cedri, limoni, naranzi, pomi adami, & innestargli ne i modi sopradetti.

Del-

Di Marco Bussato. 27

Dell'innestar gli arbori ad occhio. Cap. 40.

VOlendo innestar' ad occhio l'arbore, piglia te, come ho detto, al cap. 29. & 30. dall'arbore la palmuccia, & tagliateli per trauerso la scorza appresso al legno da ogni lato dell'occhio poco meno come è grosso vn dito di mano, & similmente tagliarete per il longo da

E 3 ogni

Figs. 3a, b

Marco Bussato, *Giardino di agricoltura,* Venice (Giovanni Fiorina) 1592. Venice, Biblioteca Nazionale Marciana

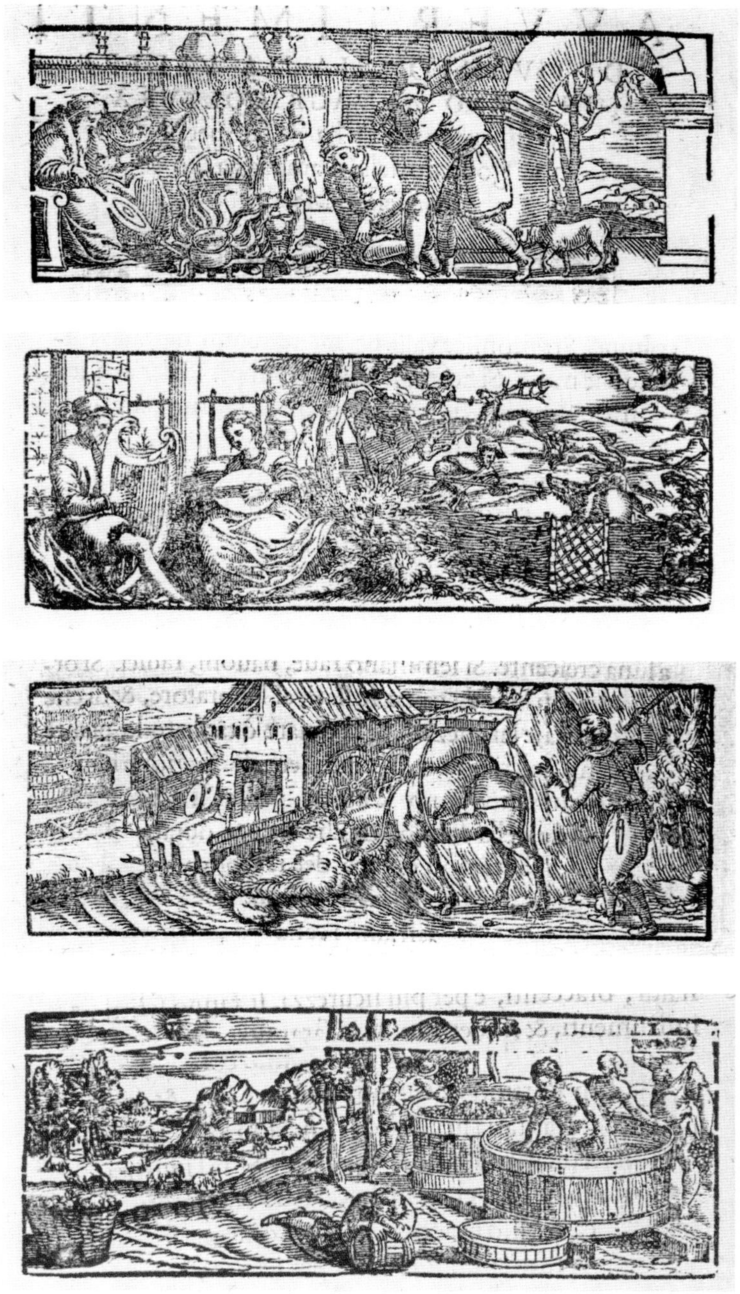

Figs. 4a–d

The Months of January, May, August, and September, in Marco Bussato, *Giardino di agricoltura ...*, Venice (Giovanni Fiorina) 1592. Venice, Biblioteca Nazionale Marciana

The nobility of agriculture and its economic potential were amplified and promulgated by a range of authors of agronomy treatises less well known than Gallo and not illustrated, like that of Giacomo Lanteri (d. 1560). In his book on domestic economy, the latter devotes many pages to showing how between 'agriculture, arms, letters, and trade' the most noble (*nobilissima*) art to which one may devote oneself is the former.[32] The Carmelite Giuseppe Falcone da Piacenza (d. 1597)[33] organizes all the material discussed by Gallo – including the construction of a fishpond and the breeding of '*bigatti*', or silkworms – around the delight and economic profit of villa life. The title is a manifesto: *La nuova, vaga, et dilettevole villa... Opera d'agricoltura, più che necessaria per chi desidera d'accrescere l'entrate de' suoi poderi, utile a tutti quelli che fanno professione d'agricoltura*.[34] The foreword *Al lettore* is programmatic and of a much more radical tone than Gallo, with a complete reversal of the concepts of *otium* and *negotium* coined by classicism. The city has become idle in the modern sense, a place of corruption, frivolity, and squalor, and is contrasted with the healthy and happy '*essercitio*' of agricultural work – and exercise/exercising are the almost obsessive refrain of the foreword.[35]

Other publications by early modern authors were of a more specialist content, and also more technical than those of Gallo and Falcone. One such was the *Giardino di agricoltura* (1592) by Marco Bussato of Ravenna (d. 1560), a concise work of just over 50 pages that concentrates on the more specific realm of tree and vine grafting techniques, exemplified with fifteen clear and useful woodcuts (figs. 3, 4).[36] The work is actually an expansion of his previous (not illustrated) *Prattica historiata dell'inestare gli arbori in diuersi modi, in varij tempi dell'anno* (Ravenna, 1578), to which he added twelve final *Avvertimenti* that are a month-by-month summary of the previously described activities, with a woodcut header portraying scenes of life opening each one. He significantly altered the title to *Giardino*. The garden was a key concept characterizing Renaissance agriculture, and the focus on fruit growing fitted well within the idea of a garden.[37] In presenting the book, the printer Fiorina particularly emphasized the pleasure the garden could afford and the differences between the mainland and Venice, where there was very little space and the salty water made planting trees and vines difficult. The *Giardino di agricoltura* was very successful and expanded in subsequent editions published until the mid-eighteenth century, at times as an independent work, at times as an appendix to new agronomy publications.[38] The woodcuts of the grafts – not the ornamental ones of the months, a legacy of an earlier way of writing about agronomy – were often re-presented in later editions, and then replaced by chalcographs. The success of the title was aided by the essential and practical nature of the text, characterized by simple and brief indications, along with the pleasing, functional illustrations, which no longer bear any similarity to those of the herbals.

Nevertheless, radical innovations in agricultural techniques were not readily taken up in everyday practice, despite the success of the agronomy books that supported them. The agronomy treatise regarded as the most innovative, the departure point of modern agriculture, is the *Ricordo d'agricoltura* by another Brescian, Camillo Tarello (d. 1573), first published in 1567 in pocket format (8°) and without illustrations.[39] Tarello knew and cited the classics of agronomy, along with Pliny and Virgil, but was at the same time aware of the innovations he intended proposing, such that he ended his introduction by putting himself on a par with 'the Genoese Columbus, discoverer of the New World, who, going beyond the Columns of Hercules, which had never been passed by the ancients, allowed the great emperor Charles V to add the motto *Plus Ultra* to his coat of arms'.[40] Such an assertion might seem somewhat immodest, but it was also an invitation to take an interest in that which, although close at hand, was as unknown as the New World – while Europeans were exploring every remote recess of the planet. Indeed, Tarello decisively abandoned Crescenzi's medieval model in the structure of the work and its substance, likewise the books by the first generation of moderns, tendentially systematic and all-encompassing. The *Ricordo d'agricoltura* is no longer an articulate and systematic treatise of humanist structure built around the useful and delightful, but a kind of technical manual containing information arranged around alphabetically ordered headwords, suited to more rapid consultation than sequential reading. Tarello's aim was to provide operational instructions, which took their cue from the need above all to increase production, improve yields, and lift the fortunes of the peasants. There are no idyllic visions of life in the fields, but mentions – often harsh – of the poverty and destitution that typified the countryside. Management systems had to be improved, by changing the contractual forms and the cultivation techniques. Tarello is owed the idea of the principle of crop rotation and the use of forage (clover) to restore the land within a four-year cycle. This agronomic innovation earned him and his descendants a special privilege from the Venetian Republic: in addition to the usual sole rights for publication obtained from the main sovereigns of Italy, the Venetian Senate granted him, at his request, the right to claim a fee from the farmers who applied his rotation method.[41] The title itself is revealing: the *aricordi* or *ricordi* (memoirs) were the technical reports submitted to the Senate in which an inventor described his invention and requested a premium and/or privilege in exchange for sharing his professional secret.[42] Undoubtedly ahead of its time, Camillo Tarello's *Ricordo* was not a great triumph in terms of practical application, despite its publishing success.[43] It was to be rediscovered only two centuries later, at the height of the Enlightenment, when the problem of the countryside became a burning issue. The *Ricordo* was actually taken up from the mid-eighteenth to the nineteenth century in various miscellaneous editions, while the treatise alone was published in Venice in 1772 in an edition on which it is worth dwelling to measure the development of the treatise genre: 'corrected, illustrated, expanded with notes, additions and plates' thanks to editing by the agronomist and scientific journalist Gian Francesco Scottoni.[44] In the *Ricordo* of 1772 the separation from any medical subject is consolidated, the two sole 'plates' announced in the frontispiece are a chart of weight equivalences and a folded chalcographic illustration intended to be made into an instrument, a wheel with concentric circles for calculating the phases of the moon from 1760 to 1801 (fig. 5). The wheel had to be cut out and glued to a rigid cardboard support, a wooden pin inserted in the centre of the wheel and a string attached in order to correctly read the indications arranged in the circles for each day of the month and year.

An engraved plate of the *Instrumento* was also sold by itself in the Venetian workshop of the Bassano painter, engraver, and publisher Teodoro Viero. Agronomy was now a mature technological subject, freed from the *materia medica*, just as botany was from pharmacopeia.

1560 and its environs, the swan song: Francesco Sansovino's publishing operation

The publishing operation of Francesco Sansovino (1521–1583) deserves a brief, special mention of its own. Popularizer, writer, and publisher, he was always ready to take on subjects of certain interest and sale, such that he could be defined as an *ante litteram* scientific popularizer.[45] Despite his legal background, letters and attendance at literary academies were always his passion. However, among the diversity of his interests, he was not averse to also concerning himself with medical-scientific production.

Fig. 5

Instrument to determine the mean age of the moon at any time, in Camillo Tarello, *Ricordo d'agricoltura … con note, aggiunte, e tavole dal padre maestro Gian-Francesco Scottoni min. conventuale*, Venice (Giammaria Bassaglia) 1772. Turin, Biblioteca della Fondazione Luigi Einaudi

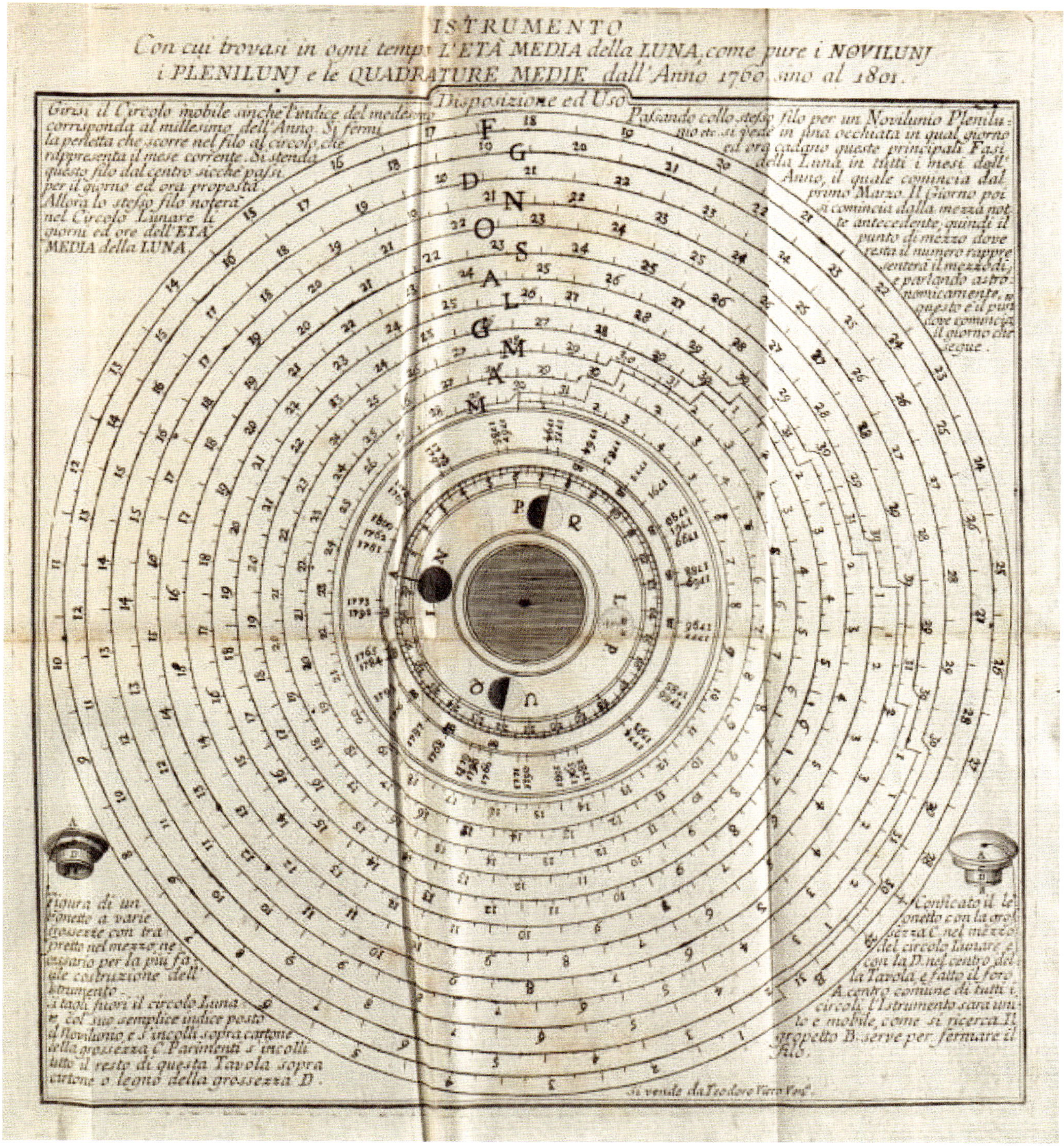

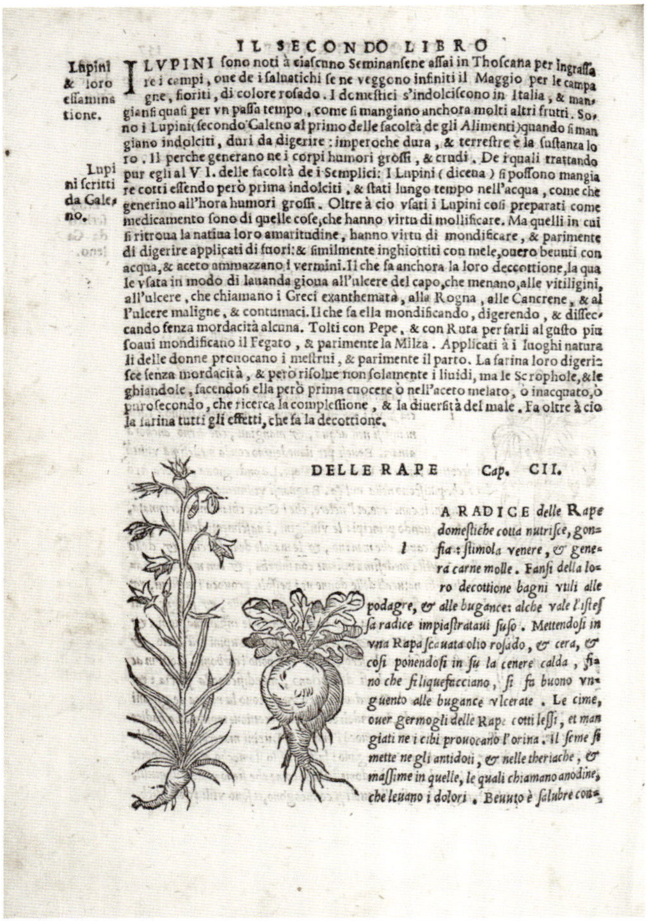

IL SECONDO LIBRO

Lupini & loro essamina tione.

LVPINI sono noti à ciascuno Seminansene assai in Thoscana per ingrassare i campi, oue de i saluatichi se ne veggono infiniti il Maggio per le campagne, fioriti, di colore rosado. I domestici s'indolciscono in Italia, & mangiansi quasi per vn passa tempo, come si mangiano anchora molti altri frutti. Sono i Lupini (secondo Galeno al primo delle facoltà de gli Alimenti) quando si mangiano indolciti, duri da digerire: imperoche dura, & terrestre è la sustanza loro. Il perche generano ne i corpi humori grossi, & crudi. De i quali trattando pur egli al VI. delle facoltà de i Semplici: I Lupini (dicena) si possono mangiare cotti essendo però prima indolciti, & stati lungo tempo nell'acqua, come che generino all'hora humori grossi. Oltre à cio vsati i Lupini cosi preparati come medicamento sono di quelle cose, che hanno virtu di mollificare. Ma quelli in cui si ritroua la natiua loro amaritudine, hanno virtu di mondificare, & parimente di digerire applicati di fuori: & similmente inghiottiti con mele, ouero beuuti con acqua, & aceto ammazzano i vermini. Il che fa anchora la loro decottione, la quale vsata in modo di lauanda gioua all'ulcere del capo, che menano, alle vitiligini, all'ulcere, che chiamano i Greci exanthemata, alla Rogna, alle Cancrene, & al l'ulcere maligne, & contumaci. Il che fa ella mondificando, digerendo, & diseccando senza mordacità alcuna. Tolti con Pepe, & con Ruta per farli al gusto piu soaui mondificano il Fegato, & parimente la Milza. Applicati à i luoghi naturali delle donne prouocano i mestrui, & parimente il parto. La farina loro digerisce senza mordacità, & però risolue non solamente i liuidi, ma le Scrophole, & le ghiandole, facendosi ella però prima cuocere ò nell'aceto melato, ò inacquato, ò puro secondo, che ricerca la complessione, & la diuersità del male. Fa oltre à cio la farina tutti gli effetti, che fa la decottione.

Lupini scritti da Galeno.

DELLE RAPE Cap. CII.

A RADICE delle Rape domestiche cotta nutrisce, gonfia: stimola venere, & genera carne molle. Fansi della loro decottione bagni vtili alle podagre, & alle buganze: alche vale l'istessa radice impiastratavi suso. Mettendosi in vna Rapa scauata olio rosado, & cera, & cosi ponendosi in su la cenere calda, fino che si liquefacciano, si fa buono vnguento alle bugance vlcerate. Le cime, ouer germogli delle Rape cotti lessi, et mangiati ne i cibi prouocano l'orina. Il seme si mette ne gli antidoti, & nelle theriache, & massime in quelle, le quali chiamano anodine, che leuano i dolori. Beuuto è salubre con-

Fig. 6

Pietro Andrea Mattioli, *Il Dioscoride,* Mantua (Giacomo Ruffinelli) 1549. Venice, Biblioteca Nazionale Marciana

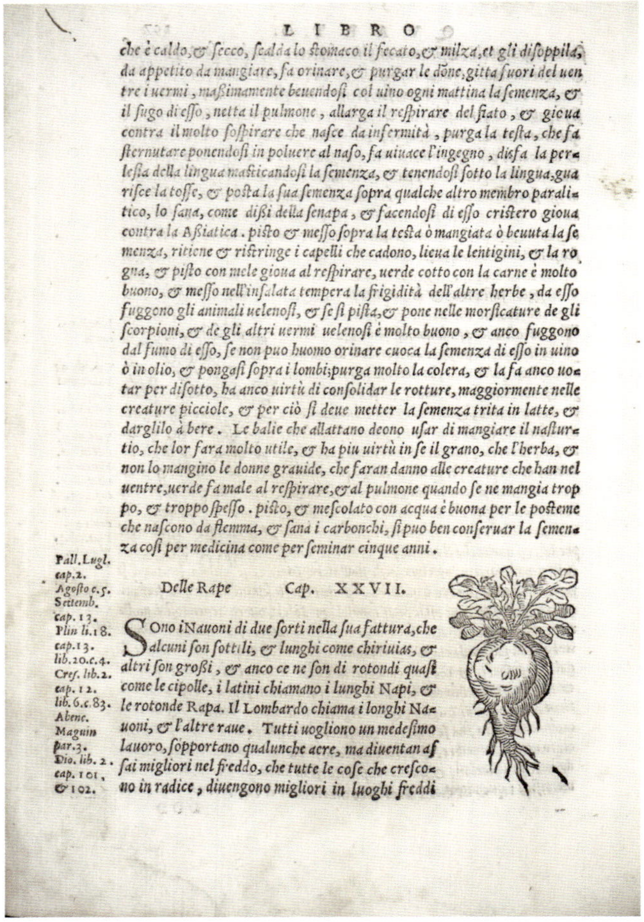

LIBRO

che è caldo, & secco, scalda lo stomaco il fecato, & milza, et gli disoppila, da appetito da mangiare, fa orinare, & purgar le dōne, gitta fuori del uentre i uermi, massimamente beuendosi col uino ogni mattina la semenza, & il sugo di esso, netta il pulmone, allarga il respirare del fiato, & gioua contra il molto sospirare che nasce da infermità, purga la testa, che fa sternutare ponendosi in poluere al naso, fa uiuace l'ingegno, dissa la perlessia della lingua masticandosi la semenza, & tenendosi sotto la lingua, guarisce la tosse, & posta la sua semenza sopra qualche altro membro paralitico, lo sana, come dissi della senapa, & facendosi di esso cristero gioua contra la Asiatica. pisto & messo sopra la testa ò mangiata ò beuuta la semenza, ritiene & ristringe i capelli che cadono, lieua le lentigini, & la rogna, & pisto con mele gioua al respirare, uerde cotto con la carne è molto buono, & messo nell'insalata tempera la frigidità dell'altre herbe, da esso fuggono gli animali uelenosi, & se si pista, & pone nelle morsicature de gli scorpioni, & de gli altri uermi uelenosi è molto buono, & anco fuggono dal fumo di esso, se non puo huomo orinare cuoca la semenza di esso in uino ò in olio, & pongasi sopra i lombi: purga molto la colera, & la fa anco uotar per disotto, ha anco uirtù di consolidar le rotture, maggiormente nelle creature picciole, & per ciò si deue metter la semenza trita in latte, & darglilo à bere. Le balie che allattano deono usar di mangiare il nasturtio, che lor farà molto utile, & ha piu uirtù in se il grano, che l'herba, & non lo mangino le donne grauide, che faran danno alle creature che han nel uentre, uerde fa male al respirare, & al pulmone quando se ne mangia troppo, & troppo spesso. pisto, & mescolato con acqua è buona per le posteme che nascono da flemma, & sana i carbonchi, si puo ben conseruar la semenza cosi per medicina come per seminar cinque anni.

Pall. Lugl. cap. 2. Agosto c. 5. Settemb. cap. 13. Plin li. 18. cap. 13. lib. 20. c. 4. Cres. lib. 2. cap. 12. lib. 6. c. 83. Abenc. Maguin par. 3. Dio. lib. 2. cap. 101. & 102.

Delle Rape Cap. XXVII.

Sono i Nauoni di due sorti nella sua fattura, che alcuni son sottili, & lunghi come chiriuias, & altri son grossi, & anco ce ne son di rotondi quasi come le cipolle, i latini chiamano i lunghi Napi, & le rotonde Rapa. Il Lombardo chiama i longhi Nauoni, & l'altre raue. Tutti uogliono un medesimo lauoro, sopportano qualunche aere, ma diuentan assai migliori nel freddo, che tutte le cose che crescono in radice, diuengono migliori in luoghi freddi

Fig. 7

Gabriele Alonso de Herrera, *Libro di agricoltura utilissimo, tratto da diuersi auttori,* Venice (Michele Tramezzino) 1557. Venice, Biblioteca Nazionale Marciana,

He translated into the vernacular and edited works on anatomy and surgery, and launched a more wide-ranging publication project specifically in the agronomic field, without neglecting the *materia medica* in a strict sense (the three natural kingdoms studied from a medico-pharmaceutical point of view).[46]

In 1560, complaining that on the subject of agronomy there was little that could be read in vernacular Italian and that the translations from Latin of Crescenzi and Columella were almost incomprehensible, he decided to produce a synthesis that would draw on the main writers of agriculture, including Crescenzi and Columella, to whom he added Pliny, Virgil, Dioscorides, and Mattioli. He divided the work into five parts and brought it out under the pseudonym Tatti Lucchese between 1560 and 1561: *Della agricoltura… libri cinque*.[47] The layout was the proven one of division into chapters (*Libri*), each with its own subject. It began with the quality of the places and the general nature of the buildings, and continued with fodder, vines and wine, vegetable gardens, trees, insects, and animals, also noxious. Oddly, the note *Ai lettori* is an *excusatio non petita*, in the sense that it forestalled the objection of anyone wishing to upbraid him for having given too much space to medicine, that is, *materia medica*:

> If you were to say that this book is more on medicine than anything else, I would reply that, as herbs have the capacity to heal the body, I thought it opportune

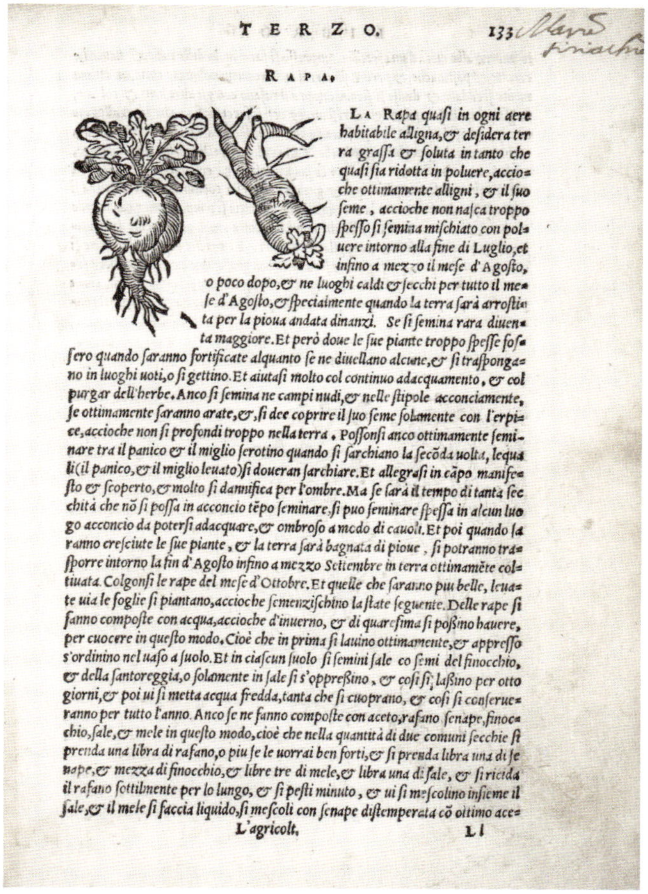

TERZO. 133

RAPA.

LA Rapa quasi in ogni aere habitabile alligna, & desidera terra grassa & soluta in tanto che quasi sia ridotta in poluere, accioche ottimamente alligni, & il suo seme, accioche non nasca troppo spesso si semina mischiato con poluere intorno alla fine di Luglio, et infino a mezzo il mese d'Agosto, o poco dopo, & ne luoghi caldi & secchi per tutto il mese d'Agosto, & specialmente quando la terra sarà arrostita per la pioua andata dinanzi. Se si semina rara diuenta maggiore. Et però doue le sue piante troppo spesse fossero quando saranno fortificate alquanto se ne diuellano alcune, & si traspongano in luoghi uoti, o si gettino. Et aiutasi molto col continuo adacquamento, & col purgar dell'herbe. Anco si semina ne campi nudi, & nelle stipole acconciamente, se ottimamente saranno arate, &, si dee coprire il suo seme solamente con l'erpice, accioche non si profondi troppo nella terra. Possonsi anco ottimamente seminare tra il panico & il miglio serotino quando si sarchiano la secōda uolta, lequali (il panico, & il miglio leuato) si doueran sarchiare. Et allegrasi in cāpo manifesto & scoperto, & molto si dannifica per l'ombre. Ma se sarà il tempo di tanta secchità che nō si possa in acconcio tēpo seminare, si puo seminare spessa in alcun luogo acconcio da potersi adacquare, & ombroso a modo di cauoli. Et poi quando saranno cresciute le sue piante, & la terra sarà bagnata di pioue, si potranno trasporre intorno la fin d'Agosto infino a mezzo Settembre in terra ottimamēte coltiuata. Colgonsi le rape del mese d'Ottobre. Et quelle che saranno piu belle, leuate uia le foglie si piantano, accioche semenzischino la state seguente. Delle rape si fanno composte con acqua, accioche d'inuerno, & di quaresima si possino hauere, per cuocere in questo modo. Cioè che in prima si lauino ottimamente, & appresso s'ordinino nel uaso a suolo. Et in ciascun suolo si semini sale co semi del finocchio, & della santoreggia, o solamente in sale si s'oppressino, & cosi si lassino per otto giorni, & poi ui si metta acqua fredda, tanta che si cuoprano, & cosi si conserueranno per tutto l'anno. Anco se ne fanno composte con aceto, rafano senape, finocchio, sale, & mele in questo modo, cioè che nella quantità di due comuni secchie si prenda una libra di rafano, o piu se le uorrai ben forti, & si prenda libra una di senape, & mezza di finocchio, & libre tre di mele, & libra una di sale, & si ricida il rafano sottilmente per lo lungo, & si pesti minuto, & ui si mescolino insieme il sale, & il mele si faccia liquido, si mescoli con senape distemperata cō ottimo ace=

L'agricolt. Ll

Fig. 8

Giovanni Tatti [i.e. Francesco Sansovino], *Della agricoltura … Ne quali si contengono tutte le cose appartenenti al bisogno della villa …*, Venice (Francesco Sansovino) 1560/61. Venice, Biblioteca Nazionale Marciana

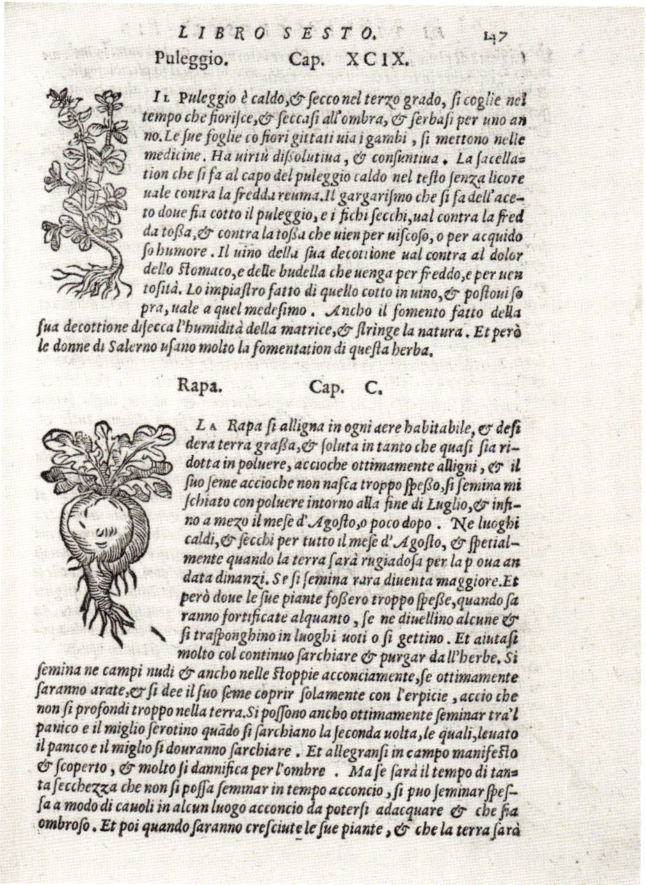

LIBRO SESTO. 147

Puleggio. Cap. XCIX.

IL Puleggio è caldo, & secco nel terzo grado, si coglie nel tempo che fiorisce, & seccasi all'ombra, & serbasi per uno anno. Le sue foglie co fiori gittati uia i gambi, si mettono nelle medicine. Ha uirtù dissolutiua, & consuntiua. La sacellation che si fa al capo del puleggio caldo nel testo senza licore uale contra la fredda reuma. Il gargarismo che si fa dell'aceto doue sia cotto il puleggio, e i fichi secchi, ual contra la fredda tossa, & contra la tossa che uien per uiscoso, o per acquidoso humore. Il uino della sua decottione ual contra al dolor dello stomaco, e delle budella che uenga per freddo, e per uentosità. Lo impiastro fatto di quello cotto in uino, & postoui sopra, uale a quel medesimo. Ancho il fomento fatto della sua decottione disecca l'humidità della matrice, & stringe la natura. Et però le donne di Salerno usano molto la fomentation di questa herba.

Rapa. Cap. C.

LA Rapa si alligna in ogni aere habitabile, & desidera terra grassa, & soluta in tanto che quasi sia ridotta in poluere, accioche ottimamente alligni, & il suo seme accioche non nasca troppo spesso, si semina mischiato con poluere intorno alla fine di Luglio, & infino a mezo il mese d'Agosto, o poco dopo. Ne luoghi caldi, & secchi per tutto il mese d'Agosto, & spetialmente quando la terra sarà rugiadosa per la p oua andata dinanzi. Se si semina rara diuenta maggiore. Et però doue le sue piante fossero troppo spesse, quando saranno fortificate alquanto, se ne diuellino alcune & si trasponghino in luoghi uoti o si gettino. Et aiutasi molto col continuo sarchiare & purgar dall'herbe. Si semina ne campi nudi & ancho nelle stoppie acconciamente, se ottimamente saranno arate, & si dee il suo seme coprir solamente con l'erpicie, accio che non si profondi troppo nella terra. Si possono ancho ottimamente seminar tra'l panico e il miglio serotino quādo si sarchiano la seconda uolta, le quali, leuato il panico e il miglio si douranno sarchiare. Et allegransi in campo manifesto & scoperto, & molto si dannifica per l'ombre. Ma se sarà il tempo di tanta secchezza che non si possa seminar in tempo acconcio, si puo seminar spessa a modo di cauoli in alcun luogo acconcio da potersi adacquare & che sia ombroso. Et poi quando saranno cresciute le sue piante, & che la terra sarà

Fig. 9

Pietro Crescenzi, *Pietro Crescentio bolognese tradotto nuouamente per Francesco Sansouino …*, Venice (Francesco Sansovino) 1561. Venice, Biblioteca Nazionale Marciana

to also give some notions of health to those who do not yet know anything of this, and who could appreciate it as much as agriculture. And in order that it be more easily comprehensible… I decided to furnish the book with pictures of herbs, plants and also animals. Anyone of good sense can see how much effort and commitment has gone into all this…[48]

Francesco Sansovino was a refined translator and good popularizer, but not being an expert on the subject, the operation he carried out with his *Dell'agricoltura* was a little anachronistic. By then, the medicinal contents, the virtues of plants, were disappearing from the agronomic treatises in favour of subjects such as grafting, the breeding of silkworms and spinning, the construction of fish ponds etc.; likewise, the illustrations of plants were increasingly making way for specialist and technical illustrations (of grafting, for example). That which Sansovino re-presented was rather too close to the contents of an illustrated *Hortus sanitatis*, an agronomy text similar to those that had only been seen in the late fifteenth century. And, indeed, the list of the *Auttori da quali si sono tratte le materie di questo libro* contains authors of both agronomy texts and of *materia medica*, such as Theophrastus, Pliny, and Dioscorides, along with his contemporary Pietro Andrea Mattioli.[49]

The woodcuts, which had cost him 'expense and effort', as he says in the note *Ai lettori*, were not made for the occasion, but were part of a set of small, reused, shared (or purchased?) blocks; in any case they had already been used by Giacomo Ruffinelli in Mantua for an edition of Dioscorides commented by Mattioli in 1549[50] and by Michele Tramezzino for his above-mentioned 1557 edition of Herrera. Not only here. Sansovino also used the same blocks in his edition of Pietro Crescenzi's work in 1561, which he presented as a new translation that finally allowed the work of the medieval author to be fully appreciated; more than a new translation, though, this was actually a profound linguistic revision that took note of the development of vernacular Italian in the last decades.[51] He was so gripped by the publishing operation of popularizing agronomic literature that he also undertook a new translation of Rutilius Palladius's *La villa* at the same time, condemning the omissions and poor Italian of the previous one, publishing it (not illustrated) in 1560/61.[52] In his mind this was undoubtedly a single project, given that in the note *A' lettori* at the beginning of Palladius's *Villa*, Sansovino speaks almost solely of the Crescenzio edition, including the decision to 'darvi in disegno le herbe, & le piante, & gli animali' ('provide in drawing the herbs and the plants and the animals').[53]

It must here be pointed out that in the years 1560–61 Sansovino embarked on a real campaign of translating/popularizing agronomy works of guaranteed success, compiling one of these himself. He did not present anything new, but restricted himself to an operation of elegant popularization, decomposing and recomposing the texts, resorting to well-tried but not particularly refined illustrations. The woodcuts depicting plants and animals are fairly small, and in the move from the Mattioli edition (Ruffinelli 1549) to that of Herrera (Tramezzino 1557), and his own in *Dell'agricoltura* (1560/61) and the *Crescentio* (1561), he limited himself to re-presenting them as such or adding them to other small blocks in his possession (figs. 6–9).[54]

The publishing operation in itself is an indication of the fact that in the 1560s a fairly extensive generic readership was also interested in reading agronomy works, regardless of whether they were actually innovative in content, as long as they were pleasantly written and well presented. Such a readership did not place great importance on illustrations of plants and that excess of medical observations by now surpassed by the agronomic genre. In this sense, Francesco Sansovino's dissemination effort can be considered the swan song of a then outdated way of producing agronomy texts and illustrations.

* This essay was written collaboratively with full agreement on the content. However, §1 was primarily drafted by M. Infelise, §2 was co-authored by both authors, and the Introduction and §3 have been mainly written by S. Minuzzi.
1 Cogliati Arano 1976; Trentini 2016.
2 Hoeninger 2006; Classen 2017.
3 For the former see essay Olmi and Tongiorgi Tomasi, p. 67.
4 Ambrosoli 1992, 17 and *passim*.
5 Derosas 2006.
6 Beutler 1973: these are probably calculations by default, given that the identification was made when online catalogues were not yet available.
7 Ambrosoli 1992; Pitteri 2006.
8 Toubert 1984.
9 Sorbelli 1933. Our essay refers to the most updated information derived from the ISTC (Incunabula Short Title Catalogue) and Edit16 (Edizioni italiane del XVI secolo).
10 Ambrosoli 1992, 52. To which a Florentine edition of 1605 must be added: http://id.sbn.it/bid/UFIE002647.
11 Compare, for example https://data.cerl.org/istc/ih00486000 and https://data.cerl.org/istc/ic00969000. On the incunabula production of *materia medica*, which also includes the *Horti sanitatis* – which are distinguished from the herbaria because they also illustrate animal and mineral substances along with vegetable – see Minuzzi 2021, 221–32.
12 Cioni 1975; cf. https://data.cerl.org/istc/ic00975000 and http://id.sbn.it/bid/VIAE011111.
13 On this image Cafà 2005, Derosas 2006, 25 and Pitteri 2006, 65.
14 Vecce 2017, 198–9.
15 See the 1511 edition attributed to Alessandro da Lessona https://edit16.iccu.sbn.it/titolo/CNCE013734 and those recomposed by Bindoni https://edit16.iccu.sbn.it/titolo/CNCE071431 and https://edit16.iccu.sbn.it/titolo/CNCE013735.
16 For example, that of Basel of 1548 http://id.sbn.it/bid/RMLE001007.
17 Apart from Jenson's edition (ISTC is00346000), the following are also recorded: is00347000 (Reggio Emilia 1482), is00348000 (Bologna 1494), is00349000 and is00350000 (Reggio Emilia 1496 and 1499).
18 Manutius 1975, I, 137–43, II, 300–5.
19 Ambrosoli 1992, 24–5.
20 Gaulin 2007. On the success of the manuscript popularizations of Palladius, in Italian and English, see Ambrosoli 1992, 19–32.
21 Palladius 1526, fol. 2r–v: 'acciò quelli che non sanno latino, fructo et gran dilecto per li suoi brevi et ordinati precepti acquistino'; 'acciochè ancora li imperiti della latinità (li quali son più che li docti) questi necessarii & dilecteuoli documenti: in piccolo, & chiaro volume collecti: possino experimentare: & da quelli incredibile & desiderato fructo: conseguire.' Pallecchi 2012.
22 Baldacchini 2011.
23 Palladius 1538, 143; Braida and Infelise 2010.
24 Herrera 1513, CLXXVII c.; fol.
25 Herrera 1557.
26 Gallo 1569.
27 Gallo 1569, 3: 'la grande utilità & il gran diletto che si cava dal coltivar la terra, la quale, come benigna Madre, non solo ci rende sopra modo de' frutti suoi, ma ci fa conoscer'anco che'l Signor Iddio ama & favorisce particolarmente tutti coloro che si occupano virtuosamente & con nobil'animo in coltivarla'.
28 Gallo 1569, 391: '...non si può trovare sorte alcuna di guadagno più honesto & più largo, né più certo né più stabile né più dilettevole o più degno d'ogni persona nobile & libera di quel che è col mezo di questa divina arte... O quanto certamente sono ciechi quei mercanti, che travagliosamente vanno d'ogni tempo per terra, per mare, per monti & per boschi, con infiniti pericoli della vita & facoltà, bramosi di guadagnare i vinti o trenta per cento: per qual cagione non lasciano quella dolorosa professione & non li donano a quest'altra, la quale non solamente rende i vinti & trenta per cento, ma quasi sempre più di cento per trenta?'
29 Benzoni 1998, Pregari 1988.
30 Gallo 1569, 2.
31 On Agostino Gallo in France see Tenenti 1988.
32 Lanteri 1560, 60 and *passim*.
33 Mensi 1899, ad vocem.
34 Falcone 1597.
35 Falcone 1597, fols. a2r–a4r.
36 Bussato 1592. On Bussato, born in Ravenna to a family originally from Ferrara, professional grafter, see Tucci 1972.
37 Samson 2012; Hyde 2013.
38 See, purely as an example: http://id.sbn.it/bid/VIAE003590, http://id.sbn.it/bid/SBLE005603, http://id.sbn.it/bid/VIAE001813.
39 Tarello 1567.
40 Tarello 1567, 10v: 'Colombo genovese inventore del Mondo Novo, che passando le colonne d'Ercole che dagli antichi non erano mai state passate, diede cagione al gran Carlo V imperatore di aggiungere alla sua impresa *Plus Ultra*'; Berengo 1975; Roveda 2012; Ciriacono 2019.
41 Poni 1970.
42 Berveglieri 1995.
43 Il *Ricordo d'agricoltura* was republished in 1577 and 1585 in Mantua http://id.sbn.it/bid/TO0E068884, http://id.sbn.it/bid/NAPE033579, in Treviso in 1601 http://id.sbn.it/bid/NAPE033579 and in Venice in 1609, 1622, 1629 http://id.sbn.it/bid/UM1E003612, http://id.sbn.it/bid/VIAE000809, http://id.sbn.it/bid/BVEE031227.
44 Cf. http://id.sbn.it/bid/SBLE001198 (1756) and http://id.sbn.it/bid/SBLE001197 (1772); on Scottoni see Infelise 2018.
45 Testa 2019.
46 In 1561 he assembled, as editor, Sansovino 1561a.
47 Tatti 1560. The frontispieces and colophons of the print run may carry the year 1560 or 1561 because of updating during printing.
48 Tatti 1560, *3r: '...se voi diceste che questo libro è più medicinale che altrimenti, vi replico che havendo le herbe le virtù che son conservative del corpo, ho giudicato che non sia se non bene l'insegnar anco a chi non sa quella parte ch'è forse non men grata a gli uomini di quel che si sia l'agricoltura, cioè la sanità. Et perché s'intendino meglio... ho voluto por sotto gli occhi le figure delle herbe, delle piante & de gli animali anchora, con quanta spesa, con quanta fatica & con quanti disturbi ogniun che ha giudicio lo può vedere...'
49 Tatti 1560, *4r, *Auttori da quali sono tratte le materie di questo libro.*
50 Mattioli 1549. This is a very incorrect and unauthorized edition of the famous physician and naturalist Mattioli, on whom see Ferri 1997 and Preti 2008. On the activity of Giacomo Ruffinelli see the entry that Pignatti 2017 dedicates to his father Venturino.
51 Crescenzi 1561.
52 Palladius 1560.
53 Palladius 1560, fol. 4*r.
54 The same blocks are used for the blackberries, figs, leeks, roses etc.; at times Sansovino associated other small blocks with those of Ruffinelli-Tramezzino, e.g. for the leeks and turnips. The direct links between Ruffinelli (who moved from Venice to Modena in 1544), Tramezzino and Sansovino can easily be shown.

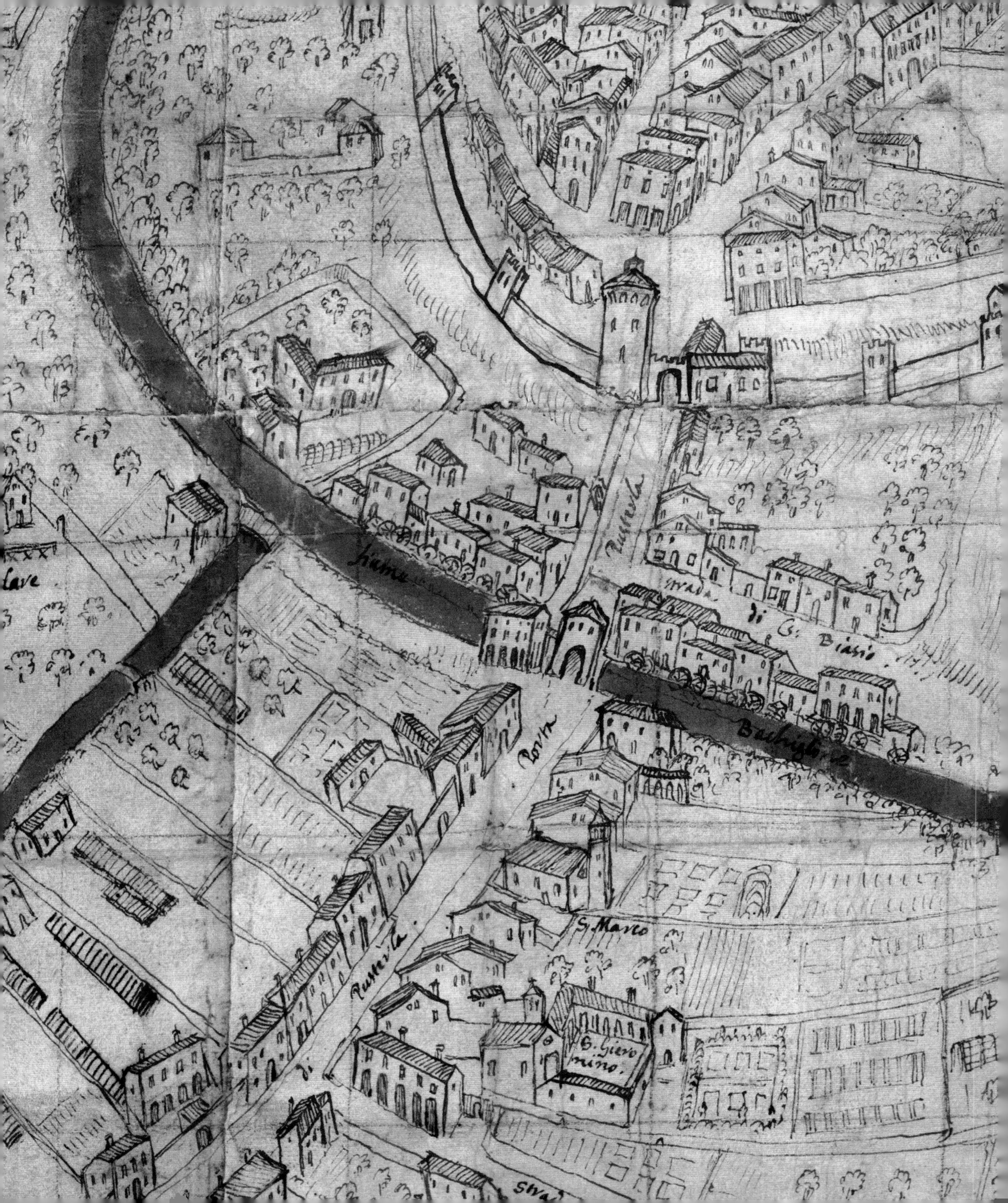

strada di S. Biasio
Bachiglione
S. Marco
S. Gierorino.
Porta

EDOARDO DEMO

An Area with a Great Manufacturing Vocation

The Economy of Vicenza and the Veneto Foothills in the Renaissance

Numerous contributions over the last thirty years have greatly expanded our knowledge of mercantile practice in the late medieval and Renaissance Venetian mainland as never before.[1] A particularly convincing picture of this has emerged, thanks to which it has been possible to define the peculiarities of a long unimagined situation marked by a very high concentration of manufacturing and commercial activities, with some sectors, above all those of wool and silk manufacture, of an absolute international level and for this very reason considered at the forefront in terms of technology and organization. It is now known with certainty that the wool and silk products made in Renaissance Veneto circulated almost everywhere in Europe and beyond, achieving considerable market success. And while the woollen mill and the silk mill may rightly be seen as the cornerstones of the pre-industrial Veneto economy, such as to constitute a reserve of fundamental technical and entrepreneurial expertise useful for explaining the subsequent stages of the region's industrial growth, the developments seen in other key sectors were of no minor importance: from mining to the processing of wood and paper; from the production of saltpetre and war materials to the tanning of hides; from metallurgy to printing. Furthermore, the same research has not only shown that Venice and the mainland were undoubtedly permeated by a great and precocious manufacturing vocation, but also that this phenomenon was not confined to the main urban centres, but involved much of the foothill or lower mountain band between the Bergamo and Feltre-Belluno regions. A vast area geographically, densely populated and generally marked by land that is poorly suited to agriculture, but rich in wood and water.

Another aspect concerning trade and investment in land is significant. Contrary to what has long been asserted by various scholars of Renaissance Veneto, who associated the oligarchic closures of the ruling groups with forms of immobility in the economic field, characterized by a gradual abandoning of trade and by a growing, at times spasmodic, interest in land, many of the recent studies recalled up to now have shown how the participants in the above-mentioned manufacturing activities and the trade generated by these were frequently not only numerous mercantile 'houses', but also different members of some of the most important families in the largest cities on the Veneto mainland. In short, several nobles did business during and after the sixteenth century. There was no lack of women, either – not just financing mercantile enterprises, but in several cases involved in the direct management of the business.[2]

The propensity for business that distinguished the Veneto mainland is particularly true of Vicenza and the surrounding foothills. Leandro Alberti of Bologna encapsulates Vicenza in his *Descrittione di tutta Italia* (1550), emphasizing its considerable wealth due to an active commercial sector and a dynamic and cultured ruling class: 'The men of this city [Vicenza] are of lively wit and great daring, and they are very disposed to letters, arms and trade. They live very civilly, dress decently and continually gather riches.'[3]

The extensive availability of raw materials, hydraulic energy and timber, along with an underemployed workforce on the upper plains and in the valleys; the readiness for business risk; the considerable international openness to trade – these are all factors that determined the powerful and long-term perseverance of manufacturing traditions in the Vicenza area. This was not static, however, but rather a play of continuities and interruptions and an alternation of favourable periods and others marked by more or less serious crises.[4] This phenomenon began in the late Middle Ages and reached its peak in the sixteenth century, in what has rightly been described as the city's golden century – that of Andrea Palladio.

One of the fundamental factors explaining the propensity for manufacturing in the Vicenza area is undoubtedly the extensive availability of water. The abundance of water was one of the principal factors, if not the principal factor, of industrial location in the centuries of the modern age. A great availability of water means having an indispensable source of energy on hand with which to power the most diverse transformation activities and so set up manufacturing companies. Almost the entire foothill area around Vicenza is very rich in water, marked as it is by the existence of numerous, complex, variegated, and linked hydrographic networks, all closely interwoven and overlapping, able, above all, to provide hydraulic energy in a different and polymorphous manner and thus support strong manufacturing growth. Vicenza itself has been described as a city 'born straddling rivers'; by the late Middle Ages, it had an astonishing number of water-wheels. Indeed, from the fifteenth century, areas near the city's two main rivers (the Bacchiglione and the Retrone) could be defined as true 'industrial zones', given the high concentration of hydraulic power plants, workshops, and factories engaged in the most diverse production activities. This is clearly visible in the famous *Pianta Angelica* of Vicenza (fig. 1), drawn up in 1580, with long lines of water-wheels marking the Borgo Pusterla, the area where the Ponte degli Angeli is now located, or that near the Ponte San Michele and the current Ponte San Paolo.[5]

It was after the very serious pandemic in the mid-fourteenth century that what had until then been defined as an '*urbicola*' or a '*parva civitas*' saw high demographic and economic growth, especially around the middle of the fifteenth century. A mercantile centre that had been anything but secondary since the late Middle Ages, Vicenza experienced a very favourable economic phase in the second half of the fifteenth century, and even more in the sixteenth, in which its population rose considerably, more than doubling in just a few decades. This did not happen in the other main cities of the Venetian mainland in the same period. From around 10,000 inhabitants at the beginning of the fifteenth century, Vincenza grew to a demographic size similar to that of Padua (about 20,000 inhabitants) by the end of the same century, though this still represented only half the population of Verona.

This upward trend continued (albeit marked by periodic shocks due to the outbreak of epidemics or subsistence crises), reaching 30,000 inhabitants by the mid-sixteenth century, 35,000 in the 1580s and almost 40,000 at the start of the seventeenth. A similar trend occurred in the surrounding region, whose population grew from 125,000 in the mid-sixteenth century to 160,000 at the start of the seventeenth. It is a region studded with large towns, some of which reached the size of small cities, at times even far exceeding 3,000 inhabitants – for example, Arzignano, Bassano, Schio, and Valdagno.[6]

This strong demographic growth went hand in hand with the considerable increase in the city's international manufacturing and commercial role, linked particularly to the great success of its silk production. Although wool was undoubtedly the most important manufacturing sector in the fifteenth century (Vicentine cloth sold by the hundreds in central and south Italy, the Balkan peninsula, the eastern Mediterranean, the German region and from

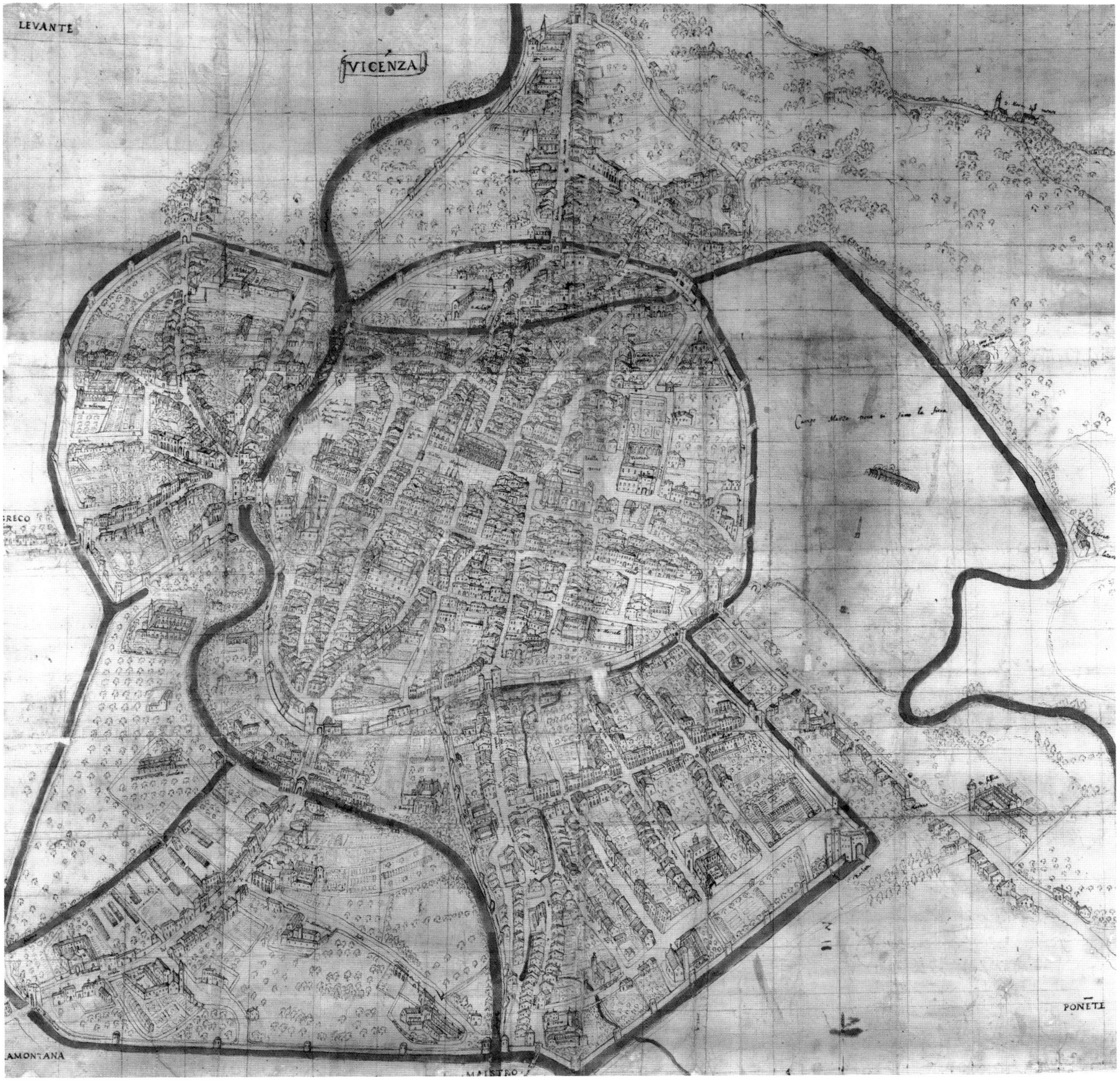

Fig. 1
The *Pianta Angelica* of Vicenza, detail, 1580. Rome, Biblioteca Angelica, Banc. Stampe N.S. 56/81

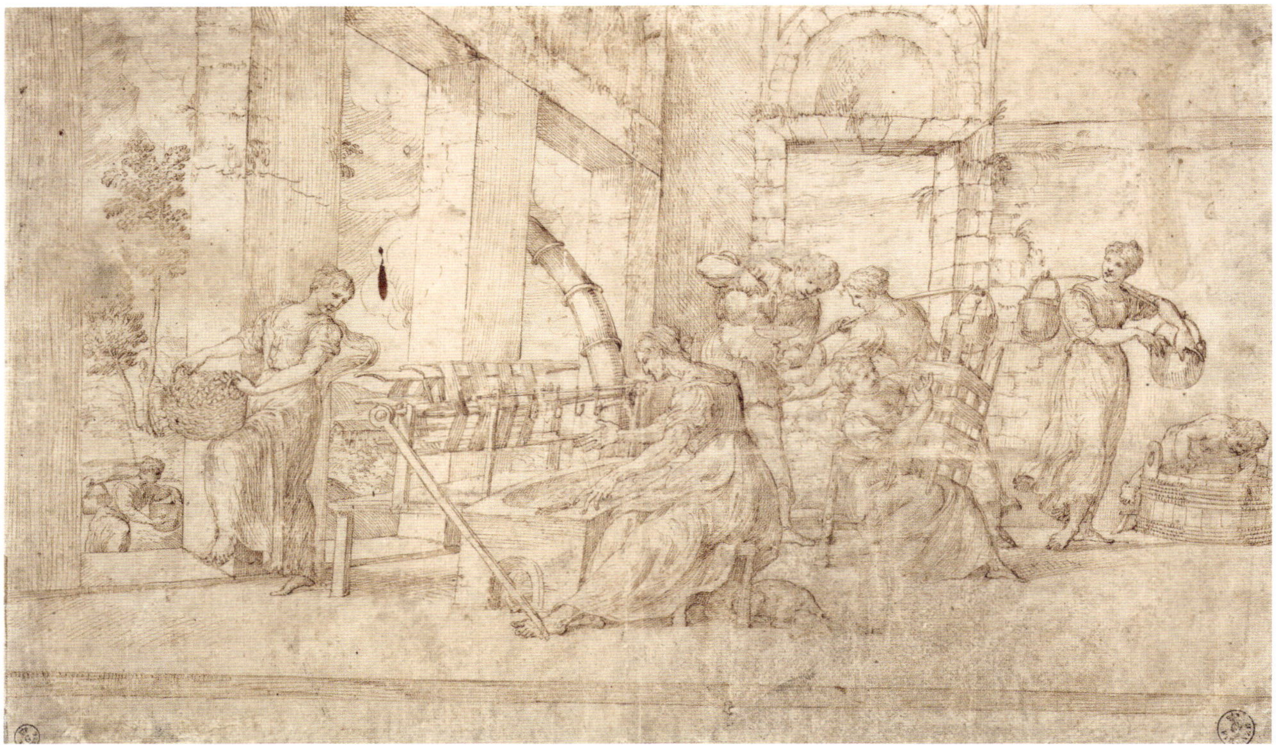

Fig. 2

Domenico Campagnola, *The Production of Raw Silk*, c.1550. Florence, Gallerie degli Uffizi, Gabinetto Disegni e Stampe, inv. 1786

Fig. 3

Andrea Palladio, Villa Almerico Capra Valmarana, called La Rotonda, 1566/67, Vicenza

there throughout central and eastern Europe),[7] in the sixteenth century there was a genuine boom in silk (fig. 2).

The production of woollen fabrics in Vicenza did not suddenly disappear, of course, as shown by Paolo Gualdo's unpublished *Rilatione*, written between 1582 and 1583, which states: 'The high-quality woollen cloths that are made in Vicenza are much esteemed and in great repute... The woollen cloths that are made for the local region are lower-quality cloths and mostly thick cloths for poor people.'[8] In the second half of the sixteenth century, more than 90 kilometres of high-quality woollen fabrics were produced in Vicenza, along with more than 420 kilometres of low-medium quality fabrics produced throughout the Vicenza region and particularly in the water-rich foothills, the same area that in subsequent centuries was crucial for Italian industrial development.

Other sectors were certainly also successfully practised, from goldsmithing/jewellery (notably, Valerio Belli, 'prince' of engravers) to glassware, with a major production, until a few years ago completely unimagined, of tumblers for use or purely decorative; from the production of paper to printing; from the tanning of hides to the working of metals, clay pottery, and timber.[9] But it was silk that became the real backbone of Vicenza's manufacturing economy, making the city one of the main production centres in Europe. Indeed, in the mid-sixteenth century more than forty per cent of all the raw silk produced on the Venetian mainland came from Vicenza, which was distinguished as the urban centre in which the greatest number of mills for the throwing of silk were operating in the entire Venetian Republic, as many as 100 in 1596. In the second half of the sixteenth century, Vicenza exported an average of eighteen to twenty tonnes of raw and semi-processed silk per year (excluding smuggled material) to every corner of Europe (France, Germany, Flanders, England...), more than any other city on the Venetian mainland. It gradually specialized in weaving, especially of plain and light cloths such as *ormesini*, which were sent in particular towards central and eastern Europe in their hundreds. In the 1560s, Vicentine silk was defined as the 'finest and in highest demand' on the Lyon market, generating at least 700,000 ducats' worth of trade per year, equivalent to the value of forty villas like Palladio's La Rotonda (fig. 3).

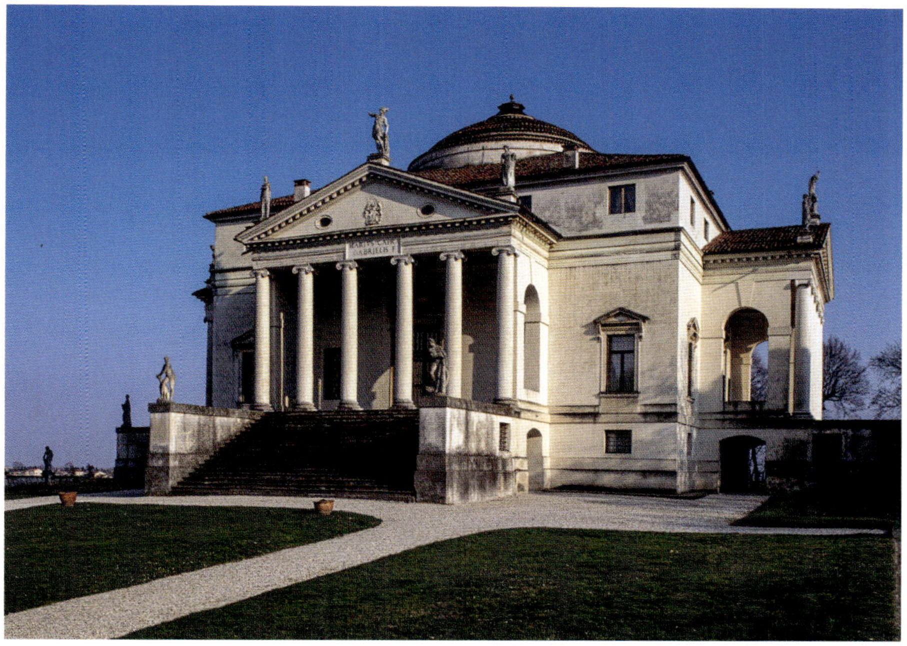

Futhermore, between the 1550s and the 1580s, dozens of companies were active internationally, alongside numerous members of the most important aristocratic families. Indeed, in the sixteenth century, Vicenza seems to have been the Venetian mainland city in which, according to current knowledge, the active participation in commerce by members of the nobility was most evident, a practice often accompanied by a fervent interest in the new ideas brought by the Protestant Reformation.[10] In Lyon, Geneva, and Basel, in Antwerp and subsequently Amsterdam, in Cologne, Leipzig, and Strasbourg, in Nuremberg, Augsburg, and Frankfurt, in London, Vienna, Prague, Cracow, Seville, Cadiz, and Lisbon, it was not uncommon to come across correspondents or branches of Vicentine companies that made the city on the banks of the Retrone a hub in a commercial network of European importance.

Among those dealing on the international markets were well-known art patrons such as Marcantonio Cogollo, who, when he commissioned Paolo Veronese to paint the *Adoration of the Magi* (Santa Corona church, Vicenza), sold silks in Lyon, Antwerp, Frankfurt, Nuremberg, Leipzig, Vienna, and Prague. They also included some of the most prestigious of Palladio's clients. Marco Antonio Thiene (who built the impressive Thiene Palazzo in Vicenza and the Thiene Villa Quinto Vicentino) sent silks to Lyon between the 1530s and 1550s. Girolamo di Nicolò Chiericati (who commissioned the Palladio palazzo in what is now Piazza Matteotti) also sold silk products of various kinds in Lyon and Antwerp at more or less the same time. He was also active in the markets of central and south Italy, selling woollen cloth he produced in Vicenza, continuing the business practised by his father and in which his brother Giovanni (builder of Villa Chiericati in Vancimuglio) was also involved. Biagio Saraceno (who commissioned the villa in Agugliaro, and relating to whom about twenty commercial letters and various extracts of accounts concerning the sale of raw and semi-processed silk to Lyon, and the marketing of cereals, have recently been found) was certainly engaged in the production of silk products and their international marketing (especially in Lyon, but also in Antwerp and the German area), as were Losco Caldogno (builder of the Palladio villa of the same name), Bonifacio Poiana (who commissioned the villa in Poiana Maggiore), and Iseppo di Gerolamo Porto (builder of the Palladio palazzo in the *contrada* of the same name; fig. 4). To note one final example, the mercantile and financial activities of the *cavaliere* Giuliano Piovene were even more extensive and diverse. Piovene, along

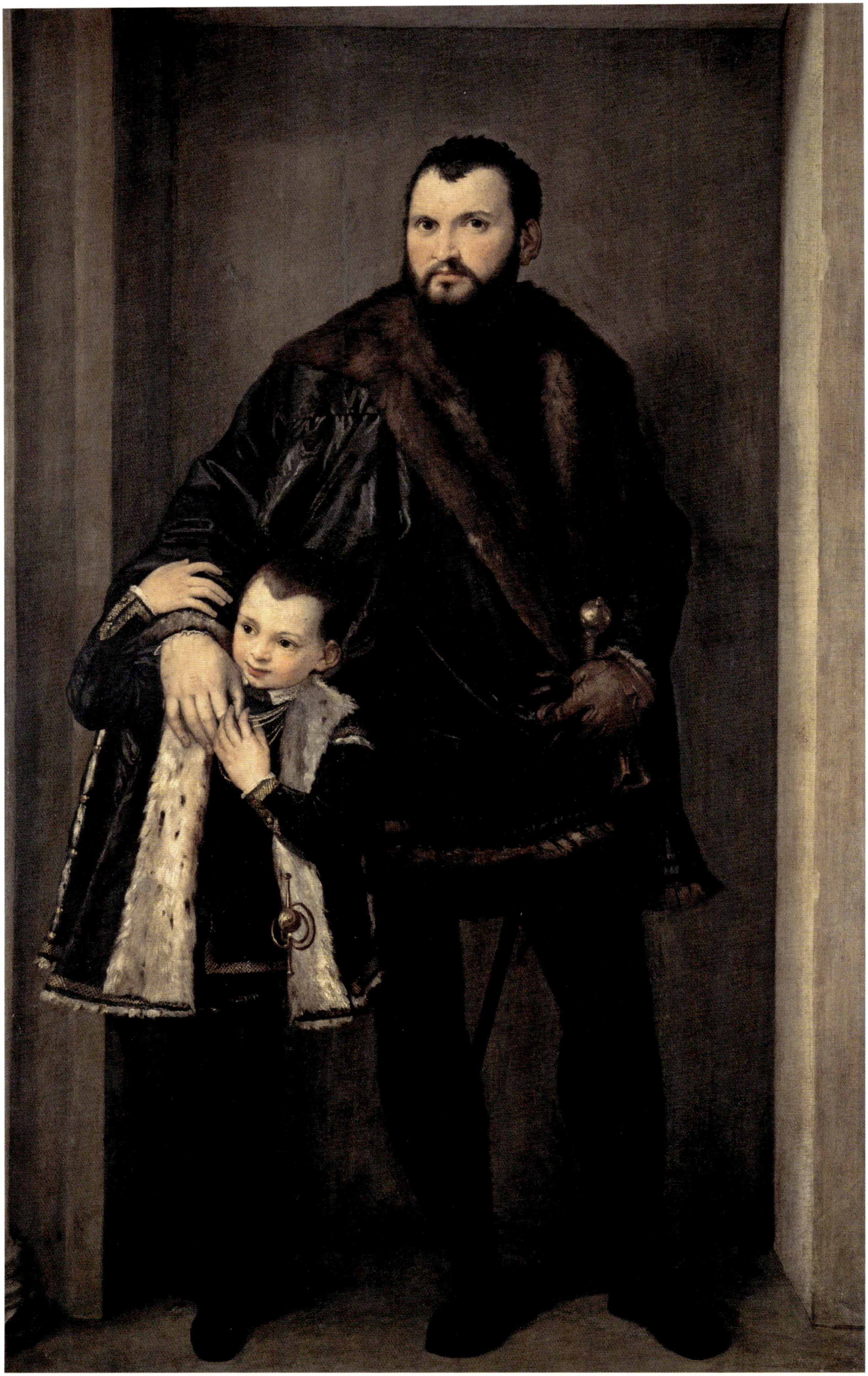

Fig. 4

Paolo Caliari, called Veronese, *Portrait of Count Giuseppe da Porto with his son, Adriano,* 1555. Florence, Gallerie degli Uffizi, inv. contini Bonacossi 16

with his brother Guido, built Palladio's 'superb palace of compelling cost' at Isola (unfortunately now destroyed) and between the 1550s and 1580s produced silk goods in Vicenza that were sent to every part of Europe. He also insured ships in Venice, set up a woollen mill and a soap works in Piedmont, and managed the mint in Mantua.[11]

The phenomenon described above was so pervasive that it is now certain that men were not alone in playing an active role in Renaissance Vicenza's world of international business. Indeed, the participation of women in the sixteenth century's lively manufacturing and mercantile world was frequent. They not only worked as financiers, but often as merchants too, directly running the business.[12] The most striking case is undoubtedly that of Bianca Nievo, wife of the Palladio patron Giacomo Angaran. A notably successful poet of rustic rhymes, a religious dissident close to Calvinism (for which she was strangled by the Inquisition in 1588), she produced light silk fabrics and marketed cloths of northern European production in the 1570s, in partnership with her daughter Cillenia. Unpublished letters from her daughter and the testimony of the master silk-thrower Iseppo Quarteri before the judge of L'Aquila (who explicitly declared that he 'does the deeds of the said lady and the work of the silk') present Bianca as an expert businesswoman who sought to obtain the best possible profit, sending what was made in Vicenza to Lyon, where her compatriot Vincenzo Pilati, one of the leading Italian silk merchants living in France at the time, worked as her agent.[13]

The expansion of silk working in the Vicenza area was so important that it also struck chroniclers and the occasional visitor. The Fano poet Gian Battista Dragonzino noted in 1525 'that from silk a great treasure is produced within the city and on all of its slopes'.[14] A few years later, Leandro Alberti (mentioned above) wrote, 'In the city as well as outside, one can see many mulberry trees for feeding the worms, from which silk is made, which is a marvellous thing' (cat. 72.1), then added, significantly, that 'the Vicentines report great gains from said silk'.[15] In the 1580s, local clergyman Paolo Gualdo noted how silk was the 'most frequented trade' by the Vicentines, adding: 'As for silk, I see two ways of trading. Some buy silk to have it made and to make from it *ormezini*, satins, velvets and other cloths, for which 200 looms were described in this city two years ago. Others buy silks to send them to France, Flanders, Germany and other foreign countries.'[16]

It is also significant that the process of exceptional economic growth in Palladian Vicenza was accompanied by equally important growth in the surrounding region. Filippo Pigafetta, Vicentine geographer and cartographer of international renown, did not hesitate to define said growth as 'beautiful for the gifts of nature and the human industry'. Thus he not only emphasized the beauty of the landscape and the fertility of the land, but also the industriousness of the Vicenza people and the propensity of the foothill towns for industrial production and the marketing of products made on distant markets, confirming a strong vocation for business.[17] Here, the scarcity of agricultural production was compensated for by an intense manufacturing activity involving various sectors, among which textiles once again stood out.

The town of Bassano played a leading role in this context. Located at the edge of the Vicenza and Treviso foothills, where the Brenta flows out of the Valsugana and on to Padua and then the lagoon, the town was distinguished from the late Middle Ages as an ideal marketplace for trading goods between the the mountains and the plain (fig. 5). Endowed with easy connections to Trento, Bolzano and the cities of southern Germany, exploiting its wealth of water and favourable geographic position on one of the most important trade routes to central Europe, Bassano developed a manufacturing activity of key importance during the Renaissance, being able to count on the extensive availability of raw materials, such as the wool and hides deriving from the sheep-rearing widely practised in the mountains, or the cocoons and silk obtained in large quantities in the foothills.[18]

The widespread practice of working wool and silk in the town on the banks of the Brenta is also shown by the presence of numerous mercantile enterprises, second only to those in Vicenza for quantity and quality. One emblematic example is that of the Brocchi brothers. Having arrived in Bassano from Piuro, a small town in the Chiavenna area, they established one of the most important trading houses in the province, able to compete in terms of invested capital and turnover with those in Vicenza. They produced raw silk, spun semi-finished products in their own watermills and dyed and wove dozens of pieces of *ormesini*, a kind of light, easily worked, smooth, silk fabric then much in demand in the German markets.[19]

The interest in the textile sector and particularly silk processing in sixteenth-century Bassano was so pervasive that it also involved the world of artists. This can be inferred from Francesco and Jacopo Bassano's second *Libro dei Conti*, which includes some accounting entries showing that the women of the family were engaged in silk-throwing, using their own silk stoves and considerably

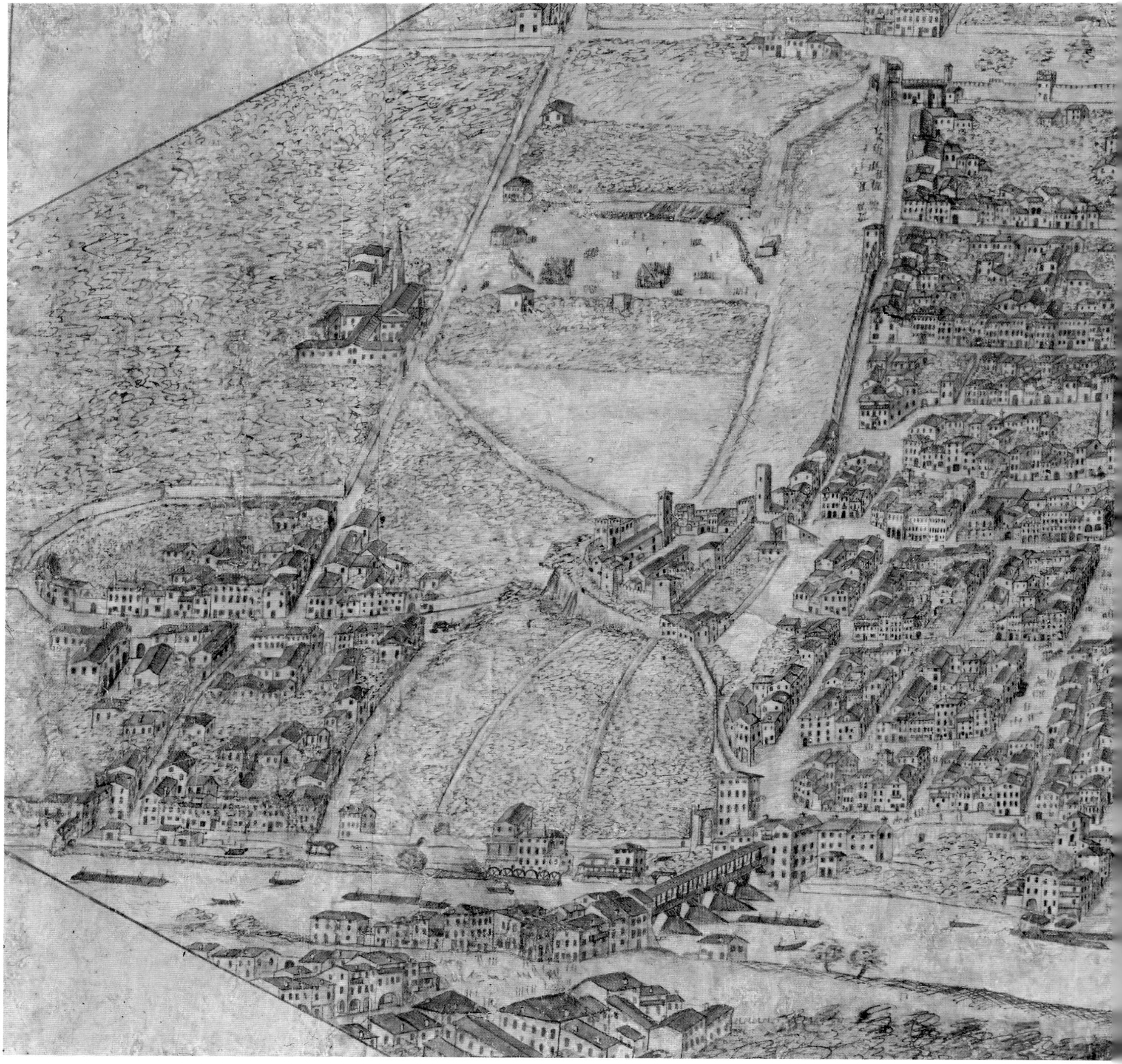

Fig. 5

Workshop of Francesco Bassano the Younger and Leandro Bassano, city map of Bassano (*Mappa dalpontiana*), 1583/1610. Museo di Bassano, inv. 10

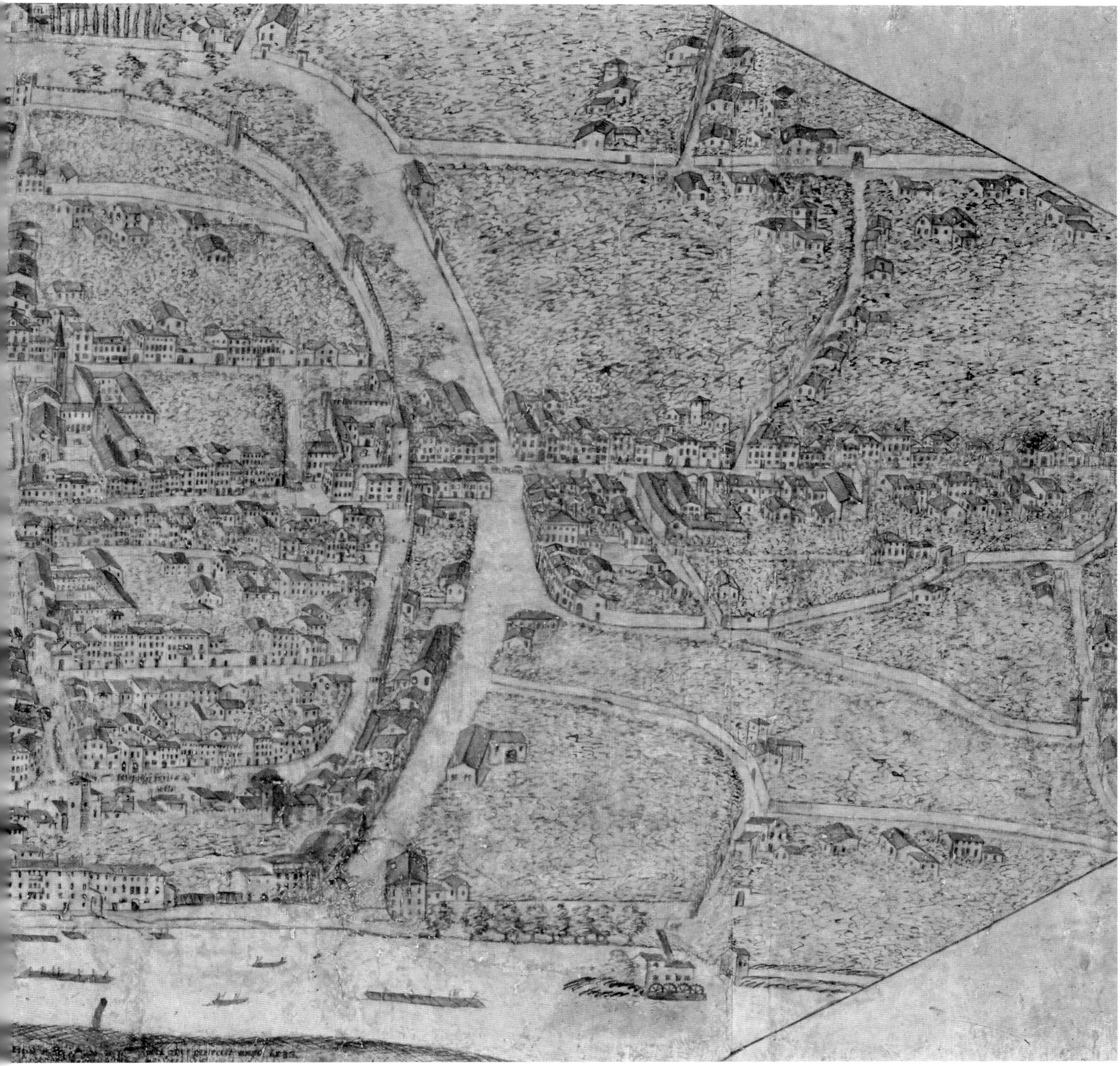

supplementing the income received from painting.[20] Such was their familiarity with the working of silk and the requisite tools that it is no surprise that, some years later, Leandro Bassano depicted, in his portrayal of the month of July, an richly detailed scene showing silk thread being extracted from cocoons (cat. 67.7)

In the words of Francesco Vianello, Renaissance Bassano 'was presented', thus, 'as a particularly significant case of a kind of urban centre of intermediate size between the cities of medium size that from the late Middle Ages had dominated the Po regions and rural villages'.[21] An 'almost city' of limited demographic size compared to nearby Vicenza, but endowed with substantial manufacturing system.

Finally, the area's long-term vocation for enterprise left significant signs in terms of the workplaces and buildings intended specifically for industrial activity, both in the city and elsewhere in the Vicenza area and, more generally, in the Venetian mainland, as shown by a recent research project supervised by Deborah Howard.[22] The case of the wool entrepreneur Antonio Pelo, to take one example, is striking. In the tax survey of 1563–64, he declared that he owned a building in Contrada di Sant'Ambrogio, Vicenza, where a good '113 of his men worked to make cloths',[23] a genuine example of a proto-factory.

A few words to conclude. An image has emerged from the previous pages of a Vicenza (and its surrounding area, especially Bassano) that experienced its golden age in the sixteenth century, thanks partly to the predominance of a particularly dynamic nobility that was distinguished by its notable economic reserves, its substantial connections to the advanced culture (both literary and artistic) of the time, and its marked ability to take a leading role beyond local limits. Important and brilliant military careers of several exponents with foreign powers such as France and Spain or at the Italian courts; a capacity for assertion in the clerical sphere beyond the local dimension, thanks to a not uncommon privileged relation with the Holy See and the Roman Curia; an openness towards cultural innovations; a tolerance and openness towards the innovations brought by the Protestant Reformation; a marked propensity for business at an international level, with manufacturing and commercial enterprises working in every corner of Europe – these are just some of the characteristics that explain the cosmopolitanism of the Vicenza ruling class of the time.[24] And that is not all. Furthermore, this also contributes to an understanding of the openness to innovation, which is iconically expressed through collaboration with the brilliant architectural and artistic ideas of Andrea Palladio, Jacopo Bassano, Paolo Veronese, and Alessandro Vittoria. So it is thanks to the presence of a group of young artists who revolutionized the very idea of art and beauty, but also of an enterprising, diligent, wealthy, cultured ruling class, open to the unusual and non-traditional proposals of the young Palladio, that Vicenza was enriched with splendid Renaissance 'factories': the Basilica Palladiana, the Teatro Olimpico and *palazzi* 'of compelling cost' (as the sources say) like Palazzo Thiene, Palazzo Barbaran, Palazzo Valmarana, Palazzo Chiericati, and the unfortunately destroyed Palazzo Piovene.

1 On the subject, the object of numerous studies, see at least Panciera 1996; Fontana 1997 (in particular the essays by Fontana himself, Salvatore Ciriacono, Walter Panciera, Giorgio Roverato and Raffaello Vergani); Molà 2000; Molà, Mueller, and Zanier 2000 (the essays by Edoardo Demo, Danilo Gasparini and Luca Molà); Demo 2001; Demo 2003; Vergani 2003; Fontana and Sandal 1997 (in particular the essays by the two editors and by Walter Panciera, Danilo Gasparini, and Maria Nicoletta Simeone); Lanaro 2003 (in particular the essays by the editor and by Edoardo Demo); Fontana and Gayot 2004 (the studies by Fontana himself, Giampaolo Cagnin, Luca Clerici, Edoardo Demo, Danilo Gasparini, Andrea Mozzato, Elisabetta Novello, Walter Panciera, Francesco Vianello, and Giovanni Zalin); Caracausi 2004; Vianello 2004; Panciera 2005; Demo 2005, 101–30; Occhi 2006; Caracausi 2008; Demo 2012; Demo 2013, 291–318; Caracausi 2014, 131–60; Demo 2014, 115–48; Demo 2021; Beltramini and Demo 2022. For other relevant bibliographic references, see Fontana 2004, esp. 174–90; Lanaro 2006 (in particular see the paper by the editor herself and the works by Edoardo Demo, Marco Belfanti, Giovanni Favero, and Francesco Vianello); Demo and Vianello 2011, 27–50; Battilotti et al. 2016. (in particular the introduction by the four editors).

2 Demo 2012, 72–8.

3 'Sono gli huomini di essa città [Vicenza] di vivace ingegno et di grand'ardire et molto disposti alle lettere, all'armi et ai trafichi. Vivono molto civilmente et vestono honestamente et di continuo radunano ricchezze.' Molà 2001, 221.

4 Fontana 2004.

5 Demo 2013a, 19–33.

6 For this and other information about demographic trends in Vicenza and the other main Veneto urban centres, based on the most recent archive acquisitions, see Battilotti et al. 2016.

7 Demo 2001, 175–93; Demo 2012, 21–8.

8 'I panni de lana che alti si fanno in Vicenza sono stimatissimi, et in molta riputatione… Li panni di lana che si fanno per lo territorio sono panni bassi et per lo più panni grossi per gente povere.' Paolo Gualdo's *Rilatione* has recently been analyzed by Andrea Savio; for citations and information see Savio 2018, 151–5.

9 Demo 2004, 21–126; Demo 2013.

10 Demo 2012, 28–38; Vianello 2004, 83–9; Molà 2000, 237–41; Demo 2006, 217–43. The introduction of mulberry sericulture in parts of the Venetian mainland, particularly Vicenza, had already occurred in the very early fifteenth century, if not the end of the fourteenth. In the mid-fifteenth century, the cultivation of mulberry trees and the breeding of silkworms were widespread, especially in the foothill band (Schio, Thiene, Marano, Valdagno, Arzignano) and in the immediate surroundings of Vicenza. In the 1480s, silk working seems to have even become intense, gradually replacing wool manufacture as the main activity of the Vicentines and being defined as the 'community treasure'. See Demo 2001, 47–52.

11 Beltramini and Demo 2022, 58–94.

12 Demo 2011, 85–95; Demo 2012, 71–2, 77–8; Beltramini and Demo 2022, 85–90.

13 Demo 2023, 89–97.

14 'che di seta produce un tesor magno la città dentro et ogni sua pendice.' Dragonzino 1981, 29.

15 'Veggonsi così nella città come fuori, tanti alberi moroni da nodrigare i vermicelli, da i quali se trae la seta, ch'ella è cosa maravigliosa'; 'ne riportano i Vicentini gran guadagno di detta seta.' Molà 2000, 221.

16 'Quanto alla seta veggo in due maniere farsi mercantie. Alcuni comprano la seta per farla ponere in opera, et farne ormezini, rasi, veluti, et altri drappi al qual effetto furno descritti già duoi anni in questa città 200 telari. Altri sono che comprano le sete per mandarle in Francia, in Fiandra, in Alamagna, et altri paesi stranieri.' Savio 2018, 153–4.

17 Valseriati 2018, 71–3.

18 Vianello 2013, Scuro 2021.

19 Vianello 2004a, 204. Other interesting examples of rural merchants are found in the same text; cf. Demo 2004 *passim*.

20 Muraro 1992, 58, 62, 68, 70, 71, 170, 171 and Demo 2021a, 269, 270. The bookkeeping items in question provide very valuable information on the active practice of commerce by the Dal Ponte family. Jacopo and Francesco negotiated the labour services with the silk merchants; the work was carried out with their own tools (silk stoves); the women of the family threw the silk. It should on the other hand come as no surprise that the Bassanese were engaged in commerce. The active practice of commerce by various fifteenth- and sixteenth-century artists working in the Veneto and Lombard areas has been widely shown. The architects Giovan Antonio Amadeo and Ludovico Beretta were involved in the sale of dyeing materials and timber; the painter Girolamo Forni in that of silk and timber; and the painter Giovan Antonio Fasolo that of silk on a large scale. In his unpublished will of August 1572, drawn up after his unfortunate fall while working on the ceiling decoration in the Loggia del Capitaniato in Vicenza, he lists several sizeable credits for the sale of silk goods, which raise some doubts as to which activity was the more lucrative, painting or commerce (Demo 2021a, 270).

21 Vianello 2013.

22 Howard 2021.

23 '113 soi lavorenti a far di panni'; Beltramini and Demo 2022, 56.

24 Beltramini and Demo 2022, 45–95.

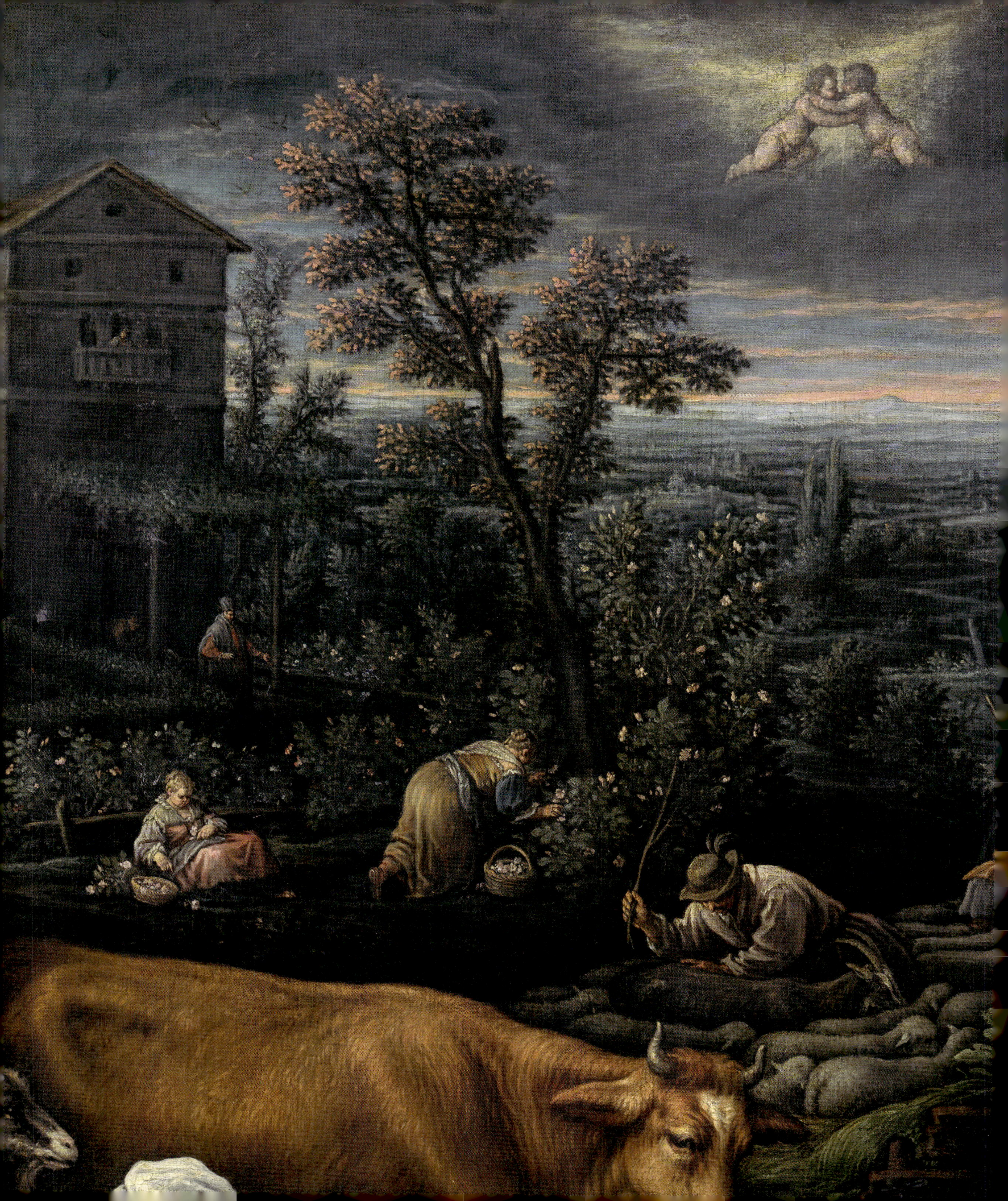

1 On the subject, the object of numerous studies, see at least Panciera 1996; Fontana 1997 (in particular the essays by Fontana himself, Salvatore Ciriacono, Walter Panciera, Giorgio Roverato and Raffaello Vergani); Molà 2000; Molà, Mueller, and Zanier 2000 (the essays by Edoardo Demo, Danilo Gasparini and Luca Molà); Demo 2001; Demo 2003; Vergani 2003; Fontana and Sandal 1997 (in particular the essays by the two editors and by Walter Panciera, Danilo Gasparini, and Maria Nicoletta Simeone); Lanaro 2003 (in particular the essays by the editor and by Edoardo Demo); Fontana and Gayot 2004 (the studies by Fontana himself, Giampaolo Cagnin, Luca Clerici, Edoardo Demo, Danilo Gasparini, Andrea Mozzato, Elisabetta Novello, Walter Panciera, Francesco Vianello, and Giovanni Zalin); Caracausi 2004; Vianello 2004; Panciera 2005; Demo 2005, 101–30; Occhi 2006; Caracausi 2008; Demo 2012; Demo 2013, 291–318; Caracausi 2014, 131–60; Demo 2014, 115–48; Demo 2021; Beltramini and Demo 2022. For other relevant bibliographic references, see Fontana 2004, esp. 174–90; Lanaro 2006 (in particular see the paper by the editor herself and the works by Edoardo Demo, Marco Belfanti, Giovanni Favero, and Francesco Vianello); Demo and Vianello 2011, 27–50; Battilotti et al. 2016. (in particular the introduction by the four editors).

2 Demo 2012, 72–8.

3 'Sono gli huomini di essa città [Vicenza] di vivace ingegno et di grand'ardire et molto disposti alle lettere, all'armi et ai trafichi. Vivono molto civilmente et vestono honestamente et di continuo radunano ricchezze.' Molà 2001, 221.

4 Fontana 2004.

5 Demo 2013a, 19–33.

6 For this and other information about demographic trends in Vicenza and the other main Veneto urban centres, based on the most recent archive acquisitions, see Battilotti et al. 2016.

7 Demo 2001, 175–93; Demo 2012, 21–8.

8 'I panni de lana che alti si fanno in Vicenza sono stimatissimi, et in molta riputatione… Li panni di lana che si fanno per lo territorio sono panni bassi et per lo più panni grossi per gente povere.' Paolo Gualdo's *Rilatione* has recently been analyzed by Andrea Savio; for citations and information see Savio 2018, 151–5.

9 Demo 2004, 21–126; Demo 2013.

10 Demo 2012, 28–38; Vianello 2004, 83–9; Molà 2000, 237–41; Demo 2006, 217–43. The introduction of mulberry sericulture in parts of the Venetian mainland, particularly Vicenza, had already occurred in the very early fifteenth century, if not the end of the fourteenth. In the mid-fifteenth century, the cultivation of mulberry trees and the breeding of silkworms were widespread, especially in the foothill band (Schio, Thiene, Marano, Valdagno, Arzignano) and in the immediate surroundings of Vicenza. In the 1480s, silk working seems to have even become intense, gradually replacing wool manufacture as the main activity of the Vicentines and being defined as the 'community treasure'. See Demo 2001, 47–52.

11 Beltramini and Demo 2022, 58–94.

12 Demo 2011, 85–95; Demo 2012, 71–2, 77–8; Beltramini and Demo 2022, 85–90.

13 Demo 2023, 89–97.

14 'che di seta produce un tesor magno la città dentro et ogni sua pendice.' Dragonzino 1981, 29.

15 'Veggonsi così nella città come fuori, tanti alberi moroni da nodrigare i vermicelli, da i quali se trae la seta, ch'ella è cosa maravigliosa'; 'ne riportano i Vicentini gran guadagno di detta seta.' Molà 2000, 221.

16 'Quanto alla seta veggo in due maniere farsi mercantie. Alcuni comprano la seta per farla ponere in opera, et farne ormezini, rasi, veluti, et altri drappi al qual effetto furno descritti già duoi anni in questa città 200 telari. Altri sono che comprano le sete per mandarle in Francia, in Fiandra, in Alamagna, et altri paesi stranieri.' Savio 2018, 153–4.

17 Valseriati 2018, 71–3.

18 Vianello 2013, Scuro 2021.

19 Vianello 2004a, 204. Other interesting examples of rural merchants are found in the same text; cf. Demo 2004 *passim*.

20 Muraro 1992, 58, 62, 68, 70, 71, 170, 171 and Demo 2021a, 269, 270. The bookkeeping items in question provide very valuable information on the active practice of commerce by the Dal Ponte family. Jacopo and Francesco negotiated the labour services with the silk merchants; the work was carried out with their own tools (silk stoves); the women of the family threw the silk. It should on the other hand come as no surprise that the Bassanese were engaged in commerce. The active practice of commerce by various fifteenth- and sixteenth-century artists working in the Veneto and Lombard areas has been widely shown. The architects Giovan Antonio Amadeo and Ludovico Beretta were involved in the sale of dyeing materials and timber; the painter Girolamo Forni in that of silk and timber; and the painter Giovan Antonio Fasolo that of silk on a large scale. In his unpublished will of August 1572, drawn up after his unfortunate fall while working on the ceiling decoration in the Loggia del Capitaniato in Vicenza, he lists several sizeable credits for the sale of silk goods, which raise some doubts as to which activity was the more lucrative, painting or commerce (Demo 2021a, 270).

21 Vianello 2013.

22 Howard 2021.

23 '113 soi lavorenti a far di panni'; Beltramini and Demo 2022, 56.

24 Beltramini and Demo 2022, 45–95.

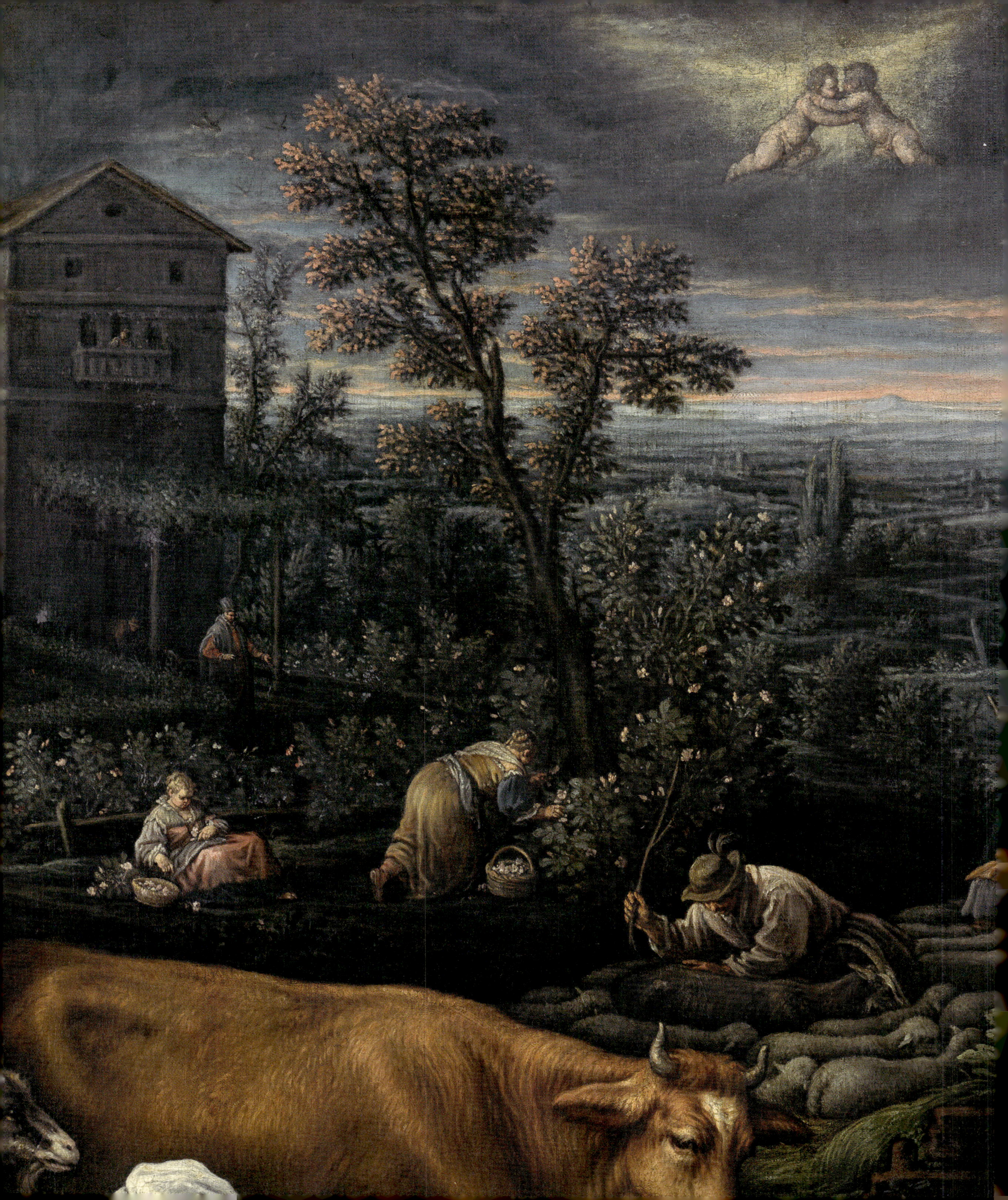

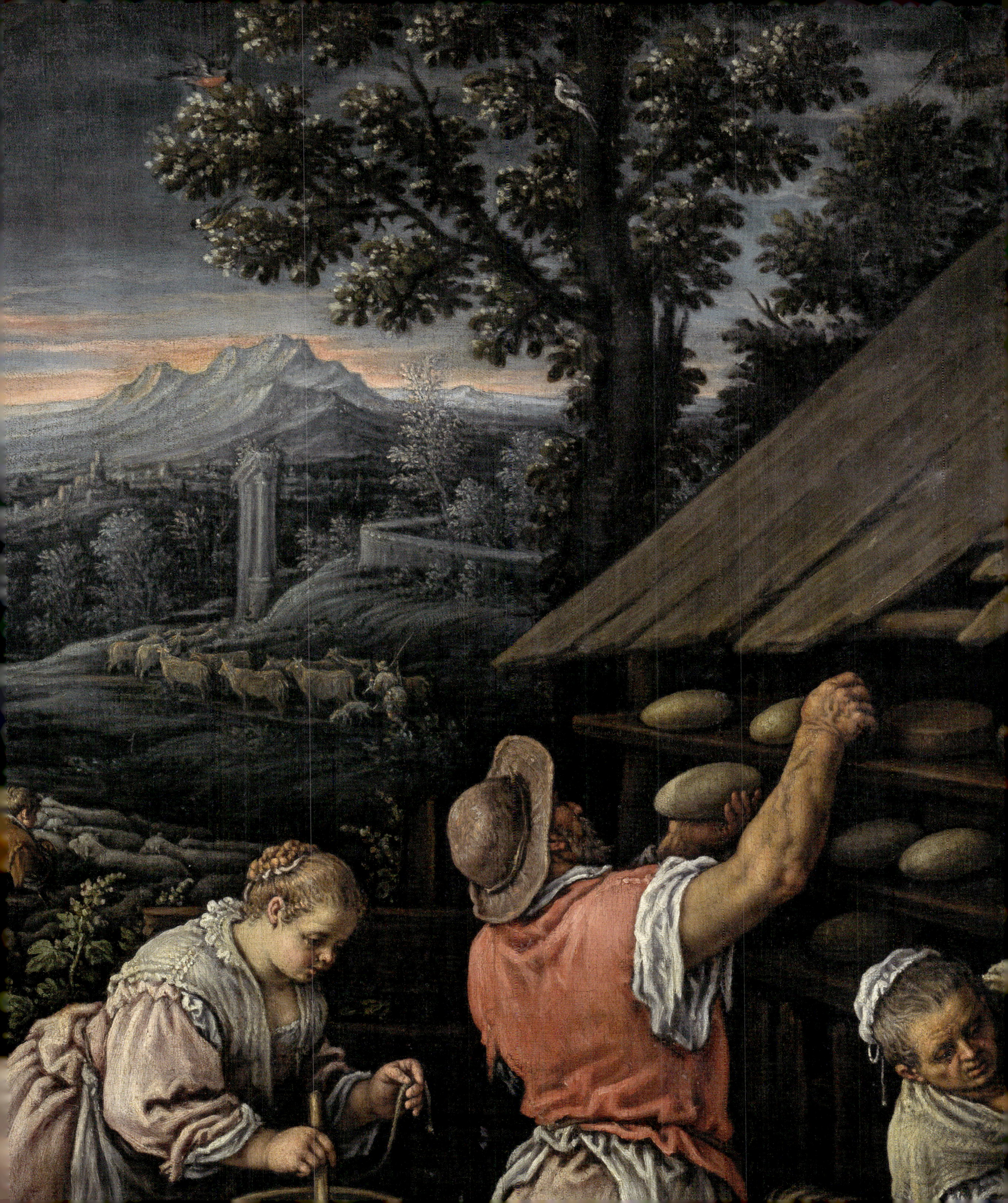

A New Perspective on Nature

(cats. 1–5)

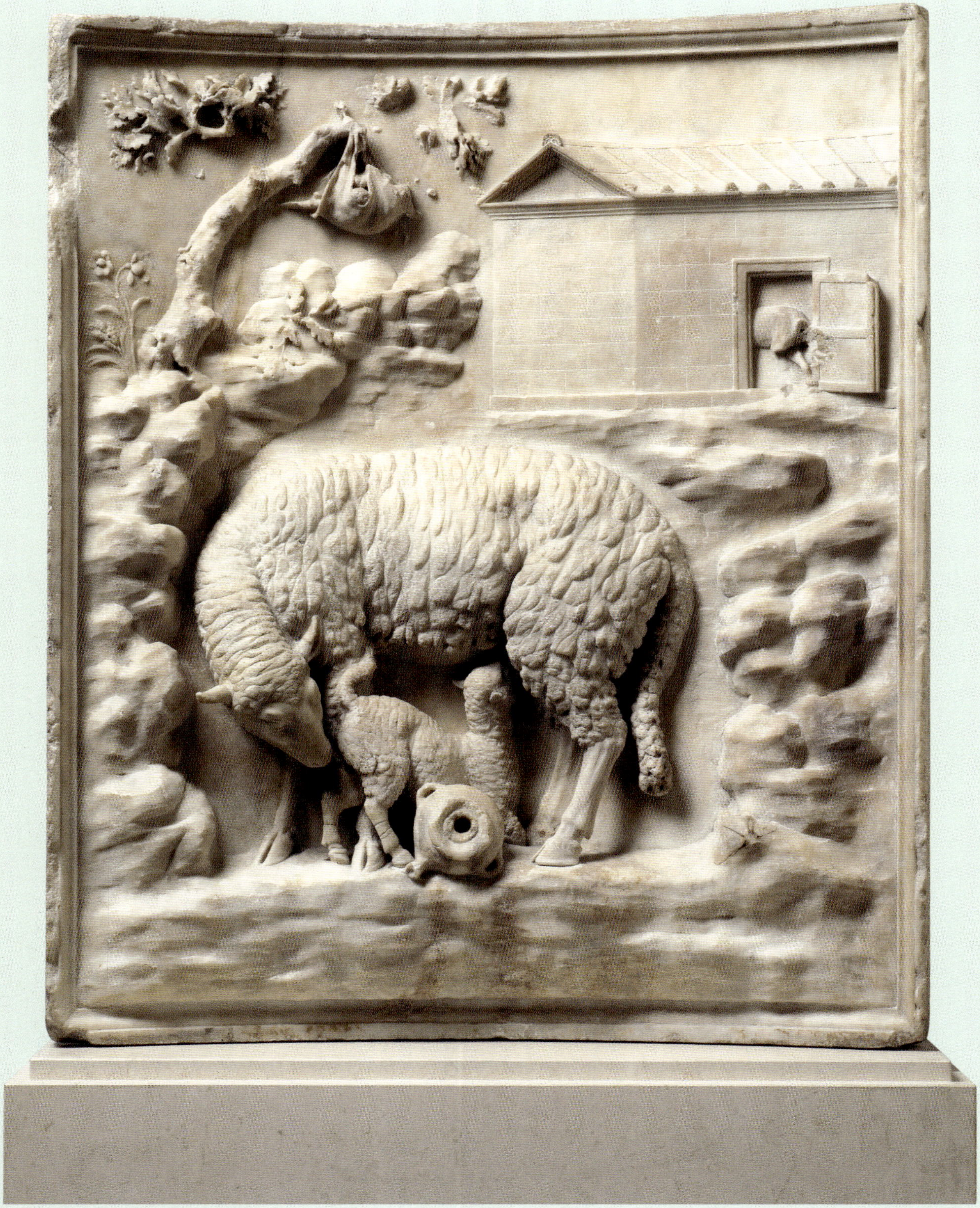

Cat. 1, Fountain Relief Grimani: *Ewe with Lamb*

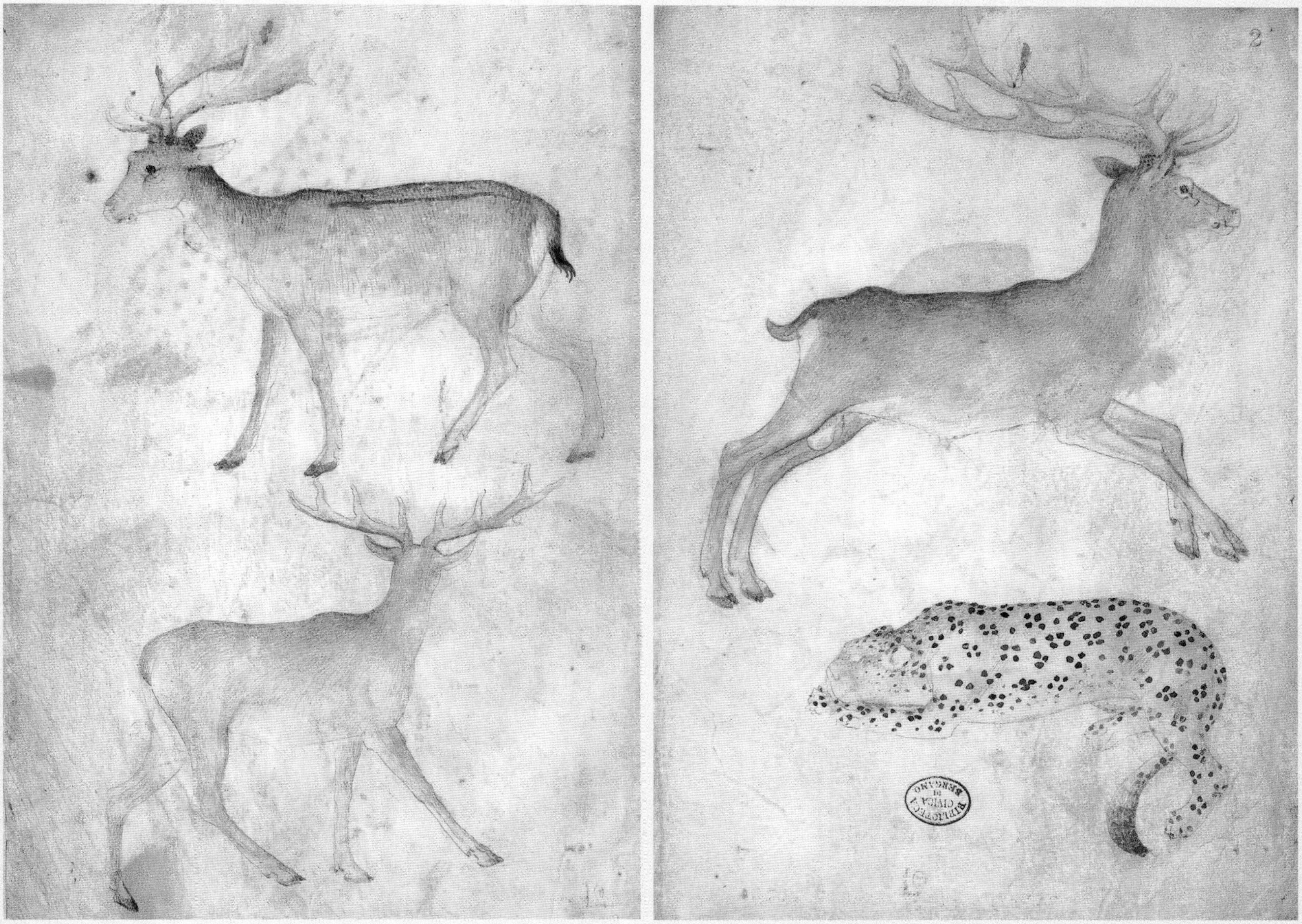

Cat. 2, Giovannino de' Grassi, *Taccuino di disegni*

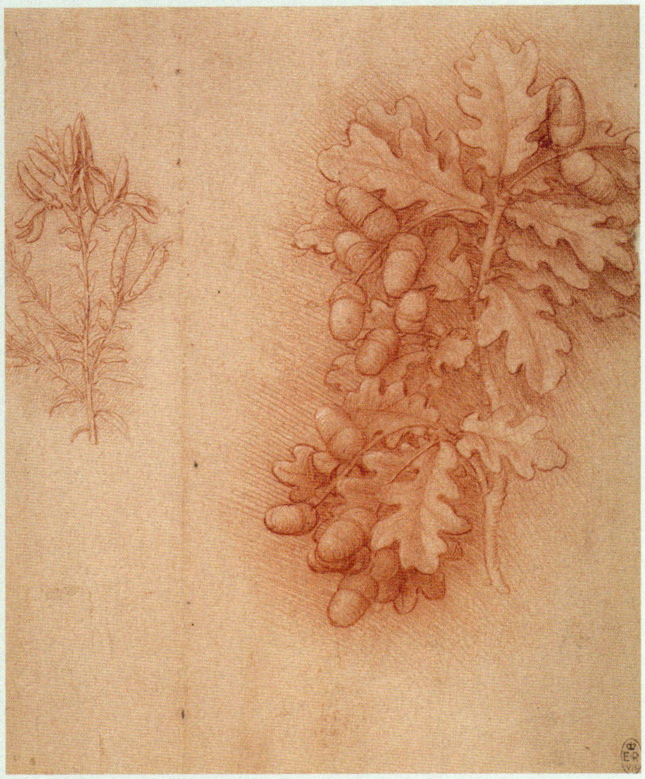

Cat. 3.1, Leonardo da Vinci *Sprigs of Oak (Quercus robur) and Dyer's Greenweed (Genista tinctoria)*

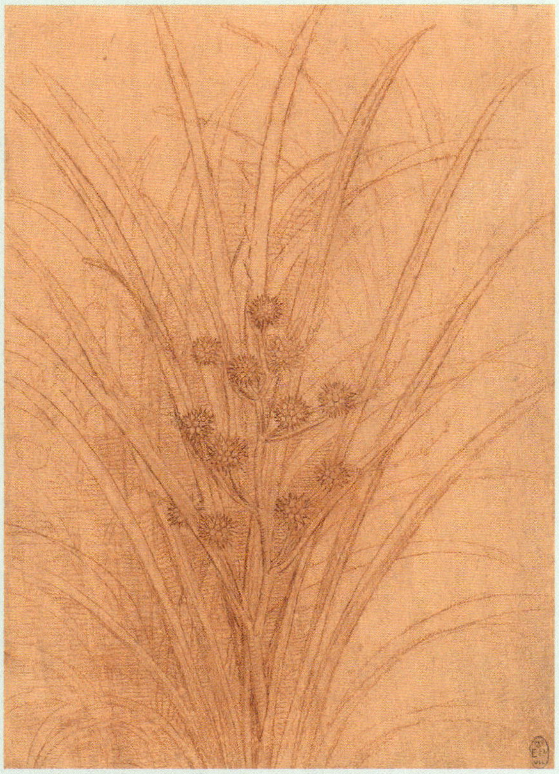

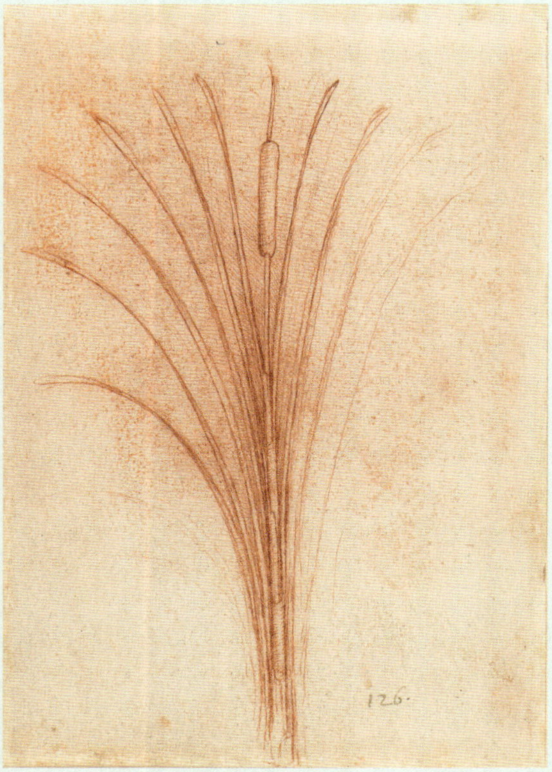

Cat. 3.2, Leonardo da Vinci, *Recto: A Branched Bur-Reed (Sparganium erectum); Verso: A Bulrush (Thypha latifolia)*

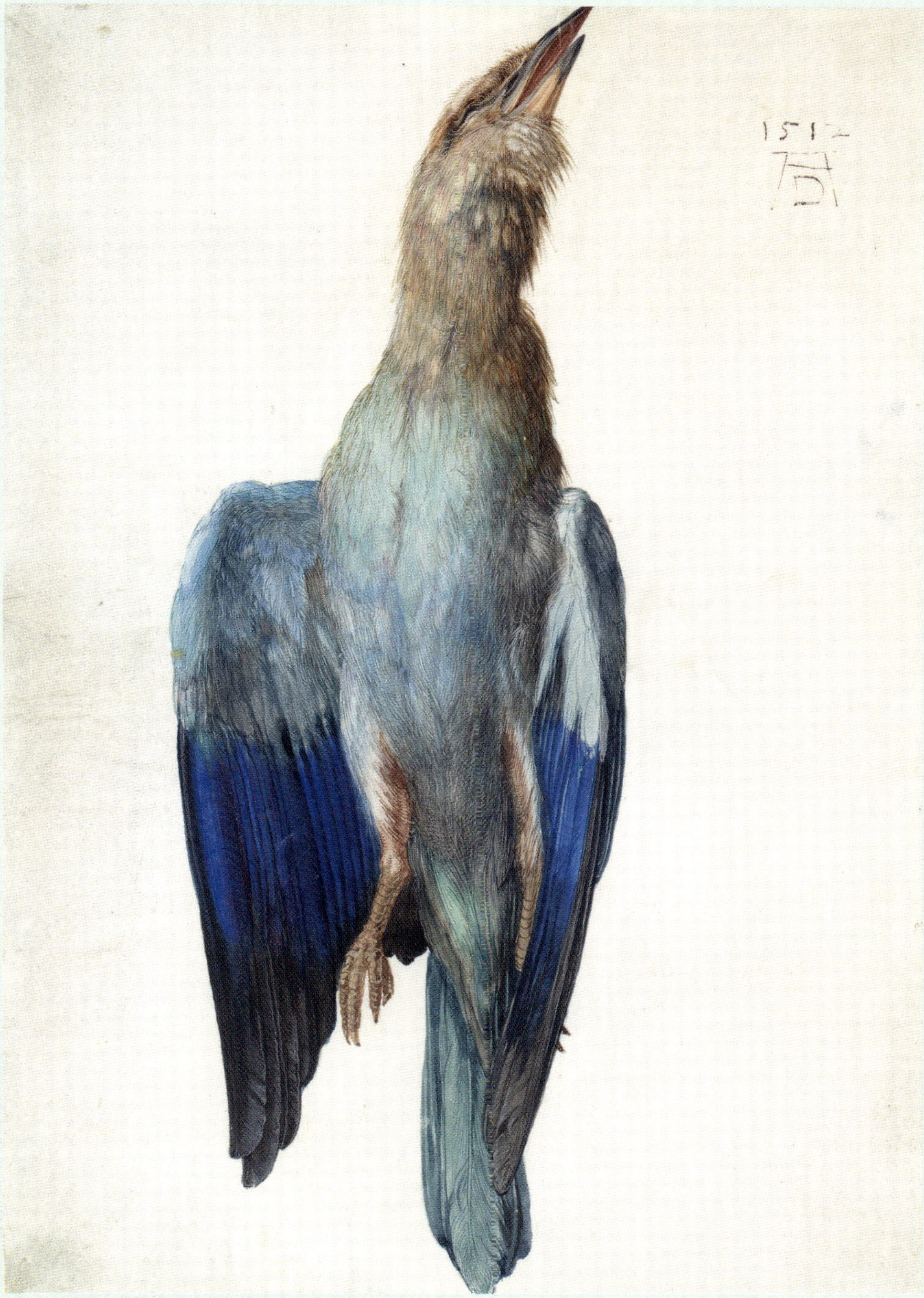

Cat. 4.1, Albrecht Dürer, *Dead European Roller*

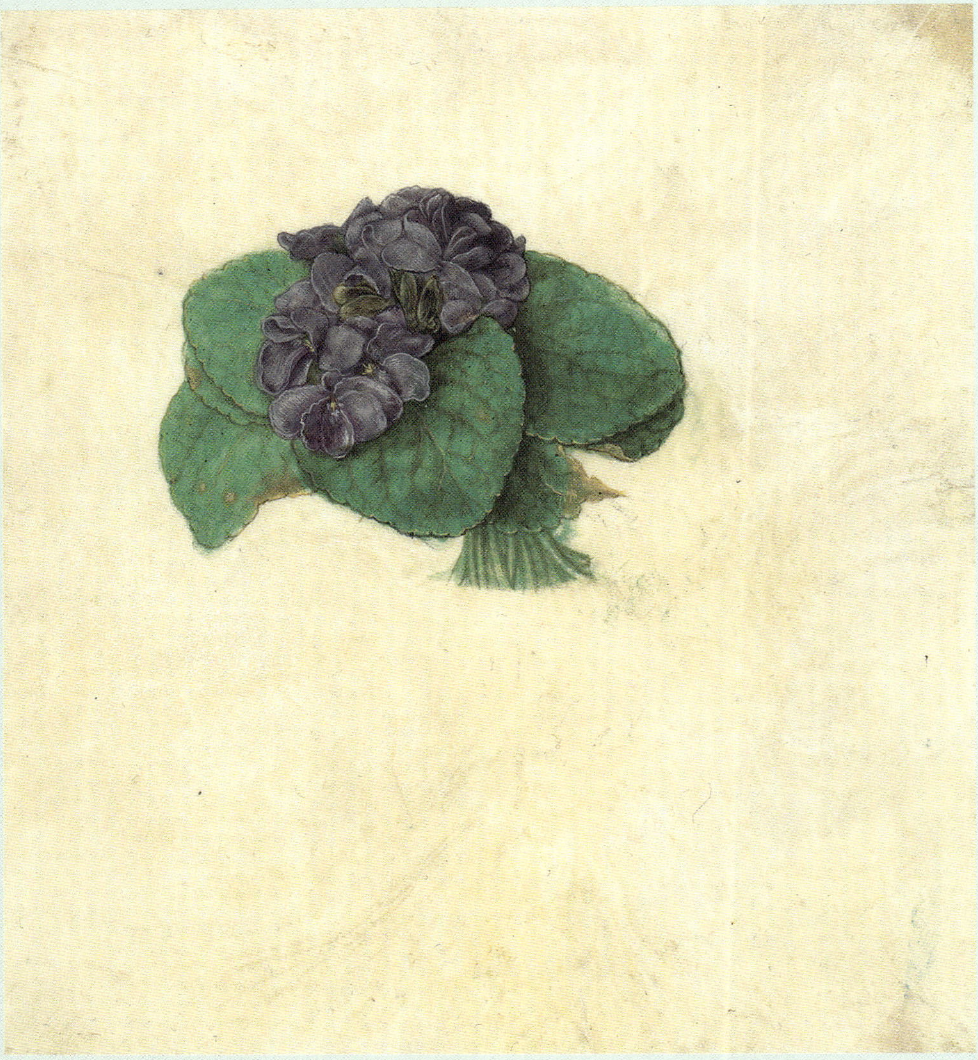

Cat. 4.2, Albrecht Dürer, *Bouquet of Violets*

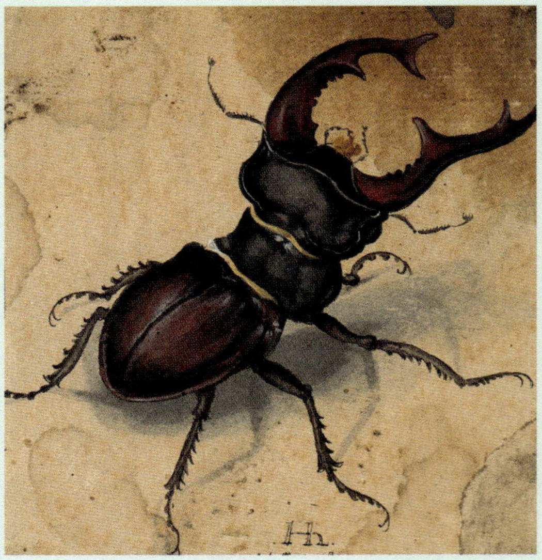

Cat. 5, Hans Hoffmann, *A Stag Beetle (Lucanus cervus L.)*

Cat. 1

Fountain Relief Grimani

Ewe with Lamb

Roman, late 1st cent. BCE
Marble; H 96 cm, W 81 cm
Vienna, Kunsthistorisches Museum, Collection of Greek and Roman Antiquities, inv. I 604

Provenance: In the Grimani Collection in Venice probably since the late 16th cent., acquired there via Michelangelo Guggenheim by Johann II Prince of Liechtenstein in 1883, and presented to the imperial collections in an exchange in 1885
Literature: Schreiber 1888; Strocka 1965; Simon 1986, 123–7; Zanker 1987, 180–2; Agnoli 2002, 207–17; exh. cat. Rome 2013, 248–9; exh. cat Vienna 2014, 10–14; Sickel 2016

At the end of the first century BCE, Emperor Augustus staged the 'Secular Games', based on old Roman custom, to celebrate the dawn of a new – golden – age. Poets such as Virgil and Horace placed themselves at the service of these celebrations and glorified the new epoch.

Augustus appeared as guarantor of perpetual peace and prosperity on the reliefs of the *ara pacis*, the altar of peace consecrated in the year 9 BCE, with Aeneas and Romulus, the mythical progenitors of Rome. The Grimani reliefs, named for the location of two of the panels in the Grimani Collection in Venice, also convey images of the Golden Age. It was not until the discovery of the third panel in 1962, in the sanctuary of Fortuna in Praeneste (Palestrina) east of Rome, that the original context was understood.

All three reliefs show suckling dams with their offspring in a bucolic landscape with stone grottos, gnarled sycamores or oaks, and flowers and reeds. A lioness with two cubs, a sheep with a lamb, and a wild sow with six piglets represent fertility and a glorious future. As with the relief here of a sheep suckling its lamb, the presence of humans is kept to the background, indicated only by the shepherd's bundle hanging on an oak.

The massive building next to the tree, where a dog is stepping out of a door, is probably meant to be a stable. The monumental construction of the building made of hewn stone with a gabled roof is confusing; one might almost think that the stone masons who worked in the imperial sculpture programme were more familiar with marble temples than with the appearance of a simple shed.

In addition to the three extant reliefs, there was probably at least a fourth. In addition to the two wild animals (a lioness and a sow) and the one domesticated animal (a sheep), one would expect a cow with her calves.

Peace, fertility, the happiness of the simple life in the Augustan Golden Age: these messages were communicated in a monument in the forum of Praeneste, where the reliefs were incorporated into a fountain. All three panels have holes drilled in them where water could flow – here, out of the overturned vessel under the sheep. The renowned *fasti Praenestini*, the Roman official and festival calendar, was probably part of the same monument. The time-honoured lists of important events in Roman history in turn contributed to the documentation of the Golden Age, here literally carved in stone.

Georg Plattner

Cat. 2

Giovannino de' Grassi (documented in Milan c.1389–1398) and Workshop

Taccuino di disegni

1385/1410
Various techniques on parchment; 32 numbered leaves; 205 × 146 mm–260 × 186 mm
Bergamo, Biblioteca Civica 'Angelo Mai' e Archivi Storici, Cassaf. 1.21, BL IV. 2r

Provenance: Leonino Secco Suardo Collection; donated to the Biblioteca on 5 May 1845
Literature: Toesca 1905, 332–9; Pächt 1950, 15–18 (new edition in Pächt 2011, 11–19); Cadei 1970, 17–36; Gatti Perer and Rossi 1989, 77–90; Rossi 1995, 45–61; Scheller 1995, 276–91; *Taccuino* 1997; *Taccuino* 1998; Bollati 2003, 297–9; Bollati 2004, 318, 320; Taccuino 2005; exh. cat Fabriano 2006, 78–9; exh. cat. Milan 2015, 156

The *Taccuino di disegni* (drawing notebook) is a rare example of a collection of models for use in a late medieval workshop, a useful repertoire for producing illuminated codices, frescoes, and sculptures. Originally (the last quarter of the fourteenth century), there were two sewn fascicles and two other loose fascicles, made up of various sized leaves. By the mid-sixteenth century, the four fascicles had been joined; to unify the sizes, the irregularly cut leaves were drastically trimmed, damaging the completeness of several figures. The leaves were numbered on the back; on many leaves the same hand has written the date 1542, to be considered ante quem of the reduction of the fascicles into a book. The red stamped numbering dates from the early twentieth century.

Writing (mostly captions for the figures) in at least five hands appears in the *Taccuino*, from between the fifteenth and the end of the sixteenth centuries. The first and oldest (at 4v) says: 'Johaninus de grassis designavit'. Generally thought to be written by the artist, this can be dated to between the end of the fourteenth century and the first decades of the fifteenth (for the codicological appearance, cf. Taccuino 2005, 9–12).

The *Taccuino*, which was already in Bergamo in the second half of the sixteenth century with the Olmo family of calligraphers, passed to the Licino family in the early seventeenth century. In the eighteenth century, before going into the Secco Suardo Collection, it was owned by Alessandro Tassi (1691–1771), where it was seen and described by Francesco Maria Tassi in his *Vite de' pittori, scultori e architetti bergamaschi* (Bergamo 1793, vol. I, 126), who attributed the drawings to Lorenzo Lotto.

Leaves 1v (*Fallow Deer* and *Stag*) and 2r (*Fallow Deer* and *Leopard*) are now unanimously considered to be by Giovannino (whose hand is recognizable up to f. 7r). The rest of the collection brings together workshop drawings, among which the fascicle of birds (the second) and the figured alphabet, partly monochrome and partly polychrome (fourth fascicle), are particularly interesting.

Created within the late fourteenth-century Milan circle, in which Giovannino was of great importance as an architect, painter, and sculptor at Milan Cathedral, and as a miniaturist for Gian Galeazzo Visconti (see the *Libro d'ore* BR 397 and LF 22 in the Biblioteca Nazionale Centrale di Firenze, with which the drawings in the *Taccuino* show many affinities), the *Taccuino* has attracted the attention of many scholars since the publication by Toesca (1905) and the unsurpassed study by Pächt (1950), for its extraordinarily lifelike depictions. In this respect, it emulates the herbals, in which the different species are easily recognisable.

Giovannino's technique, using small brush strokes that capture every detail of each animal and inserting it in a space suggested by its movement, suggests that the artist made the drawings from life ('animal portraiture' is the term used by Pächt). He captured the animal's movement through prolonged observation, in some instances by placing a dead animal in different poses, as was also suggested by his contemporary Cennino Cennini (*Libro dell'arte,* chap. CLXXXV). An artist such as Pisanello then deployed the animal's movement in his drawings with several postures.

In portraying animals in the grounds of the Visconti Castle in Pavia, Giovannino was a pioneer of the naturalism that was later to be typical of Michelino da Besozzo – who was defined as a great animal painter by Uberto Decembrio – of Gentile da Fabriano, and of his immediate followers, possibly already to be identified in the *Taccuino*, like his son Salomone, or the Maestro del Libro d'Ore di Modena (see the friezes with birds in the *Libro d'Ore di Isabella di Castiglia*, The Hague, Koninklijke Bibliotheek, MS 76 F. 6, f. 17r).

The decoration of manuscripts in medieval style, with *drôleries* and theriomorphic figures, now leave the field to unforgettable glimpses of nature (cf. *Offiziolo Visconti*, BR 397, ff. 2v, 115r; Bollati 2003), thanks to the preparatory study, which to our eyes seems like an independent study of nature.

Giulio Orazio Bravi, Maria Grazia Recanati

Cats. 3.1, 3.2

Leonardo da Vinci (1452–1519)

Sprigs of Oak (Quercus robur) and Dyer's Greenweed (Genista tinctoria)

1506/12
Red chalk, touches of white chalk, on orange-red prepared paper; 188 × 154 mm
The Royal Collection/HM King Charles III, RCIN 912422

Provenance: Bequeathed to Francesco Melzi; from whose heirs purchased by Pompeo Leoni, c.1582–90; Thomas Howard, 14th Earl of Arundel, by 1630; probably acquired by Charles II; Royal Collection by 1690
Literature: De Toni 1922, 19, fig. 15; Pedretti 1982, cat. 12422; Emboden 1987, 152; Ames-Lewis 1997, 117–24; Bird and Clayton 2017, cat. 149; exh. cat Rome 2019, 67; exh. cat. London and Edinburgh 2019/20, cat. 107

Recto: A Branched Bur-Reed (Sparganium erectum)

Verso: A Bulrush (Thypha latifolia)

1506/12
Recto: Red chalk on orange-red prepared paper; 201 × 143 mm
Verso: Red chalk on paper; 201 × 143 mm
The Royal Collection/HM King Charles III, RCIN 912430

Provenance: Bequeathed to Francesco Melzi; from whose heirs purchased by Pompeo Leoni, c.1582–90; Thomas Howard, 14th Earl of Arundel, by 1630; probably acquired by Charles II; Royal Collection by 1690
Literature: De Toni 1922, 19–20, fig. 17; Pedretti 1982, cat. 12430; Emboden 1987, 146; Ames-Lewis 1997; exh. cat. Rome 2019, 67; exh. cat. London and Edinburgh 2019/20, cat. 106

The three drawings are part of the collection of botanical sheets by Leonardo da Vinci held in the Royal Library at Windsor Castle, which contains almost all the numerous studies the artist made of the plant world, a subject that was also to appear in paintings such as the portrait of *Ginevra de' Benci* and the *Virgin of the Rocks*.

Because Leonardo's manuscripts contain numerous reflections, digressions, and notes on the subject, in addition to the drawings, it has been suggested that he had been thinking of writing a specific *Discorso sulle erbe* for artists, to be added to his treatise on painting. Indeed, a genuine interest in the most minute aspects of vegetation is a constant in Leonardo's work. It goes back to the lost cartoon of his youth (which belonged to Ottaviano de' Medici) portraying the *Earthly Paradise* in which he had painted, according to Giorgio Vasari, 'a luxuriant meadow [of which] it can truthfully be said that for diligence and faithfulness to nature nothing could be more inspired or perfect' (Giorgio Vasari, *Lives of the Artists*, vol. 1, (London, 1965, 258). Leonardo managed to add an imaginary and poetic component to the unavoidable practice of *sperientia* (experience) and the in-depth scientific expertise that gave him fundamental insights into plant anatomy, morphology, and physiology (such as the laws of phyllotaxis and the circulation of sap in plants), making him capable of translating natural reality into artistic vision.

The herbs and plants observed and portrayed from life were an absolute first, not only because of their realistic presence, but also because they had been interpreted according to a 'natural philosophy' synthesized in Leonardo's conviction that 'over time everything changes'. Unlike his near contemporary Albrecht Dürer, who preferred to depict natural subjects isolated from their environment and almost 'decontextualized', Leonardo conceived a *natura naturans* that was subject to an uninterrupted process of transformation that he managed to portray through the intuition of '*sfumato*' (that 'shade, light, lustre, and transparency' cited precisely about foliage in the *Libro di pittura*), capable of giving the sensation of an ever-changing light.

Emblematic examples of conceptual and visual rigour are offered by the three sheets, the first depicting sprigs of oak and dyer's greenweed, the second a bur-reed on the front and a bulrush on the back. The artist also reveals his technical mastery of red chalk, a medium favoured for portraying plants.

The sheet of cat. 3.2 depicts some leaves of lake plants, referring to the studies that accompanied the complex development of the lost painting of *Leda*.

On the sheet of cat. 3.1, an oak branch laden with acorns, whose lobed leaves and rough fruit capsules the artist captures in detail, emerges from the shadow on the right. The raceme of greenweed with bulging pods is more concise, but no less realistic. Branches of oak also appear in the lunettes above the *Last Supper* and an oak tree accompanies the figure of *Bacchus* (Paris, Musée du Louvre).

Giuseppe Olmi, Lucia Tongiorgi Tomasi

Cats. 4.1, 4.2

Albrecht Dürer (1471–1528)

Dead European Roller

c.1500
Watercolour and gouache on vellum, highlighted with opaque white and gold; 274 × 198 mm
Vienna, Albertina, inv. 3133

Provenance: Duke Albert von Sachsen-Teschen (Lugt 174)
Literature: Mus. cat. Vienna 1933, cat. 105; Winkler 1936–39, vol. 3, no. 615; mus. cat. Vienna 1971, cat. 34 (Walter Koschatzky); Strauss 1974, vol. 2, no. 1502/11; exh. cat. Vienna 1985, cat. 10 (Fritz Koreny); exh. cat. Vienna 2003a, cat. 72 (Heinz Widauer); exh. cat. Vienna 2019, 162–4, 168 (ill.), 451, cat. 57 (Christof Metzger)

Bouquet of Violets

1495/1500
Watercolour and gouache on vellum, highlighted with white, mounted on cardboard; 115 × 102 mm
Vienna, Albertina, inv. 3076

Provenance: Duke Albert von Sachsen-Teschen (Lugt 174)
Literature: Mus. cat. Vienna 1933, cat. 53; Winkler 1936–39, vol. 2, no. 358; mus. cat. Vienna 1971, cat. 33 (Walter Koschatzky); Strauss 1974, vol. 2, no. 1503/31; exh. cat. Vienna 1985, cat. 77 (Fritz Koreny); exh. cat. Vienna 2003a, cat. 71 (Heinz Widauer); exh. cat. Vienna 2019, 146–9, 151 (ill.), 450, cat. 48 (Christof Metzger)

No individual nature studies by northern European artists from before the end of the fifteenth century have survived. However, they must have existed in large numbers long before this time as suggested by the realistic depictions of flowers in Old Netherlandish paintings by Jan van Eyck (around 1390–1441) or Rogier van der Weyden (1399/1400–1464). Albrecht Dürer is the first artist from whom we have a large group of plant and animal studies, although the attribution of some of them remains disputed. Like the extraordinarily popular *Young Hare* (Vienna, Albertina), which is one of the works unanimously recognised as being by the Nuremberg artist, this flamboyantly colourful depiction of a (supine or hanging) dead European roller is a meticulous and masterful depiction of nature that demonstrates Dürer's superb artistic mastery. A fine, carefully smoothed and polished sheet of parchment provided Dürer with the ideal conditions for capturing with precision all the details of this migratory bird in gouache and watercolour, while delicate gold lines evoke the iridescent sheen of the turquoise breast feathers to great effect.

In another coloured study on parchment, Dürer captured the outspread wing of a European roller, which had probably been detached from the body of the same bird (also Vienna, Albertina). Both masterpieces, which resemble fine paintings rather than drawings, enjoyed extraordinary popularity after the death of their creator and were copied several times, sometimes with slight variations, by Hans Hoffmann (cat. 5). The hastily applied date '1512' (which is also the date on the blue wing) and Dürer's monogram below it on our sheet have evoked differing opinions. Although Koschatzky suspected them to be subsequent additions, these inscriptions are now considered authentic, although the interpretation of the year varies between a dating (Koreny) and a sort of inventory (Strauss and Metzger) when Dürer is said to have gone through his legacy of drawings. The latter authors wanted instead to place the two bird studies around 1500 and thus around the time of the *Young Hare*, which is dated 1502. Such an approach is also supported by the proximity of the wing study to the wings of Nemesis in Dürer's engraving of the same name from around 1501. Nevertheless, the two colourful bird studies can hardly be considered preparatory works created for such a specific purpose. As in most of Dürer's nature paintings, they are probably manifestations of his interest in the environment and his desire to explore it through drawing.

Like the *Young Hare* and the two European roller studies, the depiction of a bouquet of violets can also be traced back to the Nuremberg collection of Willibald Imhoff (1519–1580). In 1588, it was briefly described in Imhoff's so-called 'art book' as 'Gefüllt Veil auf Pergamen' ('filled violet on vellum'). Since much of Imhoff's extensive collection of drawings can be traced back to Dürer's estate, this provenance points strongly to Dürer as the artist responsible, even though this has been disputed in the past. Admittedly, the sheet is unique among the plant and animal studies associated with the artist since the depiction is not based on the original size of the model, but reproduces it in miniature. As an arrangement of individual sprigs of flowers tied together, it also has the character of a still life; Dürer's other nature paintings contain hardly any references to the presence of humans. However, in terms of technique and the masterful, extraordinarily fine execution, the *Bouquet of Violets* can easily be assigned to his group of early plant studies, probably created before 1500.

Guido Messling

Cat. 5

Hans Hoffmann (1545/50–1591/92), after Albrecht Dürer (1471–1528)

A Stag Beetle (Lucanus cervus L.)

1574
Watercolour and gouache, highlighted with white, on brownish toned paper; 96 × 94 mm
Budapest, Szépművészeti Múzeum, inv. 184

Provenance: Paulus Praun (1548–1616), Nuremberg; Nikolaus Esterházy (Lugt 1965)
Literature: Stüwe 1998, 77–8, no. A2; mus. cat. Budapest 2020, cat. 230; exh. cat. Nuremberg 2022, cat. 47 (Szilvia Bodnár); Tschetschik-Hammerl 2023, 69 (fig. 50); 70–1, 262 (no. 62)

Signed and dated 1574, this almost life-size depiction of an adult male stag beetle (*Lucanus cervus*) is the oldest of the numerous plant and animal drawings by Hans Hoffmann that we know of. It is also one of the earliest examples of his intensive involvement with the works of Albrecht Dürer (1471–1528), which runs like a leitmotif through the oeuvre of the artist who worked as court painter to Emperor Rudolf II in Prague from 1585. Like Dürer, Hoffmann was a native of Nuremberg and had admired numerous works by his famous compatriot there, such as the *Dead European Roller* (cat. 4.1) in Willibald Imhoff's collection, a painting he copied several times. The Budapest drawing was also preceded by a nature study by Dürer – it could be the sheet dated 1505 (Strauss 1974, vol. 2, no. 1505/15), now in the Getty Museum in Los Angeles, although we do not know in which Nuremberg collection Hoffmann was able to study it. The specimen was the same size, but it was not slavishly copied, as can be seen from the more prominent upper right jaw and the mandibular palps at the top of the head, which Hoffmann bends. The most striking difference, however, are the yellowish notches between the head, chest, and abdomen, which are missing in Dürer's work. They are similar to those found in nature and suggest that, in addition to the study now in Los Angeles, Hoffmann was familiar with real stag beetles from his own observations. This is also indicated by the yellowish labial palps, which Hoffmann also added between the mandibular palps.

Compared to the original, the Budapest copy has an overall rougher finish. A mirrored second version in Berlin (Tschetschik-Hammerl 2023, 262, no. 61) is evidence that Hoffmann traced it. This undated sheet, also labelled 'Hh' (ligature) at the bottom, corresponds exactly to the Budapest drawing in its contours, but falls short in its more summary execution. Years later, the Dürer insect can also be found in a book illustration in the four-volume compendium the *Four Elements* by the Flemish miniaturist Joris Hoefnagel (1542–1600) created for Rudolf II between 1591 and 1599. Details however, indicate that Hoefnagel used Hoffmann's copy, not Dürer's study.

This bizarre creature had already attracted the interest of a few painters before Dürer, as evidenced by the stag beetle in the foreground of Stefan Lochner's *Altar of the City Patrons* from around 1445 in Cologne Cathedral, where it is also viewed from above. The beetle also appears in Dürer's work before the 1505 drawing, for example in his 1504 painting *Adoration of the Magi* (Florence, Uffizi). The sheet in Los Angeles can, therefore, hardly be described as an authentic depiction of a natural specimen, but should rather be characterized as a pattern-book-like repetition of a long-established animal motif. The works of Hoffmann and Hoefnagel continue this tradition.
Guido Messling

The Development of Modern Science in the Early Sixteenth Century

(cats. 6–14)

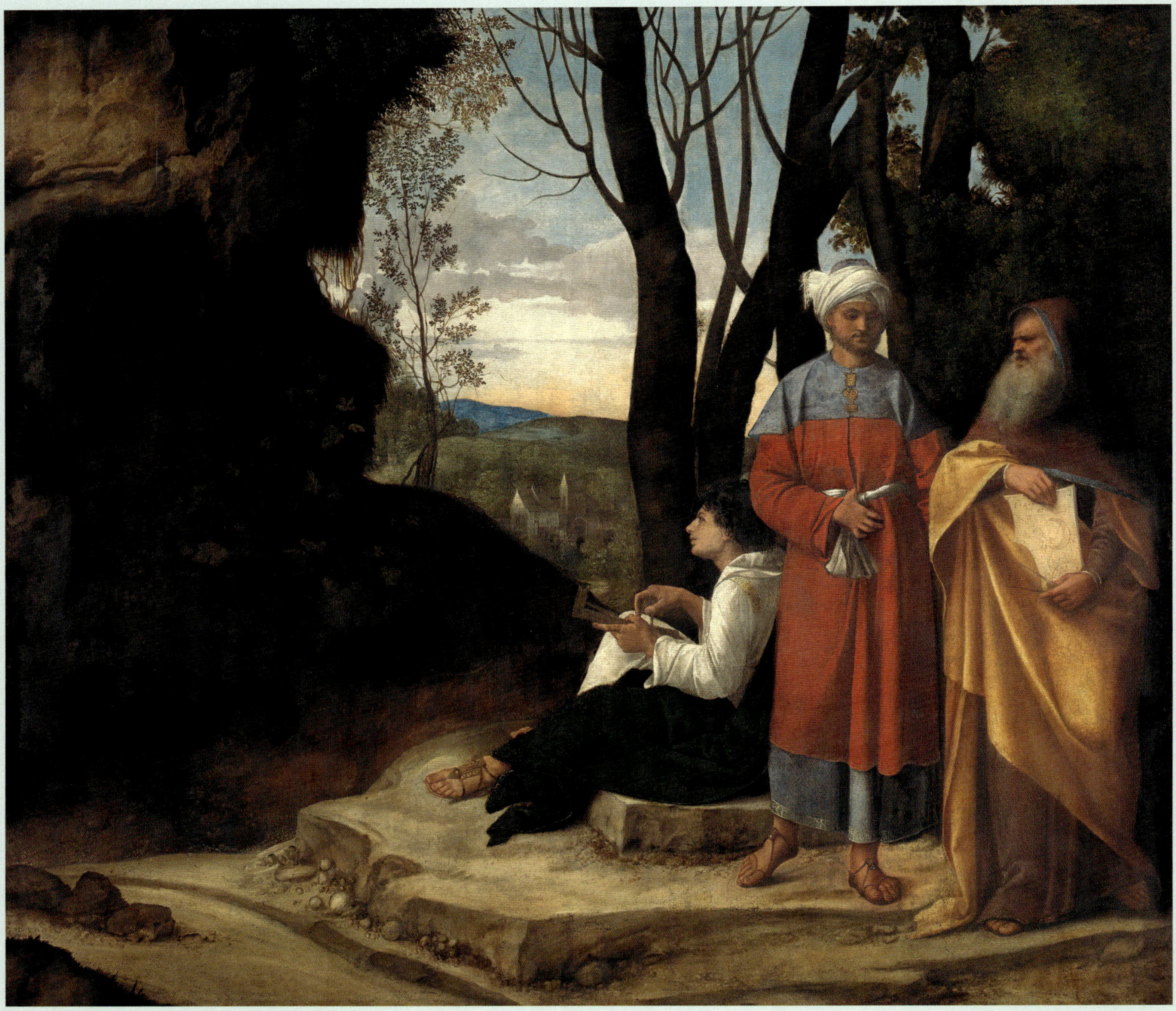

Cat. 6, Giorgione, *The Three Philosophers*

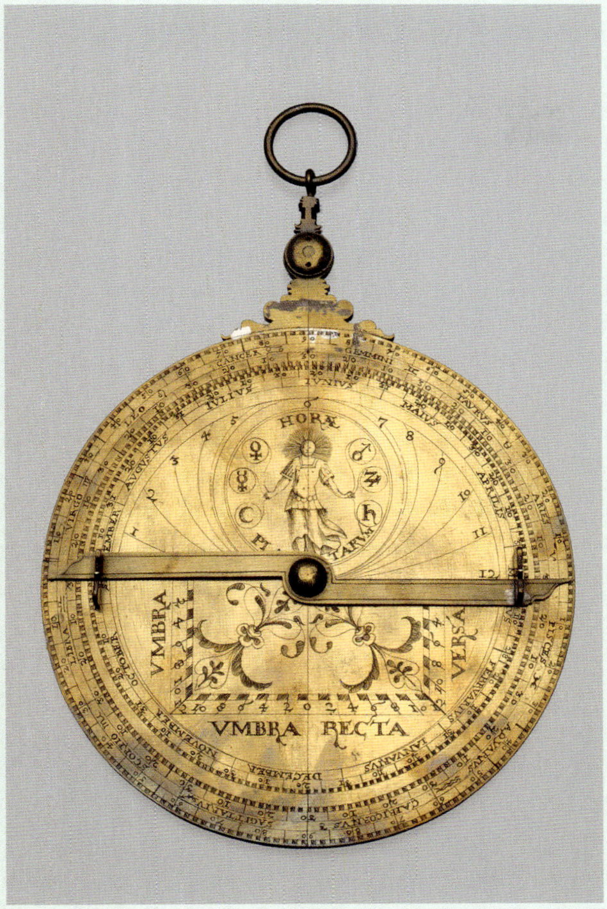

Cat. 7.1, *Astrolabe*

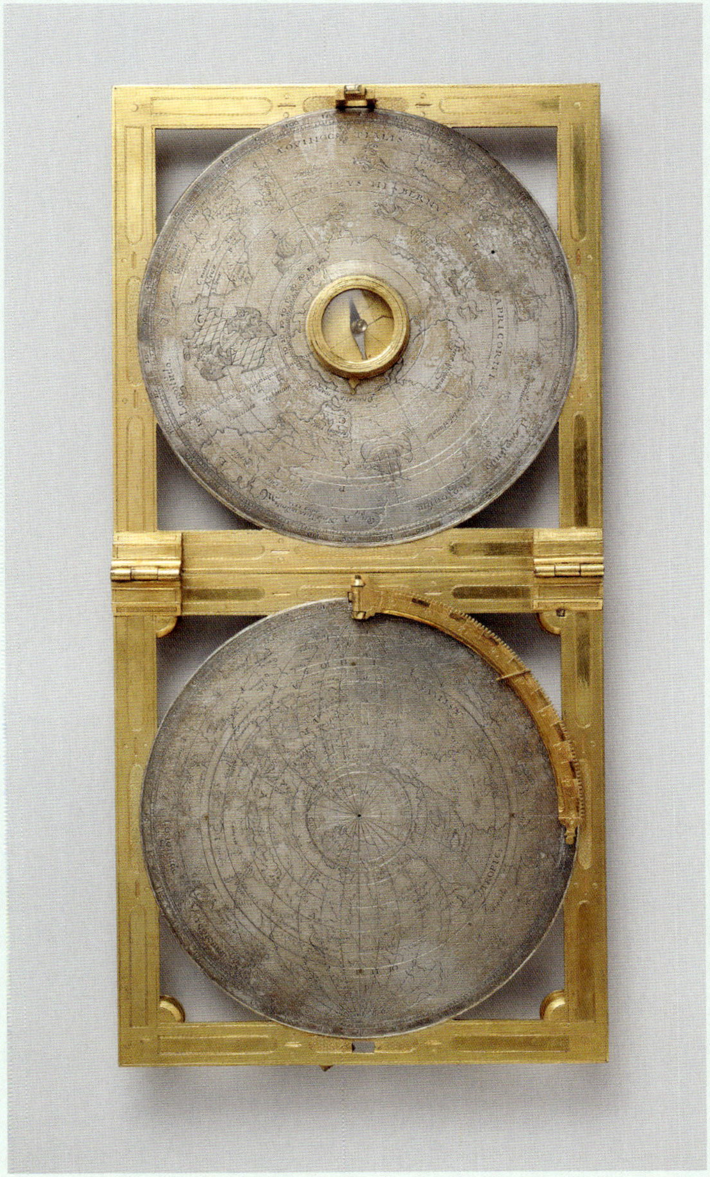

Cat. 7.2, Erasmus Habermel, *Geographical-Astronomical Compendium*

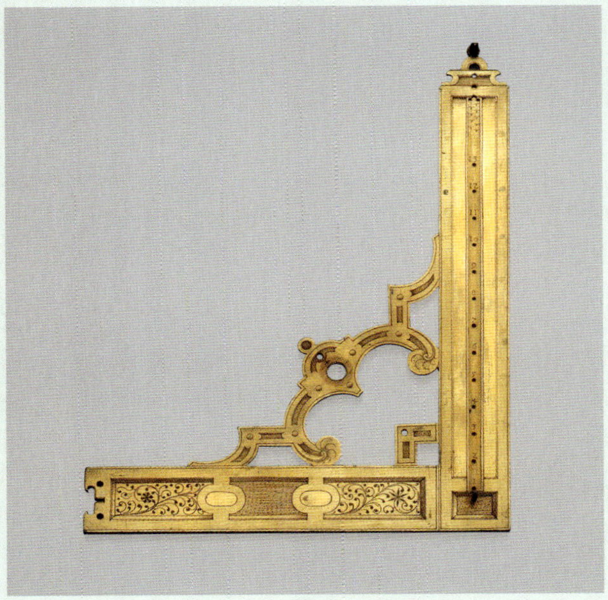

Cat. 7.3, Erasmus Habermel, *Right Angle (Calibre Scale)*

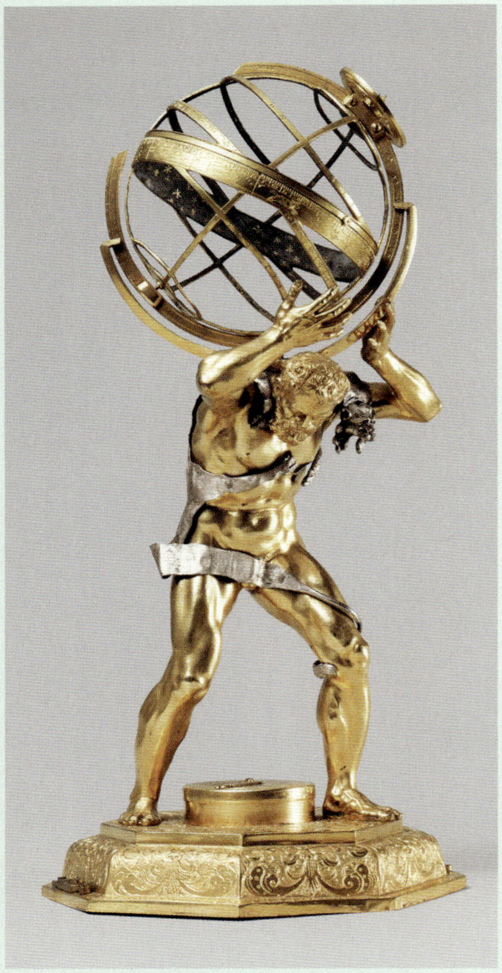

Cat. 8, *Hercules with Armillary Sphere*

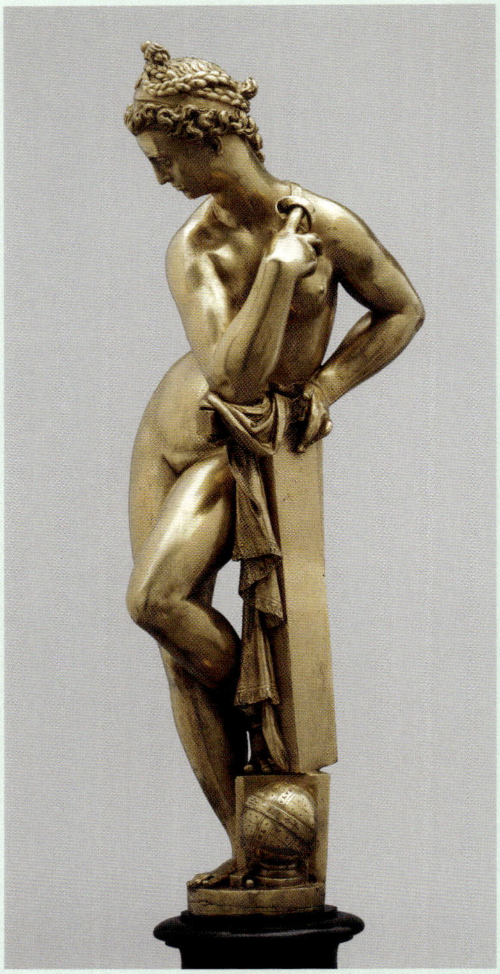

Cat. 10, Giambologna, Antonio Susini, *Allegory of Astronomy*

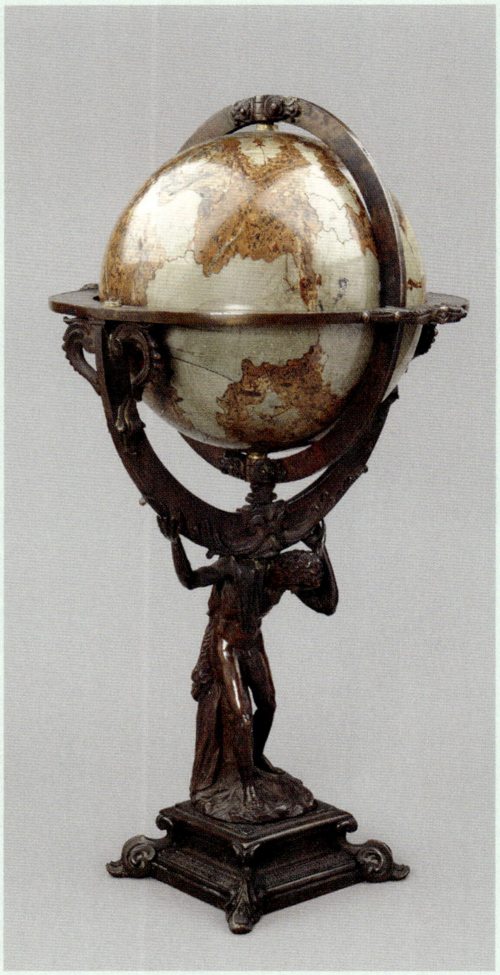

Cat. 9, *Hercules with Globe*

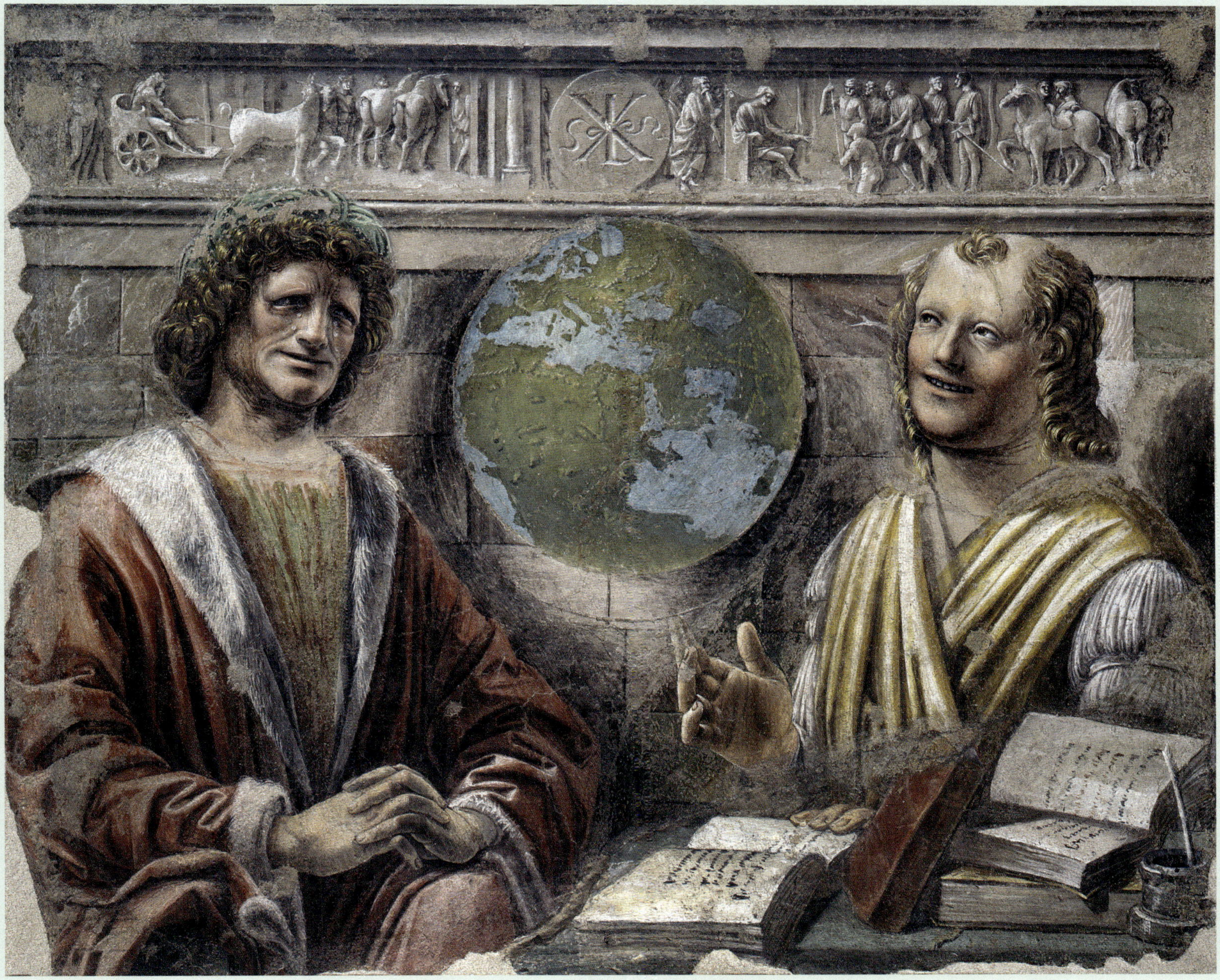

Cat. 11, Donato Bramante, *Heraclitus and Democritus*

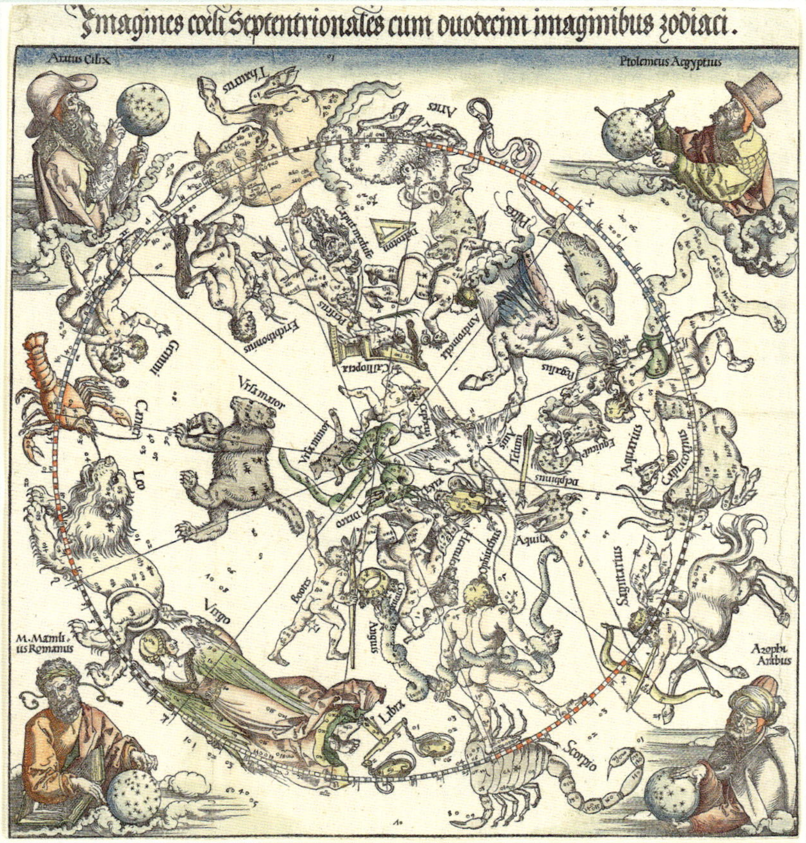

Cat. 12.1, Albrecht Dürer, *Map of the Northern Sky*

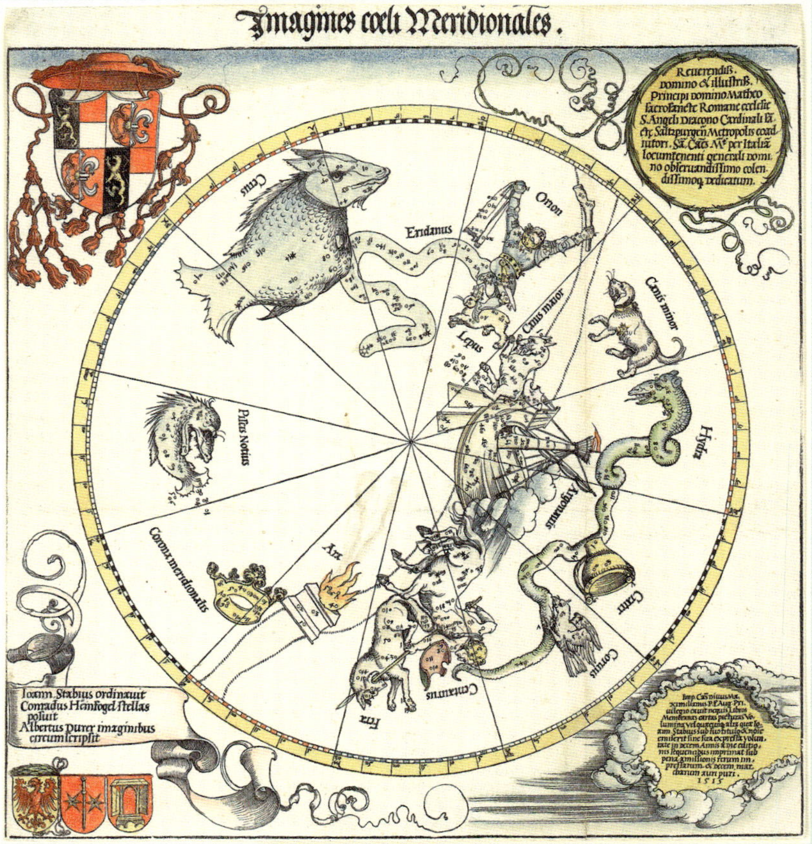

Cat. 12.2, Albrecht Dürer, *Map of the Southern Sky*

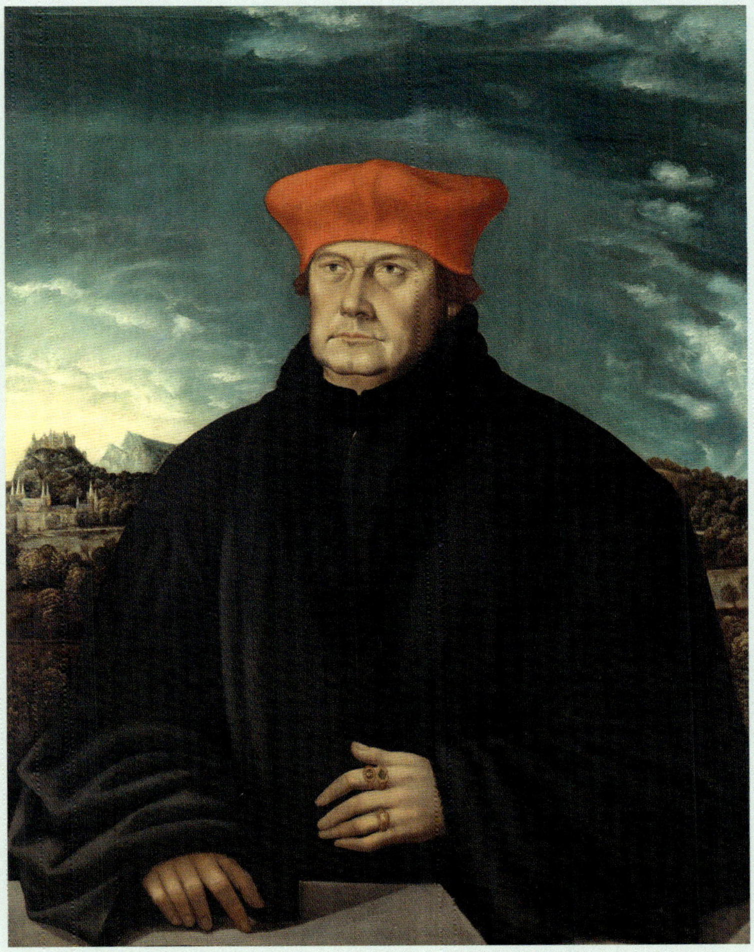

Cat. 13, *Cardinal Matthäus Lang von Wellenburg, Archbishop of Salzburg*

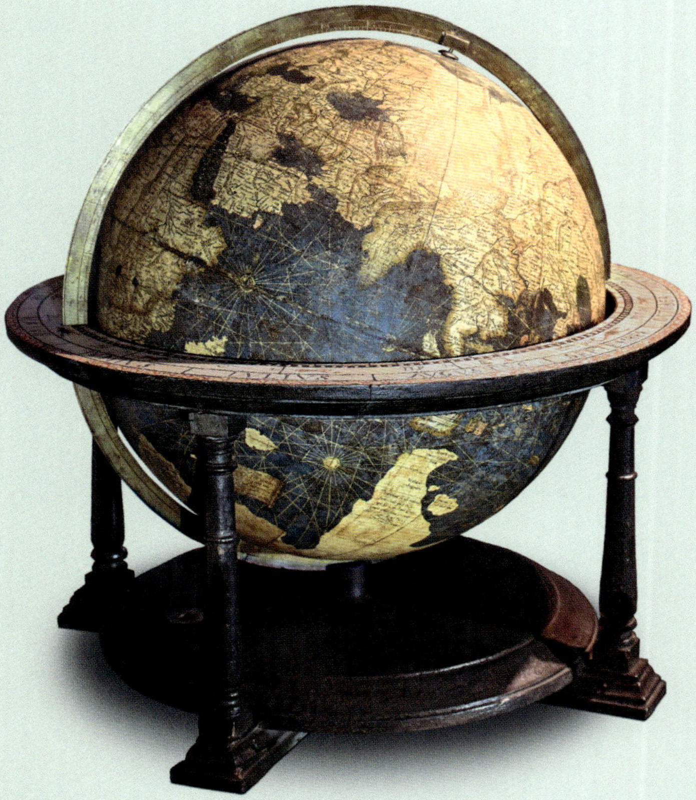

Cat. 14.1, Gerhard Mercator, *Terrestrial Globe*

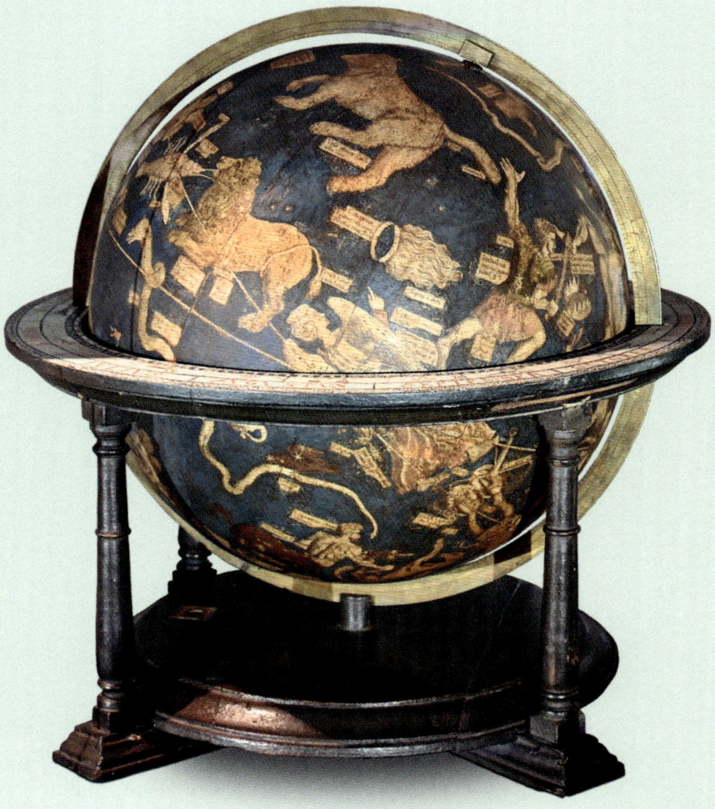

Cat. 14.2, Gerhard Mercator, *Celestial Globe*

Cat. 6

Giorgio da Castelfranco, called Giorgione (1477/78–1510)

The Three Philosophers

1508/09
Canvas; 125.5 × 146.2 cm
Vienna, Kunsthistorisches Museum, Picture Gallery, inv. 111

Provenance: 1525 Taddeo Contarini, Venice; 1545 Dario Contarini, Venice; 1636 Bartolomeo della Nave, Venice; 1638–49 Hamilton.; 1659 Archduke Leopold Wilhelm.
Literature: Exh. cat. Vienna 2004, cat. 5; Zeleny 2008; Zeleny 2008a; exh. cat. New York 2023; Zaccariotto 2024

The Three Philosophers by Giorgione is one of the most renowned and enigmatic paintings of the Venetian Renaissance. Set within a wooded landscape, enclosed on the left by a cave in which a fig tree grows, three male figures of different ages stand out on rocky terrain. From the youngest, seated, to the oldest, standing on the right, the three men are depicted as meditating and holding scientific instruments or the results of astral calculations. This has led to various interpretations of the figures as three philosophers, three astrologers, or the Three Magi observing the comet heralding the arrival of Christ.

It was recently discovered that a handwritten record dated to around 1520 exists in connection with this painting, attributed to the Venetian writer and diarist Marin Sanudo the Younger. In a miscellany of notes held in Venice's Biblioteca Marciana, at the end of a long list of images all featuring inscriptions at the bottom, Sanudo wrote: 'Subtus tres philosophi / Vivitur ingenio caetera mortis erunt' (see the recently published monograph in which this discovery is discussed; Zaccariotto 2024). The painting can be identified as the one by Giorgione that has been part of the Vienna collections since the seventeenth century. Sanudo was able to read the Latin motto when the painting was located in Cannaregio, in the Ca' Contarini owned by Taddeo Contarini (for more on the Ca' Contarini, see exh. cat. New York 2023).

The inscription is from the *Elegia a Mecenate*, a Latin text in the *Appendix Vergiliana*, a collection of compositions thought to be by the Latin poet Virgil, though later shown to be by another writer, and widely circulated in print from the end of the fifteenth century. The pentameter comes at the end of a block of verses describing the Horti Maecenatis, the pleasure gardens kept by the nobleman on Rome's Esquiline Hill, where representations of the arts and figures from mythological history coexisted in a luxuriant natural setting. The passage from the elegy is thus placed in an ekphrastic relationship with the painting, demonstrating Contarini's great literary sensitivity and classical culture, as he (almost certainly) chose the verse to link to the painting, a pentameter that can be translated as 'one lives through works of genius, death will take care of all the rest'.

Starting from Giorgione's painting, the motto had a renown linked to the world of knowledge, especially scientific knowledge. In the years immediately after Sanudo's testimony, it appeared not only with Albrecht Dürer's epigraphic portrait of Willibald Pirckheimer (1524), to note the subject's great erudition, but also in Andrea Vesalio's *Fabrica* (1543), the first anatomy treatise in the history of medicine, placed on a plinth beside a skeleton meditating on a skull. It also appeared in treatises on architecture and terrestrial and celestial measurement, such as an edition of the books of Vitruvius's *De architectura* with German commentary by Walther Hermann Ryff (1547), and especially in the *Astronomiae instauratae mechanica* by the Dane Tycho Brahe (1598), in which the pentameter is related precisely to those instruments for measuring the sky and the earth that are held by the philosophers in Giorgione's painting.

The use of the pseudo-Virgilian inscription that appeared beneath the painting in scientific treatises seems to show the noteworthiness of precisely those aspects of the image linked to science, astronomy, and mathematical knowledge that are concentrated in the attributes that denote the three wise men.

Giulia Zaccariotto

Cats. 7.1–7.3

Astrolabe

German, c.1580
Copper alloy; dia. 15.5 cm
Vienna, Kunsthistorisches Museum, Kunstkammer, inv. KK 800
Provenance: 1788 Ambras Inventory, XIV, 347, no. 100
Literature: Exh. cat. Vienna 1973, 19, cat. 61; exh. cat. Vienna 1978, 34; exh. cat. Krems 1999, 232, cat. 55

Erasmus Habermel (1538–1606)

Geographical-Astronomical Compendium

Prague, 1592/94
Copper alloy, gilt, silver; H 37 cm, W 15.5 cm, D 15.5 cm
Vienna, Kunsthistorisches Museum, Kunstkammer, inv. KK 7246
Provenance: Acquired from Karl Ullmayer, Vienna (O.K.A. 696, 7.3.1913)
Literature: Zinner 1967, 329–46; Eckhardt 1976, 21, 55–92; Eckhardt 1977, 22, 41, cat. 72; exh. cat. Essen 1988, 540, cat. 432; exh. cat. Prague 1997, 620, cat. IV. 70

Erasmus Habermel (1538–1606)

Right Angle (Calibre Scale)

Prague, c.1600
Copper alloy, gilt; H 19.5 cm, W 15.3 cm
Vienna, Kunsthistorisches Museum, Kunstkammer, inv. KK 790
Provenance: 1788 Ambras Inventory, XIV, 326, no. 36
Literature: Zinner 1967, 344; Eckhardt 1977, 22, 56–7, cat. 125

Various scientific instruments were necessary in order to discover nature and to explore and survey the earth. Some of these instruments, such as rulers, sundials, and compasses – both the aid to drawing and to geographical orientation – have been known in unaltered form since ancient times. One of these is the astrolabe, which can be termed a multifunctional tool. This circular instrument was used to determine the points of the compass and the positions of the stars, as well as to measure altitude and time. The astrolabe was of great use in surveying land; improvements for nautical use are attributed to Martin Behaim from Nuremberg and Prince Henry the Navigator in the fifteenth century. Both Bartolomeu Dias and Vasco da Gama used the device on their voyages of discovery. The drawing set with square and rulers was used for making geometric drawings and maps.

A special version of such intruments is the calibre scale, which was used to determine the weight of stone, iron, or lead bullets of different diameters. The compendium has several functions. It can show the time of sunrise and sunset as well as the length of day and night. Inside are geographical maps of the two hemispheres of the earth, north and south. Basic geographical knowledge is particularly evident in the precise reproduction of the outlines of the continents.

The Electoral *Kunstkammer* of Augustus of Saxony and the *Kunstkammer* of Emperor Rudolf II in Prague had a rich collection of assorted astronomical and mathematical devices, around 120 in all. The most important of these works were produced by the imperial instrument maker Erasmus Habermel, and attracted the admiration of Danish astronomer Tycho Brahe, who also worked at the court of Rudolf II. The elaborate decoration, including gilding, chasing, and engraving, show that such devices were not only useful for understanding the world, but could also be considered works of art in their own right.

Thomas Kuster

Cat. 8

Hercules with Armillary Sphere

Southern Germany (?), Vienna (?), 1st half 17th cent.
Silver, brass, partially gilt and painted; H 36.4 cm
Vienna, Kunsthistorisches Museum, Kunstkammer, inv. KK 862

Provenance: 1750 Imperial Treasury inventory, box 9, 417, no. 50; 1875 Imperial Treasury inventory, XIV, 66, 309; 1890 from Imperial Treasury
Literature: Exh. cat. Nara and Tokyo 1995/96, 197–8, cat. 73; exh. cat. Krems 1999, 226–7, cat. 52

This object skilfully combines the finest goldsmithing, mythological content, and a sophisticated scientific apparatus. Its theme is the ancient myth of Hercules, who temporarily carried the vault of heaven for Atlas, while the latter, who had been given the burden as a punishment, stole the golden apples of Hesperides for Hercules. The muscular hero, whose precisely rendered body testifies to a study of anatomy, holds the globe, which takes the form of an armillary sphere. This is an astronomical instrument consisting of rotating metal rings (circles) that simulate the orbits of the stars and planets and was used to determine the position of celestial bodies. A prototype was created by the ancient scholar Ptolemy. His knowledge, preserved in the Arab world, became available again in Christian central Europe, through the study of relevant sources during the period of Renaissance humanism. The pioneering studies of Nicolaus Copernicus revolutionized the previously accepted world view. Previously, it was assumed that the earth was at the centre of the cosmos (geocentrism), but his observations showed that the sun was at the centre, with all the planets orbiting around it (heliocentrism). This armillary sphere, which does not have the earth at the centre, reflects those new scientific investigations. The circles connected to the meridian circle represent the equator, the poles with the polar axis, the polar circles and tropics, and the circle of the horizon. The thickest metal ring provides information about the annual calendar and the respective signs of the zodiac; the days of the calendar could be set using this ring. At Hercules' feet is a round cover on which the signs of the zodiac and the twelve months are marked. The position of the sun in the zodiac could be determined using the pointer like a sundial.

Thomas Kuster

Cat. 9

Hercules with Globe

Italy (Tuscany?), 1st half 17th cent.
Bronze, limestone (ruin marble, landscape marble); H 53.1 cm (total), globe dia. 21 cm
Vienna, Kunsthistorisches Museum, Kunstkammer, inv. KK 6010

Provenance: 1879 Ambras Collection, XIV, 94, p. 15
Literature: Haag, Kirchweger, and Rainer 2015, 15, 61; Rainer 2016, 45; for ruin marble in general: Lergier and Börner 2001; Gehring 2020

As with the armillary sphere (cat. 8), it is the ancient hero Hercules who bears the globe with his superhuman strength. This time his burden is a globe. With its three-dimensional form, the globe is a spatial model for understanding the world. With its detailed reproduction of the map of the world, the armillary sphere reflects the expansion of and changes to the world view as well as the rapid development of seafaring in the course of European exploration. The discovery of the world and the discovery of nature picked up speed. It was primarily Dutch mariners, cartographers, and printers who produced globes of various sizes modelled on precise world maps such as those by Gerhard Mercator of Flanders. The designs of the Langren and Blaeu families of Amsterdam were considered particularly innovative. Magnificent examples of such globes can be found in the Austrian National Library in Vienna.

In the present case, the stone properties of a special limestone were part of the cartographic design. Its grain and different colours made it possible to depict the continents and their distinctive coastlines. This is an impressive example of work by creative individuals who – almost like gods – utilised nature and its products to create and convey knowledge artistically. The structure of limestone was also used to depict landscapes, city skylines, and buildings until the Baroque period. As inlays on objects of applied art, they created interesting views in terms of perspective.

Thomas Kuster

Cat. 10

Giovanni da Bologna, called Giambologna (1529–1608), model; Antonio Susini (1558–1624), bronze cast

Allegory of Astronomy

c.1585
Bronze, fire gilded; H 38.3 cm
Vienna, Kunsthistorisches Museum, Kunstkammer, inv. KK 5893

Provenance: Old imperial holdings, first identified in the inventory of the Imperial Treasury 1750
Literature: Dhanens 1956, 184–5, no. XXXII; exh. cat. Edinburgh, London, and Vienna 1978/79, 92–3, cat. 12 (Manfred Leithe-Jasper); Avery 1987, 259, no. 55; exh. cat. Florence 2006, 204–6, cat. 22 (Manfred Leithe-Jasper); exh. cat. Vienna 2006, 234–7, cat. 16 (Claudia Kryza-Gersch); mus. cat. Vienna 2010, 142, no. 61 (Franz Kirchweger), exh. cat. Mannheim 2012, 144, cat. III.3 (Claudia Kryza-Gersch); Kryza-Gersch 2015

In the sixteenth century, astrology was a popular science that was practised at royal courts throughout Europe. As it was not yet distinct from astronomy as an interpretation-free, mathematical observation of the stars, it was studied even by astronomers as famous as Tycho Brahe and Johannes Kepler. As part of the *artes liberales*, it was also depicted in painting and sculpture.

This sculpture of the personification of astronomy is a signed masterpiece by the Flemish artist Giambologna. His fame as court sculptor to the Medici spread throughout the Western world thanks to his bronze statuettes. Unlike monumental sculptures, they were easy to transport and affordable for bourgeois collectors. They were also used by the Medici as diplomatic gifts, and Emperor Rudolf II (1552–1612), an admirer of Giambologna who was known to have a liking for female nudes, is considered to have been the recipient of *Astronomy*. Nonetheless, the sculpture cannot be identified with certainty in the inventories of Rudolf's collection. This may be due to difficulties created by the interpretation of the iconography.

Unique to the Vienna cast are stars, symbols of the zodiac, meridians, and the planetary names 'VENNVS', 'SOL', and 'IVNNA' engraved on the sphere at the feet of the figure, which explicitly characterise it as a celestial globe. However, these may be later additions. The female figure of the personification of astronomy holds a ruler and dividers in her left hand, while a large set square rests on the elongated support, which has been interpreted as a straightedge or a board for drawing charts and building plans. As the artist usually designed figure supports as real-life objects, the prism on which her free leg rests has been interpreted as an open book (Kryza-Gersch 2015, 68–70). This would also characterise the statuette as a personification of a science. The ambiguity of the attributes means the sculpture could also refer to the related subject of geometry, which is essential for calculating the positions of stars and planets. An indication that it was nevertheless understood as astrology by contemporaries can be found in the list of bronzes owned by Markus Zäch, the reason being that these titles presumably reflect those under which his father had acquired them in Florence.

The artist focused on the young female figure, depicted in an elegantly twisted pose and *ponderation*. Some elements are already present in Giambologna's creations from the 1570s, such as the *Fiorenza* and the *Grotticella Venus*. His *Apollo* (1573/74) for the Studiolo of Francesco I de' Medici is understood to be its compositional mirror image. Since the emergence of a long-unknown cast of *Astronomy* (Hill Art Foundation, New York), considered to be the direct predecessor of the Vienna version, this is now considered to date from around 1585. The balanced composition leads the eye around the figure in a flowing movement. *Astronomy* is, therefore, not only a high point among Giambologna's artistic achievements, it is also an outstanding example of the *figura serpentinata* that was so characteristic of his time.
Alexandra Sattler

Cat. 11

Donato Bramante (c.1444–1514)

Heraclitus and Democritus

1486/87
Fresco detached and transferred on to canvas; 102 × 127 cm
Milan, Pinacoteca di Brera, inv. Reg. Cron. 1240

Provenance: Milan, Palazzo di Gaspare Ambrogio Visconti in Pietro in Camminadella parish church (building now destroyed, formerly located in current Via Lanzone); detached and taken to the Pinacoteca di Brera, 1901–1902.
Literature: Lomazzo 1584 (1973/74), vol. II, 335; Ferri Piccaluga 1988; Kiang 1992; Schofield 2013; exh. cat. Lugano 2014/15, 100–5, cat. 6 (Edoardo Rossetti); exh. cat. Milan 2014/15, 195, cat. III.9 (Matteo Ceriana & Edoardo Rossetti)

Donato Bramante painted effigies of the Greek philosophers Heraclitus and Democritus between 1486 and 1487 as part of an extensive decorative programme for the Milan palazzo of the aristocratic poet Gaspare Ambrogio Visconti (see Albonico and Moro 2020). The painting was already recorded by Lomazzo as a work by Bramante (Rosetti, in print). In the eighteenth century it was mentioned as a door mantel (which had probably been created by closing an open portico) in an upper-floor room, illustrated with images of philosophers. The *Men of Arms* cycle, also painted by Bramante, was in the adjacent room (Rossetti, in print).

The choice of subject must have been borrowed from the Florentine *Gymnasio* by Marsilio Ficino (Hankins 1991, 448). The two philosophers are depicted surrounded by books against a variegated marble wall. A frieze above probably portrays scenes of triumph and justice with the letters X and L in a central *clypeus*, possibly the initials of *luctus* and χαρά (*gaudium*), referring to their philosophical reflections (Schofield 2013, 7, note 20). A globe suspended between the thinkers is one of the most up-to-date maps extant at this time, probably derived from the Ulm edition of Ptolemy, with plates, published by Lienhart Holl in 1482 (Kiang 1992). The latter was partly financed by the Milanese merchant Ambrogio Caimi, who was close to Visconti (Rossetti 2021). A more schematic version of the planisphere also appears on the frontispiece of the edition of a text on Democritus by Antonietto Fregoso, who was a friend of Visconti (Fregoso 1506; Ferri Piccaluga 1988, Berra 2020). The popularity of the subject in Milan is attested to by a later painting, with the philosophers portrayed in a different pose but with a similar globe suspended between them; a copy of this is known, with a controversial attribution to one of the Figino (Pavesi 2017, 556–8, no. E.2).

The presence of the detailed globe is linked to the geographical interests of Visconti's cultural circle, which also included Bramante and Leonardo, in which the study of the Earth was part of an interesting philosophical-religious ferment (Pederson 2020; Rossetti 2020). One of the first printed topographical representations of Lombardy appeared in a book by the Visconti household's tutor (Maccaneo 1490; Schofield 1995). The Visconti villa was entirely decorated with urban views (Buganza 2020). A printed planisphere was glued to a bench in the study, which contained various books on geographical subjects (Rossetti 2012). They even included the *Codex Arcerianus*, one of the most valuable illuminated codices on land surveying, which had belonged to Petrarch and later passed into the hands of Erasmus (Wolfenbüttel, Herzog-August-Bibliothek, cod. Guelf. 36,23A; Marshall 2024).

Edoardo Rossetti

Cats. 12.1, 12.2

Albrecht Dürer (1471–1528)

Map of the Northern Sky

1515
Woodcut, coloured; 450 × 433 mm
Staatliche Graphische Sammlung München,
inv. 118931 D

Map of the Southern Sky

1515
Woodcut, coloured; 455 × 433 mm
Staatliche Graphische Sammlung München,
inv. 118930 D

Provenance: Bayerische Hof- und Staatsbibliothek Munich, transferred from there around 1835
Literature: Meder 1932, 244, cat. 260 (I), 307, no. 127, plate XIX, fig. 127, 'from 1471 to 1524'; Schoch, Mende, and Scherbaum 2002, 430–5, cat. 243 (with catalogues raisonnés and older literature, Rainer Schoch); Wörz 2007, 156–95; exh. cat. Cambridge and Evanston 2011/12, 86–9, cat. 15 (Marisa Mandabach), 90–3, cat. 16 (Marisa Mandabach)

Two large-format sheets, each printed from a single block, show the stars of the northern and southern night sky in stereographic projection. Divided into two halves, they depict the celestial sphere, imagined as an enormous hollow sphere that surrounds the earth. The division between the two sheets does not run north and south of the equator, as one might expect, but above and below the ecliptic, the apparent path of the sun as seen from Earth over the course of a year. Corresponding to the annual cycle, the circle is divided into twelve equal phases, each representing a 30° segment. Each phase is assigned to the zodiac sign in which the sun is positioned during that period. These constellations are formed by connecting the fixed stars – which do not change their positions but remain in the same position relative to one another – into figures using imaginary lines. This knowledge was indispensible as an astronomical aid for dividing the year into months and for navigation at sea. This set of maps, published in Nuremberg in 1515, brought together astronomical knowledge in printed form for the first time. The woodcuts, which could be reproduced many times over, were met with great interest and were reprinted several times.

The starting point was two maps drawn in 1503, which can be considered the work of the Nuremberg astronomer Conrad Heinfogel (d.1517). Using knowledge from ancient and Arabic traditions, they link the calculations of important astronomers from Nuremberg, which at this time was also a centre for the production of astronomical measuring instruments.

Idealized portraits of four forefathers of astronomy – Aratos of Soloi (author of the didactic poem *Phaenomena*), Marcus Manilius (author of the Latin poem *Astronomica*), Abd ar-Rahman as-Sufi (representative of Persian-Islamic astronomy), and Ptolemy, mathematician and astronomer par excellence – appear in the corners of the map of the northern firmament. The constellations on the printed maps are based on the constellation catalogue in the eighth and ninth books of Ptolomy's compendium *Almagest*. Various symbols distinguish the stars according to their brightness.

Conrad Heinfogel is one of the three authorities mentioned by name to whom we owe these pioneering star maps. He is responsible for the information on the position of the celestial bodies. The cartographer, astronomer, and historiographer Johannes Stabius (after 1460–1522), professor of mathematics in Ingolstadt and adviser to Kaiser Maximilian I, acted as publisher. Finally, Albrecht Dürer was responsible for the graphic design. This must have been more than just an artistic challenge for the '*Pictor doctus*', who was interested in science his entire life, particularly in problems of geometry, proportion, and perspective.

The signs of the zodiac are memorably designed. At first quite abstract, they are ultimately fleshed out from a few individual points with captivating naturalness and supported here by refined colouring. Strikingly, the anthropomorphic figures are depicted from behind. They indicate that viewers of the map are seeing the firmament from the outside, not from Earth. These early Dürer maps were the prerequisite for later print versions from an exterior point of view, which in turn first made possible three-dimensional celestial globes, such as those of Gerhard Mercator (cat. 14).

The map of the southern firmament bears a dedication to Cardinal Matthäus Lang von Wellenburg (see cat. 13), one of the most influential Catholic clerics, chamberlain to Maximillian I, and a brilliant diplomat, who was named coadjutor to the prince-archbishop of Salzburg in 1512. Johannes Stabius's dedication was addressed to this former

fellow student in Ingolstadt, who was a friend of the humanist and astronomer Georg Tannenstetter (1482–1535), who taught in Vienna. Albrecht Dürer made a portrait of the cardinal, who was also interested in scientific questions, at the Diet of Augsburg in 1518 (Basel, Kupferstichkabinett).
ACHIM RIETHER

Cat. 13

Cardinal Matthäus Lang von Wellenburg, Archbishop of Salzburg

Salzburg (?), 1528 dated lower right
Parchment on mahogany; 76.5 × 61 cm
Vienna, Kunsthistorisches Museum, Picture Gallery, inv. 5636

Provenance: 1663 verified in Ambras
Literature: Legers 1906, 494; Hugelshofer 1939; mus. cat. Salzburg 1962, no. 182; exh. cat. St Florian and Linz 1965, 146–7, cat. 361 (Franz Fuhrmann); Löcher 1965, 346; Bonorand and Haffter 1983, 327–9; Sallaberger 1997; exh. cat. Vienna 2003, 524, cat. X.7 (Karl Schütz); Juffinger and Plasser 2007, 181; Müller 2011; Moosleitner 2017

This portrait of a man dressed in black with a cardinal's biretta has been frequently cited as the work of a master of the Danube school, with well-known names such as Wolf Huber and Albrecht Altdorfer mentioned in this connection. Thus far, none of these suppositions have been adequately substantiated. However, the literature does agree on the identity of the sitter: Cardinal Matthäus Lang von Wellenburg (1468–1540), Archbishop of Salzburg, behind whom can be seen various buildings in Salzburg, including the Hohensalzburg Fortress with the 'Hoher Stock'.

In 1494, Lang became one of the secretaries of the future Emperor Maximilian I, a career move that would shape his life. Within a few years, he had become *the* secretary of the emperor. As a diplomat, he negotiated on behalf of Maximilian, travelled, and fought alongside him, and even brokered the Habsburg–Jagiellonian marriage treaty of 1515. His service – 'mit unmentschlichen Fleyß' ('with inhuman industry') as he described it himself – was rewarded with privileges and titles, from his appointment as Bishop of Gurk and Provost of Augsburg Cathedral to a noble title, a knighthood, and an honorary doctorate to his consecration as Archbishop of Salzburg. Lang is seen, on the one hand, as one of the most intransigent persecutors of Protestants and, on the other, as the complete humanist Renaissance ruler, a friend of the arts and sciences. He supported literary figures, musicians, and visual artists such as Hans Burgkmair the Elder and Albrecht Dürer. The latter made a portrait sketch of Lang and designed a throne for the splendour-loving cardinal (Brunswick, Herzog Anton Ulrich-Museum, inv. Z32). Dürer was also responsible for the graphic realisation of Johannes Stabius's maps of the world and stars (cats. 12.1, 12.2), which he dedicated to Lang. The cardinal was the addressee of many such dedications, including a horoscope by Johannes Stabius, an early report on Magellan's circumnavigation of the world, and a treatise on possible cures for syphilis.
EVELYN KLAMMER

Cats. 14.1, 14.2

Gerhard Mercator (Gerhard Kremer, 1512–1594)

Terrestrial Globe

1541
Sphere: wood, plaster, paper; support: wood, brass; H 56 cm (total), dia. 41 cm, circ. 129 cm
Inscribed: 'Lovanij an. 1541'
Cremona, Biblioteca Statale, inv. Beni mob. 183

Celestial Globe

1551
Sphere: wood, plaster, paper; support: wood, brass; H 56 cm (total), dia. 41 cm, circ. 129 cm
Inscribed: 'Lovanij anno Domini 1551 mense Aprili'
Cremona, Biblioteca Statale, inv. Beni mob. 182

Provenance: Historical holdings
Literature: Ceradini 1889–1891; Buonanno 1890; exh. cat. Cremona 2016/17, 243–6, cat. 35 (Marica Milanesi)

Mercator's terrestrial globe stands out from sixteenth-century map production due its wealth of information, fidelity of reproduction, and rigorous control of sources. It is thus one of the most important stages in the development of modern cartography.

The globe was made in 1541 on the meridian of Fuerteventura, the largest of the Canary Islands, and divides the world into five parts: Europe, Africa, Asia, America, and the Southern Land. Mercator made use of the latest information and thus depicted the New World quite accurately. As in his chronological and biblical studies, Mercator critically compared the traditional sources and checked them against new information. For obvious reasons, he made use of recent geographical reports following the discovery of the New World and subsequent exploratory travels, especially for the terrestrial globe. Among the many cartouches, one with the Granvelle coat of arms and a dedication to Nicola Perrenot, chancellor to Charles V, stands out; the signature of Gerhard Mercator and the date 1541 appear in another; a third lists 65 of the most notable cities in Europe in three columns; other cartouches contain various explanatory notes. Specimens of marine fauna and rare, little-known, or recently discovered species are also illustrated, but Mercator's cartographic skill is primarily revealed in his description of the fourth part of the world (America), due to his capacity for describing sources and his intuition in resolving contradictory information.

The fourth part ('AME/RI/CA a multis hodie Nova India/dicta') is represented with incomparable precision for the time. Florida is named 'HISPANIA MAIOR capta anno 1530'; Mexico ('HISPANIA NOVA') is distinguished by a mountain range, with its capital 'Temistian' (Mexico City) and other coastal places, including the city of 'Almeria' or Vera Crux 'founded by Cortes'. The mouth of the Amazon is shown among the dense indications of settlements on the Brazilian coast, which then continues to the Strait of Magellan. Peru ('nova Castilia omnium / auro ditissima') and other places are shown on the Pacific coast. The wealth of toponyms, the precision of topographical detail, and greater cartographic accuracy mark the difference from previous representations of the world.

Mercator depicted fifty constellations on his celestial globe of 1551, dedicated to George of Austria, bishop of Liege. They include the 48 traditional (Ptolemaic) ones, plus two others that, although also coming from classical antiquity, were later additions: Cicinnus (Coma Berenices – in honour of Queen Berenice of Egypt who, according to legend, cut off her hair as an offering for her husband's return from war); and Antinous – in honour of Hadrian's beloved companion who drowned in the Nile and was subsequently deified by the emperor. The stars, recognizable in six orders of magnitude, are positioned according to the equinox of 1550. The design of the constellations (as for all the similar celestial globes and maps to come) was inspired by two famous woodcuts by Albrecht Dürer from 1515 (cat. 12). The background to Mercator's work was not so much astronomical as astrological.

The globes are made of plastered wood and mounted on a perfectly preserved wooden support. Paper lozenges are glued to the surface, with two circular caps at the ends to close the joins between the lozenges. The original horizon is missing from the Cremona globes, which is crudely reproduced and lacks much of the data contained in the print. The meridians are original, but the hour dial is missing, though its ancient setting is visible. The most original feature of the Cremona globes is their vivid colouring, with extensive use of pure gold to mark the stars of the celestial globe and many other details, such as the loxodromic (rhumb) lines of the terrestrial globe, with a uniform background (probably lapiz lazuli blue) to distinguish the celestial vault and the sea.

The globes have always belonged to the Biblioteca Statale of Cremona, having arrived when it was still the library of the Jesuit College, probably part of the legacy of Bishop Cesare Speciano (1539–1607). He was apostolic nuncio (1586–88) at the court of Philip II in Spain and, at the request of Pope Clement VIII, again a papal diplomat (1592–98) with Rudolf II in Prague. Speciano brought the Jesuits to Cremona, began building the college and church, and bequeathed the college his own remarkable library of more than 1,200 manuscripts and very valuable editions, which formed the original nucleus of the Biblioteca Statale. It is important to note that the globes probably belonged to Speciano (who could have known the then elderly Mercator at the Habsburg court), because his collection is distinguished by remarkable geographical works, many of which have similar characteristics to the globes in question. Strangely, though, it was only at the end of the nineteenth century that the globes were recognized for what they were: the work of Mercator.

Raffaella Barbierato

Courtly Banquets and Conversations

(cats. 15–39)

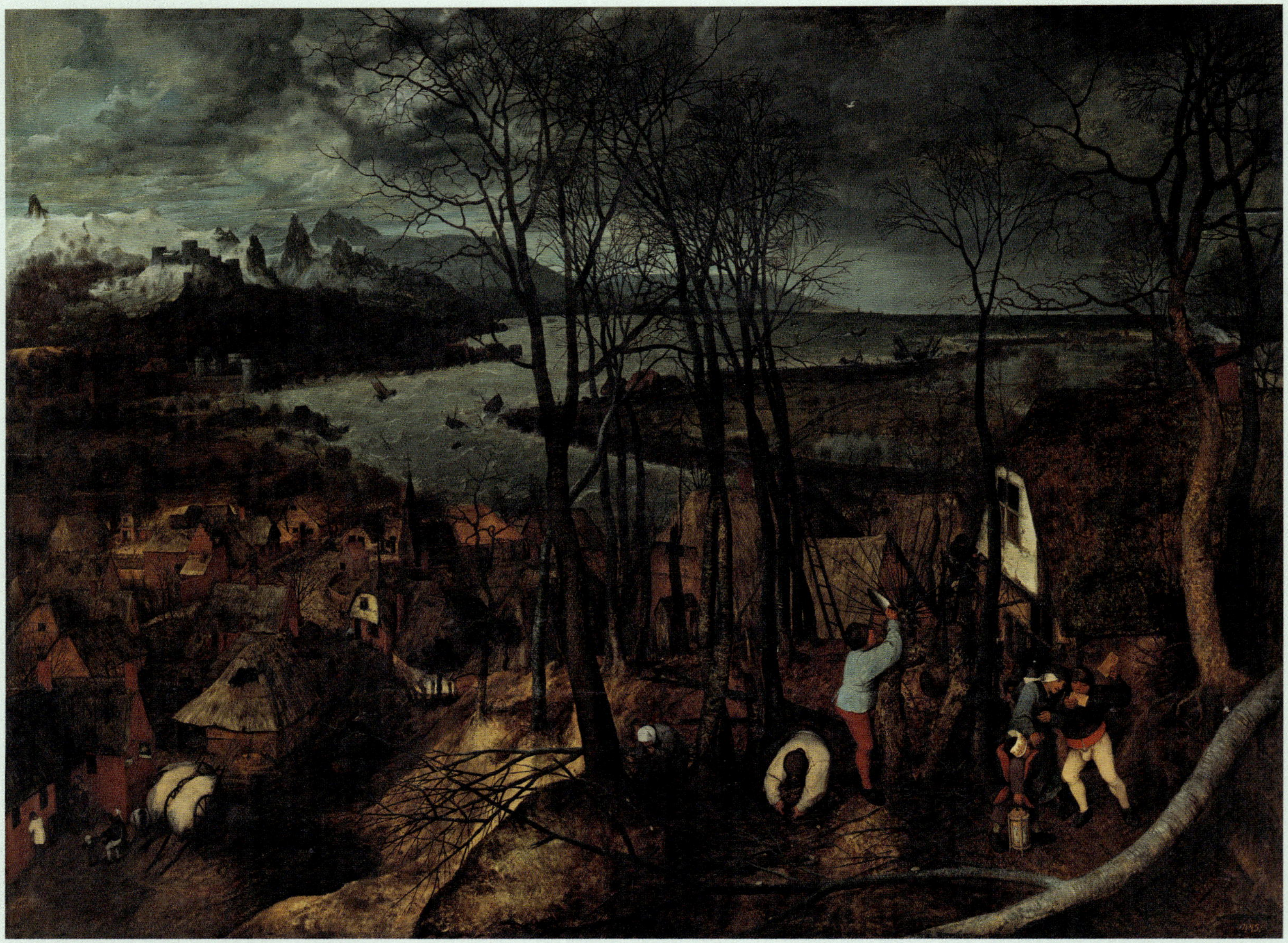

Cat. 15.1, Pieter Bruegel the Elder, *The Gloomy Day (Early Spring)*

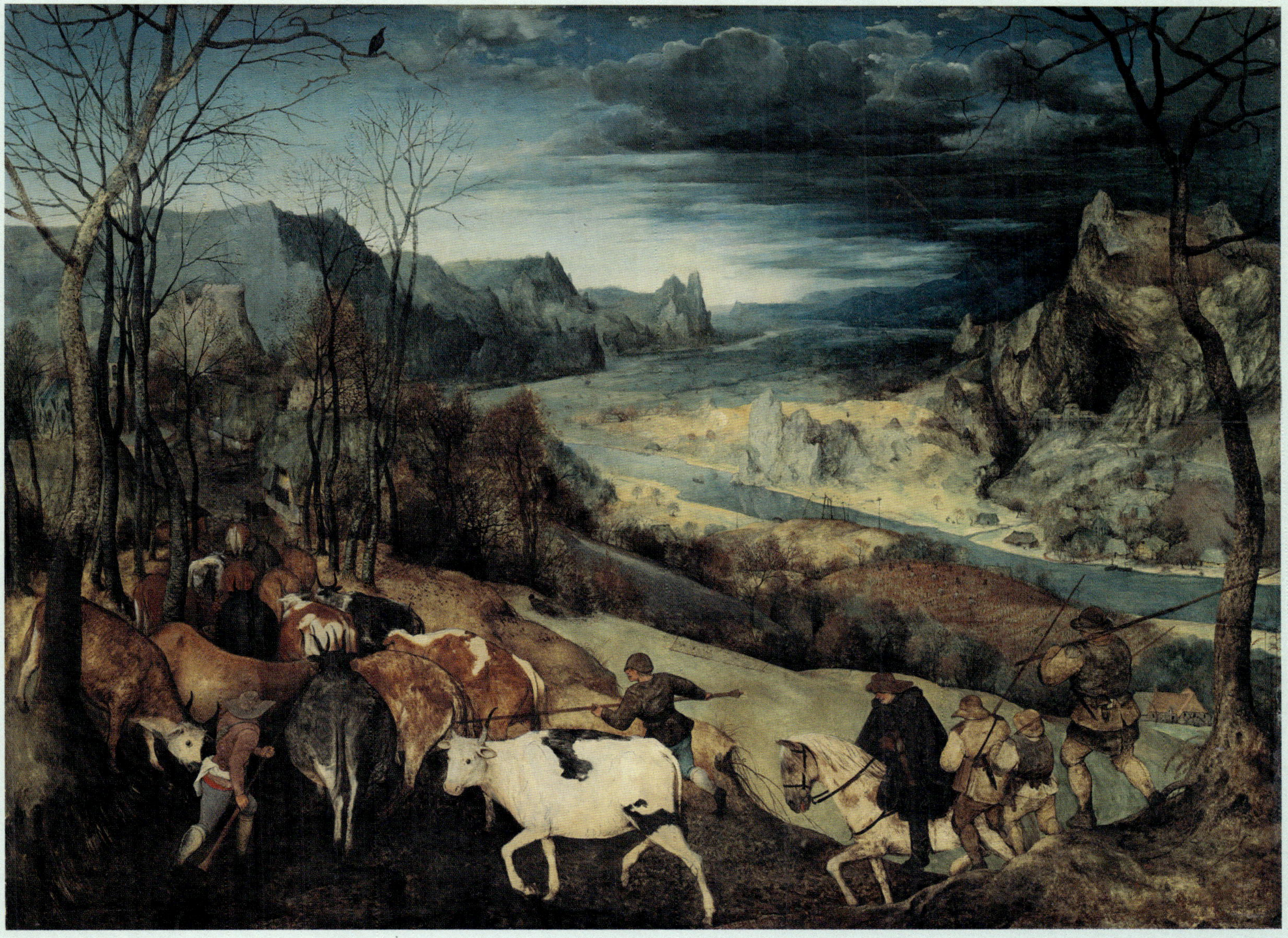

Cat. 15.2, Pieter Bruegel the Elder, *The Return of the Herd (Autumn)*

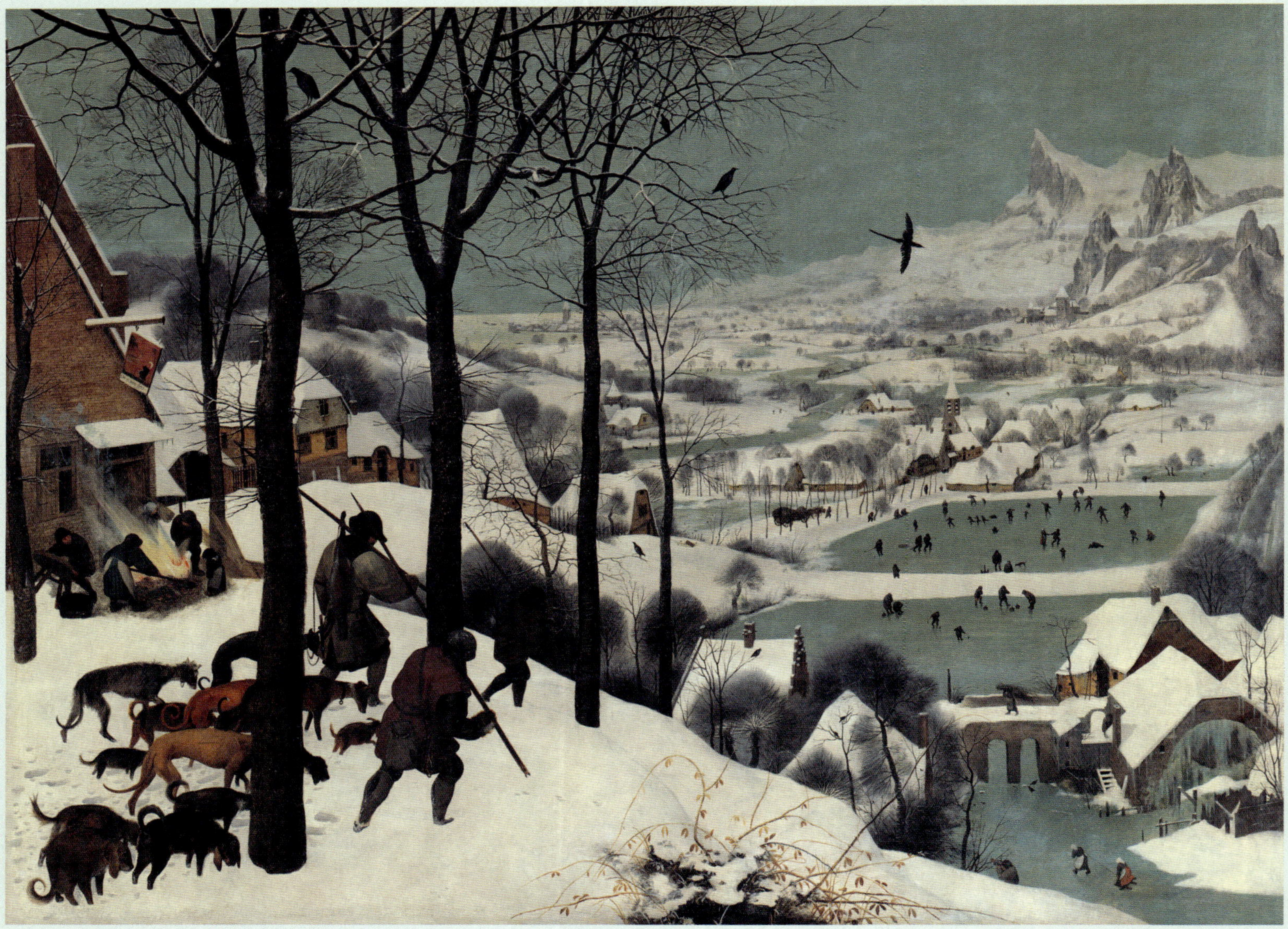

Cat. 15.3, Pieter Bruegel the Elder, *Hunters in the Snow (Winter)*

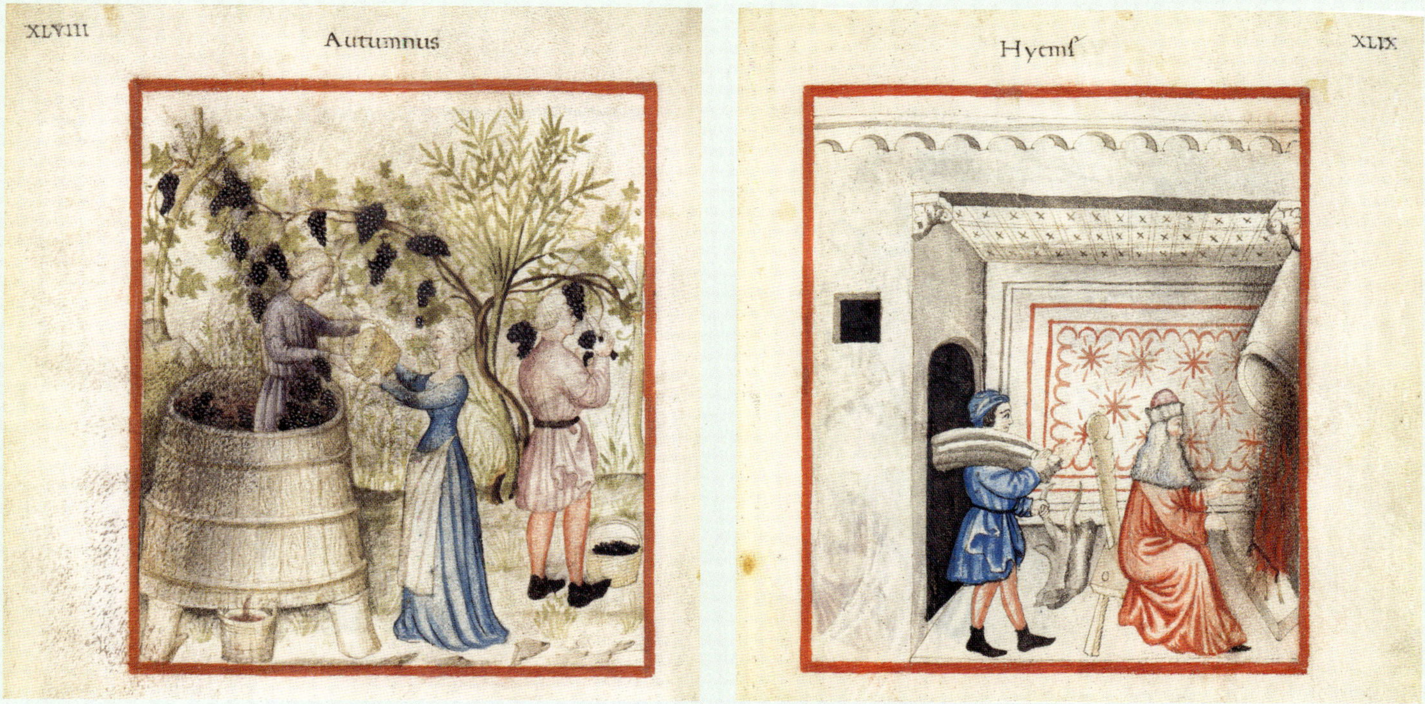

Cat. 16, *The Liechtenstein Tacuinum Sanitatis*

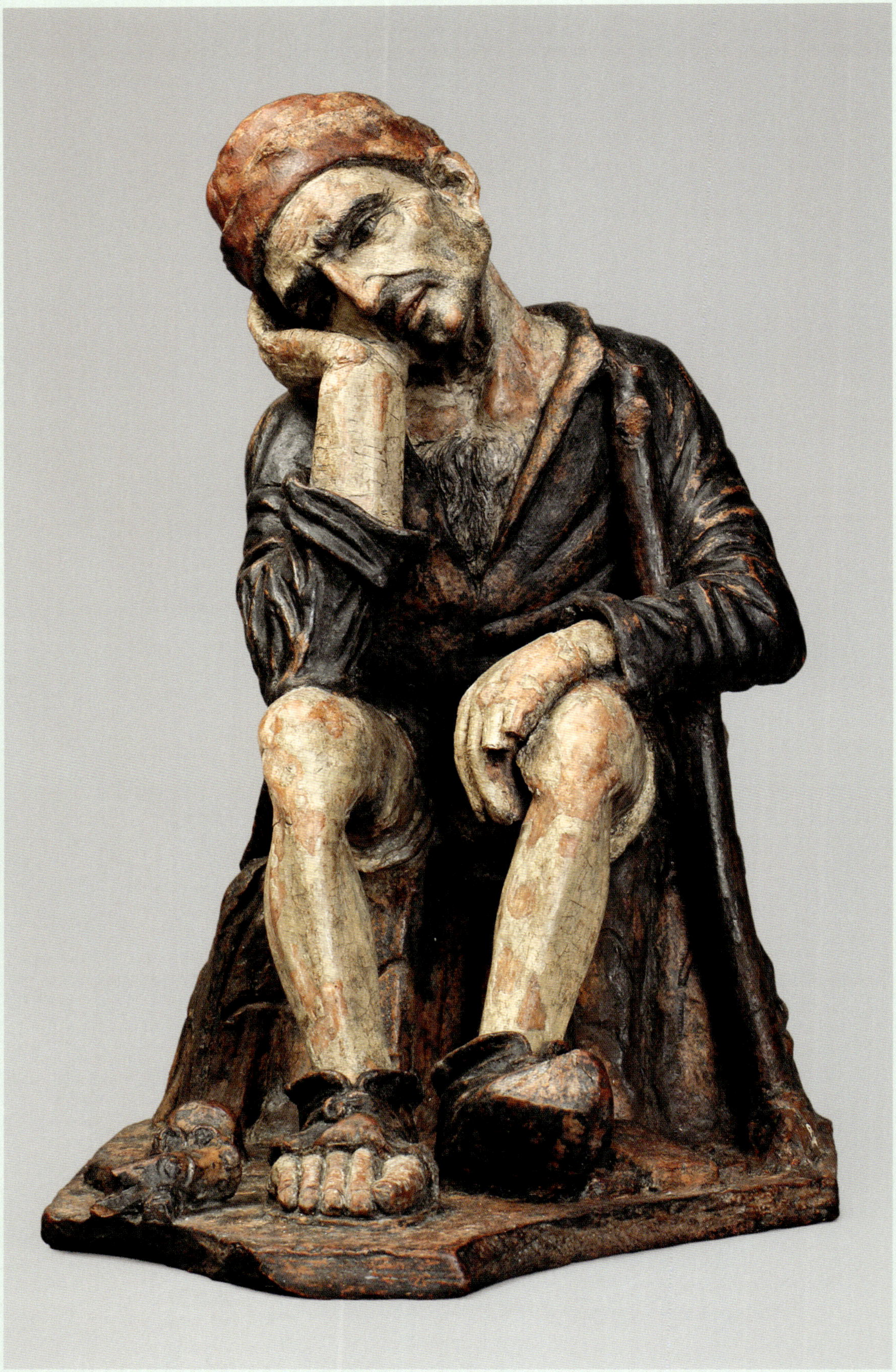

Cat. 17, Andrea Riccio, *Mower at Rest*

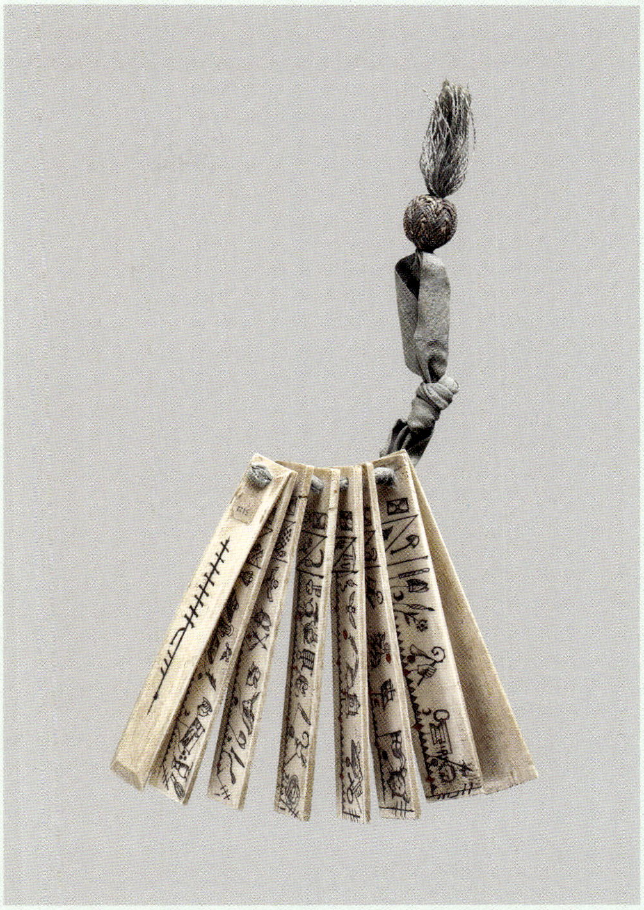

Cat. 18.3, *Farmer's Calendar ('Mandlkalender')*

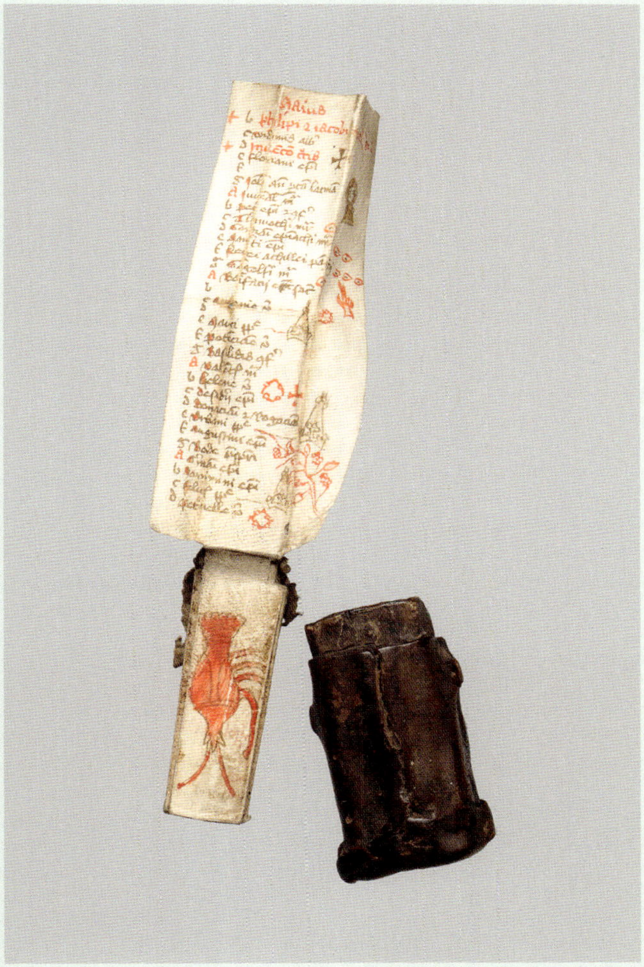

Cat. 18.1, *Calendar*

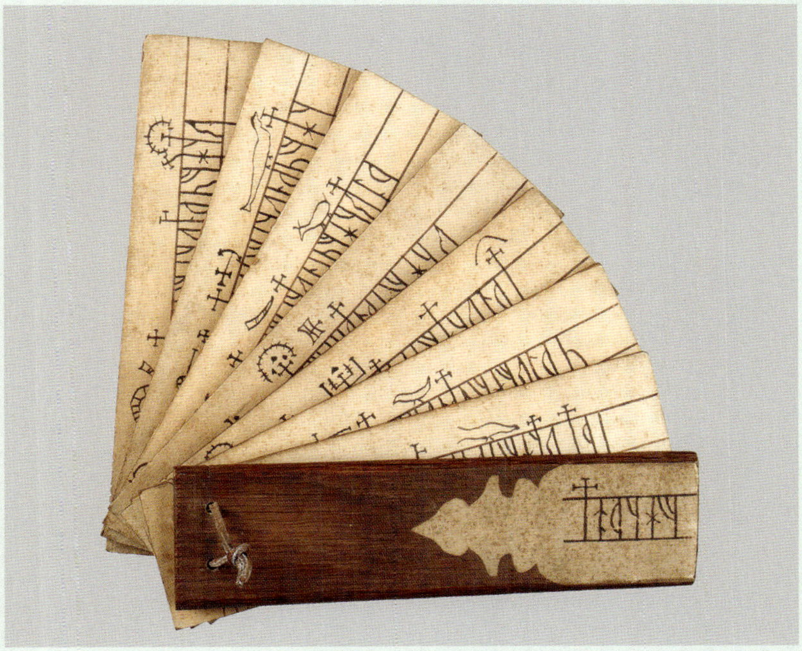

Cat. 18.2, *Farmer's Calendar (Runic Calendar)*

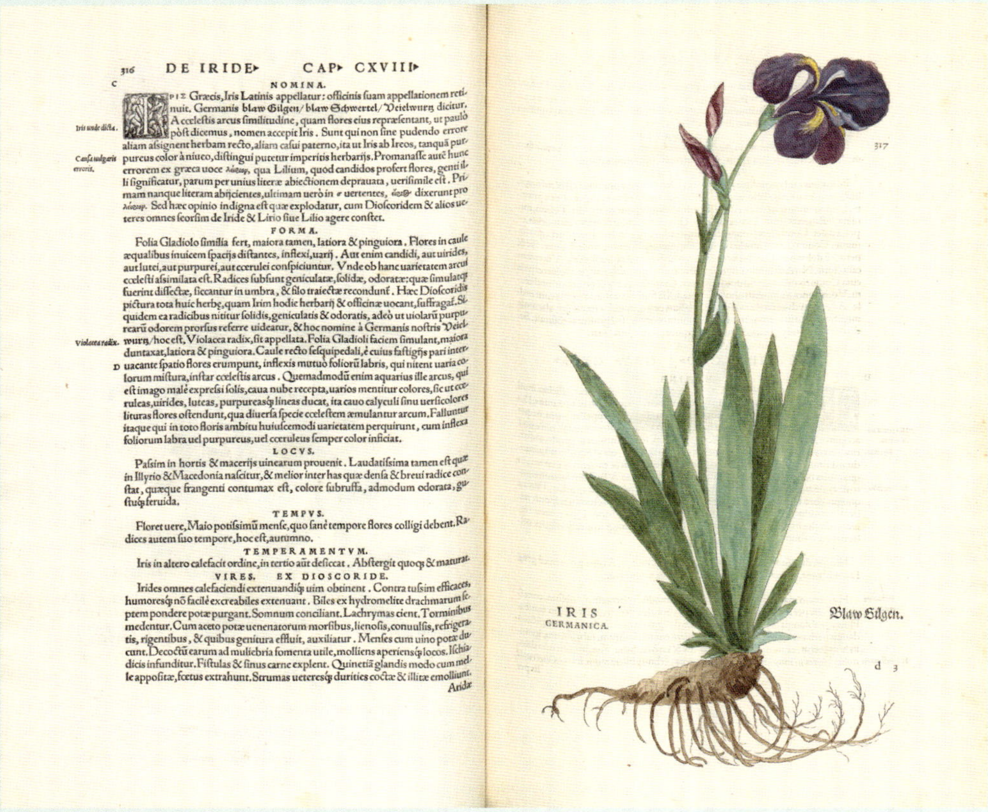

Cat. 19, Leonhart Fuchs, *De historia stirpium commentarii*

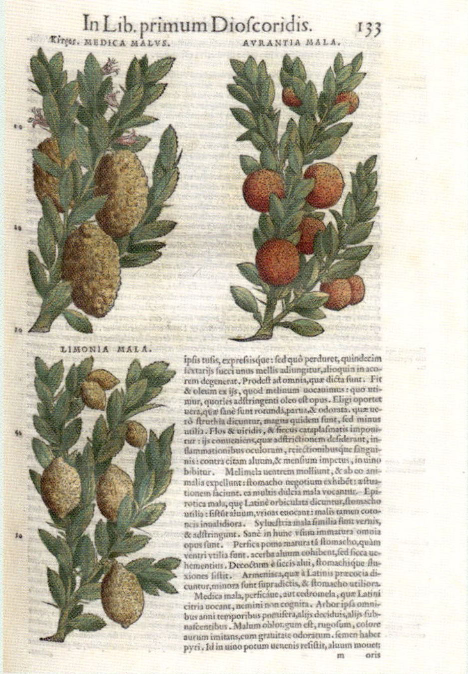

Cat. 20.1, Pietro Andrea Mattioli, *Commentarii, In Libros Sex Pedacii Dioscoridis Anazarbei, De Medica materia*

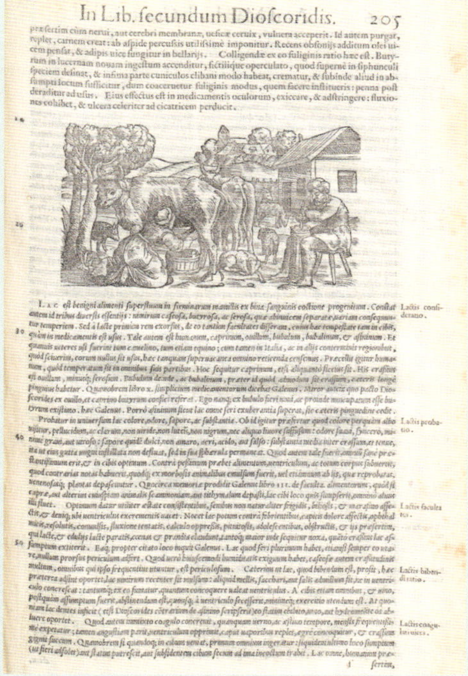

Cat. 20.2, Pietro Andrea Mattioli, *Commentarii, In Libros Sex Pedacii Dioscoridis Anazarbei, De Medica materia*

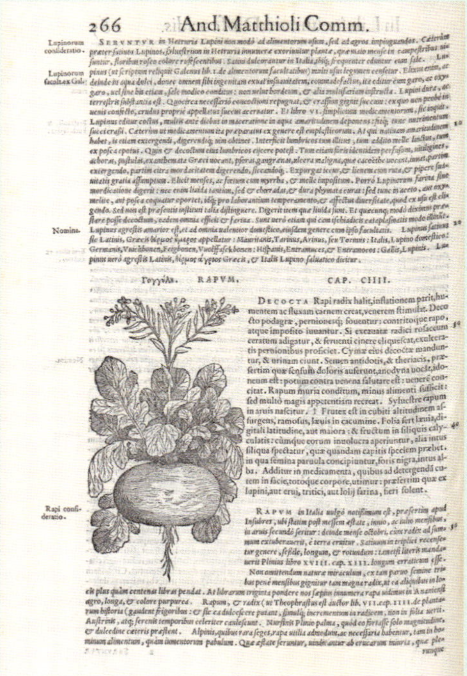

Cat. 20.3, Pietro Andrea Mattioli, *Commentarii Secvndo Avcti, In Libros Sex Pedacii Dioscoridis Anazarbei De Medica materia*

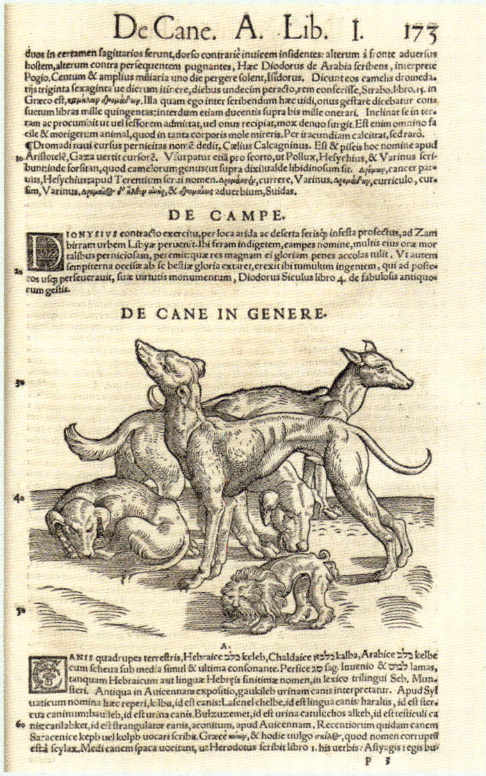
De Cane. A. Lib. I. 173

DE CAMPE.

DE CANE IN GENERE.

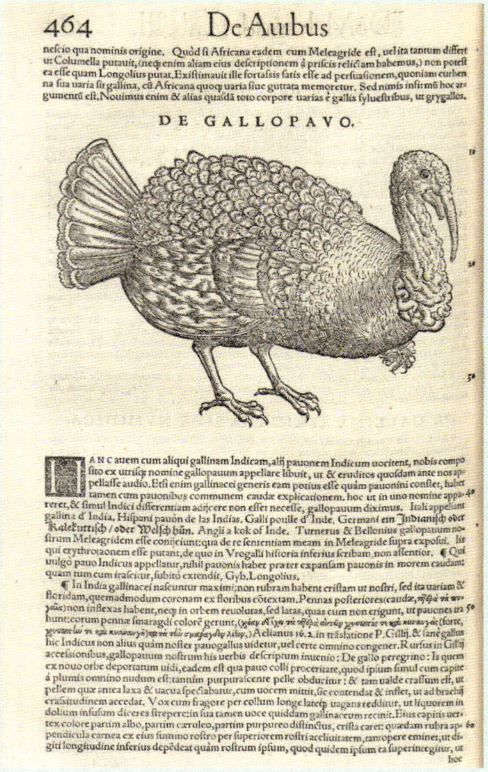
464 De Auibus

DE GALLOPAVO.

Cat. 21.1, Conrad Gessner, *Historiae Animalium, Liber I. de Quadrupedibus viviparis*

Cat. 21.2, Conrad Gessner, *Historiae Animalium, Liber III. de Avium natura*

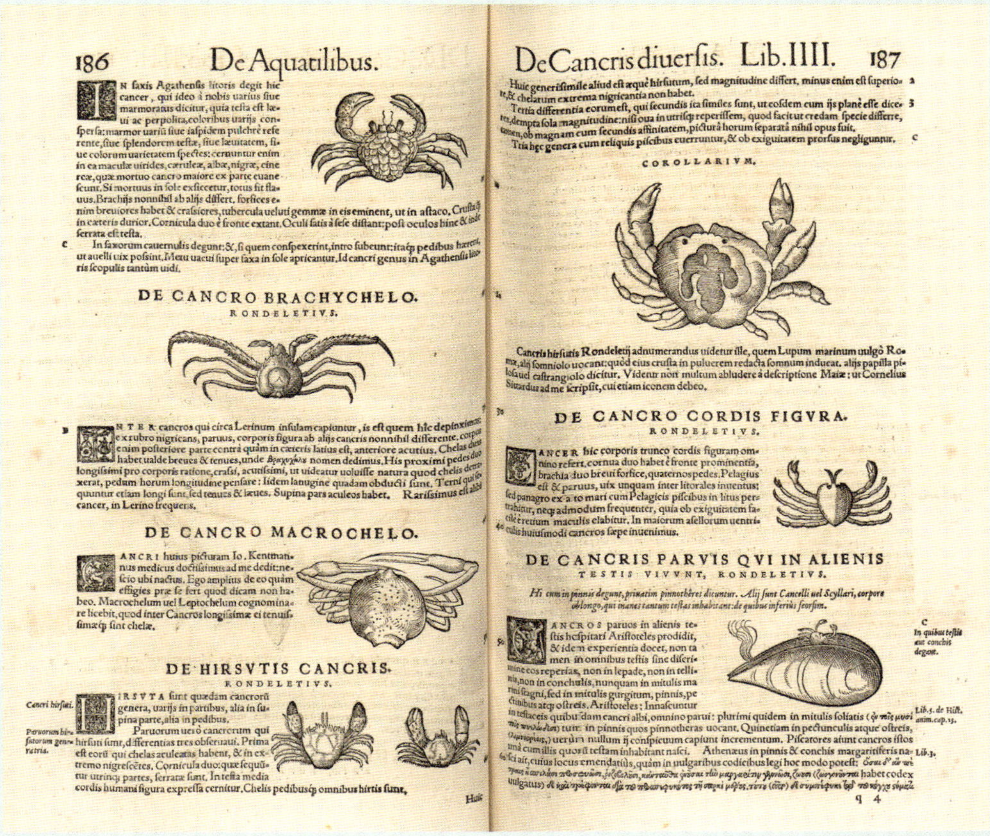
186 De Aquatilibus.

DE CANCRO BRACHYCHELO. RONDELETIVS.

DE CANCRO MACROCHELO.

DE HIRSVTIS CANCRIS. RONDELETIVS.

De Cancris diuersis. Lib. IIII. 187

COROLLARIVM.

DE CANCRO CORDIS FIGVRA. RONDELETIVS.

DE CANCRIS PARVIS QVI IN ALIENIS TESTIS VIVVNT, RONDELETIVS.

Cat. 21.3, Conrad Gessner, *Historiae Animalium, Liber IV. de Piscium & Aquatilium animantium natura*

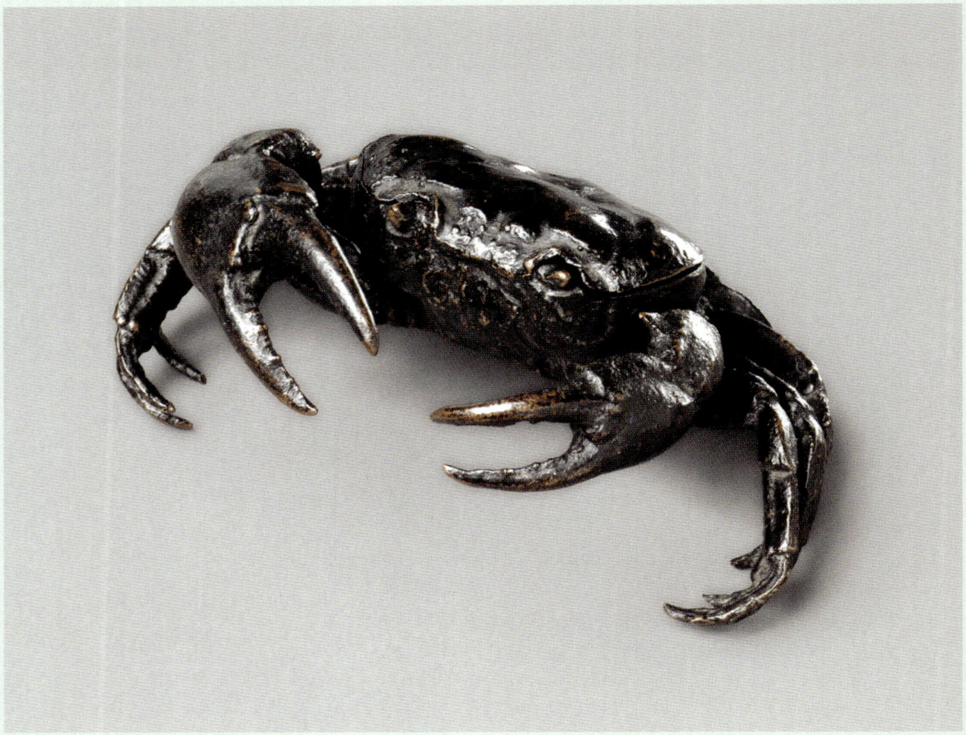

Cat. 22.1, *Crab*

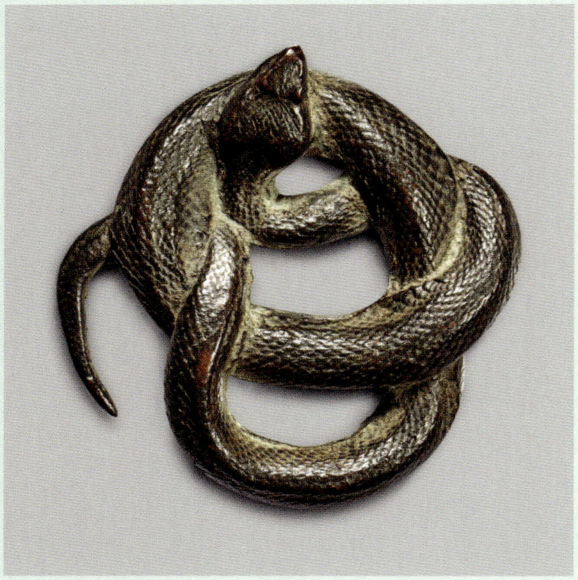

Cat. 22.2, *Snake*

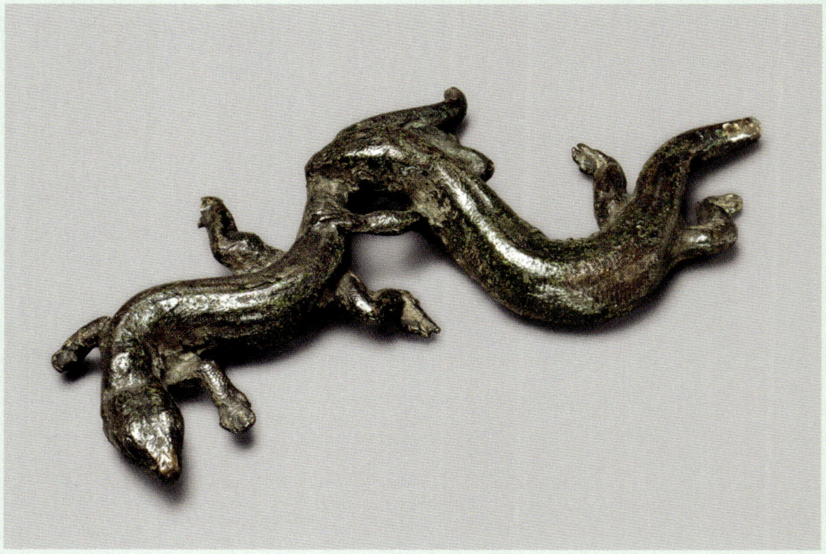

Cat. 22.3, *Two Lizards*

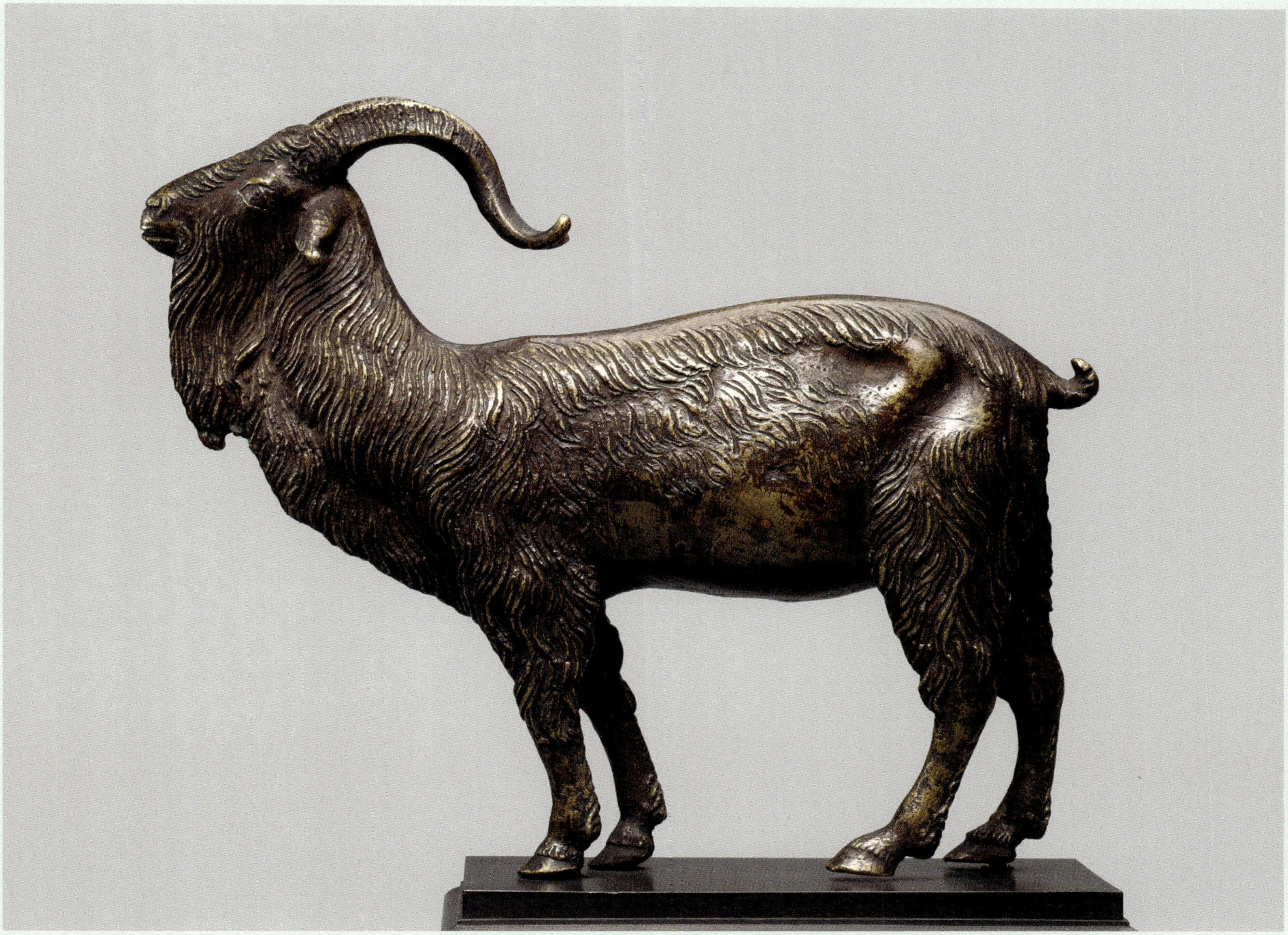

Cat. 23, after Andrea Riccio, *Billy Goat*

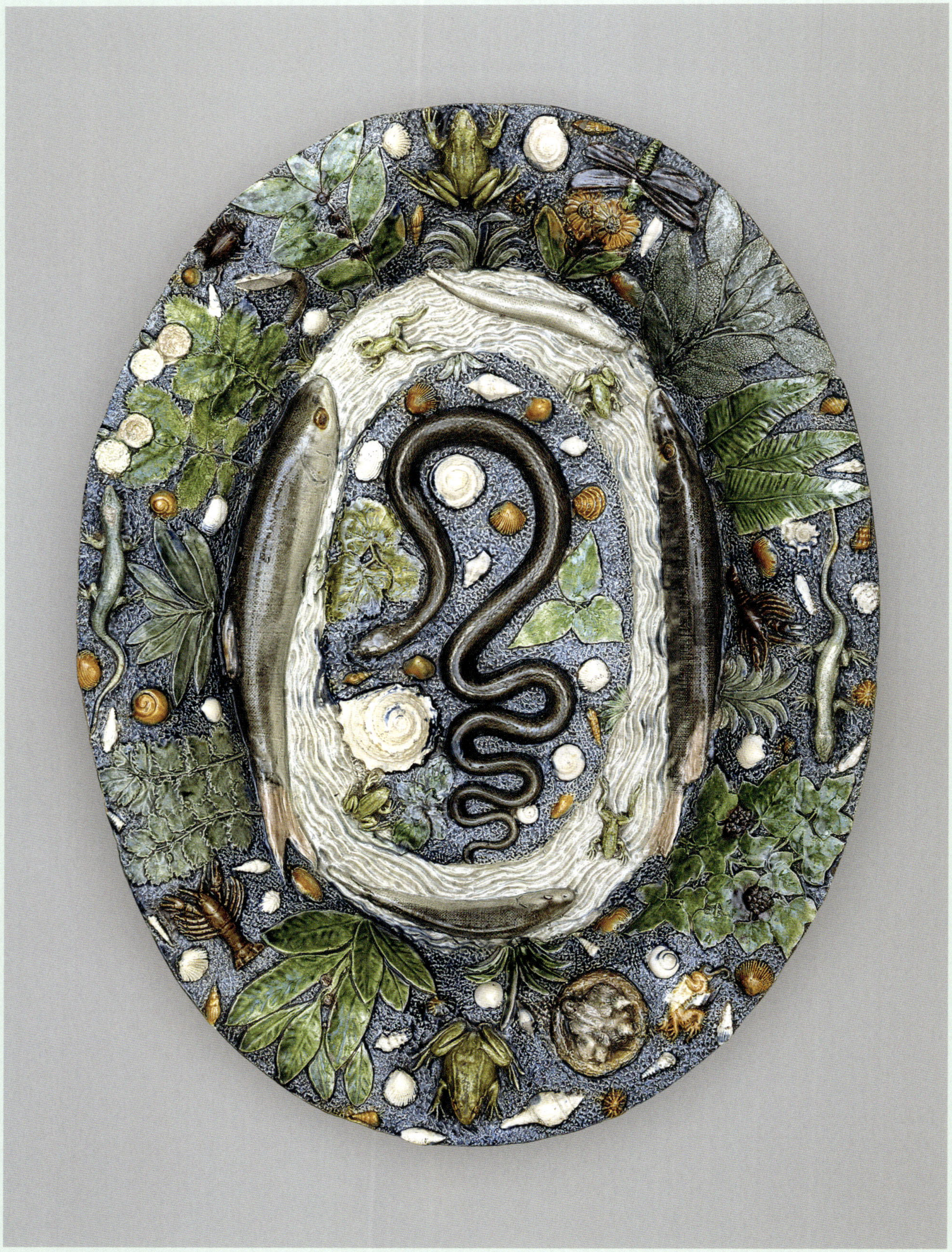

Cat. 24, Bernard Palissy (attributed), *Faience Bowl with Natural Casts*

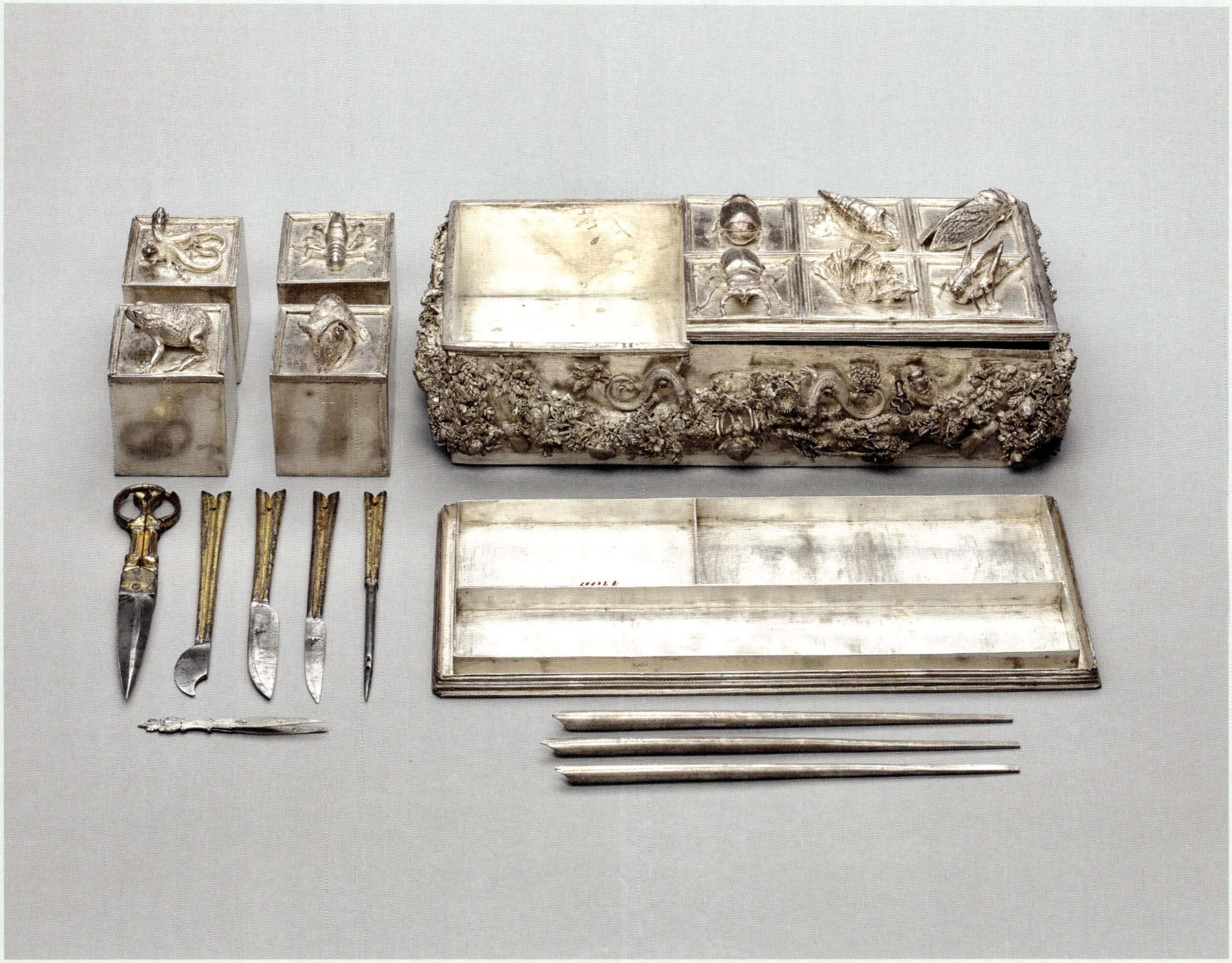

Cat. 25, Wenzel Jamnitzer, *Writing Box*

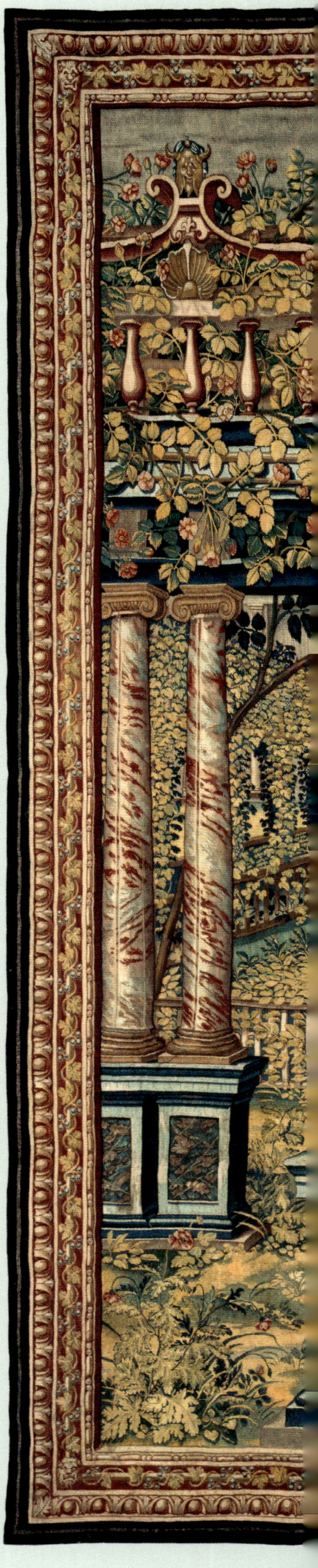

 Cat. 26, workshop of Willem de Pannemaker, *Garden Veduta with Porticoes*

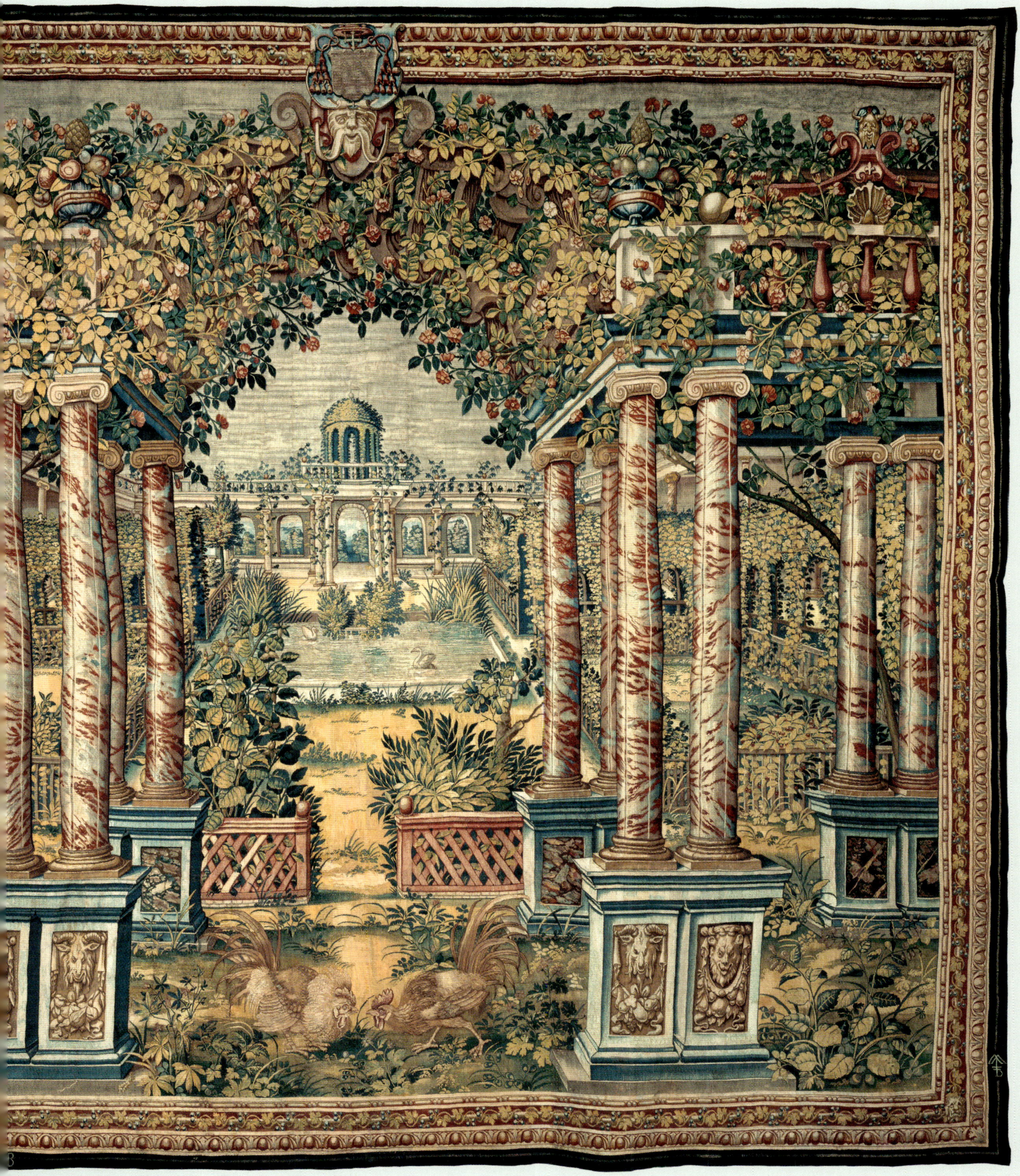

Cats. 15.1–15.3

Pieter Bruegel the Elder (1525/30–1569)

The Gloomy Day (Early Spring)

1565
Oak panel; 118 × 163 cm
Signed and dated lower right: 'BRVEGEL MCCCCC LXV'
Vienna, Kunsthistorisches Museum, Picture Gallery, inv. 1837

The Return of the Herd (Autumn)

1565
Oak panel; 117 × 159.7 cm
Traces of a signature lower left: 'BRVEGE[L]'
Vienna, Kunsthistorisches Museum, Picture Gallery, inv. 1018

Hunters in the Snow (Winter)

1565
Oak panel; 116.5 × 162 cm
Signed and dated lower middle: 'BRVEGEL. M.D.LXV'
Vienna, Kunsthistorisches Museum, Picture Gallery, inv. 1838

Provenance: Probably 1566 with Nicolaes Jongelinck, Antwerp; 1 July 1594 purchase by the City of Antwerp from Hane van Wijk and presented as gift to Archduke Ernst; 1595 Archduke Ernst's estate; 1659 already reduced to five paintings by Archduke Leopold Wilhelm

Literature: Buchanan 1990; Sellink (2007) 2011, nos. 134–8; exh. cat. Amsterdam 2009, 59–61; exh. cat. Vienna and Zurich 2011/12, 141–5, cat. 20–22 (Sabine Pénot); Kaschek 2012 (with additional literature); Meganck and Sprang 2018; Pénot and Oberthaler 2018/19

Pieter Bruegel the Elder created panoramic views of expansive landscapes in large-format panel paintings. Some are dated 1565 and together they form a cycle of the seasons. The series, originally of six parts, is not only unique within the Flemish artist's oeuvre, it also represents the culmination of an artistic interest in the cycles of the year that can be traced back to antiquity. The cycle was, in addition, groundbreaking for the development of European landscape painting (exh. cat. Vienna and Zurich 2011/12, 229). The cycle was probably commissioned by the merchant banker and art collector Nicolaes Jongelinck, who had the paintings made for his country house 't'goed ter Beke' outside Antwerp, probably for the dining room. The three works in the Kunsthistorisches Museum have borne the titles *Gloomy Day (Early Spring)*, *The Return of the Herd (Autumn)*, and *Hunters in the Snow (Winter)* since the beginning of the twentieth century. These paintings, together with the works *Haymaking (Early Summer)* in the Lobkowicz Collection in Prague (see essay Pénot, p. 39, fig. 1) and *The Harvesters (Late Summer)* in the Metropolitan Museum of Art in New York (see essay Pénot, p. 39, fig. 2) as well as a depiction of spring that is considered lost, were part of a series conceived as a cyclical frieze. The division into six seasons was quite common in the Netherlands at the time, as a distinction was made between early spring and spring as well as between early summer and late summer.

The three paintings in the Kunsthistorisches Museum display different traits for each season, characterised in the depiction of different activities, qualities of the landscape, and, in particular, varying weather conditions. *Gloomy Day* marks the beginning of the new year. The early spring landscape still bears traces of a harsh winter, evident in the snow-covered mountain peaks in the background and elsewhere. In addition, the mood is made threatening by the overcast sky, the rough waters – which have capsized a boat and left behind a flooded headland – and the dominant brown tones of the landscape. In the scene's right foreground, farmers cut willow rods and collect firewood. The new year is marked by the carnival group near the farmers, in particular the boy with the paper crown.

Bruegel characterises autumn with *The Return of the Herd*, which takes as its main theme the so-called Almabtrieb, in which herds are driven from their mountain pastures to winter in the valley. In the foreground, a group of farmers are driving a herd of cows to the village. Apart from the horseman in the foreground on the right, the people are predominantly repoussoir figures depicted in a standardized manner. In contrast, a cow in the foreground makes direct eye contact with the viewer. Barely discernible figures who almost merge with the landscape are busy harvesting grapes on a hill in the middle distance. Threatening clouds loom behind the mountains on the right, and death is also thematised by the gallows and hanged man in the distance.

The year ends with *Hunters in the Snow*, one of the earliest large-format winter landscapes, which introduced this pictorial theme to European painting. Here too, Bruegel masterfully captures the atmosphere of the time of year with the mood of the light determined by snow. A contrasting group of hunters, followed by their dogs, strides over a snow-covered hill, with a view that opens out over the valley. At the left edge of the picture, people in front of an inn are lighting a fire to roast pigs. A bird trap in the middle ground also takes up the hunting theme. Like the standardized figures, the bare trees also function as a repoussoir directing the view into the village. There, people are engaged in various recreational activities on the ice, from ice skating to the popular sport of colf (a kind of ice golf).

In this series of paintings, Bruegel addresses the relationship between the changing seasons and the cycle of human life. His observations of nature, animals, and humans and their relationship to one another are groundbreaking for the landscape and genre painting that was then emerging. The cyclical sequence of the images becomes particularly impressive when one assumes that the panels were originally mounted as a frieze, without either beginning or end of the direction of reading. Reflecting on the original group of recipients and the socio-historical context is also informative for the understanding and significance of the pictures. Based on the size of the panels, which hung on at least three walls of a room, the seasonal cycle as a whole offers an impressive, imagined world landscape, which must have contrasted sharply with the actual views from the dining room (see essay Pénot, p. 39).

Angelina Illes

Cat. 16

The Liechtenstein Tacuinum Sanitatis

Padua (?), c.1450
Illuminated manuscript on vellum, 68 folios; 160 × 170 mm
Basel, Courtesy of Dr. Jörn Günther Rare Books

Provenance: Before 1838, split into two volumes, bound and sold separately; 1838, untrimmed volume purchased by Rouen Bibliothèque municipale (now MS 3095); 1948 Princely Library, Liechtenstein, sold by Prince Joseph II to H.P. Kraus, New York; sold to Carleton R. Richmond, Boston (bookplate on the front pastedown); Sotheby's, New York, 30 October 1981, lot 48; H.P. Kraus, New York, cat. 165, sold to a private collector; Sotheby's, London, 17 December 1991, lot 50; Sam Fogg, London, 2005; private collection, Rick Adams, US (bookplate)

Literature: Cogliati Arano 1976; Kraus 1978, 1978a; Sotheby's New York 1981, lot 48; Sotheby's London 1991, lot 50; Moly Mariotti 1993, 32–39; Bovey 2005

The *Tacuinum Sanitatis*, a guide to health and well-being, was a popular text copied and widely read throughout medieval Europe. This medical handbook, with 130 illustrations, is also a unique mirror to life in fifteenth-century Padua. Four books use the same models and visual language, one of which has been securely linked to the city through the inclusion of a coat of arms (the other manuscripts are: Vienna, Österreichische Nationalbibliothek, cod. S.n. 2644; Rome, Biblioteca Casanatense, cod. 4182; Paris, Bibliothèque nationale de France, Ms. Nouv. Acq. Lat. 1673, this one with secure Lombardy provenance; and Rouen, Bibliothèque municipale, MS 3054, the other section of the Padua book).

In the codex we find depictions of everyday life: a man camouflaged with twigs hunts turtle doves; two women make pasta in a kitchen; a camel is led to slaughter; and a man samples dried figs in a shop. In between the illustration of basil and crocus (from which saffron is derived) a man is harvesting a mythological mandrake, and towards the end of the codex are depictions of the four cardinal winds. Originally written in Arabic by Ibn Butlān in the eleventh century, the text was translated in the thirteenth century to Latin, and made available to European audiences in different versions. Drawing on the Galenic medical tradition, the text explains how to adjust the internal humours through diets and adjusting other aspects of a person's life. The humours were believed to fluctuate by day and night, as a person aged, and as the seasons changed. Thus, four fascinating illustrations of the seasons are included: in summer, a man and woman harvest wheat against a dark green landscape; in autumn, a group of men and women harvest grapes and make wine; in winter, an old man warms his hands in front of a fire while a servant approaches; and in spring a group of young men and women congregate in a verdant landscape. It is likely that these motifs, alongside other depictions of daily life (found in this and the other four manuscripts in the same group) inspired and influenced the frescoes depicting the cycle of the twelve months that were painted on the walls of Torre Aquila, the palace of the Prince-Bishop, probably before 1407. The springtime lovers in this manuscript are particularly closely echoed in the depiction of men and women exchanging flowers in a verdant May landscape.

Sara Öberg Strådal

Cat. 17

Andrea Briosco, called Riccio (1470–1532)
Mower at Rest

Padua, c.1500
Terracotta, painted; H 37 cm, W 25 cm, D 31.5 cm
Vienna, Kunsthistorisches Museum, Kunstkammer, inv. KK 7345

Provenance: Padua; acquired by Carlo Zuber in Venice; collection Guido von Rho; collection Dr Heinrich Studer; 20 July 1920 gift of Prince Johann II of Liechtenstein
Literature: Beitl 1995; exh. cat. Trento 2008, 61, 73; exh. cat. Trento 2018, 38, 42, 48; Schlegel 2022, 14–17

He is visibly exhausted and slumps in a sleepy, pensive position. His tools have been laid to the side. Is this a man taking a well-earned break or is his daily work finished? The sculpture provides a haunting image of a farm labourer whose striking, individual face is touching. As in the detailed pictures from Labours of the Months cycles, this mower's clothing also provides clues to his social status. They are work clothes and the accoutrements of common people, far removed from the stately portraits of nobility with which we are so familiar. We see a loose shirt open at the front, revealing a bare, hairy chest. No trouser legs are visible, but the mower could be wearing shorts. His feet are in coarse leather shoes with straps tied very simply around the ankles. One shoe is already so worn – perhaps from the hard labour – that his toes are sticking out. His head is covered by a flat-brimmed hat, which provides protection from the hot, merciless, summer sun.

The man's seated posture is particularly striking. This is a pose that can be found in medieval works of art depicting 'Christ at Rest'. In this sculpture, however, the religious subject is transformed into a secular one. This reflects a break with society's previous spiritual worldview. The visual arts of the Renaissance discovered people's everyday lives, took their ordinary activities as themes, and provided glimpses into their world. Such genre scenes, with their interiors and still lifes, were in great demand among the affluent upper middle class and the elites of the time. Thus, art also provided a 'look through the keyhole' at an uncomfortable and unknown world. The Paduan sculptor Riccio may have modelled his resting mower on a typical farm worker of the Venetian Terraferma, growing grain in the hinterlands of the Serenissima.

Thomas Kuster

Cats. 18.1–18.3

Calendar

Tirol, 16th cent.
Leather, vellum, closed; H 8.2 cm, W 5.2 cm, D 3 cm
Ambras Castle Innsbruck, inv. KK 5368
Provenance: 1821 Ambras Inventory, no. 22
Literature: Exh. cat. Innsbruck 2012, 85, cat. 2.5

Farmer's Calendar (Runic Calendar)

German, 2nd half of 16th cent.
Wood, paper; H 21.2 cm, W 5.6 cm
Ambras Castle Innsbruck, inv. KK 5431
Provenance: 1847 from the Antikenkabinett; 1875 Ambras Collection, X, 82, S. 262
Literature: Exh. cat. Innsbruck 2012, 85, cat. 2.5

Farmer's Calendar ('Mandlkalender')

Augsburg (?), 1588
Ivory, silk, silver thread; H 10.3 cm, W 2.2 cm
Ambras Castle Innsbruck, inv. KK 5422
Provenance: 1847 from the Antikenkabinett; 1875 Ambras Collection, IX, 183, 230
Literature: Schindler 1964; Hallonquist 2010

Astronomical calendars are not based on arithmetical rules, but astronomical events, such as the phases of the moon, the position of the sun, or the positions of celestial bodies. In the sixteenth century they were used, for example, to determine the best time to treat various diseases or for personal hygiene, or to determine the appropriate time for planting, sowing, felling, ploughing, or spreading manure. In humor–pathological theory a distinction was made between signs of the zodiac that were dry (such as Aries, Capricorn, Leo) and and those that were wet (Pisces, Aquarius, Cancer). The most suitable constellations for bathing were those when the moon was in the moist signs of the zodiac; Leo and Virgo were particularly suitable for haircuts and shaves. The best months for bloodletting, for prophylactic, therapeutic, or diagnostic purposes, were April and December, as were certain days counted after the full moon: the 6th, 11th, 17th, 18th, 21st through 26th, and 28th. If something had to be done at another time, a calculation was made based on the location to determine which days were advisable for bloodletting and which points on the body were most suitable. The symbols on individual days of the calendar could also provide information about the phases of the moon, weather, signs of the zodiac, planets, and which days were favourable for eye remedies, purging, or weaning children.

The open page of the *Calendar* (inv. KK 5368) shows the month of May with various symbols; the folded page is marked by the zodiac sign Cancer as the following month of June. Each of the six ivory panels of the *Farmer's Calendar* (inv. KK 5422) is engraved with two months from the year 1588. From left to right, information is given about the length of a day, the sign of the month, the sign of the zodiac, the number of days in the month, festivals, and the phases of the moon. A precursor to this calendar was probably the so-called *Runic Calendar* (inv. KK 5431) made of wood and paper. A Swedish tradition was thought to be the origin of these 'perpetual calendars' that spread throughout northern Europe between the late thirteenth and the middle of the eighteenth century. Runic calendars comprised three lines each: the first line contained important saints' days and other crucial days for agriculture. The second stood for the dating of the Sundays in a year. There, the first seven runes were repeated 52 times for the 52 weeks; a specific rune represented a specific day of the week in each year. The third line marked the date of the lunar phases, the so-called 'golden numbers', on which the best times for sowing and harvesting were based.

Katharina Seidl

Cat. 19

Leonhart Fuchs (1501–1566)
De historia stirpium commentarii

Basel (Michael Isingrin) 1542
Vienna, Austrian National Library, Picture Archives and Graphics Department, 263875-D FID, 316–7

Literature: Exh. cat. Innsbruck and Vienna 2006/07, 56–7, cat. 2.7 (Katharina Seidl); Kusukawa 2012

Leonhart Fuchs's *De historia stirpium* of 1542 represented an important milestone in the science of botany. The physician and botanist wanted to revitalise the medical knowledge of the ancients with this universal history of plants. Unlike texts by classical authors such as Pliny the Elder, Pedanius Dioscorides, or Galen, images were an integral part of Fuchs's scientific argument. He commented on their significance in the foreword: 'Who, I ask, will with reason despise the image, which certainly depicts things much more clearly than any words, even the most eloquent words, can capture.' ('Quis quaeso sanae mentis picturam contemneret, quam constat res multo clarius exprimere, quam verbis ullis, etiam eloquentissimorum, delineari queant.')

For the illustrations, Fuchs favoured a detailed drawing (*ad vivarum stirpium lineamenta et effigies*), free of any artistic fancies (*neque passi sumus ut sic libidini suae indulgerent artifices*). Each kind of plant was recorded 'as complete as possible' (*absolutissima*) on one sheet, i.e., from the root to the leaf and showing all stages of growth – from the seed to the buds and flowers to the fruit.

The woodcuts of the exhibited example were hand-coloured. The subsequent colouring may have been an integral part of the original design, as the woodcuts show only slight shading. The less well-off reader, however, had to be satisfied with the non-standardized colour terminology and a description of variations in colour in the text.

With more than 500 woodcuts of European and exotic plants, *De historia stirpium* bears witness to the new relationship between art and the natural sciences. The botanist paid tribute to the artists in the unusual portraits on the last page: Albrecht Meyer (*pictor*) draws a plant, which Heinrich Füllmaurer (*pictor*) transfers to the wooden block, which in turn is cut by Veit Rudolf Specklin (*sculptor*). Fuchs's praise of the block cutter's skills in his preface, who has so skilfully expressed the outlines of each picture by carving (*sculpendo*) that he seemes to compete with the painter for glory and victory, recalls the Renaissance topos of *paragone*.

The Latin edition of the book was followed in 1543 by the simplified German-language *New Kreüterbuch* ('New Herb Book') for the 'common man' and in 1545 by a version reduced to the woodcuts and plant names, which could be used outdoors thanks to its handy octavo format.

Alexandra Sattler

Cats. 20.1–20.3

Pietro Andrea Mattioli (1501–1577)

Commentarii, In Libros Sex Pedacii Dioscoridis Anazarbei, De Medica materia

Venice (Vincenzo Valgrisi), 1554
Vienna, Austrian National Library, Department of Manuscripts and Rare Books, 69.P.32 Alt Prunk, 132–3; 68.B.17 Alt Prunk, 204–5

Commentarii Secvndo Avcti, In Libros Sex Pedacii Dioscoridis Anazarbei De Medica materia

Venice (Vincenzo Valgrisi), 1558
Vienna, Austrian National Library, Department of Manuscripts and Rare Books, 69.A.85 Alt Prunk, 266–7

Literature: Ferri 2001; Omodeo 2001; Tongiorgi Tomasi 2001; Tosi 2001; exh. cat. Innsbruck and Vienna 2006/07, 57–60, cat. 2.8 (Margot Rauch); exh. cat. Innsbruck 2015, 262–3, cat. 6.2 (Katharina Seidl)

The natural scientist Pietro Andrea Mattioli of Siena enjoyed great success with his publication of *Materia Medica* by the Greek physician Dioscorides, a foundational work on herbal, animal, and mineral medicine and their use that dated back to the first century CE. Mattioli translated the book, along with commentaries, from Greek to make its knowledge available to his contemporaries. He found the ideal conditions for this work first in 1527, when he was physician and adviser at the court of Bishop Bernardo Clesio in Trento, and later in 1542 as the city physician of Gorizia. He made studies of native plants while on research trips that took him as far as the Alps and Monte Baldo, Lake Garda, and along the Adriatic coast of Trieste and Istria. Mattioli sought out samples from the Middle East in apothecary's shops in the harbour cities of Venice and Naples. To observe how the plants grow, he planted a garden in Gorizia and visited those of specialists.

The first edition of the book, titled *Discorsi*, was published in 1544 in the Italian vernacular *volgare*; it was intended for practical use by physicians and pharmacists. Nevertheless, the work also attracted the interest of scientists working with medicinal plants, particularly professors at the University of Padua. From that point on, Mattioli would receive unidentified plants and information about them and he began corresponding with individuals such as Luca Ghini, Ulisse Aldrovandi, Francesco Calzolari, Giacomo Antonio Cortuso, and Ogier Ghislain de Busbecq. Over the years, they contributed new findings, which were reflected in ever-expanding new editions.

Worth mentioning is the first Latin edition of 1554, now titled *Commentarii*, that made the work known to an even broader, now also international audience and was the first to feature magnificent woodcuts. Originally, natural scientists believed that a precise mastery of medicinal plants could not be achieved through pictures, since the plants were not represented in all stages of their development. From this edition on, however, Mattioli spared no effort or expense to supplement the text with drawings *dal vivo*.

Mattioli must have relied on several artists for the 600 or so woodcuts, though he only mentions two of them in his preface. The talented young painter Giorgio Liberale made drawings of the herbal and animal remedies on paper and Wolfgang Meyerpeck from Meissen carved them into the wooden moulds. Copies intended for illustrious personages were coloured and decorated with gold and silver, such as the copy Mattioli sent to the Hapsburg monarch Ferdinand I. In 1555, Mattioli was appointed physician at the court in Prague, where he became acquainted with new plants and medical practices in Bohemia, Germany, Austria, and Hungary. Giorgio Liberale remained a great help with the new illustrations, drawing plants as well as live animals with 'arte' (art), 'ingegno' (genius), and 'patientia inestimabile' (inestimable patience) (see *Epistola* of the 1555 Valgrisi edition). Under Habsburg patronage, Liberale contributed full-page plates to the Prague edition of the *Commentarii*. These were integrated into the prestigious Latin edition of 1565, which comprised around 900 plant and 100 animal illustrations.

The plates on the health effects of animal products show the creatures in their natural environment or during the making of these products. Thus, scenes from rural life such as milking cows, making butter, or shearing sheep are depicted. Dioscorides had discussed honey, milk, fats, and animal feed; Mattioli supplemented that knowledge with vivid descriptions of the animals' habits, which he had observed during his excursions.

Just as in science, themes of peasant and pastoral life also attracted the attention of renowned artists such as Lucas van Leyden (cat. 57) or Titian (cat. 58). The plates of the *Commentarii* were not only studied by scholars, they obviously also served as models for painters. Corn and an aubergine, for example, can be found in Giuseppe Arcimboldo's *Summer* (cat. 29.1).
Alexandra Sattler

Cats. 21.1–21.3

Conrad Gessner (1516–1565)

Historiae Animalium, Liber I. de Quadrupedibus viviparis

Zurich (Christoph Froschauer) 1551, 2°
Vienna, Austrian National Library,
Picture Archives and Graphics Department,
252193-D.1 FID, vol. I, 173

Historiae Animalium, Liber III. de Avium natura

Zurich (Christoph Froschauer) 1555, 2°
Vienna, Austrian National Library,
Picture Archives and Graphics Department,
252193-D.3 FID, vol. III, 464

Historiae Animalium, Liber IV. de Piscium & Aquatilium animantium natura

Zurich (Christoph Froschauer) 1558, 2°
Vienna, Austrian National Library,
Picture Archives and Graphics Department,
252193-D.4 FID, vol. IV, 186–7

Literature: Exh. cat Innsbruck and Vienna 2006/07, 87, cat. 2.35 (Katharina Seidl); Fischel 2009, 18–73; Kusukawa 2010; Kusukawa 2012; Egmond 2013; exh.cat. Innsbruck 2015, 264–5, cat. 6.3 (Katharina Seidl); Egmond and Kusukawa 2016

Swiss physician Conrad Gessner is considered one of the founding fathers of modern zoology. In his encyclopaedic work the *Historiae animalium*, published in Zurich between 1551 and 1558, he compiled all the knowledge of fauna available at the time. He based his classification on ancient authors, in particular Aristotle's standard work of the same name. Gessner divided the animal world into four volumes in which the animals are organised alphabetically: *Quadrupedes vivipares* (live-bearing quadrupeds, 1551), *Quadrupedes ovipares* (egg-laying quadrupeds, 1554), *Avium natura* (birds, 1555), and *Piscium et aquatilium animantium natura* (fish and aquatic animals, 1558).

An important innovation of Gessner's was an iconographic apparatus that allowed the animals with his compendium of over 3,500 folios to be viewed 'quovis tempore et perpetuo' (at any time and forever) and 'absque labore, absque periculo' (without effort, without danger). Gessner placed the illustrations of the animals at the beginning of each chapter under their Latin names. At the time, printed pictures were expensive, which is why wood blocks were usually reused for other books, and pictures were copied. Gessner, in contrast, used his own funds to commission woodcuts in order to guarantee a consistent image–text relationship and to ensure that the animal depictions were true to life. During his research, he compiled a cabinet of naturalia with a collection of pictures, of which only a few animal drawings have survived (Felix Platter estate).

Since it was impossible for one man to have personally observed all the fauna in the world, Gessner turned to naturalist friends – including Ulisse Aldrovandi, whom he regarded as the most diligent and successful collector of natural specimens. In the preface to his first volume, he mentions around fifty contemporaries who contributed depictions or descriptions of animals. In addition, he used other scientific treatises as sources or relied on works of art, the most famous of which is probably Albrecht Dürer's *Rhinoceros*. In addition, he had pictures made *ad vivum* by painters, of whom Lucas Schan and Jos Murer are known by name. To ensure that the illustrations were as accurate as possible, he doublechecked the received templates and made corrections. He attributed possible errors to the large number of painters and the fact that the publisher supervised the work's production, as a result of which, for example, pictures were not arranged in the correct order.

The naturalist regretted that the illustrations could not be printed in colour, which plays an important role in distinguishing species. However, for those willing to pay more, a hand-coloured copy could be purchased from the publisher Froschauer. Even though Gessner provided a coloured master copy 'ad archetypum', he had to complain about incorrect reproduction by the painter, saying that due to the printer's avarice he had applied the paint 'negligenter' (carelessly) and 'defunctorie' (perfunctorily).

As early as 1560, Gessner had his woodcuts reprinted without text as *Icones Animalium*. They were no longer arranged alphabetically but in supposedly 'natural' order, according to their living conditions or cultural contexts. Many artists used his plates as models for animals they could never observe themselves. Thus, Gessner's animals can be found in stained-glass art, tapestries, metalwork, paintings, and even the embroidery of Mary, Queen of Scots.
Alexandra Sattler

Cats. 22.1–22.3

Crab

Northern Italy, 1st half 16th cent.
Bronze; H 7 cm, W 13 cm, D 12.5 cm
Vienna, Kunsthistorisches Museum,
Kunstkammer, inv. KK 5922
Provenance: 1880 Ambras Collection, VI, 513
Literature: Planiscig 1924, IV, 39, cat. 64; Kris 1926; exh. cat. Vienna 1987, 367, cat. VIII/64; exh. cat. Innsbruck and Vienna 2006/07, 103, cat. 2.46; exh. cat. Paris and Vienna 2007/08, 198, cat. V.7 (Kryza-Gersch); exh. cat. Innsbruck 2015, 244–5, cats. 5.10.1–2

Snake

Northern Italy, 1st half 15th cent.
Bronze; H 2.5 cm, W 10.5 cm, D 10.3 cm
Vienna, Kunsthistorisches Museum,
Kunstkammer, inv. KK 5929
Provenance: 1880 Ambras Collection, VI, 519
Literature: Planiscig 1924, IV, 37, cat. 61;
exh. cat. Frankfurt 1985, 204, 543, cat. 277;
exh. cat. Innsbruck 2015, 244–5, cat. 5.10.1;
exh. cat. Tokyo 2017, 118–9, cat. III.13;
exh. cat. Rome 2017/18, 109, cat. III.2.3

Two Lizards

Northern Italy, 1st half 15th cent.
Bronze; H 2 cm, W 8 cm, D 18 cm
Vienna, Kunsthistorisches Museum,
Kunstkammer, inv. KK 5920
Provenance: 1821 inventory, I, S.179 ('von Wutky'); 1880 Ambras Collection, VI, 470
Literature: Planiscig 1924, IV, 39; exh. cat. Schallaburg 1976, 105, cat. 137 (M. Leithe-Jasper); exh. cat. Vienna 1987, 367, cat. VIII/65A; exh. cat. Innsbruck 2015, 244–5, cat. 5.10.2

A crab, a snake, and two lizards cast from nature. This technique has its origins in the death masks made in antiquity, a custom that came into the service of portrait sculpture in the fifteenth century. At the same time, the perfected technical possibilities were also applied to other areas. In an attempt to imitate nature as closely as possible, smaller and smaller plants and animals were cast. To achieve this, a dead animal or plant was placed in the desired position by the caster and coated with a wet clay-water mixture in order to preserve even the finest details. After an additional coating of firmer clay, it was fired at a high temperature until the model inside was burnt to ash, thus leaving a hollow mould for casting. This refined technique, the result of a demand for the most precise observation of the natural model possible, found its philosophical foundation in the Aristotelian principle of the imitation of nature.

The writings of the painter Cennini, who had already described the technique of natural moulding around 1390, influenced the establishment of large production facilities, particularly in Italy – for example, Andrea Riccio's foundry in Padua.

Only one natural cast could be produced using this process since the mould was destroyed after casting. In order to save material and reduce manufacturing costs, the hollow casting process was developed, in which impressions of the animal were made in two or more parts. The partial moulds were filled with liquid wax so that a thin layer of wax remained. The excess wax was poured away. The form with the thin layer of wax was filled with a core of clay and completely covered with clay. The wax was then melted out and the mould filled with molten metal. Because such partial forms necessary for the impressions could be reused, it was possible to make several identical casts of a subject.

Natural casts were coveted collector's items in courtly Chambers of art and wonders. Emperor Rudolf II, for example, owned numerous silver casts of various animals, which are listed in the inventory of his *Kunstkammer* compiled between 1607 and 1611.

Katharina Seidl

Cat. 23

After Andrea Briosco, called Riccio (1470–1532)

Billy Goat

Padua, 16th cent.
Bronze; H 16.5 cm, W 20 cm
Vienna, Kunsthistorisches Museum,
Kunstkammer, inv. KK 5707

Provenance: 1750 in the Imperial Treasury
Literature: Zimmermann 1889, 10, CCCX, cat. 33; Planiscig 1924, IV, 40, cat. 70; Planiscig 1927, 197; Cessi 1965, 104; exh. cat. New York 2008, 128, cat. 6.2

A small billy goat made of light-coloured bronze is depicted standing with its head raised. Its shaggy coat and curved horns are naturalistically modelled; it looks as if the goat is catching a scent. Its solid stature and massive backward-curving horns, as well as the unusually short hair on its belly, suggest that it could be a Valdostana goat. This breed was used for show fights in the Alpine region (especially Italy's Valle d'Aosta) as early as the sixteenth century. The Kunsthistorisches Museum also holds another very similar work, albeit with an open mouth (inv. KK 5705).

Goats were among the most popular motifs in animal sculpture during the Renaissance. They offered an opportunity to translate newly acquired knowledge about locomotion into artistic form. Goats and sheep were probably the most important farm animals for milk production in the sixteenth century. The royal courts of the Renaissance kept goats for agricultural purposes, in addition to deer, hares, rabbits, and pheasants.

Depictions of goats also served as a reminder of bucolic antique models. In Greek mythology, the nymph Amaltheia, in the form of a goat, nursed the newborn Zeus after his mother Rhea abandoned him on Crete to protect him from his father Kronos. He received ambrosia and nectar from Amaltheia's horns. To show his gratitude, Zeus placed her in the sky as the star Capella (Latin for 'little goat'). He also transformed her broken horn into a cornucopia, which became a symbol of the fertility of nature and an attribute of blessings bestowed by the deities.

Katharina Seidl

Cat. 24

Bernard Palissy (1510–1589), attributed

Faience Bowl with Natural Casts

2nd half 16th cent.
Faience, adorned, glazed, and painted;
H 53 cm, W 40 cm, D 7 cm
Vienna, MAK – Museum of Applied Arts,
inv. KE 3694

Provenance: Acquired 1891
Literature: Exh. cat. Schallaburg 2024, 223

This oval bowl is decorated with foliage and a myriad of aquatic animals in colourful glazed relief. Like an aqua-terrarium, it reveals a unique world of extremely naturalistic animals and plants, among which a trout and pike, as well as a grass snake – the central motif – frogs, lizards, dragonflies, shells, snails, crayfish, ivy foliage with berries, burnet leaves, sage and fern leaves (hart's-tongue?) can be clearly identified. In order to achieve this degree of fidelity to nature, the French scientist, stained-glass artist, and potter Bernard Palissy developed his own ceramic process, which worked with casts of actual small animals, plants, snails, and mussels.

This so-called 'rustic' ware enjoyed great popularity in the sixteenth century. It is often difficult to distinguish pieces from Palissy's own workshop from those of a series of successors who quickly adopted his style. Imitations and variations of his works were produced in France until around 1800 and experienced a renaissance in the nineteenth century.

In addition to his sixteen years attempting to recreate Chinese porcelain, Palissy is also known for his contributions to the natural sciences, particularly for his discovery of various principles of geology, hydrology, and the formation of fossils.

Palissy was imprisoned for his Protestant faith during the turbulent French Wars of Religion and sentenced to death. He died in 1589, before his planned execution, as a result of his maltreatment in the Bastille.

Katharina Seidl

Cat. 25

Wenzel Jamnitzer (1507/08–1585)

Writing Box

Nuremberg, c.1560/70
Silver; H 6 cm, W 22.7 cm, D 10.2 cm
Vienna, Kunsthistorisches Museum, Kunstkammer,
invs. KK 1155–1164

Provenance: 1596 listed in the estate inventory of Archduke Ferdinand II at Schloss Ambras, fol. 356v: 'Ain schöner silberner alter schreibzeug mit vil luckhen, darauf allerlai keferwerch, auf den seiten mit gegossnem laub[w]erch, wigt 10 markh 12 lot' ('A pretty, old, silver writing box with many sections, with various small animals and insects, with cast leaves on the side, weighs 10 mark, 12 lot'); 1621 Ambras Inv., fol. 125v/126r; 1821 Ambras Inv., 506, no. 10; 1875 Ambras Castle., XVIII, 66, 336
Literature: Exh. cat. Paris and Vienna 2007/08, 200–1, V.10; mus. cat. Vienna 2010, 120, cat. 50

The lid of this simple, rectangular, silver writing box is divided into ten square panels. A section of the lid comprising six panels can be opened; the other four can be removed individually. Inside are several compartments and a pounce pot. Three silver quill pens, three small knives, an etching blade, scissors with a gold-plated handle, and tweezers are stored in four compartments in the false bottom, from which the main box can be separated.

The distinctive feature of the box is its elaborate decoration. On the lid's ten panels are natural casts, in silver, of small creatures, specifically a grasshopper, a butterfly, two snails, three different beetles, a small mouse, a toad, and two lizards. The sides are also decorated with similar natural casts (crayfish, frogs, lizards, spiders, etc.), and grasses and blossoms spread out like garlands.

Wenzel Jamnitzer, born in Vienna, started working as a goldsmith some time in or before 1534. In addition to commissions from wealthy citizens and secular and ecclesiastical princes, he also did work for Emperor Ferdinand I, Emperor Maximilian II, and Archduke Ferdinand II. He conducted a lively correspondence with the latter regarding a silver fountain with a depiction of the creation of Adam and Eve in Paradise, a piece he was supposed to make but which remained unfinished. Ferdinand II placed particular importance on natural casts. He even asked Jamnitzer to send a specialist who could teach him, the archduke, the technique. As well as the high quality of artistic execution, it was this close contact between artist and archduke that led the writing box to be attributed to Jamnitzer, despite it missing the usual Jamnitzer stamp.

Katharina Seidl

Cat. 26

Workshop of Willem de Pannemaker (c.1510–1581)

Garden Veduta with Porticoes. In the Foreground Two Fighting Cocks

Series title: *Garden Landscapes*
Brussels, 1564
Wool, silk; H 376 cm, W 423 cm
Vienna, Kunsthistorisches Museum, Kunstkammer,
inv. T LXVI/6

Provenance: Antoine Perrenot de Granvelle (1517–1586; patron); from the estate of Emperor Rudolf II
Literature: Piquard 1950; Bauer 2000, 151–4, 361–3, nos. 160–1; exh. cat. Lemgo and Antwerp 2002, 210–11, no. 33 (Thomas Fusenig); Schmitz-von Ledebur 2024, *74–85*

In the Renaissance, that age of humanist scholars and the revival of antiquity, artfully designed gardens and cabinets of curiosities were regarded as microcosms of divine creation. Their diversity of familiar and exotic flora and fauna provided ample material for empirical knowledge. As a result, well-designed gardens gained enormous importance in the context of courtly representation. We also know that Cardinal Antoine Perrenot de Granvelle, a cultured statesman and diplomat in the service of the Habsburgs, was a passionate enthusiast of gardens. He had an equally great interest in tapestries. Of particular importance is a commission for a series of six tapestries depicting extensive gardens, which combined his passion for tapestries with his passion for nature.

In 1564, the popular Brussels manufactory of Willem de Pannemaker undertook to make the tapestries, which – executed with technical perfection – convey a deceptively realistic impression. The compositions, which were based on ancient writings as well as contemporary architectural treatises, may also have appealed to the scholarly interests of the humanistically educated cardinal. Their symmetrical structure and their design, which adheres to the laws of proportion and central perspective, mark the idealized gardens depicted in the tapestries as artificial objects. The native and exotic plants and animals also do justice to the representative, costly appearance of the tapestries.

This tapestry with two fighting cocks is dedicated to the principle of Ionic architecture. The cock symbolises the sunrise and vigilance; here, it also symbolises pugnacity. The marbled columns with Ionic capitals are particularly graceful. Roses, a symbol of innocence and beauty, as well as being a token of the Virgin Mary since the Middle Ages, entwine the arched entrance to the garden. Together they accentuate the subtle yet dignified character of this composition.

Katja Schmitz-von Ledebur

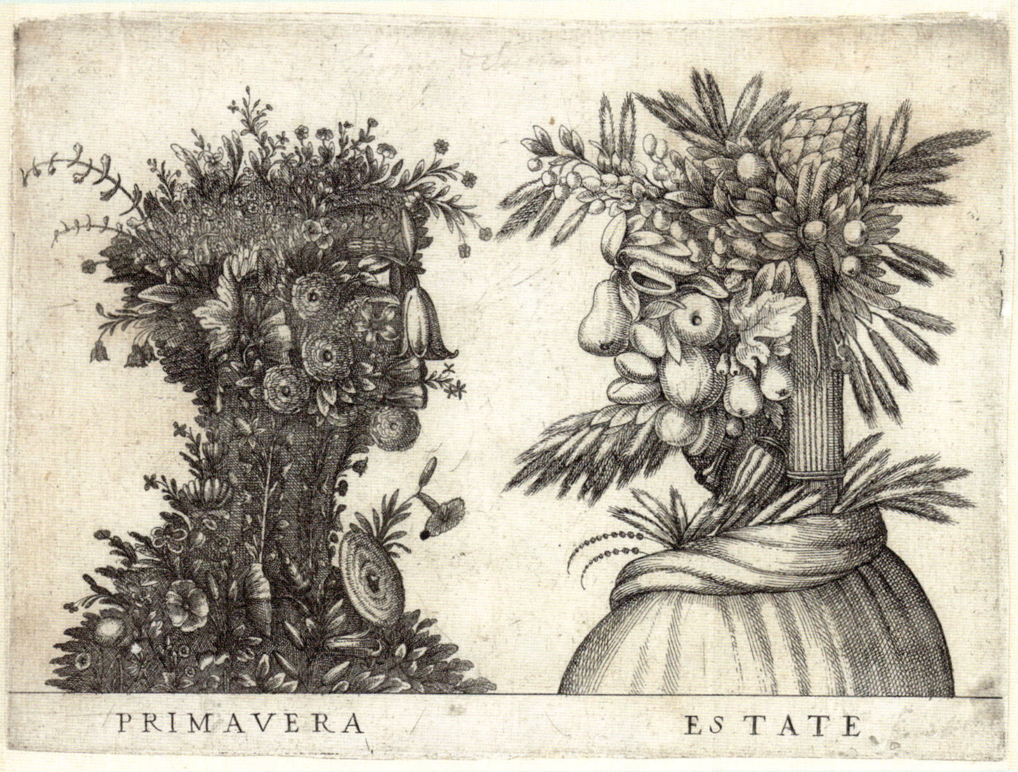

Cat. 27.1, after Giuseppe Arcimboldo, *Allegory of the Four Seasons: Spring and Summer*

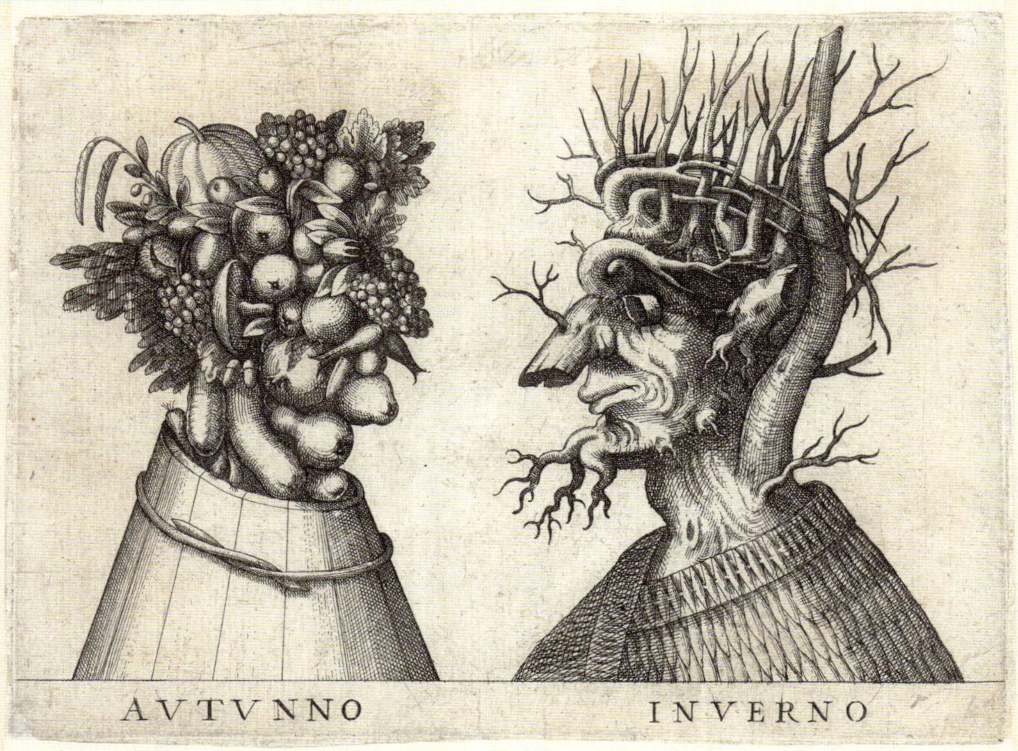

Cat. 27.2, after Giuseppe Arcimboldo, *Allegory of the Four Seasons: Autumn and Winter*

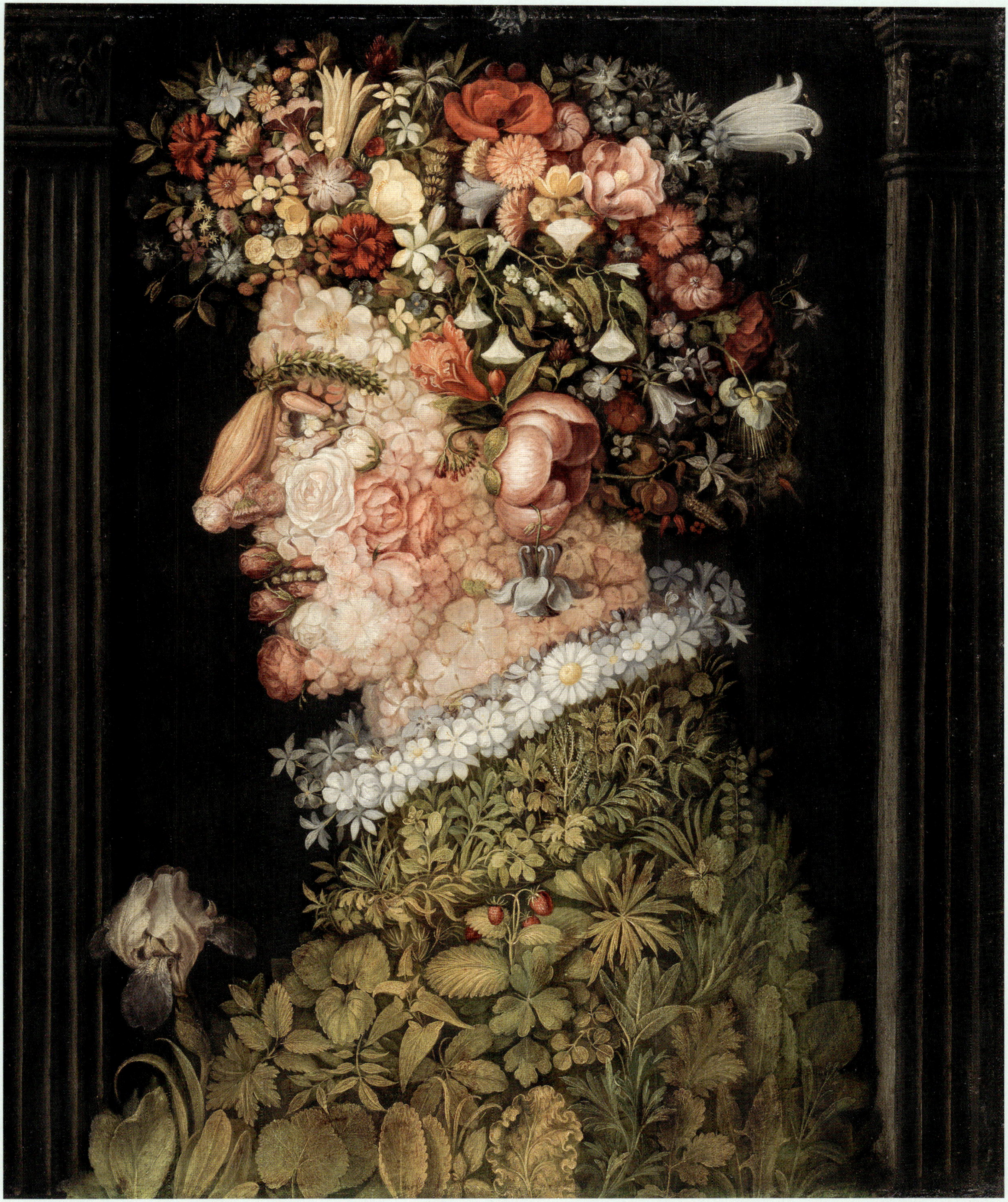

Cat. 28.1, Giuseppe Arcimboldo, *Spring*

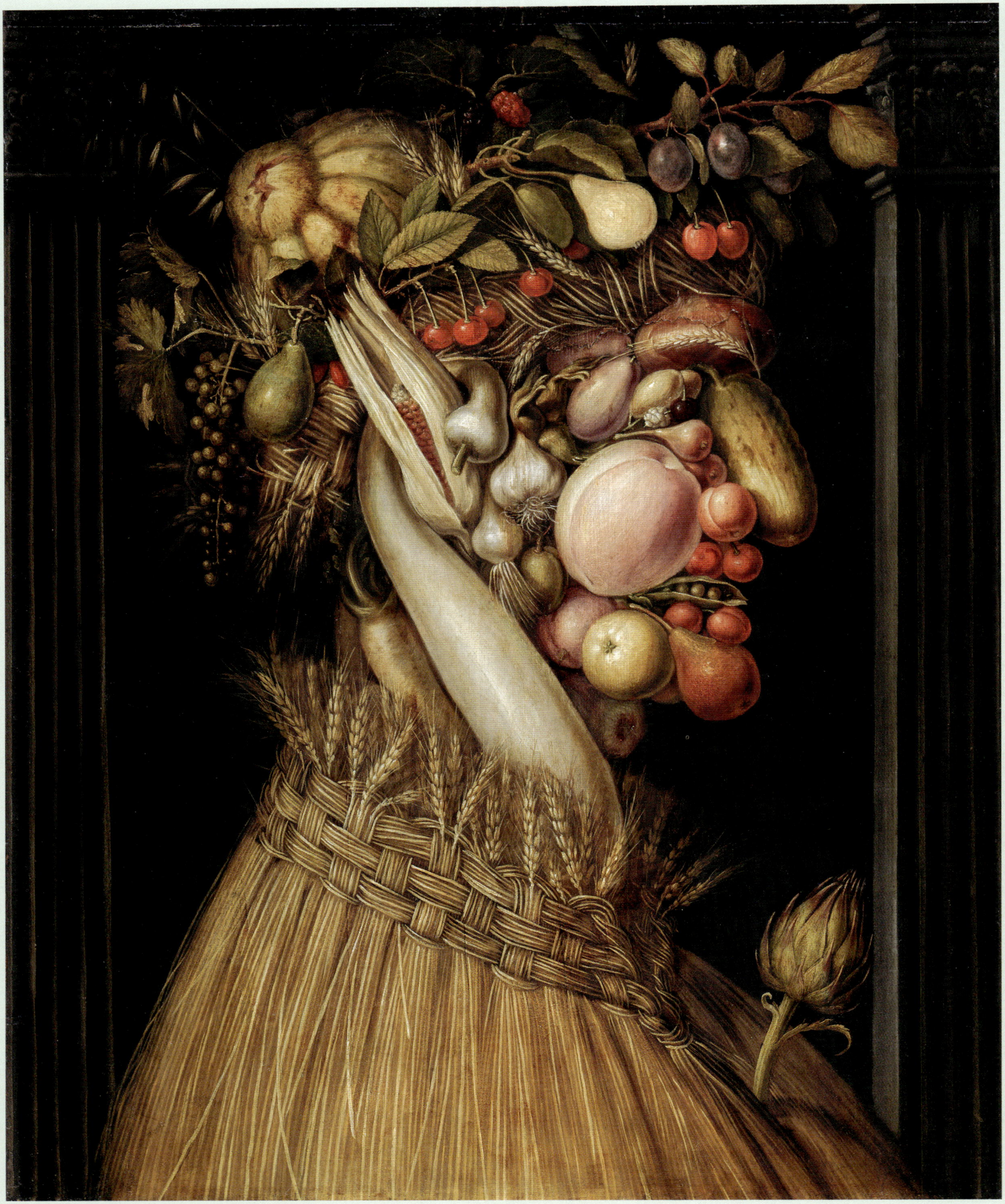
Cat. 28.2, Giuseppe Arcimboldo, *Summer*

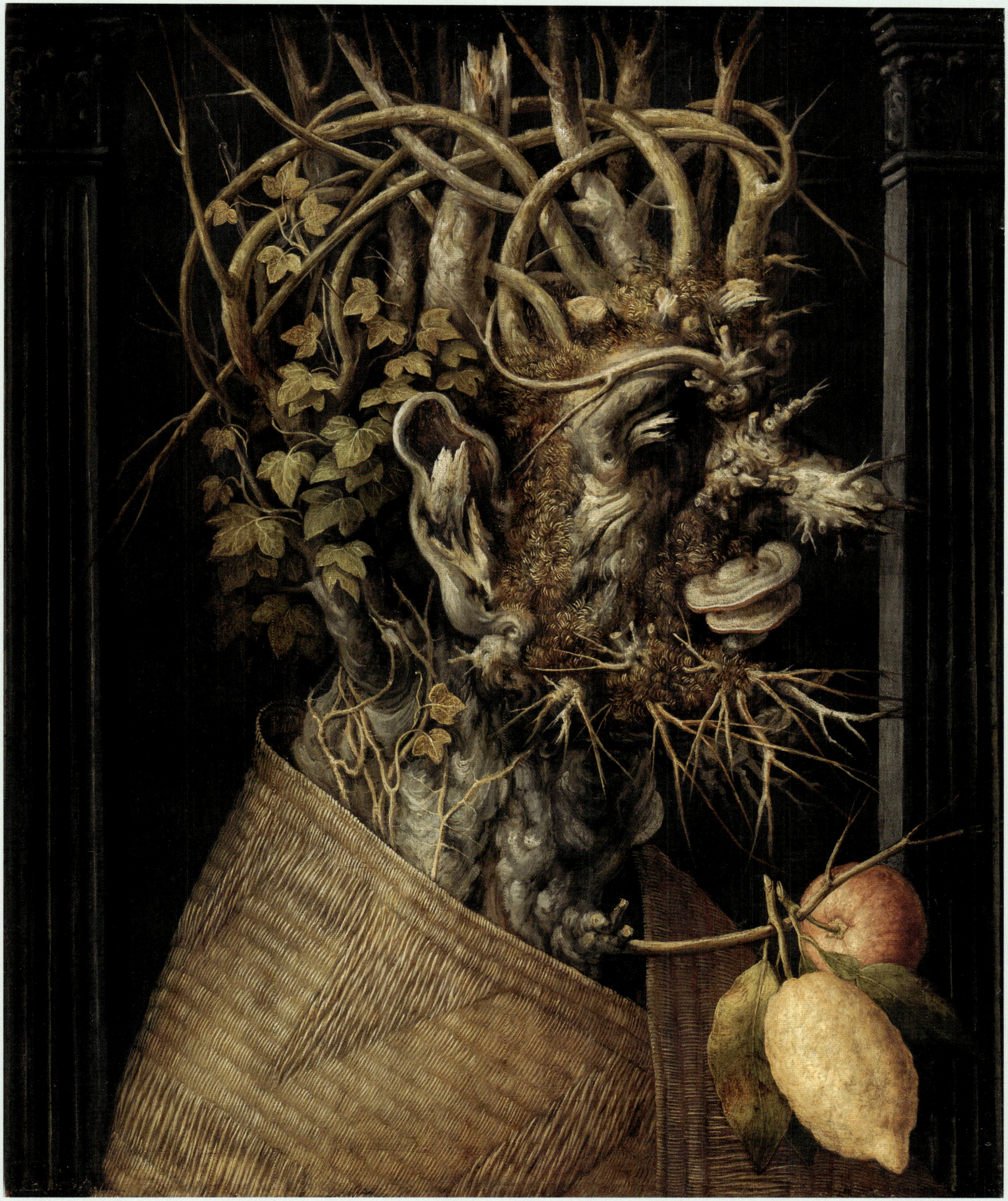

Cat. 28.3, Giuseppe Arcimboldo, *Winter*

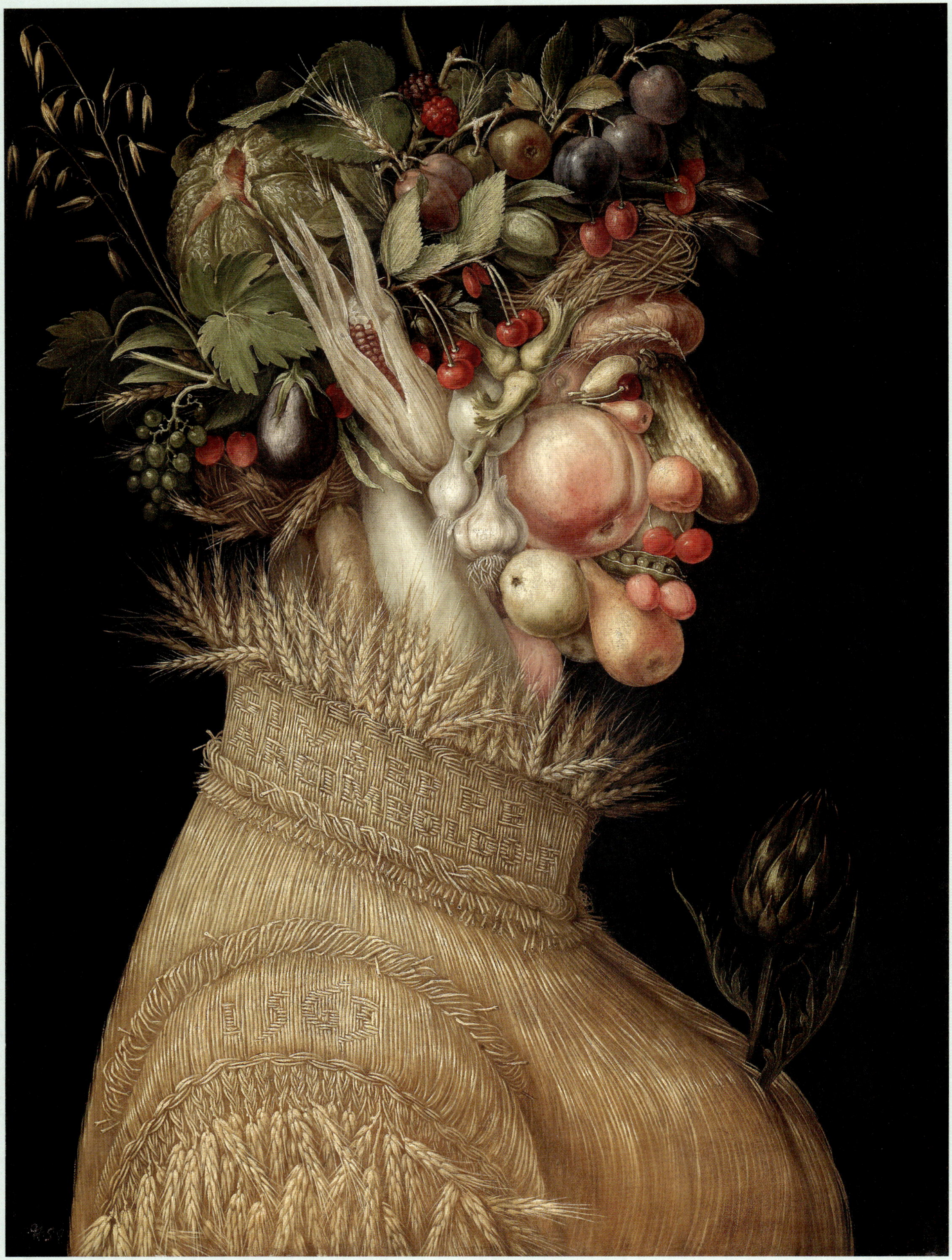

Cat. 29.1, Giuseppe Arcimboldo, *Summer*

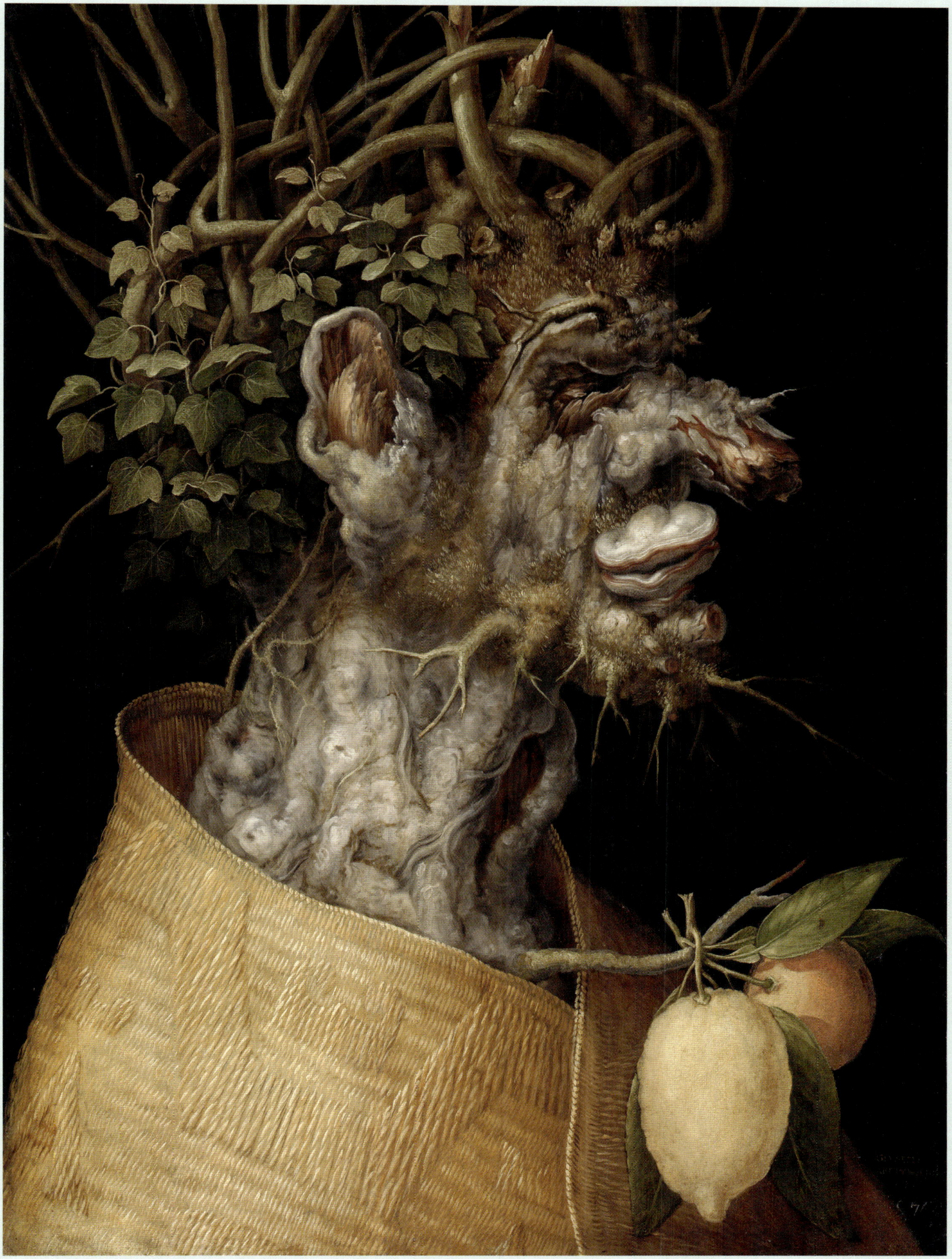

Cat. 29.2, Giuseppe Arcimboldo, *Winter*

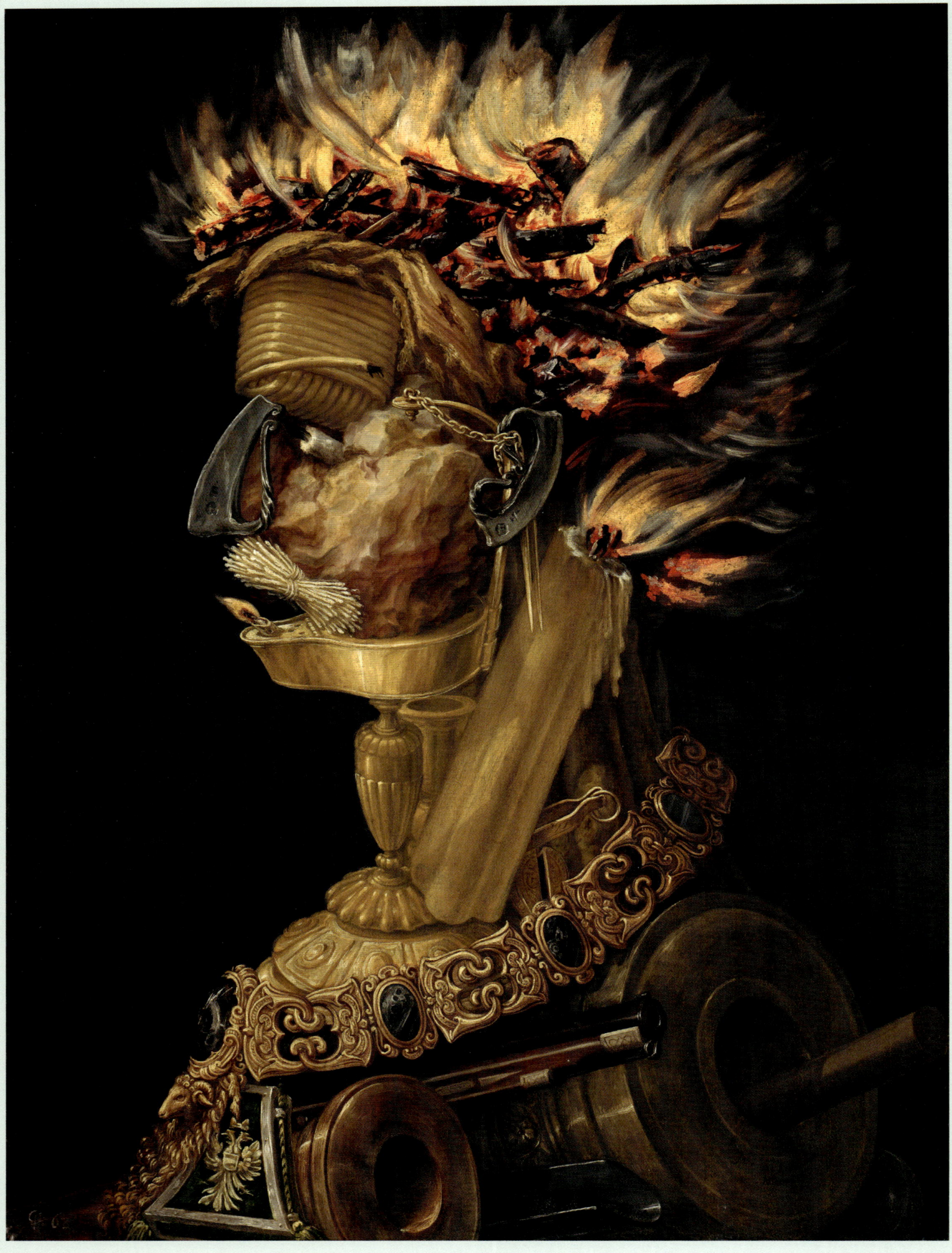

Cat. 30.1, Giuseppe Arcimboldo, *Fire*

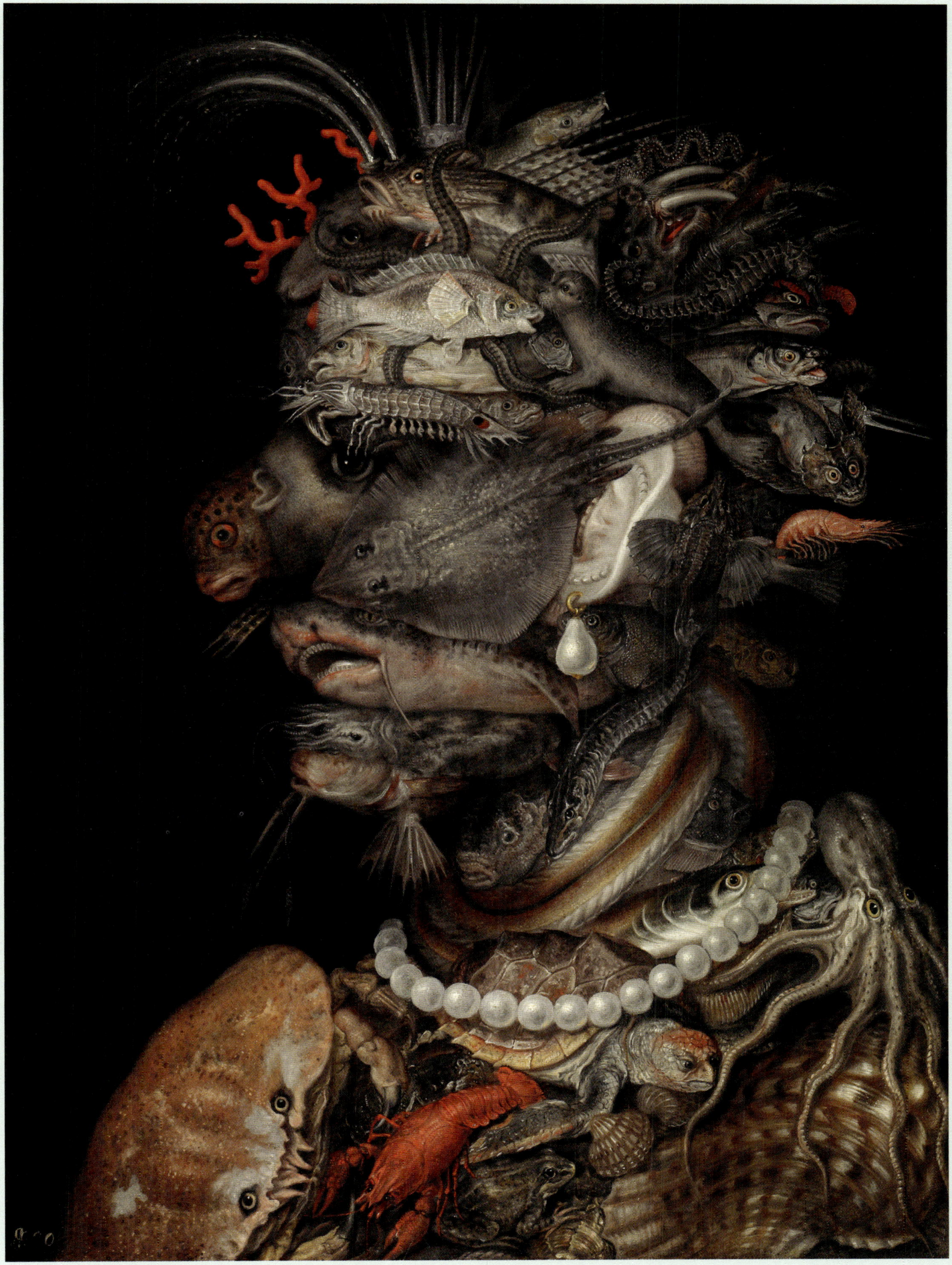

Cat. 30.2. Giuseppe Arcimboldo, *Water*

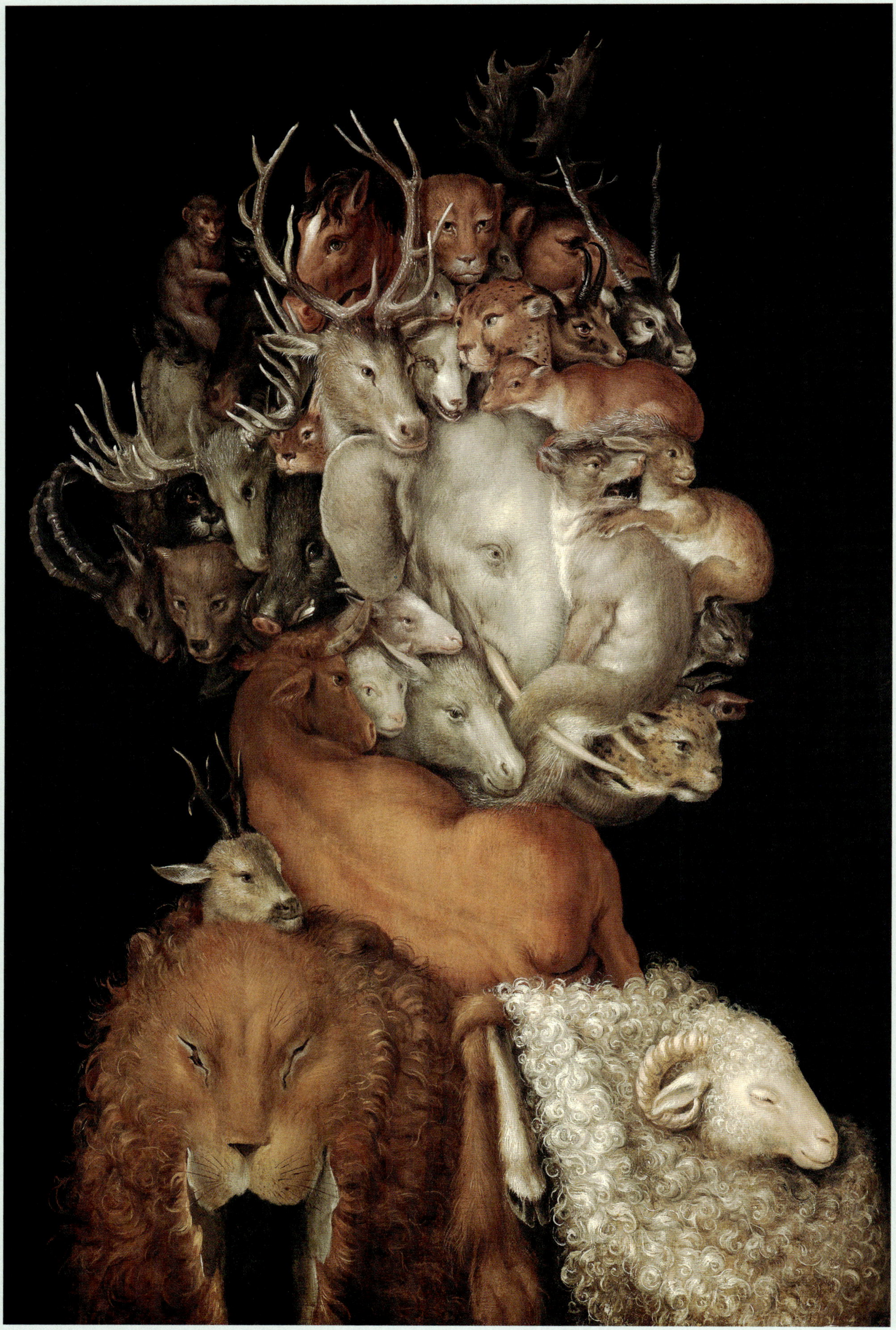

Cat. 30.3, Giuseppe Arcimboldo, *Earth*

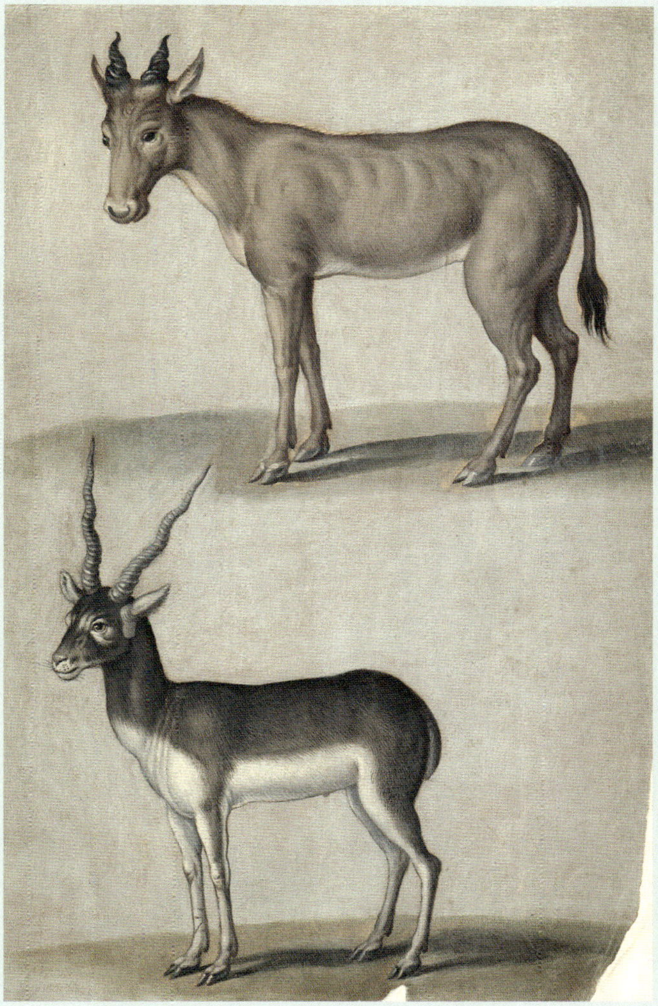

Cat. 31.1, Giuseppe Arcimboldo, *Hartebeest (Alcelaphus) and Blackbuck (Antilope cervicapra)*

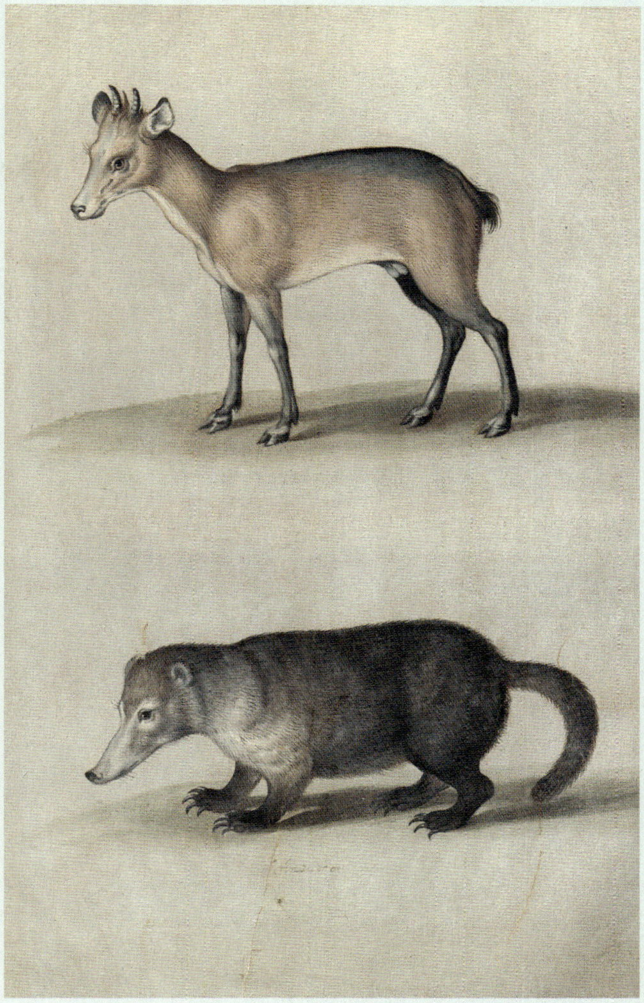

Cat. 31.2, Giuseppe Arcimboldo, *Red-flanked Duiker (Cephalophorus rufilatus) and Western Mountain Coati (Nasua olivacea)*

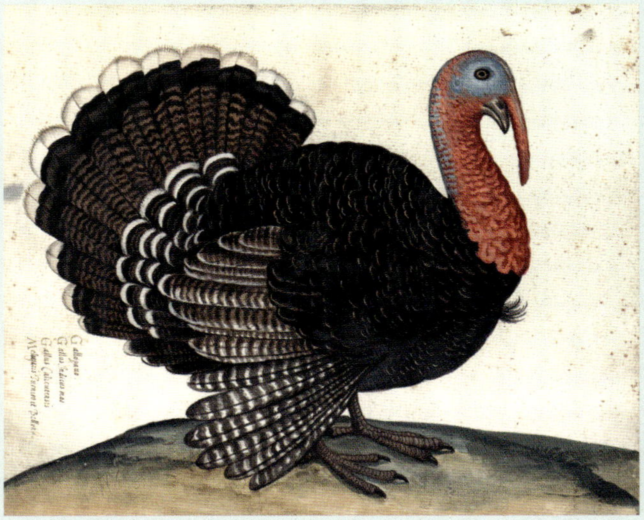

Cat. 32, *Turkey* (*Meleagris gallopavo*)

Cat. 33, Giuseppe Arcimboldo, *Vertumnus*

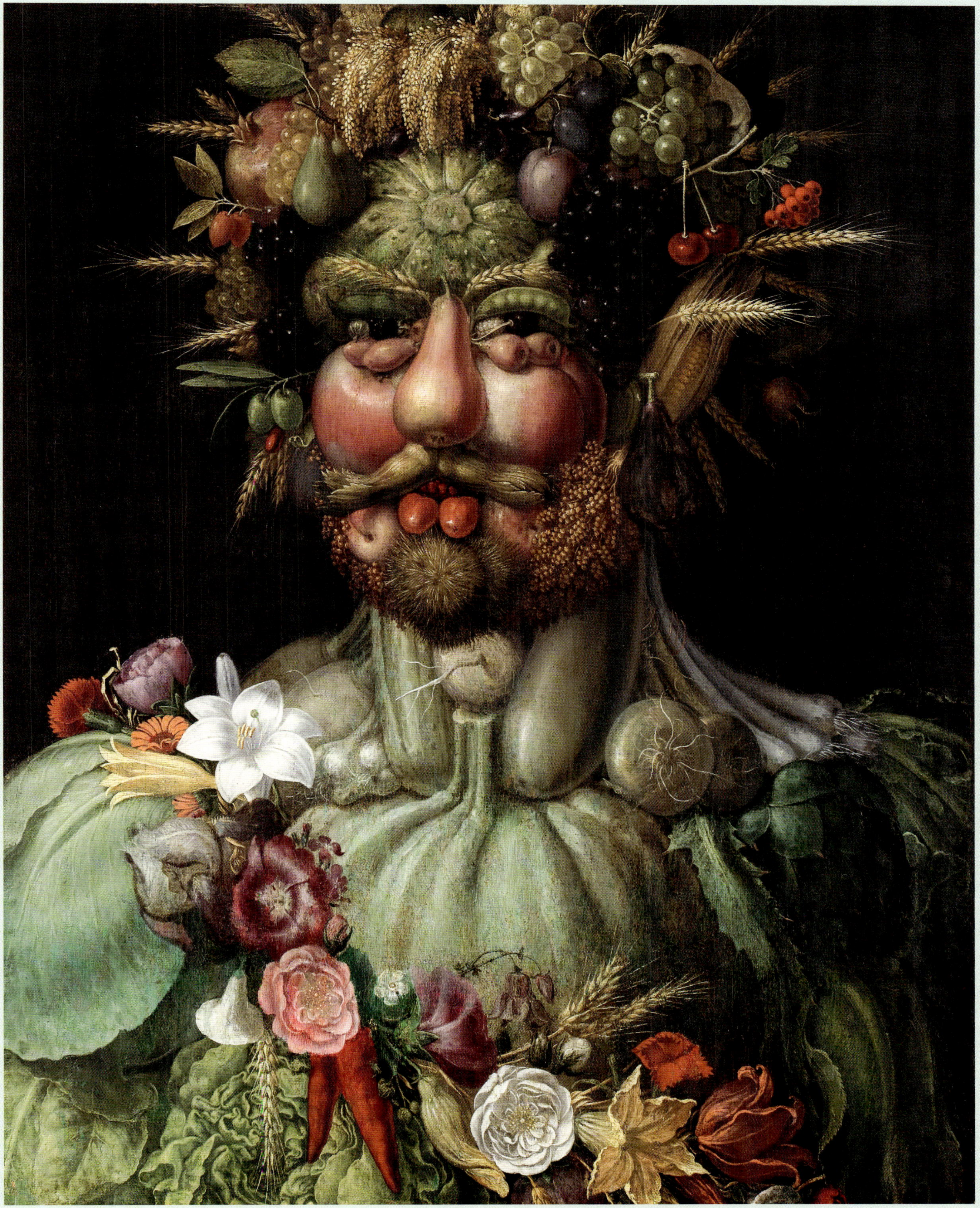

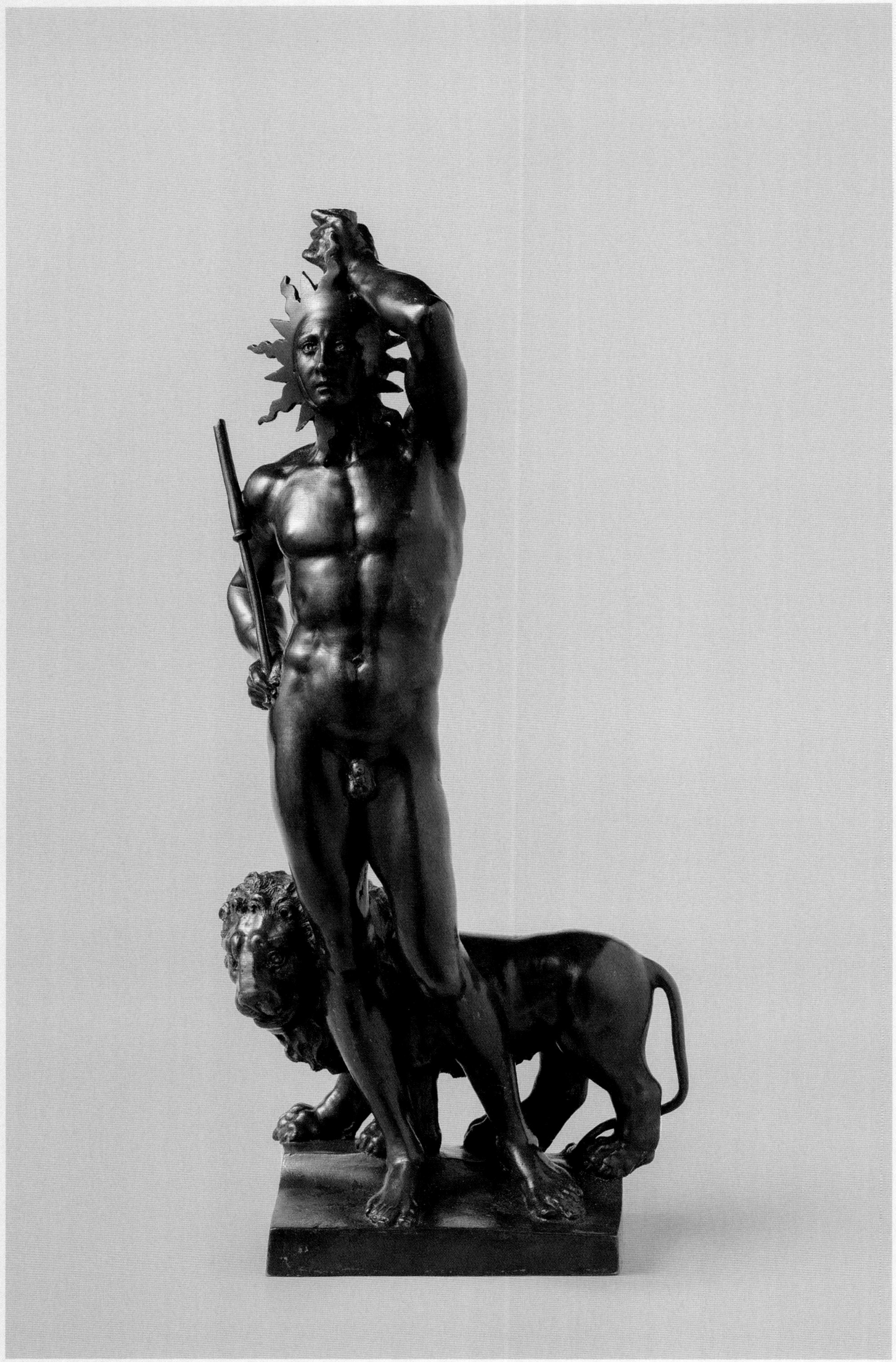

Cat. 34.1, Johan Gregor van der Schardt, *Sol*

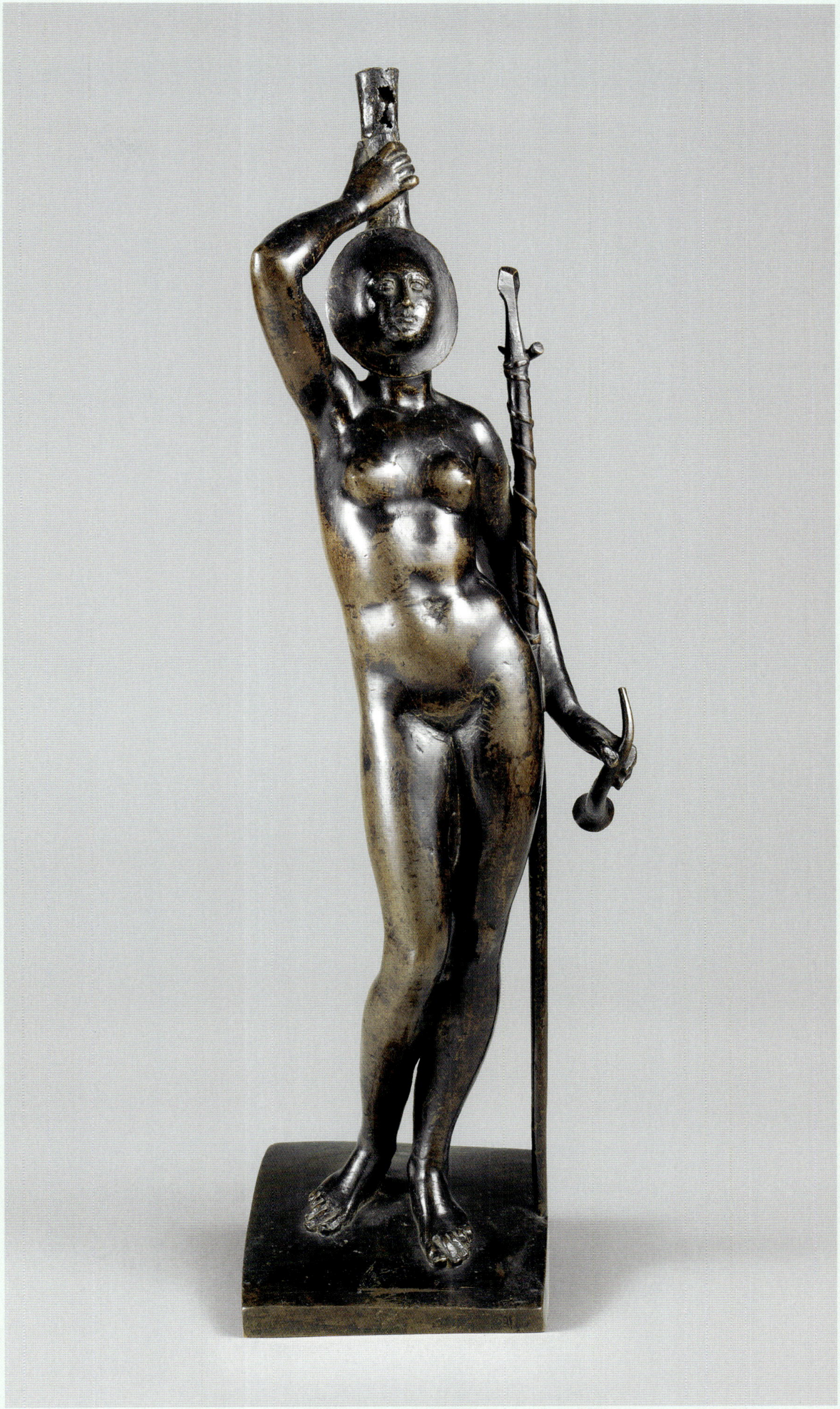

Cat. 34.2, Johan Gregor
van der Schardt, *Luna*

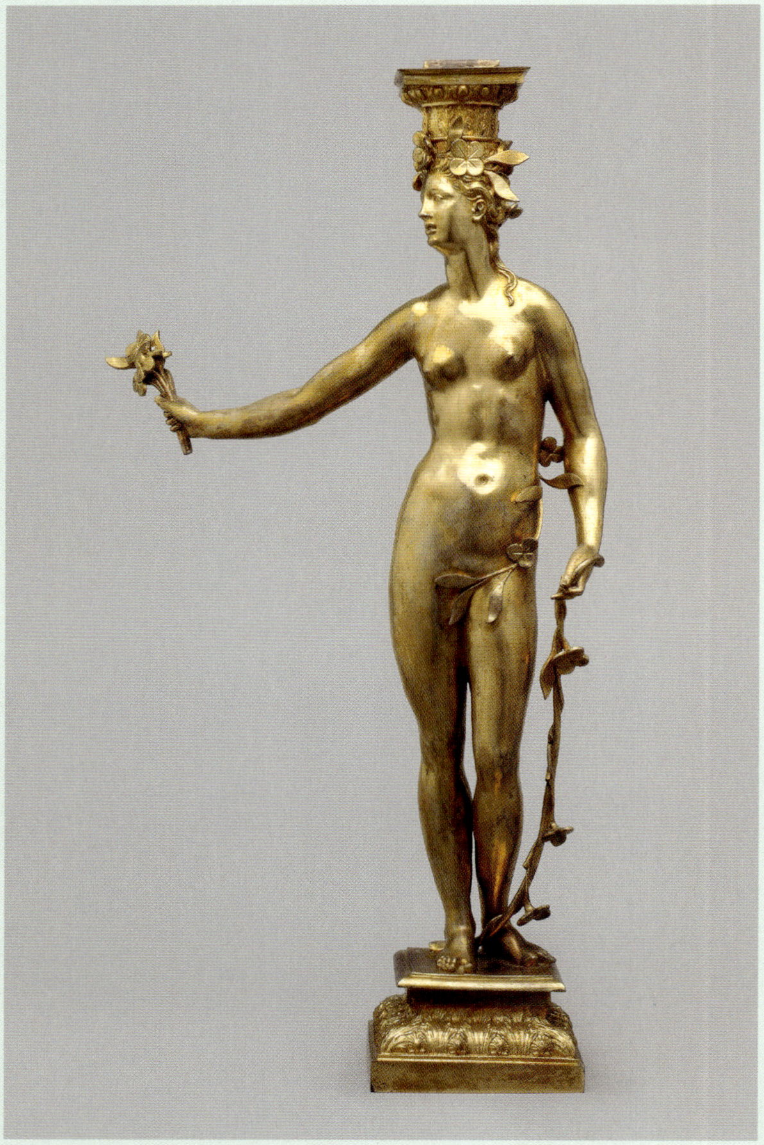

Cat. 35.1, Johan Gregor van der Schardt; Georg Labenwolf, *Flora*

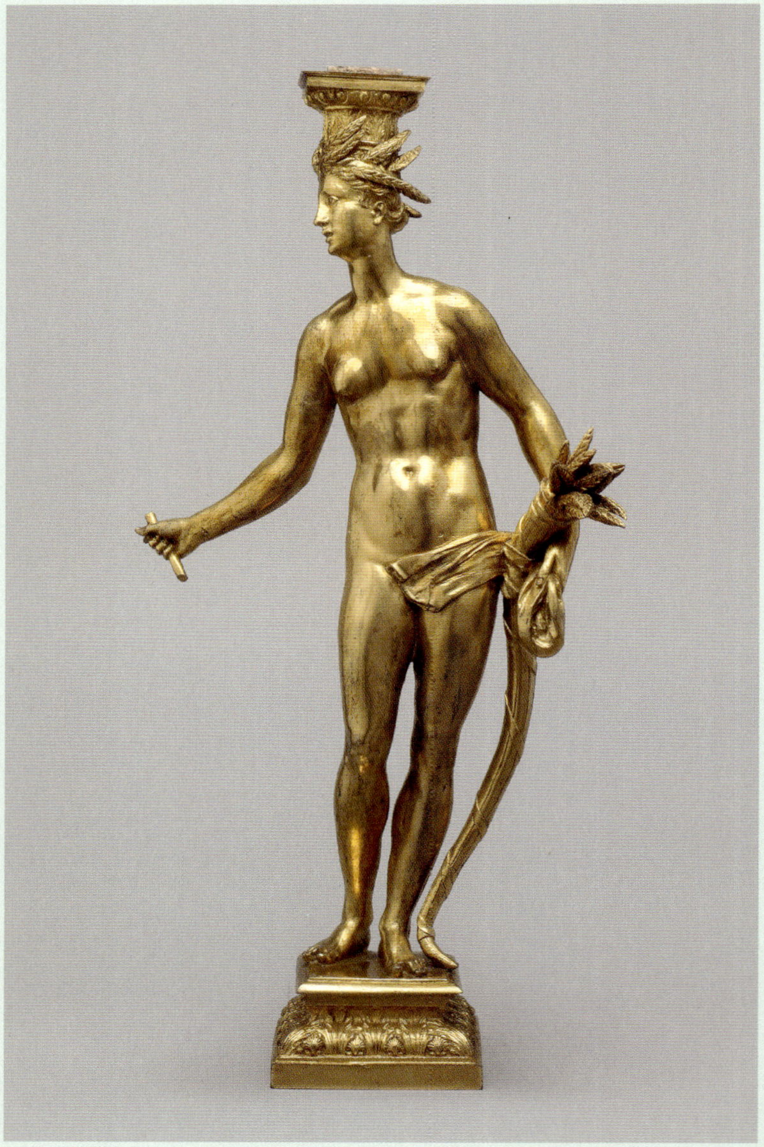

Cat. 35.2, Johan Gregor van der Schardt; Georg Labenwolf, *Ceres*

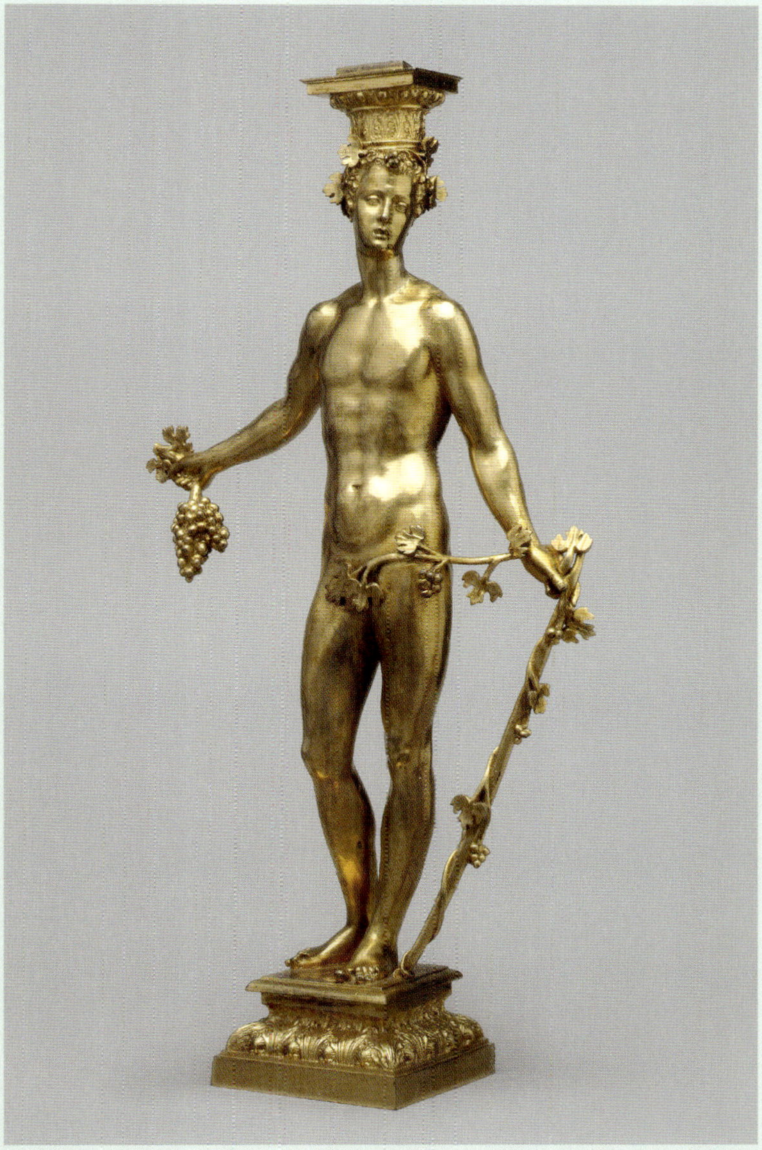

Cat. 35.3, Johan Gregor van der Schardt; Georg Labenwolf, *Bacchus*

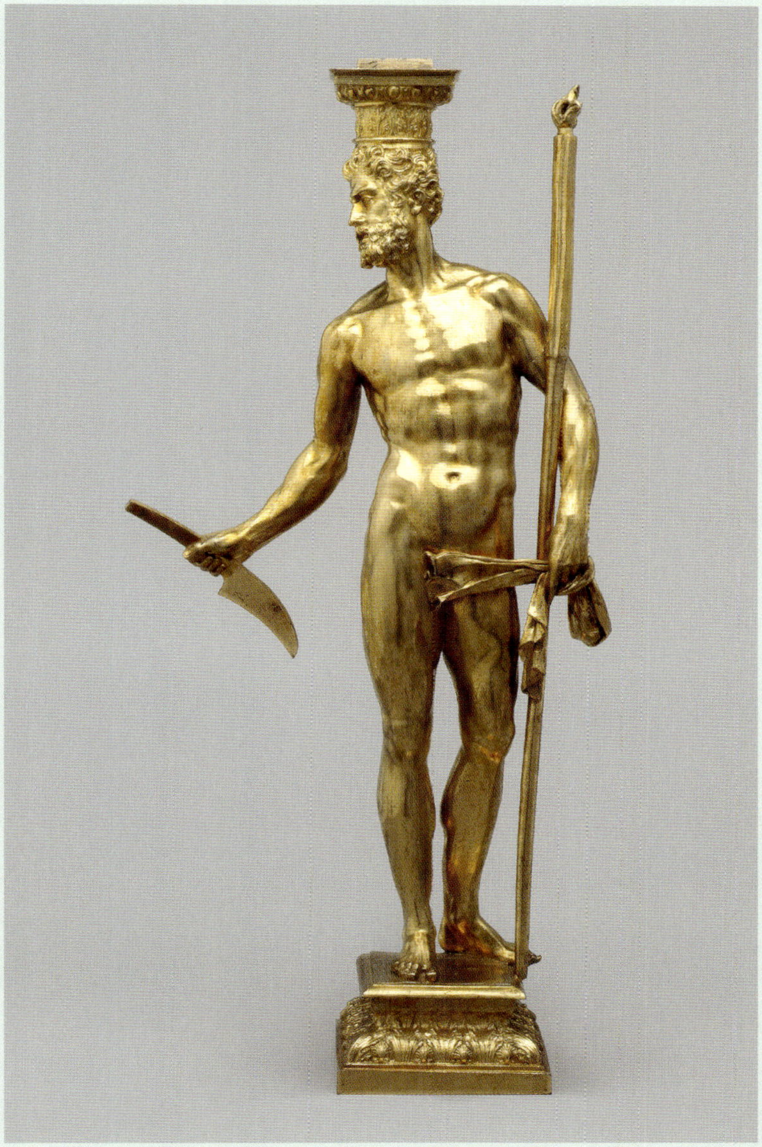

Cat. 35.4, Johan Gregor van der Schardt; Georg Labenwolf, *Vulcan*

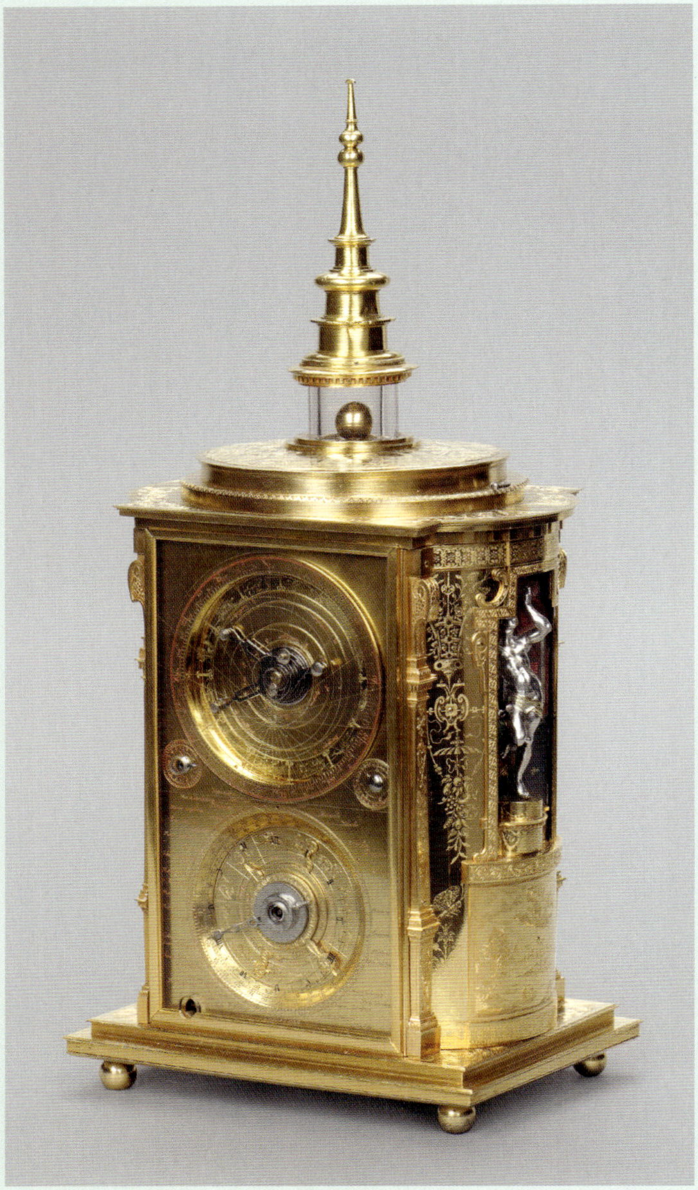

Cat. 36, Jobst Bürgi, *So-called Viennese Planetary Clock*

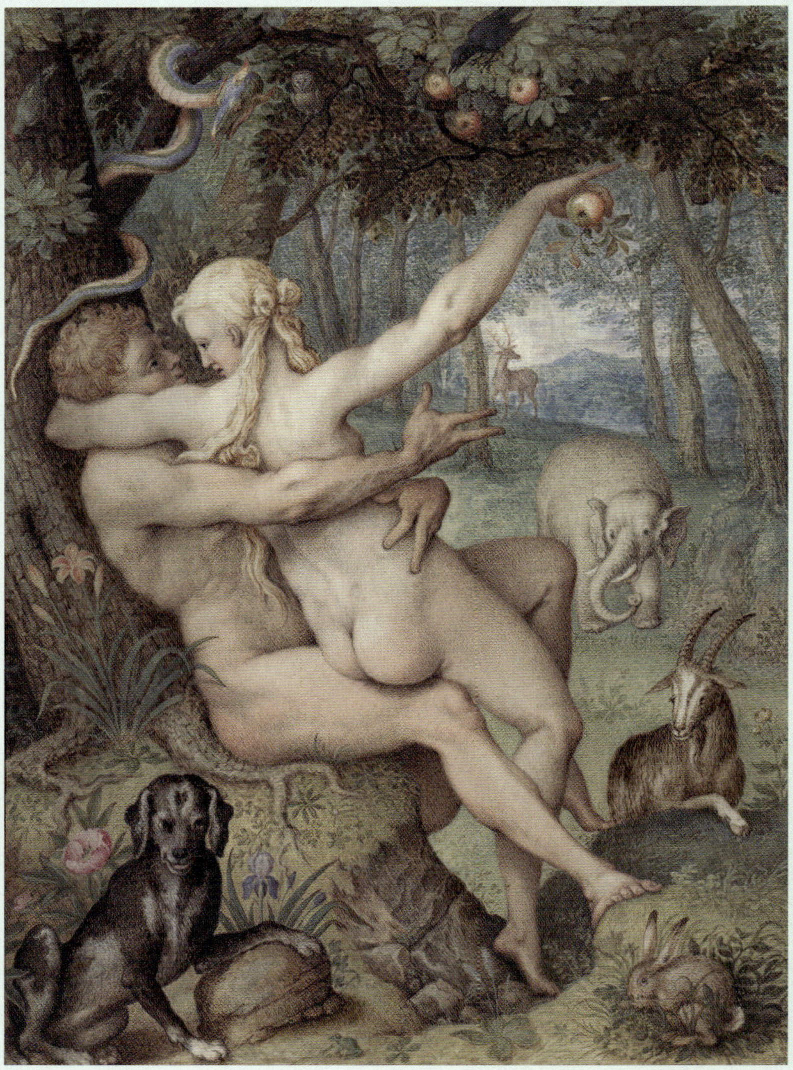

Cat. 37, Daniel Fröschl, *The Fall from Grace*

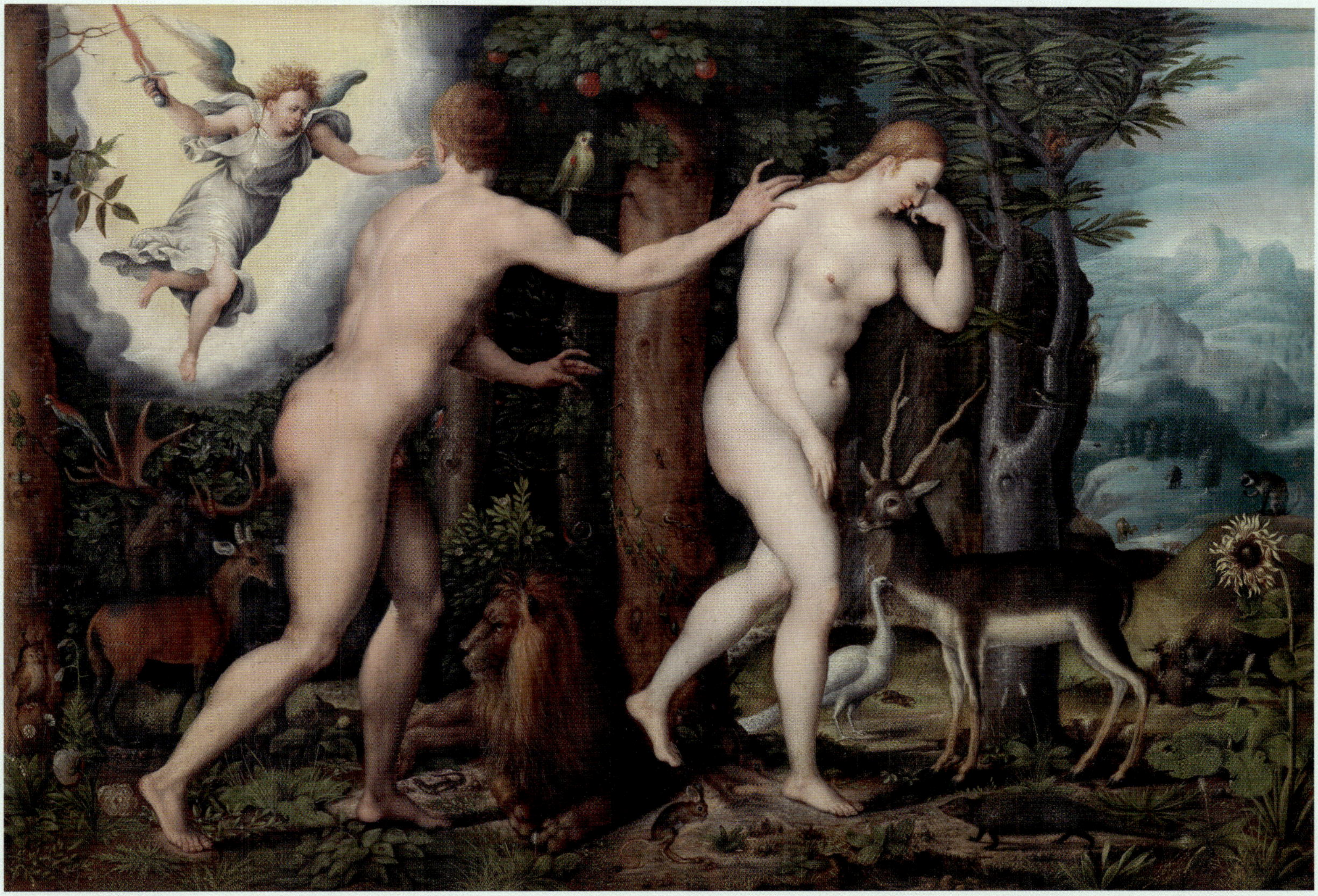

Cat. 38, Hans Hoffmann, *The Expulsion from Paradise*

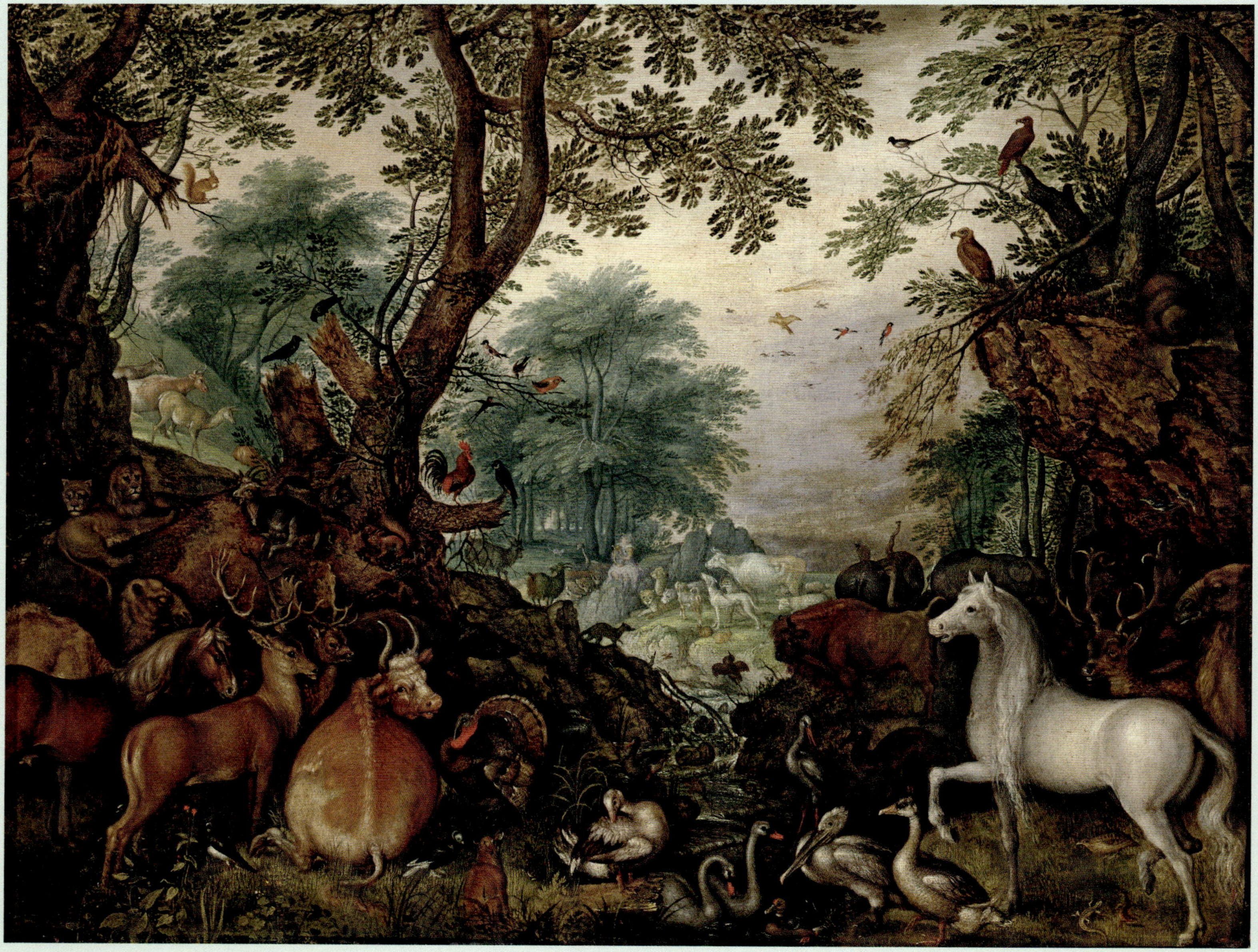

Cat. 39, Roelant Savery, *Orpheus with the Animals*

Cats. 27.1, 27.2

After Giuseppe Arcimboldo (1526–1593)

Allegory of the Four Seasons: Spring and Summer

c.1580
Etching; 175 × 235 mm
Amsterdam, Rijksmuseum, inv. RP-P-2017-1116-1; purchased with support of the F.G. Waller-Fonds

Allegory of the Four Seasons: Autumn and Winter

c.1580
Etching; 175 × 242 mm
Amsterdam, Rijksmuseum, inv. RP-P-2017-1116-2; purchased with support of the F.G. Waller-Fonds

Provenance: 2017 purchased
Literature: Exh. cat. Venice 1987, 170, 350–1; exh. cat. Milan 2011, cats. 200, 201 (Francesco Porzio); Porzio 2011, 230; exh. cat. Tokyo 2017, cats. I.10a/b, I.11a/b of a series in Oxford (Francesca Del Torre Scheuch)

Each of the two etchings show two anthropomorphic profile busts composed of objects that – as the inscription confirms – are allegories of the seasons. The heads look at each other and form a pair. The etchings are neither signed nor dated and there is no indication of the engraver or publisher. They are similar to the so-called *teste composte* ('composite heads') by the Milanese artist Giuseppe Arcimboldo, who painted several series of depictions of the seasons, the most famous for the imperial court in Vienna, where he moved in 1562 (cats. 29.1, 29.2).
In comparison to the Vienna cycle, which represents a highpoint of the anthropomorphising of nature and objects and harmoniously unites all the objects in a 'natural' manner, the composition of the individual objects in the etchings is more awkward, coarser, and features more exaggerated natural forms. In *Winter*, a gnarled tree stump forms the backbone from which the neck and head are formed; the branches are the hair that reaches upwards. Thicker roots grow wildly from the chin. In *Spring*, the flowers and leaves show less variation – for example, in the formation of the ear, neck, and clothing. *Summer* appears more rigid and instead of the humanised fruit and vegetable head of a young woman, which would correspond to the interpretation of the four seasons as the four ages of man (see cat. 29.1), it is here presented with coarse facial features and the protruding chin of a man.

In any case, the composition alludes to Arcimboldo. The etchings have always been associated with Giovanni Ambrogio Brambilla, who is known to have lived in Milan between 1560 and 1591. He was a painter, engraver, scholar, and the creator of numerous popular engravings, such as the caricature heads of Olympian gods (Florence, Gabinetto dei Disegni e delle Stampe degli Uffizi), and he was probably known to Arcimboldo.

Or do the etchings represent a version that precedes the painted *Seasons* cycle in Munich (cats. 28.1–28.3), as Porzio 2011 has surmised? There, too, the natural shapes from which the anthropomorphic heads are formed are modelled in a coarser and harsher manner than the Vienna series. According to recent research, the Munich pictures are probably the earliest surviving series of seasons that Arcimboldo already painted while he was in Milan, probably in 1555/60, thus pre-dating the series he made for the emperor in Vienna.

Accordingly, the etchings may be evidence of an earlier, simplified version of the Munich cycle and also of an attribution of the pictorial idea to Arcimboldo, as is assumed for this seasonal series. The universal character of the etchings would also speak in favour of an earlier 'experimental series'. Like the ones in Munich, and in contrast to those in Vienna as well as the series created after Vienna, they are not signed or dated, nor do they bear any information that would associate them in any way with a person, for example, a coat of arms.

The etchings were successful. Further series were reprinted, albeit in a modified form and at a later date, with profile busts scaled down in order to accomodate poems about the season underneath (Oxford, Ashmolean Museum). Thanks to their reproduction, Arcimboldo's pictorial idea found a wide audience and was no longer – as was the case for the Vienna paintings – reserved for a select courtly elite. The Arcimboldo effect still has an impact today – regardless of who the inventor of this series might have been.
Wencke Deiters

Cats. 28.1–28.3

Giuseppe Arcimboldo (1526–1593)

Spring

1555/60
Panel; 68.3 × 57 cm
Munich, Bayerische Staatsgemäldesammlungen, Alte Pinakothek, inv. 2037

Summer

1555/60
Panel; 67.5 × 57 cm
Munich, Bayerische Staatsgemäldesammlungen, Alte Pinakothek, inv. 2038

Winter

1555/60
Panel; 67.5 × 57 cm
Munich, Bayerische Staatsgemäldesammlungen, Alte Pinakothek, inv. 2040

Provenance: Since 1598 documented in the Munich Kunstkammer
Literature: Kriegeskorte 1986, 64, 66, 68 (original Arcimboldo); Sangl 2004, 74–5 (after Arcimboldo); exh. cat. Paris and Vienna 2007/08, cats. IV.12–14 (Alexander Wied; 'workshop member'); Porzio 2011, 221–30 (Arcimboldo); exh. cat. Rome 2017/18, 42–1, cats. I.26, I.27 (Sylvia Ferino-Pagden; Arcimboldo); Ferino-Pagden 2023, 80, 87, 93 (Arcimboldo)

A series of Arcimboldo's *Four Seasons* has been documented in the *Kunstkammer* of the House of Wittelsbach in Munich since 1598. (*Autumn* is not included in the exhibition due to its state of preservation.) This series was long regarded as a variant of the Vienna cycle (cats. 29.1, 29.2) dated 1563, which was created for the Holy Roman Emperor Maximilian II. This had consequences for the attribution of the Munich paintings. With a few exceptions, they were judged to be workshop works or copies. In Vienna, only *Summer* and *Winter* have survived, although *Spring* (Madrid, Museo Nacional del Prado) is also considered part of this series.

However, new findings suggest that Arcimboldo had already executed the Munich series while he was in Milan, that is, before his move to the imperial court in Vienna and Prague in 1562 and thus before the Vienna series (Porzio 2011).

The profile busts, composed of various objects associated with their respective seasons, are framed by fluted pilasters. *Summer* and *Winter* face right, *Spring* and *Autumn* left. In contrast to the corresponding Vienna pictures and other surviving seasons, *Summer* is neither signed nor dated, and there is no information on *Winter* that would associate the series with a person, for example, with a coat of arms – aspects that lend the Munich cycle a universal character.

A comparison of the series in Munich and Vienna/Madrid reveals further differences. The natural shapes that comprise the anthropomorphic heads are modelled relatively more coarsely and harshly in Munich – for example, in the gnarled stump of the tree in *Winter* from which the neck and head are formed, the thicker branches of the hair, and the beard made of moss. The same is true of the flowers and leaves in *Spring* and the fruit and vegetables in *Summer*. In the latter, moreover, the pictorial transitions between the objects are less fluid and there are occasional gaps, such as between the peach and aubergine that form the face and neck of *Summer*.

The fact that the version completed for Maximilian II is more varied in its execution and more homogeneous in terms of the shaping of the profile busts suggests that the Munich series was created before the one in Vienna (Porzio 2011). It represents a high point in the anthropomorphisation of nature. Arcimboldo probably fulfilled the expectations of the imperial court, thanks in part to his experience with the Munich series. Information from Paolo Morigia (1592), a friend of Arcimboldo's, also speaks in favour of dating the Munich paintings to the Milan years. Morigia reported that Arcimboldo had already developed the first *teste composte* ('composite heads') before his appointment to the Vienna court. The series is an example of his painting from the 1550s of which only a few works are known and the reason that Porzio (2011) suggests a date around 1555/60.

In February 1564, the Elector of Saxony's personal physician Johannes Neefe reported that the ailing Emperor Ferdinand I had shown him a series of four seasons composed of composite heads in the Vienna Hofburg. Karl Rudolf assumes that Neefe saw the Vienna cycle (Rudolf 2015, 134–5). However, since the doctor – despite examining the paintings carefully – does not mention the name of the artist, the question arises: might this not have been the unsigned Munich series (Ferino-Pagden 2023)? If we assume that it was created in the 1550s, then it was completed during Ferdinand's lifetime and may have been sent in advance or brought by the artist to the Viennese court. Although the Vienna *Summer* is dated 1563, the series as a whole was not presented to Emperor Maximilian II until 1569 (cats. 29.1, 29.2).

But how did the Munich series end up in the *Kunstkammer* of the Wittelsbachs? Maximilian could have given it to Albrecht V of Bavaria in 1571 to strengthen the friendship between the two dynasties – perhaps on the occasion of the marriage of Albrecht's daughter Maria Anna to Archduke Charles II, the son of Emperor Ferdinand I (Porzio 2011, 230). The Wittelsbachs thus received the 'first' version, which would explain the universal character of the depictions. It would also have been the first of further gifts of the *Seasons*, which were subsequently based on the Vienna series, created, and personalised in the course of the 1570s (see cats. 29.1, 29.2).

Wencke Deiters

Cats. 29.1, 29.2

Giuseppe Arcimboldo (1526–1593)

Summer

1563

Lime panel; 67 × 50.8 cm

Signed as pattern in the straw weave of the collar and shoulder: 'GIVSEPPE/ARCIMBOLDO F'; dated: '1563'; date and title on the back in old lettering: '1563. AESTAS'

Vienna, Kunsthistorisches Museum, Picture Gallery, inv. 1589

Winter

1563

Lime panel; 66.6 × 50.5 cm

Signed lower right: 'GIVSEPPE/ARCIMBOLDO F.'; on the back in old lettering: '1563 HJEMS'

Vienna, Kunsthistorisches Museum, Picture Gallery, inv. 1590

Provenance: Painted for Archduke Maximilian, later Kaiser Maximilian II (?); from Rudolf II's Kunstkammer; 1748 to the Vienna Treasury; from 1830 in the Picture Gallery

Literature: Exh. cat. Paris and Vienna 2007/08, cats. IV.3, IV.4 (Alexander Wied), with earlier lit.; DaCosta Kaufmann 2008a, 277–8; exh. cat. Milan 2011, cats. 206, 208 (Sylvia Ferino-Pagden); Porzio 2011, 221–30; Ferino-Pagden 2023, 82–7, 93–4

Summer and *Winter* are part of a series of four seasons begun in 1563 by Giuseppe Arcimboldo for Emperor Ferdinand I (1503–1564) and completed after his death for Maximilian II (1527–1576). The Milanese artist was appointed to the court in Vienna in 1562. *Spring* (now in Madrid, Museo Nacional del Prado) is also attributed to this series; *Autumn* is considered lost.

The profile busts, assembled from objects associated with the seasons, comprise allegories that were described by Gian Paolo Lomazzo (1590) as *teste composte* ('composite heads'). Both heads face to the right.

Summer consists of grains and fruits that symbolize the richness of the season, including a peach as a cheek, a cherry as an eye, two pears as eyelids, and a cucumber as the nose. A pea pod is an open mouth between cherries, while a white aubergine, among other things, forms the neck. Instead of an ear, there is an ear of corn – a botanical rarity, as maize was only brought to Europe by Columbus at the end of the fifteenth century. The corn can also be seen as part of the hat's ear flap, which is made of fruit, vegetables, and leaves, including cherries, plums, grapes, and a head of lettuce. The husks of the corn form the hat's plume, a fashionable accessory that suits the straw coat with its silken sheen. *Summer* is the only picture from the series that is signed and dated (1563). An artichoke protruding upright from the chest serves as jewellery.

Winter's face and neck are formed from a gnarled tree stump, his nose and ear from the stumps of branches, his eye from an opening in the bark, his mouth from two bracket fungi, and his hair from a wild outgrowth of branches that form a kind of crown. A branch with two lemons grows just above the chest. In the straw garment, the woven 'M' and firesteel refer to Emperor Maximilian and the Order of the Golden Fleece, the house order of the Habsburgs, whose heraldic collar is worn by *Fire* (cat. 30.1) in the *Four Elements* series that complements the *Seasons*. Although the *Elements* were not created until three years later, the two series correspond with each other.

Additional arguments have been put forward in recent years that confirm the assumption that the Vienna *Seasons* series was created after the one in Munich (cats. 28.1–28.3) and does not, as long thought, represent the prototype. There are few differences between the two versions in terms of the objects used, but in the Vienna version created for the emperor the design of the profile busts exhibits more variation. In *Summer*, for example, the shoulder and upper sleeve of the straw coat with their silky sheen are more finely executed. After the experience gained with the earlier Munich version, Arcimboldo adapted his profile busts to the expectations of the imperial court, for an emperor who was keenly interested in the observation of nature. In the Vienna series, the anthropomorphisation of nature and objects reaches a high point (Porzio 2011, 226). The objects seem to be joined in a 'natural' way, as if any other combination would be unthinkable.

The artist took inspiration for his composite heads from his milieu, for instance from Leonardo da Vinci's treatise on painting or his nature studies (cats. 3.1, 3.2, 30.1–30.3).

Arcimboldo's *teste composte* suggest different readings, for example, the four ages of life: childhood (spring), youth (summer), adulthood (autumn), and old age (winter). The Vienna series also has an allegorical-symbolic character. On New Year's Day 1569, the cycle of the *Seasons* and *Elements*, then still in eight parts, was presented to Maximilian II, together with a panegyric by the humanist Giovanni Battista Fonteo. The poem is an explanatory commentary on the paintings (DaCosta Kaufmann 1976), which allude to Maximilian and the House of Habsburg (in contradistinction to the cycle in Munich). The emperor rules not only over people, but also over nature, with the ever-recurring seasons symbolising the eternal rule of the Habsburgs.

After receiving the series, Maximilian commissioned further *Seasons* for diplomatic gifts or gave parts of them as gifts to recipients that included the Elector of Saxony, one of the emperor's electors (today in Paris, Louvre), and his cousin Philip II in Spain. The Vienna series was the prototype for these paintings, entirely in keeping with the emperor's taste.

WENCKE DEITERS

Cats. 30.1–30.3

Giuseppe Arcimboldo (1526–1593)

Fire

1566
Lime panel; 66.6 × 50.8 cm
Signed lower right: 'Josephus Arcimboldus/ Milensis F'
Inscribed and dated on the back: 'IGNIS 1566'
Vienna, Kunsthistorisches Museum, Picture Gallery, inv. 1585
Provenance: Painted for Emperor Maximilian II (?); from the Kunstkammer of Emperor Rudolf II; 1748 in the Imperial Treasury; from 1830 in the Picture Gallery

Water

1566
Alder panel; 66.5 × 50.5 cm
Inscribed on the back: 'AQUA'
Vienna, Kunsthistorisches Museum, Picture Gallery, inv. 1586
Provenance: Painted for Emperor Maximilian II (?); from the Kunstkammer of Emperor Rudolf II; 1748 in the Vienna treasury; from 1830 in the Picture Gallery

Earth

c.1566
Panel; 70.2 cm × 48.7 cm
LIECHTENSTEIN, The Princely Collections, Vaduz – Vienna, inv. GE 2508
Provenance: Commissioned by Emperor Maximilian in 1566; 1872 presented by Emperor Franz Joseph I as gift to Sammlungen des Joanneum (Graz) (from the storerooms of the Kunsthistorisches Museum); privately owned since the 1950s; since 2005 in The Princely Collections as permanent loan; 2015 acquired by Hans-Adam II, Prince of Liechtenstein

Literature: Exh. cat. Paris and Vienna 2007/08, cats. IV.18, IV.21 (Fire, Earth; Alexander Wied), cat. IV.20 (Earth; Thomas DaCosta Kaufmann); DaCosta Kaufmann 2008a, 277–8; exh. cat. Milan 2011, cats. 213, 214 (Sylvia Ferino-Pagden); exh. cat. Tokyo 2017, cat. II.19 (Earth; Shinsuke Watanabe); Ferino-Pagden 2023, 83–8

Fire and *Water* are part of a series of elements, originally of four parts, created by the Milanese court artist Giuseppe Arcimboldo in 1566 for Emperor Maximilian II. *Earth* is in the Princely Collections of Liechtenstein; *Air* is lost but survives in copies. The series dates from three years after the *Seasons* (cat. 29), which were also created for the Viennese court.

The artist created allegories from various objects associated with the respective elements in the form of anthropomorphic profile busts, a form described by Gian Paolo Lomazzo (1590) as *teste composte* (Italian for 'composite heads') and the result of 'great care and immeasurable study'.

In *Fire*, a flint forms the cheek, a candle stub the eye, two fire strikers the nose and ears. A torch and oil lamp make up the neck, with the body and nozzle of the lamp forming the chin and lower jaw. The moustache is created from a bundle of kindling, the forehead from a long, coiled fuse, and the hair from burning logs. The chest and shoulders consist of firearms: a mortar, a cannon barrel with a powder ladle, and the barrel of a pistol. Around the neck is the heraldic collar of the Order of the Golden Fleece, the house order of the Habsburgs, together with the imperial double eagle, both references to the recipient of the series.

The overwhelming biodiversity of *Water* is astonishing. More than sixty aquatic creatures – fish, amphibians, reptiles, mammals, crustaceans and so on – make up the bust whose components have been itemised by DaCosta Kaufmann (1987). Not every animal can be identified. All come from the Mediterranean, with the exception of the sea moth (behind the ear) from the Indian Ocean. The absence of typical ocean and freshwater fish, such as herring or trout, is conspicuous. The eye is a moonfish, the cheek a ray, the nose a Mediterranean moray, the mouth that of a shark. The ear is the shell of an ark clam from which a pearl earring hangs; the necklace is also made up of pearls, and a crown of sea urchin spines sits on the head. The chest and shoulders consist primarily of crustaceans, parts of which resemble armour. A crab covers the chest; the shoulder consists of a Triton's trumpet. An octopus spreads its tentacles over the shoulder, resembling an epaulette. The Triton's trumpet, a rare species of snail, illustrates how coveted Habsburg collector's items (Vienna, Kunsthistorisches Museum, inv. KK 6863) were incorporated into the composite heads. It is not by coincidence that the pike in the neck area has too many gills and resembles a gorget (the collar piece of armour). The size ratio of the creatures to each other is also of secondary importance. A relatively large sea horse above the ear nestles up to a small seal. Despite these artistic liberties, Arcimboldo's interest in a detailed depiction of nature is obvious and is part of his recipe for success.

We have numerous study drawings for *Earth* (see essay Ferino-Pagden, p. 27, fig. 5). The emperor's menagerie was certainly a rich source for studies from nature. The allegory consists of mammals that allude to the Habsburg imperial family. The ram's skin (chest) refers to the Order of the Golden Fleece, the lion's skin (back) to Hercules, the family's mythical ancestor. The head is adorned with a crown of antlers, which also identifies the Habsburgs as lords of nature. According to contemporary sources, the arrangement of the animals derives from an ancient description in Pliny the Elder, which indicates a comparison (*paragone*) of Arcimboldo and antiquity. It is possible that *Earth* was made somewhat later than *Water* and *Fire* since its dimensions are different.

The *Elements* series corresponds to the four temperaments: air – sanguine, fire – choleric, earth – melancholic, water – phlegmatic. The four elements are associated with contrary pairs of properties, such as warm/cold, moist/dry. They can also be assigned to the seasons. Under this interpretation, damp/cold corresponds to winter and water, warm/dry to summer and fire. In Arcimboldo's work, the heads face each other in pairs that form units. The theory of the elements goes back to the ancient philosopher Empedocles and was the subject of intense discussion at the Renaissance court of Ferdinand I, the father of Maximilian II (Rudolf 2015, 141 and note 56).

On New Year's Day 1569, the eight-part cycle was presented to Emperor Maximilian, together with a poem of homage to the 'good government' of the house of Habsburg. The poem, written by Giovanni Battista Fonteo, was also an explanatory commentary on the paintings (DaCosta Kaufmann 1976). The emperor is not only the representative of secular and spiritual power, he is also the universal ruler over mankind, nature, and the elements. His rule is harmonious, like the unity of seasons and elements, and is eternal, like the ever-recurring seasons.

WENCKE DEITERS

Cats. 31.1, 31.2

Giuseppe Arcimboldo (1526–1593)

Hartebeest (Alcelaphus) and Blackbuck (Antilope cervicapra)

c.1580
Tempera and watercolour on paper; 430 × 285 mm
Alma Mater Studiorum – Università di Bologna, Biblioteca Universitaria di Bologna, Ms Aldrovandi, *Tavole di animali*, vol. V, fol. 20

Red-flanked Duiker (Cephalophorus rufilatus) and Western Mountain Coati (Nasua olivacea)

Tempera and watercolour on paper; 427 × 290 mm
Alma Mater Studiorum – Università di Bologna, Biblioteca Universitaria di Bologna, Ms Aldrovandi, Tavole di Animali, vol. VI, fol. 87

Provenance: Fondo Ulisse Aldrovandi
Literature: Ferino-Pagden 2008; Staudinger 2008; DaCosta Kaufmann 2009, passim; Olmi 2010, 69–71; Olmi and Tongiorgi Tomasi 2011

Among sixteenth-century naturalists, Ulisse Aldrovandi of Bologna was certainly one of the most convinced of the need to illustrate his books so that readers could also know what the animals, plants, and minerals described in the text looked like. In his lifetime, he managed to collect 8,000 tempera and watercolour painted sheets, many of which were used for the woodcuts in his books. In order to achieve his grandiose project of depicting the whole of nature, Aldrovandi employed painters, draughtsmen, and engravers, whose work he personally supervised. Those who worked most closely with the Bolognese scholar were the painter Giovanni Neri, the draughtsmen (*delineatores*) Cornelio Schwindt of Frankfurt am Main and Lorenzo Benini, and the carver Cristoforo Coriolano (Lederlein) of Nuremberg, who over a period of more than fifteen years produced most of the woodcut blocks.

As he was unable to observe directly 'in the field' (as he would have wished) all the specimens from the three kingdoms of nature, especially those in the recently discovered New World and other distant lands, Aldrovandi used the colour illustrations he was collecting to familiarise himself with those animals, plants, and minerals that he had not seen in person or that were not present in his museum; or which, if present, were badly deteriorated and therefore unrecognizable. At the time, it was particularly difficult, if not impossible, to preserve whole specimens from the animal world, so the Bolognese scientist often ended up owning small or rather insignificant parts of them (usually the so-called 'hard' parts): beaks, feathers, horns, teeth, fangs and so on.

Aldrovandi received many painted sheets thanks to his dense network of correspondents and associates, which extended from Italy to many European countries; a network of princes, patricians, clergymen, physicians, apothecaries, university teachers, travellers, and others who were simply curious about nature. Various paintings of 'foreign animals' by Giuseppe Arcimboldo came to him from Prague. He did not receive these directly from the painter, but from Francesco Padovani, a physician originally from Forlì, who gravitated towards the imperial court and had been Aldrovandi's pupil at Bologna University. Only three of these sheets have come down to us. In addition to the two displayed here, the other probably depicts a small African rodent, the jerboa, though it is seriously deteriorated. They are, however, sufficient to confirm that Arcimboldo's expertise as an illustrator of plants and animals, as demonstrated in his famous heads, derived from or was accompanied by analytical observation of nature. All five of the exotic animals depicted on these three sheets are copies of images in the Cod. min. 42 and the Cod. min. 129 and 130 in the Austrian National Library of Vienna, the last two known under the name 'Museum of Emperor Rudolf II'.

GIUSEPPE OLMI, LUCIA TONGIORGI TOMASI

Cat. 32

Turkey (Meleagris gallopavo)

16th cent.
Tempera and watercolour on paper; 474 × 372 mm
Alma Mater Studiorum – Università di Bologna, Biblioteca Universitaria di Bologna, Ms. Aldrovandi, *Tavole di animali*, vol. I, fol. 69

Provenance: Ulisse Aldrovandi
Literature: Aldrovandi 1600, 35–45; Olmi 1992, passim; Olmi 2015; Olmi 2015a

The flora and fauna specimens or illustrations that Ulisse Aldrovandi most wished to own were those of distant and (for him) inaccessible lands. To him, the most fascinating of these was the recently discovered New World, which, according to the first reports, was distinguished by an extraordinarily exuberant nature, rich in mysterious and wonderful specimens. Although there were still many things to be discovered in Asia, Africa, and Europe, in America everything was new and different to what had been written about by ancient and medieval authors, and so was yet to be fully revealed. The Bolognese scholar's efforts to educate himself about the lands discovered by Christopher Columbus (which Aldrovandi described as 'almost another world') are testified to by the numerous books on the subject in his very rich library, often in Italian translations printed in Venice – such as *Navigationi et viaggi* by G.B. Ramusio, *Delle cose che vengono portate dalle Indie Occidentali pertinenti all'uso della medicina* by Nicolás Monardes, *Historia del mondo nuovo* by Girolamo Benzoni, and *Historia naturale e morale delle Indie* by José Acosta.

Aldrovandi came into possession of numerous images of American plants and animals, such as the pineapple, the rooster and hen 'from the Indies', as well as the agouti received as a gift from Francesco I de' Medici, Grand Duke of Tuscany, and painted by Jacopo Ligozzi, or, as seems more likely, by Ligozzi's cousin Francesco di Mercurio. Other images included the two splendid parrots that lived in the apartment of Eleonora Gonzaga, Duchess of Mantua, painted by Theodoro Ghisi; the *Reversus indicus aculeatus* sent by the Roman collector Tommaso de' Cavalieri, a friend of Michelangelo; and the *Berberis America* and *Acacia Americana* received from Lisbon.

The painter of the plate depicting a turkey is unknown; he may have been Giovanni Neri. The bird had already been portrayed in 1555 in the *Histoire de la nature des oyseaux* by Pierre Belon and in the *Historiae Animalium Liber III: Qui est de Avium natura* by Conrad Gessner. The bird was also painted by Jacopo Zucchi and associates in the Stanza degli Uccelli in Villa Medici, Rome, in 1576/77. Aldrovandi published a woodcut of the male turkey, and another of the female, in the second volume of his *Ornithologia* (1600). He claimed that the bird, seen by him directly ('touched with the hand'), was already widely known among European people and, although he stated that it had arrived from 'new India' about eighty years before, was reluctant to rule out that it had already been known to the ancient Greeks and Romans.

Giuseppe Olmi, Lucia Tongiorgi Tomasi

Cat. 33 (not included in the exhibition)

Giuseppe Arcimboldo (1526–1593)

Vertumnus

c.1590
Lime panel; 68 × 56 cm
Bålsta, Skokloster Castle

Provenance: 1621 Emperor Rudolf II, Prague; 1648 Hans Christoffer von Königsmarck; 1680, 1728 Bogesund Castle (?); 1845 Skokloster Castle
Literature: Exh. cat. Paris and Vienna 2007/08, 186, cat. IV.38 (Thomas DaCosta Kaufmann); Nardelli 2014, 75–82; Ferino-Pagden 2017/18, 157

When Arcimboldo returned to his native Milan, Emperor Rudolf II, a collector of art, requested further works from his former court artist and is said to have eagerly awaited this painting in Prague (Lomazzo 1590 & 1973/74, vol. 1, 364). When the picture reached him, it was accompanied by an explanatory poem by Gregorio Comanini (*Il Figino*, Comanini 1591 & 1962, 268–7). It stated that the painting was a double portrait – Rudolf II as the ancient god Vertumnus (from the Latin *vertere*, 'to change'), the god of transformation, agriculture, and the seasons. All of the latter can be found in the composite head, which is made up of different kinds of fruit, vegetables, grains, and flowers. Rudolf's distinguishing features – plump cheeks (apple, peach), bags under the eyes (pears), a beard (nuts, chestnuts; millet clusters as jowls or mutton chops?) – are also represented. There are also cherries, grapes, a fig, and a sash of flowers (carnation, rose, tulip, etc.), all in full ripeness or bloom.

The double portrait refers to the cycles of the *Seasons* (cats. 29.1, 29.2) and the *Elements* (cats. 30.1–30.3) which Arcimboldo had made for the Viennese imperial court, although with the difference that here the ruler's iconography is merged into one portrait – Rudolf is equated with the god of the seasons. He possesses not only worldly power, he also rules over nature (Fischel 2009, 137). This changes under the influence of the elements (water, air). Fruits ripen and flowers bloom, a process of transformation that was also associated with alchemy – a subject Rudolf harboured a passion for and to which the *Vertumnus* double portrait might also allude (Nardelli 2014).

Arcimboldo was probably inspired by the ancient poet Propertius (DaCosta Kaufmann 1993, 129–35), who maintained that Vertumnus reigned all year round. Propertius lived and worked in a period of flourishing literature under Emperor Augustus, when Rome, after years of civil wars, was experiencing a time of peace, the so-called Golden Age. Rudolf II saw himself as Augustus's successor and after the Ottoman Wars presented himself as the preserver of prosperity. At the same time, Comanini also referred to the *Vertumnus* – probably in jest – as a 'monster' and a 'hieroglyph', although from a European point of view a hieroglyph is a pictorial script with a hidden meaning. Perhaps this is the key to a deeper understanding that stretches back to antiquity, when hybrid creatures, including monsters, were described as 'humorous pictures' (DaCosta Kaufmann 2008, 100). The multiple meanings were certainly to Rudolf's taste – in 1592 he rewarded Arcimboldo, naming him a count palatine.

Wencke Deiters

Cats. 34.1, 34.2

Johan Gregor van der Schardt (1530–after 1581), models, attributed

Sol

1570/81
Bronze (hollow, indirect cast with 78 % copper, 10.1 % tin, 6.9 % lead, 3.2 % zinc); H 45.7 cm
Amsterdam, Rijksmuseum, inv. BK-1977-24
Provenance: Heim Gallery, London, 1977
Literature: Halsema-Kubes 1989, 182–4; exh. cat. Vienna 1987, no. I.9; Honnens de Lichtenberg 1991, 104–11, figs. 59–62; Scholten, Van Langh, and Verber 2005, cat. 35 (Frits Scholten), 165 (no. 35, Robert van Langh), figs. 35a–b; Scholten 2013, 135, 136, fig. 2; Scholten 2015, no. 101; exh. cat. Potsdam and Paris 2023, 79, no. 4

Luna

1570/81
Bronze (hollow, indirect cast with 84 % copper, 7.6 % tin, 3.6 % lead, 3.6 % zinc); H 51 cm
Vienna, Kunsthistorisches Museum, inv. KK 5511

Provenance: Archduke Leopold Wilhelm (1614–1662)
Literature: Stampart and Prenner 1735, 30; Weihrauch 1967, 143, fig. 163; exh. cat. Vienna 1987, no. I.10; Honnens de Lichtenberg 1991, 104–11, figs. 59–62; Scholten, Van Langh, and Verber 2005, 112, 115; Scholten 2013, 135, 136, pl. 2

This masked pair personifies the celestial bodies Sol (Sun) and Luna (Moon). Before *Sol* rose from the darkness of history in 1977, only *Luna* was known in art historical literature and attributed to the Venetian sculptor Danese Cattaneo. Both statuettes were then linked by Anthony Radcliffe (former keeper of the sculpture collection of the Victoria & Albert Museum in Londen) and ascribed to a sculptor of Dutch origin, Johan Gregor van der Schardt, who worked in Nuremberg in the service of Emperor Maximilian II from 1570 onwards (Halsema-Kubes 1989, 184, note 3). That attribution has since been widely accepted. The stylistic and iconographic connection between the two sculptures is underscored by the strong similarities in alloy composition (information kindly provided by Arie Pappot, Rijksmuseum).

Sol and Luna are traditionally part of a larger cosmological allegory, reflecting the universe. This allegorical system includes the six other celestial bodies of our solar system, each of which was assigned to a classical god or goddess: Mercury, Saturn, Mars, Venus, Jupiter, with Earth (or Cybele) in the centre of this universe. Supplemented by the four elements, this created a series of twelve that also corresponded to the twelve signs of the zodiac. According to Platonic and Pythagorean ideas, which were still very much alive in the early modern period, these celestial bodies and constellations governed and influenced the course of everything on earth. As such Sol appears opposite to Tempus, the personification of Time, in an engraving by Maarten de Vos from c. 1585, depicting the cycle of the vicissitudes of human life (Hollstein 1996, Nr. 1266). Within this cosmological ensemble, Sol and Luna also represent Day and Night and are associated with the gods Apollo (Phoebus, the radiant one) and Diana. The bronze *Luna* therefore also carries the goddess's hunting attributes, the horn and spear. Moreover, the pair were linked to the signs of the zodiac. A lion (the sign of Leo) stands behind the figure of *Sol*, while a now-missing crab (representing Cancer) may have stood behind Luna, fixed in a square hole in her right calf.

It has been assumed that both bronzes were originally intended for a large table fountain in which the seven planets were united; such cosmological waterworks enjoyed a certain popularity among the sixteenth- and early seventeenth-century German nobility. Like caryatids, the bronzes would have carried a basin into which water would have flowed from the pipes that both figures hold above their heads. With their irregular, block-shaped plinths, they were then sunk into the base of the waterwork. Recent technical research demonstrated, however, that it is unlikely that *Sol* ever functioned as a fountain figure. Contrary to earlier reports there is and was no pipe leading up through his body and head to the partially cut-off top, since the lower half of the figure is a solid cast. It is possible that the lion originally contained a pipe, as part of an internal water system that led up through the animal's left front leg through its head and out of its open mouth. The opening for the pipe is still visible on the underside, and part of the pipe's path can be seen on radiography images. In addition, the pipe surmounting *Luna*'s head has no open connection to an eventual internal water system; instead, it appears to have been unintentionally sealed shut during the casting process. All this suggests that the fountain was never completed, with the two realized statues treated as autonomous works thereafter. Perhaps initially they were seen as a pair, but have been separated at least since the seventeenth century, since only *Luna* appears in Archduke Leopold Wilhelm's inventory, and she is also depicted – on her own – in a 1735 engraving with statues from the archduke's collection.

The similarities in pose and attributes between *Sol* and *Luna* with the same personifications in the series of monumental bronze planets made by the Antwerp sculptor Jacques Jongelinck around 1570 (and reproduced in print by Philips Galle in 1585) are so great that there must have been a common source or some form of interdependence. The fact that the alloy compositions of both statuettes show strong similarities to alloys of Jongelinck's bronzes may not be without significance in this context and calls for further investigation (information kindly provided by Arie Pappot, Rijksmuseum). Since both Van der Schardt and Jongelinck worked in Habsburg service, it is not inconceivable that they were aware of each other's work – perhaps through plaster casts of Van der Schardt's inventions? In any case, the motif of the raised arm, which figures prominently in both artists' works, appears to be an invention of Van der Schardt's given its functionality: the raised hands hold the pipes coming out of the heads of *Sol* and *Luna* through which the fountain water was to be led upwards.

Frits Scholten

Cats. 35.1–35.4

Johan Gregor van der Schardt (1530–after 1581), models; Georg Labenwolf (?–1585), casts

Flora, Ceres, Bacchus, and Vulcan, representing the Four Seasons

1570/76
Gilt-bronze; H 72 cm
Vienna, Kunsthistorisches Museum, Kunstkammer, invs. KK 1118, KK 1122, KK 1126, KK 1130

Provenance: Emperor Rudolf II, Prague, 1578
Literature: Exh. cat. Nuremberg 1985, cats. 27–30 (Klaus Pechstein); Schürer 1986; Honnens de Lichtenberg 1991, 97–104, figs. 49–58; exh. cat. Berlin 1995, cats. 94–97 (Ursel Berger); Hauschke 2002, 250–5; Scholten 2013, 135, 136, pl. 1

In the summer of 1569, the Dutch sculptor Johan Gregor van der Schardt exchanged Venice for Nuremberg where, on the recommendation of Daniele Barbaro, the Venetian theologian and translator of Vitruvius, he entered the service of Emperor Maximilian II. He had then worked for at least a decade in various places in Italy and had developed into a versatile sculptor in bronze, stone, terracotta, and stucco. Vasari, in his 1568 *Vite*, praised 'Giovanni di Sart di Nimega' as a 'scultore studiosissimo e diligente', and two years earlier Lodovico Guicciardini called him 'Ian de Sart de Nimmeghe, excellent sculpteur' (Honnens de Lichtenberg 1991, 15). Moreover, in 1587, Gabriel Kaltemarckt in Dresden ranked Van der Schardt among the sculptors whose work absolutely should not be missing from a *Kunstkammer* (Scholten 2013, 134). Probably shortly after his arrival in Nuremberg, Van der Schardt became involved in one of the most ambitious imperial commissions of the time: a partially gilt-silver table fountain that would become known as the *schöne Brunnen* or *Prager Brunnen*. It had been commissioned from Nuremberg's leading silversmith, Wenzel Jamnitzer, in 1568. Ten years later, the project was completed and delivered to the new emperor, Rudolf II, in Prague.

For the complex programme centred on the glorification of the Habsburg emperor within the whole cosmos, Jamnitzer was probably advised by humanists at court, including his neighbour Jacopo Strada (Jansen 2019, I, 96–9). More than three metres high, the fountain had the shape of an open-work spherical Habsburg imperial crown, decorated with many coats of arms and composed inside of several tiers, each corresponding to one of the four elements. Numerous moving figures and flowing water made it a huge spectacle that was characterized by a contemporary as something 'das ichs nit describiren kann' ('something that I cannot describe'; exh. cat. Nuremberg 1985, 231). The huge waterwork rested on four gilt-bronze caryatids, arranged in a circle of around one and a half metres in diameter and connected by a brass cross on the floor. They depict two classical gods and two goddesses, as personifications of the four seasons: Flora as Spring, Ceres as Summer, Bacchus as Autumn, and Vulcan as Winter. Standing on square bases and crowned by capitals, they form the anthropomorphic shafts of four columns in the Tuscan order. Amid them, on the brass cross, originally stood a lion with the coats of arms of Burgundy and Austria. Within the entire iconographic programme, the four sculptures represent the element of time, both the continuous cycle of emergence, growth, flowering, and decay of the seasons and the ages of men.

It is generally assumed that Van der Schardt was responsible for this sculptural component, but whether he also participated in the modelling of the fountain's numerous other figures, including statues of Cybele, Neptune, Mercury, and Jupiter, is unknown. The four bronzes – the only part of the fountain remaining after the precious metal parts were melted down between 1747 and 1750 – unmistakably show his style, shaped by the graceful elegance of late-Cinquecento Venetian sculpture of Alessandro Vittoria and his contemporaries. It cannot be ruled out that Van der Schardt spent some time working with Vittoria before settling in Nuremberg. Characteristic of this *bellissima maniera* are the elongated bodies, the small, high breasts of the women, the slight curve of the hips, and the graceful poses that give the carrying figures, despite their heavy task, a somewhat relaxed and light-footed air. Their sideways gazes and outstretched arms, with which they offer each other useful products, visually link the foursome and create a circular movement that reflects the cyclical aspect of the seasons. The sculptor allowed himself slight variations in the poses here and there – Bacchus/Autumn, for instance, looks with his face in the opposite direction to the other three. Such variations lend a certain liveliness to the ensemble and may also subtly express the unstable nature of the seasons.

Frits Scholten

Cat. 36

Jobst Bürgi (1552–1632)

So-called Viennese Planetary Clock

Prague, c.1605
Brass, gilt, silver, gouache, rock crystal, glass (clockwork: iron, brass); H 39.3 cm
Vienna, Kunsthistorisches Museum, Kunstkammer, inv. KK 846

Provenance: 1621 Imperial Treasury, no. 275; 1633 Imperial Treasury, no. 17; 1750 Imperial Treasury inventory, no. 24; 1875 Imperial Treasury inventory, II, 51, 36; 1890 from the Imperial Treasury
Literature: Mus. cat. Vienna 2012, 224–5; mus. cat. Vienna 2013, 160–1, no. 70; exh. cat. St Gallen 2023, 124–7, cat. BWV 5

This clock is the product of an intense and fruitful cooperation between (artistic) handcraft and science. Imperial clockmaker Jobst Bürgi made use of the most up-to-date findings of court astronomer Johannes Kepler on the heliocentric system of the planets. The intricacies of the mechanism can be seen in the dials, the hands, and the rotating ball in the turret. The most important technical innovation was the use of a mechanism to wind the clock. This lifted a weight that then powered the clockwork as it descended. The constant force that resulted made possible a running time of several weeks. In addition to showing the time, the device can also display the motions of the planets known at the time of its creation: Mercury, Venus, Mars, Jupiter, and Saturn. Interestingly, alongside the new heliocentric system, the traditional geocentric system was also visualized.

The niche-shaped side sections and the lid of the housing are decorated with intricate engravings. The motifs range from fruit garlands and flower vases to butterflies. The subjects are reminiscent of the delicate Dutch miniature paintings of the time, which were masterfully produced by, for example, Georg Hoefnagel. A thorough study of nature was required for such precise depictions with their almost scientific naturalism. The grown interest in botanical and zoological studies influenced the development of natural history and propelled it forward. As a result of Bürgli, Kepler, and Hoefnagel's activities at his court in Prague, Emperor Rudolf II, with his affinity for art, created fertile ground for developments in which technology, nature, and the human will to create were intertwined.

Thomas Kuster

Cat. 37

Daniel Fröschl (1563–1613)

The Fall from Grace

1604
Gouache on paper; 241 × 180 mm (with gold border)
Vienna, Albertina, inv. 3352

Provenance: Duke Albert von Sachsen-Teschen (seal unclear)
Literature: Boeheim 1889, XIV, no. 5630; mus. cat. Vienna 1933, 457; exh. cat. Stuttgart 1980, vol. 2, 170; DaCosta Kaufmann 1985, 218; Tongiorgi Tomasi and Garbari 1995, 37; Knedlik 2005, 380–1; exh. cat. New York 2014, 224–6, cat. 135, fig. 53; exh. cat. Hradec Králové 2021, 52–3; Tschetschik-Hammerl 2023, 294; sincere thanks to Christof Metzger for his information

Born in Augsburg and the son of a lawyer who was knowledgable about art, Daniel Fröschl came into contact with international works of art at an early age. His lifelong interest in depictions of nature may have been rooted in his years of study in Nuremberg, where he received drawing lessons from no less a figure than Wenzel Jamnitzer. After his first professional experience in Heidelberg, he travelled to Italy – financed by the Fugger family – where he became a miniaturist at the Medici court and produced illustrations of the collection of the Pisa botanical garden. Thus, Fröschl became part of the scholarly culture that was widespread in various European courts around 1600 'in which interests in natural history, collecting, and art were symbiotically intertwined'. In 1604, he became the official painter of miniatures at Emperor Rudolf II's court in Prague, where from 1607 he worked as an *antiquarius* on the inventory of the emperor's *Kunstkammer*. This inventory reveals Fröschl's profound knowledge of the fine arts as well as natural history.

This monogrammed, small-format composition of Adam and Eve in the Garden of Eden is based on a drawing by Bartholomäus Spranger. Eve hands Adam the fateful apple under the watchful eye of Satan in his guise as the serpent. The massive tree trunk that Adam is leaning against appears to be covered in dense scales. The miniaturist technique used here by Fröschl is borrowed from Giulio Clovio. The pictorial elements are set off from each other by filigree lines of different colours; the use of tiny dots and strokes disguises the individuality of the artist's hand. Fröschl may have used this technique to create the impression that his works were not produced by human craftsmanship, but, like the natural phenomena he valued so highly, in an almost miraculous manner (for Vasari's assessment of Clovio's technique, see Vasari 1568 (1880), vol. 6, 217). Another sheet in a private collection shows the same motif, framed by detailed depictions of nature, which may have been made by Jacob Hoefnagel, the son of Joris Hoefnagel.

Evelyn Klammer

Cat. 38

Hans Hoffmann (1545/50–1591/92)

The Expulsion from Paradise

1580/90
Lime panel; 30.5 × 44.5 cm
Vienna, Kunsthistorisches Museum, Picture Gallery, inv. 917

Provenance: 1772 verified in the gallery
Literature: Pilz 1962; DaCosta Kaufmann 1982; Koreny and Segal 1989/90; Hendrix 1997; Stüwe 1998; DaCosta Kaufmann 2009, 146; exh. cat. Milan 2011, cat. 170 (Giuseppe Olmi and Lucia Tongiorgi Tomasi); exh. cat. Innsbruck 2015, 190–1, cat. 4.2 (Annemarie Jordan Gschwend); exh. cat. Nuremberg 2022; Doosry 2022; Tschetschik-Hammerl 2023

Hans Hoffmann, who is known to have been in Nuremberg from the 1570s onwards, was regarded by his contemporaries as a gifted Dürer adept. His abilities secured him the favour of influential patrons, including Emperor Rudolf II, who summoned him to the court in Prague in 1585 (presumably mediated by the art agent Jacopo Strada). There, in addition to portraits, Dürer studies, and scientific depictions, Hoffmann increasingly devoted himself to complex artistic tasks. *The Expulsion from Paradise* is one such example and illustrates Hoffmann's working method.

The painting was compiled from a variety of sources. His elements – human figures, plants, and animals – are closely interwoven in the style of Dürer. On the right, the pictorial space opens up into a world landscape modelled on Dutch painting. The group of figures, Adam, Eve, and the Archangel Michael, is a direct adaption of a composition by the Italian Girolamo Siciolante. Hoffmann did not rely on his own observations in his depictions of animals, for which he would have found many models in the emperor's menagerie in Prague. Instead, he consulted studies by other artists. Some of the animals are clearly references to Dürer, such as the reclining lion, the parrot, or the hare seen from behind near the right-hand edge of the picture. The jerboa under Eva's left foot and the prominently placed gazelle are, however, in all probability quotations from Giuseppe Arcimboldo, who worked for Emperor Rudolf II in Prague – overlapping with Hoffmann for two years – and had previously made studies of animals belonging to Maximilian II in Vienna.

The flora and fauna are not completely true to life, although Hoffmann would undoubtedly have been capable of rendering them accurately. It is possible that the artist trusted his models blindly – in the truest sense of the word – and, in the context of a panel painting, attached greater importance to artistic re-creation than to the truthful reproduction of the natural objects.

Evelyn Klammer

Cat. 39

Roelant Savery (1576/78–1639)

Orpheus with the Animals

1625/28
Copper; 27.5 x 36 cm
Vienna, Kunsthistorisches Museum, Picture Gallery, inv. 3534

Provenance: 1783 Vienna Gallery
Literature: Müllenmeister 1988, 299, pl. 214; exh. cat. Cremona and Vienna 2000/01, 178–9, cat. II. 29 (Alexander Wied); exh. cat. Tokyo and Kobe 2004, 188, cat. 13 (Karl Schütz); exh. cat. Innsbruck 2015, 196–7, cat. 4.5 (Karl Schütz)

This painting by Flemish artist Roelant Savery depicts an idyllic landscape, where trees and rock formations frame a peaceful coexistence of various animals. Alongside European animals, such as deer, squirrels, horses, and dogs, the imaginary scene includes exotic species, including lions, dromedaries, elephants, and ostriches. The focus of most animals is directed towards Orpheus, sitting on a rock in the middle ground of the picture, playing his lyre. In Greek mythology, Orpheus ventures into the underworld to bring back his deceased wife, Eurydice. Moved by his music, the gods agree to her return, but only if Orpheus refrains from looking back at her until they reach the world of the living. Unable to resist, he glances back, and Eurydice disappears forever. Heartbroken, Orpheus retreats into nature, where his music is so captivating that it enchants trees and tames wild beasts. In the late sixteenth and seventeenth centuries, Flemish painters revived the theme of Orpheus surrounded by animals in a paradise-like setting. As the emphasis shifted towards scientifically accurate depictions of animals, the mythological aspect receded, leading Savery to produce multiple versions of the scene. His meticulous attention to detail and use of vibrant earth tones in painting the animals and trees highlight his extraordinary skill as a nature painter. From 1603/04, Savery worked for Emperor Rudolf II in Prague, and later in Vienna, before moving to Utrecht in 1619. The court of Rudolf II housed not only the greatest art collection of its time but also an impressive array of exotic plants and animals. In the imperial menageries, Savery created study drawings of many of the rare species featured in his paintings, some of which – like the turkey – were being seen in Europe for the first time. During his productive career, Savery evolved into a remarkably versatile artist, celebrated for creating the Netherlands' first floral still life and his famous depictions of the now-extinct dodo.

Charlotte Roosen

Humankind Through the Passage of Time

(cats. 40–44)

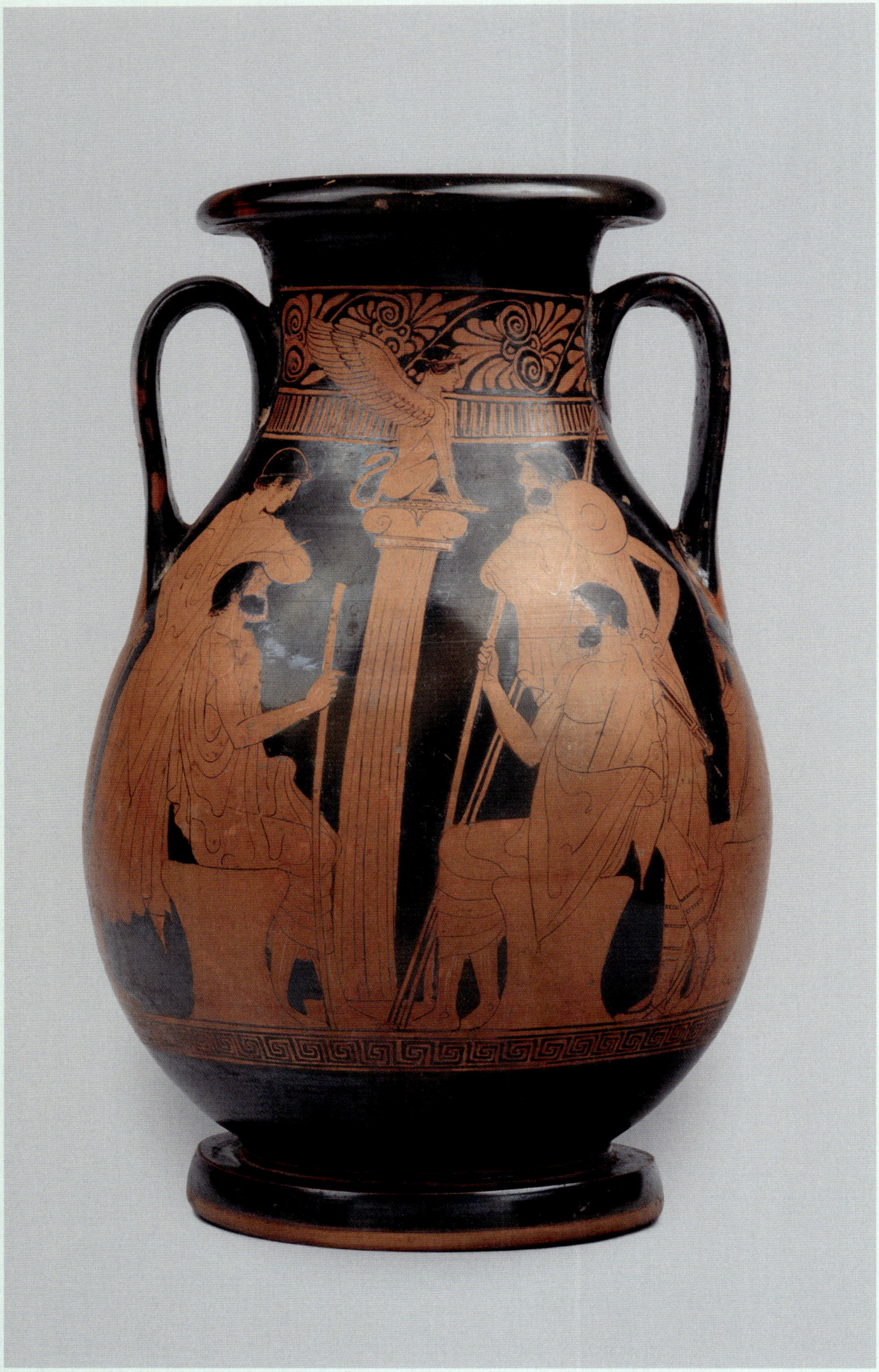

Cat. 40, Hermonax, *Pelike: Oedipus and the Sphinx*

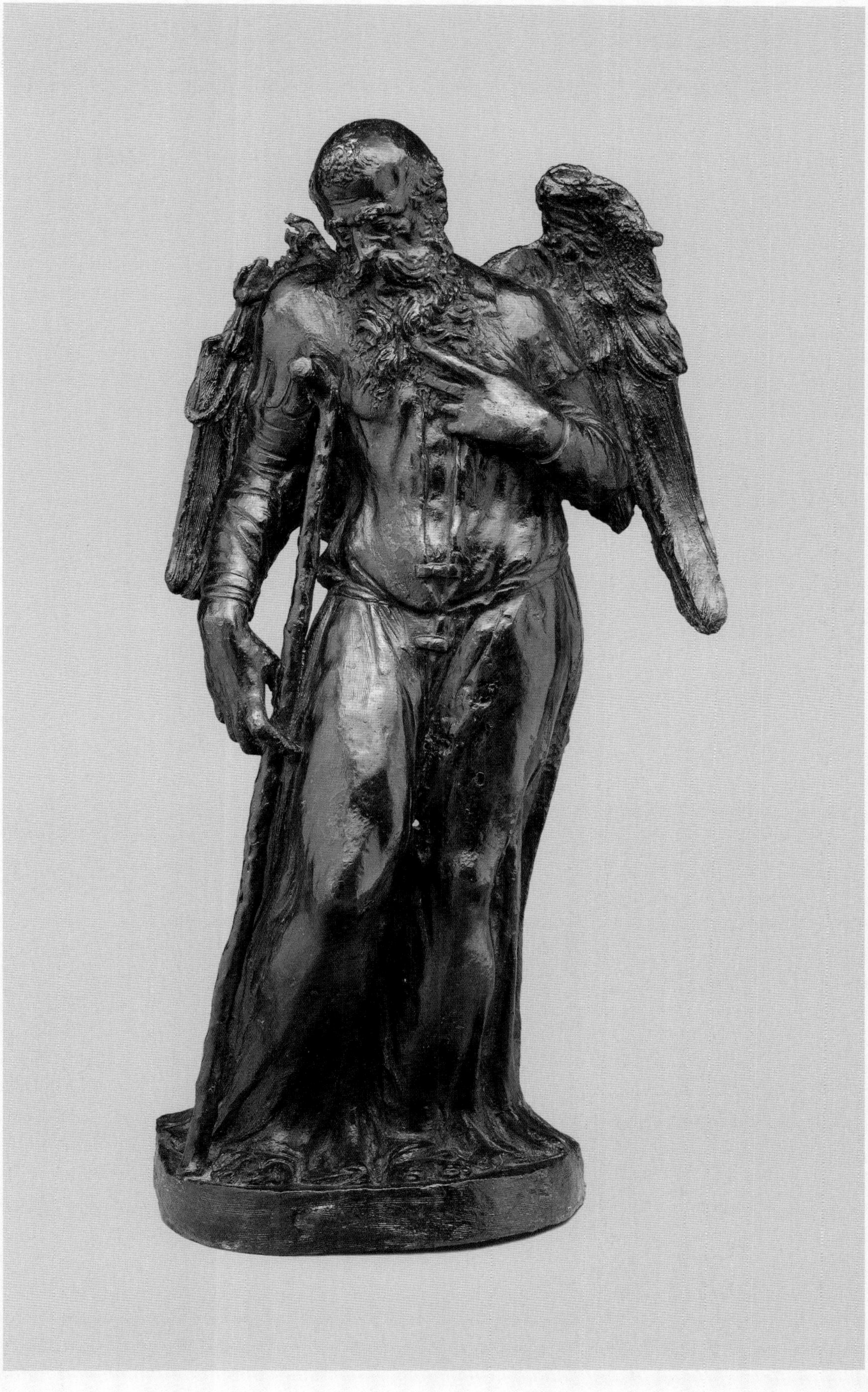

Cat. 41, Agostino Zoppo, *Chronos*

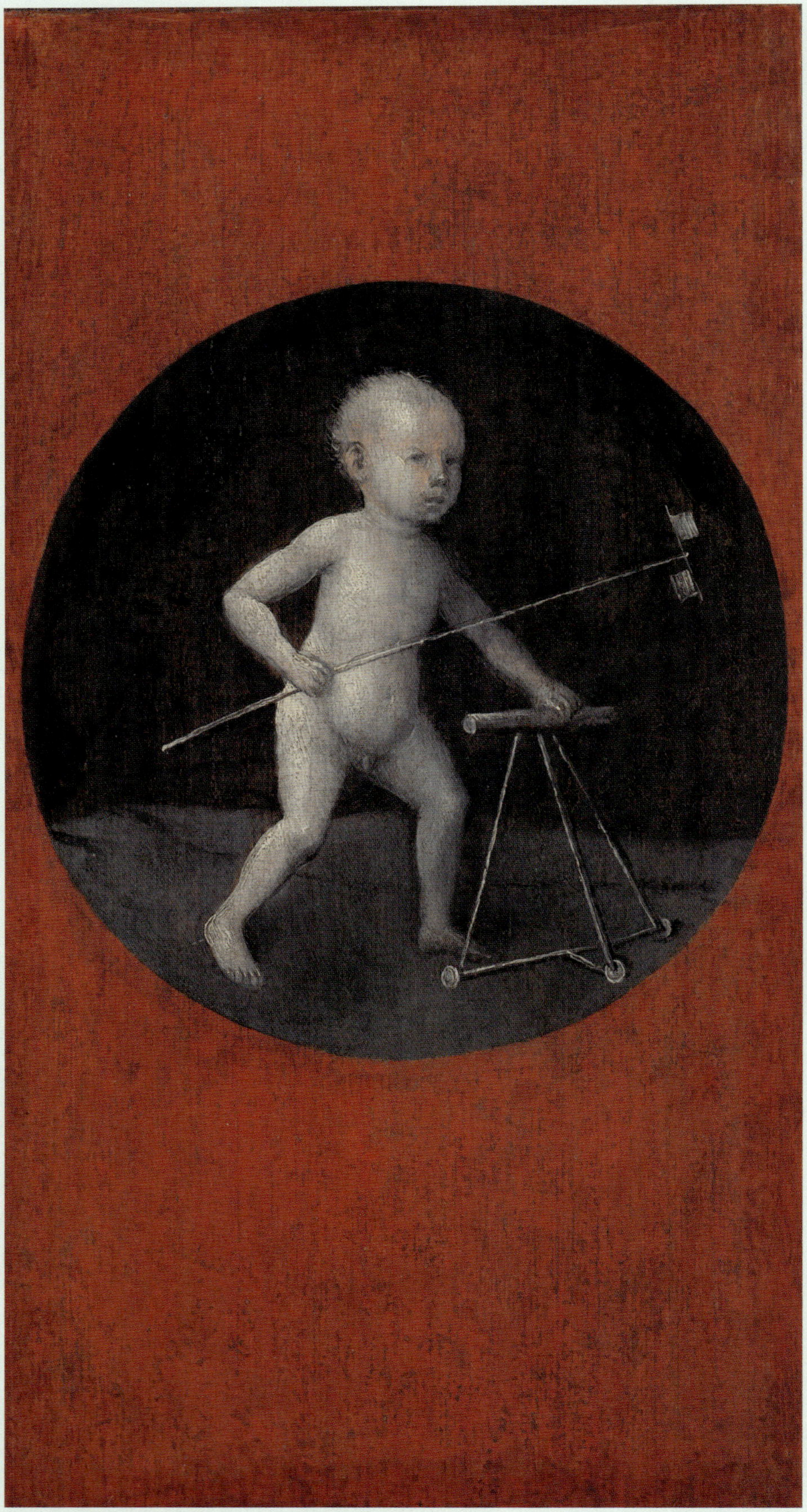

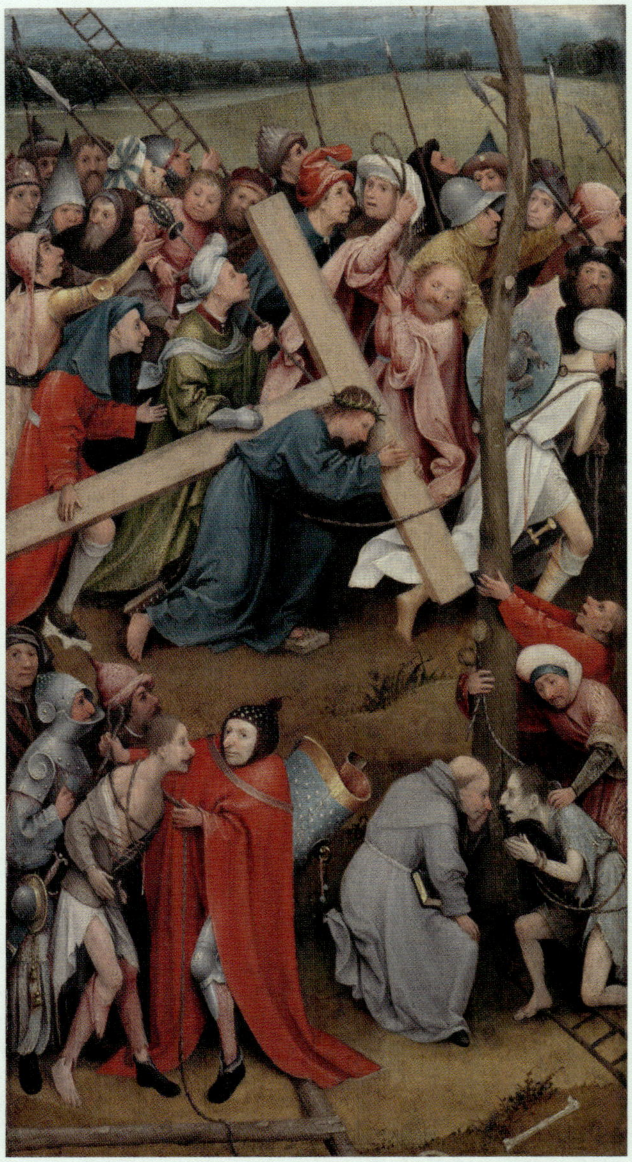

Cat. 42, Hieronymus Bosch, Left wing of a triptych with *Christ Child* and *Christ Carrying the Cross*

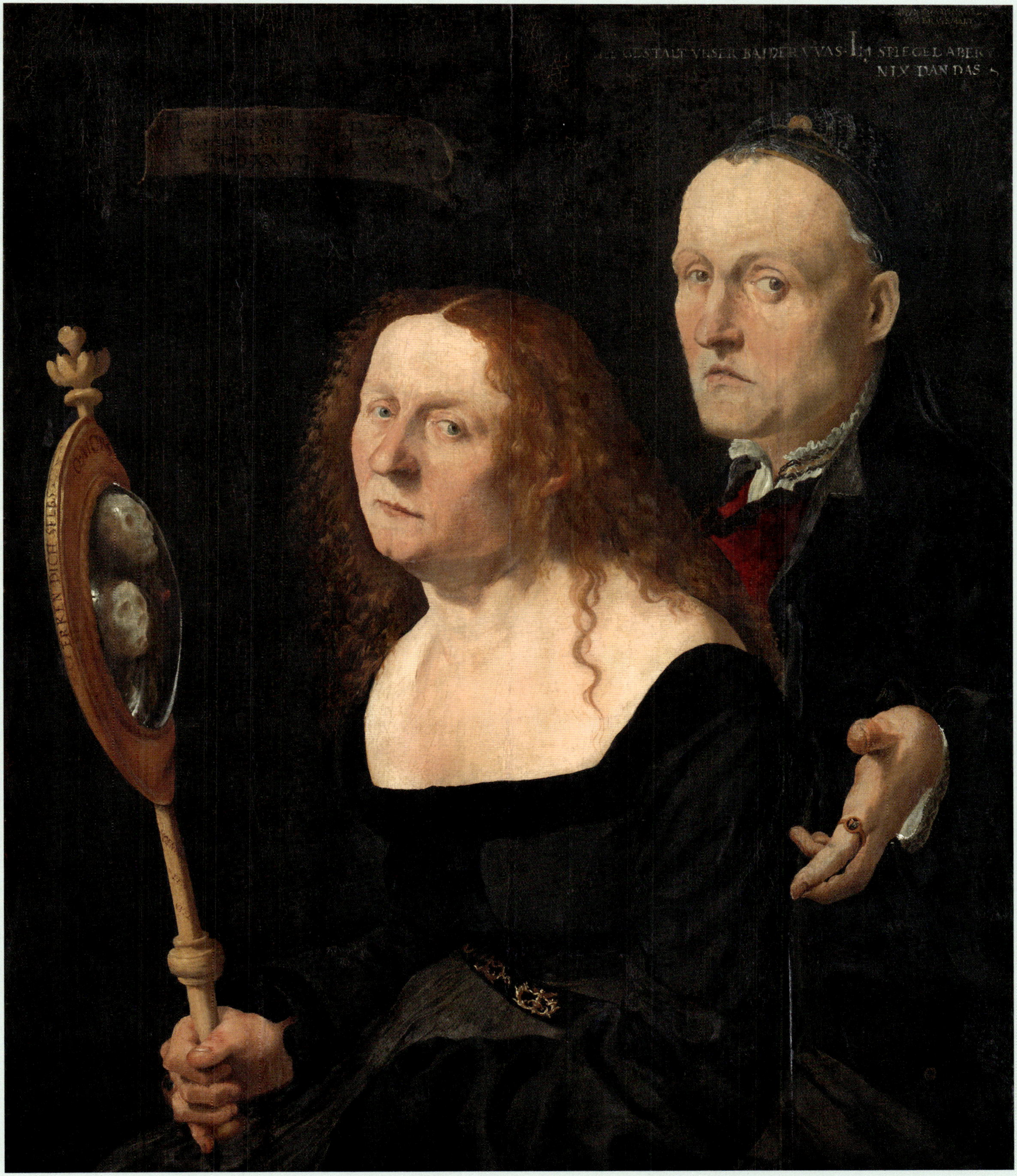

Cat. 43, Laux Furtenagel, *Portrait of Hans Burgkmair the Elder and his Wife Anna née Allerlay*

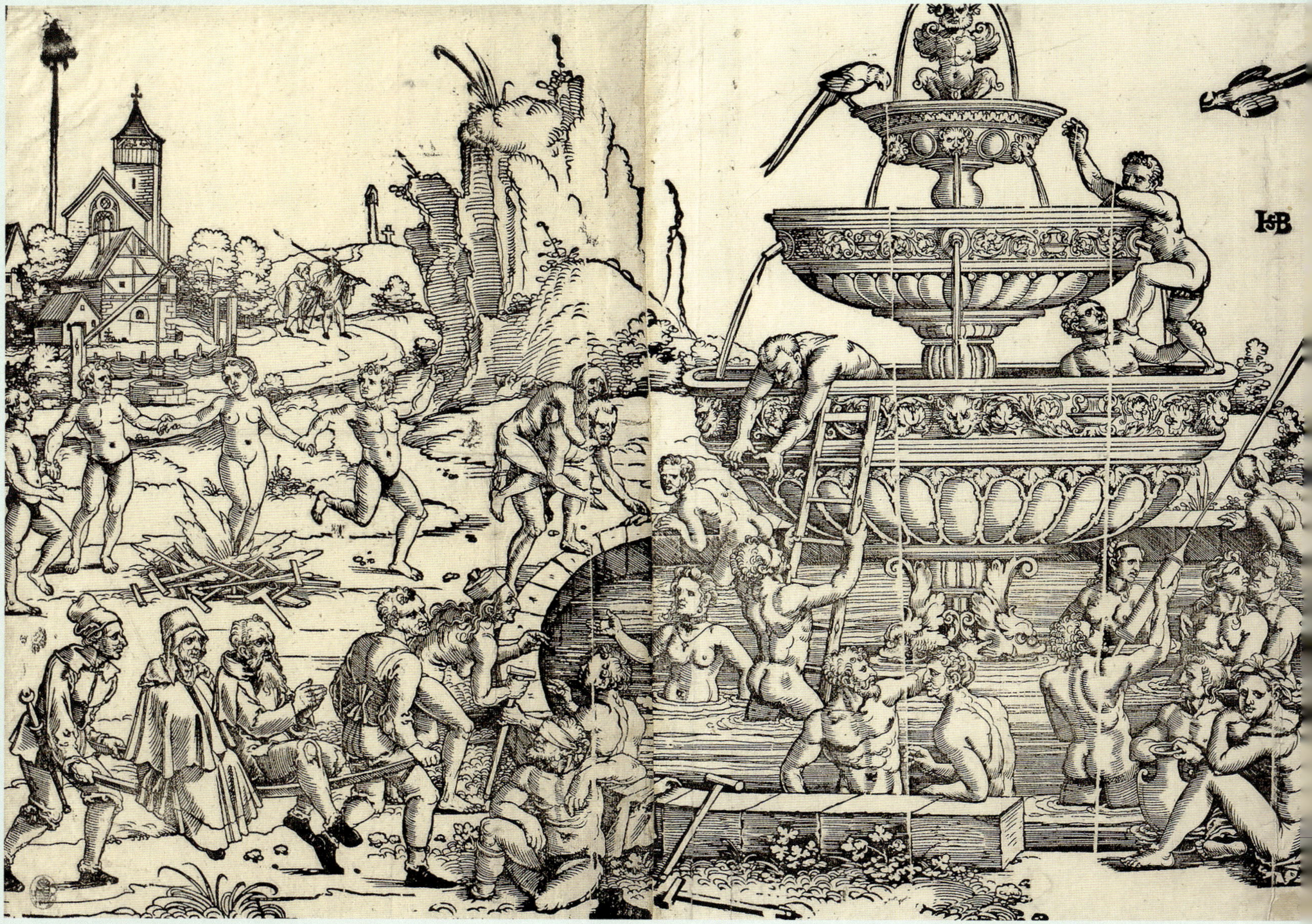

Cat. 44, Sebald Beham, *The Fountain of Youth*

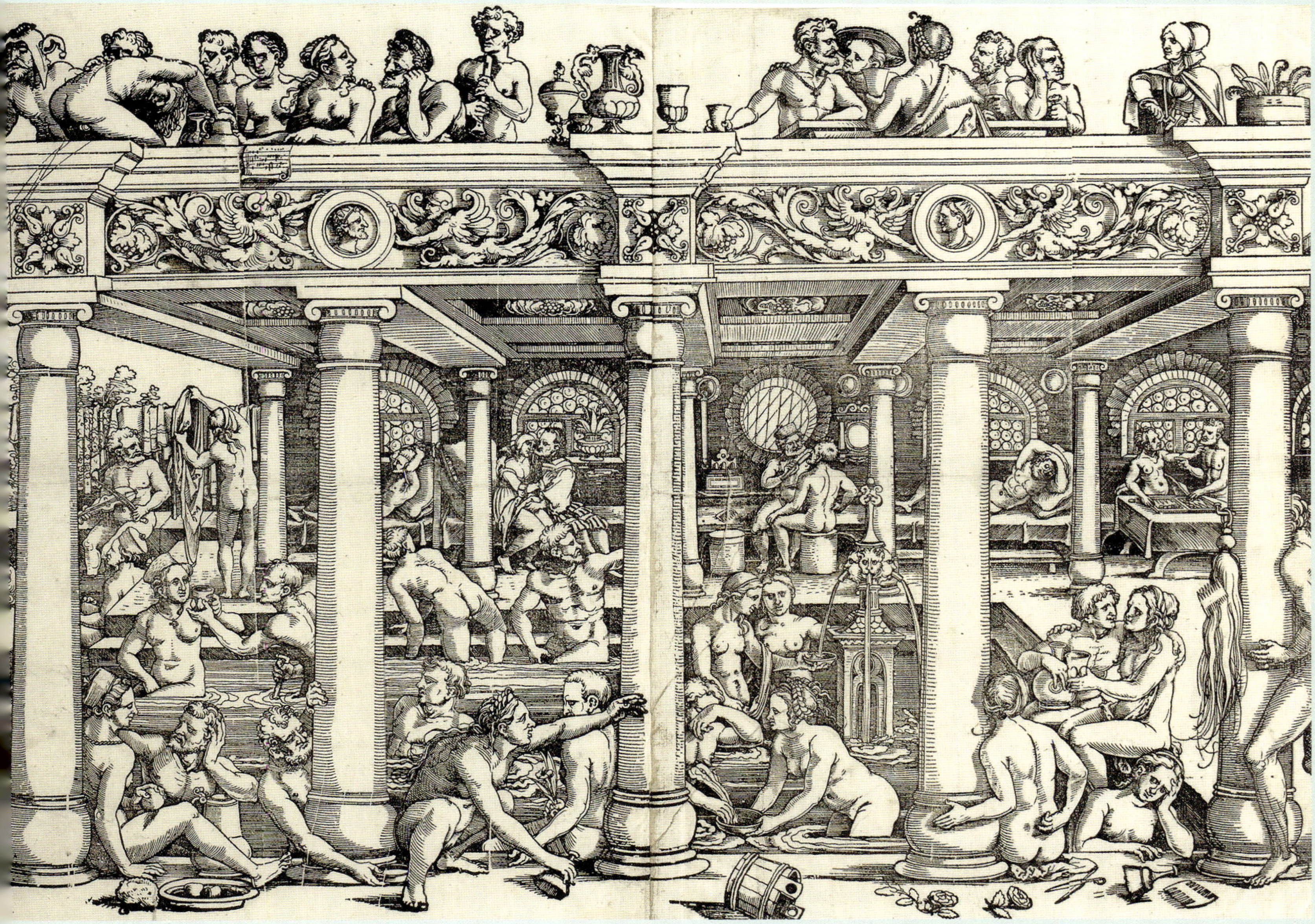

Cat. 40

Unknown potter, Hermonax (painter, active 470–440 BCE in Athens)

Pelike: Oedipus and the Sphinx

Classical Greek, Attic, red-figured, 470–460 BCE
Clay; H 39.5 cm, dia. 26.5 cm; inscription: 'Hermonax'
Vienna, Kunsthistorisches Museum, Collection of Greek and Roman Antiquities, inv. IV 3728

Provenance: Discovery site, Caere (Cerveteri, Italy); 1865 purchase from A. Castellani collection, Rome; 1940 acquired from Österreichisches Museum für Kunst und Industrie
Literature: *Tabula Cebetis* 1497; Diodorus 1508, fol. XCVIr; Alciato 1542, 46; Alciato 1602, 844–50; CVA Österreich 1959, pl. 74; Beazley 1963, 485, no. 24; Hausmann 1972, 14–15, figs. 5-7; Moret 1984, 49, no. 71, pls. 40, 41; mus. cat. Vienna 2009, 112, no. 43 (A. Bernhard-Walcher)

A famous scene from the Theban sagas appears on this pelike (a jar used to hold wine or oil). The city of Thebes is being ravaged by the Sphinx, a monstrous hybrid creature with the body of a lioness, the head of a woman, and the wings of a bird. According to a prophecy, the Thebans will only be liberated from her when they solve her riddle: "What is it that has one voice and soon becomes four-footed, two-footed, and three-footed?" The answer is a human being, who crawls on all fours as a child, then walks on two legs, and finally needs a cane as a third leg.

Unfortunately, many men fail to solve the riddle and are devoured by the Sphinx. The king, Creon, promises dominion over Thebes and the hand of his widowed sister to whoever can save the city. Enter Oedipus, who, it was prophesied after his birth, would kill his father and marry his mother. He is indeed able to solve the riddle (the Sphinx, enraged, plunges to her death), but he does not escape his fate. Unbenownst to him, he had already killed his father, Laius, the previous king of Thebes. He will later marry his mother, Laius's widow, Jocasta. In the end, when he realizes the connections to his family, he will put out his own eyes in despair.

The depiction on the vase shows the Sphinx crouching on a high Ionic column painted in the so-called 'red-figure' pottery technique against a black background. She is surrounded by a group of men pondering the riddle. Oedipus's hat, short cloak, and boots show him to be a traveller.

Riddles were already regarded as metaphors in ancient times. The Sphinx herself was considered a symbol of death. Indeed, the Sphinx has been a popular decorative motif since the early modern era; the riddle, however, was not depicted in the pictorial arts until much later.

In the literary reception of the sixteenth century, the riddle – handed down by the Greek playwrights Aeschylus and Sophocles as well as in Diodorus's historical work – is not only an allegory of the passage of time, but above all reveals the path to Delphic self-knowledge.

Andrea Alciato, for example, dealt with the subject in his *Emblematum libellus* under the motto 'Uncertainty must be eliminated': the Sphinx is a monument to ignorance that prevents one from achieving self-knowledge. There are three reasons for this which correspond to the Sphinx's three forms: lust (the female bust), recklessness (the wings), and arrogance (the lion's body).

Conclusion: Whoever solves the riddle, knows themselves and lives happily afterwards. Whoever is too stupid, gets eaten.

Manuela Laubenberger

Cat. 41

Agostino Zoppo (c.1520–1572)

Chronos

c.1550
Bronze; H 47 cm, W 25.4 cm, D 12.7 cm
New York, The Metropolitan Museum of Art, inv. 1997.512; Edith Perry Chapman Fund, 1997

Provenance: Private collection, Europe; sold to Metropolitan Museum of Art on 10 December 1997, Bonhams, Knightsbridge, London, lot 172
Literature: Draper and Zappo 1998; mus. cat. New York 2022, no. 32, 139–43

This small bronze depicts winged Chronos, the personification of time, as a venerable figure. His classical attributes, the scythe and hourglass, are clearly recognizable. What was new in the Renaissance interpretation was the clear humanization of the divine figure by means of mild, introverted, contemplative features. Since Chronos is depicted as an old man with a long beard, the bronze also conforms to the familiar, traditional image of God the Father. In this respect, the artistic execution of Chronos clearly differs from the fearsome, threatening Grim Reapers of the Middle Ages, which were usually portrayed as skeletons. This work also reflects the change in worldview of an entire society, from the otherworldliness of the cleric to a life-affirming worldliness of here and now.

The conception of time and its accompanying transience was omnipresent for people around 1500 and determined everyday life much more intensively than it does today. While nowadays we have various technical means of tracking time at our disposal – which often make us restless – the ever-recurring days and seasons along with associated customs gave the common man of that period a set of rules and an orientation that provided routine. Paintings of the months and seasons, in particular, such as those by Jörg Breu, Pieter Bruegel, and Leandro Bassano, are dedicated to these recurring periods and address such cycles artistically.

Over the course of Renaissance humanism, the human drive to research and develop led to innovative new devices for recording time. On the one hand, their development was made possible by the study of relevant ancient writings on mechanics and technology; on the other by means of the latest discoveries around 1500. Magnificent clocks, the most refined mechanisms, and beautifully decorated scientific instruments bear witness to these efforts, which by reason of their novelty and exclusivity are frequently considered elaborate works of art (cats. 7–9, 36). It is therefore not surprising that measuring devices and instruments – the masterpieces among them were produced by masters in Augsburg and Nuremberg – found prominent homes as highly desirable collectors' objects in early modern cabinets of curiosities.

Thomas Kuster

Cat. 42

Hieronymus Bosch (c.1450–1516)

Left wing of a triptych with *Christ Child* (back) and *Christ Carrying the Cross* (front)

1490/1510
Panel; 57 × 32 cm (top originally a quarter circle closed; top c.20 cm, bottom trimmed slightly)
Vienna, Kunsthistorisches Museum, Picture Gallery, inv. 6429

Provenance: English art trade; art dealer Frederik Muller & Cie, Amsterdam, January 1923; 1923 acquired by Goudstikker family, Amsterdam; since 1923 property of the Kunsthistorisches Museum
Literature: Silver 2006, 189–93; exh. cat. Bruges 2011/12, 84, cat. 18; Koreny 2012, 28, 406; Fischer 2013, 245–6; exh. cat. 's-Hertogenbosch 2016, 70–72, cat. 15; exh. cat. Madrid 2016, 227, cat. 19; BRCP 2016, 236–47, cat. 12

This panel painting by Hieronymus Bosch, painted on both sides, was originally the left wing of a triptych that no longer exists. The back of the retable features a naked boy in semi-grisaille, framed in a circular medallion or tondo that stands out sharply from the red background; the front depicts Christ carrying the cross. The right wing of the altar was presumably of similar design; it is thought that the back depicted the young John the Baptist as a counterpart to the Christ Child, while the front might have been a picture of the Entombment or Resurrection. The central theme of the middle panel was probably the Crucifixion. Reconstruction attempts also assume that the top of the triptych was originally arched and that the panel has been trimmed by about 20 cm.

The painting on the panel's back depicts a small boy carrying a toy windmill in one hand while his other grasps a three-wheeled walker as he tries to take his first steps. The figure is moving towards the right half of the picture, with the path already travelled shown in the lower third of the circular scene. The figure of the child has been interpreted as an allegory of the lack of understanding, but also identified as the Christ Child, as his attributes refer to Christ's Passion. In addition, the genre-like character of the scene has also been underscored.

The two sides of the retable wing can be linked, especially since the pose of the Christ Child corresponds to that of Christ carrying his cross on the front. The two periods in Christ's life could not be more different, however. On the front, Christ, brought to his knees by the weight of the cross, is also moving towards the right side of the picture, to meet his fate on Mount Golgotha. Viewed together, the wing's two sides represent Christ's predetermined path of life and suffering, which began innocently with the young boy's first steps. The temporal or cyclical aspect of the scenes is further evoked by the movement of the wing when the retable was opened and closed.

Angelina Illes

Cat. 43

Laux (Lucas) Furtenagel (1505–c.1550)

Portrait of Hans Burgkmair the Elder and his Wife Anna née Allerlay

1529
Lime panel; 59.7 × 52 cm
Vienna, Kunsthistorisches Museum, Picture Gallery, inv. 924

Provenance: 1685 Prague (Prague Inventory 1685, no. 43); 1781 Pressburg/Bratislava; 1783 documented in the gallery
Literature: Baldass 1936; Falk 1968, 9, 53, 60; Hinz 1974, 167–72, fig. 30; Reitzenstein 1975; mus. cat. Vienna 1991, 60, plate 576; Birnfeld 2009, 187–93, 214–16, no. 11, fig. 158; exh. cat. Frankfurt and Vienna 2023/24, cat. 2.006 (Guido Messling)

The mirror is considered the classic symbol of Vanitas (transience), for life itself is as fleeting as the vain image in the mirror. However, it can at the same time symbolize self-knowledge. These layers of significance are combined in this double portrait, in which the Augsburg painter Hans Burgkmair (1473–1531) and his wife Anna (1477–1554) have seen their inevitable end in the form of two death heads, which appear opposite them in a convex mirror. The couple's plaintive gaze and the man's gesture are an unmistakable call for every observer to take note of the inevitability of their own death. This all-encompassing memento mori idea is echoed in inscriptions on the mirror and at the top of the picture. They also provide information about the age of the individuals depicted and the date the portrait was painted, 1529.

For a long time, the painting was considered Burgkmair's self-portrait until, in the course of a restoration in 1933, the signature of the little-known Laux Furtenagel was uncovered in the upper right corner. The painter, who refers to himself as a *Junger* ('young man', presumably also meaning 'pupil'), was born in Augsburg. Nothing is known of his relationship to Burgkmair. In the Vienna painting, which was first documented in the imperial collections in 1685, Furtenagel apparently copied, with slight variations, a self-portrait of Burgkmair and his wife, today lost. This is most likely identical with a painting that was etched in reverse in 1766 by the Augsburg artist Georg Christoph Kilian (1709–1781) and which can still be traced in Augsburg in 1788. In view of the personally coloured message and the unembellished depiction of Anna with her hair down, there can be no doubt that Burgkmair is indeed the author of the image. Inspired by the Vanitas/Prudentia allegories of Titian's circle and the depictions of skulls on mirrors that were particularly widespread in the north, the Augsburg artist created a complex work, in its content and form, that is unique among both self-portraits and portraits of married couples. What remains unclear, however, is the motivation for the resigned tone. Did the painter, who died two years later, already saw his vitality waning or did other events fuel his premonition of death?

Guido Messling

Cat. 44

Sebald Beham (1500–1550)

The Fountain of Youth

1531
Woodcut (from four blocks), 2nd state;
378 × 1,139 mm
Staatliche Kunstsammlungen Dresden,
Kupferstich-Kabinett, inv. A 3016

Provenance: Historical holdings
Literature: Pauli 1901, no. 1120; New Hollstein S. Beham, no. 402; Stewart 1989; exh. cat. Dresden 2005, cat. 32 (Claudia Schnitzer); Müller 2007; Mentzel 2011; Yasui 2016

Water can give life, cleanse, and heal. In the high Middle Ages these attributes gave rise to the dream of a bath that could restore youth (Rapp 1976). And the earliest pictorial depictions of such a fountain of youth make it clear that along with a lust for life, a lust for love should return too. In Sebald Beham's large, frieze-like woodcut, which could be considered the most significant and complex depiction of the subject in the Renaissance, numerous pairs of lovers frolic in and around a bathhouse, a magnificent Renaissance loggia that takes up the entire right half of the sheet. With this unusual element, Beham complemented the actual fountain of youth next door, which is the first destination for the elderly and infirm who approach it from the left.

The *Jungbrunnen* ('fountain of youth') is one of Sebald Beham's most spectacular creations, an artist who otherwise made primarily small-format engravings and woodcuts. For this reason, like his younger brother Barthel, he was considered one of the 'Little Masters' (*Kleinmeister*). As with many other works by these artists, this extremely detailed composition exhibits numerous figures borrowed from Raphael and Michelangelo, whom Beham had become familiar with from prints. A first state of the woodcut (a unique impression in Oxford) is accompanied by a text at the bottom, dated 1531. In it, a certain Albrecht Glockendon describes the pleasurable but ultimately futile goings-on in the fountain of youth. This text is missing from every existing copy of the second state. There, Glockenson's name above the fountain was replaced by Beham's monogram; the stream of urine from the woman squatting in front of the loggia was removed. However, even without this drastic detail, the observer who lets his eye wander through the picture will discover many other indications that reveal this picture of regained youth and love's lust to be foolish wishful thinking ultimately worthy of damnation. This is most clearly demonstrated by the jester standing on the far top left of the loggia next to someone whose backside, stretched out towards us, is being sprayed with an enema syringe. In addition to this main message, other elements of the image have inspired further interpretations of the picture. For example, the church in the background to the left and the cross worn by a woman in the basin of the fountain of youth could also be read as a reference to baptism, a bath that, according to Christian belief, promises true salvation.

Guido Messling

Humankind in the Universe – Myth and Poetry

(cats. 45–50)

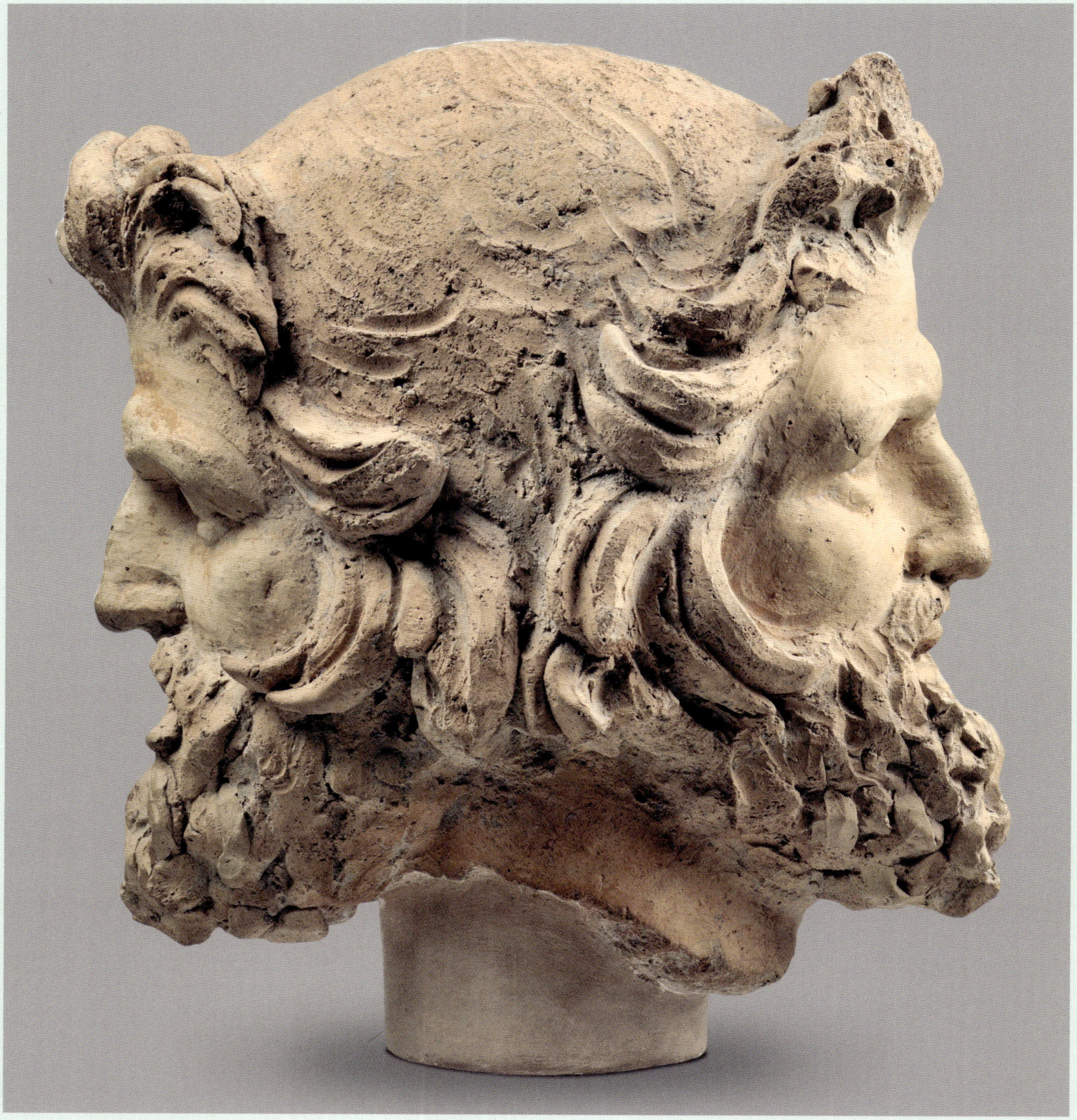

Cat. 45, *Double-Faced Janus*

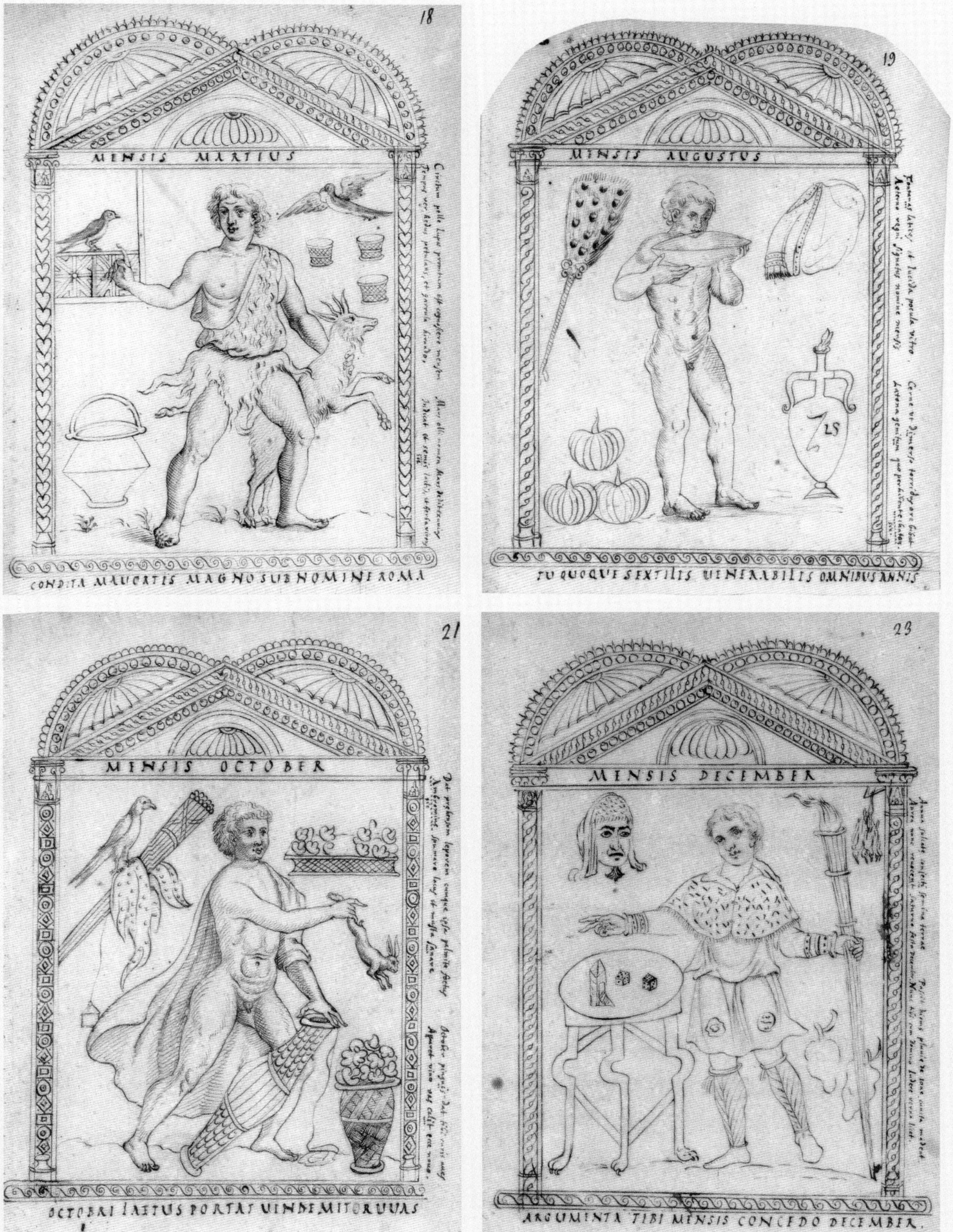

Cats. 46.1–46.4, *Chronograph of 354: March, August, October, December*

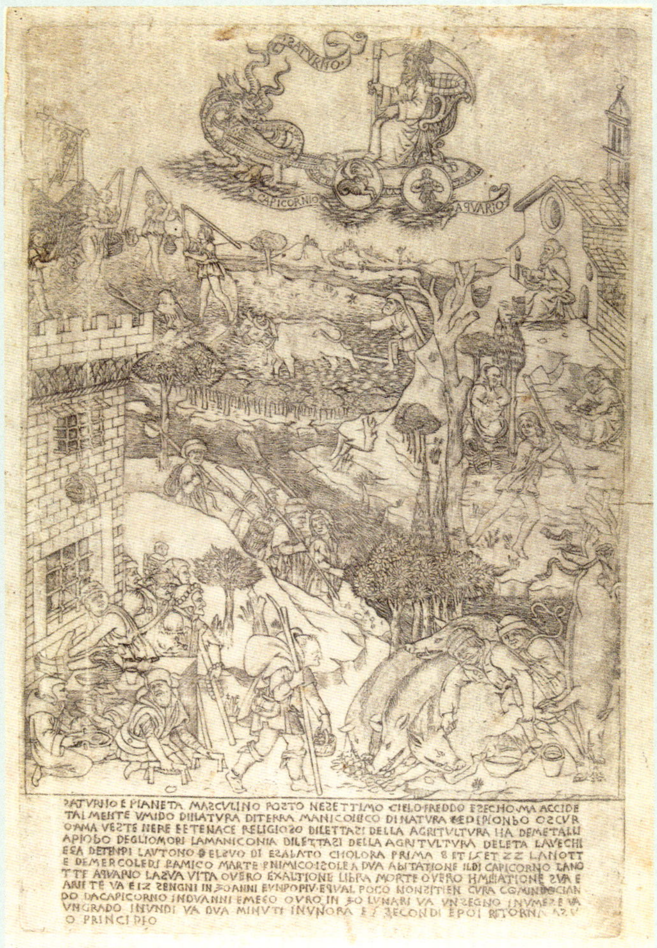

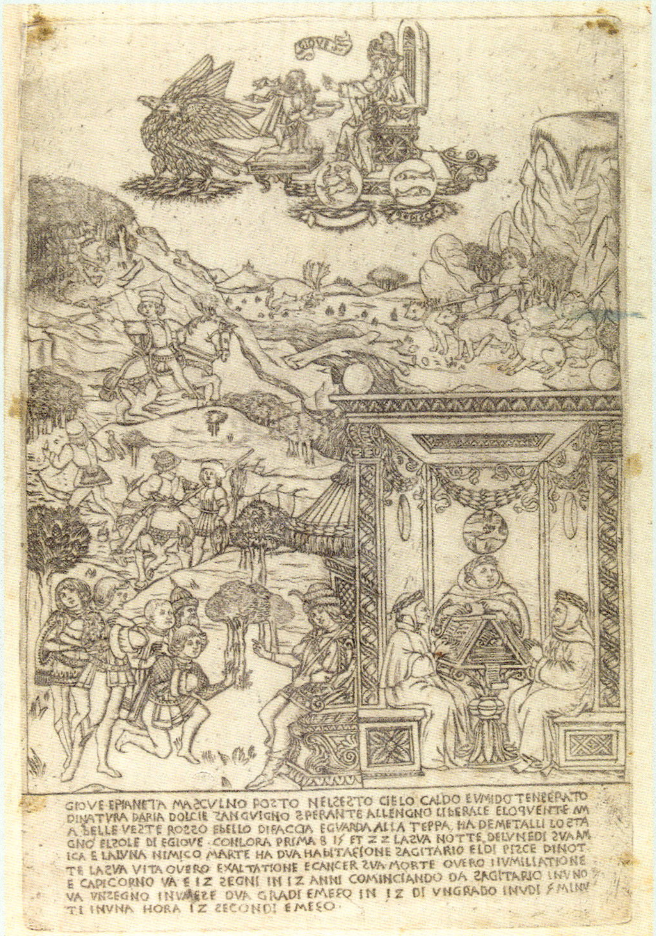

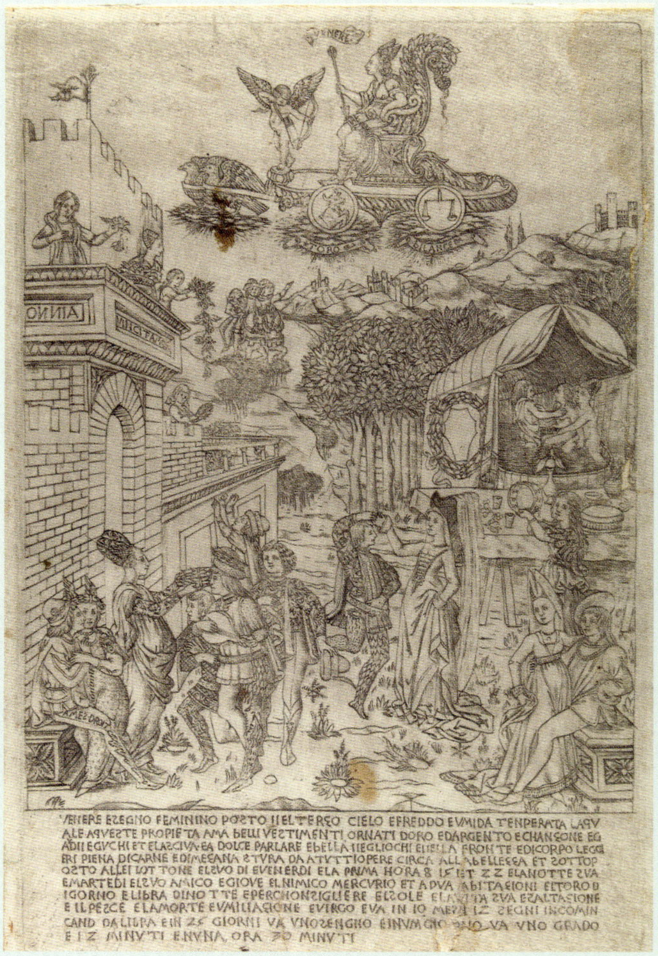

 Cats. 47.1–47.7, Baccio Baldini, *The Seven Planets*

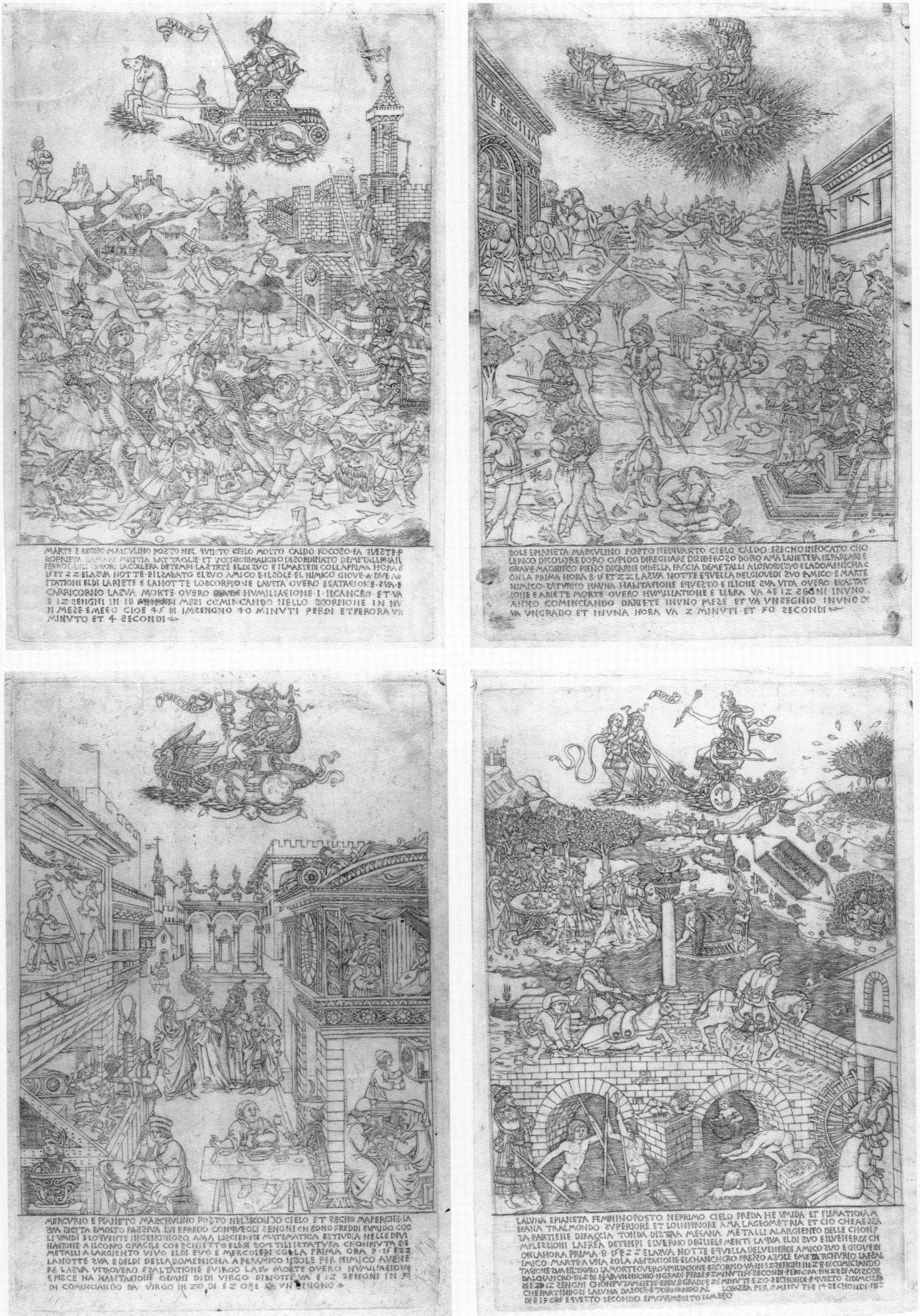
MARTE
MARTE E SEGHO MASCULINO POSTO NEL QUINTO CELO MOLTO CALDO FOCOSO EA QUESTE P
CARRICORNO LASUA MORTE OVERO HUMILIACIONE I ILCANCRO ET VA
N MESE EMEZO CIOE 45 DI IMSENGNO 40 MINUTI PERDI ETPERORA VN
MINUTO ET 4 SECONDI
SOLE EPIANETA MASCULINO POSTO NELQUARTO CIELO CALDO ESECHO INFOCATO CHO
GRAVE MAGNIFICO PIENO DICARNE DIBELLA FACCIA DEMETALLI ALORO EDISUO ELADOMENICHA C
ON LA PRIMA HORA 8 15 ET 22 LASUA NOTTE EQUELLA DELGIOVEDI SUO AMICO E MARTE
IOUE EARIETE MORTE OVERO HUMILIATIONE E LIBRA VA 4E 12 SEGNI INUNO
ANNO COMINCIANDO DARIETE INUNO MESE ET VA UNSEGNIO INUNO DI
VA UNGRADO ET INUNA HORA VA 2 MINUTI ET
MERCURIO E PIANETO MASCHULINO POSTO NELSECONDO CIELO ET SECHO MAPERCHE LA
LANOTTE SUA EDELDI DELLADOMENICHA
DI COMINCIANDO DA VIRGO IN 20 DI
LALUNA EPIANETA FEMMINO POSTO NEPRIMO CIELO FREDA HE UMIDA ET FLEMATICHA M
REANA TRALMONDO SUPERIORE ET LOINFERIORE AMA LAGEOMETRIA ET CIO CHEAESSA
ONLAHORA PRIMA 8 15 E 22 ELASUA NOTTE EQUELLA DELVENERDI AMICO SUO E GIOVE IN
DI E 13 ORE EQUESTO SECONDO EMOVIMENTO DIMEZO

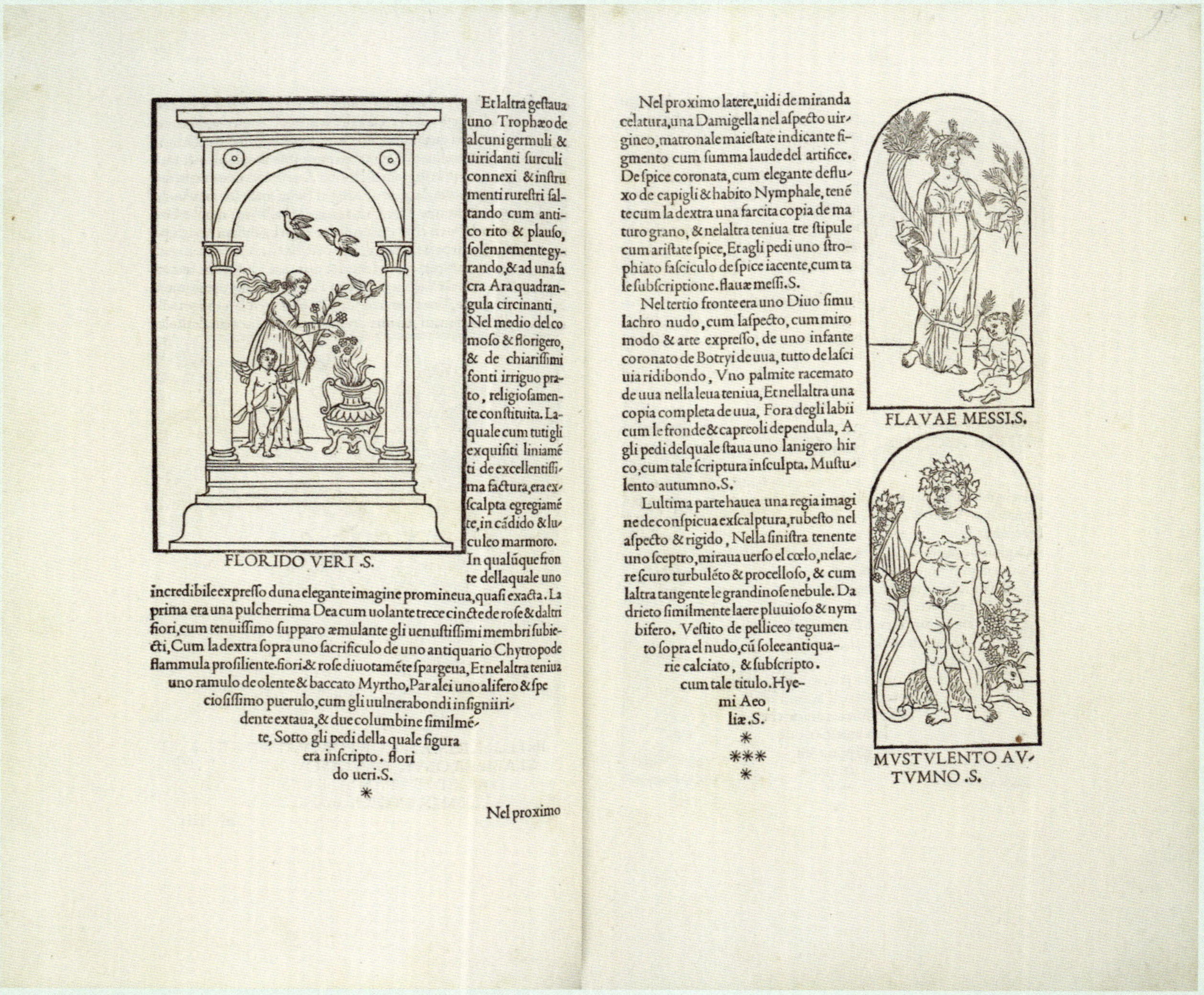

FLORIDO VERI .S.

Et laltra geſtaua uno Trophæo de alcuni germuli & uiridanti ſurculi connexi & inſtrumenti rureſtri ſaltando cum antico rito & plauſo, ſolennemente gyrando, & ad una ſacra Ara quadrangula circinanti, Nel medio del comoſo & florigero, & de chiariſſimi fonti irriguo prato, religioſamente conſtituita. Laquale cum tuti gli exquiſiti liniamẽti de excellentiſſima factura, era exſcalpta egregiamẽte, in cãdido & luculeo marmoro. In qualũque fronte dellaquale uno incredibile expreſſo duna elegante imagine promineua, quaſi exacta. La prima era una pulcherrima Dea cum uolante trece cincte de roſe & daltri fiori, cum tenuiſſimo ſupparo æmulante gli uenuſtiſſimi membri ſubiecti, Cum la dextra ſopra uno ſacrificulo de uno antiquario Chytropode flammula proſiliente. fiori & roſe diuotamẽte ſpargeua, Et nelaltra teniua uno ramulo de olente & baccato Myrtho, Par alei uno alifero & ſpecioſiſſimo puerulo, cum gli uulnerabondi inſignii ridente extaua, & due columbine ſimilmẽte, Sotto gli pedi della quale figura era inſcripto. flori do ueri. S.

*

Nel proximo

Nel proximo latere, uidi de miranda celatura, una Damigella nel aſpecto uirgineo, matronale maieſtate indicante figmento cum ſumma laude del artifice. De ſpice coronata, cum elegante defluxo de capigli & habito Nymphale, tenẽte cum la dextra una farcita copia de maturo grano, & nelaltra teniua tre ſtipule cum ariſtate ſpice, Et agli pedi uno ſtrophiato faſciculo de ſpice iacente, cum tale ſubſcriptione. flauæ meſſi. S.

Nel tertio fronte era uno Diuo ſimulachro nudo, cum laſpecto, cum miro modo & arte expreſſo, de uno infante coronato de Botryi de uua, tutto de laſciuia ridibondo, Vno palmite racemato de uua nella leua teniua, Et nellaltra una copia completa de uua, Fora degli labii cum le fronde & capreoli dependula, A gli pedi delquale ſtaua uno lanigero hirco, cum tale ſcriptura inſculpta. Muſtulento autumno. S.

Lultima parte hauea una regia imagine de conſpicua exſcalptura, rubeſto nel aſpecto & rigido, Nella ſiniſtra tenente uno ſceptro, miraua uerſo el cœlo, nelaere ſcuro turbulẽto & procelloſo, & cum laltra tangente le grandinoſe nebule. Da drieto ſimilmente laere pluuioſo & nymbifero. Veſtito de pelliceo tegumento ſopra el nudo, cũ ſolee antiquarie calciato, & ſubſcripto. cum tale titulo. Hyemi Aeoliæ. S.

*

***

*

FLAVAE MESSI.S.

MVSTVLENTO AVTVMNO .S.

Cat. 48, Francesco Colonna, *Hypnerotomachia Poliphili* …

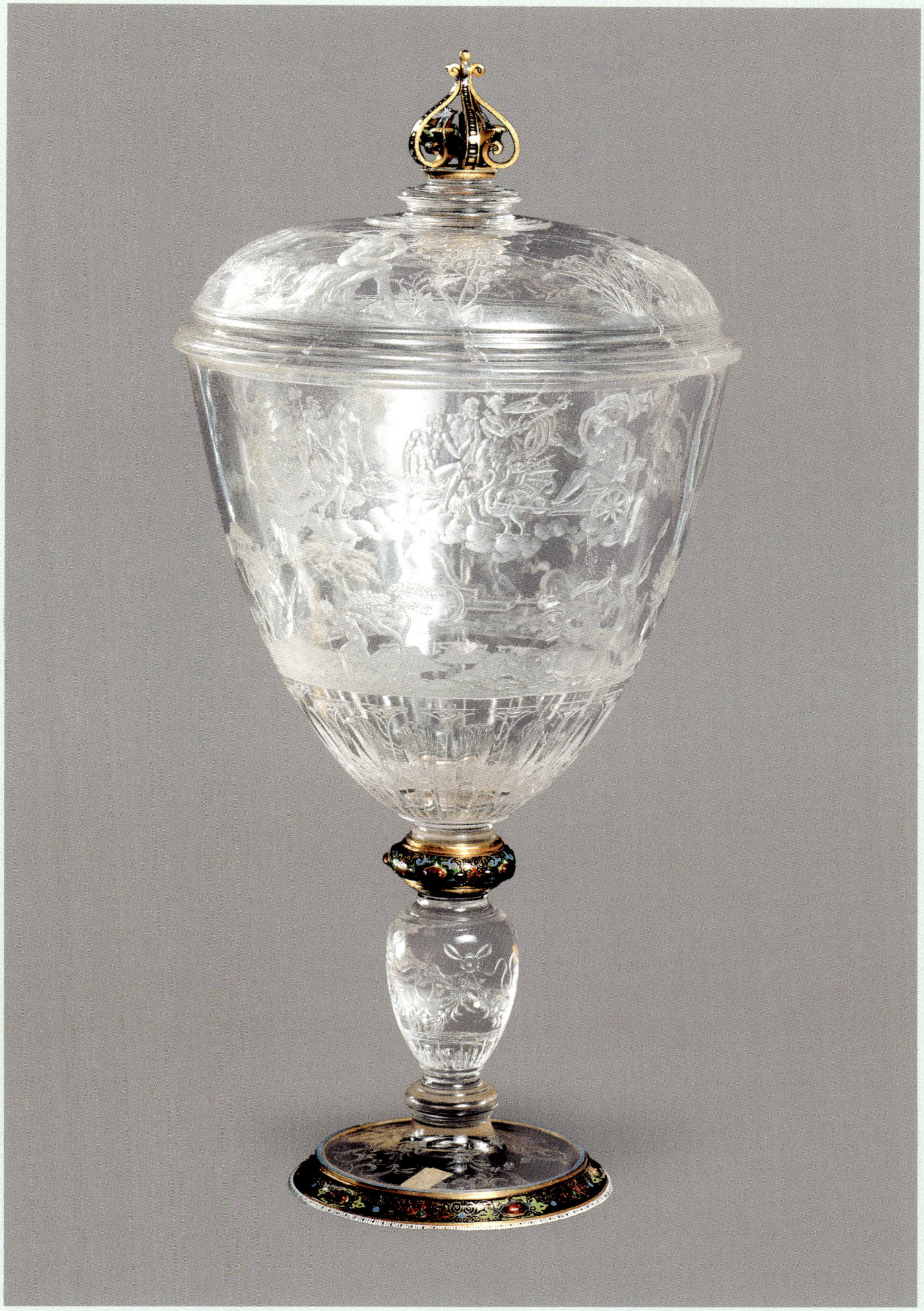

Cat. 49, Annibale Fontana, *Lidded Cup Depicting the Myth of the Creation of the Seasons*

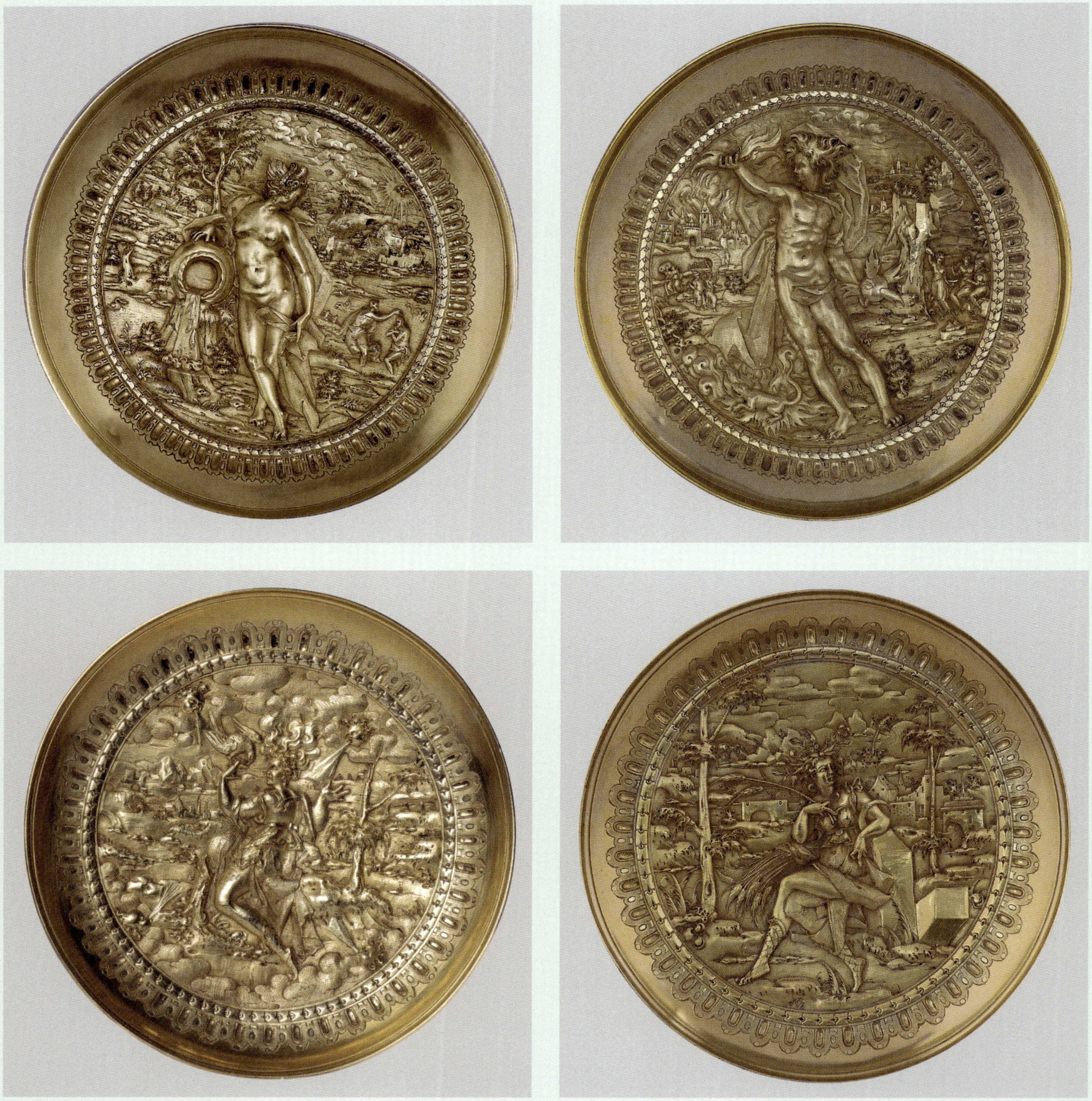

Cats. 50.1–50.4, Paul Hübner, *Tazze with Allegories of the Elements: Water, Fire, Air, Earth*

Cat. 45

Double-Faced Janus (Etruscan: *Culsans*)

Discovered in Vulci in ancient Etruria (Viterbo Province, Latium, Italy), 2nd cent. BCE (Hellenistic) Terracotta with few remains of red painting, neck modernly reconstructed in painted plaster, a few missing parts; H max. 29 cm, W max. 26 cm; Rome, Museo Nazionale Etrusco di Villa Giulia, inv. 59737

Literature: Pettazzoni 1956; Schilling 1960; Radke 1965, 147–9; Pfiffig 1975, 246–7, Simon 1990, 88–93, esp. 91; Simon 1990a; Pautasso 1994, 29–32, 114–15, pl. 9b; Krauskopf 1997, 33; De Grummond 2006, 147–8; Belfiore 2015, 152, 155–6; Calapà 2022, 150–1

This head with two bearded faces looking in opposite directions comes from a votive hoard of an ancient sanctuary, discovered near the north gate (Porta Nord) of the Etruscan metropolis Vulci. An identification with the Etruscan god *Culsans* (comparable with the ancient Roman *Ianus*) is extremely probable since among the Etruscan-Italic gods it was mainly Culsans who was depicted with two (or, in rare cases, four) faces. As his name indicates in both languages, he is an old gatekeeper diety. Both the Latin *ianua* and the Etruscan *culs* mean 'entrance', 'gate', 'door'. Thus, he is a god who protects (spatial and temporal) transitions, responsible for entrances and exits, and, in a metaphorical sense, for beginnings and endings, past and future. In particular, he plays an important role for beginnings of every sort (for example, of sacrificial rituals, a new life, or a war).

The inspiration for the – otherwise unusual in ancient Italy – double-faced depiction of the god, who in Etruria was sometimes shown beardless, probably came originally from the ancient Near East, later supplemented by influences from Greek herm iconography. However, the Greeks did not have a diety that corresponded to *Ianus*, a fact emphasized by the Roman poet Ovid in his calendar of the Roman festival days (*Fasti* 1, 90). Our quite expressive *Ianus bifrons* ('double-faced Janus') dates from the second century BCE, that is, a time when the once powerful Etruscans were under Roman domination, which had led to an alignment of their ways of life.

Ianus and the Latin name of the month *Ianuarius* (January) have the same etymology. In his *Fasti* Ovid starts the year with this month and describes the god and his cults (I, 89–293). This idea is, in any case, secondary, even if it has given rise to many allegories. The ancient Roman year originally began with *Martius* (March) – *Ianuarius* was therefore the penultimate (i.e. the eleventh) month. Not until the calendar reform of 153 BCE did the year start with *Ianuarius*. Still today, the numbers in the names of the months September (7), October (8), November (9), and December (10) recall the old order.

The old *Ianus* sanctuary on the Forum Romanum was famous for its bronze statue of the god, more than two metres high, with his attributes staff and (appropriate for a god of gates) key. Its gates were closed only in times of absolute peace, which was seldom the case during the Roman Republic. However, it occurred three times under the reign of Augustus (*Res Gestae* 13), which was supposed to symbolize the peace and prosperity of the Augustan period.

Petra Amann

Cats. 46.1–46.4

Chronograph of 354

Transcription of a Carolingian copy, 1620/21
Vatican City, Biblioteca Apostolica Vaticana, Barb.lat.2154.pt.B

March

Ink on paper; 297 × 232 mm
fol. 18r

August

Ink on paper; 282 × 235 mm
fol. 19r

October

Ink on paper; 305 × 240 mm
fol. 21r

December

Ink on paper; 309 × 228 mm
fol. 23r

Provenance: 1620/21 Hieronymus Aleander the Younger; Biblioteca Barberini; since 1902 Biblioteca Vaticana

Literature: Mommsen 1850; Strzygowski 1888; Levi 1941; Stern 1953, Salzmann 1990; Divjak and Wischmeyer 2014; Rüpke 2015

The *Chronograph* is an ancient calendrical handbook from the year 354, which was dedicated by the calligrapher Furius Dionysius Filocalus to a private individual named Valentinus. Using pictures, lists, and poetic texts, Filocalus helped to organise the public life of the urban Roman upper throughout the year by recording cultic traditions, senate sessions, festivals, emperors' birthdays, and astrological events. Today, we only know of many of these dates thanks to the *Chronograph*. It also provides information about the empire and ways of thinking during the late Constantinian era, in which pagan and Christian elements intermingled.

A picture of the ancient original is provided only by fragmentary copies that complement each other in content and date back to two lost intermediate copies from the ninth century. The *Codex Barberini* on display is considered one of the most comprehensive and faithful copies. At the end of 1620, the humanist Nicolas-Claude Fabri de Peiresc (1580–1637) ordered copies to be made of an intermediate Carolingian manuscript for Hieronymus Aleander the Younger (1574–1629) and provides detailed information about this earlier work in letters.

Seven images (*February*, *March*, *August*, *September*, *October*, *November*, *December*) and eight pages of text (now *Codex Vaticanus Latinus* 9135) were preserved from the calendar section of the months. On the right side were the monthly *dies fastus* in black and red ink, where the days listed were divided into the systems in use in this period (nundinal cycle, lunar system, and fixed days such as Kalends, Nones, Ides) and labelled with events. On the left side, the months were depicted as human figures in black ink with descriptive distichs and tetrastichs. These verses probably originated in a completely independent tradition, as their connection to the picture is not always obvious and they are not part of the decorative scheme. Peiresc had the framework copied for all pages with figures, but in *October* and *November* only for the text pages due to time constraints. The zodiac tondi, which marked the sun's entry into a new sign of the zodiac, were also left out and they were subsequently sent to Aleander on a single sheet.

The pictorial symbolism in the labours of the months combines aspects of the seasons with pagan elements. *March* appears as a young man dressed in a belted coat and is thus identified as a shepherd. Following a Roman tradition of representation, he is considered to be Romulus, who in turn refers to the cult of his father Mars, with whom the month was associated. His gesture, pointing at a woodpecker, could be a reference to the myth of Rome's founding. He is joined by the messengers of spring in the form of a leaping goat, swallows, budding greenery, and vessels for milk, which is now abundantly available.

The focus of *August* is the prevailing heat. A youth has already taken off his clothes and drinks water from the glass cup and has a *flabellum* (fan) of peacock feathers to further cool him down. Three melons, fruits that ripen this month, are also depicted.

October represents the start of the hunting season. The hunter, semi-clothed in a cape, pulls a hare out of a basket trap. On the left, a falcon, a stick smeared with birdlime, a net, and a hanging cage allude to bird hunting.

December is dedicated to the Saturnalia, a time of celebratory drinking and dice games. During this festival, the usual order of social classes was suspended, so masters traded roles with their slaves and adults with children. The birds hanging on a hook could refer to a supply of food for the winter.

The months were a popular subject in ancient art, in connection with both the seasons and the calendrical context. Typically, there are pronounced reference to areas of ancient religious life, in particular the festivals. The *Chronograph* is considered one of the primary examples of this genre because, unlike many frescoes and mosaics, it has survived in its entirety. Here, the characteristics that originated in the belief in the gods have still been preserved for individual months. In later Christian depictions, they were to make way for purely agrarian picture cycles featuring rural activities over the course of the year.

Alexandra Sattler

Cats. 47.1–47.7

Baccio Baldini (c.1436–1487), attributed

The Seven Planets

c.1460
Burin on paper; Saturn: 348 × 237 mm, Jupiter: 344 × 236 mm, Mars: 342 × 231 mm, Sun: 340 × 230 mm, Venus: 335 × 237 mm, Mercury: 342 × 237 mm, Moon: 341 × 232 mm
Pavia, Musei Civici del Castello Visconteo, inv. St. Mal. 1585–1591

Provenance: 1812 acquired by Marquis Malaspina from Abbot Mauro Boni
Literature: Malaspina di Sannazzaro 1824, 29; Lippmann 1895; Hind 1910, 48–61; Spike and Zucker 1993, 94–126; Blume 2000, 183–91; exh. cat. Pavia 2003/04, 105–7, cats. 38–44 (Vera Segre); Gray 2012; Pezzuto 2015; Baroni Vannucci 2017; Tarabochia Canavero 2021

In the fifteenth century, interest in astronomy and astrology led to a rapid increase in the dissemination of both ancient writings and contemporary treatises. In the fine arts, this was reflected in the popularity of the depiction of zodiac signs, constellations, and planetary deities. Artists based their work on the ancient Ptolemaic conception of the universe, in which all celestial bodies revolved around the Earth. Earth was surrounded by the spheres of water, air, and fire, followed by the seven known planets (Moon, Mercury, Venus, Sun, Mars, Jupiter, Saturn), the starry firmament, the crystal heaven, and the Primum Mobile.

Character traits were ascribed to the planets according to their namesake deity. These traits were believed to influence the fate of individuals and to rule over entire groups of people, depending on the prevailing celestial constellation. They conferred temperaments upon their 'children' that were associated with certain professions, occupations, and social circumstances.

The particular type of planets shown here started appearing in graphic art around the middle of the fifteenth century. All seven depictions follow the same compositional principle and are accompanied at the bottom of the picture by a text on astrological teachings, the nature of the planets, and their astronomical movements.

As a personification in a fantastic costume and supplied with attributes, the respective planet moves in its orbit across the sky in a chariot. Saturn is assigned a two-headed dragon biting its own tail to pull his chariot. Jupiter has two eagles, Mars two horses, the Sun four horses, Venus two doves, and Mercury two birds of prey. In Luna's case, they are replaced by two nymphs of Diana. The chariot wheels display the signs of the zodiac in which the respective planet has its houses.

In the lower area, the human activities under the influence of the deities are embedded in a landscape or city. Saturn rules men of low status who live from farming or as hermits; they also include beggars, cripples, prisoners, and the hanged. In the scene under the influence of Jupiter, a judge gives an audience, while the aristocratic pastime of hunting with hounds and falcons can be seen in the background. Three scholars identified with the leading figures of Italian poetry – Dante, Petrarch, and Boccaccio – sit around a lectern in a Renaissance building. The children of Mars are warriors, robbers, and the violent, illustrated in a scene of wild fighting and plunder. Under the influence of Sol (Sun), men engage in swordplay, wrestling, stone throwing, and archery for the entertainment of their enthroned ruler. In the background, three pilgrims kneel before an image of the Madonna. Lovers, ruled by the planet Venus, enjoy themselves bathing, making festive music, and dancing while Cupid, blindfolded, aims his arrows at them. The busy and industrious children of Mercury are destined for art, science, and invention, which they pursue in a cityscape that recalls important buildings in Florence. The scene influenced by the moon goddess Luna, in keeping with her element, is characterised by flowing water that stimulates fishing, swimming, and working the water-powered mill.

The human activities and pastimes, like the armour and clothing of the figures, allude to the customs and traditions of the Florentine Renaissance. The costumes and decorated chariots of the planets are borrowed from the festive processions of that time. The architectural and ornamental embellishment and the drawing of the figures also correspond to this cultural setting, which is why the *The Seven Planets* has been attributed to Baccio Baldini. According to Vasari, he was one of the first to practise the art of engraving in Florence, but his identity is still in dispute.

The artist could rely on a tradition of depiction north of the Alps from the first half of the fifteenth century, which translated popular songs and verse about the planets and their spheres of influence into pictures. Inspired by Boccaccio's *Genealogia deorum gentilium*, he supplemented the personifications with attributes and the motif of the chariot, and in doing so created a prototype that was to become the next main iconographic model.

ALEXANDRA SATTLER

Cat. 48

Francesco Colonna (1433–1527)

Hypnerotomachia Poliphili

Venice (Aldus Manutius for Leonardo Crasso)
1499, 2°
Venice, Biblioteca Nazionale Marciana,
394.D.290, fols. m4v, m5r

Literature: IGIISTC No. ic00767000; Colonna 1964 (1980); Colonna 1999

A masterpiece of Venetian publishing, the *Hypnerotomachia* is the fruit of a refined, syncretic and multilingual humanist culture (the text includes Latin, literary *volgare*, Venetian with vernacular incursions, Greek, artificial and invented languages such as 'polifilesco' and hieroglyphics, and brief citations in Arabic and Hebrew). The Dominican monk Francesco Colonna remains the most credible author of the work among the many that have been proposed – as referred to by the acrostic (made up of the figured initials of the book's 38 chapters: POLIAM FRATER FRANCISCUS COLUMNA PERAMAVIT (Brother Francesco Colonna has dearly loved Polia)) and documented by sources both historic (Leandro Alberti, Apostolo Zeno, Giusto Fontanini, Tommaso Temanza) and modern (Casella-Pozzi, Edoardo Fumagalli, Ariani-Gabriele), which invalidate other and confusing proposals

The 172 magnificent woodcuts that illustrate the book are from the Venetian studio directed by the anonymous masters [b] and [•b•], who worked for various printers and publishers from at least 1490 to 1536, producing numerous vignettes: the frequent, alleged attributions to famous artists of the time are thwarted by the final date of this chronology. Some drawings and sketches by the author himself are included in the iconographic apparatus.

The work is a philosophical romance in which Polifilo, both protagonist and narrator, recalls his dream-like journey, a *visio in somniis*. Through various events, in changing and harsh erotic battles between body and soul (hence the title: *Hypnerotomachia Poliphili*, meaning 'battle of love in Polifilo's dream'), he is led to purification and knowledge of the mysteries of Venus, the cosmic mother. It is a journey of the soul towards understanding of the arcane enigma of Eros and his dual power: sensual and spiritual, licentious and chaste. Polifilo's purpose is to dissolve this antithesis, for which he must convert the two aspects to *medietas amoris*: a condition in which such extremes are mitigated, reconciled, generating pure love (*amor purus*), the ultimate aim of noble lovers. This is the message developed in the work, defining it not only on the ethical-erotic level of the medieval and humanist art of love (*ars amandi*) – with the courtly precepts that govern the knight who wants to conquer his beloved to pursue prudence and temperance – but also and especially in a more universal, philosophical, cosmological, and mysteriosophic perspective of neo-Platonic coinage (such as the enigmatic Trinitarian monument symbolizing *coeleste harmonia*). It is a perspective in which direction and sovereignty is devolved to a *religio Veneris*, which, with its rites, mythical figures, Cupid's triumphs, and sacred Templar architecture, shapes the design of the romance. The plot develops through a sequence of imaginary buildings, symbolic monuments, and utopian gardens inspired by the classical world, but new in their distinctive original plastic, material, and architectural inventions. An allegorical language of wonderful forms that was to be so successful in subsequent centuries is thus conceived.

The book includes pictures of the seasons that decorate the four sides of the altar of ithyphallic Priapus, custodian of the gardens (*horti*) and symbol of the fertilizing power of Nature, whose incessant generative rhythm is testified by the seasons themselves.

MINO GABRIELE

Cat. 49

Annibale Fontana (1540–1587)

Lidded Cup Depicting the Myth of the Creation of the Seasons, so-called Proserpina Cup

Milan, before 1569
Rock crystal; setting: gold, enamelled; H 24.6 cm, dia. 12.3 cm
Vienna, Kunsthistorisches Museum, Kunstkammer, inv. KK 1415

Provenance: From the Imperial Treasury
Literature: Exh. cat. Vienna 2002/03, 125–7, cat. 45; Distelberger 2002/03, 86; exh. cat. Paris and Vienna 2007/08, 214–15, cat. V29 (Franz Kirchweger); mus. cat. Vienna 2010, 106, no. 43 (Thomas Kuster); exh. cat. Vienna and Zurich 2011/12, 130–1, cat. 12 (Paulus Rainer); Rainer 2016, 32–3

The origin of the four seasons was explained in ancient times by the Roman myth of Proserpina (Ovid, *Metamorphoses* V, 341–571). Struck by the arrows of Cupid, the god of erotic love, Pluto abducted Proserpina on his chariot and took her to the underworld. Ceres, the goddess of agriculture, furious at the theft of her daughter, deprived the earth of its fertility and slew the farmers and cattle of Sicily. She took her case to Jupiter, who heard her lament and divided the year into two parts: during the half when Proserpina is with her mother, the earth blossoms, and spring and summer reign in the land. But when the daughter returns to her consort Pluto in the underworld, Ceres' grief gives rise to autumn and winter.

This precious goblet tells the story of Proserpina, carved into a single piece of rock crystal as an intaglio of the highest quality. The narrative unfolds in successive scenes around the entire vessel, with the two zones of events, earthly and Olympian, artfully intertwined. The myth is completed by the personifications of the four seasons on the lid. Spring, surrounded by blooming flowers, is followed by summer, symbolized by a disk of sunlight. Autumn appears with a grape vine, while winter has wrapped itself in a cloak.

The stylistic affinity with the *Proserpina-Kanne* (Proserpina pitcher) in the Munich Schatzkammer has made it possible to identify Annibale Fontana as the creator of the meticulously modelled and manneristically animated figure scenes. This is the earliest known evidence of his work in the *arte minuta*. Demonstrating a perfect mastery of anatomy, he placed the outline of the figures on the polished area to accentuate them. His virtuosity comes through in the individual forms and the way details are positioned to follow the grain pattern of the stone. The carver also made use of the stone's natural colouring by carving Jupiter's thematically significant judgement into the goblet's wall, where it stands out in colour caused by inclusions in the rock crystal.

With this lidded goblet, Fontana created an exquisite collector's item for the princely *Kunstkammer*, one in which nature and art merge, and which – in keeping with the Mannerist demand for a view from all angles – can only be grasped in its full complexity by turning it or walking around it.

ALEXANDRA SATTLER

Cats. 50.1–50.4

Paul Hübner (c.1550–1614), attributed

Tazze with Allegories of the Elements

1585/90
Augsburg hallmark (Rosenberg 3/I no. 130), maker's mark PH of Paul Hübner (Rosenberg 3/I no. 410)

Water, Fire

Silver, gilt; each H 16.5 cm, dia. 22.3 cm
Florence, Palazzo Pitti, Museo degli Argenti, inv. A.s.e 1911, n. 20 (water), n. 22 (fire)

Air, Earth

1585/90
Silver, gilt; each H 14.7 cm, dia. 18.7 cm
Florence, Palazzo Pitti, Tesoro dei Granduchi, inv. A.s.e 1911, n. 50 (air), n. 56 (earth)

Provenance: 1590 and 1594 acquired by the Archbishop of Salzburg, Wolf Dietrich von Raitenau; 1612 in inventory of the silver collection of the Archbishop of Salzburg; in inventories of 1772 and 1786; in 1814 probably brought to the Palazzo Pitti by Archduke Ferdinand III of Tuscany; traceable in the inventories of the Palazzo Pitti since 1861.

Literature: Morassi 1963, 36–39; Rossacher 1966, 142–5, nos. 62–85; exh. cat. Salzburg 1967, 66–7, no. 56a; mus. cat. Florence 1967, 163–4, nos. 609, 611, 630, 632; Weber 1970; exh. cat. Salzburg 1987, 358–9, cat. 138, 139 (K.R.); Tait 1988, 160–84, nos. 24–35; Mosco and Casazza 2003, 203; Ramharter 2011

These four serving *tazze* with allegories of the elements are the work of a virtuoso goldsmith and in keeping with the tastes of Mannerist court art. The shape of the *tazza* developed in Italy in the early Renaissance, and it became a popular vessel for drinking and presenting fruit. From the second half of the sixteenth century, the flat area of the *tazza* bowl was embellished with relief scenes. Princely banquets undoubtedly required large sets of tableware, and these vessels were once part of larger sets that belonged to the Archbishop of Salzburg, Wolf Dietrich von Raitenau. Acquired in Regensburg in 1590, *Fire* and *Water* were part of a 36-piece set with depictions of the twelve months, twelve scenes from the Old Testament, and a set consisting of the four elements, the four cardinal virtues, and the three theological virtues, supplemented by Patientia/Innocentia. Four years later, during the Imperial Diet of Regensburg, the Archbishop had silver merchant Bartholomäus Fesenmayr purchase another twelve-piece set with the same allegories of the elements and virtues, but in a smaller format, from which *Earth* and *Air* can be seen here.

Despite the variety of subjects, the 48 *tazze* form a visual unity in which the moulded relief images are framed by simple, classic ornamentation. The allegories consist of female or male personifications with corresponding attributes. As is common in the goldsmith's art, the figurative compositions are based on pictorial inventions of artists from other disciplines that had later been spread through engravings. These depictions were translated into silver in Paul Hübner's workshop with a certain degree of independence or combined to create new compositions. The four elements were a popular theme for which there were numerous models because, according to the ancient teachings still widespread at the time, the entire world was formed of earth, water, fire, and air in specific proportions (see essay Gabriele, p. 19).

In the large set, the main figures are taken from a series of engravings of the elements (c.1586) by Hendrick Goltzius and set in an original landscape. The female personification of *Aqua* (Water; cat. 50.1), crowned with a shell, leans with her right arm on an urn from which water and fish are streaming. Her sharply turned head directs the viewer's gaze to the background, where the biblical scene of Christ's baptism is assigned to the element.

Ignis (Fire; cat. 50.2) with lightning and fireball in his hands has also been taken completely from Goltzius. Part of the puffed-up cloak has been extended to cover the pubic area, and the salamander as the elemental spirit of fire has gained in realism. In the left background of the relief, a sacrificial scene has been replaced by Sodom afire, from which Lot and his family are led by an angel. On the right, the story continues with the seduction of Lot by his daughters.

The smaller *tazze* take a different approach in their figural depiction and highly stylised landscapes. In addition, the religious dimension in the background has been dispensed with. The personifications here can be traced back to Jost Amman's *Kunstbüchlin*.

Holding two ears of corn in her right hand and a sickle in her left, *Terra* (Earth; cat. 50.3) sits on a stone seat on which lies a stalk of grain. In Amman's work, she is the goddess Ceres (fol. 40r), who symbolizes earth in allegories of elements and summer in the context of seasons. In a departure from the original, the female figure has been provided with clothing and is more elegant due to her elongated proportions.

The personification of *Aer* (Air; cat. 50.4) is considered a variation on various sheets from which the Mannerist devices of the contrapposto and the back turned towards the viewer have been adopted. In order to identify her as the element air, the figure in the relief is supplied with the typical trappings that are also found in Goltzius, for example, the four winds, hair as clouds, and a bird.

ALEXANDRA SATTLER

Venice on the Mainland and the Development of Agronomy in the Sixteenth Century

(cats. 51–56)

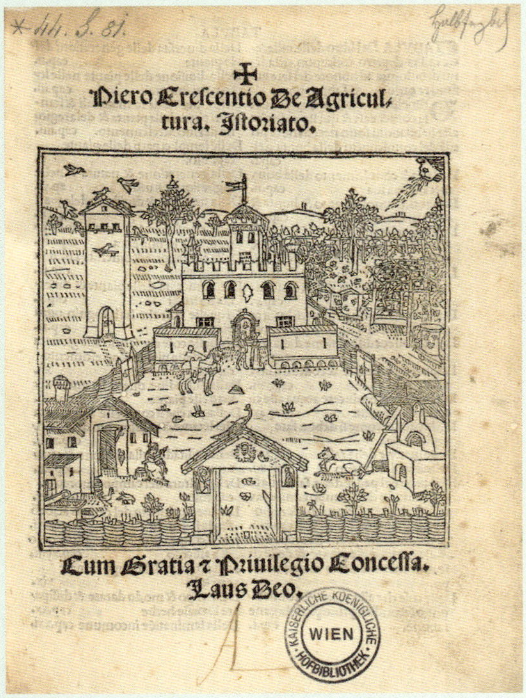

Cat. 51.1, Pietro Crescenzi, *De Agricultura. Istoriato*

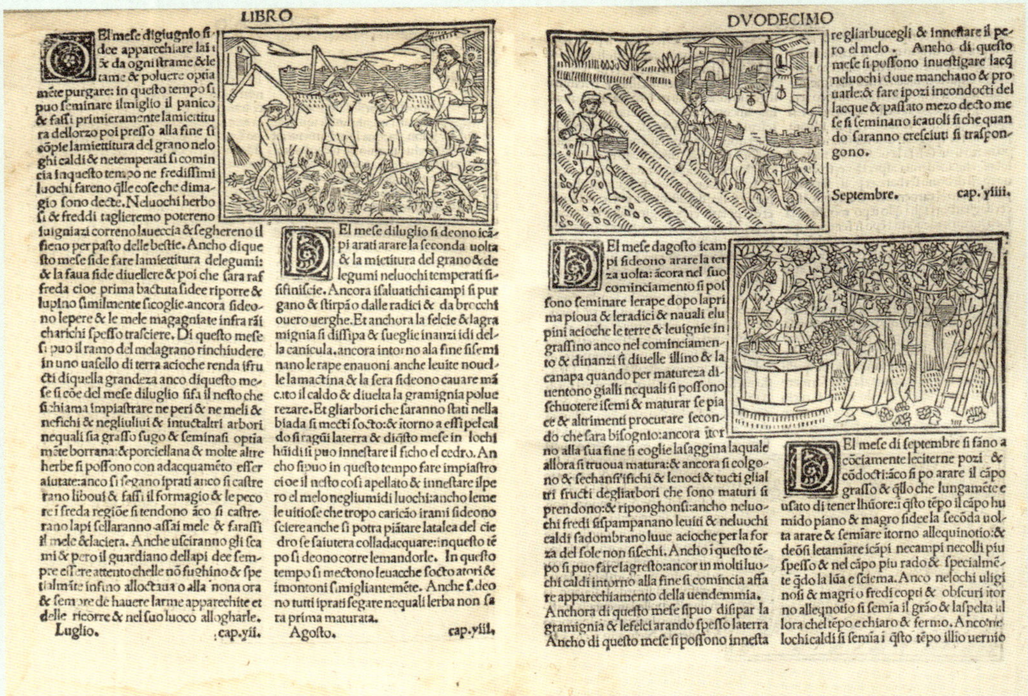

Cat. 51.2, Pietro Crescenzi, *De Agricultura*

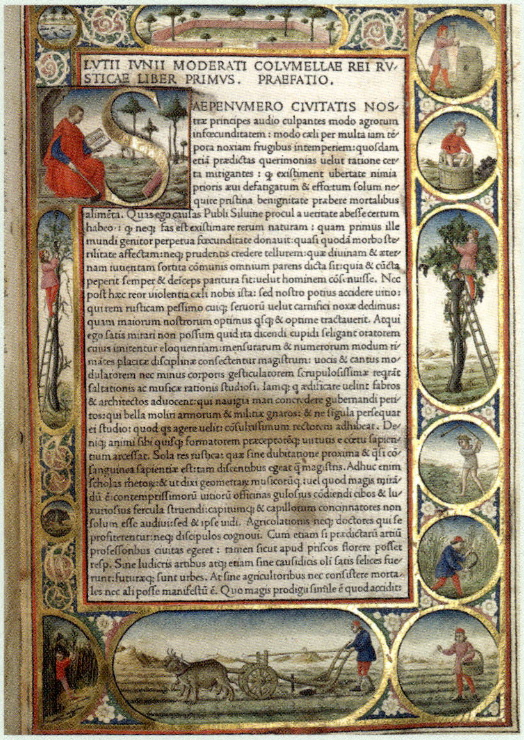

Cat. 52, Marcus P. Cato the Elder et al., *Scriptores rei rusticae*

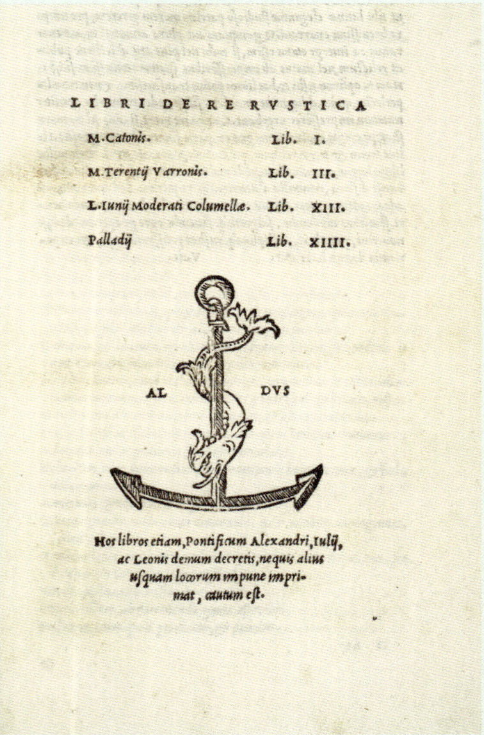

Cat. 53.1, Marcus P. Cato the Elder et al., *Libri de re rustica*

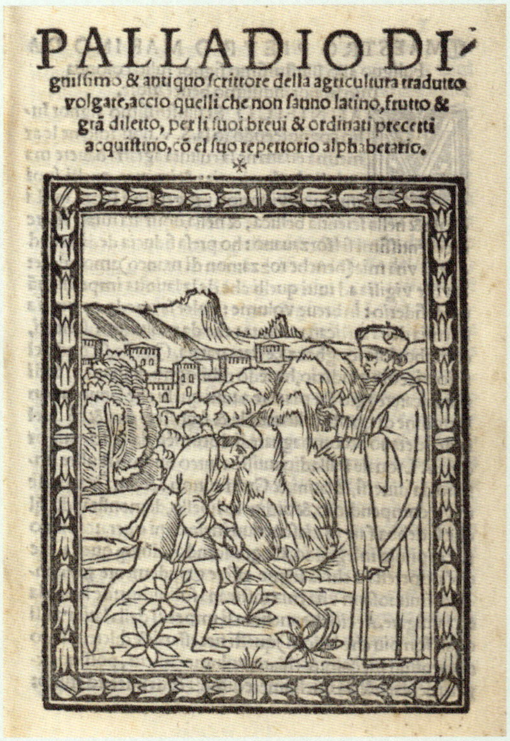

Cat. 53.2, Rutilius T. A. Palladius, *Della agricultura tradutto volgare*

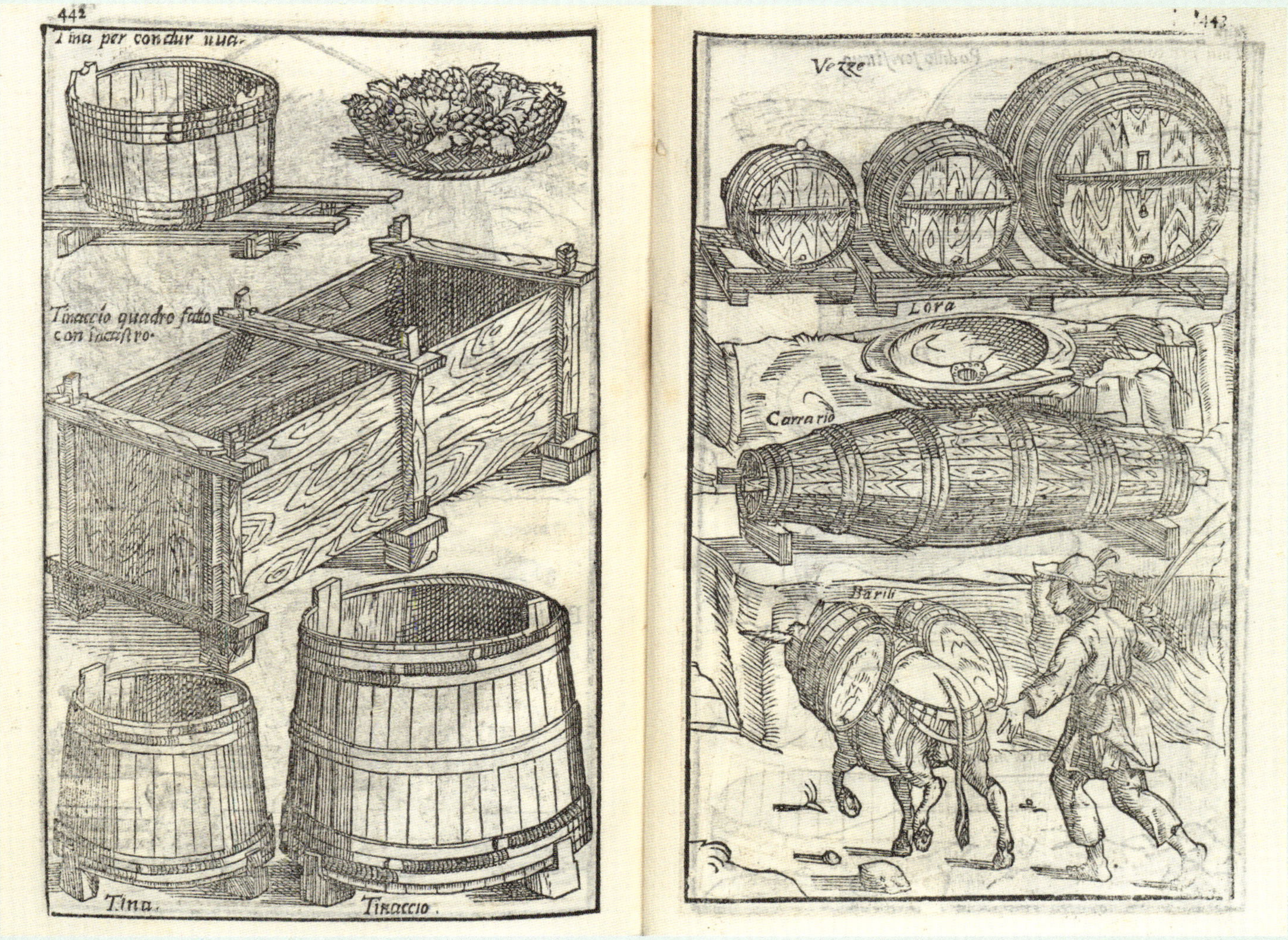

Cat. 54, Agostino Gallo, *Le vinti giornate dell'agricoltura*

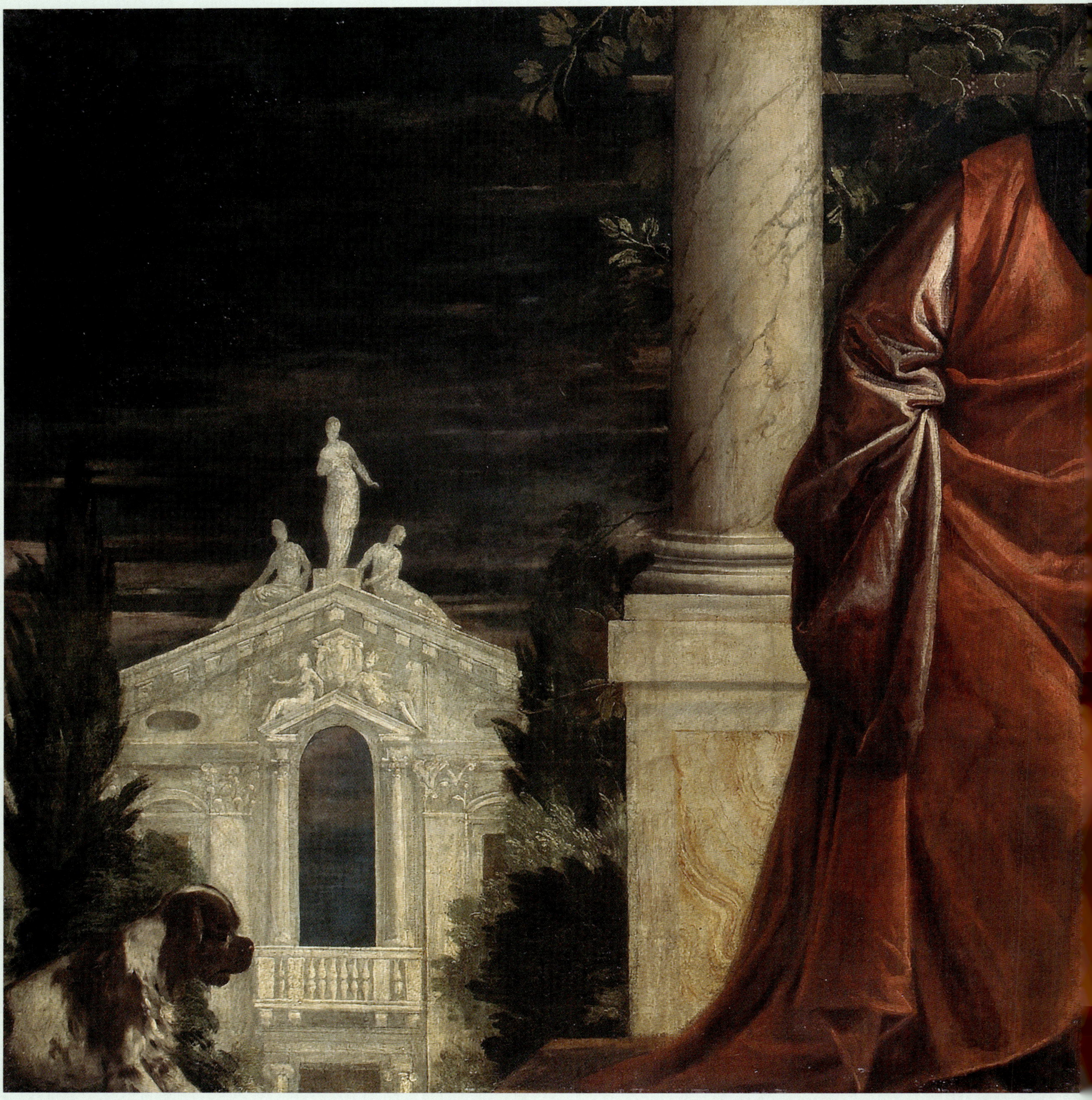

Cat. 55, Veronese, *Susanna and the Elders*

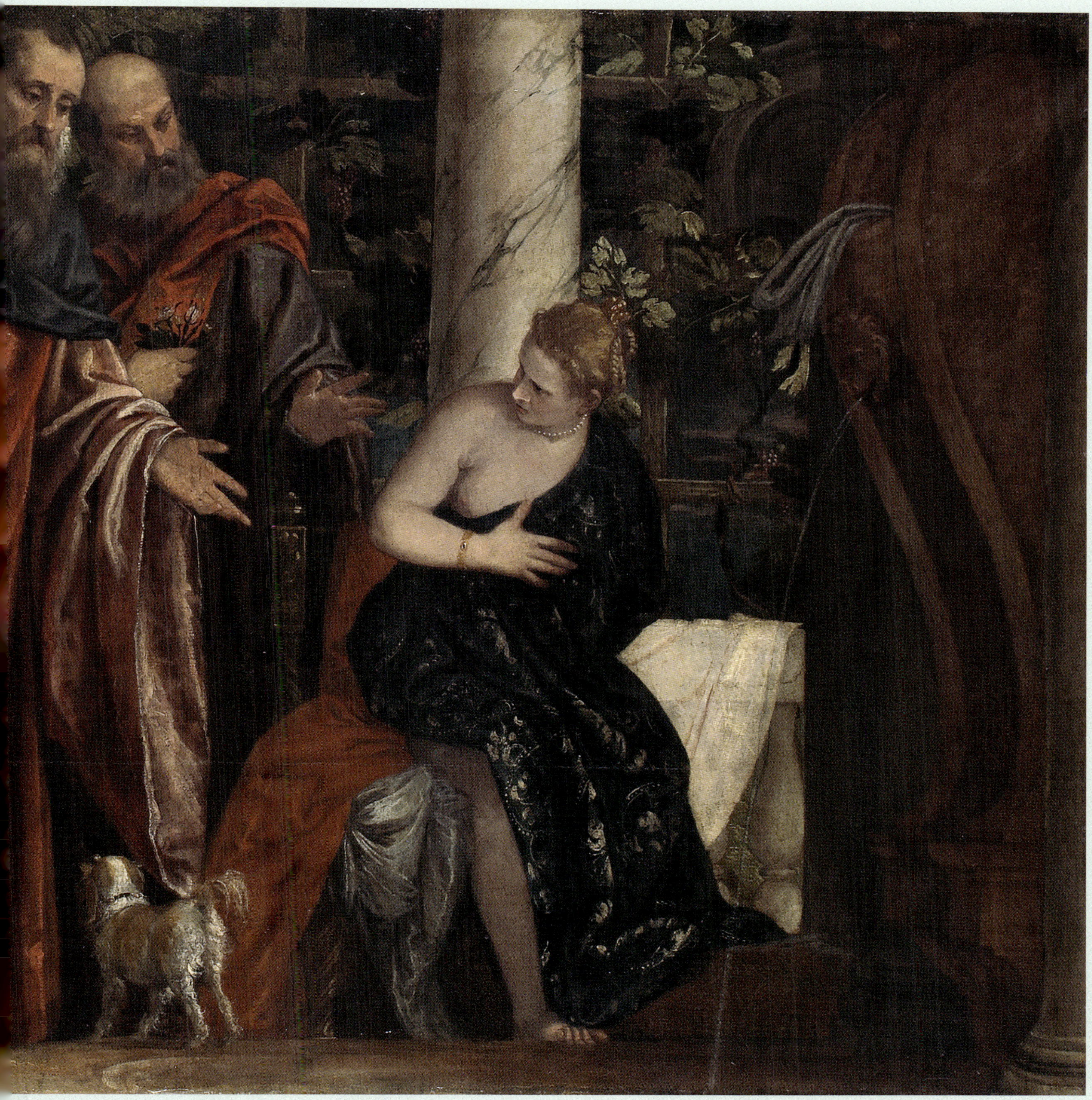

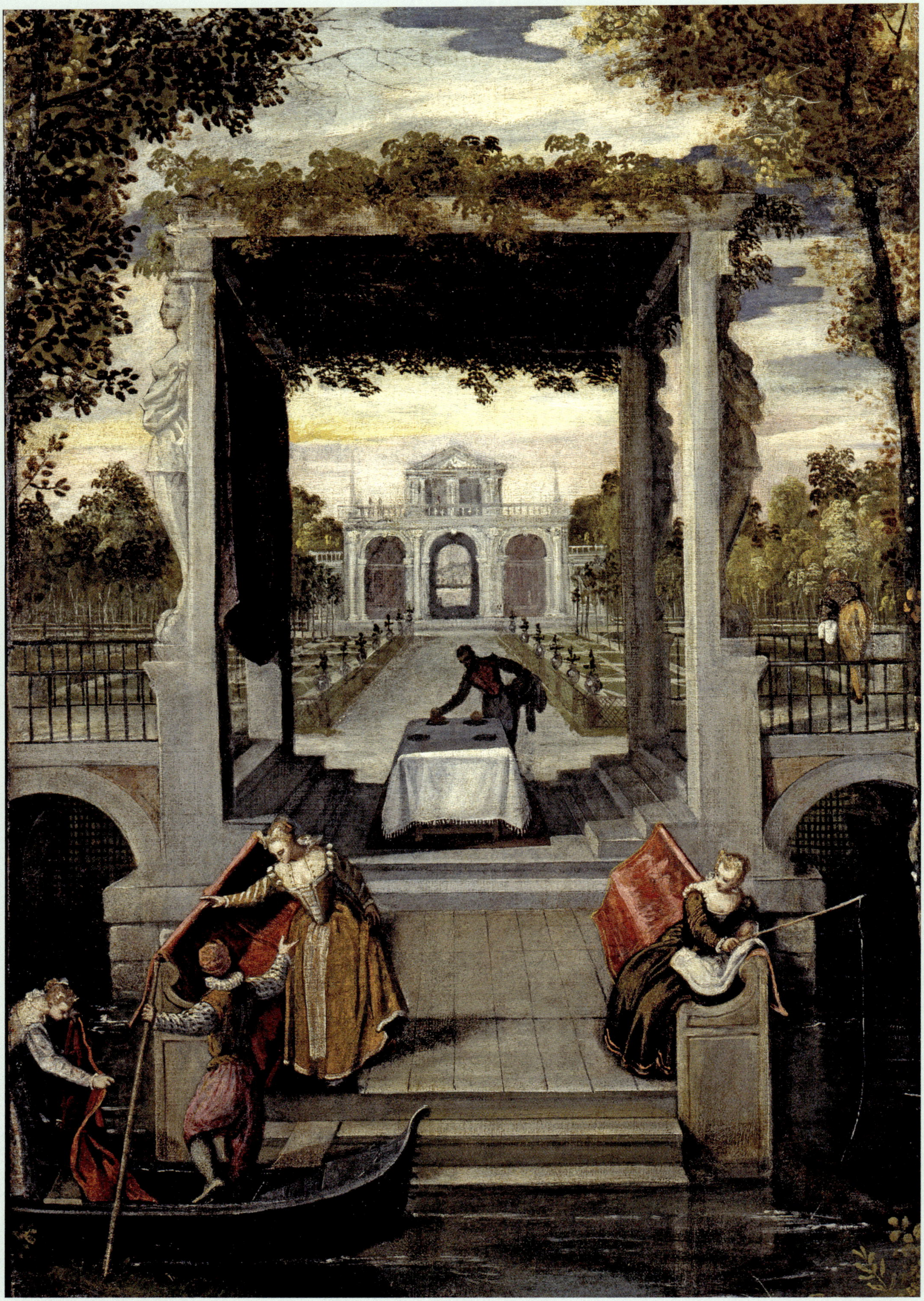

Cat. 56, Benedetto Caliari, *View of a Veneto Villa with Figures*

Cats. 51.1, 51.2

Pietro Crescenzi (c.1233–c.1320)

De Agricultura. Istoriato

Venice 1504; 4°
Vienna, Austrian National Library, Department of Manuscripts and Rare Books, *44.S.81 Alt Prunk, frontispiece

De Agricultura

Venice 1505; 4°
Vienna, Austrian National Library, Department of Manuscripts and Rare Books, *44.S.76 Alt Prunk, 360–1

Literature: Toubert 1984; Ambrosoli 1992

Between 1304 and 1309, Pietro Crescenzi composed his *Ruralia commoda* (titled *De Agricultura* since the late fifteenth century), the most important example of the medieval agronomy treatise, which had a rich tradition first in manuscript and then in print, in Latin and several European languages.

Having studied law and natural philosophy at Bologna University, Crescenzi travelled extensively for his work as a judge and consultant accompanying the *podestà* and high officials in the Lombard, Emilia, and Romagna areas. His travels allowed him to directly observe agricultural techniques, crops, and rural landscapes in northern Italy, furthering his own interests as a naturalist. When he retired from public life in 1298, he lived between Bologna and his country home in Villa dell'Olmo (Rubizzano, Bologna), where he devoted himself to farming and writing his *Ruralia commoda*. His sources were ancient and modern authors, and personal experience.

He produced an original, practical encyclopaedia intended for affluent readers who had invested their wealth in rural land and wished to learn how to manage it. Divided into twelve books, in a sophisticated didactic style, the *Ruralia commoda* covers soil qualities and climates, rural crops, horticulture, knowledge of herbs and their medicinal properties, the garden and its architecture, animal husbandry, veterinary treatments, hunting and fishing. Crescenzi listed the different botanical varieties for each plant, the techniques suited to its cultivation, the harvesting and conservation of the product and finally its alimentary and medicinal uses. The last chapter, a summary of activities month by month, is a legacy from the *Tacuina sanitates*: Crescenzi expanded this concept into a highly practical calendar, which became a staple of agronomic literature.

The first printed editions of the *Ruralia* resembled herbals in their appearance: they featured Gothic typeface text arranged in two columns, and included woodcuts depicting plants and fieldwork, which were sometimes repeated within just a few pages. Anticipating the future evolution of the agronomic literature genre, a more practical quarto format with a simplified illustrative apparatus became the standard in Italy for Crescenzi's work. Small woodcuts, occasionally repeated, served as a concise and effective visual complement to the text.

Sabrina Minuzzi

Cat. 52

Marcus P. Cato the Elder, Marcus T. Varro, Lucius J.M. Columella, Rutilius T.A. Palladius

Scriptores rei rusticae

Venice (Nicolas Jenson) 1472; 2°
Stuttgart, Württembergische Landesbibliothek, 14564, vol. 1, fol. 1r

Literature: Lowry 1991; Armstrong 2003, 233–8; Pennuto 2007; Fabbri 2022, 131–8; the author thanks Helena Szepe and Federica Toniolo for having checked through Lilian Armstrong's papers

This copy of the *Scriptores rei rusticae* is one of the most representative witnesses of the transition from manuscript to printed book, from both a technical and artistic perspective as well as in terms of publishing. The contents were assembled, with the meticulous philological expertise of the humanist Giorgio Merula, by Nicolas Jenson, a French printer-publisher-bookseller active in Venice (1470–80), who was the first to launch this highly successful title. The volume, in an impressive large format, gathered the agronomic works of four classical authors – Columella, Rutilius Palladius, Cato, and Varro – and offered them to a readership of new landowners keen to learn how to manage their estates more effectively.

The publication, like the subsequent editions of the *Scriptores rei rusticae*, emerged from the printer's workshop without illustrations but with wide blank margins and spaces reserved for the intervention of a miniaturist (such as the initial letters marking significant divisions in the text). Many copies of the *Scriptores rei rusticae* remained unadorned, but this one was lavishly illustrated by the miniaturist identified as the Pico Master, as noted by the scholar Lilian Armstrong, who recently passed away. It is through her studies that we can confirm the collaboration of the Pico Master in completing this incunabulum. The anonymous hand of the Pico Master is recognizable in the decorative apparatus of more than a hundred manuscripts and incunabula; he was active first in Ferrara and later in Venice between 1469 and 1495. He often collaborated with Nicolas Jenson – booksellers frequently connected their wealthy clients with miniaturists capable of transforming printed books into magnificently illustrated copies akin to manuscripts.

In the *Scriptores rei rusticae* now preserved in Stuttgart, Columella's text opens with a page framed by a series of scenes that are echoed, with variations, in the subsequent illuminated initials: pruning vines, cutting wood for winter, plowing with oxen, sowing, harvesting and threshing grain, grape harvesting of the 'married' vine (grown clinging to upright trees), grape pressing, wine storage, a fenced garden, and a fishpond. The page that begins Cato's text is also fully illuminated, framed by architectural elements with a rural scene in the background of a vineyard. Nineteen historiated initials punctuate the text with agronomic subjects (beekeeping, peacocks and other domestic animals, a 'flowery' woman, a man warming himself by the fire, a woman milking a goat, and so on), with white-vine borders extending along the margins of the pages. Many other initials are more simply decorated, inscribed in gold within alternating pink-crimson and blue squares.

The miniatures were realized shortly after the book's publication (1472) and belong to the early period of the Pico Master's career. These are the clues that reveal his hand: the predominance of pink and light crimson tones, even in the architecture, as well as in the human figures' clothing and decorations; roundels with monochrome heads punctuating the white-vine borders; and slender putti with wispy blonde hair and heavy eyelids (as seen in the frontispiece of Cato's text).

In the preliminary pages, at the *bas-de-page* of Columella's work summary, there is an erased illuminated coat of arms, probably linked to one of the noble Venetian families that constituted the typical clientele of the Pico Master in the early 1470s. Some marginal notes, written in Latin by an early owner, are consistent with the period and the Venetian area – a reader deeply engaged with the content, who could afford the privilege of studying it in a lavishly illustrated copy crafted by a master of miniature art such as the Pico Master.

Sabrina Minuzzi

Cats. 53.1, 53.2

Marcus P. Cato the Elder, Marcus T. Varro, Lucius J.M. Columella, Rutilius T.A. Palladius

Libri de re rustica

Venice (Aldus Manutius and Andrea Torresano) 1514; 4°
Venice, Biblioteca Nazionale Marciana, 386.D.132, fol. 9r

Rutilius T.A. Palladius

Della agricultura tradutto volgare

Venice (Bernardino de Viano) 1538; 8°
Vienna, Austrian National Library, Department of Manuscripts and Rare Books, *44.X.80 Alt Prunk, frontispiece

Literature: Renouard 1834; Manutius 1975; Lowry 1979; Lowry 1991; Lugato 1994; Pagliara 2001; Lannier 2011

Publishers were quick to turn their attention to the Latin agronomists. This was a logical reflection of humanist interests, but also a natural consequence of the new interest in the countryside shown by the urban ruling classes. In 1472, Nicolas Jenson published in Venice the first edition of the Latin agronomists under the title *Scriptores rei rusticae*; it contained the works of Marcus Porcius Cato, Marcus Varro, Lucius Columella, and Rutilius Palladius (cat. 52). Numerous versions of the collection were produced in Italy, Germany, and France between the fifteenth and sixteenth centuries. Among these, the quarto edition published in Venice in May 1514 by Aldus Manutius stands out, and was noted for its significant new additions. The book was introduced with a dedication by Pietro Bembo to Pope Leo X and a brief preface by the great humanist, architect, and architectural theorist Giovanni Giocondo da Verona (c.1443–1515). In it, he recalls the immense delight he felt with the agronomic studies, 'because the pleasures that are drawn from them seem to come as near as possible to the life of the wise man. I am in harmony with the land, which never rejects rule and never returns what it has received without interest.' This was Giocondo's last engagement in Venice, as he was about to move to Rome to work with Raphael on the new building for St Peter's Basilica.

Giocondo's preface was followed by two fine introductions by Manutius. In the first, the publisher explains to readers the important results of Giocondo's philological efforts: he had realized for the first time that Columella's Book III on trees was not actually his own work, but that of another unidentified author. In the second, taking his cue from the writings of Rutilius Palladius, he provides a series of tables and information on the division of the day into twelve or twenty-four parts, as well as on the gradual lengthening and shortening of the days throughout the year, according to the seasons.

Mario Infelise

Cat. 54

Agostino Gallo (1499–1570)

Le vinti giornate dell'agricoltura

Venice (Camillo and Rutilio Borgomineri) 1575; 4°
Vienna, Austrian National Library, Department of Manuscripts and Rare Books, 53.S.15 Alt Prunk, 442–3

Literature: Benzoni 1998; Minuzzi 2017

Agostino Gallo was one of the most successful early modern agronomy authors. A textile merchant from Brescia, he owned a twenty-hectare estate in Borgo di Poncarale, just outside the town, where he cultivated wheat, flax, forage, and timber. It was there that he pursued his aspiration to master the art of land management. From 1552, he devoted himself enthusiastically to writing his agronomy treatise, synthesising insights gained from books and his own practical experience. Unfortunately, his trading business yielded little profit, ultimately forcing him to sell his cherished estate. Despite this setback, Gallo continued his work on the treatise with renewed fervour.

In December 1564, he asked the Republic of Venice for a ten-year privilege to protect the work he had just printed for the first time in Brescia, under the title *Le dieci giornate della vera agricoltura e de' piaceri della villa*. It was an immediate success, as shown by the three unauthorized editions that came out over the next nine months, full of 'scorretioni' and with 'infiniti errori'. As a result, in March 1566, Gallo decided to request a twenty-year privilege in Venice, which, promptly granted, raised the fine from 300 to 500 ducats for anyone daring to publish what had become an expanded version, covering twenty rather then ten days. Finally, in 1569, an edition appeared that aligned with the author's intentions and was personally overseen by him: *Le vinti giornate di agricultura e de' piaceri della villa*. This edition cited the Venetian privilege – the longest-lasting one – alongside privileges from other Italian states.

Each of the twenty days covered a specific subject, in the form of a dialogue between gentlemen clarifying the advantages of agriculture that was well run, rationally and wisely organized and open to innovation; a 'divine art' capable, in the words of the author, of returning much greater profits than those of trade.

A distinctive feature of the mature agronomic genre, now fully separated from the representation of materia medica with which it initially shared some characteristics, is the choice of a reduced and strictly technical illustrative apparatus. The book concludes with nineteen, full-page woodcuts, depicting the tools essential for carrying out agricultural tasks: ploughs, harrows, shovels, wine-making vats, and every other necessary implement.

Sabrina Minuzzi

Cat. 55

Paolo Caliari, called Veronese (1528–1588)

Susanna and the Elders

c.1585
Canvas; 140 × 280 cm
Vienna, Kunsthistorisches Museum, Picture Gallery, inv. 3676

Provenance: c.1613 Charles de Croy, Duc d'Arschot, Beaumont Castle; before 1635–48 Buckingham Collection; acquired 1649
Literature: Faßbinder 1971, 20; Pignatti 1976, no. 301; exh. cat. London 2009, 129, cat. 69 (Sergio Marinelli); 114–17, cat. I.2 (Howard Burns)

Susanna and the Elders by Veronese is part of a series of ten paintings of scenes from the Old and New Testaments. Chapter 13 of the Book of Daniel (considered part of the Apocrypha) relates how the beautiful, God-fearing Susanna is molested during her daily bath by two old judges who have secretly crept into her garden. She refuses their advances even though they threaten to accuse her of adultery, which is punishable by death. Only the judgement of the prophet Daniel saves her, after the two elders become entangled in contradictions.

With one foot touching the fountain on the right edge of the picture, Susanna is about to enter her bath. The two men in the centre, large and imposing, one of them holding a small bouquet of flowers, harass and solicit her. Susanna tries to hide her nakedness under a brocade towel. A spaniel standing in front of the two elders, its tail raised and barking, expresses its anger at the intruders, while another dog watches the scene suspiciously from the side.

The oppressive moment is heightened by the architecture. Two marble columns rise directly behind the scene, backed by a pergola lattice. The narrowness of the space shows the hopelessness of the situation – all escape is barred to the young woman.

Veronese provides a view of a garden in the background and a white facade with pointed gables and pilasters of colossal order; in the centre is a high arched window with a balcony. The literature points out its similarity to the facade of the central wing of the Villa Barbaro in Maser (Faßbinder 1971; exh. cat. London 2009, 129, cat. 69; 114–17, cat. I.2), designed by Andrea Palladio, the most important Renaissance architect in northern Italy. The villa is considered a prime example of a country house on the Venetian mainland, the Terraferma, where the representative requirements of the urban nobility were combined ideally with a profit-oriented agricultural use of the country estate. The painting of its interior (1560/61) was done by Veronese. In his depictions there, which are framed by mock architecture, his theme is a harmonious world order that applies to nature and the virtuous family, among other things.

The facade in the Vienna painting is also mock architecture (exh. cat. London 2009, 129), although here it is intended to conjure up a deceptive rural idyll. The 'illusionistic' window offers a view of a sky streaked with clouds, which highlight the scene's drama.

Wencke Deiters

Cat. 56

Benedetto Caliari (c.1538–1598)

View of a Veneto Villa with Figures

1565/80
Canvas; 85 × 60 cm
Bergamo, Fondazione Accademia Carrara, inv. 81 LC 00181

Provenance: 1834 Guglielmo Lochis
Literature: Frizzoni 1897, 67–8; Peltzer 1924, 149–50; Coletti 1925/26, 407, 408; Fiocco 1928, 151; Peltzer 1933, 726; Buscaroli 1935, 191; Fiocco 1955, 272; Menegazzi 1957, 174–5; Pedrocco 1990; Rossi 2000; Rallo 2022

The authorship of this painting is debated. It entered the Accademia Carrara in 1866 with an attribution to Paolo Veronese, and was then assigned to Lodevijk Toeput, called Pozzoserrato, a Flemish painter long active in Venice. Finally, it was attributed to Paolo Veronese's younger brother Benedetto Caliari, but cautiously, given the difficulty of distinguishing the latter from his sibling, with whom he worked closely.

Historic sources indicate Benedetto's specialization in fresco painting and particularly architectural and landscape backgrounds. These indications are confirmed in the works attributed to the artist, among which is the decoration of the Salone del Vescovado in Treviso, distinguished by airy landscape views framed by mock-classical architecture. These are also present in this painting, which is unusual in that the landscape is not the background to a biblical or literary story, but the central feature of the scene on a par with the episode of contemporary life that animates it.

A gondola is moored at the jetty in the foreground; two servants are helping an elegantly dressed woman get into the boat. On the opposite side, another lady is fishing. Behind them, beneath a broad pergola supported by caryatids, a servant is laying a table, while on the right the artist has inserted a male figure leaning on a balcony. In the background is an elegant Italian garden, with a broad path down its centre, which is closed off by a porticoed building in an explicitly Palladian style.

The artist has portrayed one of those mainland villas built by the Venetian aristocracy as a place of leisure and amusement, which, over the course of the sixteenth century, became actual centres of agriculture and land management, at a time when Venice was abandoning its original trading vocation. They were complex sites with cottages, gardens, orchards, and places of amusement as well as the landlord's residence, and their construction was accompanied by a comprehensive campaign to transform the land and the landscape. This painting by Caliari is exemplary and rare testimony of this period.

PAOLO PLEBANI

Jacopo Bassano and the Representation of the Seasons in Venice

(cats. 57–62)

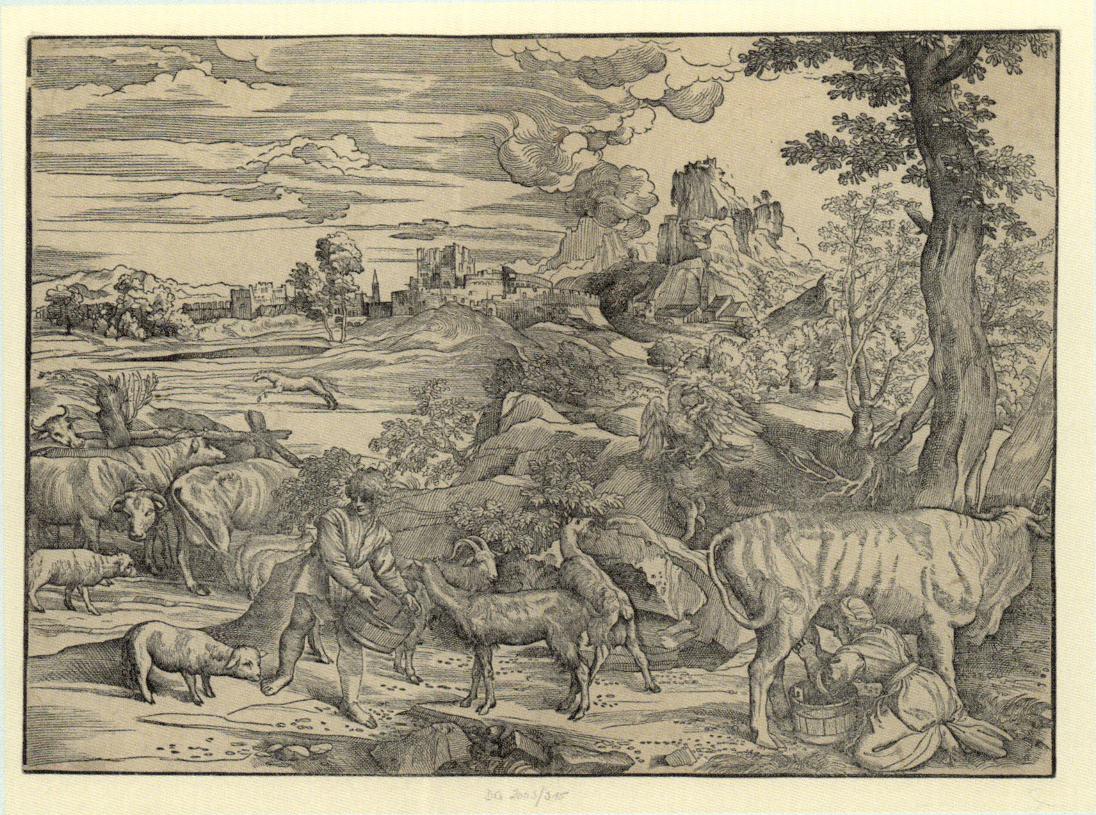

Cat. 57, Lucas van Leyden, *The Milkmaid*

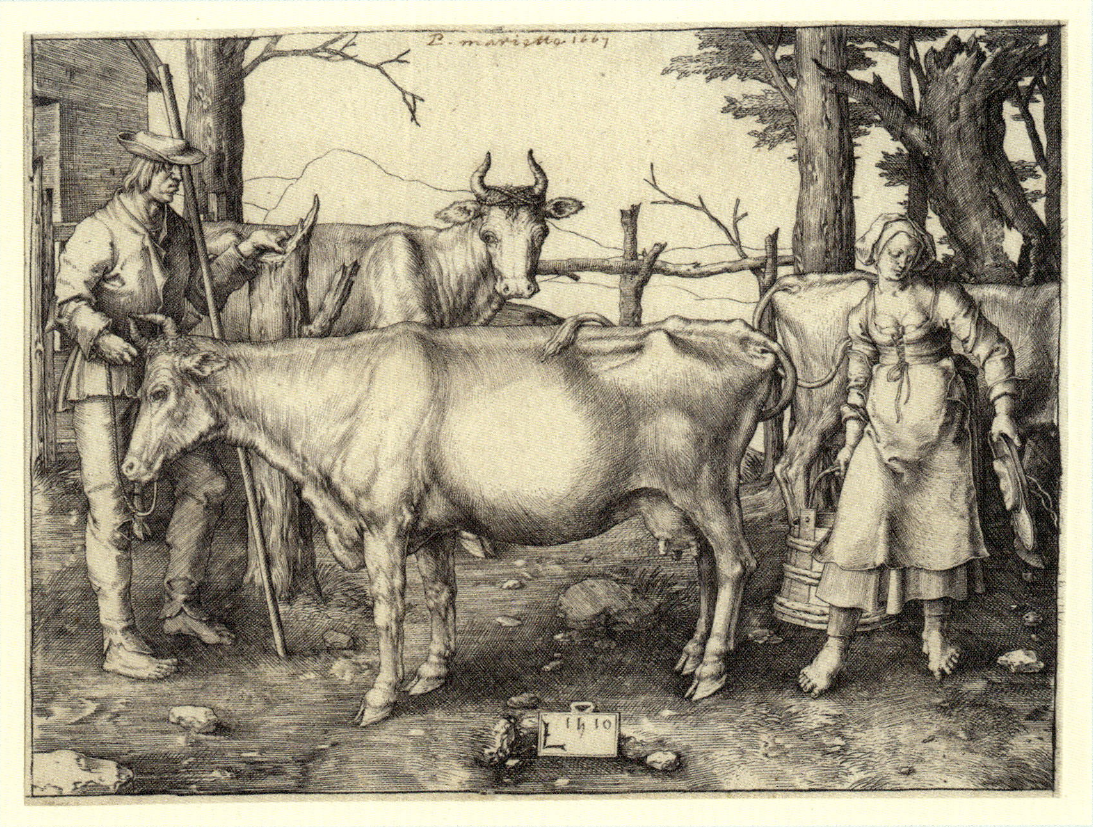

Cat. 58, Niccolò Boldrini after Titian, *Landscape with a Milkmaid*

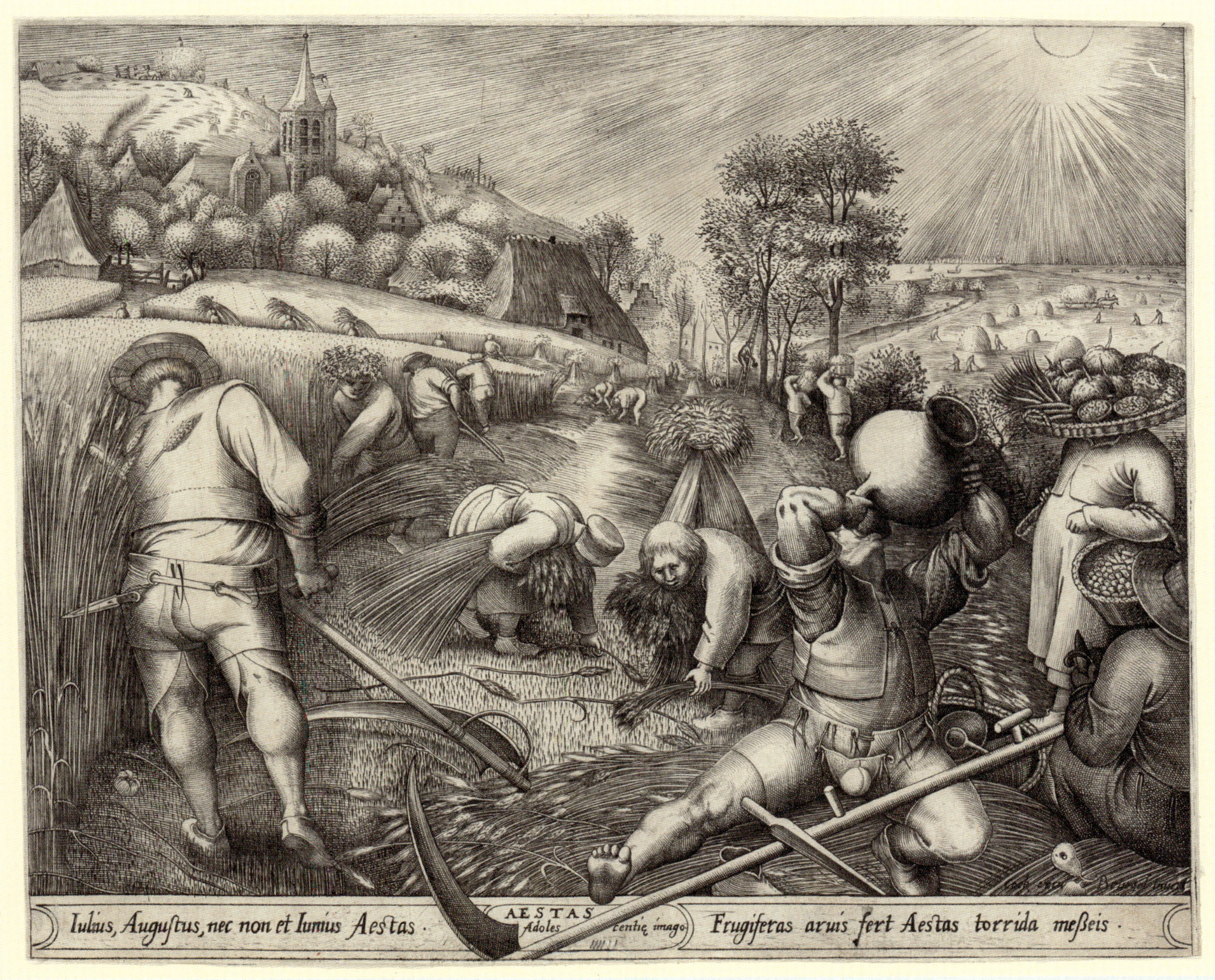

Cat. 59, Pieter van der Heyden after Pieter Bruegel the Elder, *Aestas (Summer)*

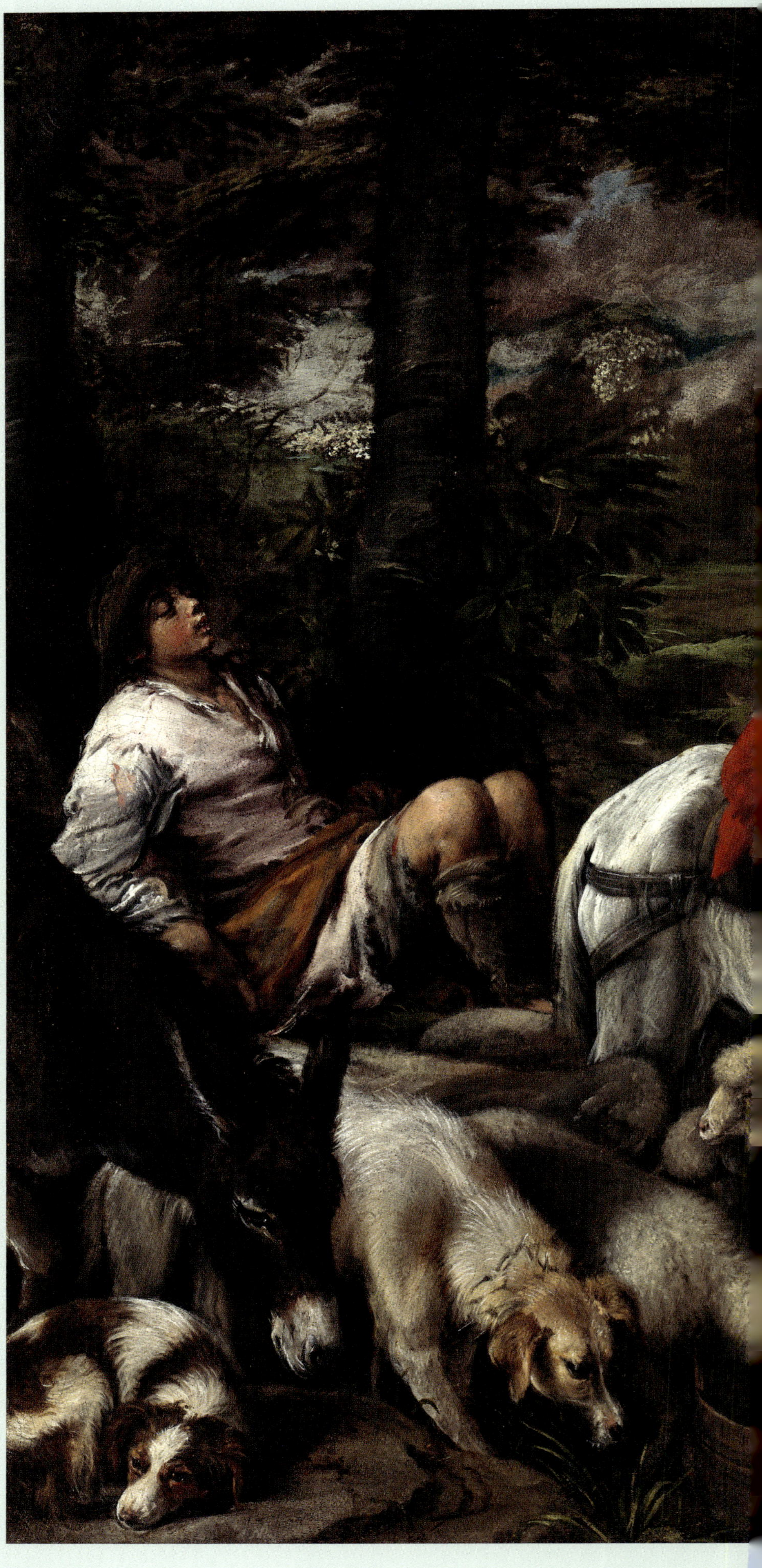

 Cat. 60, Jacopo Bassano, *Sleeping Shepherd*

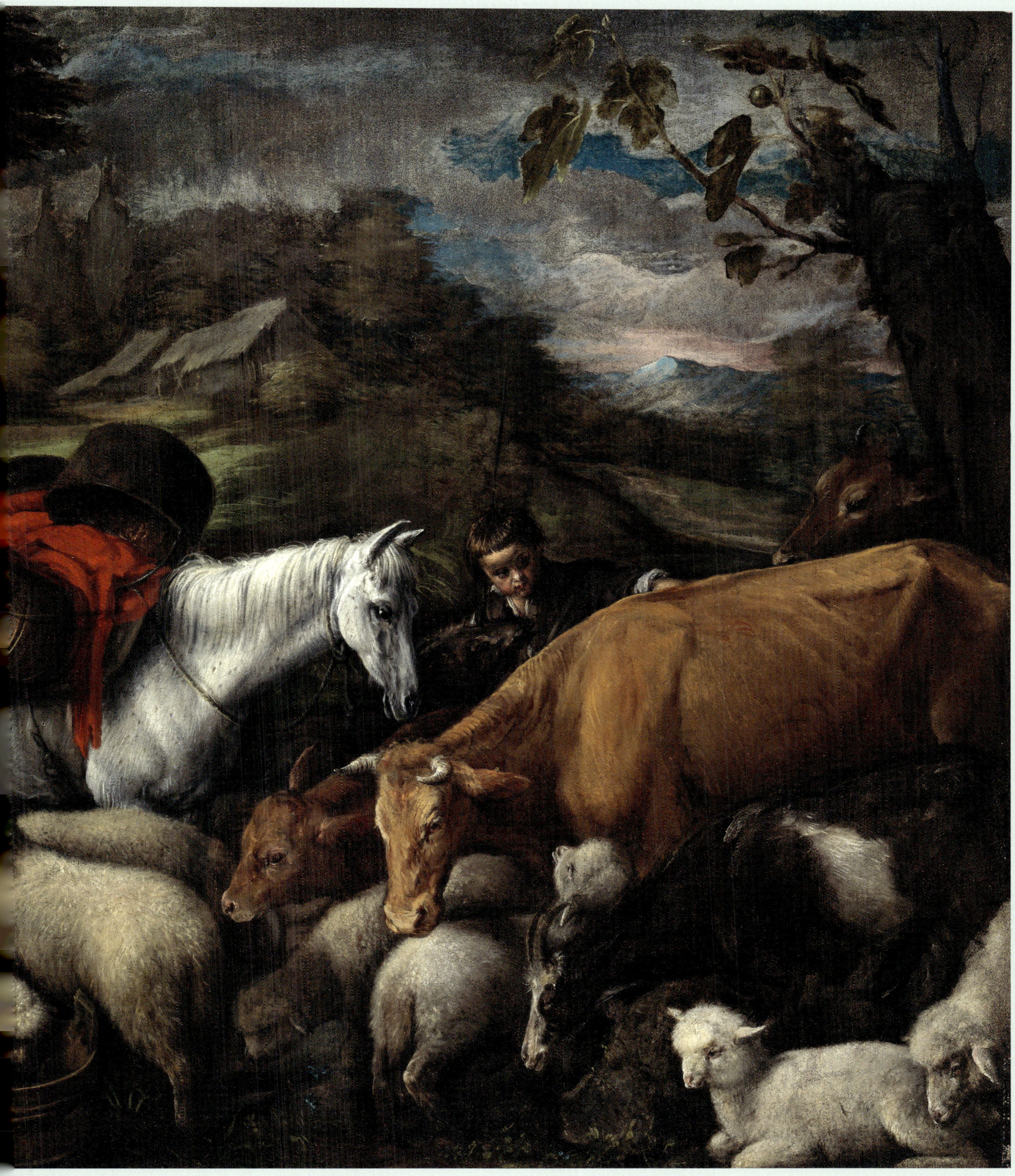

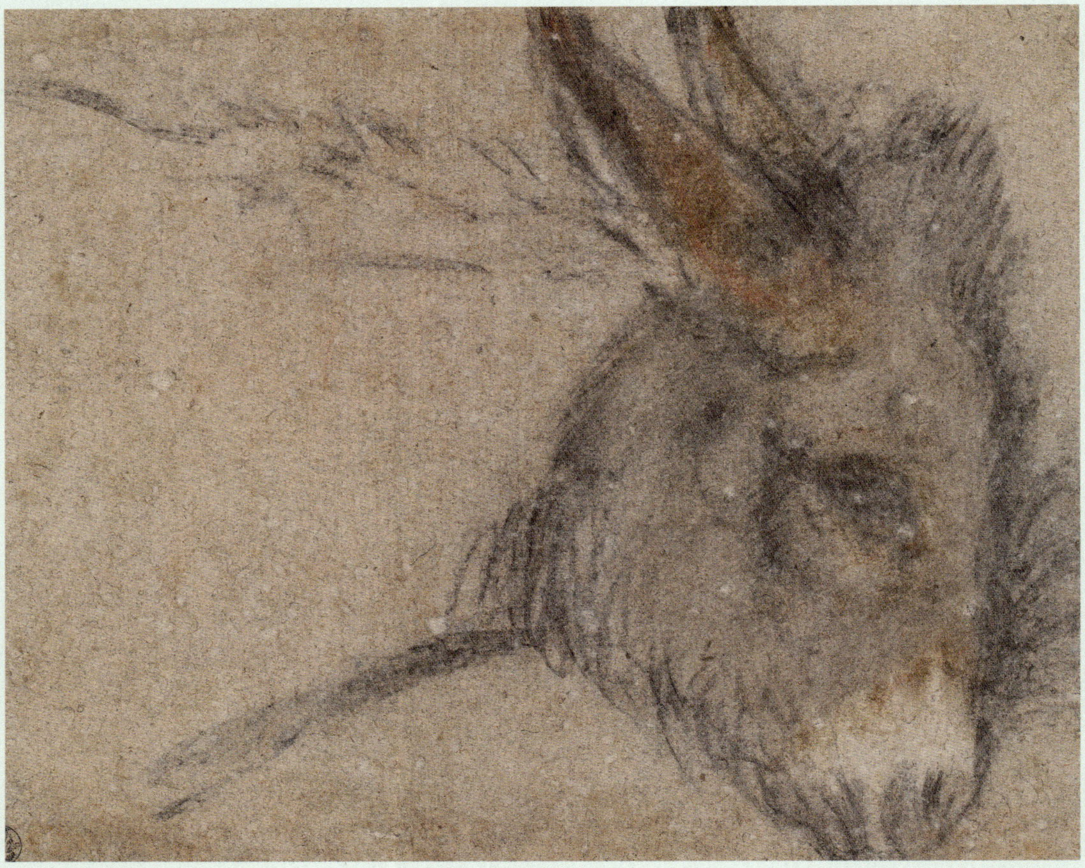

Cat. 61, Jacopo Bassano, *Head of a Donkey*

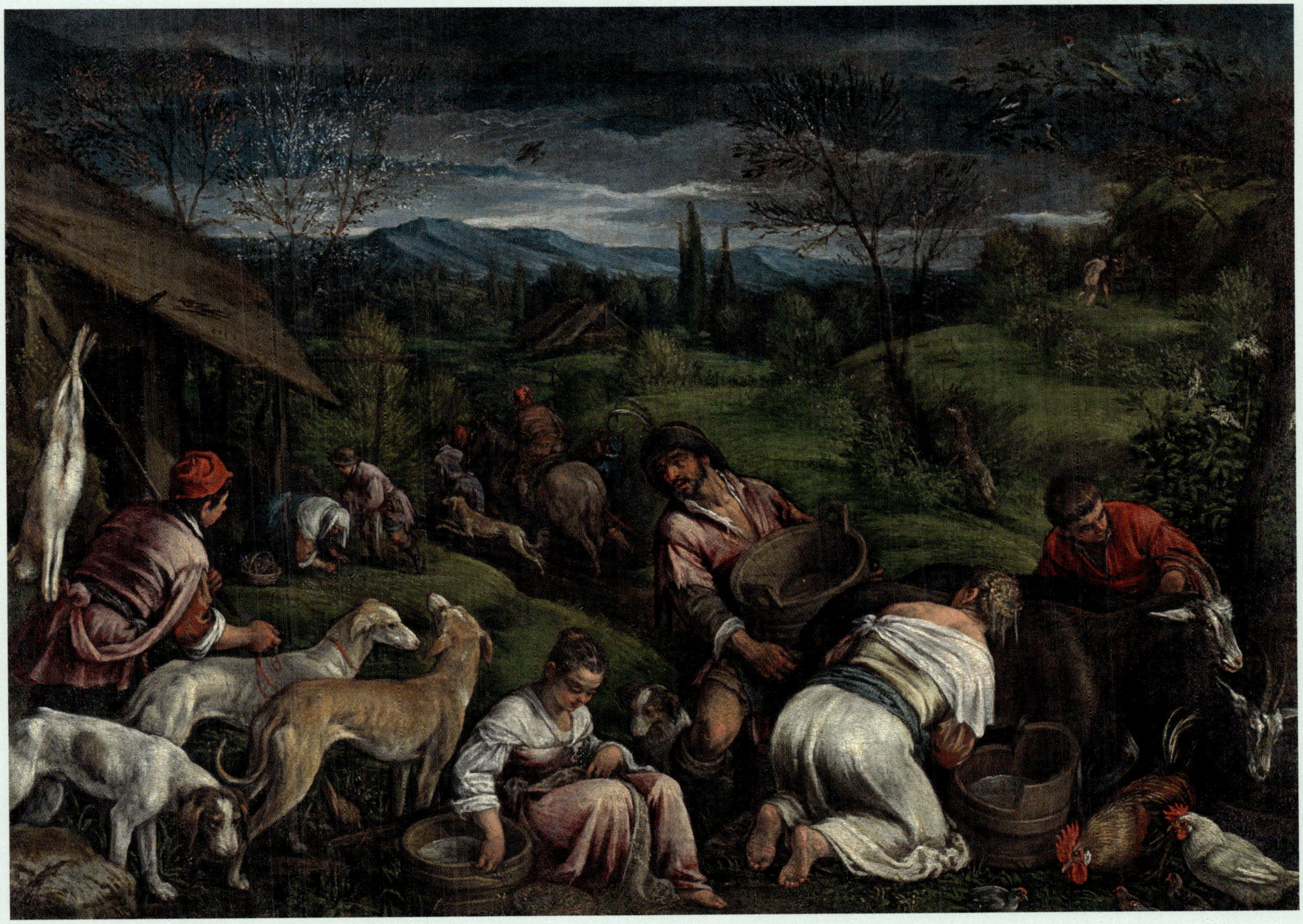

Cat. 62.1, Jacopo Bassano, *Spring (Expulsion from Paradise)*

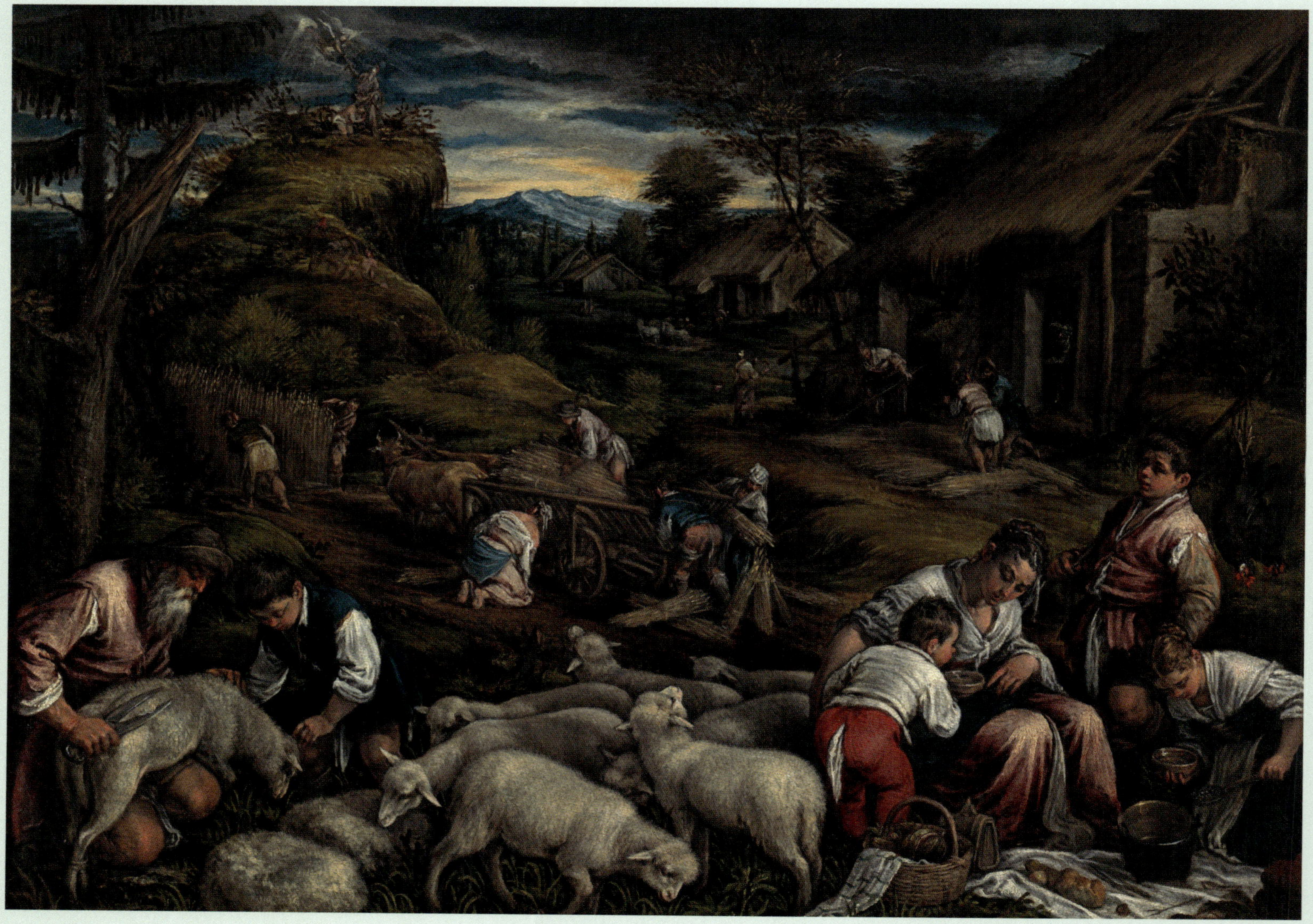

Cat. 62.2, Jacopo Bassano, *Summer (Sacrifice of Isaac)*

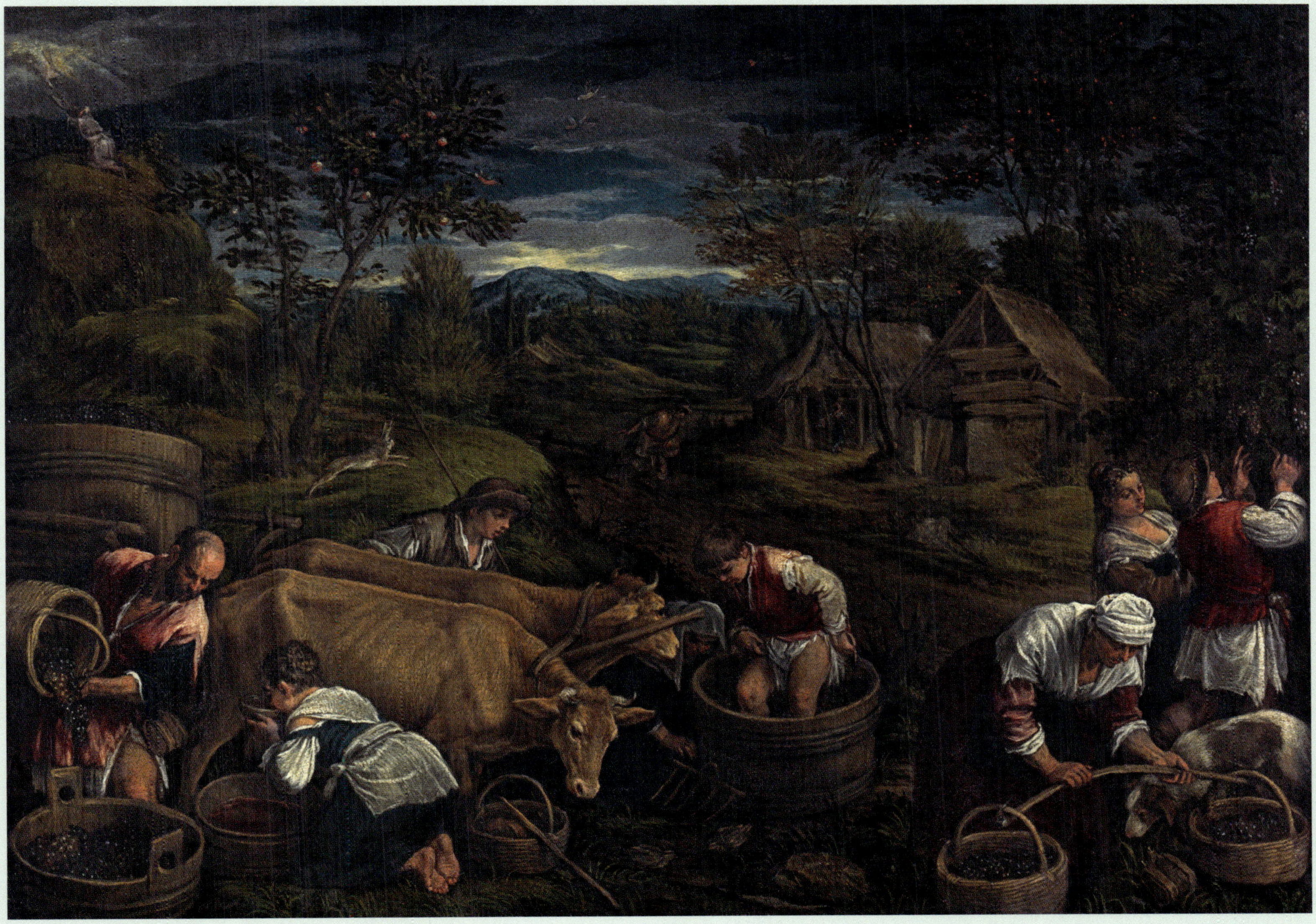

Cat. 62.3, Jacopo Bassano, *Autumn (Moses Receives the Tablets of the Law)*

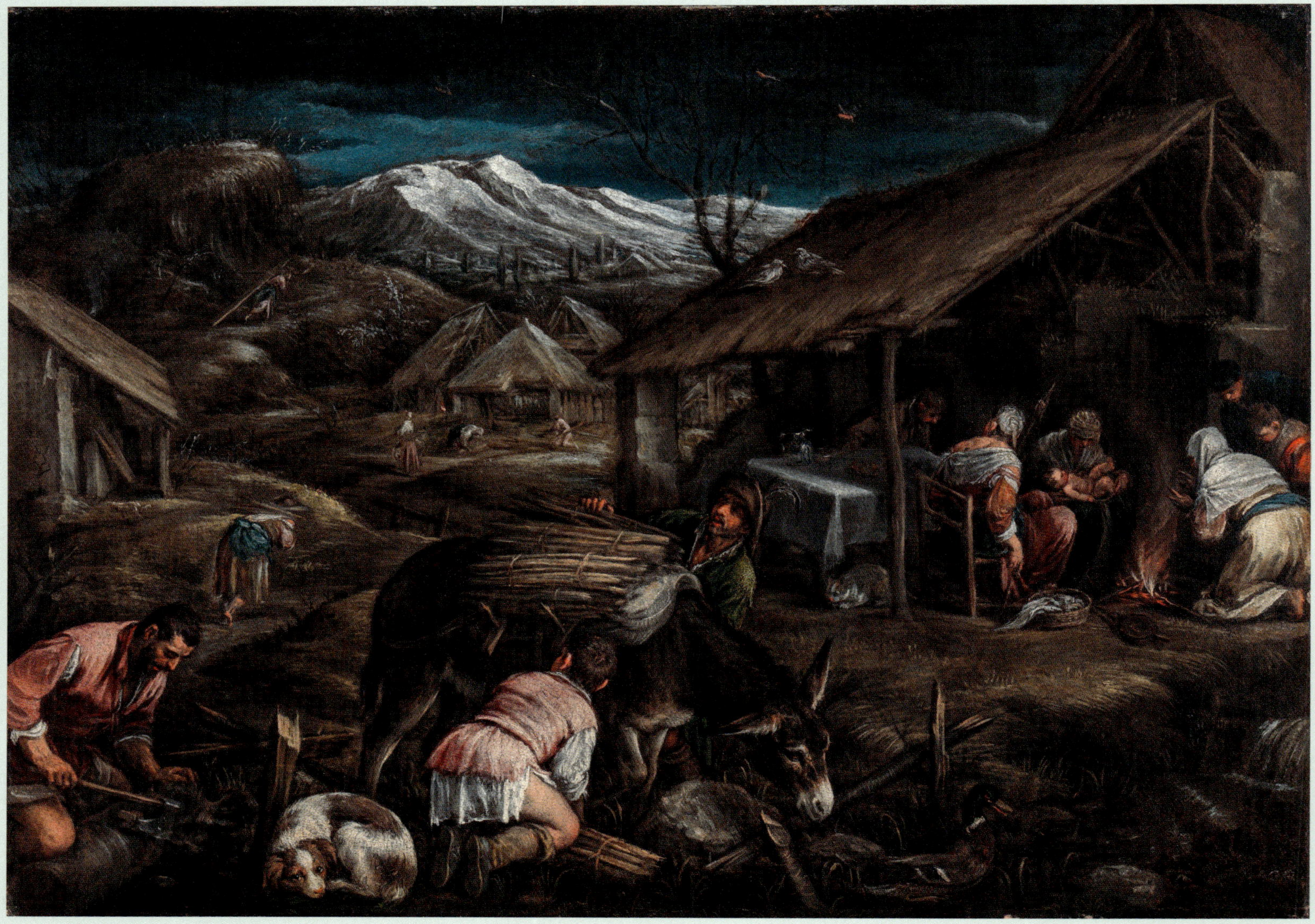

Cat. 62.4, Jacopo Bassano, *Winter (Christ Carrying the Cross)*

Cat. 57

Lucas van Leyden (1494–1533)

The Milkmaid

1510
Engraving; 115 × 157 mm
Signed and dated lower middle: 'L 1510'; upper middle in brown ink: 'P. Mariette 1667'
Vienna, Albertina, inv. DG1926/2060

Provenance: Vienna, Court Library
Literature: Van Mander 1604, fol. 212v–213r; exh. cat. Amsterdam 1978, 32; Van der Coelen and Lammertse 2019, 1–32; exh. cat. Leiden 2011, 247, cat. 46; exh. cat. Rotterdam 2015, 86, cat. 21; mus. cat. Vienna 2022, no. 51

This copperplate engraving by Lucas van Leyden, dated 1510, is considered to be the first depiction of a milkmaid and illustrates the emerging interest that illustrations of peasant life were to acquire as a subject for art in the sixteenth century. The single sheet from the Albertina bears the addition 'P. Mariette 1667' in brown ink in the upper margin, linking the engraving to the seventeenth-century printmaker and publisher Pierre Mariette II.

Two figures in peasant dress and three cows are depicted outdoors in a fenced-in area. In the centre of the sheet is a dairy cow in full-length profile. Another cow behind it looks directly at us. The cow in the centre is flanked by the two figures. On the left, a man stands with a long staff and a rope tied to the animal's horns; on the right, a woman holds a milking bucket and wide-brimmed hat. The maid, visibly tired from her work, looks down at the ground. The farmer, on the other hand, focuses his gaze on the woman, whose décolleté is accentuated by her tightly laced bodice. Together with the suggestive interpretation that the activity of milking has in the Dutch language, the pictorial theme has sexual connotations. The lifelike depiction of the dairy cows is impressive. The convincing anatomical structure and the detailed modelling with its cross-hatching show clearly that the animal interested the artist. In comparison, the mountainous view suggested by fine lines in the scene's background appears to be more of an artistic fantasy (the Dutch landscape is famously flat). The scene is framed by trees and a stable, which reinforce its rural setting. Karel van Mander mentions an engraving with a maid and cows by Lucas van Leyden in his *Schilder-Boek* and praises its technical execution.

Lucas van Leyden is one of the most important pioneers of genre pictures, which developed in particular from printmaking, and he was most likely responsible for popularizing them. The emerging interest in pictures of everyday life was remarkable, because previously only biblical histories or portraits had been considered worthy of depiction.

Angelina Illes

Cat. 58

Niccolò Boldrini (early 16th cent.–after 1566) after Tiziano Vecellio, called Titian (c.1488–1576)

Landscape with a Milkmaid

1525/30
Woodcut; 373 × 525 mm
Vienna, Albertina, inv. DG2003/315

Provenance: 1678 Pierre II Mariette (1634–1716), Paris; Albertina historical holdings
Literature: Exh. cat. Vienna 1966, cat. 176 (Konrad Oberhuber); Muraro and Rosand 1976, 101–2; mus. cat. Venice 1982, 31–2, no. III (different version); Borea 2009, vol. 1, 66, 145, vol. 2, fig. XIII/22; Lüdemann 2016, 120–2

From the 1530s onwards, Titian sought new means of expression in landscapes, which became the primary subject in his figurative depictions. One example is this woodcut, a peasant scene in a landscape. A shepherd boy feeds his animals in the midst of grazing cows, goats, and sheep, while a woman, seen from behind, milks a cow. Further back an eagle sits on a tree stump. A foal gallops across a gently rolling landscape. A fortified city can be seen on the horizon. Mountains rise up in the distance. Clouds tower over one of them and drift towards the city, while on the right half of the picture, the landscape is bathed in sunlight from a clear sky.

Titian may have been inspired by Lucas van Leyden's engraving *The Milkmaid* (cat. 57), in which the female protagonist, surrounded by cows, is eyed by a young man and the 'milking' given erotic allusions. In Titian there is no eye contact between the shepherd and the maid. Each just goes about their business, symbolic of the peaceful coexistence of humans and animals in an idyllic rural setting captured in a variety of atmospheric moods. But the idyll is deceptive. The eagle with its outstretched wings resembles a heraldic animal and is interpreted as an allusion to the emperor's intervention in the *Pax Veneta*, the Peace of Venice.

According to Vasari, Titian depicted 'many landscapes' (*molti paesi*) in his woodcuts (Vasari 1568 & 1880, V, 433). In relation to Titian, Ridolfi also mentions 'some pastorals and animals' (*alcuni pastorelli et animali*), an allusion to the pastoral landscapes typical of Venice, which – inspired by ancient bucolic poetry – praise the peaceful life of shepherds in nature with a romanticized idea of the rural world, a contrast to the busy city life at a time of political unrest (Ridolfi 1648, Part I, 156). It is natural to see our woodcut in this context. Its execution has been attributed to Niccolò Boldrini or Giovanni Britti, among others. However, the latter is only known to have been in in Venice from 1536, which speaks against him (Muraro & Rosand 1976).

There are preparatory drawings, including one in the Louvre in Paris (inv. 3422) that has also been discussed as copy or workshop work (Muraro & Rosand 1976; Lüdemann 2016). However, it is missing the eagle, among other things, which may have been prepared in a different drawing (Muraro & Rosand 1976). Perhaps the various preparatory studies can also be understood as evidence of how much Titian was preoccupied with the discovery of landscape in his works.

Wencke Deiters

Cat. 59

Pieter van der Heyden (c.1530–after 1572) after Pieter Bruegel the Elder (1525/30–1569)

Aestas (Summer)

1570
Engraving, 1st state; 223 × 285 mm
Signed lower right: 'Cock excu Bruegel Inuet'
Inscription lower centre: 'AESTAS / Adoles centie imago.' ('Summer / Image of youth.'); below: 'Iulius, Augustus, nec non et Iunius Aestas. Frugiferas aruis fert Aestas torrida meßeis.' ('Summer reigns in July, August and also June. Hot summer brings bounteous harvests to the fields.')
Vienna, Albertina, inv. DG1955/128

Provenance: Vienna, Court Library
Literature: Bastelaer 1908, 202.A; Hollstein, Veldman, and Luijten 2006, 62.30 I; Sellink (2007) 2011, no. 150 (about a copy in a different collection); exh. cat. Chemnitz 2014, 162–3, cat. 44 (Bertram Kaschek; about a copy in a different collection); Michel 2017, 67–71, 93 (fig)

Summer, together with *Spring,* is part of an unfinished series of engravings of the seasons, based on drawings by Pieter Bruegel the Elder. He died in 1569, so was unable to complete *Autumn* and *Winter.*

In 1565, with his painted *Seasons* (cats. 15.1–15.3), which included *Haymaking* (see essay Pénot, fig. 1) and *The Harvesters* (see essay Pénot, fig. 2), Bruegel created the first large-format labours of the months in painting and established the landscape as an independent genre. There are references here to motifs in these two works.

The theme, as stated in the inscription, is the bountiful harvest in the hot months of summer. The sun stands high in the sky, its rays of glistening light stream across the sky. As in the painted cycle, Bruegel creates an atmospheric mood that characterises the season. This is also true of the integration of various agricultural activities into a panoramic landscape, especially the grain and hay harvest near a village. A repoussoir figure in the left foreground – the farmer seen from behind cutting grain – serves as an introduction and lends depth to the scene. The positions of his head and arm resemble a reaper in *The Harvesters.* The farmer in the foreground on the right, on the other hand, is resting. He drinks from a jug and stretches his bare foot towards the viewer. Along with his scythe, it juts out of the picture into the caption, 'an overstepping of the pictorial border that is unique in Bruegel's graphic work' (Michel 2017, 71). Both peasants are modelled on figures in Michelangelo's *Last Judgement* (Rome, Sistine Chapel, 1534–41): the labourer on St Andrew, the drinker on one of the resurrected (Kaschek 2012, 94ff.). In Bruegel's work they are transformed, probably ironically, into farm workers, 'to satisfy supremely earthly needs', among other things (exh. cat. Chemnitz 2014, 163).

Otherwise, ears of corn are reaped and carried away; in the background the hay harvest is being organised. A shooting competition is probably taking place in the distance to the right of the church tower (exh. cat. Chemnitz 2014), similar to *Haymaking.* As in that painting, a so-called 'basket head' (Pénot and Oberthaler 2018/19, 226) is depicted in the foreground. The head has been completely replaced by a richly filled basket symbolizing the unity of man and nature.

The Latin caption recognises youth in summer (see also cat. 29.1). It is intended for the educated upper classes, who were only able to admire Bruegel's painted landscape cycle in small private circles. Thanks to printmaking, his revolutionary pictorial ideas were then available to a wider audience. Hieronymus Cock was aware of their significance when he made the decision to add *Autumn* and *Winter.*

WENCKE DEITERS

Cat. 60

Jacopo dal Ponte, called Bassano (1510/12–1592)

Sleeping Shepherd

c.1568
Canvas; 99.5 × 137.5 cm
Budapest, Szépművészeti Múzeum, inv. 119

Provenance: Esterházy Collection; 1871 Szépművészeti Múzeum
Literature: Exh. cat. Turin 1990, 144; mus. cat. Budapest 1991, 5; exh. cat. Bassano del Grappa and Fort Worth 1992/93, 369–71, no. 45; Rearick 1993, 126; Aikema 1996, 96–7; Lichner 2001, 91–114, 207–19; Caramanna 2004, 180–4; Ballarin 2007, 33–4, 40–3, fig. 2; Mason 2009, 16-17; mus. cat. Budapest 2024, 25

Since representation without narrative is unprecedented in Jacopo Bassano's oeuvre, this enigmatic work has sparked intense discussions. Theories from the past thirty years – which have suggested the subject of the painting to be mythological themes related to Mercury, the month of August, the contrast of virtuous and vicious activities, or the duality of active and contemplative lifestyles – although ingenious, have failed to provide a satisfactory explanation. Thus, we are compelled to accept the painting's peculiar lack of subject.

The first printed catalogue of the Esterházy Collection (written in German, 1812) listed 'Shepherd asleep amidst his flock' as the work of Jacopo Bassano, but for long it was considered to be a workshop creation. Alessandro Ballarin reinstated the piece into the master's œuvre, dating it around 1568.

In the second half of the 1560s, while studying the nuances of light effects and nature, Bassano developed a classical style with a sense of monumentality and tranquility. This gave a new tone to his biblical-pastoral paintings – a genre created by combining a desire for rural simplicity and a nostalgia for antiquity based on Virgil's *Georgics* with Old Testament themes. The *Sleeping Shepherd* is a most perfect culmination of these years' efforts.

The turquoise blue of the sky (most probably painted with azurite) blends into crimson hues; the lights of dusk fill the composition. The domestic animals and plants (an elder bush on the left and a fig tree far right) are treated with the same attention as human figures, conveying a harmonious coexistence in nature.

The Budapest painting has two known copies. One, which appeared on the Hungarian art market in 2008 and 2014 (Nagyházi Gallery, 27 May 2014, lot 89), exactly reproduces the composition. Interestingly, the other copy's landscape includes a biblical scene, the Call of Abraham (Stalker & Boos, 26–28 July 1975). However, technical studies on the thin layers of the heavily abraded background have shown no evidence of such an insertion in the autograph work.

Csenge Júlia Béres

Cat. 61

Jacopo dal Ponte, called Bassano (1510/12–1592)

Head of a Donkey

1565/70
Black pencil, red chalk, brown and white chalk on brownish coloured paper; 222 × 281 mm
Staatliche Museen zu Berlin, Kupferstichkabinett, inv. KdZ 15655

Provenance: Vincenzo Pacetti
Literature: Rearick 1989, III, no. 11

Jacopo Bassano's long career was marked by curiosity and a natural openness to artistic innovations, both in the planning design stage and the painting itself. He used coloured chalks in his drawings from the 1540s, intensifying their use around the end of the 1560s in compositional and life studies. His choice of this medium makes him a true innovator, who sought new means of expression to convey his fundamentally chromatic view of reality.

This study in coloured chalks was first published and discussed by Roger Rearick in his 1989 examination of Jacopo Bassano's drawings. Less well known than the animal studies in the Uffizi or the Louvre, it is worthy of attention for the spontaneity and speed of its execution, suggesting a study from life.

It depicts a donkey, facing to the right; its head and neck are visible, the latter only in outline. Jacopo concentrated on the animal's muzzle with rapid strokes of black chalk, building it up by effectively integrating the paper into the chromatic portrayal of the subject. The depiction of the shaggy, bristly hair, suggested with rapidly traced signs, is remarkable, as is the look of the moist eyes that speak of the animal's patient nature, while its long ears are bent as if listening.

Thus, the sheet has the flavour of a study from life and shows the versatility of the artist, who used direct observation of nature for his compositions as well as the models contained in the illustrated treatises that were in wide circulation in the second half of the century. This flexible approach was due to the increasing need to provide his workshop with useful material to meet the exponential growth in demand for biblical scenes on the art market.

Indeed, it was in precisely the years 1565–70, when the production of paintings with Old Testament subjects set in rural landscapes intensified, that Rearick, followed by Romani (exh. cat. Bassano del Grappa and Fort Worth 1992/93, 258), placed the creation of this sheet, linking it to Jacopo's painting *The Animals Entering Noah's Ark* (Madrid, Museo Nacional del Prado).

Francesca Del Torre Scheuch

Cats. 62.1–62.4 (62.4 not included in the exhibition)

Jacopo dal Ponte, called Bassano (1510/12–1592)

Spring (Expulsion from Paradise)

1570/75
Canvas; 83 × 115 cm
Vienna, Kunsthistorisches Museum, Picture Gallery, inv. 4303

Summer (Sacrifice of Isaac)

1570/75
Canvas, top and bottom extended; 78.5 × 110.5 cm
Vienna, Kunsthistorisches Museum, Picture Gallery, inv. 4302

Autumn (Moses Receives the Tablets of the Law)

1570/75
Canvas; 75.7 cm × 109 cm
Vienna, Kunsthistorisches Museum, Picture Gallery, inv. 4304
Provenance: collection of Archduke Leopold Wilhelm, inventory of 1659, 330–5

Winter (Christ Carrying the Cross)

1570/75
Canvas; 75. 8 × 107.8 cm
Mexico City, Museo Soumaya, inv. 58341
Provenance: Imperial Collections (?); Sotheby's London 12 December 2002, lot 118; Dorotheum 10 November 2021, lot 28

Literature: Ridolfi 1648, 398; Baldass 1949, 212–13 (Francesco); Ballarin 1968, 240–1; mus. cat. Vienna 1991, 26, tab. 82; exh. cat. Bassano del Grappa and Fort Worth 1992/93, 139–42, cats. 50, 51 (Livia Alberton Vinco da Sesso); exh. cat. Venice 1999, 568–70, cats. 169, 170 (Stefania Mason); Ballarin 2004, 70–100; exh. cat. Budapest 2009/10, 352, cat. 104, (Francesca Del Torre Scheuch); exh. cat. Helsinki 2024, 97–111 (Kirsi Eskelinen)

Six paintings depicting the seasons are listed in Archduke Leopold Wilhelm's inventory of 1659, four of which were engraved by David Teniers the Younger for his *Theatrum Pictorium*. The paintings *Spring*, *Summer*, and *Autumn*, which were in Prague from the beginning of the eighteenth century, were brought to Vienna in 1894. *Winter*, thought to be lost, might be identifiable as the painting in the Museo Soumaya in Mexico City.

The series depicts the four seasons through the agricultural work typical of each respective time of year. The compositions are characterised by a slightly elevated viewpoint, which offers a view of a tree-covered landscape with huts where the farmers live. There is a mountain on the horizon that could be Mount Grappa. Small biblical scenes, simply rendered, can be made out in the background. Each of the four depictions has its own unique lighting.

The return from the hunt is shown in *Spring*. Vividly depicted hunting dogs accompany a servant in the foreground. A hunter on horseback has already ridden past the hut. In the foreground and in the background, farmers are collecting flowers. On the right side they are busy with their goats. The expulsion of Adam and Eve from Paradise can be seen in a clearing in the background on the right. The trees are in full bloom and the numerous birds perched on the branches recall a Paradise-like landscape in the early morning light.

Sheep shearing and the preparation of a rustic meal are depicted in the foreground of *Summer*. Allusions to the summer season include small scenes in the middle ground of mowing, harvesting, and threshing of wheat, as well as a warm light that envelops the figures and lends the colours a special intensity. On a hill on the left, the sacrifice of Isaac, a prefiguration of Christ's fate, has been sketched in quick brushstrokes.

The harvest and grape pressing are the focus of *Autumn*. The light's warm but gloomy mood is characteristic of this time of year. The narrative unfolds from right to left. Two farmers harvest grapes, which will be carried in baskets by another woman to the farmer on the left. He pours the fruit into a tub, which is then emptied into a large wine barrel on a wagon to which two oxen are hitched. A barefoot child presses the grapes. A girl kneels and tastes the sweet grape juice. In the background, a sower scatters seed on the field. On the hill on the left, Moses can be seen receiving the tablets of the law, as described in the Bible.

Winter is marked by a break in work on the farm. The farmers are busy collecting wood. Their animals stand by patiently. A family warms themselves at a fire in a shed to keep the cold at bay. The Passion of Christ as he carries his cross is depicted in the snow-covered landscape in the background.

The presence of a biblical theme in the background of all the paintings led to a religious interpretation of the series. Scholars considered it the path of humanity from the Fall of Man (spring) to Christ's Way to Calvary (winter). Similarly, Rearick interpreted the series (1992, CLX–CLXII) as a depiction of the history of man from the loss of God's grace to the hope of redemption through the sacrifice of Christ. Kirsi Eskelinen recently returned to the significance of the religious scenes; in her view, the paintings visualise the Quatuor Tempora ('Four Times') or Ember Days, four Catholic feasts associated with liturgical celebrations and fasting.

Indeed, the dignity and seriousness of the paintings' protagonists convey a religious mood. In this, they reflect a development that is typical of post-Tridentine culture and lends a sacred meaning to the everyday lives of the faithful (Bortolotti 1999, 166). Aikema (1996, 137) attributes a moralising character to these representations, which is expressed through a contrast: leading an ideal life (biblical scene) and the inability of people to recognise salvation because they are distracted by everyday activities. However, we have the impression that underlying these depictions is the harmonious coexistence of the figures with nature expressed by the almost sacred solemnity of their gestures.

Due to their varying states of conservation, the paintings were attributed alternately to Jacopo or Francesco Bassano, but the high and homogeneous quality of the painting has become increasingly apparent following recent restorations. The refinement of Jacopo's colour palette and painting technique is particularly evident in the impasto white of the fabrics, the touches of light applied with the tip of the brush, the rendering of the various textures, and the naturalistic liveliness of the depiction.

The Seasons are among the artist's most successful paintings. Repeated in countless variations by the Bassano workshop and its successors, they owe their success to the original invention of a new pictorial subject that harmoniously combines everyday life with deep religiosity. Prints, especially those by the Sadeler family, also spread these creations north of the Alps, where they were received with great approval and served as a model for countless variations in the seventeenth century.

Francesca Del Torre Scheuch

Influences from the North

(cats. 63–65)

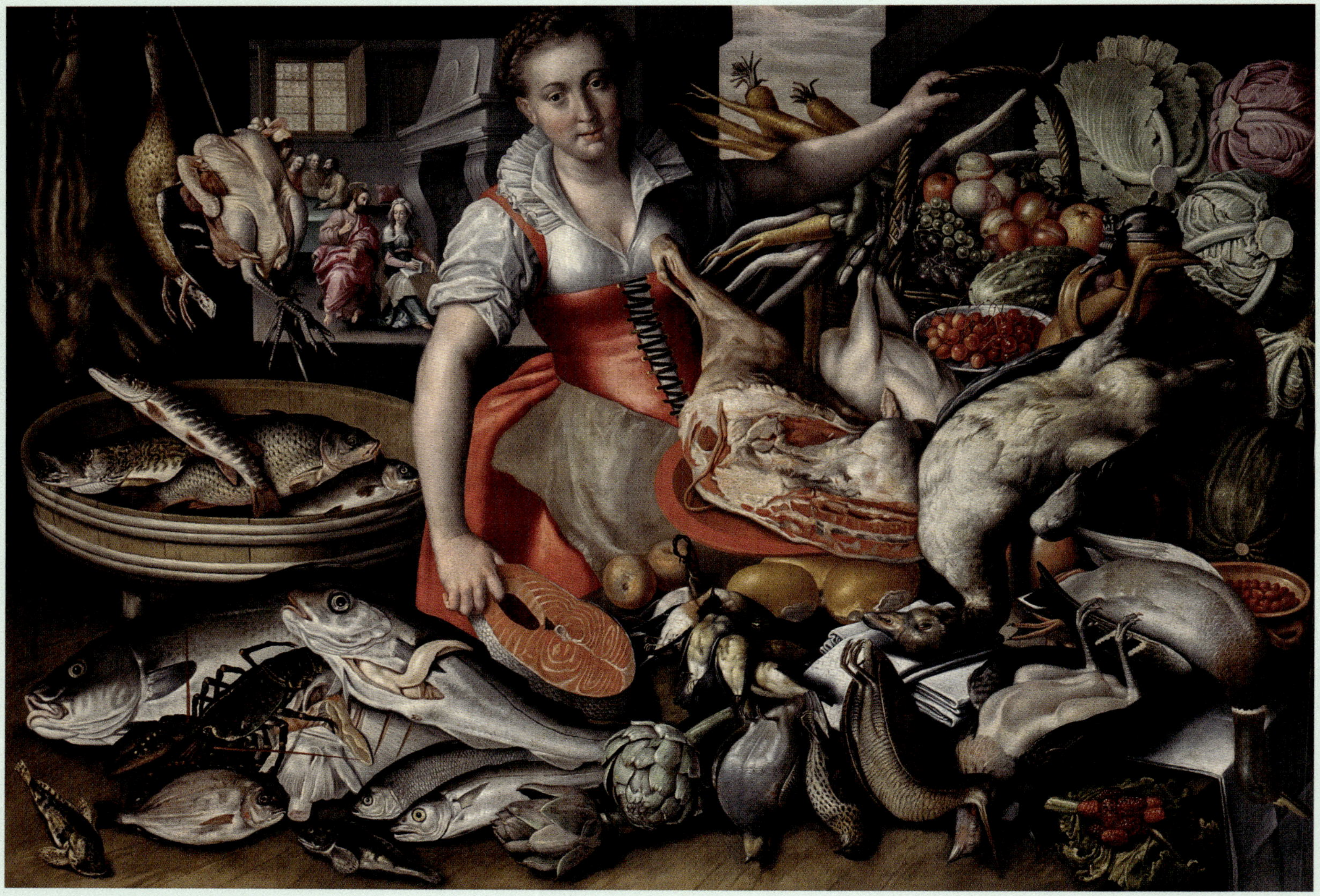

Cat. 63, Joachim Beuckelaer, *Market Scene with Meat and Fish Seller*

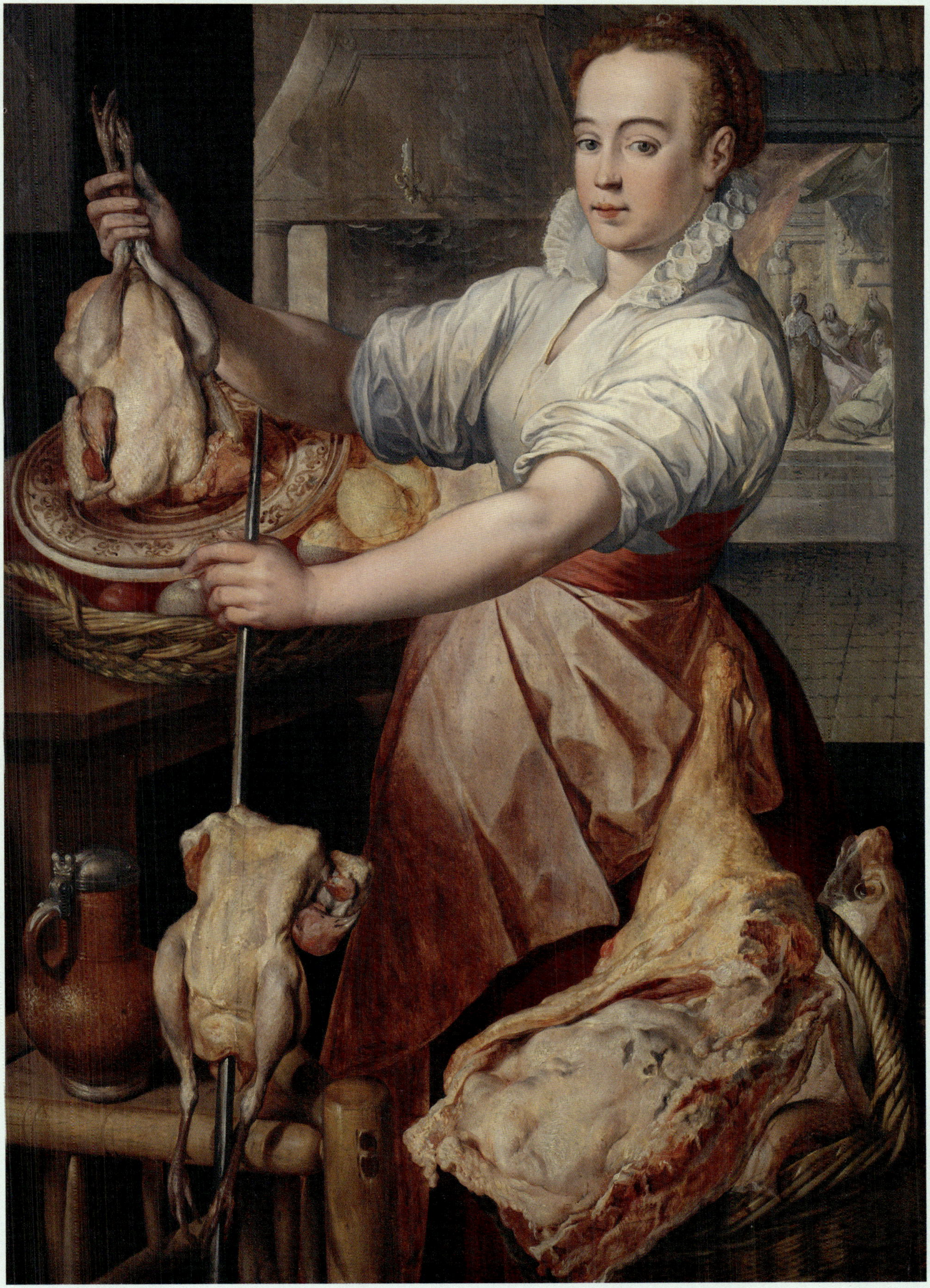

Cat. 64, Joachim Beuckelaer, *The Cook*

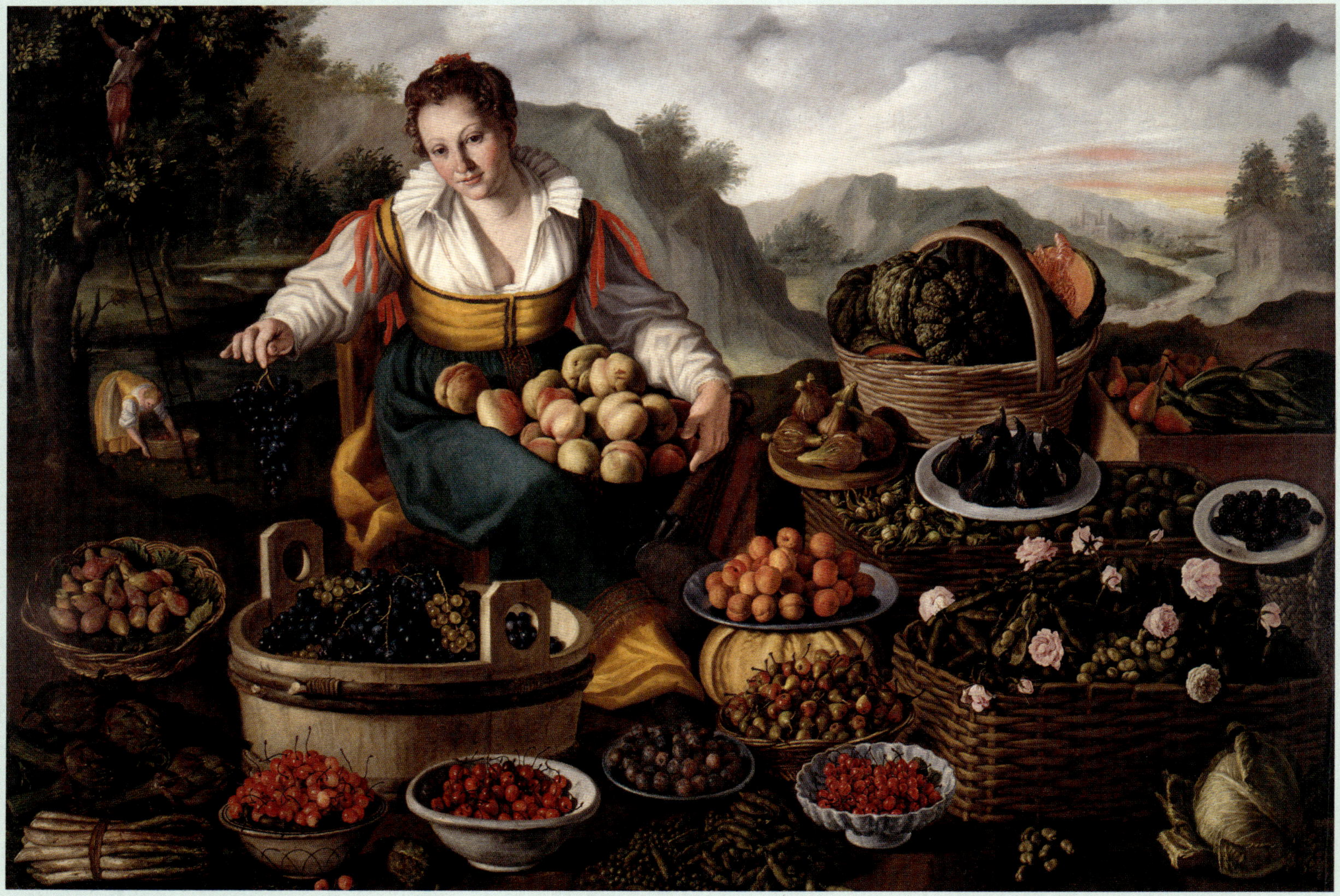

Cat. 65, Vincenzo Campi, *The Fruit Seller*

Cat. 63

Joachim Beuckelaer (c.1530–c.1574), attributed

Market Scene with Meat and Fish Seller, in the Background Christ in the House of Martha and Mary

Last quarter 16th cent.
Canvas; 127.5 × 187.5 cm
Modena, Gallerie Estensi, inv. R.C.G.E. 4195; granted in concession with the Ministry for Cultural Heritage, Activities, and Tourism

Provenance: Marquis G. Campori (1894); attributed to Vincenzo Campi da R. Pallucchini (1945)
Literature: Van Mander 1604, fol. 238r; Baldass 1923, 19; Emmens 1973, 93–101; Moxey 1977; exh. cat. Ghent 1986/87, 148, cat. 22; Falkenburg 1989; Hammer-Tugendhat 2001, 389

In this market scene, Joachim Beuckelaer uses an innovative but unusual compositional structure. Although the scene is dominated by a market stall with a maid in the foreground, the narrative action has been pushed into the background – in the distance in small format is the story of Christ with Mary and Martha from the Gospel of Luke (10:38–42).

The still life is characterized by an impressive variety of food, depicted in great detail. Different kinds of fish and birds, poultry and meat that are ready to be cooked, as well as fruit and vegetables, are arranged opulently on a wooden table. A roasting spit leaning against the wall and partially blocking the biblical scene is present in other works of Beuckelaer (cat. 64). Regarding the observation of nature evident in Beuckelaer's work, Karel van Mander writes in his *Schilder-Boek* that during the artist's apprenticeship with his uncle Pieter Aertsen, he learned 'to paint all things from life, such as vegetables, fruits, meat, poultry, fish, and similar things…'.

Clearly inspired by his teacher's pictorial invention, Beuckelaer also merges biblical history with genre depiction and still life – although still lifes without human figures did not become a pictorial tradition until the seventeenth century. The relationship between the scenes in the foreground and background gave rise to different interpretations. In older art historical interpretations, for example, the small-format Bible story gave the still life its legitimacy. However, the integration of the sacred narrative cannot only be understood as part of the still life's pictorial space. Its withdrawn, sometimes ambiguous location in the architectural setting, also led to an interpretation of it as a picture within a picture. The biblical scene in which Christ praises Mary, who listens to him attentively while her sister Martha devotes herself to everyday activities, was seen as a kind of commentary. In addition, iconographic approaches interpret the opulent still life as an antithesis to the biblical scene, and suggest a moral interpretation. Others explain the different proportions of the two scenes in terms of a shift from the sacred to the profane in the religious and socio-historical context of the time, or question the potential target audience of such paintings. The kitchen and market pieces of both Beuckelaer and Aertsen reveal the recurring preoccupation with this pictorial invention, which was taken up and further developed by artists into the following century.

Angelina Illes

Cat. 64

Joachim Beuckelaer (c.1530–c.1574)

The Cook

1574
Panel; 112.3 × 81.3 cm
Vienna, Kunsthistorisches Museum, Picture Gallery, inv. 6049

Provenance: 1907 acquired from the art dealer Schwarz
Literature: Emmens 1973, 95; Moxey 1976, 166; Moxey 1977, 98–99; mus. cat. Vienna 1981, 139, pl. 141; exh. cat. Ghent 1986/87, 155, cat. 28, fig. 1; Tholen 1987, 293, cat. 31; exh. cat. San Francisco, Baltimore, and London 1997/98, 222, cat. 30, fig. 1 (Anne W. Lowenthal)

The painting depicts a lively kitchen where a confident maid, absorbed in preparing capons for the spit, engages the viewer. The linear architecture connects the foreground's still life to a background kitchen, where Christ visits Martha and Mary. Popularized by Joachim Beuckelaer and Pieter Aertsen (c.1508–1575) in the 1550s, this composition places a contemporary kitchen in stark contrast to a biblical narrative, thematically blending the everyday with the divine. The modestly dressed maid represents the household virtue of diligent service, performing the daily labour for the upper class. Beyond this simple narrative, viewers of the time would have recognized a deeper symbolism in the food displayed. To the maid's right, a jug of wine hints at both inebriation and the spiritual significance of the Eucharist, reinforced by Christ's partaking in bread and wine in the background. The painting's focal points are two capons and a basket holding a sheep's hindquarter, symbols of luxury and abundance. In elite circles, meat was highly prized, though the Church imposed abstinence from eating land animals on Wednesdays, Fridays, and during Lent, permitting only fish like the cod here discreetly placed in the basket (Van Winter 1986, 63–4). The biblical scene from Luke 10:38–42 highlights Christ's praise for Mary's quiet devotion over Martha's busy service, offering a moral lesson on prioritizing spiritual over material concerns. The reduced biblical scene, set behind the richly detailed foods, subtly invites reflection on the moral choice between moderation and excess. Any suggestion of an erotic undertone in the act of skewering capons, linked to the colloquial *vogelen* (to fornicate), is unlikely, as no interaction between the maid and a man occurs in this work (Moxey 1976, 166). The animals are depicted with lifelike precision, the cook illuminated in warm tones, while the background schematically rendered in pastels adds a dreamlike quality.

Charlotte Roosen

Cat. 65

Vincenzo Campi (before 1536–1591)

The Fruit Seller

1578/81
Canvas; 143 × 213 cm
Milan, Pinacoteca di Brera, inv. 397

Provenance: From the monastery of San Sigismondo in Cremona to the Pinacoteca di Brera in 1809
Literature: Wind 1975, 71, fig. 2; exh. cat. New York, Tulsa, and Dayton 1983, 22–6, cat. 1 (John T. Spike); exh. cat. Cremona 2000/01, 152–5, cat. 4 (Franco Paliaga); Klerck 2000/01; Paliaga 2000/01; Paliaga 2000/01a; McTighe 2004; Tanzi 2004, 32–3

In the sixteenth century, Flemish genre painting began spreading south of the Alps. Vincenzo Campi – during the same time as the Bassanos – was one of the first Italian artists to take up the new pictorial themes, which he may have encountered as a result of contacts between his native Cremona and Flanders. He may even have been familiar with works of Joachim Beuckelaer (cats. 63, 64) in the Farnese Collection or in the collection of the Affaitati banking family.

Campi allows the fruit and vegetables arranged in containers by the *Fruttivendola*, all rendered in tangible naturalism, to become the painting's protagonists. The variety of produce puts the richness of his homeland on display and reflects the new view of nature, which was characterised by upheavals in agriculture and trade. At the same time, the painting testifies to the encyclopaedic interests of the Renaissance, which catalogued and depicted the flora known at the time.

Biblical scenes in the background still gave the Flemish models a moralising dimension, but Campi seems to concentrate on the depiction of the rural world. Nevertheless, lost meanings were sought in his market and kitchen scenes. For example, since many genre scenes from north of the Alps were based on folk wisdom, the grapes being proffered were read as an allusion to easily lost virtue in the sense of the proverb 'Non tutti i grappoli vengono al torchio' ('Not all grapes go to the press'; McTighe 2004). In Italy, a parallel can be drawn with the *pittura ridicola* (Wind 1975, McTighe 2004, Klerck 2000/01), which aims to provoke laughter at the comical ostentation of ordinary citizens. In the case of *The Fruit Seller*, the irony is not to be found in her posture, but in the contrast with the fruit, which at the time were reserved for the upper classes (McTighe 2004).

Another interpretation sees the painting as part of the four elements or seasons, because it was located in the monastery of San Sigismondo near Cremona until the late eighteenth century alongside three other paintings by Campi depicting a *Kitchen*, *Fishmongers*, and *Poultry Sellers*. Given the abundance of fruit, *The Fruit Seller* would then represent the element of earth (AK New York & Tulsa & Dayton 1983), or the harvest season in late summer (Klerck 2000/01), or autumn (Wind 1975). However, without information about the original commission, the question of whether Campi conceived the paintings as a group remains open. It is possible that they were created for personal reasons over a period of several years since they remained in his studio until his death in 1591 (Klerck 2000/01).

Even if Campi's everyday scenes represent only a brief intermezzo in his oeuvre around 1580, they attracted the interest of important patrons such as Hans Fugger and Emperor Rudolf II. They were objects of frequent copying and exerted great influence as precursors to the emergence of autonomous still life painting in seventeenth-century Italy.

Alexandra Sattler

Francesco and Leandro Bassano and the Viennese Cycle of the Months

(cats. 66–73)

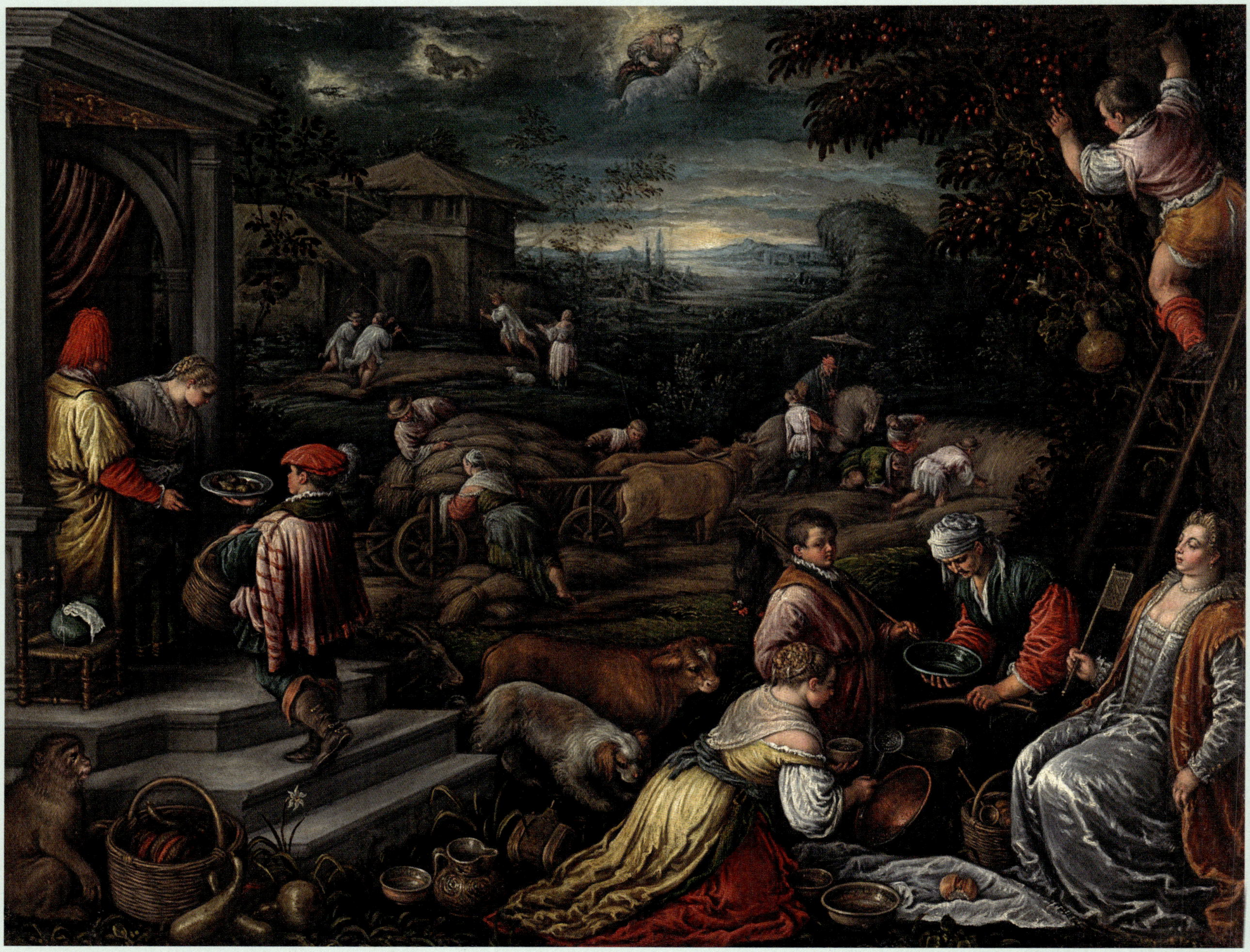

Cat. 66.1, Francesco Bassano, *Summer*

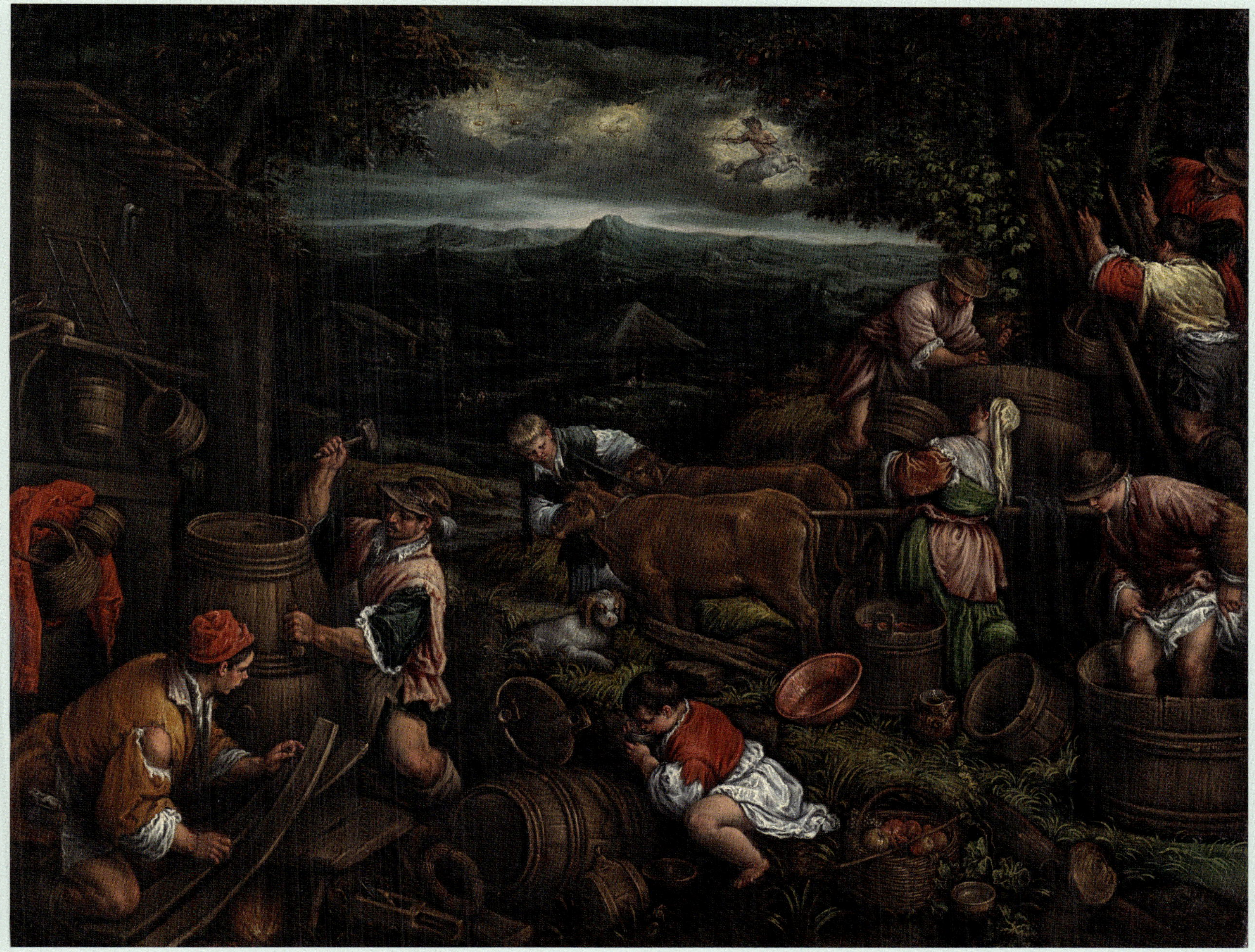

Cat. 66.2, Francesco Bassano, *Autumn*

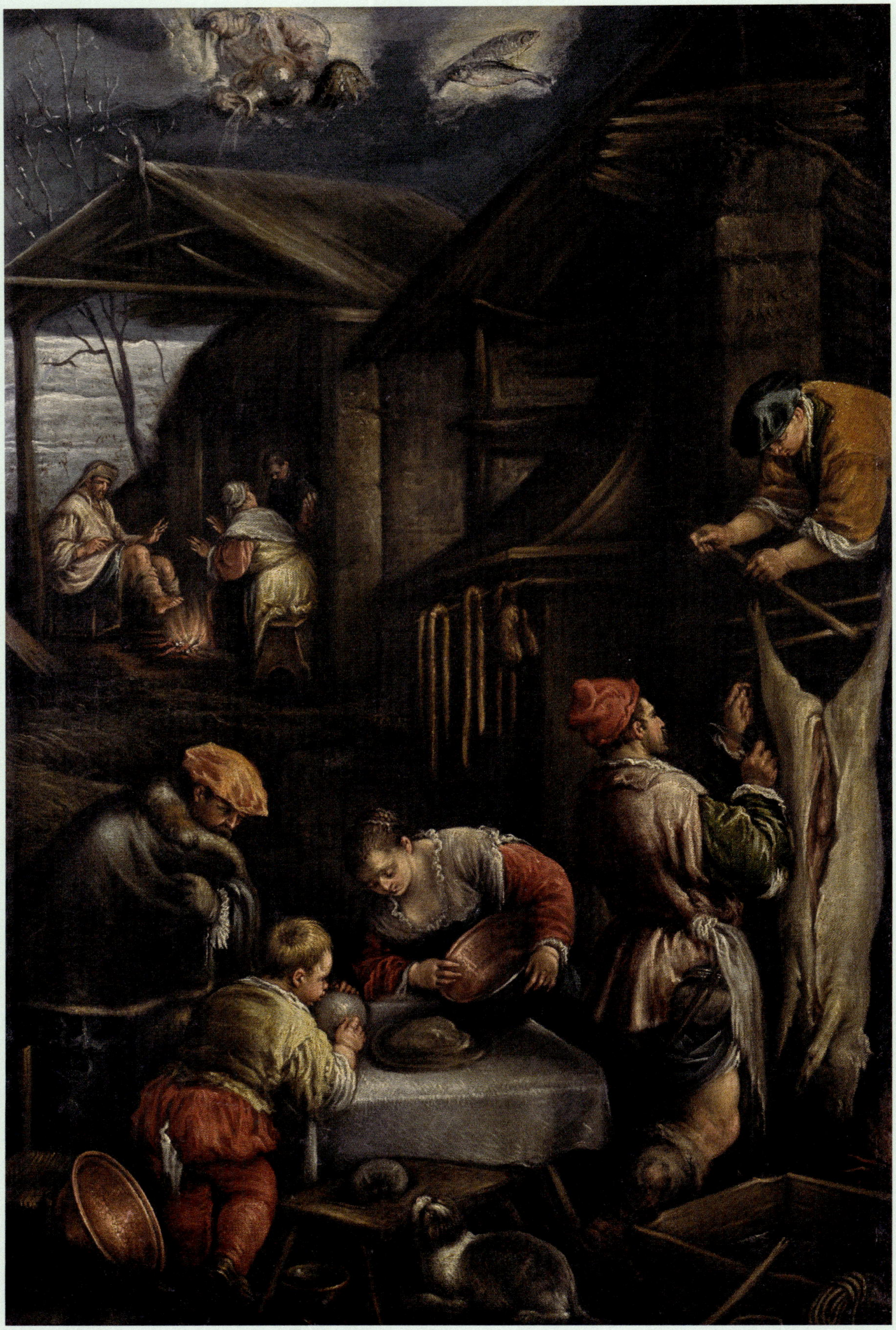

Cat. 66.3, Francesco Bassano, *Winter*

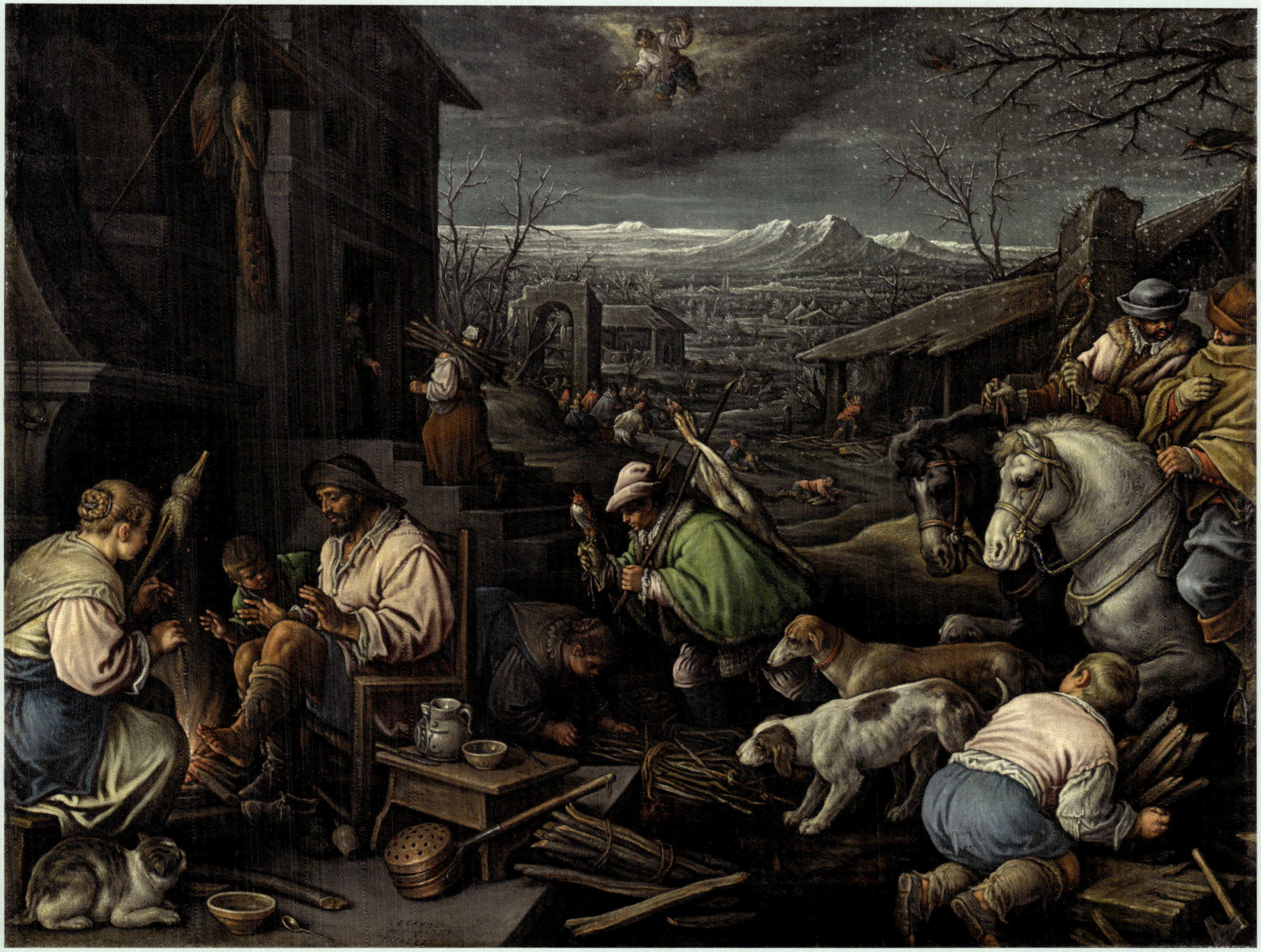

Cat. 67.1, Leandro Bassano, *January*

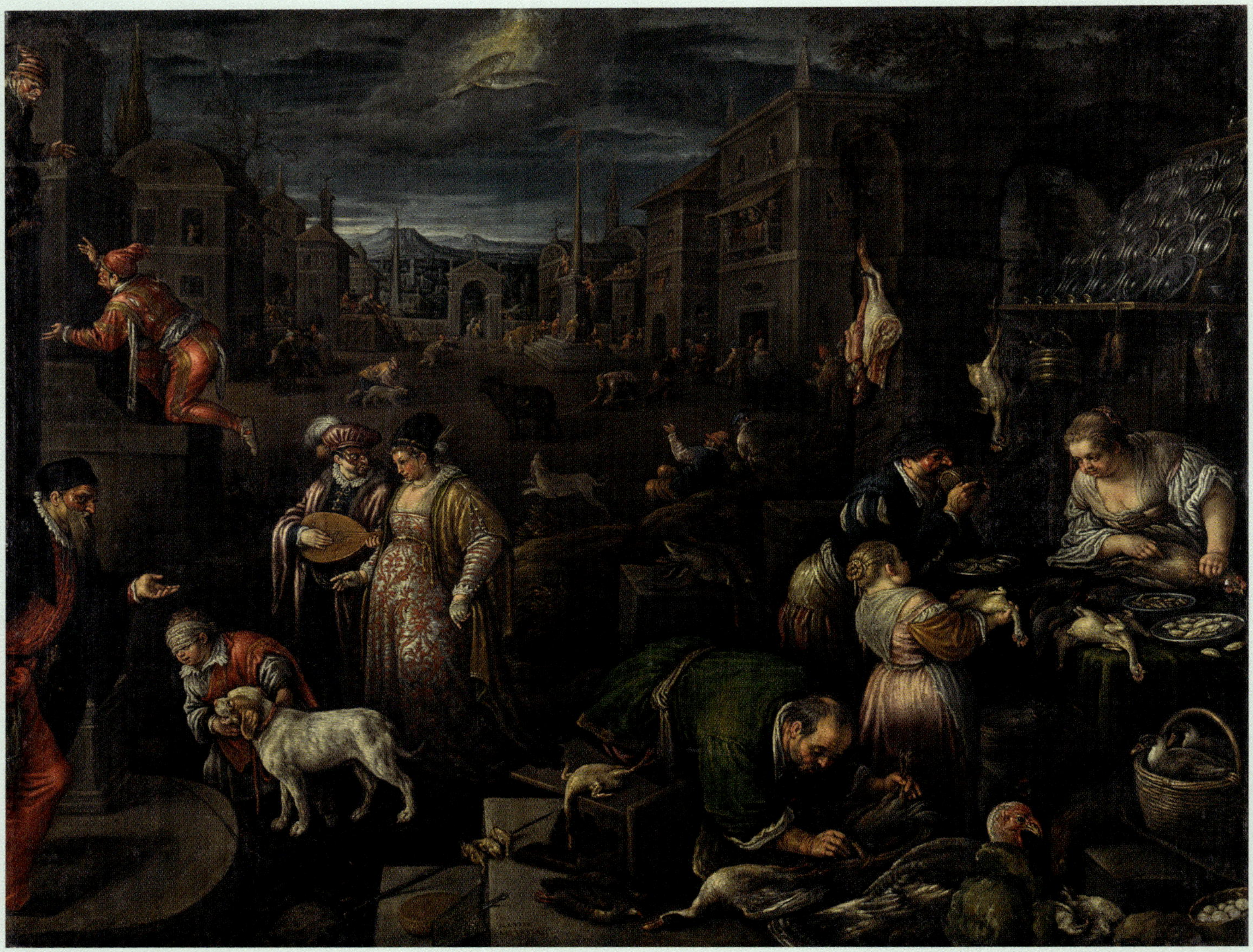

Cat. 67.2, Leandro Bassano, *February*

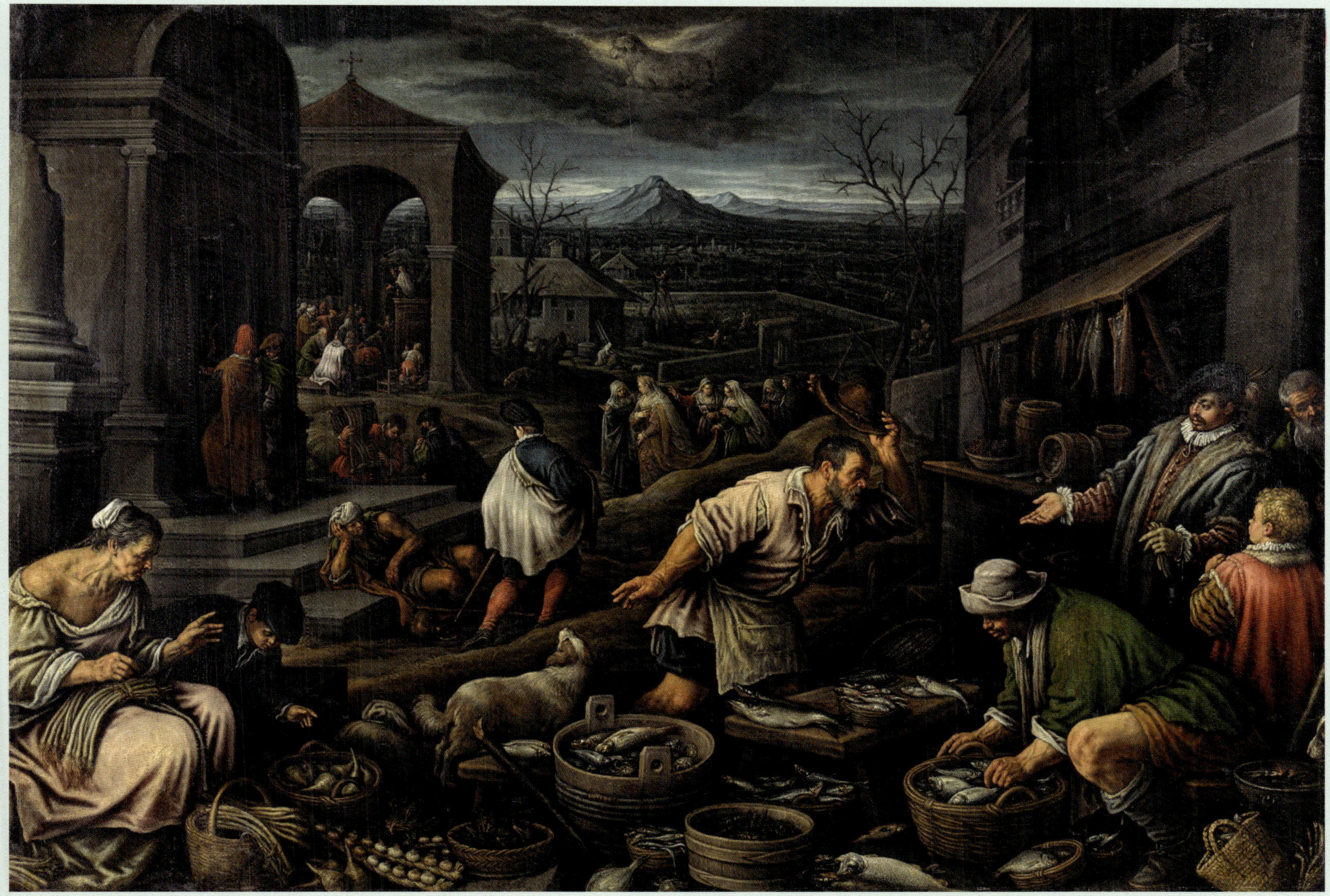

Cat. 67.3, Leandro Bassano, *March*

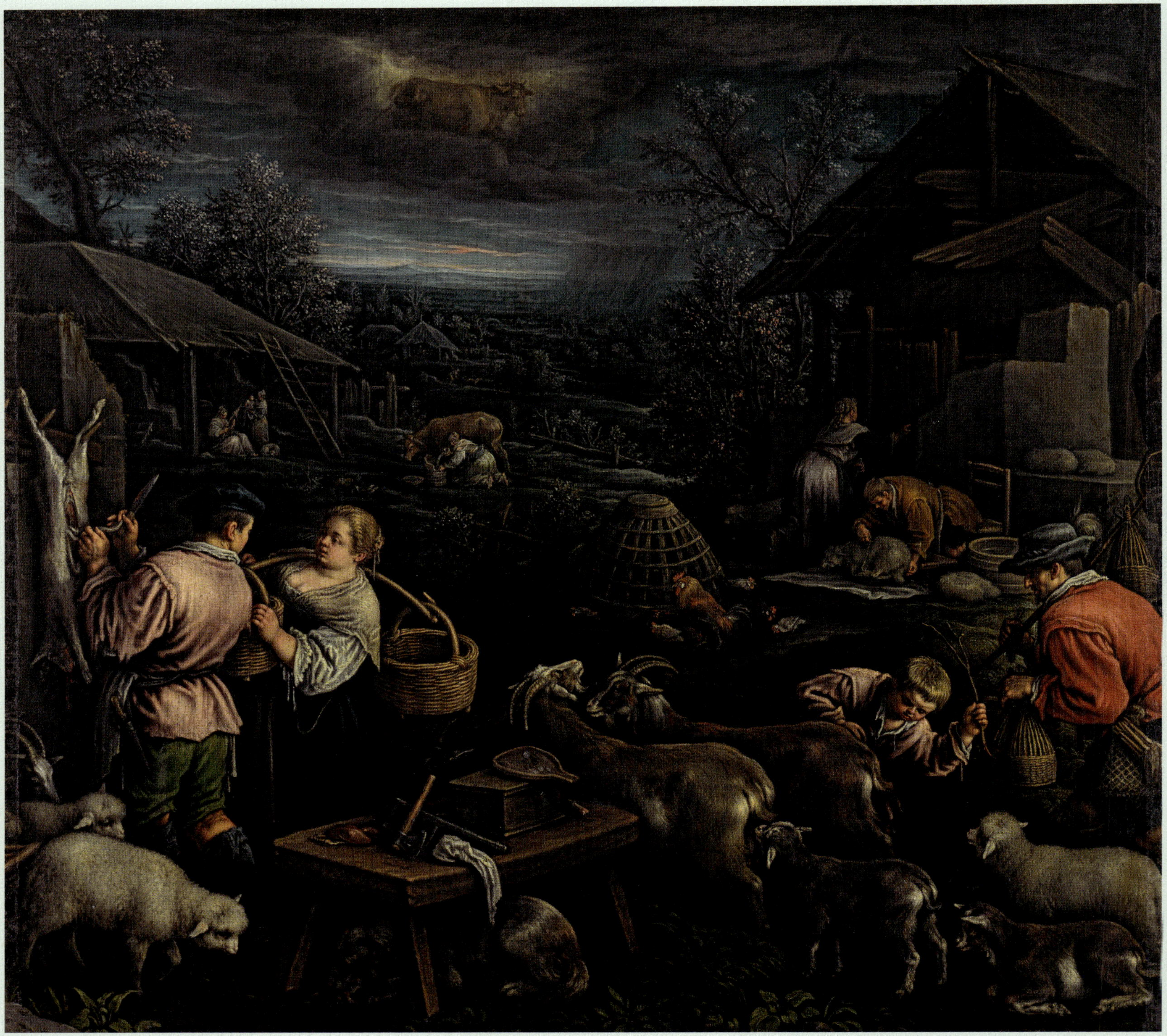

Cat. 67.4, Leandro Bassano, *April*

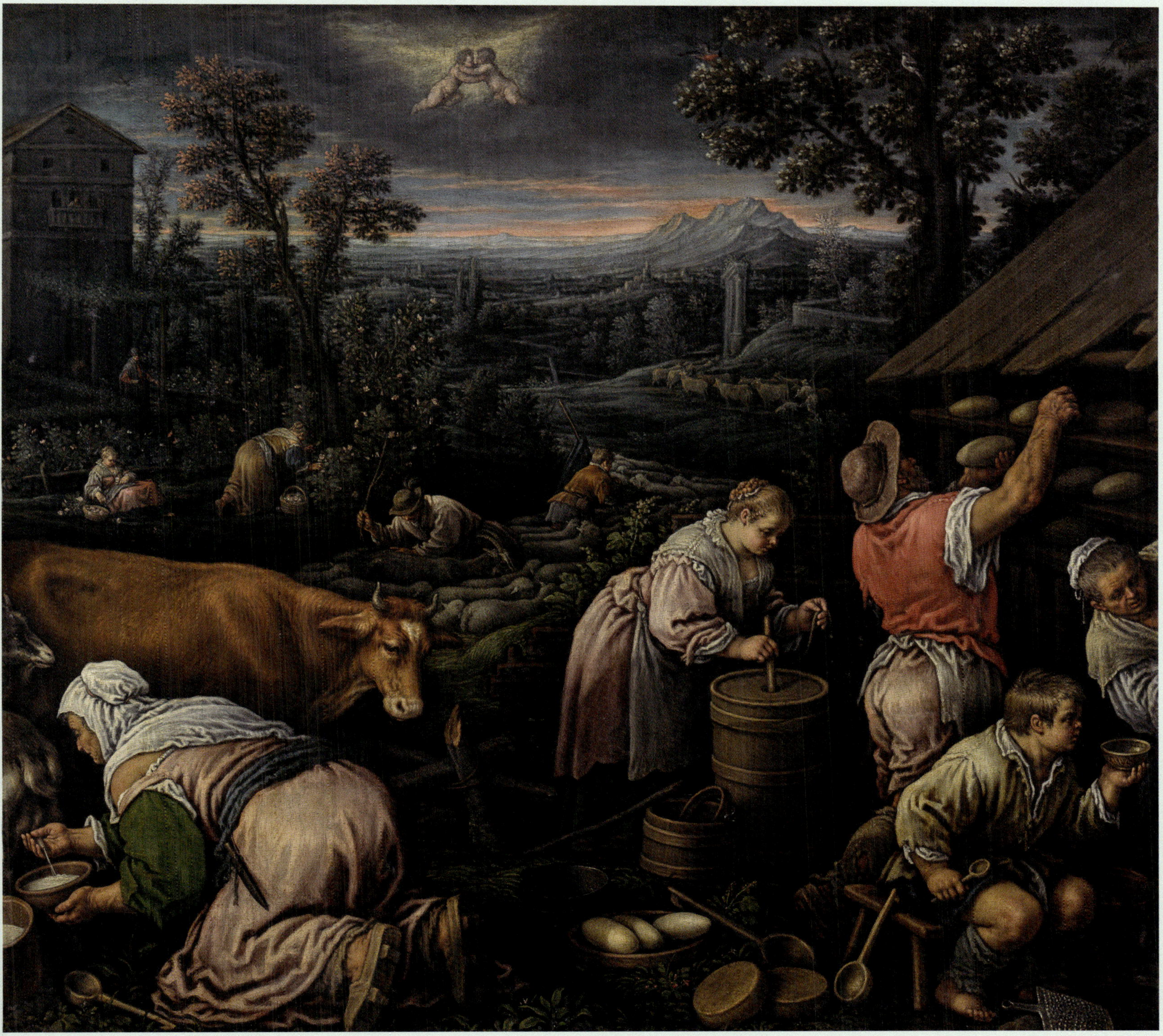

Cat. 67.5, Leandro Bassano, *May*

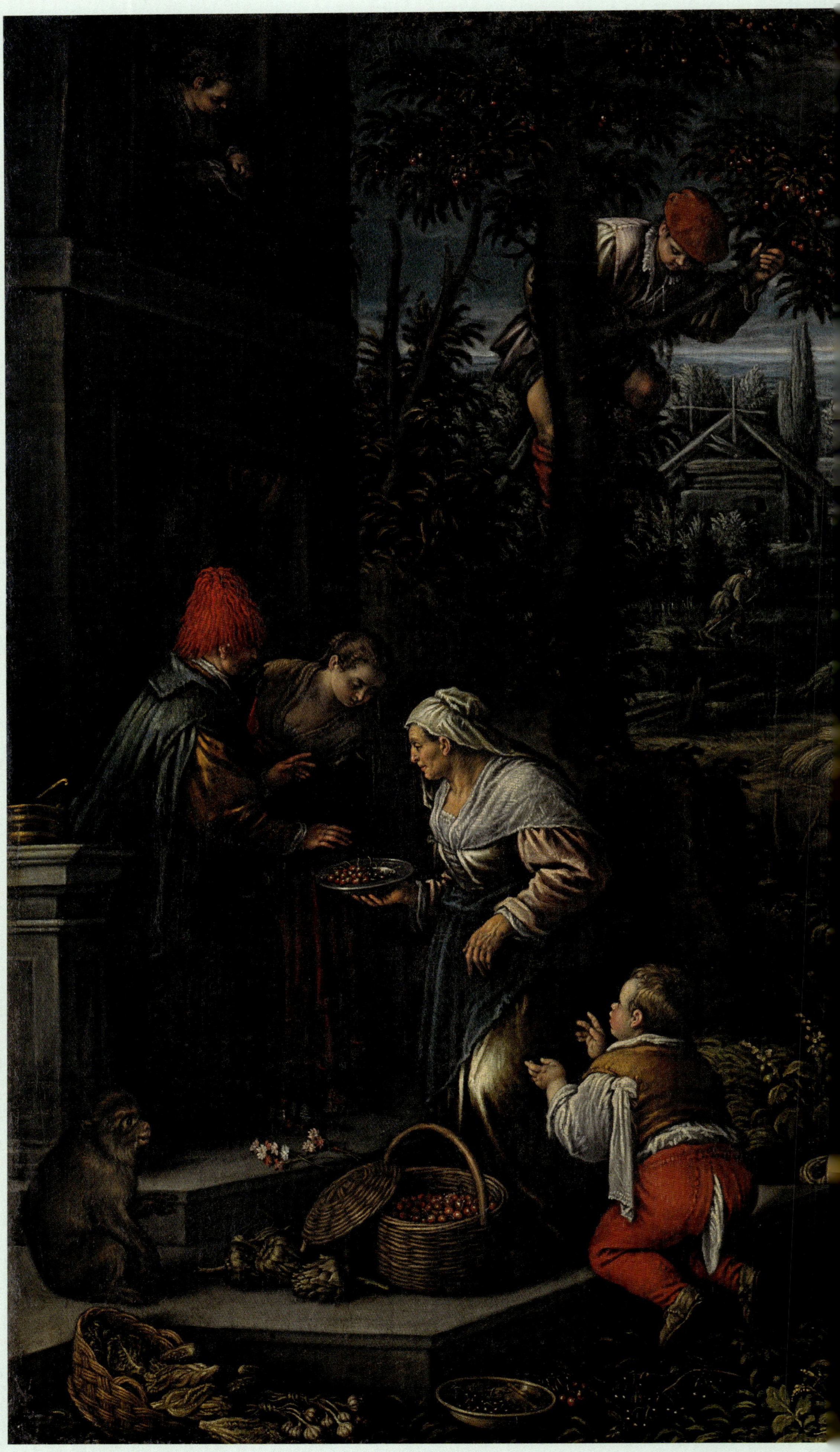

 Cat. 67.6, Leandro Bassano, *June*

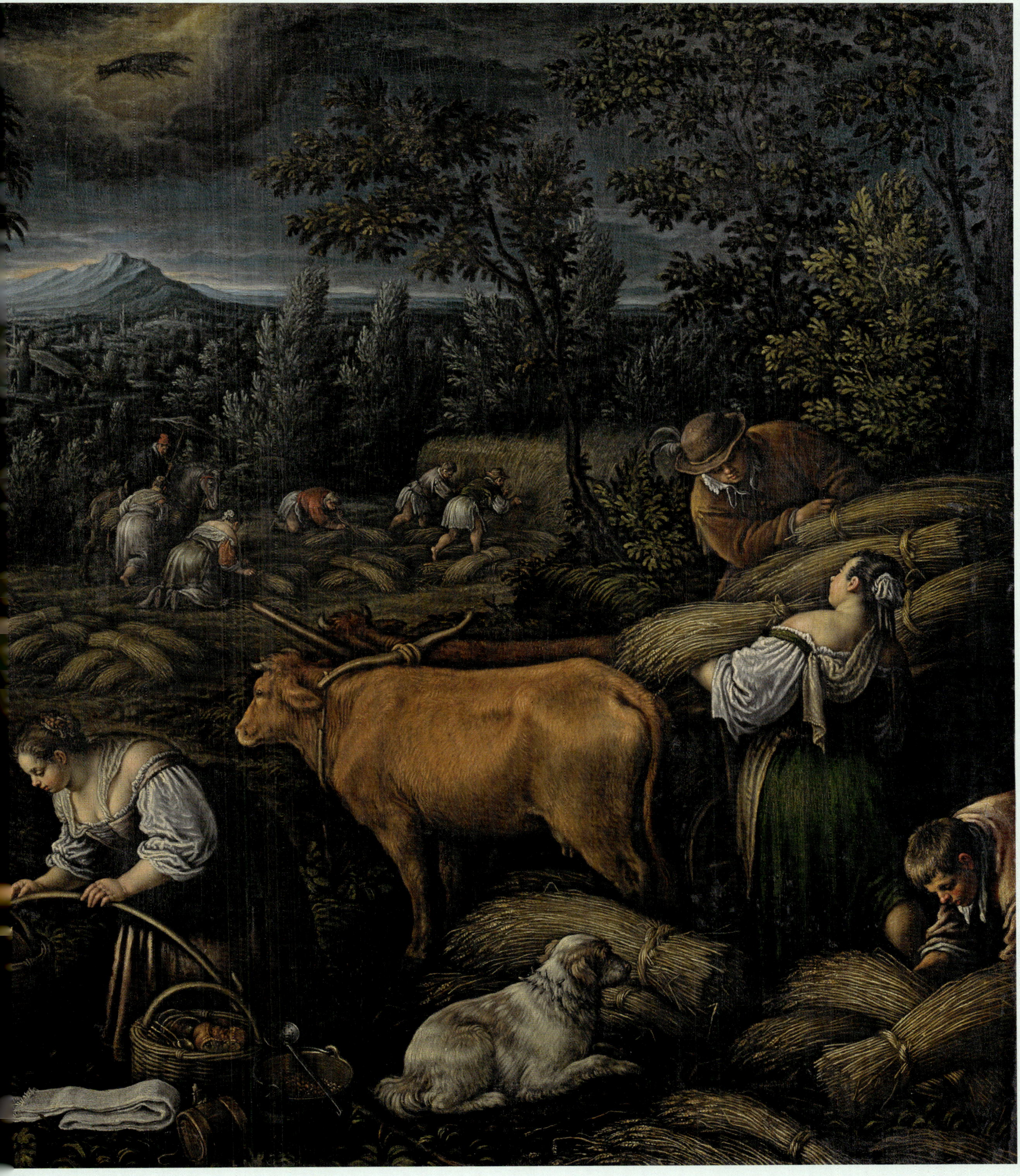

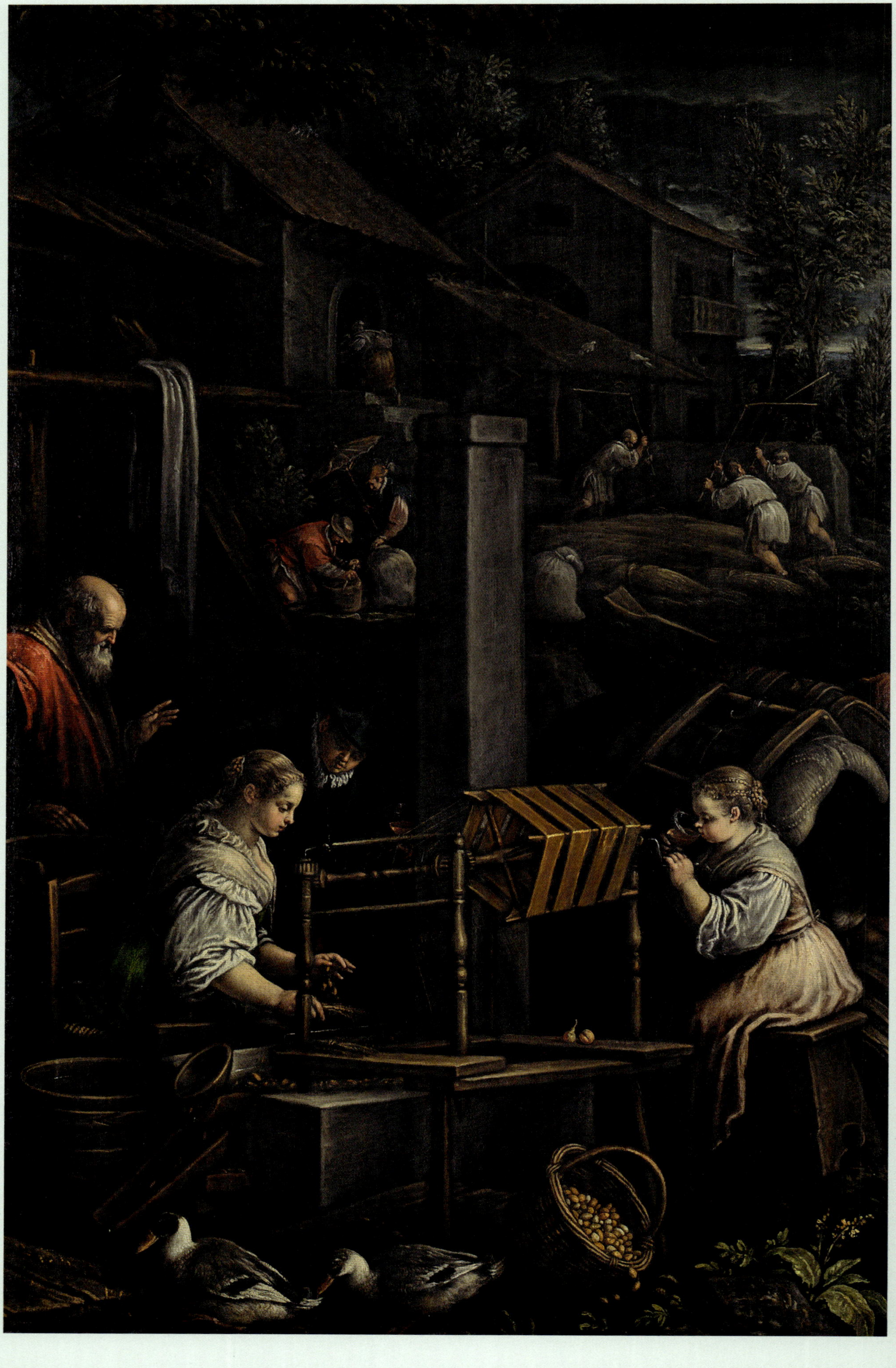

Cat. 67.7, Leandro Bassano, *July* *(Spinning and Weaving)*

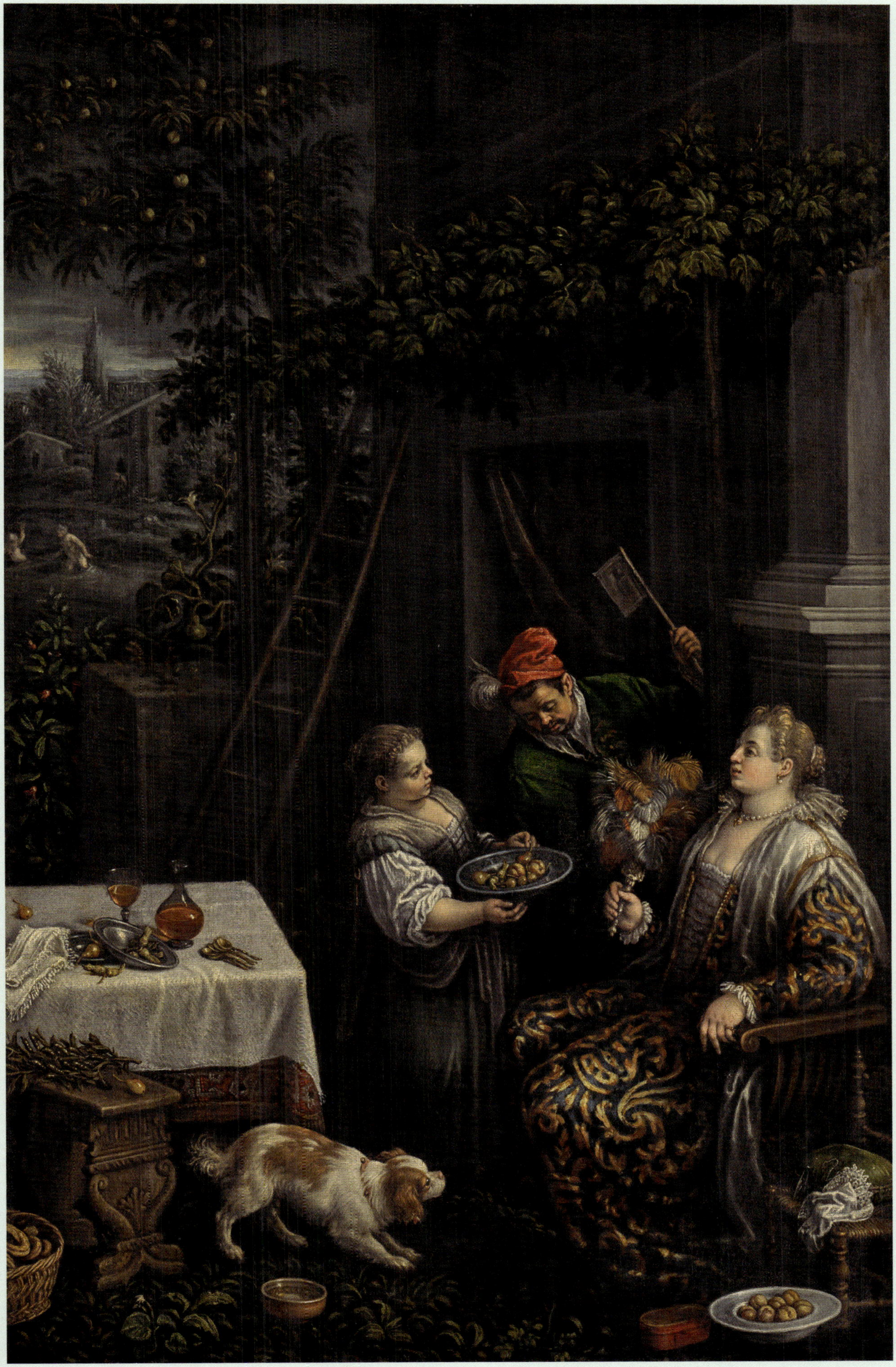

Cat. 67.8, Leandro Bassano, *July*

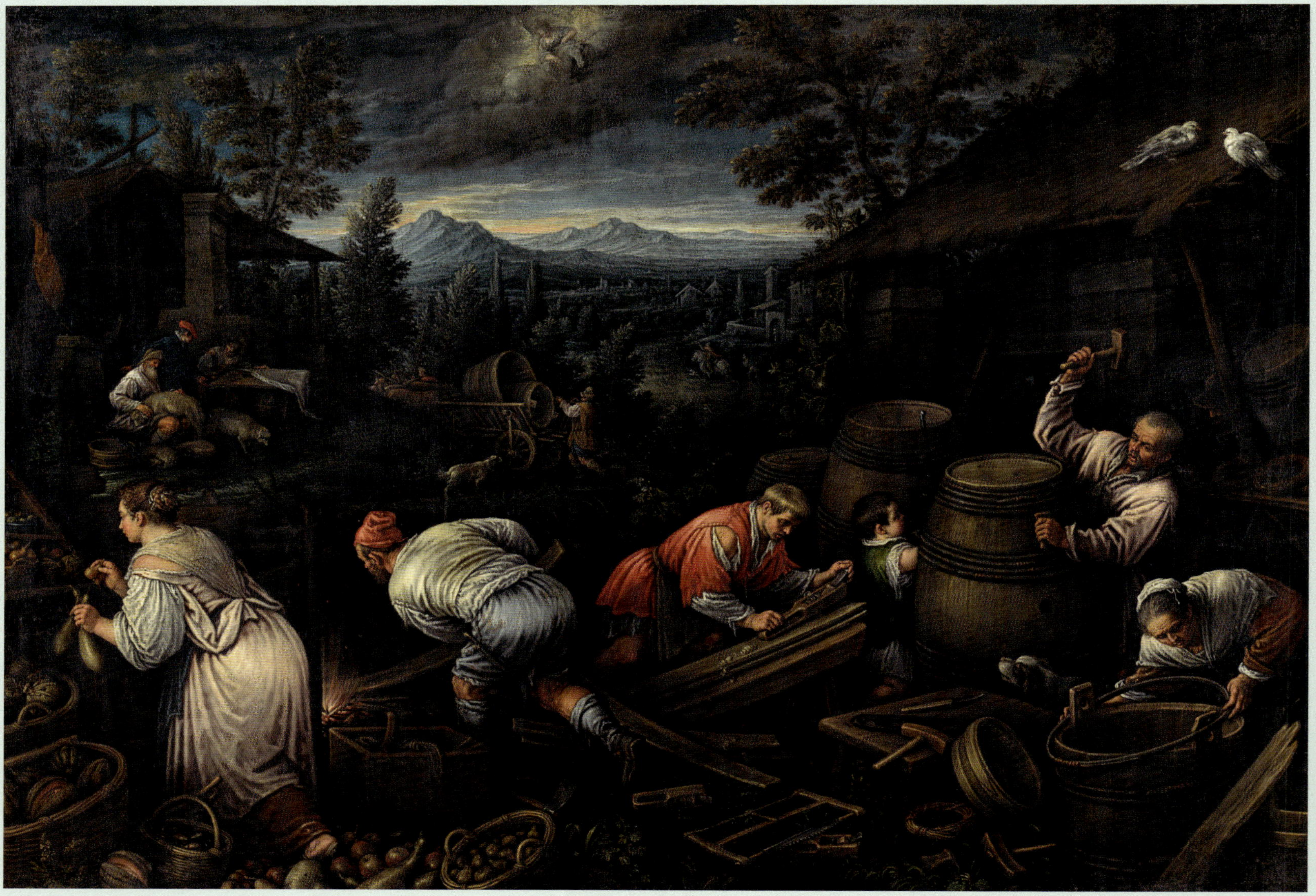

Cat. 67.9, Leandro Bassano, *August*

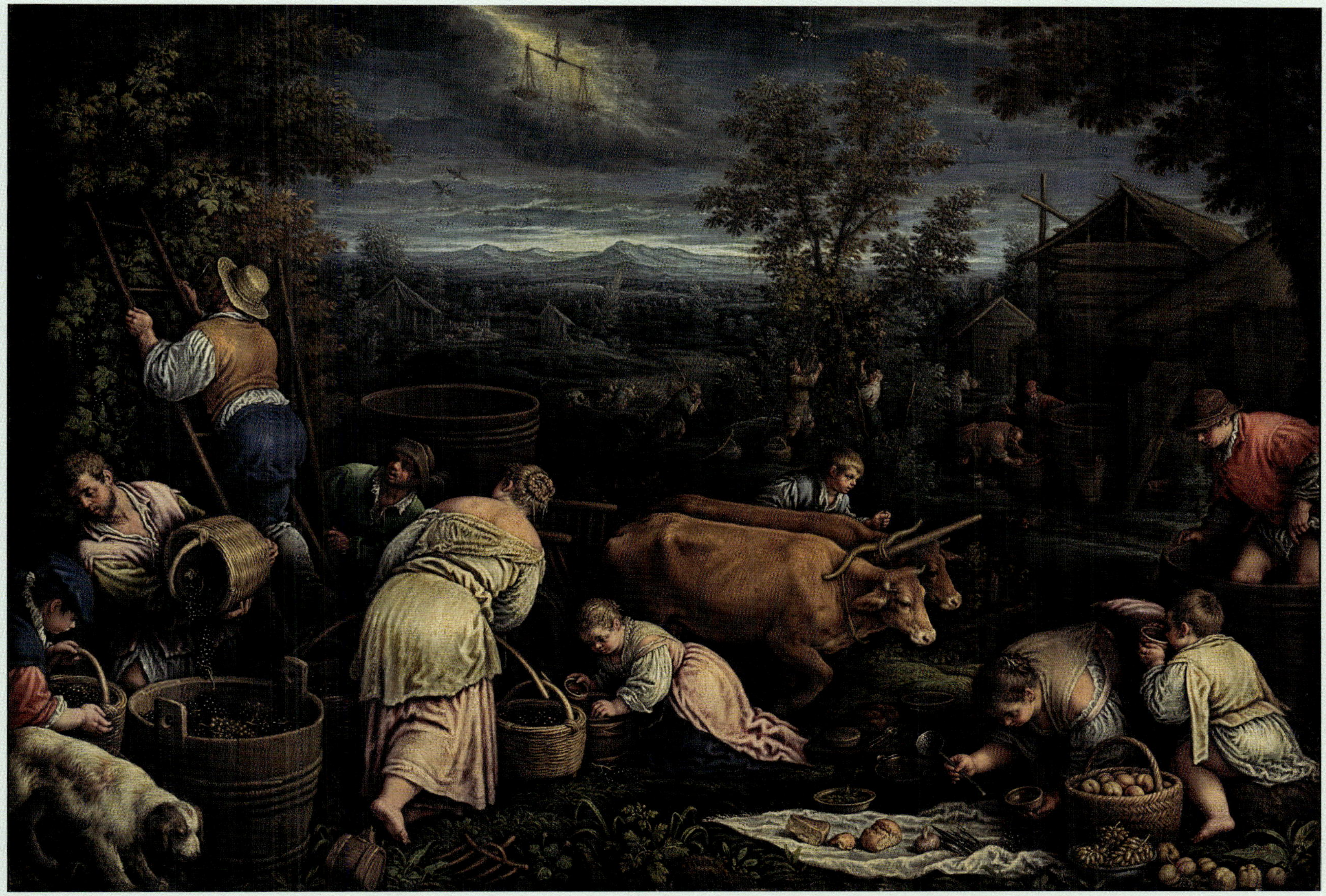

Cat. 67.10, Leandro Bassano, *September*

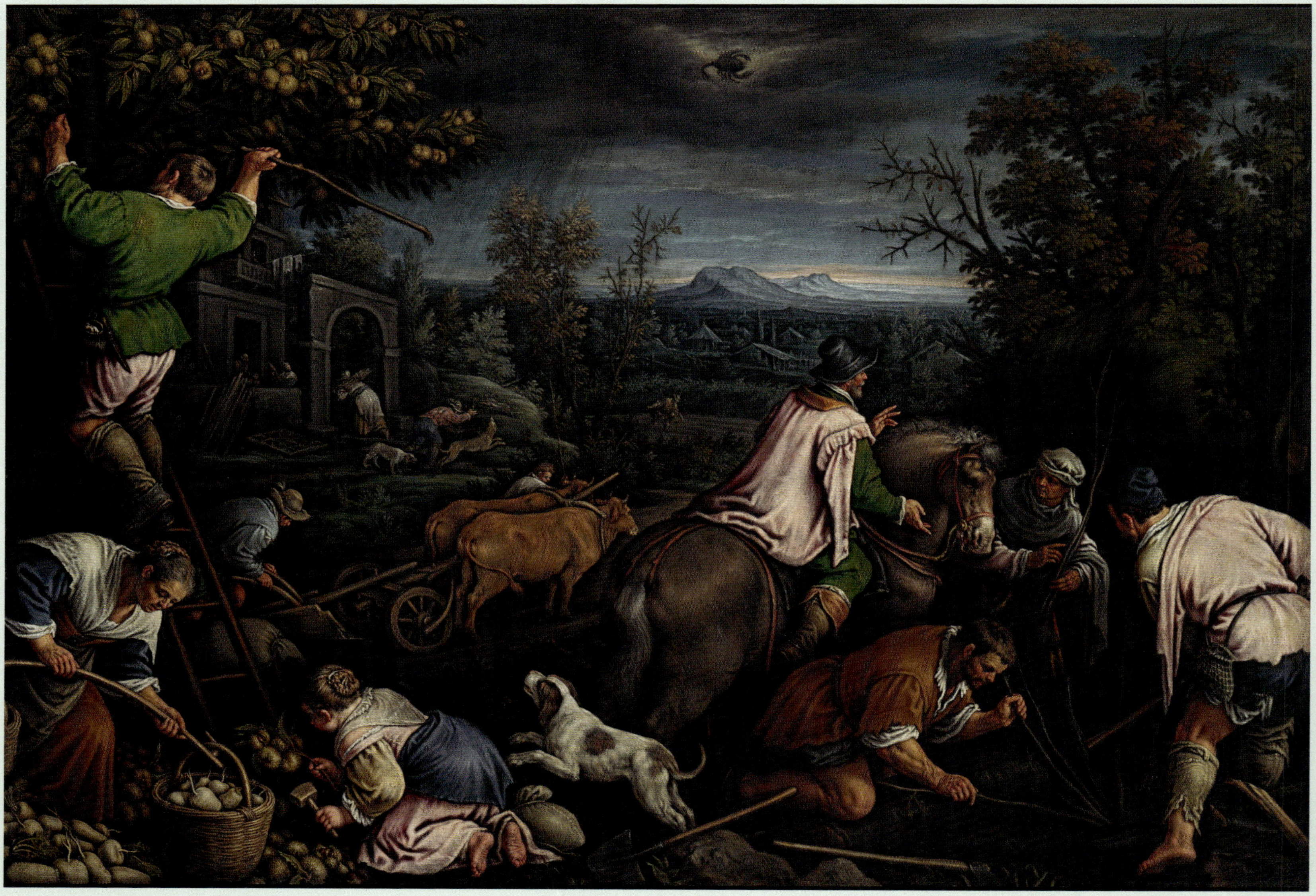

Cat. 67.11, Leandro Bassano, *October*

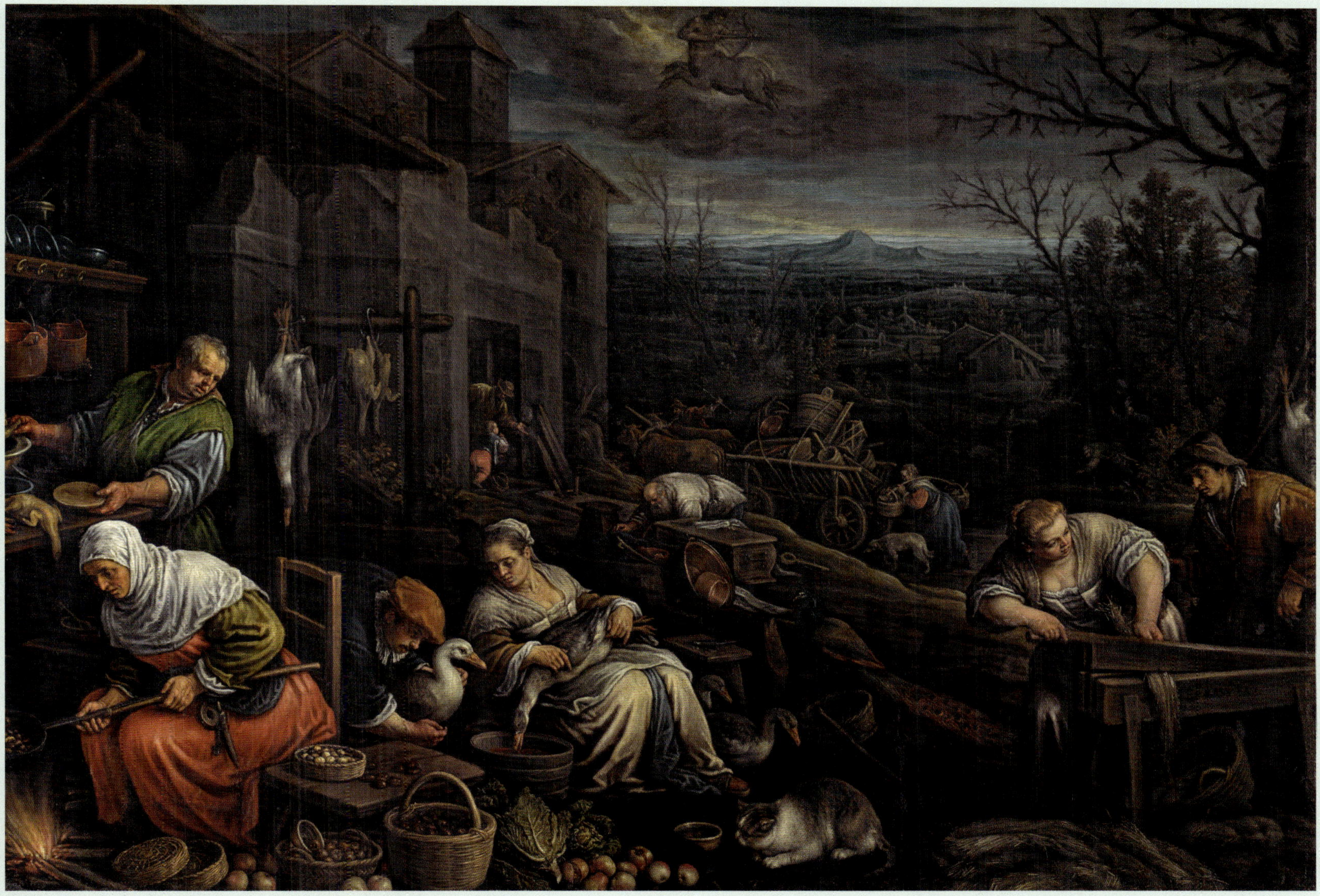

Cat. 67.12, Leandro Bassano, *November*

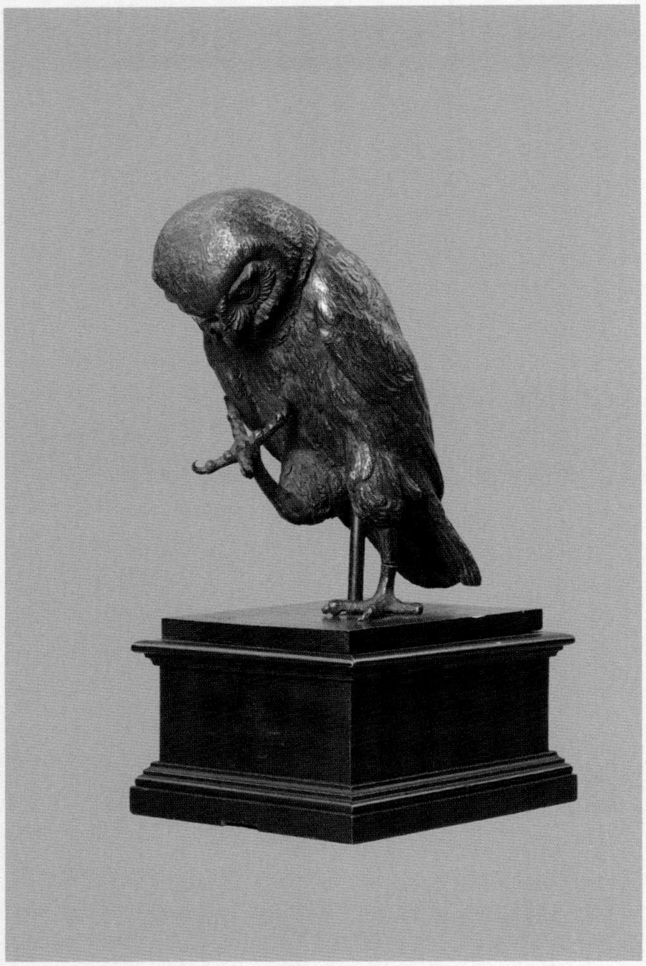

Cat. 68, *Owl*

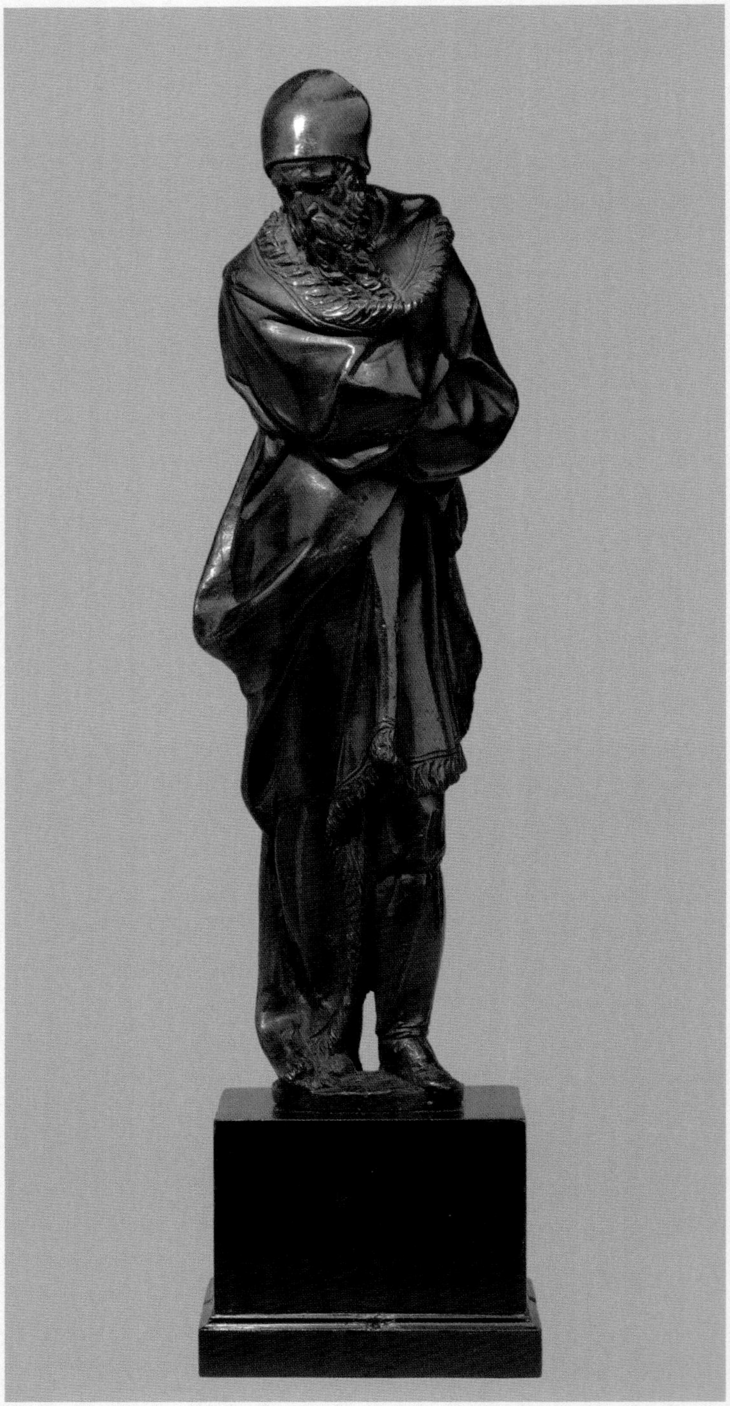

Cat. 69, Alessandro Vittoria, *St Zachariah? – Allegory of Winter?*

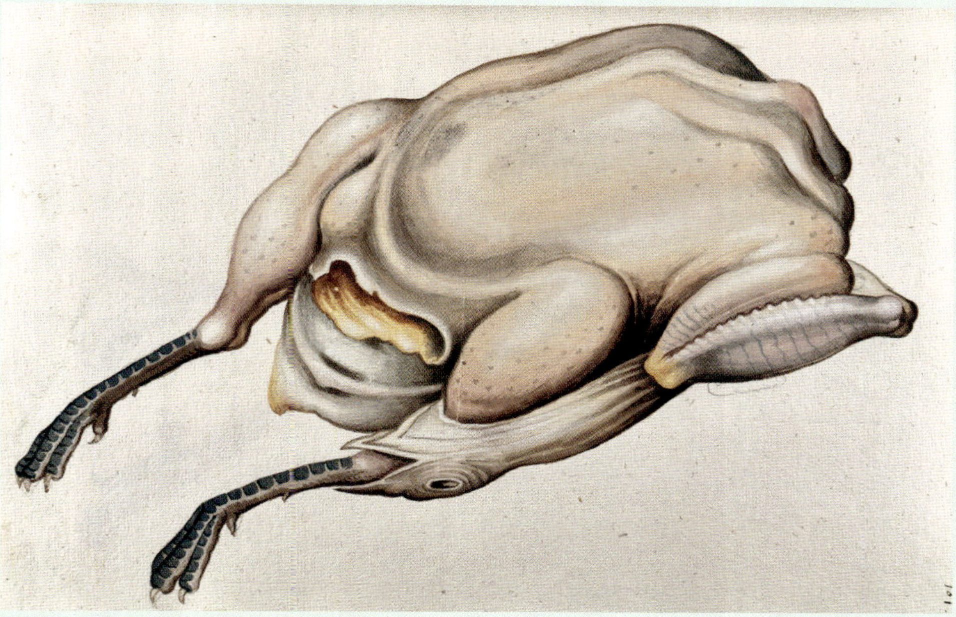

Cat. 70, Daniel Fröschl, *Plucked Chicken*

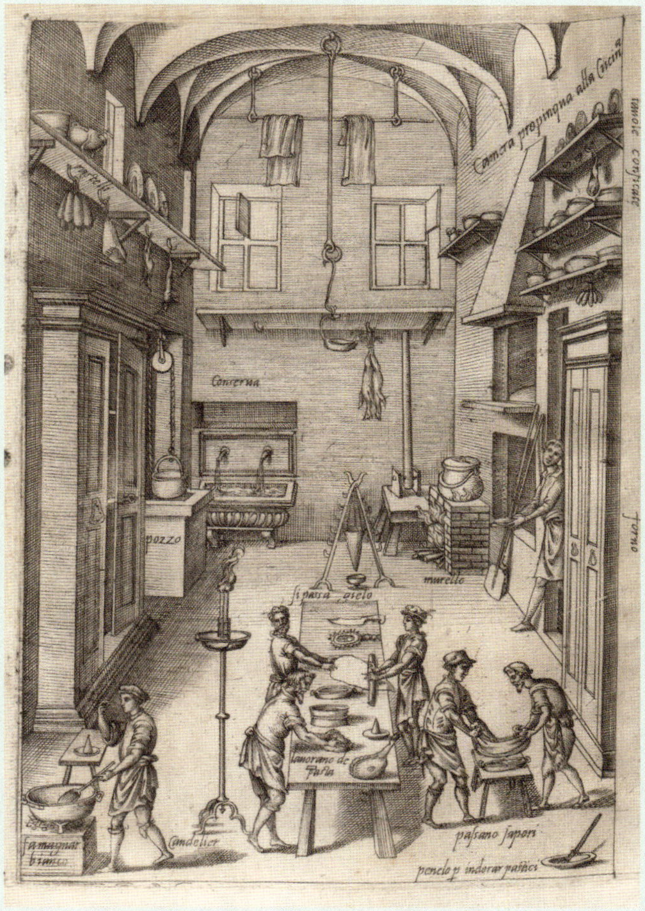

Cat. 71, Bartolomeo Scappi, *Opera di M. Bartolomeo Scappi, Cuoco Secreto di Papa Pio V. divisa in Sei Libri*

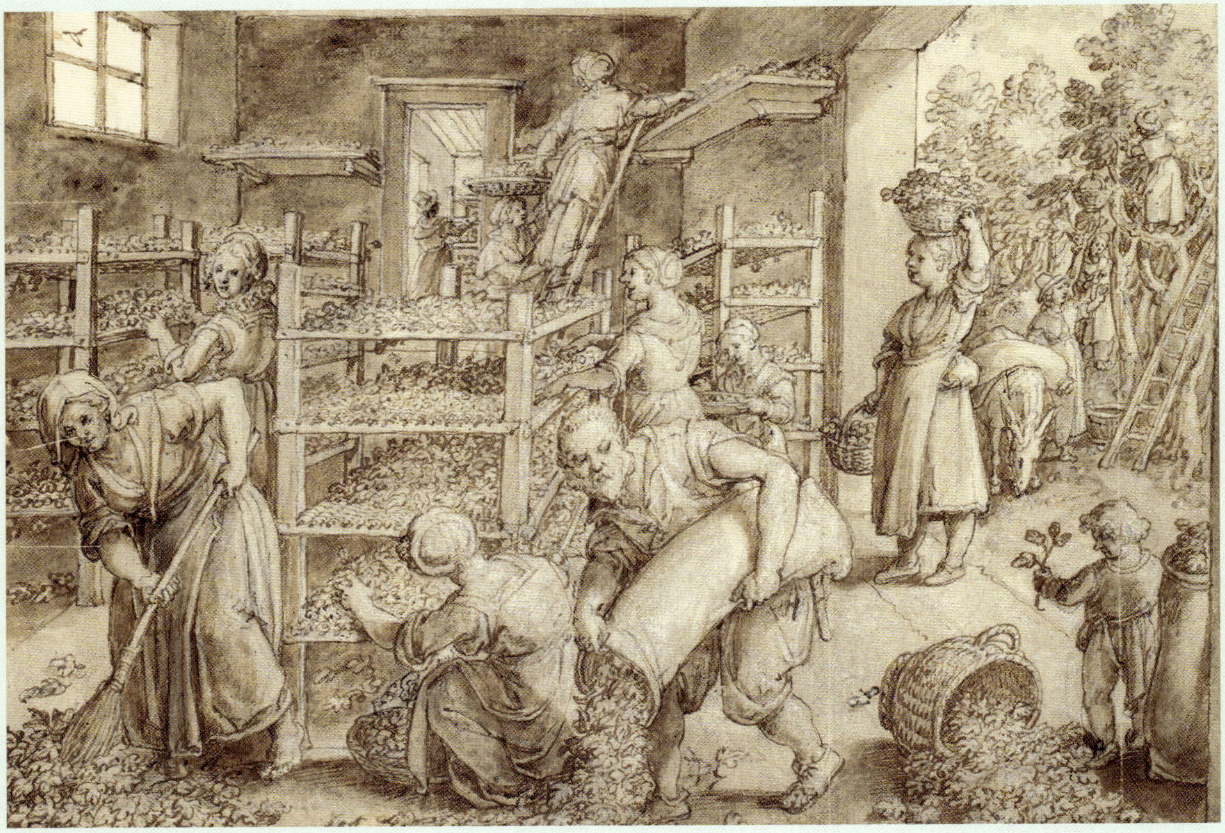

Cat. 72.1, Johannes Stradanus, *Feeding the Silkworms (II)*

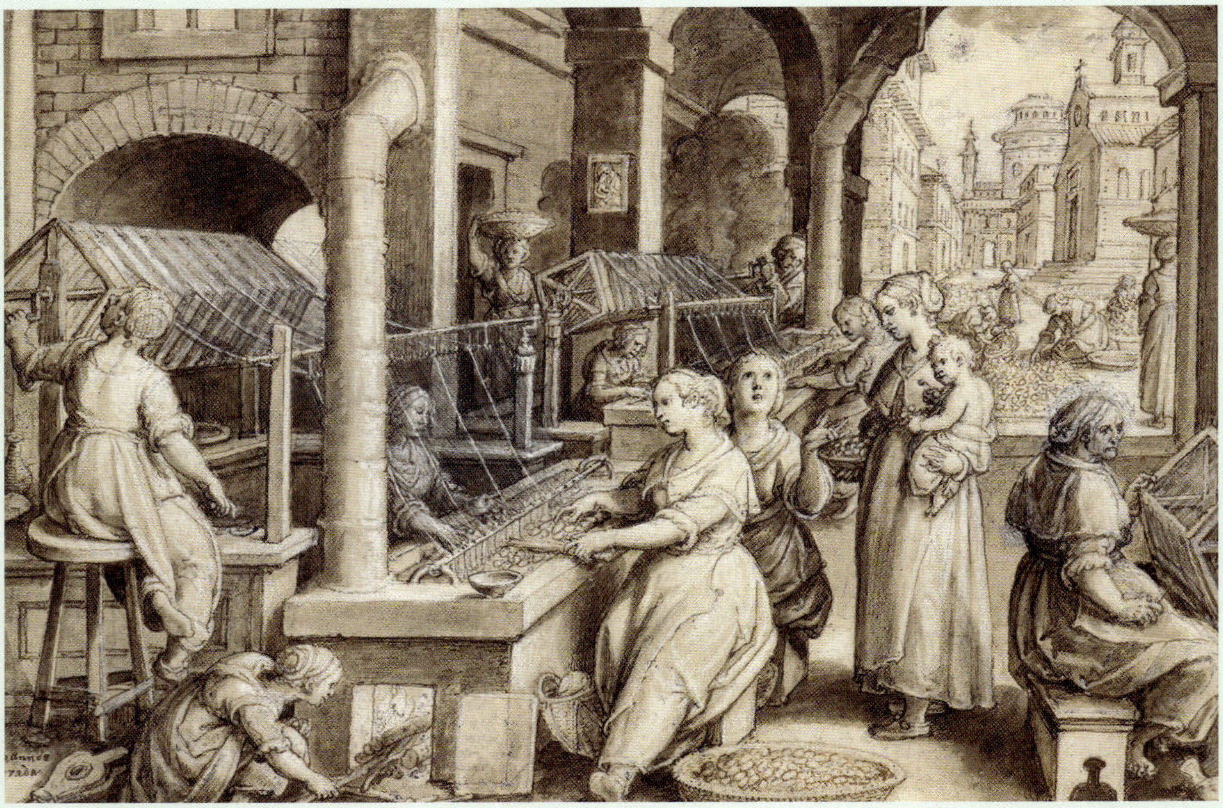

Cat. 72.2, Johannes Stradanus, *Women Reeling Silk*

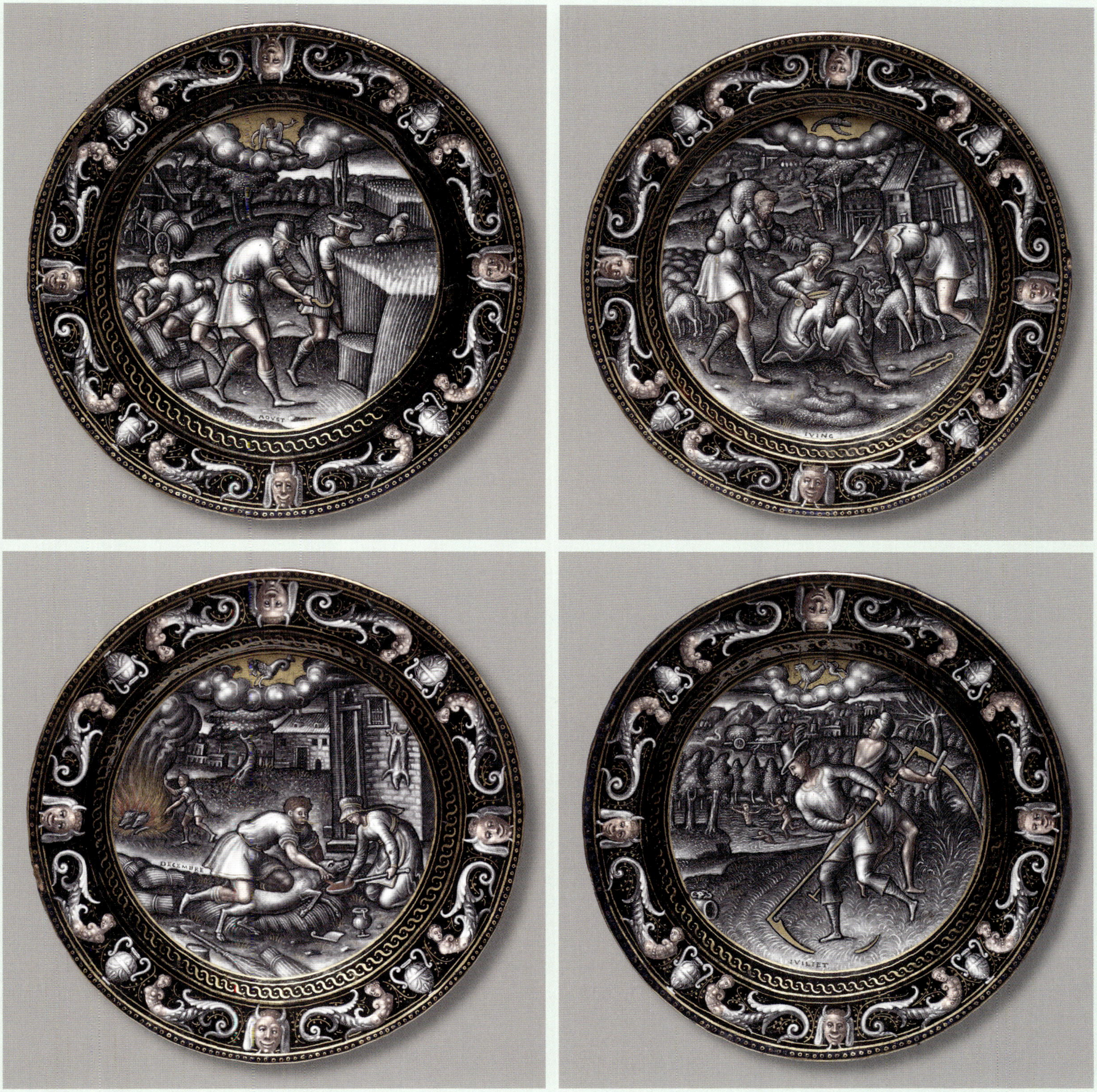

Cats. 73.1–73.4, *Four Plates with Depictions of the Months: June, July, August, December*

Cat. 66.1–66.3

Francesco dal Ponte, called Bassano (1549–1592)

Summer

c.1580
Canvas; 111 cm × 145.5 cm
Signed bottom left: 'FRANC. BASS'
Vienna, Kunsthistorisches Museum, Picture Gallery, inv. 4289

Autumn

c.1580
Canvas; 111 cm × 146 cm
Signed bottom right: 'FRANC BASS'
Vienna, Kunsthistorisches Museum, Picture Gallery, inv. 4287

Winter

c.1580
Canvas; 111 cm × 73 cm
Signed to right: 'FRANCvs BASS is F'
Vienna Kunsthistorisches Museum, Picture Gallery, inv. 4288

Provenance: Archduke Leopold Wilhelm 1659
Literature: Baldass 1949, 209–10; Baldass 1955; mus. cat. Vienna 1991, 27, pl. 85; exh. cat. Las Vegas 2002/03, 125 (Karl Schütz); exh. cat. Treviso 2019/20, 32–6, cats. 2–4 (Francesca Del Torre Scheuch)

Archduke Leopold Wilhelm bought this cycle of seasons, considered to be a work by Jacopo Bassano in the *Theatrum Pictorium* (1660), compiled by David Teniers the Younger. The series is listed with the same attribution in the inventory drawn up in 1659 after the transfer of the collection from Brussels to Vienna, and in the Prague inventory of 1718. Three paintings, *Summer*, *Autumn*, and *Winter*, returned to Vienna in 1894, the latter in the form of a fragment because the left half of the composition had been cut off. All trace has been lost of *Spring*.

As in Jacopo's *Seasons* (cats. 62.1–62.4), Francesco developed the composition on parallel planes sloping down towards the background and kept the episodes from his father's repertoire, though he made significant changes. In *Summer*, the shearing of sheep is replaced by a scene around an elegant country house, where servants receiving baskets of fruit look out from a stone doorway. An elegantly dressed lady sitting by a tree is cooling herself with a fan and perhaps waiting for the peasant women to lay out a rustic lunch at her feet. The repertoire of baskets of fruit and vegetables, animals, and everyday objects is enriched with new details such as the bobbin embroidery left on a chair, the ceramic and copper dishes, and the basket of pumpkins watched over by a monkey. The usual scenes of reaping and threshing grain appear in the middle distance, though under the supervision of the farmer on horseback, who is protecting himself from the heat with a parasol.

Francesco dedicated the narrative on the right side of the painting to the picking and pressing of grapes, the main occupations in autumn. On the left, though, he added a new scene with two men constructing barrels. One is bending the staves in the fire, the other is completing the hooping. This activity offered the chance to arrange several objects and tools in the foreground near the farm building on the left: planes, saws and mallets depicted with remarkable documentary precision (Wharf 1999, 19).

Winter also presents an innovation: in the landscape stiffened by frost and snow a pig is being butchered in a kind of open-air kitchen. The dead animal is about to be dismembered by two men while a woman at the table attends to the offal. A boy is inflating the animal's bladder – a motif inspired by painting from northern countries – while a man wearing a fur-lined cloak and gloves, clothing in clear contrast with that of the peasants, is approaching the table. People warming themselves at a sheltered fire, a traditional element of winter iconography, can be seen in the middle distance. The zodiac sign of Capricorn, now no longer visible, was in the missing part of the painting, whose original appearance is recorded in the *Theatrum Pictorium* engraving.

These paintings mark a fundamental stage in the iconographic development of the first series of *Seasons* through large-format variants, as shown for example by the paintings in the Galleria Borghese. Although the biblical scene is still present in the background of the Rome works, a new iconographic element appears in these paintings, cutting off links with the religious meaning in previous versions. Arranged along a precise trajectory, the signs of the zodiac emerge in a beam of light from the clouds in the three pictures: Gemini, Cancer, and Leo in Summer, Libra, Scorpio, and Sagittarius in Autumn, and Aquarius and Pisces in Winter. Drawing on the ancient astrological tradition, Francesco thus opted for a 'worldly' representation of the seasons, paving the way for the sumptuous cycles of the *Months* (cats. 67.1–67.12). These paintings suited the taste of a sensitive, cultivated public interested in the depiction of natural elements. The choice of a larger format than Jacopo's first version favoured the narration of genuine still-life passages with animals, fruit, and plants, along with items of everyday use. Such paintings were suitable for decorating sumptuous rooms in patrician homes with pleasing portrayals of the rural activities conducted on the mainland estates, as confirmed by the presence of the richly dressed lady in *Summer* and the cloaked man in *Winter* (see essay Del Torre Scheuch, p. 49).

Francesca Del Torre Scheuch

Cats. 67.1–67.12

Leandro dal Ponte, called Bassano (1557–1622)

January

1581/87
Canvas, both sides trimmed slightly;
146 × 192.5 cm
Inscribed lower left: 'LEANDER BASSANENSIS'
Vienna, Kunsthistorisches Museum, Picture Gallery, inv. 4292

February

1581/87
Canvas, left side trimmed slightly;
144.5 × 190 cm
Inscribed lower centre: 'LEANDER BASSANENSIS F.'
Vienna, Kunsthistorisches Museum, Picture Gallery, inv. 4293

March

1581/87
Canvas; 145.5 × 216 cm
Inscribed lower edge: 'LEANDER'
Vienna, Kunsthistorisches Museum,
Picture Gallery, inv. 4296

April

1581/87
Canvas, both sides trimmed (the left by more);
145.5 × 164.5 cm
Remains of an inscription lower left
Vienna, Kunsthistorisches Museum,
Picture Gallery, inv. 4298

May

1581/87
Canvas, both sides trimmed;
145.5 × 164 cm
Vienna, Kunsthistorisches Museum,
Picture Gallery, inv. 4299

June

1581/87
Canvas; 145 × 216 cm
Inscribed lower left on the step:
'LEANDER BASSANENSIS FACIEBAT'
Vienna, Kunsthistorisches Museum, Picture
Gallery, inv. 4294

July (Spinning and Weaving)

1581/87
Canvas, fragments; 132 × 89.5 cm
Vienna, Kunsthistorisches Museum,
Picture Gallery inv. 4309

July

1581/87
Canvas; 130 × 86 cm
Vienna, Kunsthistorisches Museum,
Picture Gallery, inv. 4308

August

1581/87
Canvas; 145 × 213 cm
Inscribed lower left on the tool case:
'LEANDER BASSis FAC. EBAT'
Vienna, Kunsthistorisches Museum,
Picture Gallery, inv. 4295

September

1581/87
Canvas; 145 × 213 cm
Inscribed lower centre:
'LEANDER BASSANENSIS'
Prague, Castle Gallery, inv. O 22

October

1581/87
Canvas, 146 × 216.7 cm
Inscribed lower centre on the stone:
'LEANDER BASSANENSIS'
Prague, Castle Gallery, inv. O 21

November

1581/87
Canvas, both sides slightly trimmed;
145 × 216 cm
Inscribed on the breaking frame:
'L. ER BASS. FAT.'
Vienna, Kunsthistorisches Museum,
Picture Gallery, inv. 4297

Provenance: Emperor Rudolf II; Archduke Leopold Wilhelm

Literature: Woltmann 1877, 47; Neumann 1966, 102–9; mus. cat. Vienna 1991, 28, fig. 92–3; exh. cat. Belluno 1994, 25–31, 62–5 (Paola Marini); exh. cat. Madrid 2002, 125–33 (Falomir); Del Torre Scheuch 2009, 121–31

According to the painter and art writer Carlo Ridolfi (1648), Jacopo Bassano sent Emperor Rudolf II in Prague a series of paintings depicting the twelve months. However, the paintings do not appear in the Prague inventories. They may have been brought to Vienna when Rudolf's estate was divided among his siblings. They are first recorded in Archduke Leopold Wilhelm's inventory (1659), where they are listed as works by the 'young Bassano'.

Almost the entire series is still preserved in Vienna; *September* and *October* are in the Castle Gallery in Prague, and *December* is lost. The journey of the paintings through the imperial collections left them with comparatively few traces, and the series is generally well preserved. The month of *July* was cut into two parts, possibly for decorative reasons. Other changes in size are found in *January*, *February*, *April*, and *May*. The Vienna and Prague paintings have been reunited for the first time since the nineteenth century in this exhibition. Today, we can once again enjoy the unity of style and content of this important cycle.

Leandro depicts the activities of the figures with great care and precision in the reproduction of details, from tools and objects to clothing, with the result that the paintings also have considerable documentary value. The viewer is pleasantly entertained. Some people probably recognised themselves in the scenes: for example, on horseback in the hunting party in *January*; in the richly dressed lady to whom crops are presented; in the lord of the manor who inspects the work and the harvest with his estate manager. Leandro innovatively combined diverse activities in front of both rural and urban backdrops, and created varied and detailed narratives. The signs of the zodiac at the top of the pictures complete the compositions. The cycle of the months has its roots in an iconographic tradition from the Middle Ages, and has the character of a vividly illustrated calendar.

In fact, the paintings reflect the refined tastes of an aristocratic audience. Their highly decorative qualities and large dimensions attest to the fact that they were intended to adorn a sizeable, stately room. Francesco Bassano himself mentioned an important commission in a letter to the Florentine art connoisseur Niccolò Gaddi (1581). The artist wanted to create the twelve months, which he had been thinking of painting for some time, for the palace of a certain 'Signori' (Bottari 1821, CX).

At least two series of months were created in the 1580s, one signed by Francesco (partly preserved in the Museo del Prado in Madrid), the other, the Vienna series, signed by Leandro.

Using compositional schemes and figure groups from the repertoire of the family studio, Leandro developed the narrative from month to month with creative enthusiasm and a natural talent for storytelling. Through a brilliant use of colours and an analytical approach to the reproduction of objects and natural components, the scenes provide an impressive insight into sixteenth-century life.

The urban context in the first three months of the year provides an appropriate framework for the narrative. In *January*, a peasant family warms themselves by the fire. The woman works a hand spindle; the man has taken off his left shoe and is drying his foot by the fire. Others tie firewood into bundles and take them to the manor house, while a page with a falcon and carrying game accompanies a hunting party. Two gentlemen with fur-trimmed coats ride towards the centre of the picture from the right. In the snowy landscape in the background, several small figures are chopping and collecting wood. A few well-to-do individuals hurry through the scene as snowflakes fall on huts and farmhouses at dusk.

February is represented by the very first depiction of Carnival in Italian Renaissance art. Pantalone, on the left, is approached by a blindfolded child with a dog, and a richly dressed, masked couple. These two personify the lovers (*Innamorati*), standard characters of the Commedia dell'Arte, the professional comedy born in the second half of the sixteenth century (Katritzky 2006, 12–32; Moldovan 2021, 119–20). On the right, a woman sells poultry from behind a counter on which goods are displayed. A man and a girl are there too. An elongated square surrounded by buildings is the setting for a bull fight, which traditionally took place on Shrove Thursday.

March depicts a market scene in a city during Lent. A fishmonger welcomes a prominent customer who admires the variety of fish and shellfish. A woman offers products typical of the season; spring onions, turnips, onions, and spinach, as well as fish, are some of the foods permitted during Lent, the forty-day period of fasting that follows Carnival. In the background, a priest gives a sermon in an open temple. On the left side of the painting, a lady accompanied by other women is on her way into the church, where a beggar is sprawled on the steps.

From *April* onwards, the agricultural world around Bassano del Grappa, characterised by a charming, lush, hilly landscape, forms the backdrop for the many activities of farmers. In *April*, the lambs are slaughtered and the sheep shorn. The main protagonists are the animals, which dominate the foreground. Small marginal scenes can be seen in the the middle ground and background. A farm woman milks a cow; two women, one holding a child, chat under a hut's roof. An unexpected rain shower, typical of the changeable weather in April, is also depicted.

Farmers are shown making butter and cheese in *May*. The cheese moulds are placed on wooden shelves to dry. A rose garden is in bloom in front of a stately villa in the background. Two women are picking roses, which are used not only for decoration, but also in countless recipes, for cooking as well as medicinal purposes. In the centre, one can see the departure of the herd, which is driven out to pasture at this time of year.

June is harvesting time for cherries and grain. A farm woman offers her cherries for tasting at the manor house. A young woman has just brought out baskets with lunch for the farm workers. Some are busy loading the wagon with sheaves of grain; others are harvesting the grain, which women tie into large sheaves and place in orderly piles on the ground.

Two fragments of the month of *July* depict – with Bassano's customary care – a phase of silk production in a household setting. On the left, the cocoons are heated in a boiler, where the minerals on the surface of the cocoon are dissolved by hot water and the silk thread unwound. The rejected cocoons are eaten by the ducks. Two figures in the courtyard in the right background are threshing grain, which also takes place in July. The warm time of year is an occasion for refreshment. On the left, workers are offered wine, a lady sitting under an arbour (in the fragment on the right) is offered fruit. In the background, women refresh themselves by bathing in a pond or river.

August is characterised by preparations for the grape harvest. Wooden staves are heated and bent, then planed and bound with willow hoops, to create wine barrels.

The barrels are used for the grape harvest in *September*. The farmers pick the grapes from the vines, which are tied to the trees, and fill their baskets and barrels with the fruit. The wine pressing takes place on the right side of the picture. A rustic picnic is served.

In *October*, chestnuts are harvested, and the fields are ploughed and sown with seed. A steward on horseback supervises the farmers' work.

No farm work is done during the winter months. The workers' contracts expired on 11 November – the feast of St Martin – and, as shown in the scene in the background of *November*, they are loading a wagon with their belongings to return to their villages. In the foreground, a kitchen scene is depicted where poultry are being prepared and a goose slaughtered. On the right side, flax is being broken with a breaking frame.

The year ends in December. The pig slaughter and associated work are characteristic of this month's depiction, known both from the painting preserved in Madrid and from various small-format replicas (Monastery of Seitenstetten; Schwarzenberg Castle of Hlúboka; Tula Museum of Fine Arts).

Francesca Del Torre Scheuch

Cat. 68

Owl

Florence, before 1596
Bronze; H 15.8 cm (in total c.22 cm), pedestal W 10 cm, D 13 cm
Vienna, Kunsthistorisches Museum, Kunstkammer, inv. KK 5841

Provenance: 1596 in the estate inventory of Archduke Ferdinand II in Schloss Ambras
Literature: Planiscig 1924, IV, 167, cat. 272; mus.

cat. New York 1984, 174, no. 92; Krahn 1988, 42, 82ff; exh. cat. Innsbruck 2015, 236–7, cat. 5.6

In the princely chambers of art and curiosities of the Renaissance, naturalistic depictions of animals served not only as an aesthetic pleasure, but also as an opportunity for scientific examination of the natural world. This small bronze figure depicts a small owl looking at the feathered toes of its raised right leg. Based on its size and the shape of its head, it is probably a little owl (*Athene noctua*), a short-tailed owl species of the family of true owls (*Strigidae*). The bird was regarded as a symbol of wisdom in ancient Greece, which is also indicated by its zoological name, a reference to Athena, the goddess of wisdom. The phrase 'carrying owls to Athens', which originates with the Greek comic playwright Aristophanes, refers to the depictions of little owls on ancient obols (coins) that were in circulation from around 525 BCE. These bore an image of Athena on the obverse side, and a little owl with an olive branch in its beak on the reverse. The phrase did not refer to the futility of bringing wisdom to the city of Athena, it expressed the absurdity of sending money to Athens, which was already rich.

As early as the fourth century BCE, Aristotle described the so-called 'hatred' of songbirds for owls in his *Historia animalium*. The way that owls flew mock attacks to drive off potential enemies was also used for hunting in the sixteenth century. Especially during the migration season in spring and autumn, the owls were tied with a long fetter to a perch on a pole near a camouflaged hunter's blind. While larger owls such as eagle owls primarily attracted other birds of prey and crows, the little owl attracted smaller songbirds. As soon as the 'hating' birds flew by, they got caught in traps or on hidden rods covered with birdlime, or were shot by the hunter from the blind. This widely known form of bird hunting was probably also the reason why attempts were made to breed little owls in captivity in pre-Christian times. Pliny the Elder also describes the little owl, along with the eagle owl and barn owl, in his *Historia naturalis* (around 77 CE).

Katharina Seidl

Cat. 69

Alessandro Vittoria (1525–1608)

St Zachariah? – Allegory of Winter? (formerly: *The Scythian Philosopher Anacharsis*)

Venice, c.1585
Bronze; H (without pedestal) 33.4 cm
Vienna, Kunsthistorisches Museum, Kunstkammer, inv. KK 5664

Provenance: Imperial Treasurer Joseph Angelus de France (Martini 1781); 1808 acquired for the k. k. Münz- und Antikencabinet; 1880 Ambras Collection
Literature: Leithe-Jasper 1963, 207–8; Bode 1980, 107; exh. cat. Trento 1999, 360–4, cat. no. 81 (Manfred Leithe-Jasper); exh. cat. Parma 2003, 399–400, cat. no. 3.5.6; mus. cat Vienna 2010, 136, no. 58; exh. cat. Schallaburg 2011, 186, 230, no. II.100; mus. cat. Vienna 2012, 158–9; mus. cat. Vienna 2013, 62 (Konrad Schlegel)

This masterfully modelled statuette was probably made by sculptor Alessandro Vittoria, one of the most significant creators of small bronze sculpture in the sixteenth century. The silhouette of a bearded figure with a slightly lowered head rises above a base. He appears to have wrapped a coat protectively around himself; its folds lend physicality and movement to his elongated silhouette. Conveniently sized bronzes of this kind were autonomous works of art intended to be experienced tactilely and studied in detail. The virtuoso sculptural shaping also speaks to Vittoria's knowledge of monumental sculptures.

The fact that the figure appears to be freezing as he wraps himself in his coat has led to it being seen as a personification of winter. As a rule, however, such depictions are usually part of a group of four, each dedicated to one of the seasons. Since there is no evidence of that in Vittorio's case, this interpretation has found little acceptance. The same fate has befallen the designation of this piece as a philosopher, which was made on the basis of an inventory from 1781, in which it is referred to as the legendary Scythian philosopher Anacharsis.

In the end, stylistic elements, such as the leg coverings fastened with bands beneath the knee, which is also a characteristic of the monumental statue *Moses* by Michelangelo (San Pietro in Vincoli, Rome), have suggested it might be a biblical figure, such as St Zachariah, the father of John the Baptist. Zachariah refused to believe an angel of God who prophesied that his wife Elizabeth, despite her advanced age, would give birth to a son. When he asked for a sign in confirmation, he was temporarily struck dumb. It is not odd that Vittoria would devote himself to this rarely depicted saint since two other depictions of Zachariah can be found in his oeuvre.

Katja Schmitz-von Ledebur

Cat. 70

Daniel Fröschl (1563–1613)

Plucked Chicken

End of 16th cent. to 1630
Tempera on paper; 201 × 316 mm
Pisa, Biblioteca Universitaria, Ms. 514, *Disegni di animali*, fol. 161r

Provenance: Antico giardino dei Semplici di Pisa
Literature: Tongiorgi Tomasi 1980, 574; Tongiorgi Tomasi 2024, pl. 20–1

This sheet, in a miscellaneous codex of 426 zoological plates, once belonged to the collection of Pisa's ancient botanical garden, the Giardino dei Semplici. In the garden's 1672 inventory, it is cited as 'another book of various animals and birds' ('un altro libro d'Animali e Uccelli diversi').

Notes relating to the names of the animals depicted appear frequently on the sheets, mostly in Italian, Latin, and German. The plates were made or assembled between the end of the sixteenth century and 1630, when the institution was under the direction of Giuseppe Casabona (Joseph Goedenhuize, 1592–95) and Francesco Malocchi (1596–1613), for whom Daniel Fröschl worked. He was sent to the botanical garden to paint plants and animals by the Grand Duke Ferdinand I de' Medici.

The codex is characterized by a striking unevenness both in the sequence of the animal groups (birds, mammals, fish, insects, and reptiles), and in the style and execution of the temperas. The German miniaturist to whom the ornithological plates in particular are ascribed used a less refined technique than that used for the Habsburg temperas (cf. Vienna, Austrian National Library, cod. min. 42, fol. 54r).

Among the numerous hens, three sheets stand out, depicting a chicken and two turkeys, gutted and plucked. These are followed by a plate with a pig's head and trotter, and another large one with a slice of beef – all subjects gathered from market stalls that interested the naturalists for the anatomical information they provided.

The iconography has an intriguing correspondence with the contemporary market and kitchen paintings, for which the Flemish artists Pieter Aersten and Joachim Beuckelaer, and Vincenzo Campi of Cremona were renowned. The latter painted a scene of *Poulterers* (c.1580, conserved in Milan, Accademia di Belle Arti di Brera) and copied it for the German banker Hans Fugger. Alongside the numerous hanging birds (which take up to an iconography expressed by Jacopo dei Barbari, Albrecht Dürer, and Lucas Cranach), the poulterer in the foreground is holding a turkey he has just plucked.

Giuseppe Olmi, Lucia Tongiorgi Tomasi

Cat. 71

Bartolomeo Scappi (1500–1577)

Opera di M. Bartolomeo Scappi, Cuoco Secreto di Papa Pio V. divisa in Sei Libri …

Venice (Michele Tramezzino) 1570
Vienna, Austrian National Library, Department of Manuscripts and Rare Books, *44.G.99 Alt Prunk, fol. 442

Literature: Luccichenti and Di Schino 2007; Scully 2008; Krohn 2008/09; exh. cat. Vienna 2016, 109, cat. 10 (Katharina Seidl); Di Schino 2019; exh. cat. Venaria 2023/24, 89, cats. I.12–14 (Alessandra Rodolfo)

During the Renaissance, Italy experienced a flowering of treatises on the art of dining. Of particular importance is *Opera* by Bartolomeo Scappi, who worked as a cook for cardinals and popes in Venice and Rome. First published by Tramezzino in Venice in 1570, the treatise was reprinted several times until 1643.

Over almost 500 pages, the author described the culinary world in its entirety, covering 1,017 recipes for local and exotic foods as well as topics such as kitchen equipment, the sequence of courses, serving, and the profession of chef. After an introductory *Ragionamento* on the art of cookery (Book I), Scappi divided his work into dishes made from quadrupeds and poultry (Book II), fish and dishes for fasting (Book III), pasta (Book V), and food for the sick and convalescent (Book VI). Particularly noteworthy is the fourth book, which lists the courses of famous banquets for princes to papal coronations over the course of the year. Scappi reports, for example, on the splendour of a banquet for Charles V in Trastevere (1536), which was elevated to an art form by dishes made of gold, silver, and majolica, sculptures made of sugar, butter, and *pasta reale*, and musical performances.

A new feature of the *Opera* was the 28 illustrated panels on cooking and the preparation of food at the Renaissance court. Elements such as fireplaces for cooking can be found in illuminated manuscripts such as the *Tacuinum sanitatis* (cat. 16) as early as the late fourteenth century as settings for seasonal activities or the preparation of particular foods. Illustrations had adorned the frontpieces of cookbooks since the late fifteenth century. But in the *Opera*'s illustrations, the world of cookery was presented for the first time using a didactic approach. The plates section opens by presenting the layout and features of the ideal kitchen and its adjoining rooms, where kitchen workers demonstrate the use of specific implements for the preparation of specific dishes. This is followed by the methodical depiction of cooking utensils and containers. Thanks to the wealth of visual detail and the written explanations, Scappi created a pictorial archive of historical practices and kitchen utensils, some of which no longer exist.

From the mid-sixteenth century onwards, alongside the growing scientific interest in the culinary world, kitchens and food emerged as important themes in genre painting. They illustrated a variety of stories, from biblical parables to moral allegories, first in the Netherlands and then in Italy (cats. 63–67, 89).

Alexandra Sattler

Cats. 72.1, 72.2

Johannes Stradanus (1523–1605)

Feeding the Silkworms (II)

c.1580
Pen and brown ink, brown and gray wash, traces of black chalk, white highlights; 182 × 270 mm
The Royal Collection/HM King Charles III, inv. RCIN 904764

Women Reeling Silk

c.1590
Pen and brown ink, brown and gray wash, traces of black chalk, white highlights; 178 × 269 mm
The Royal Collection/HM King Charles III, inv. RCIN 904766

Provenance: 1810 mentioned in inventory of the Royal Collection for the first time
Literature: DaCosta Kaufmann 1993, 152–3; White and Crawley 1994, 170–1; Morel 2008; exh. cat. Rome 2017/18, cat. I.20 (Sylvia Ferino-Pagden)

These sheets are two of the surviving preparatory drawings by Johannes Stradanus, after which Philipp Galle commissioned Karel van Mallery to make engravings for a six-part series entitled *Vermis Sericus* (Latin for 'silkworm'). Galle was a successful publisher and the founder of one of the most important Dutch engraving workshops in Antwerp. He probably published the series at the end of the 1590s. The engravings with their explanatory notes describe the history of the introduction of the silkworm to the West by Emperor Justinian, the various phases of its rearing, and the production of silk, from harvesting the larvae to unwinding the thread and spinning the precious cloth.

Johannes Stradanus, or Jan van der Straet, was a Flemish painter and draughtsman from Bruges. He is documented as a master craftsman in Antwerp in 1545. He travelled to Italy, where he worked for the Medici and private clients in Florence and elsewhere. Italy was a leader in the production of silk in Europe during the Renaissance and in the sixteenth century, and Florence was one of the most important centres for its processing and production. After its start in southern Italy, where the climatic conditions and soil were ideal for growing the mulberry trees needed, production gradually shifted to central and northern Italy.

Stradanus's drawing *Feeding the Silkworms* shows various steps in the breeding of silkworms, and combines agricultural and craft activities. A large room opens on to a plantation of mulberry trees, the leaves of which were used to feed the silkworms up to ten times a day. Women and men can be seen harvesting the leaves. A donkey is being loaded with a sack for further transport, and a woman carries a basket of leaves on her head into the building. In the foreground, a man pours a sack of mulberry leaves on to the floor; behind him, several women spread them out to dry on meshwork surfaces on shelves. This is the preparatory drawing for plate five of the series of engravings.

The sheet *Women Reeling Silk*, the model for plate six of the series, offers a glimpse into a silk manufactory, which opens in the background on to a Renaissance town. Outside, the cocoons are spread out on the street and then collected again. Inside the factory, the various stages of silk processing can be seen taking place in a large room. In the centre, seated women place the silkworm cocoons into heated basins of water and wind the thread from the cocoon on to reels. In the foreground, a woman adds wood to the fire that warms the basins. A woman with a child brings her colleagues a basket with more cocoons to be processed.

The two sheets are closely related to a series of thirteen drawings by Giuseppe Arcimboldo, in which the individual steps of silk processing are recorded and explained (Boston, Museum of Fine Arts, inv. 50.6.15). In 1587, when he was a court artist to the Habsburgs in Vienna and Prague, Arcimboldo presented the drawings to Baron Ferdinand Hoffmann, the president of the imperial Hofkammer, as decorative designs for his palace in Prague (Baroni Vannucci 1997, 289–91, 397, 401–2; McGinty 1998, 116–22). Philippe Morel believes the series of engravings *Vermis Sericus* 'was probably commissioned by Costanza Alamanni towards the end of the 1580s (similar to the decorations planned for Baron Hoffmann)' (Morel 2008, 236).

The *Gelsomania cinquecentesca* – that is, 'mulberry mania' – with the attendant breeding of silkworms and the production of silk led to various related publications in the sixteenth century, including a series of pictures in the *Nova Reperta* ('New Discoveries', 1597). There, the production of silk – along with the discovery of America – ranks as one of the most important achievements. Costanza's brother, Luigi Alamanni, commissioned the *Nova Reperta* series and its publisher was once again Philipp Galle, with Johannes Stradanus also producing the preparatory drawings.

Wencke Deiters

Cats. 73.1–73.4

Four Plates with Depictions of the Months: June, July, August, December

From a series of 12 plates
Limoges, second half 16th cent.
Enamel painting on copper (two-sided);
dia. 19.7–19.8 cm
Vienna, Kunsthistorisches Museum,
Kunstkammer, invs. KK 3203, KK 3234,
KK 3235, KK 3248

Provenance: 1619 Prague Rebelleninventar; 1648 Prague Inventory; 1750 Imperial Treasury: set into the ceiling of the Goldkabinett as a decorative element; 1871 removed from the Imperial Treasury; 1875 Ambras Collection

Literature: Ilg 1884, I, 111–28.; mus. cat. Baltimore 1967, 329; mus. cat. Berlin 1999, 78–82; exh. cat. Vienna and Zurich 2011/12, 120–3, no. 7 (Katja Schmitz-von Ledebur)

The art of enamelling has been practiced in Limoges since the Middle Ages, but the city, which is located in the north-west corner of France's Massif Central, is particularly famous for the Limoges painted enamel technique that take its name. This decorative form finds special expression in the grisaille technique, which was probably developed in the workshop of Jean Pénicaut (active in the first half of the sixteenth century) and involves applying white enamel paint to a dark enamel base. Objects made using this method were particularly popular at the court of King Francois I. Pierre Reymond's prolific studio in Limoges made a name for itself with objects decorated using this technique, which was based primarily on graphic models.

The series of twelve plates in the collection of the *Kunstkammer* in Vienna was also made in Limoges and decorated in grisaille. Each plate depicts a different month, whose sign of the zodiac is enthroned on a bank of clouds at the upper edge of a scenic depiction. Each plate shows several figures engaged in an activity characteristic of the season or month.

The pictorial representation of the months has a long tradition. The ancient Roman *Calendarium rusticum* linked the months to aspects of everyday life, especially rural life. Therefore, it is not surprising that over time each month was assigned a specific agricultural activity (Schmitz-von Ledebur 2011/12, 68).

The four plates represent the months of June, July, August, and December. In June, (inscription: 'IVING'), a shepherd tends his flock in the background under the sign of Cancer while in the foreground three people are busy shearing sheep. July (inscription: 'IVILIET') combines both pleasurable and work-related aspects of the month under the sign of Leo. At the front, two men are mowing a meadow with scythes; in the background, hay is being brought in. Some children are also taking a refreshing swim in a tree-lined pond.

The activity in August (inscription: 'AOVST') is also an arduous one. The end of summer is drawing near under the sign of Virgo. A reaper uses a sickle to harvest grain, which is tied into sheaves and taken away on a cart. As in the July plate, the dynamism of the figures' movements is striking.

Finally, December (inscription: 'DECEMBRE') has a motif closely associated with winter. A farmer is slaughtering a pig under the sign of Capricorn. An already eviscerated animal hangs on the wall of the house on the right of the picture, while in the left background the bristles are being flayed off two other pigs. The edge of every plate is lined with a grotesque row of sirens, horned masks, and vases.

A series of engravings by Étienne Delaune, published in 1568, served as a model for the figurative scenes on the plates – though they were altered slightly. Delaune's ornamental engravings were often used as models in the decorative arts, as they were in Pierre Reymond's enamel paintings. A series of month plates with the initials 'P.R.' that were also made after engravings by Delaune can be found in Paris (Musée des Arts Décoratifs). The plates in Vienna are not signed. They were never intended for everyday use – they served purely representative purposes. They were inlaid in the wooden ceiling of the Goldkabinett ('gold cabinet') of the treasury for a time as decorative elements along with majolica and faience.

Katja Schmitz-von Ledebur

Leandro Bassano and His Patrons in Padua

(cats. 74–80)

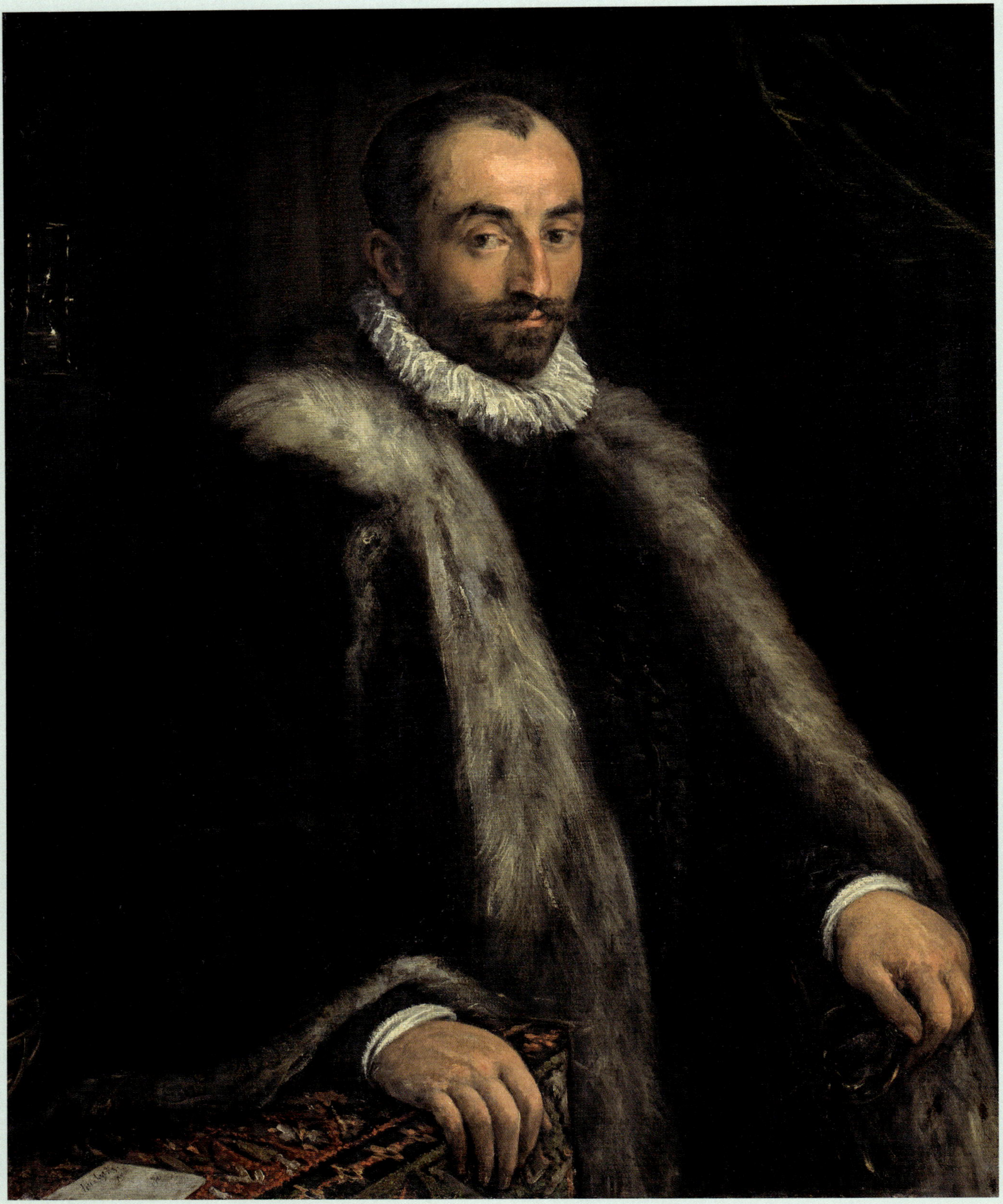

Cat. 74, Francesco Bassano, *Portrait of a Bearded Man with Hourglass and Celestial Globe*

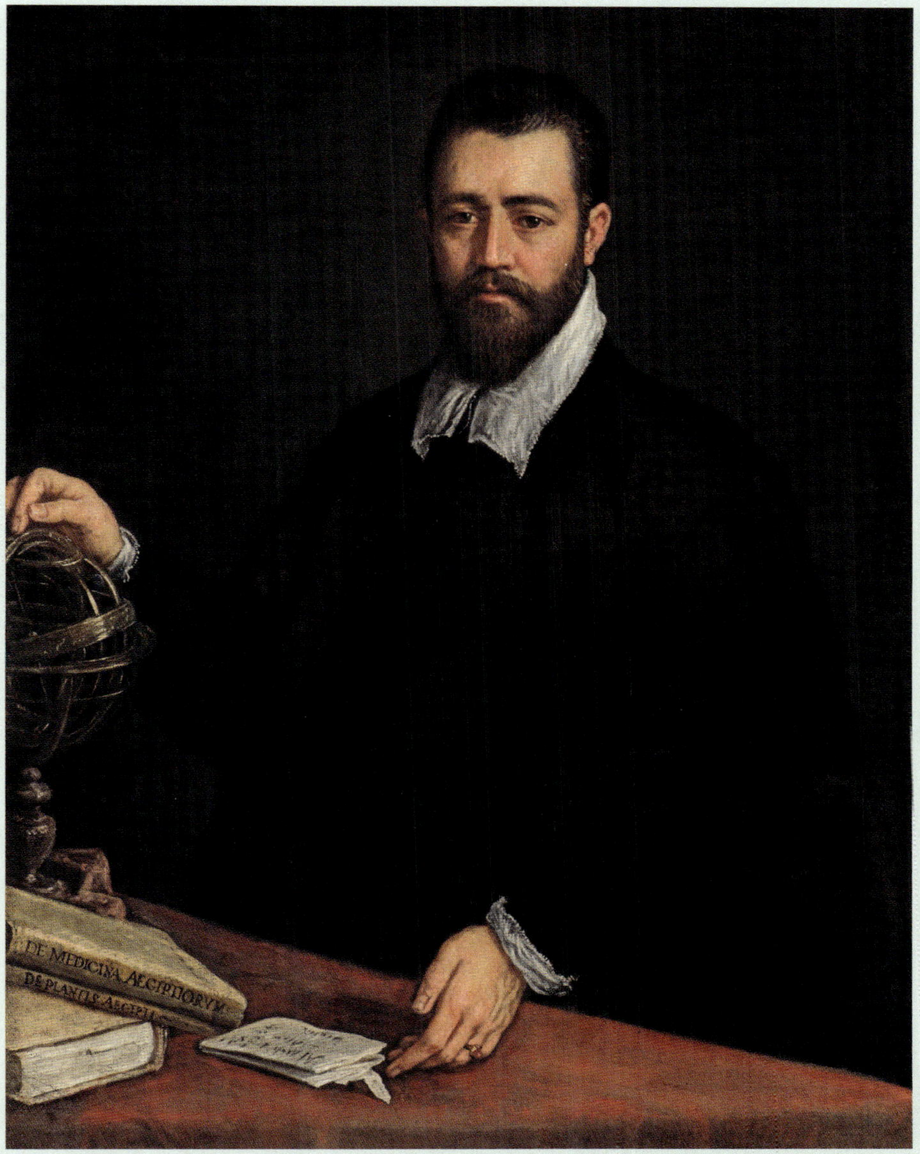

Cat. 75, Leandro Bassano, *Portrait of Prospero Alpini*

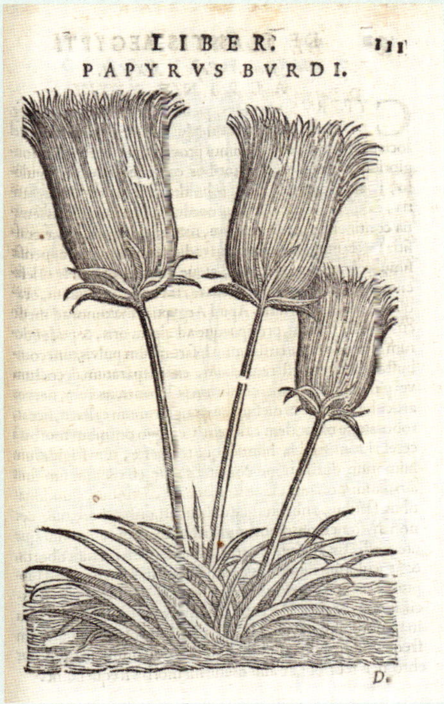

Cat. 76, Prospero Alpini, *De plantis Aegypti liber*

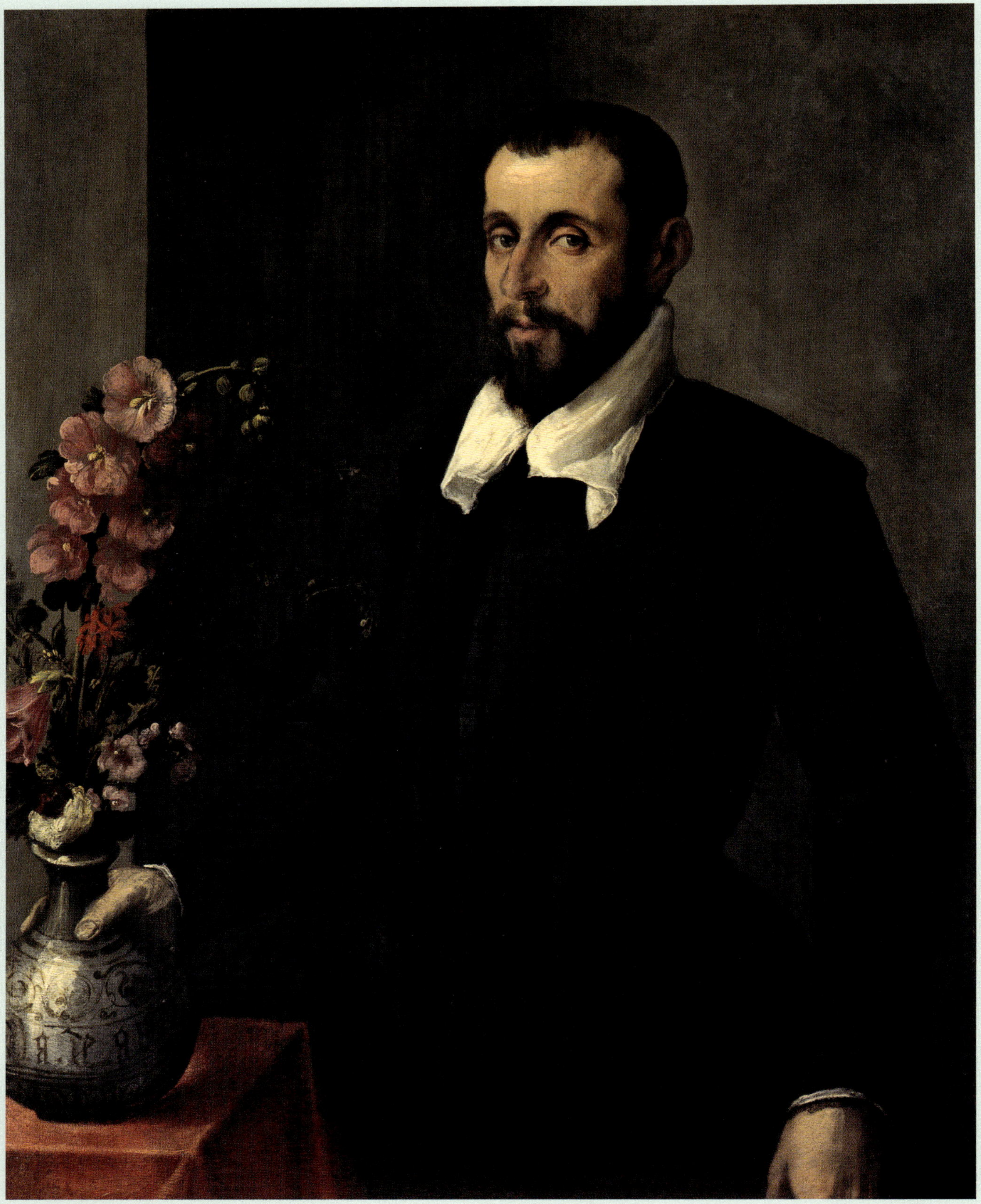

Cat. 77, Leandro Bassano, *Portrait of a Man*

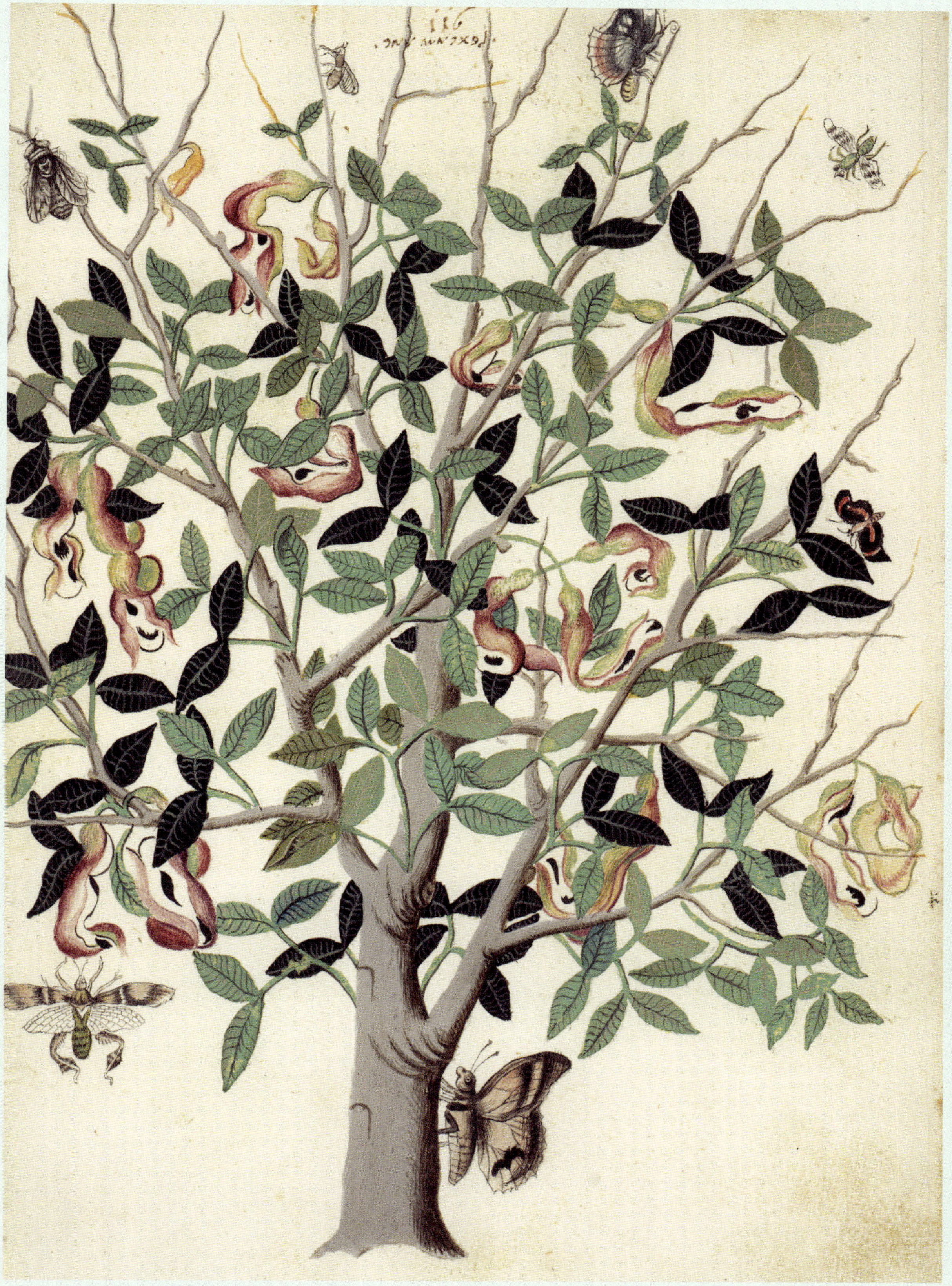

Cat. 78, Pietro Antonio Michiel, *I cinque libri di piante. Libro Azzurro*

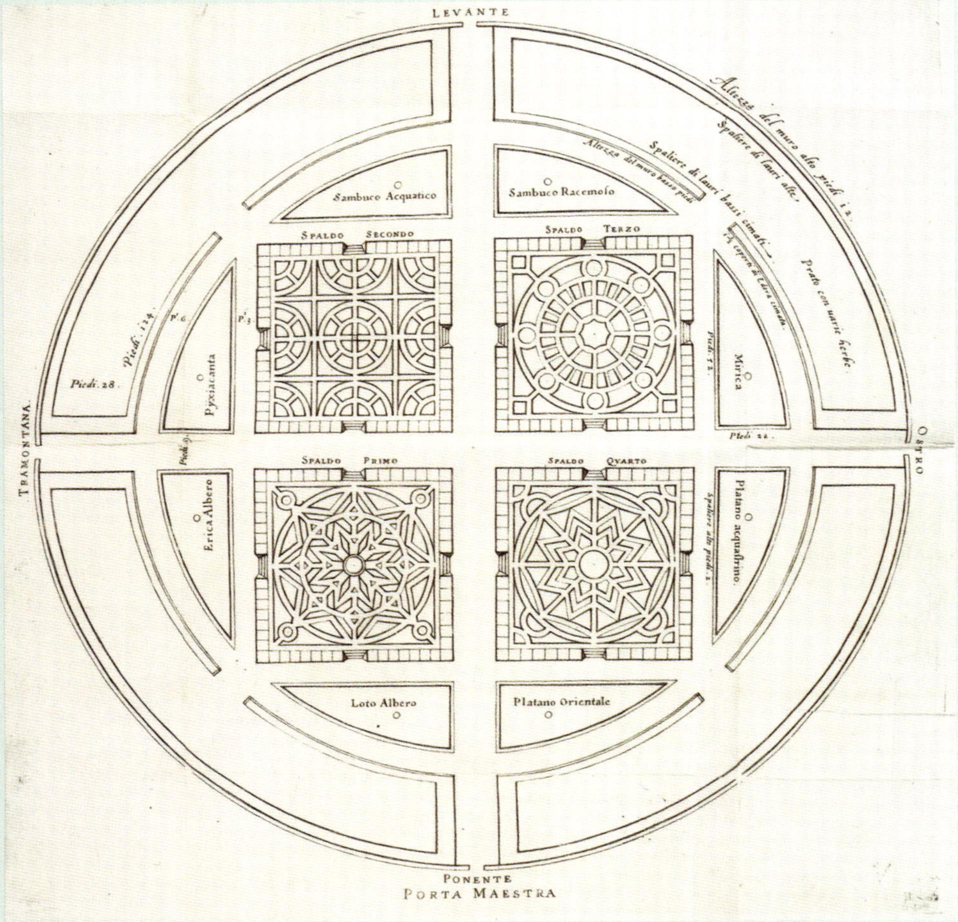

Cat. 79, Giacomo Antonio Cortuso, *L'Horto de i semplici di Padova*

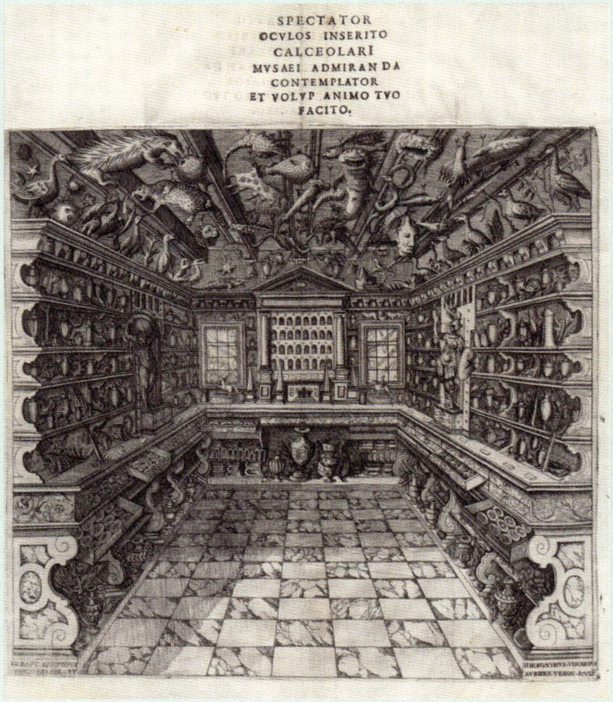

Cat. 80, Benedetto Ceruti, Andrea Chiocco, *Musaeum Franc. Calceolari Iun. Veronensis*

Cat. 74

Francesco dal Ponte, called Bassano (1549–1592)

Portrait of a Bearded Man with Hourglass and Celestial Globe (Joseph Justus Scaliger?)

c.1580
Canvas; 106.3 cm × 89.8 cm
Vienna, Kunsthistorisches Museum, Picture Gallery, inv. 5775

Provenance: Ambras Inventory 1663 no. 234; Ambra Inventory 1773, no. 78
Literature: Primisser 1819, 146, no. 2 (Tintoretto); mus. cat. Vienna 1938, 12, no. 321A (Leandro Bassano); mus. cat. Vienna 1954, 7 (Francesco Bassano); mus. cat. Vienna 1991, 26; Swoboda 2004/05, 295; exh. cat. Innsbruck 2009, 129, cat. 2.6 (Del Torre Scheuch)

This portrait of a scientist is documented from 1663 in the Ambras Collection. It was for centuries ascribed to Tintoretto, but since 1954 has been unanimously attributed to Francesco Bassano. Scholars propose dating it to the 1580s, when the painter had moved to Venice. Francesco's stylistic maturity is expressed in a very dense, soft application of the paint and a self-assured play of transparency. This style is evident in the iridescent white ruff and the fur trim on the sober black gown of the figure, who is certainly of high lineage due to the sword belted at his side. The hourglass behind him and the armillary sphere on the table at the left, mostly cut away following a reduction in the size of the painting, testify to the subject's scientific interests.

The identity of the man in the portrait is unknown. However, his facial features undoubtedly resemble those of the Italian-born French humanist Giuseppe Giusto Scaligero (Joseph Justus Scaliger, 1540–1609), portrayed at the age of 35 by Hendrick Goltzius in a later engraving (1592/93; see Vam Ommen 2016). This opens new research perspectives on the possible commissioner of the work in light of the Bassano family's relations with various exponents of the University of Padua.

Gian Vincenzo Pinelli, a humanist, bibliophile, and collector of Genoese origin, lived in Padua from 1558 and frequented university circles, and was also known for his portrait gallery of distinguished men (Raufei 2018). It may be inferred from the letters consulted to date that in around 1578 Pinelli had a particular interest in Scaliger, who at the time was working on astronomy and astrology: first on the edition of *Astronomica* by Manilius (Paris, 1579), then on the definition of the Julian day number, and on studies on ancient chronology that were soon to be published in the *De emendatione temporum* (Paris, 1583). It's only natural to ask whether Pinelli's collection would have been without a portrait of one of the most learned men of the time, who excelled in ancient literature and the medical, mathematical, and astronomical sciences, and whether this may, in fact, be that portrait.
Sofia Magnaguagno

Cat. 75

Leandro dal Ponte, called Bassano (1557–1622)

Portrait of Prospero Alpini

1585, most likely 1594 reworked by the artist
Canvas; 107.8 × 85 cm
Staatsgalerie Stuttgart, inv. 143

Provenance: 1852 acquired with the Barbini-Breganze Collection, Venice
Literature: Morgagni 1763, 7–8; Verci 1775, 188; Zanotto 1850, 68, 173; mus. cat. Stuttgart 1907, 177, no. 471 Ma.; Ongaro 1961/62–1962/63; exh. cat. Stuttgart 1982/83, 10–12, cat. 1 (Gerhard Ewald); Gamba 1984; Ongaro and Gamba 1994/95; exh. cat. Crema 1999, 68–71 (Livia Alberton Vinco da Sesso)

Numerous portraits of important scholars and dignitaries by Leandro Bassano have been preserved. Ridolfi stressed the painter's importance as an outstanding portraitist (Ridolfi 1648, 165). Bassano's portraits are characterised by their sober, unemotional depiction of the sitter – as in this portrait. A decorously dressed, middle-aged man stands behind a diagonally positioned table before a dark background. He regards us with a calm, confident gaze. Only an armillary sphere and three books hint at his profession. The titles of two books are visible; these provide information about his identity. It is the physician and botanist Prospero Alpini.

A 1732 letter from Giovanni Battista Morgagni to Hieronymus David Gaub is a key source for the provenance, authorship, and dating of the painting (Morgagni 1763). It quotes a Latin inscription (which has not been preserved) on the back of the painting (mus. cat. Stuttgart 1907, 177, no. 471 Ma.). This stated that Leandro Bassano painted a portrait of the 41-year-old Alpini in February 1586, immediately after the scientist's return from Egypt. Morgagni correctly notes that, at the time, Alpini was actually ten years younger. The inscription contains a further error. Alpini was born in 1553, so the painting must have been completed in 1584 – not 1586. Since until 1797 the year in Venice began on 1 March, the portrait must be dated to the year 1585. At that time, however, Alpini had not yet published any of the writings depicted in the painting. Infrared reflectography carried out in October 2024 clarified this discrepancy. It showed that there was originally only one book leaning on the lower volume. On it could be read 'HERE.FRACANTORIUS'. This refers to the famous Italian physician and polymath Girolamo Fracastoro, who was clearly an important role model for Alpini. The size of the book was enlarged later to provide enough space for the long title *De medicina Aegyptiorum*; the second book with the title *De plantis Aegypti* (cat. 76) was also added. Macroscopic examinations have shown that the tablecloth, which is now red, was originally a light beige colour.

On the basis of the new findings (presented here in very abbreviated form), it can be concluded that Bassano completed the painting in February 1585 and modified it a few years later. This probably occurred in connection with Alpini's appointment as professor of herbal medicine and pharmacy at the University of Padua on 19 April 1594. The new chair holder proudly presents

his writings published in 1591 and 1592. In this context, the red colour of the tablecloth is to be interpreted as a token of dignity and an affirmation of his newly acquired academic and social status.
CHRISTINE FOLLMANN

Cat. 76

Prospero Alpini (1553–1616/17)

De plantis Aegypti liber

Padua (Typis Pauli Frambotti Bibliopolæ) 1640, 4°
Vienna, Austrian National Library, Department of Manuscripts and Rare Books, BE.4.O.31 Alt Prunk, 111

Literature: Ongaro 1961/62–1962/63; Tongiorgi Tomasi and Willis 2009, 95–9; Ongaro 2016

In 1580, two years after graduating in philosophy and medicine from Padua University, Prospero Alpini left for Egypt, as personal physician to the nobleman Giorgio Emo, who had been appointed Venetian consul in Cairo. During the three years he spent in Egypt, Alpini intensively studied nature and local medical practices. After returning home, he worked as a professional physician for several years in various places, among them Bassano, where he also treated members of the Dal Ponte family of famous painters. In 1594, he was appointed chair of what we could now call pharmacological botany (*Lectura simplicium*) at Padua University. In 1603, he was also appointed prefect of the city's botanical garden. Such prestigious positions were entrusted to him not only because of the fame he had acquired as a physician, but also thanks to the books he had begun to publish. These were mainly the result of the naturalist and medical (and also ethnographic, historical, and archaeological) observations he had made in Egypt. *De medicina Aegyptiorum libri quatuor* (in which, among other things, the scarification of the legs by Egyptian physicians is described, accompanied by a picture) and *De balsamo dialogus* were both published in 1591; *De plantis Aegypti liber* in 1592. After these came other medical works, while *De plantis exoticis Libri Duo* (1627) and *Rerum Aegyptiarum Libri Quatuor* (1735) were published posthumously.

The posthumous 1640 edition of *De plantis Aegypti liber*, edited and expanded by Johannes Wesling, is displayed in this exhibition. It describes numerous plants, 'in particular trees and shrubs, wild or cultivated, most widely used in Egyptian medical treatments' ('in particolare alberi e arbusti, spontanei o coltivati, di più largo uso nella terapeutica egiziana'). These include banana, papyrus, tamarind, and *Coffea arabica*, whose seeds were used to make coffee, a drink that Alpini says was widespread in Egypt under the name 'Caova' and whose curative properties he praised. The work is furnished with 49 woodcuts; we know that at least one of these, depicting balsam, was taken from a drawing made by Joachim Jungermann, nephew of the great Nuremberg physician and naturalist Joachim Camerarius II.
GIUSEPPE OLMI, LUCIA TONGIORGI TOMASI

Cat. 77

Leandro dal Ponte, called Bassano (1557–1622)

Portrait of a Man

c.1610
Canvas; 100 × 83 cm
Milan, Pinacoteca del Castello Sforzesco, inv. PIN 7

Provenance: Camillo Tanzi
Literature: Mus. cat. Milan 1915, 8; Berenson 1932, 61; Arslan 1960, I, 354; mus. cat. Milan 1987, 117, no. 179 (Maria Teresa Fiorio & Mercedes Garberi); mus. cat. Milan 1998, 52 (Valerio Guazzoni)

The attribution of this painting to Leandro Bassano dates from 1932, when Bernard Berenson removed it from the generic Venetian School label under which it had gone into Milan's civic collections and included it in a list of works by the Bassano del Grappa painter. Although Arslan favoured Francesco Bassano's circle, Fiorio and Garberi and, finally, Guazzoni, expressed their preference for Leandro.

A bearded man of about thirty in a black gown is portrayed in a room without any marked architectural or decorative connotations, but a beam of light from the left reveals the presence of a window. The neutral background allows concentration on the figure, captured half-length with slight foreshortening, dressed in a waisted tunic. The soft, wide collar of the white shirt, in vogue between the end of the sixteenth and the early seventeenth century, mediates the change of brightness between the face and the tunic. The subject's warm gaze leads our attention to the majolica vase on which he rests his right hand, placed on a small table. A bouquet of flowers, among which a stem of double mallows can be distinguished, is casually arranged in the vase without any attention paid to the aesthetic effect, as if just picked from the garden. Attempts to decipher the Gothic characters painted on the bowl of the vase are inevitable, but they cannot be related to any meaningful words. The eloquent presence of the flowers, particularly the mallow, very realistically depicted and very common in gardens, especially the double variety like the one portrayed, suggests we should identify the figure as the owner of a garden and a botanist. Or, considering the proven benefits of mallow for the intestines and its anti-inflammatory properties, as a physician or pharmacist, professions to which the type of vase decoration could also allude.

This portrait seems close to that of Alvise Corradini (Musei Civici, Padua) in its composition and style of dress. It is distinguished by a less graphic and softer touch, compatible with a dating to around the first years of the seventeenth century. The calibrated colouring that accentuates the figure's intellect and character closely matches the celebrated talent of Leandro Bassano, a portraitist sought after not only by rulers and powerful men, but especially by scholars and intellectuals who frequented Padua University.
FRANCESCA DEL TORRE SCHEUCH

Cat. 78

Pietro Antonio Michiel (1510–1576)

I cinque libri di piante. Libro Azzurro

16th cent.
Paper; 315 × 230 mm
Venice, Biblioteca Nazionale Marciana, It. II, 30 (=4864), pl. 116

Provenance: Pietro Antonio Michiel; in the possession of the Michiel family since 1576; Giovanni Marsili, 18th cent.; Giuseppe Antonio Bonato; in the Biblioteca Marciana in Venice since 1796
Literature: De Toni 1940; Minelli 2010; Mason and Pardo Tomás 2020

The sixteenth century (the first century of the modern age) was distinguished by widespread enthusiasm for *materia medica* – the therapeutic properties of the three natural kingdoms – not only among physicians and apothecaries, but also laymen, thanks to the burgeoning printing industry. Numerous fifteenth- and sixteenth-century herbals, held in libraries in both manuscript and printed form, document the transmission and gradual enrichment of knowledge inherited from antiquity and the Middle Ages concerning the medicinal properties of these plants and herbs. But above all they explain the explosion of interest in the natural world, of which there was (and still is) much to be discovered.

At the same time as the first botanical gardens were opened at public request for the purpose of teaching *materia medica* to medical students (in Pisa and Padua, in 1543–44), many individuals created their own botanical gardens. Even in Venice, despite the salty lagoon waters not favouring cultivation, several people who owned plots of land attempted to grow plants and trees, both known and unknown varieties. The nobleman Pietro Antonio Michiel was typical: a modest and enthusiastic amateur naturalist, he often made botanical expeditions in the lands occupied by the Republic of Venice (La Serenissima), while diplomat and traveller friends sent him rare plants from the New World, northern Europe, and the Far East. Rich only in children, as he described himself in his unpublished will, Michiel studied plants in books and especially by direct observation: he tried to get many to take root in his own garden at San Trovaso in Venice, to better study their morphological characteristics and medicinal or toxic properties.

While he was cultivating his garden – which, according to his contemporaries, was one of the most beautiful and richest in botanical varieties in the lagoon area – Michiel was also compiling an illustrated herbal in five volumes. In it, he personally described 1,028 plant species, most of which were portrayed by the painter Domenico dalle Greche. Each plant is illustrated on the front of a page, followed on the back by its description arranged under a series of headings (names by which it is known, place of origin, morphology, reproduction, sources and opinions, medicinal virtues). The manuscript herbal was itself a means of investigation, with which Michiel managed to identify at least 150 plant species, either before or better than other contemporary botanists.

The fruit tree 'Cua muchel' shown here is one of eleven American plants that Michiel could only have copied from illustrations made in Mexico by indigenous painters. His friend Antonio Da Mula, the Venetian ambassador to the Spanish court, provided him with drawings from which to make a copy for his own herbal. The depictions – populated with lepidoptera, other insects, and birds – are magnificent, though in some cases invented. It was only in 2020 that the 'Cua muchel' was identified as guamúchil, or *Pithecellobium* Mart., a robust, leafy, perennial shrub belonging to the legume or bean family (Leguminosae), which reaches a height of twenty metres and produces edible pods.

Sabrina Minuzzi

Cat. 79

Giacomo Antonio Cortuso (1513–1603)

L'Horto de i semplici di Padova

Venice (Girolamo Porro) 1591
Venice, Biblioteca Nazionale Marciana, 168.D.221, pl. 16-2r

Literature: Azzi Visentini 1984; Azzi Visentini 1986; Minelli 1995

In 1533, a rather important new addition was made to the courses available at Padua University and, more specifically, the field of medical studies. Francesco Bonafede, until then a lecturer in practical medicine, received, partly at the explicit request of his students, the new chair of 'reading medicinal matter' (*lettura della materia Medicinale*); this consisted of illustrating the plants, animals, and minerals that could be advantageously used in medical treatments. The establishment of such a position, like the similar one assigned to Ulisse Aldrovandi at Bologna University in 1561, marked the first recognition of natural history as a separate discipline, although the links to medicine continued to be quite strong. Some years later, with the support of other lecturers and the students, Bonafede requested that the university set up a botanical garden, in connection with his teaching, so that theoretical lessons could be followed by direct observation of the plants. It was finally decided to construct this garden in 1545 by senatorial decree. Giacomo Antonio Cortuso, who worked with the most important naturalists of the time, was the garden's third director, from 1590 to 1603. He probably drew the work shown here, comprising a circular plan of the garden with its four square central beds (*spaldi*), which contained 576 smaller beds (*areole*), and, finally, an index of all the plants cultivated in the garden in the year 1591. It also contains boxes, corresponding in number to the *areole*, ready to be completed by the students with the names of the plants seen at the time of their visit.

Giuseppe Olmi, Lucia Tongiorgi Tomasi

Cat. 80

Benedetto Ceruti (?–1620), Andrea Chiocco (1562–1624)

Musaeum Franc. Calceolari Iun. Veronensis

Verona (Angelus Tamus) 1622, 4°
Vienna, Austrian National Library, Department of Manuscripts and Rare Books, BE.11.J.26 Alt Prunk, folding plate

Literature: Tergolina Gislanzoni Brasco 1934; Franchini et al. 1979; Fahy 1993; Olmi 2007

Francesco Calzolari owned an apothecary's shop in the centre of Verona. His skill in the preparation of medicines and his deep knowledge of nature, especially plants, acquired mainly 'in the field', earned him great renown among scholars of the time (many of whom established working relations with him) and the gratitude of illustrious people, including the duke of Mantua, Vincenzo Gonzaga. Calzolari set up a museum above his shop that presented some of the typical encyclopaedic peculiarities of the time, but was focused on naturalist research and the practices of the pharmaceutical profession. A catalogue of the museum, described by Ulisse Aldrovandi as an 'ocean of nature', was published by the physician Giovanni Battista Olivi in 1584, and reprinted in 1593. When Calzolari died, the museum (and the apothecary's shop) passed into the hands of his nephew, also called Francesco, who further enriched it with new finds. He promoted the publication of a new catalogue in 1622 – richer in information and more sumptuous – engaging the physician Benedetto Ceruti to write it and, after his death, another physician, Andrea Chiocco, to complete it. The 800-page book contains 44 engravings, which illustrate some of the finds in the collection. It opens with an illustration printed on different paper than the rest of the edition (and thus conceived to be also circulated separately), offering a panoramic view, probably idealized, of the museum. The plate is the only one on which its authors are named: the designer Giovanni Battista Bertoni and the engraver Girolamo Viscardi.

Giuseppe Olmi, Lucia Tongiorgi Tomasi

Nature Studies Between Prague and Florence

(cats. 81–87)

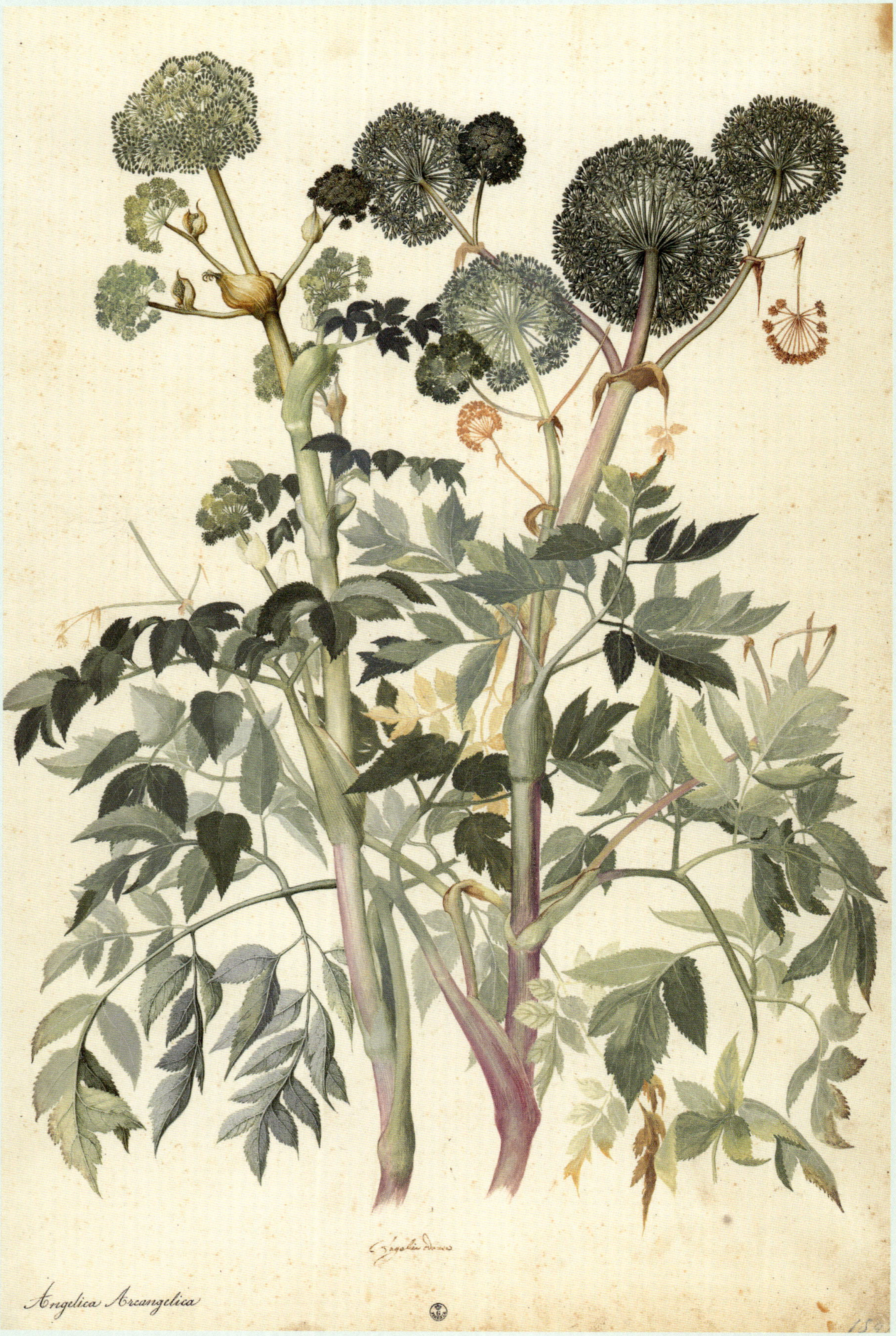

Cat. 81, Jacopo Ligozzi, *Angelica (Angelica arcangelica)*

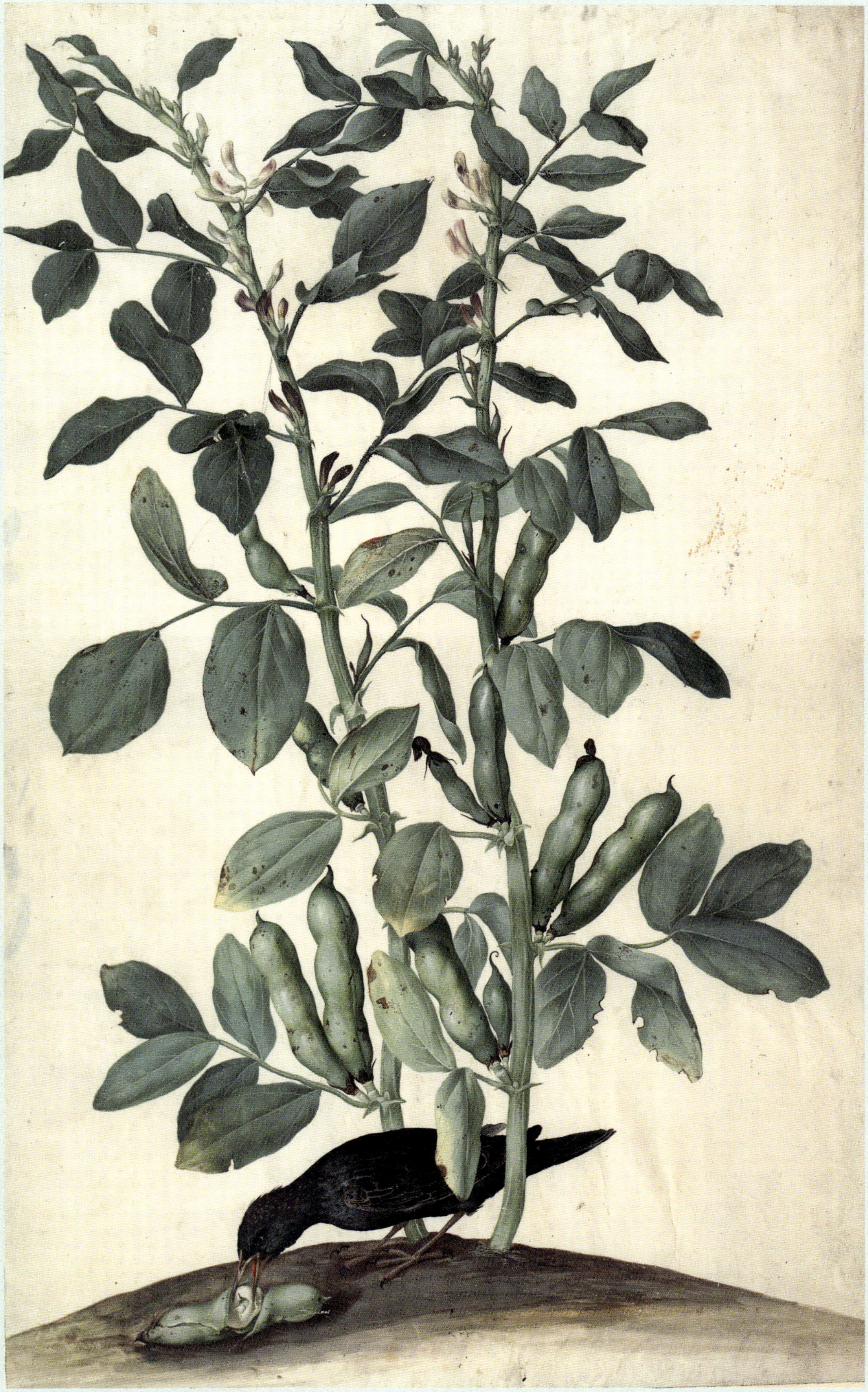

Cat. 82, Francesco and Jacopo Ligozzi, *Two Broad Bean Plants and a Bird*

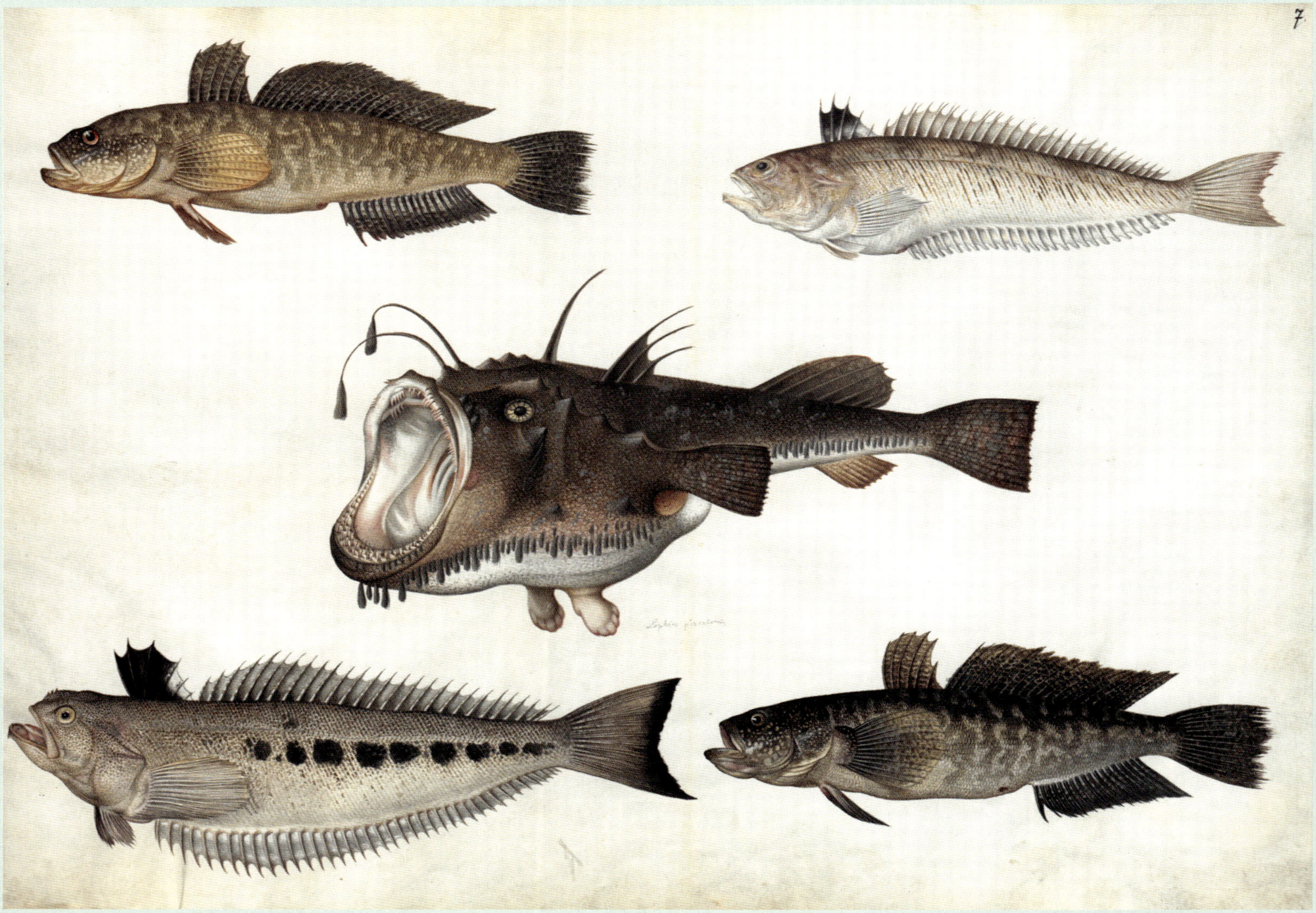

Cat. 83, Jacopo Ligozzi, *Anglerfish, Two Gobies, and Two Weever Fish*

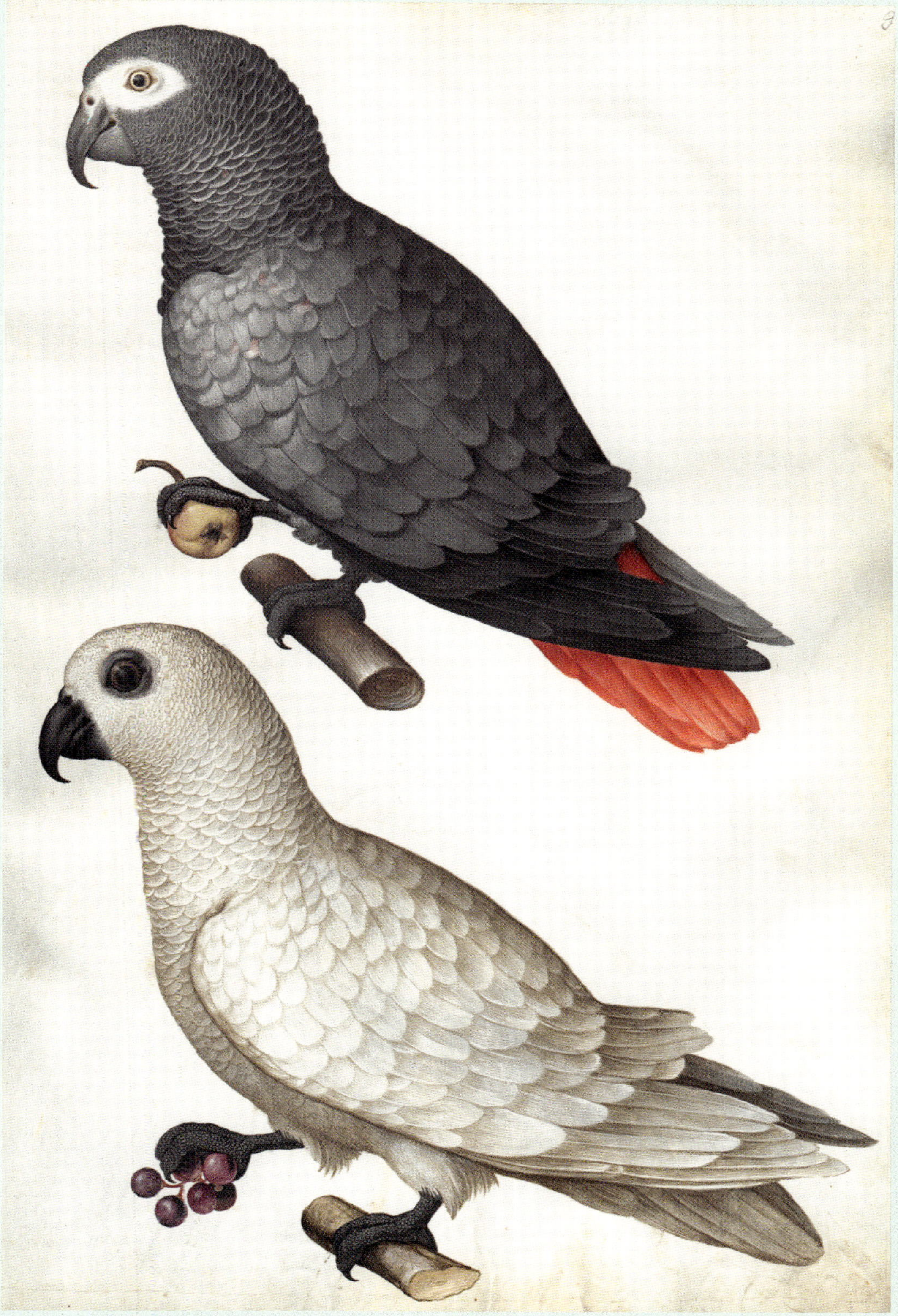

Cat. 84, Francesco and Jacopo Ligozzi, *Grey Parrot and Albinotic Grey Parrot (Psittacus erithacus)*

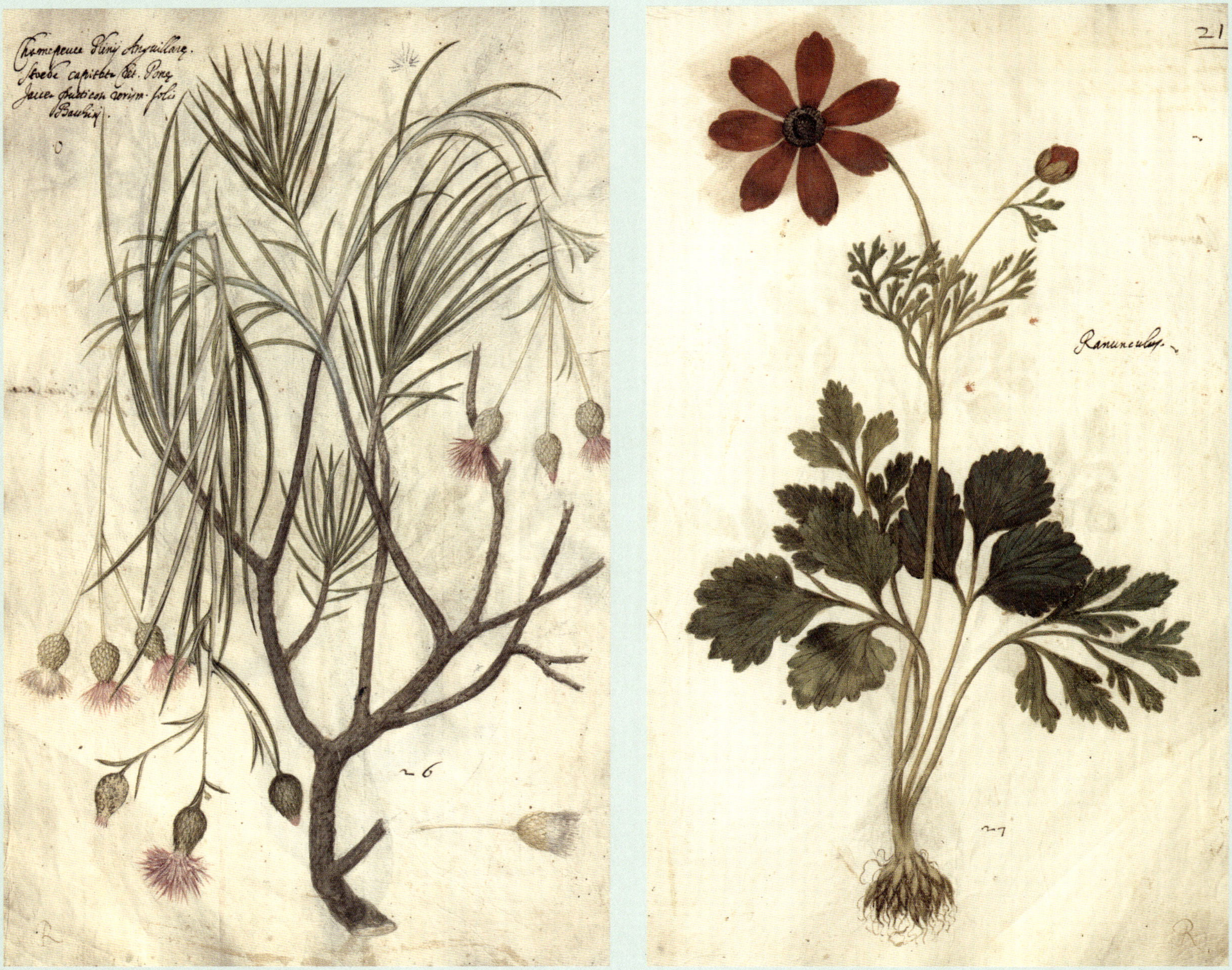

Cat. 85, Georg Dyckman, *Ptilostemon Casabonae and Ranunculus creticus*

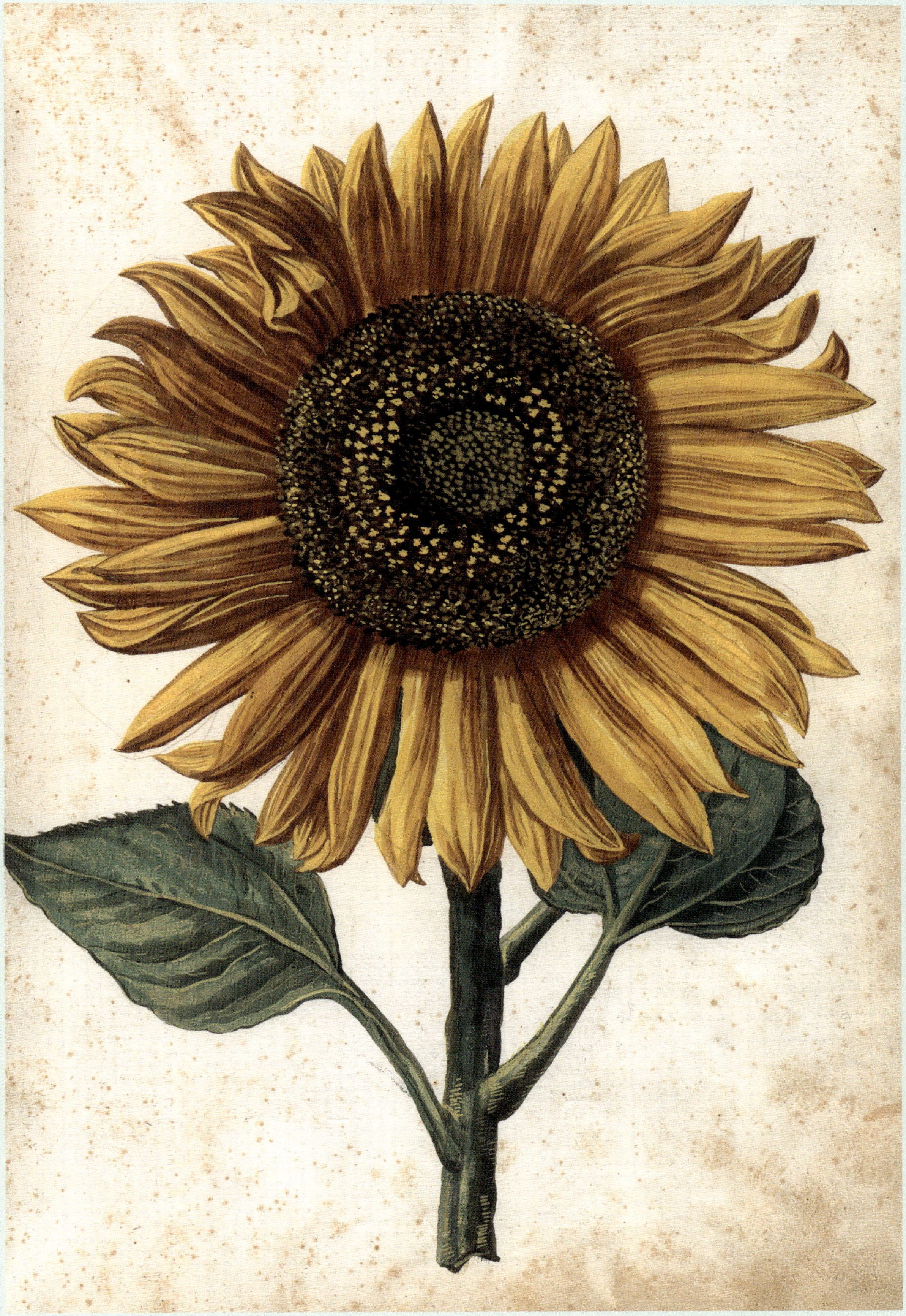

Cat. 86, Daniel Fröschl, *Sunflower (Helianthus annuus)*

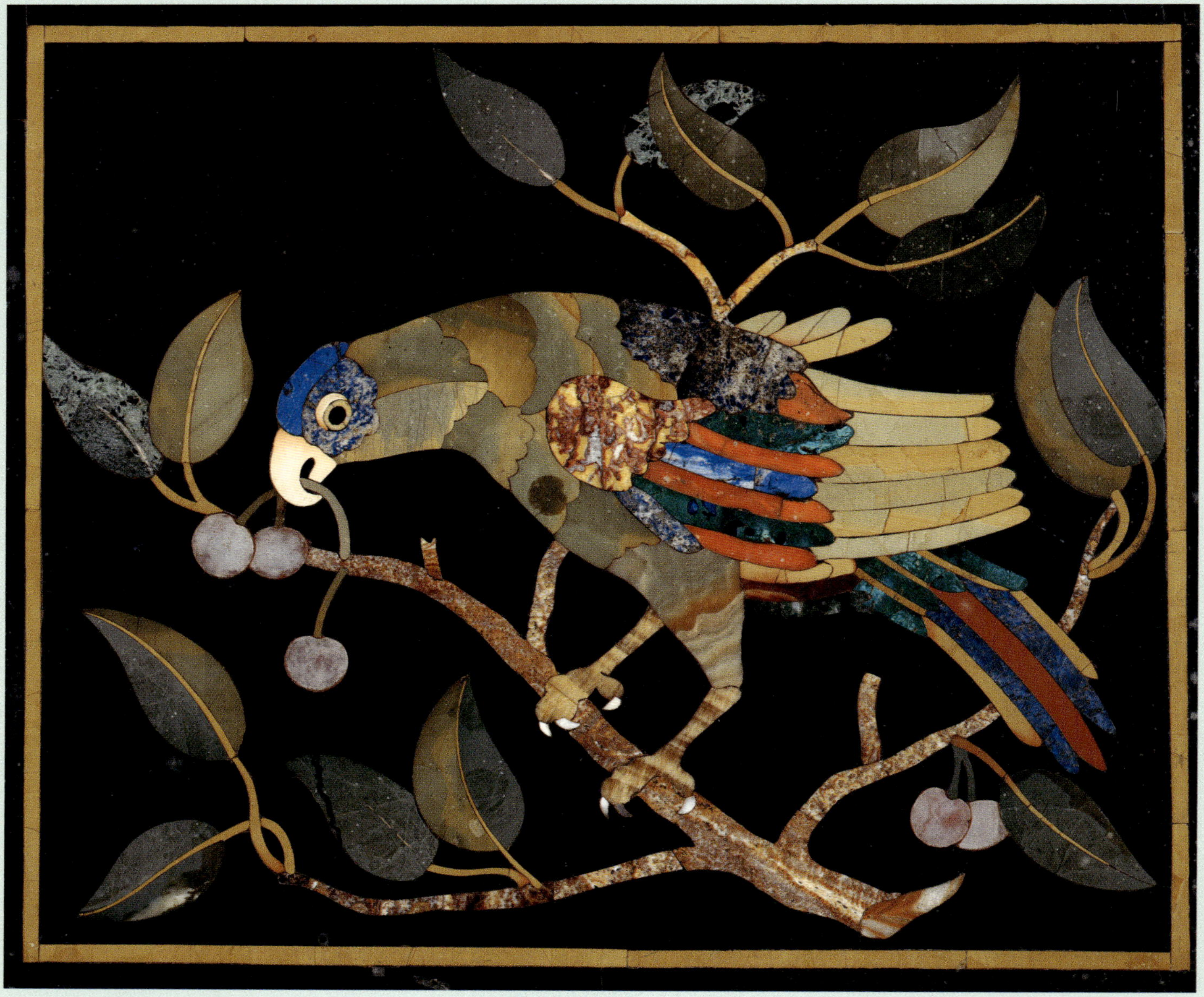

Cat. 87, *Parrot*

Cat. 81

Jacopo Ligozzi (c.1547–1627)

Angelica (Angelica arcangelica)

c.1583
Tempera on paper; 680 × 460 mm
Florence, Galleria degli Uffizi, GDS Ornato, n. 1897

Provenance: Fondo Mediceo
Literature: Exh. cat. Florence 1961, 25; Tongiorgi Tomasi 1993 (pl. and cat, n.n.); Tosi 1989, 278

This tempera is part of the collection of large botanical and zoological plates painted by the Veronese artist Jacopo Ligozzi in Florence, starting in 1577. This was on the instruction of Francesco I de' Medici, who had assigned him a studio in Casino di San Marco, defined as the 'house of nature' by the Bolognese scientist Ulisse Aldrovandi. It was here, facing the Giardino dei Semplici, that Aldrovandi himself, accompanied by the grand duke, was able to admire the work of the 'new Apelles' and ventured to ask for some copies of his works for his own collection.

The talent and sensitivity expressed in this substantial corpus of highly formal, scientific iconography suggests that Ligozzi was already known as a skilled painter of naturalist subjects and had been called to the Tuscan grand duchy precisely because of his expertise in this area.

Portraying the plant *ad vivum*, the artist depicts this impressive plant over the entire surface of the sheet, precisely reproducing its sturdy, branched stem marked by reddish veins, with lighter green leaves in the lower part of the sheet, and yellow-greenish flowers arranged in umbels and presented in various stages of flower. He also depicted with great accuracy the close tangle of stems and the downward curve of the heavy flowerheads.

A list of plant essences attached to a letter of 26 April 1583 from Aldrovandi to Francesco I, in which 'Angelica flo[re]albo' is mentioned, could perhaps suggest the date of the tempera. Unknown to Greek and Roman physicians, angelica was considered a 'divine' plant in the Middle Ages because it was related to a legend about the archangel Raphael. Widely used for its sedative and expectorant medicinal properties, it was also the object of an extensive commentary by Pietro Andrea Mattioli, who describes two varieties of it in his *Discorsi* (also known as *Commentarii,* see cat. 20): 'Angelica selvatica' (a smaller version) and 'Angelica domestica'. He also states that 'according to the opinion of modern physicians... [it is] appetizer, desiccant, resolutive... of use... against poisons [and] good... for protection against plague' (Venice, Valgrisi 1568, 1229–30). Mattioli offers fine images of the two varieties with roots, certainly taken from the drawing by Giorgio Liberale of Udine translated into an engraving by the German Wolfgang Meyerpeck.

Giuseppe Olmi, Lucia Tongiorgi Tomasi

Cat. 82

Francesco and Jacopo Ligozzi (c.1547–1627), attributed

Two Broad Bean Plants and a Bird

c.1600
Tempera on parchment; 617 × 387 mm
Inscribed on bottom left; 'War in dem Cod. Min. 83. auf dem Deckel aufgeklebt'
Vienna, Albertina, inv. 25163

Provenance: Vienna, Hofbibliothek, Cod. Min. 81.2; 1920/21 to the Albertina
Literature: Unterkircher 1959, 133; Da Costa Kaufmann 1985, 144; Conigliello 1991; exh. cat. Vienna 2011/12, 194–9

The inscription at bottom left alludes to the collecting history and provenance of this sheet, which originally decorated the cover of the Cod. Min. 83 now held in the Austrian National Library.

This is a broad bean plant (*Vicia faba*) emerging from the ground, whose erect stem, transparent, vivid green leaves (though some appear yellowed or damaged by insect attack), rosy flowers sprouting from the leaf axils, and pods in various stages of ripening are all well depicted. Although the medicinal – especially relaxant and sedative – virtues of the legumes have always been known, legend records Pythagoras's aversion to this not easily digested plant. This concept was only partly taken up by Dioscorides, as inferred from the *Discorsi* by Pietro Andrea Mattioli (also known as *Commentarii*, see cat. 20), who dedicated several pages to its properties and the culinary recipes that transformed it, along with two fine engravings, the work of Giorgio Liberale and Wolfgang Meyerpeck (Venice, Valgrisi 1568, 444–8).

Although the accurate depiction from life, the expert use of pigments and the elegance of the plant are in Jacopo's style, the general compositional layout, the association of the plant with a bird, and some less successful details suggest that here the artist worked with one of his relatives, who used to assist him in his illustrations of subjects from nature. It was possibly his brother Francesco, who was able to mimic Jacopo's methods and techniques in depicting plants and animals better than the others.

Sometimes the Verona artist liked to place birds next to plants – see, for example, the imaginative composition of the fig tree on which some birds of paradise are perched (Uffizi, GDS, 1958 Orn); the *Iberis* with partridge (GDS, 1947 Orn); the budgerigar on a plum branch (GDS, 1952 Orn) and the oak branch with some birds (GDS, 1962 Orn), but in this case the association is not entirely harmonious and the depiction of the plant emerging from the ground is uncertain.

The bird, clearly identifiable as a starling – note the elongated, pointed shape of the beak, the lustrous metallic effects of the plumage and, especially, the dappled feathers of the head – is vividly naturalistic and finely executed, as is the bean pod whose whose textural consistency is perceived, torn by the hungry bird in search of its juicy seeds.

Giuseppe Olmi, Lucia Tongiorgi Tomasi

Cat. 83

Jacopo Ligozzi (c.1547–1627)

Anglerfish, Two Gobies, and Two Weever Fish

1590/1610
Tempera on paper; 600 × 815 mm
Vienna, Austrian National Library,
Department of Manuscripts and Rare Books,
Cod. Min. 83, fol. 7

Provenance: Kunstkammer of Emperor Rudolf II. in Prague; in the Imperial Treasury in Vienna, after 1612; transferred to the Court Library in 1783
Literature: Conigliello 1991; Hendrix 1997, 150–71; exh. cat. Vienna 1988/89, 135–8; Tongiorgi Tomasi 2014, 12

Like the parallel manuscript 131 (cat. 84) with images of birds, this one with marine organisms held in the *Wunderkammer* of Emperor Rudolf II was also presented in the Viennese *Prague Around 1600* exhibition (Kunsthistorisches Museum, 1988) as a work by Jacopo Ligozzi; an attribution confirmed by its high stylistic quality. The codex contains twenty plates depicting numerous Mediterranean species, along with an exotic lizard – a monitor, initially mistakenly identified as an iguana. Two plates feature crustaceans (fols. 2, 3) and three individual fish (fols. 6, 12, 20); various species are portrayed in harmonious compositions in the other plates.

Folio 7 is particularly fascinating. The focus is on the centre where there is an anglerfish (*Lophius piscatorius*) with gaping jaws, accompanied by two gobies (*Gobius sp.*) at top left and bottom right, and two weever fish: a greater weever (*Trachinus drago*) at top right and a spotted weever (*Trachinus araneus*) at bottom left.

This extraordinary series of fish was probably painted by Jacopo Ligozzi *ad vivum* in the Serenissima before 1577, when he went to the Medici court in Florence, where he settled and continued to paint fish specimens, usually one per plate. Some copies of these were sent to Ulisse Aldrovandi in Bologna.

Fish iconography was very popular throughout Europe from the mid-sixteenth century, circulated in printed works by Conrad Gessner, Guillaume Rondelet, Pierre Belon, Ippolito Salviani, and Ulisse Aldrovandi. Historical sources show that painters specializing in fish images were particularly appreciated in Veneto; indeed, a large number of marine species could be observed in the port and markets of Venice. These were much sought after by collectors and naturalists, who ordered reproductions of them for their studies. One extraordinary example is provided by the 100 tempera paintings of life-size fish that Archduke Ferdinand of Tyrol kept in his *Wunderkammer* (Vienna, Austrian National Library, Cod. Min. 2669), produced by the Udine painter-engraver Giorgio Liberale, who was also an active associate of Pietro Andrea Mattioli (cat. 20).
Giuseppe Olmi, Lucia Tongiorgi Tomasi

Cat. 84

Francesco and Jacopo Ligozzi (c.1547–1627), attributed

Grey Parrot and Albinotic Grey Parrot (Psittacus erithacus)

1600/11
Tempera on paper; 600 × 500 mm
Vienna, Austrian National Library, Department of Manuscripts and Rare Books, Cod. Min. 131, fol. 9

Provenance: Kunstkammer of Emperor Rudolf II in Prague; after 1612 in the Imperial Treasury in Vienna; transferred to the Imperial Fideicommiss Library (no. 6383) after 1785; in 1926 part of the Cimelia Palatina Collection of the National Library (C.P. 2.A.13); in 1978 transferred to the Manuscript Collection
Literature: Hendrix 1997, 150–71; exh. cat. Vienna 1988/89, 135–8; Conigliello 2014; Tongiorgi Tomasi 2014, 12

Attention was drawn to this extraordinary codex containing 52 folios with 134 images of birds (and to the parallel codex 83 with images of marine organisms; see cat. 83) by the *Prague Around 1600* exhibition at Kunsthistorisches Museum in 1988. There, on the basis of an inventory drawn up by Daniel Fröschl in 1607–11, the illustrations were attributed to Jacopo Ligozzi, a renowned naturalist painter in Medici Florence between the sixteenth and seventeenth centuries. The two manuscripts were part of Emperor Rudolf II's outstanding collection of images of the natural world.

Although the lack of further information on the two codices makes it difficult to reconstruct their history and provenance (the artist's temporary presence in the Habsburg sphere has been suggested), their aesthetic quality is undeniable, as is a clear affinity with the 'miniaturist' style and technique of the Veronese artist. However, in the light of Ligozzi's overall production, this ornithological collection does not seem entirely his, being only partly ascribable to his youthful brushes and, more likely, those of his close 'family-associates', particularly his brother Francesco.

The 'miniated' birds (often a male example is accompanied by the female) are portrayed *ad vivum* with an extraordinary accuracy that reveals the artist's marked naturalist sensitivity to detail, as shown by fol. 9, where a grey parrot stands out with its neck feathers slightly raised in a behaviour typical of the species. The same species is portrayed below, but with a leucistic mutation of the plumage. Both examples (like other birds in the manuscript) grasp small fruit that clearly show their feeding habits and enliven the compositions.

The species portrayed are Italian, suggesting that the work was produced in Italy, probably in Venice, where the young Jacopo and his brother Francesco are known to have stayed: for example, two sparrows (*Passer italiae*) appear at the top of fol. 13, a species not found north of the Alps, where instead there is the house sparrow (*Passer domesticus*). The same plate shows two common linnets (*Linaria cannabina*) and, on the right, a male and female pair of yellowhammers (*Emberiza citrinella*).
Giuseppe Olmi, Lucia Tongiorgi Tomasi

Cat. 85

Georg Dyckman (recorded 1590/91 in Crete)

Ptilostemon Casabonae and Ranunculus creticus

1590/91
Tempera on paper; 440 × 294 mm
Pisa, Biblioteca Universitaria, Ms. 462, *Icones variarum plantarum*, fols. 20v, 21r

Provenance: Historical holdings
Literature: Tongiorgi Tomasi 1980, 570–1; Tongiorgi Tomasi 1984, 61–84; Olmi 1991, 1–31; Tongiorgi Tomasi, Garbari, and Tosi 1991, 39–45; Tongiorgi Tomasi and Garbari 1995; Olmi 2015b; 12–14; exh. cat. Pisa 2024, 38–3

These two temperas are part of a codex containing 35 endemic plants from the island of Crete, for centuries Venice's Mediterranean outpost and traditionally considered a 'botanical paradise', which Giuseppe Casabona (Joseph Goedenhuize), the third director of Pisa's botanical garden, the Orto dei Semplici, commissioned between 1590 and 1591.

A lively report written by the herbalist and sent to his colleague Ulisse Aldrovandi in Bologna has come down to us from the botanical expedition to Crete ordered by Ferdinando I de' Medici, which left Venice on the galley of the nobleman Girolamo Cappello (BUB, MS. Aldrovandi 138, XVIII, fol. 52). There are also numerous letters sent to various European botanists informing them of the discoveries made on the island. Casabona also wrote to the secretary of state, Belisario Vinta, to solicit financial support. In a letter of 1 January 1591, he informs him of 'a wonderful stroke of luck, namely a young German, whom I have arranged to accompany me for the whole of this journey with expenses and a fair price, who paints all the plants from life for me on royal paper and is very skilful in that profession and I hope will do beautiful work and it will be with all his descriptions that I hope to honour your lordship' ('una bellissima ventura cioè un giovane Tudisco il quale ho accordato meco per tutto questo viaggio con le spese et honesto prezzo il quale tutte le piante me depinge in Carta reale al vivo et è assai valente in quella professione et spero farà una bellissima opera et sarà con tutte le sue Descrittioni che spero di far honore a VSS'; Florence, Archivio di Stato, *Guardaroba Mediceo*, 813, fol. 1).

A letter sent to his German colleague Joachim Camerarius also tells us that the 'German painter' (*pittore tudisco*) was not a professional artist, but rather a simple but talented soldier 'whom I keep with me and take around the island, who is rather a good man ... by the name of Georgious Dyckman' ('quale io tengo meco et io lo meno per l'isola, che è assai valenthuomo ... per nome Georgius Dyckman').

Having returned to Pisa to resume his care of the Giardino dei Semplici, Casabona also sent some reproductions of Cretan plants to Aldrovandi and Carolus Clusius, director of Leiden's botanical garden. These were accurate copies of the originals, which were later bound into a volume that was added to the Pisa garden's library.

These copies still exist, held in the Aldrovandi iconographic collections in Bologna and Leiden. The wild plants portrayed in pasty temperas and in great detail (for example, the crumpled leaves, the bent or broken branches, and the fresh roots just taken from the ground) include *Paeonia peregrina*, *Fagonia cretica*, *Euphorbia spinosa* and various examples of red and yellow *Ranunculus asiaticus*. A red ranunculus is portrayed on fol. 21r, while on fol. 20v is a *Ptilostemon chamaepeuce*, a thorny herbaceous plant with rosy corollas, now rightly known as *Ptilostemon casabonae* in honour of the Flemish-Pisan herbalist.

Giuseppe Olmi, Lucia Tongiorgi Tomasi

Cat. 86

Daniel Fröschl (1563–1613)

Sunflower (Helianthus annuus)

End of 16th cent. to 1630
Tempera on paper; 430 × 310 mm
Pisa, Biblioteca Universitaria, Ms. 513Bis, *Codice Casabona*, fol. 45r

Provenance: Giardino dei Semplici di Pisa
Literature: Tongiorgi Tomasi 1988, 289–98; Tongiorgi Tomasi and Garbari 1995; Olmi and Tongiorgi Tomasi 2011, 122

The codex was part of the library at the historic botanical garden in Pisa, as shown by a contemporary loose sheet added to the 1672 inventory, which mentions: 'a big book of illuminated figures by Daniel Frocel in red leather'. The Florentine monk Agostino del Riccio also recalls in his *Agricoltura sperimentale* that the director of the Pisa garden, Giuseppe Casabona, had instructed the Augsburg artist to portray 'all the herbal simples and plants in the Garden on imperial sheets, but that he should paint them when they were flowering, and with their bulbs...' (Florence, Biblioteca Nazionale, Ms. Targioni Tozzetti, 56, 1, c.75v).

This illuminated herbal of 153 folios, bought by the Italian state in 1992 for the Pisa University Library, can be linked to Casabona (whose Flemish surname Goedenhuize was variously translated as 'Casabona' or 'Benincasa') precisely because of the Pisan Benincasa family's coat of arms (though the family had nothing to do with the herbalist) on the boards with red leather bindings. (The boards were made at the start of the seventeenth century.) Further proof comes in the paper, made in neighbouring Lucca, and the fact that it depicts mainly plants with bulbs and roots. The stylistic affinities to numerous plates by Fröschl in manuscripts 513 (*Diverse figure di piante*) and 514 (see cat. 70) are also noteworthy.

Daniel Fröschl worked at the Pisa garden for several months between 1594 and 1595, as deduced from a letter in which Casabona urged the Medici government to honour the payment to 'm. Daniele Fruscel German illuminator already [in] service for a year and a half' ('m. Daniele Fruscel tudisco miniatore già [in] servitio un anno e mezzo'; Florence, Archivio Mediceo, 860, fol. 380). The letter is dated 4 August 1595.

The codex, which documents the plants cultivated in the Pisa garden at the end of the sixteenth century, begins with the image of two rare tulips 'da Bruseles in Fiandra' and continues with numerous bulbous plants, a dragon lily, tobacco, and rattan (the latter is also in the *Libro Verde* of the herbal by Pietro Antonio Michiel).

The folios 45 and 46 are particularly significant, as they present the image of a remarkable sunflower (*Helianthus annuus*), shown front and back. The *Asteracea* from Peru, described for the first time by the Spanish physician Francisco Hernandez, had already been cultivated in Padua's botanical garden in 1568, while one of the first illustrations of the flower was also held in the iconographic collection of Ulisse Aldrovandi (BUB, MS. Aldrovandi, Tavole di piante, fiori e frutti, vol. 1, carta 76).
GIUSEPPE OLMI, LUCIA TONGIORGI TOMASI

Cat. 87

Parrot

Florence (?), 17th cent. (before 1666)
Pietra dura; lapis lazuli, malachite, marble, agate, chalcedony, slate plate, wood; H 37 cm, W 43 cm
Ambras Castle Innsbruck, inv. PA 872

Provenance: 1666 inventory of Ambras Collection
Literature: Exh. cat. Innsbruck and Vienna 2006/07, 168–9, cat. 3.12; exh. cat. Innsbruck 2015, 256–7, cat. 5.16; exh. cat. Innsbruck 2022, 170–1, cat. 113

This mosaic shows a parrot with a blue head sitting on a branch, nibbling on cherries, and looking to the left. Parrots were already known in ancient times, especially small green Indian parakeets. Knowledge of the diversity of the species increased as a result of the voyages of discovery of Christopher Columbus, who brought the first macaw to Europe in 1493. From the second quarter of the sixteenth century onwards, other East Indian parrot species were imported by Portuguese merchant ships. The birds were valued for the impressive colours of their plumage, but also for their ability to imitate the human voice.

Since the survival rate of the birds fluctuated during transport due to improper care and feeding, some people, including Emperor Rudolf II and his uncle, Archduke Ferdinand II, collected stuffed parrots, the skins of other birds, individual feathers, or artistic depictions in the form of paintings, miniatures, and stonework. The specialized mosaic form, which used (semi-) precious stones in the Florentine *pietra dura* technique, developed to a high level of artistry. This special craft received additional support in Prague under Rudolf II. In contrast to classic mosaics, pieces were not cut into cubes but into strips. In this picture, lapis lazuli, malachite, marble, agate, and chalcedony were used. Pietra dura was used in furniture ornamentation, table tops, and murals, with subjects ranging from landscapes and portraits to flora and fauna motifs. The extremely realistic scenes created in the process required a thorough study of nature and precise observation of the human environment. The depiction of a sitting parrot seems to have been one of the most popular subjects. This decorative method showed how man succeeded in getting as close as possible to nature with the help of art and its associated techniques, depicting nature realistically and at the same time staging and deliberately changing it according to human will.
THOMAS KUSTER

Epilogue

(cats. 88–90)

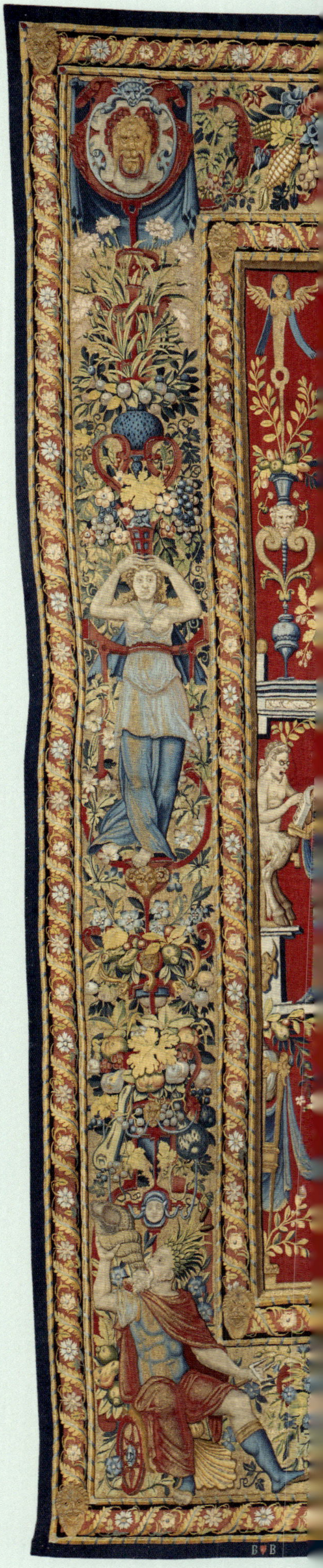

Cat. 88, *June – Mercury with the Sign of Cancer*

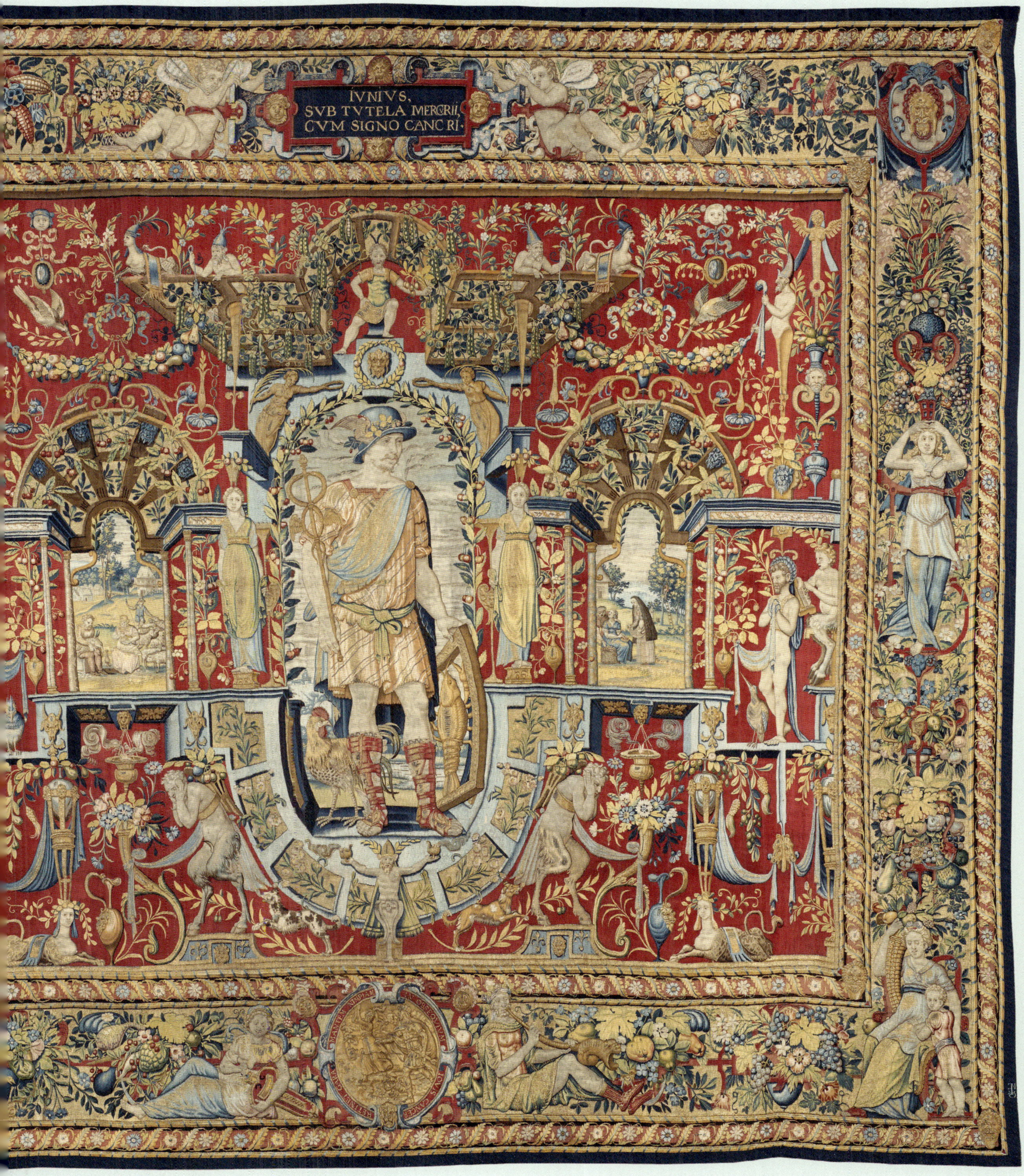
IVNIVS,
SVB TVTELA MERCVRII,
CVM SIGNO CANCRI.

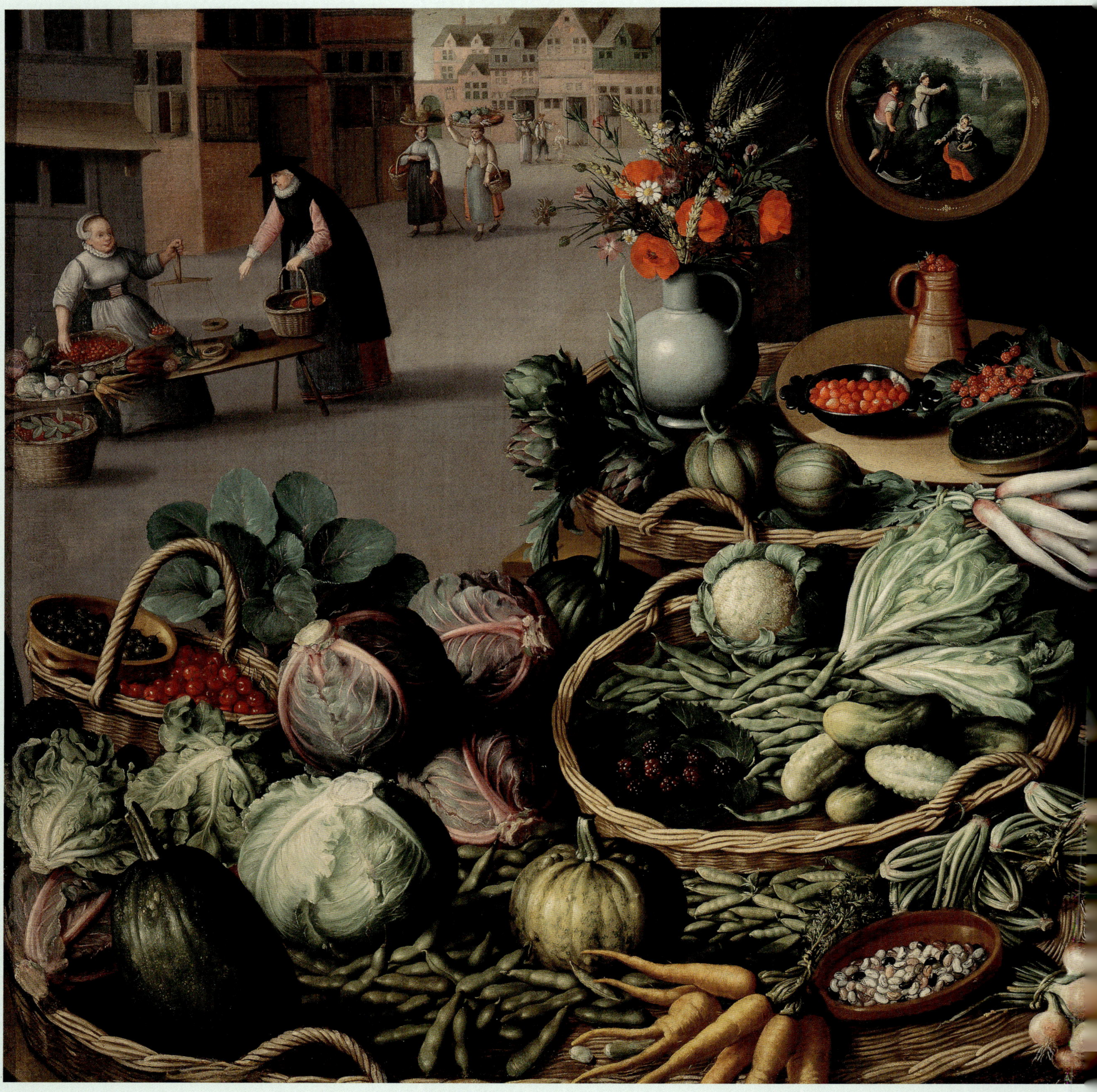

Cat. 89.1, Jan Baptist Saive the Elder, *Vegetable Market (July–August)*

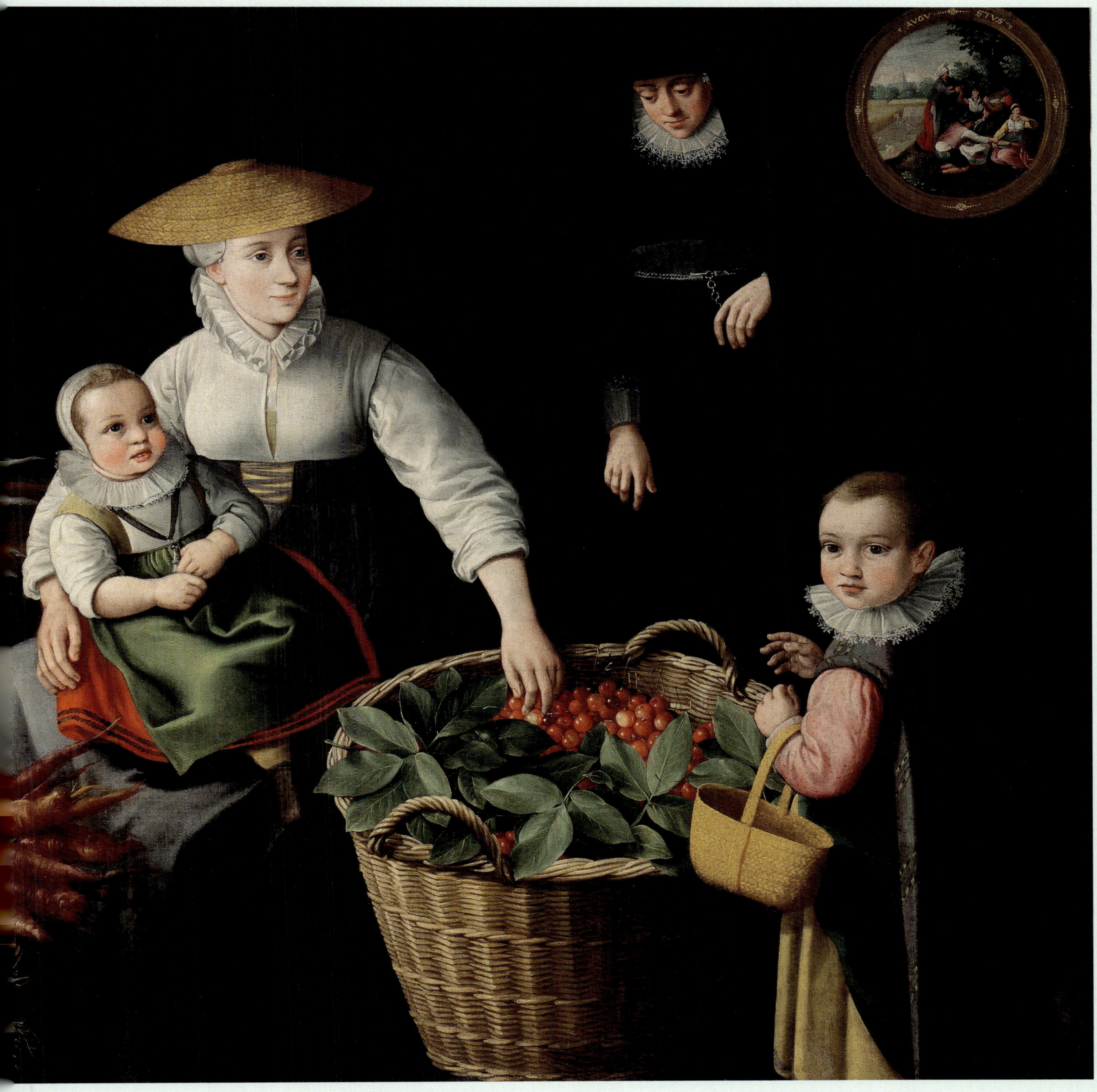

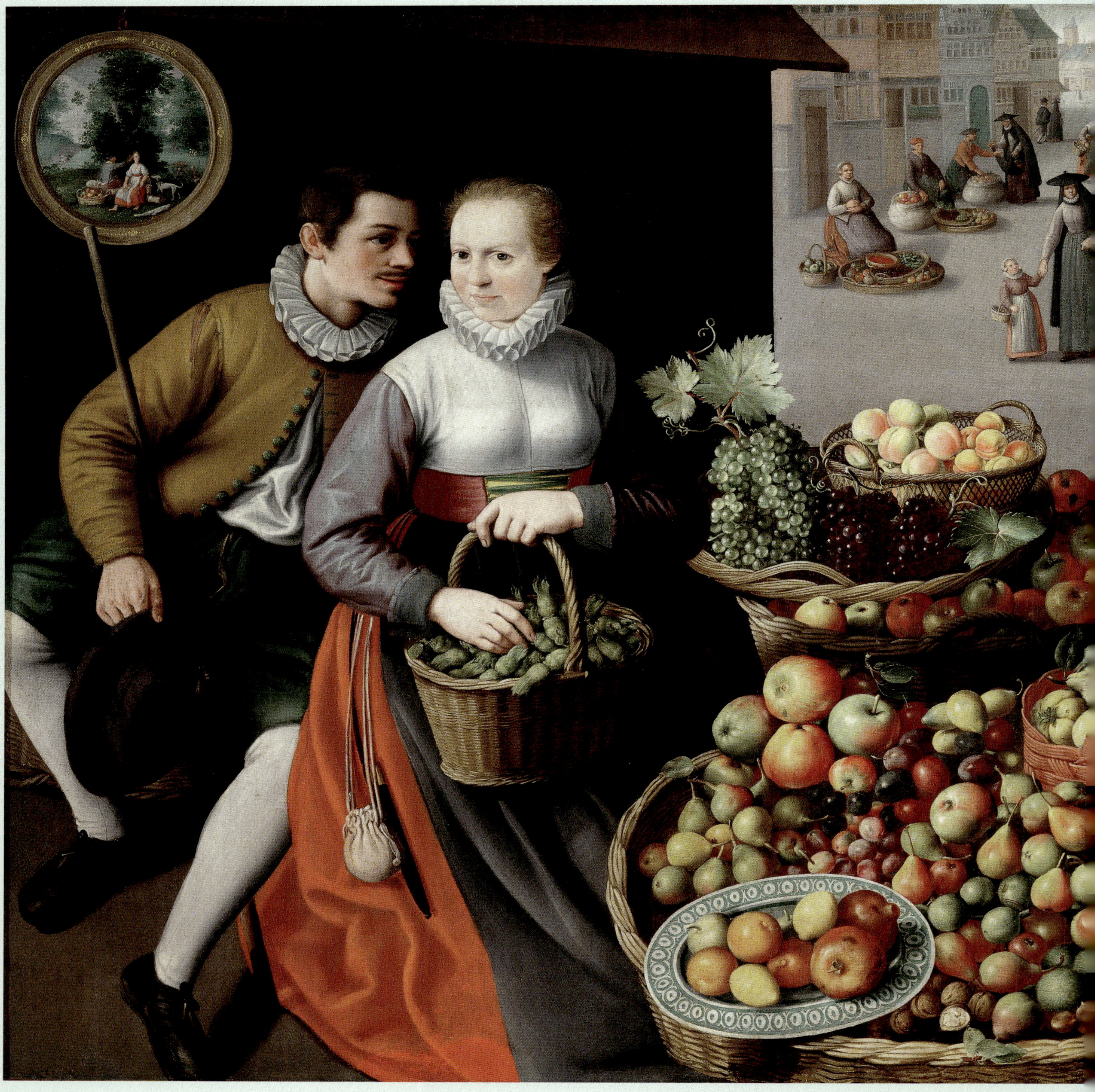

Cat. 89.2, Jan Baptist Saive the Elder, *Fruit Market (September–October)*

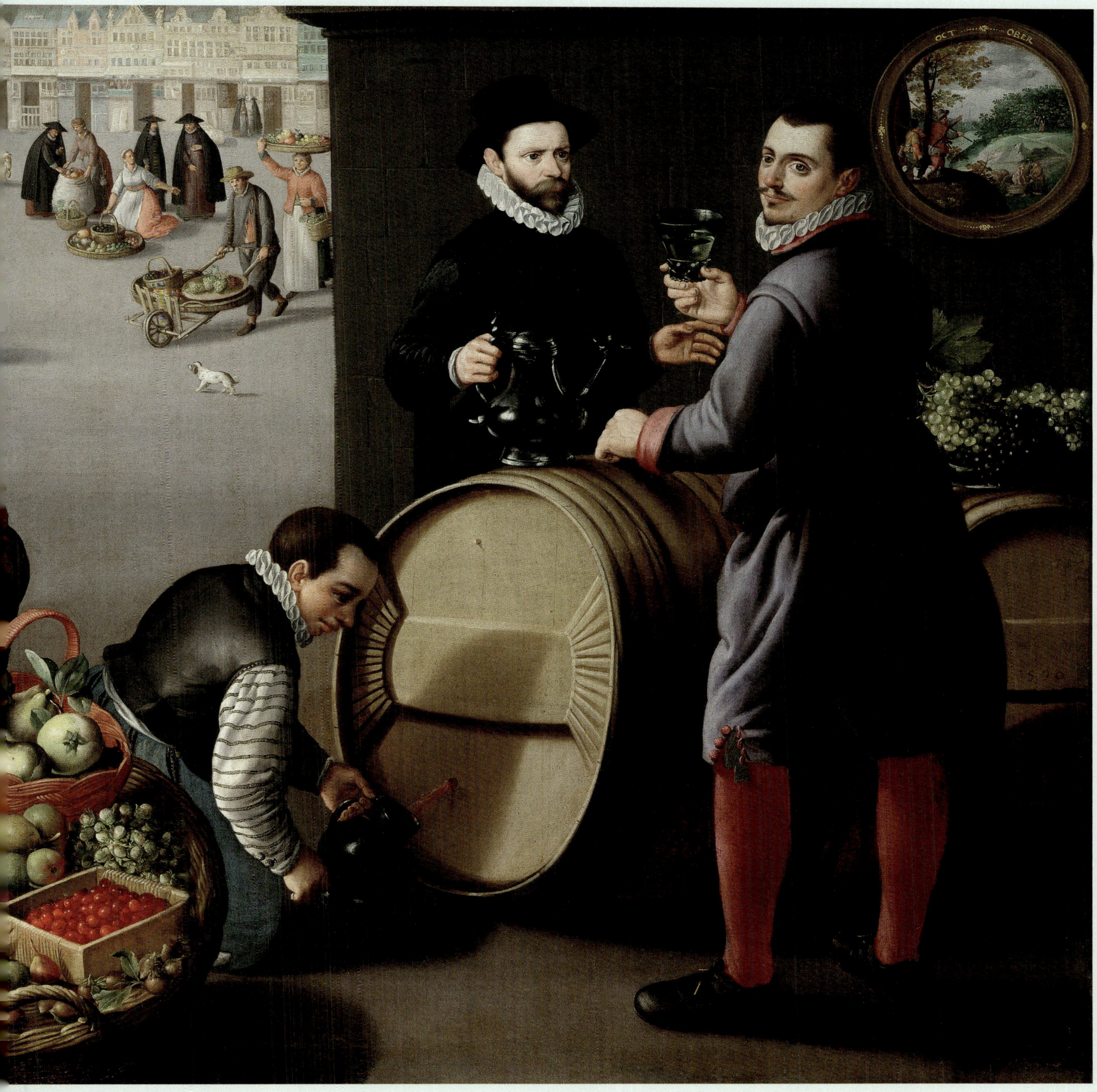
OCT OBER

Cat. 90, Giuseppe Arcimboldo, *Four Seasons in One Head*

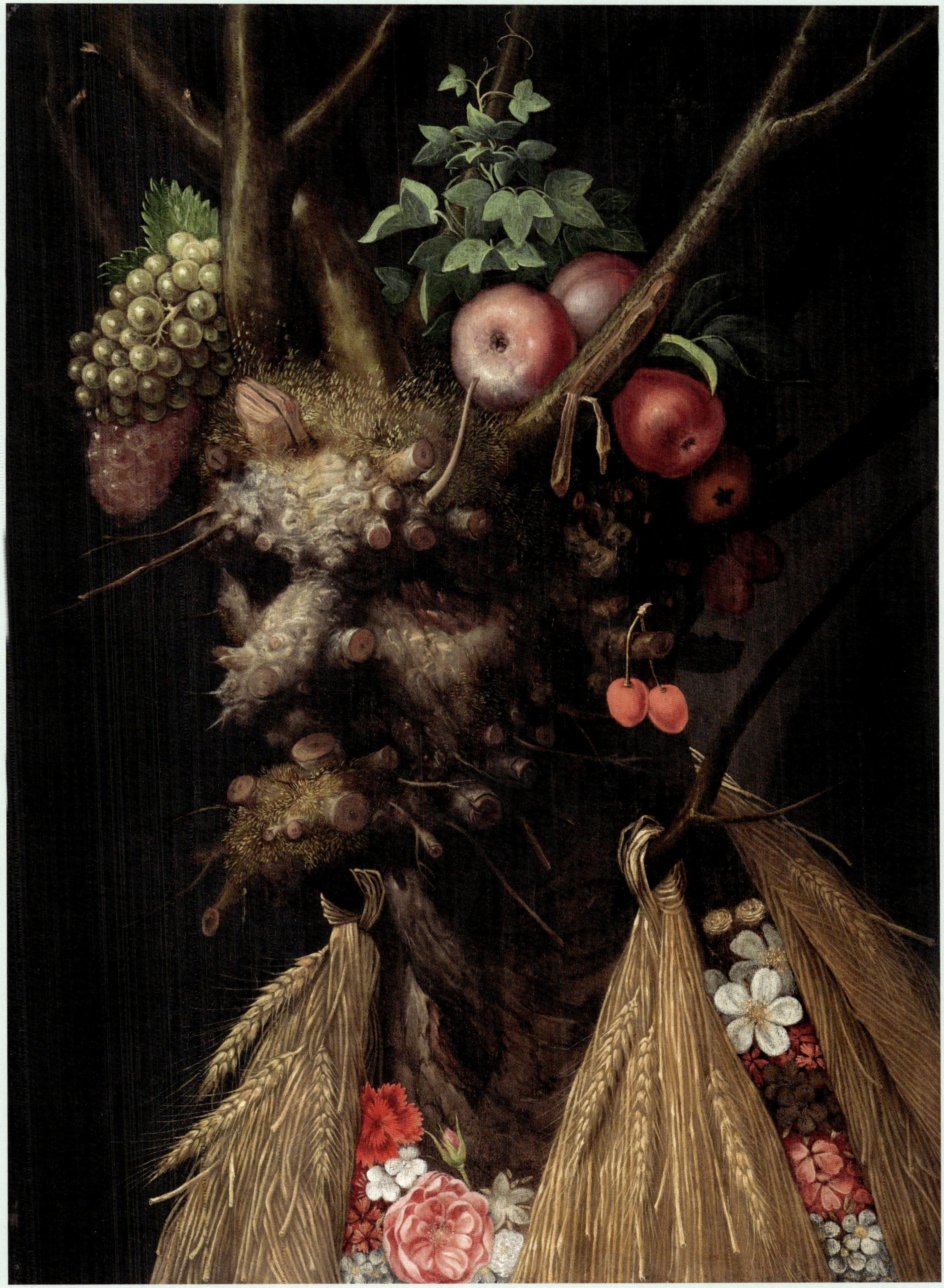

Cat. 88

June – Mercury with the Sign of Cancer

Series title: *The Twelve Months*, so-called *Grotesque Months*
Conception: after 1556; execution: Brussels, 1560/70
Wool, silk, gold and silver threads; H 419 cm, W 468 cm
Inscription: 'IVNIVS, / SVB TVTELA MERCVRII / CVM SIGNO CANCRI' ('under the protection of mercury / with the sign of cancer')
Vienna, Kunsthistorisches Museum, Kunstkammer, inv. KK T XI/6

Provenance: Inventory of the furnishings of the ducal palace in Nancy and other residences of the Dukes of Lorraine between 17 May 1575 and 22 January 1606
Literature: Scheicher 1973, 55–84; exh. cat. Vienna 2015, 142–53 (Katja Schmitz-von Ledebur), cat. 9; exh. cat. Vienna and Zurich 2011/12, 70–1 (Katja Schmitz-von Ledebur)

The pictorial portrayal of the months has a long tradition. The Greeks, for example, had a festival calendar in the third century BCE, where an allegorical depiction of the months could be found. Over time, special aspects and activities were assigned to the individual months, as well as a comprehensive astrological system according to which each month was associated with a sign of the zodiac under the protection of an ancient deity.

The perennial relevance of the seasons and months made it inevitable that they would become subjects for monumental tapestries. These tapestries found special expression in bringing together grotesque motifs. The grotesque, an ornamental composition often enlivened with animals, mythical creatures, and half-humans, developed against the background of the rediscovered ancient wall decorations in the Roman grottos of Nero's Domus Aurea.

The twelve tapestries in Vienna that depict the months are of this type. In the centre of each is an Olympic deity under a delicate canopy or arbor-like structure. In the present instance, it is the Roman god Mercury, behind whom the pictorial field opens up into a broad landscape. Of the once lavish attributes of the messenger of the gods, only his winged helmet and caduceus remain. In his left hand he holds the sign of Cancer. A rooster is next to him, which can be interpreted as a symbol of the early rising of eager students, which the humanists of the time thought was one of the essential disciplines of a successful course of study. In this sense, the rooster symbolizes the indispensable basis for learned research and is directly linked to Mercury, the patron of scholarship. However, the rooster is also associated with the vigilance of traders, as Mercury was also considered the god of trade.

The small scenes to the left and right of Mercury depict the shearing of sheep, which Mercury was said to have invented, and a cherry harvest. The delicate architecture surrounding them, together with the elements framing the deity, form a three-gated triumphal arch.

There are parallels between the Viennese tapestries and the famous Gods sequence of the Flemish painter Léonard Thiry (1490–1550) published in 1540, as well as with the graphic works of Cornelis Floris II (before 1514–1575) and the Flemish artist Cornelis Bos (1506/10–before 7 May 1555). The draughtsman must, therefore, have been familiar with the printmaking techniques then known in the Netherlands. It is possible that several artists were involved in the development of the series, since, unlike the grotesques, the personified deities are more reminiscent of Michiel Coxcie (1499–1592) and his circle.

Katja Schmitz-von Ledebur

Cat. 89.1, 89.2

Jan Baptist Saive the Elder (c.1540–1624)

Vegetable Market (July–August)

c.1590
Canvas; 108 × 220 cm
Vienna, Kunsthistorisches Museum, Picture Gallery, inv. 7626

Fruit Market (September–October)

Dated 1590
Canvas; 108 × 220 cm
Vienna, Kunsthistorisches Museum, Picture Gallery, inv. 2204

Provenance: 1590 probably on commission from Archduke Ernst; 1591 sent to Schloss Karlau in Graz as gift to Maria von Bayern, widow of Archduke Karl of Inner Austria; 1748 transported to Vienna
Literature: Wied 1990, 37, 38, figs. 12, 13; mus. cat. Vienna 1991, 88, pl. 373; Wied 1997; Honig 1998, 126–33, pl. 12, fig. 51; Wied 2002, 180–1, cat. 57; Wied 2008, 40–1; Wied 2010, 222, note 227; Deiters 2019, 50–2, cat. 9

The *Vegetable Market (July–August)* and the *Fruit Market (September–October)* are two works in a series of six that depicts the cycle of the year in paintings representing two months each. The Kunsthistorisches Museum still owns three of them, January–February and March–April are now in private hands, May–June is lost. The series was created at the royal court in Brussels. In 1590, Saive, also known as Jan de Namur, was court painter to Alessandro Farnese, the governor of the Spanish Netherlands; he was also employed there temporarily as cellar master ('concierge du Vignoble'; Thieme-Becker 1935, 330). Archduke Ernst did not pay for the series until 1594, when he became governor in Brussels, but had probably commissioned it and sent it to Graz (Schloss Karlau) as a gift to Archduchess Maria as early as 1591.

The more unusual combination of two rather than three months per picture probably goes back to Pieter Bruegel the Elder's series of seasons (cat. 15), which he devoted entirely to realistic depictions of peasant life. Saive, on the other hand, combines an everyday scene with an opulent still life in the foreground. Small circular pictures (tondi) hang on dark walls. In addition, a view of an urban space usually opens up. Through this compositional structure, the cycle merges various traditions of depicting the months and seasons with market and kitchen pieces. The detailed everyday stories told almost make one forget the allegorical character of the scenes. The small circular pictures with their inscriptions clearly name the months and show corresponding work, but there is no personified allegory or zodiac sign. Such *tondi*, mostly wooden, have survived to this day (for example, in the Stedelijk Museum Alkmaar; see Gruber 2011, 157; exh. cat. Vienna and Zurich 2011/12, 117–19).

In the *Vegetable Market (July–August)*, a farmer's wife with a child on her lap stands out clearly against the dark wall. The baskets to her right are full of various vegetables and fruits. She reaches with her left hand for cherries in a basket, which the woman in traditional Antwerp garb next to her is pointing at. In the city view on the left, another woman is weighing cherries for a customer.

The two circular paintings in the vegetable market refer to peasant work during the hay and grain harvests, which is not directly related to the goods shown in the foreground of the painting. The July picture shows a man with a scythe harvesting hay; a woman is helping him, piling up the hay to dry, while a second woman is sitting on the haystack. In the August picture, a group of farmers take a midday break – four sit beside a picnic blanket where food is being passed around, a fifth is already asleep under a tree – while in the background grain is being harvested. Here too Saive seems to be following the tradition of Bruegel, whose painting *The Harvesters* (see essay Pénot, fig. 2) also depicts people eating and resting under a tree.

In the foreground of the *Fruit Market (September–October)* various containers are brimming with fruit. A woman sits to the left of them, with a basket of hazelnuts in her lap, while a man leans against her familiarly. On the right, a cask of apparently new wine is being tasted – a reference to Saive's position as cellar master? The depiction of the tasting is unusual. Leandro Bassano gives a detailed description of wine production in his September picture (cat. 67.10), but there is no wine tasting there. The *tondo* of September on the left behind the couple shows the apple harvest, the prelude to the main scene, as it were. A woman sits next to a basket that is already very full; the man behind her has stretched out his right hand towards the tree to pick an apple. In the October *tondo*, two hunters, a man and a boy, are walking down a hill. They point at a man in a vat at the foot of the hill in the middle ground, who – assuming a connection to the main scene – is probably crushing grapes. The two hunters resemble an autumnal version of Bruegel's *Hunters in the Snow*, even though it is not clear whether Saive might have actually seen Bruegel's paintings in the collection of the Antwerp merchant Nicolaas Jonglinck.

Gerlinde Gruber

Cat. 90

Giuseppe Arcimboldo (1526–1593)

Four Seasons in One Head

Poplar panel; 60.4 × 44.7 cm
Washington, National Gallery of Art, inv. 2010.77.1; Paul Mellon Fund

Provenance: inventory of the collection of Giovan Pietro Cortoni, Verona, 1656, fol. 1: 'Arcimboldo pezzi uno – n.o 1 Le quattro Stagioni che formano una testa, Largo P. 1 o 4 alto P.1 o 9'
Literature: Comanini 1591 (1962), 268–9; Campori 1870, 192–202; Montanari 1994, 44; Berra 1996 (Paragone), 116–7 for Comanini's description; exh. cat. Paris and Vienna 2007/08, 144–6, cat. IV.15 (Ferino-Pagden); Ferino-Pagden 2010,18–9, fig. 27; Berra 2011, 316–7

Don Gregorio Comanini's dialogue *Il Figino*, published in 1591, states clearly that Arcimboldo dedicated this painting to him (see essay Ferino -Pagden, p. 27). Comanini lists the work after the paintings *Flora* and *Vertumnus* (cat. 33), which Arcimboldo sent to Emperor Rudolf II in 1589 and 1591 respectively, after he had returned to Milan. One could therefore assume that this was one of Arcimboldo's last paintings.

Too little is known about Don Gregorio Comanini's life, property, or last will and testament to determine the whereabouts of this work with any certainty. However, the painting *Le quattro Stagioni che formano una testa* (literally 'The four seasons forming a head') mentioned in the 1656 inventory of Giovan Pietro Cortoni's famous Veronese collection could be identical to this painting, a possibility furthermore suggested by its comparable dimensions.

During the preparations for the Arcimboldo exhibition in Paris and Vienna in 2007/08, I was shown the painting. I immediately recognised it as an authentic work of Arcimboldo's and included it in the catalogue. On the occasion of the Arcimboldo exhibition at the National Gallery of Art in Washington in 2010/11 (*Arcimboldo 1526–1593: Nature and Fantasy*, 19 September 2010 – 9 January 2011), the museum's curator of Italian painting, David Allan Brown acquired it for the institution.

In all of Arcimboldo's versions of *Winter* – in Munich (cat. 28.3), Vienna (cat. 29.2), and Paris – the head consists of a gnarled, moss-covered tree stump with scaly bark. The set-up is similar in this picture, in which the wintry elements form the basic structure. In contrast to the profile heads of the *Seasons* or *Elements* series, however, this is an *en face* depiction with a slight three-quarter turn to the left. In no other painting by Arcimboldo does the head stand out so effectively and vividly from the background.

The mysterious chiaroscuro modelling intensifies the expression of gentle melancholy and evokes immediate associations with Leonardo's works – more so than with any of the master's other creations. In this picture, it is almost as if one is looking at an old person painted by Leonardo, but a person covered in tree bark. In particular, one is reminded of the drawing of an old man (albeit a reverse image) in the Istituto Centrale per la Grafica in Rome (inv. D-FN4r).

This union of the *Four Seasons* in a single painting constitutes (as I wrote more than fifteen years ago) a sort of summary of all of Arcimboldo's previous naturalistic and artistic experiences, the quintessence of the interests to which the artist devoted his life. Two shreds of peeling bark hang from the branch protruding from the top right of the head. Arcimboldo's carved signature 'ARCIMBOLDUS P.' can be seen on the exposed wood.

Sylvia Ferino-Pagden

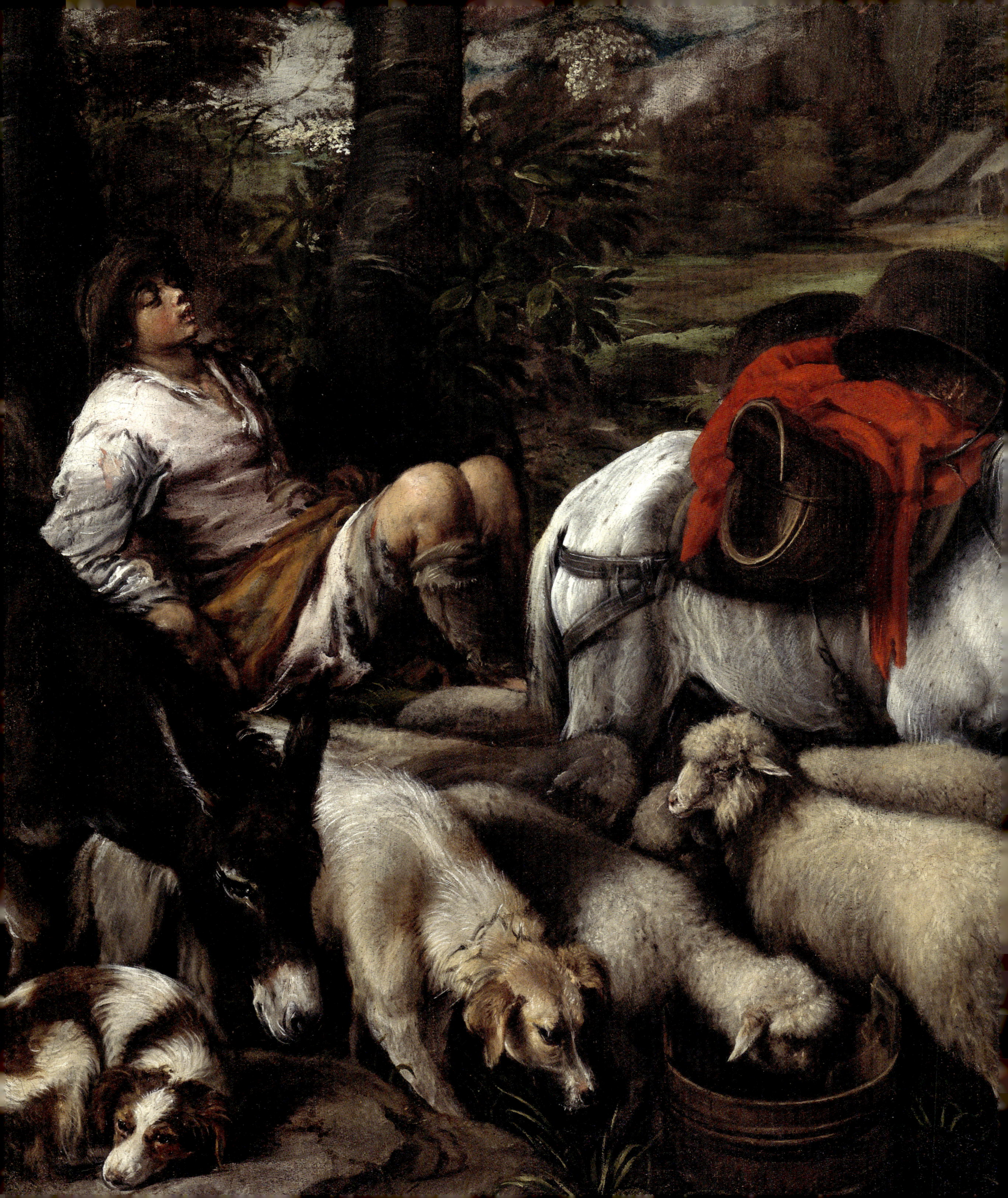

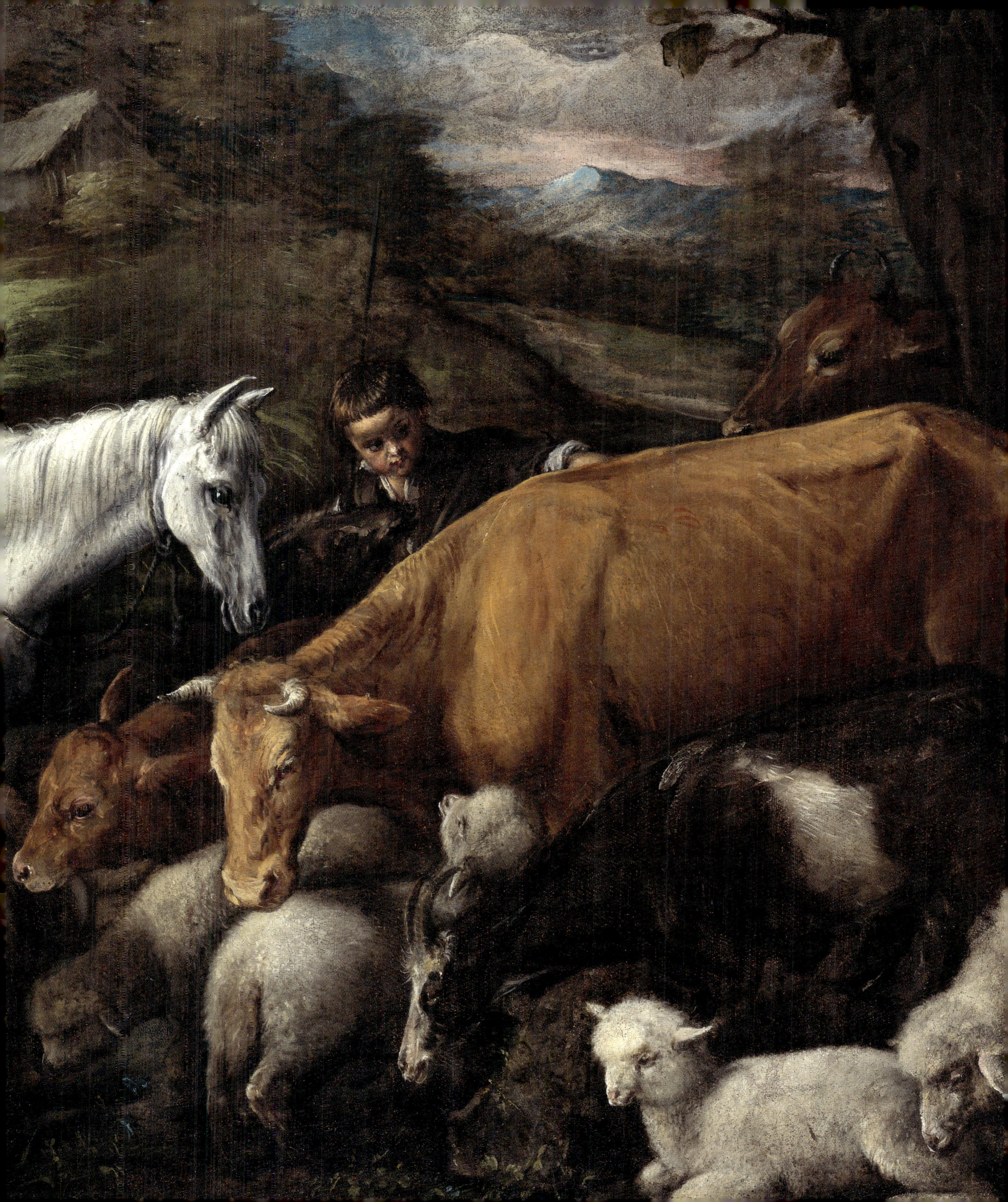

Reference List

Abbreviations

DBI: *Dizionario Biografico degli italiani*
www.treccani.it/biografico

EDIT16: *Edizioni Italiane del XVI Secolo*
edit16.iccu.sbn.it

IGI: *Indice Generale degli Incunaboli*

ISTC: *Incunabula Short Title Catalogue*
data.cerl.org/istc

SBN: *Servizio Bibliotecario Nazionale*
opac.sbn.it

EXHIBITION CATALOGUES

Exh. cat. Amsterdam 1978
Lucas van Leyden (1489 of 1494–1533). Grafiek: met een complete oeuvrecatalogus van zijn gravures, etsen en houtsneden, ed. Filedt Kok and Jan Piet, Amsterdam (Rijksmuseum) 1978

Exh. cat. Amsterdam 2009
Hendrick Avercamp. Master of the Ice Scene, ed. Pieter Roelofs and Jonathan Bikker, Amsterdam (Rijksmuseum) 2009

Exh. cat. Bassano del Grappa 2010
Jacopo Bassano e lo stupendo inganno dell'occhio, ed. Alessandro Ballarin and Giulia Ericani, Bassano del Grappa (Museo Civico) 2010

Exh. cat. Bassano del Grappa and Fort Worth 1992/93
Jacopo Bassano c. 1510–1592, ed. Beverly L. Brown and Paola Marini, Bassano del Grappa (Museo Civico) and Fort Worth (Kimbell Art Museum) 1992/93

Exh. cat. Belluno 1994
Capolavori della pittura veneta dal castello di Praga, ed. Eliška Fučiková, Belluno (Palazzo Crepadona) 1994

Exh. cat. Berlin 1995
Von allen Seiten schön. Bronzen der Renaissance und des Barock, ed. Volker Krahn, Berlin (Staatliche Museen zu Berlin, Skulpturensammlung), 1995

Exh. cat. Bologna 2004
Rappresentare il corpo. Arte e Anatomia da Leonardo all'Illuminismo, ed. Giuseppe Olmi, Bologna (Palazzo Poggi) 2004

Exh. cat. Bruges 2011/12
Fürstlich gesammelt. Van Eyck, Gossaert, Bruegel. Meisterwerke des Kunsthistorischen Museums Wien, ed. Sylvia Ferino-Pagden, Till-Holger Borchert, and Manfred Sellink, Bruges (Groeningemuseum) 2011/12

Exh. cat. Budapest 2009/10
Botticelli to Titian. Two Centuries of Italian Masterpieces, ed. Dóra Sallay, Vilmos Tátrai, and Axel Vécsey, Budapest (Szépmuvészeti Múzeum) 2009/10

Exh. cat. Cambridge and Evanston 2011/12
Prints and the Pursuit of Knowledge in Early Modern Europe, ed. Susan Dackerman, Cambridge (Harvard Art Museum) and Evanston (Block Museum of Art) 2011/12

Exh. cat. Caserta 2022
Frammenti di paradiso. Giardini nel tempo alla Reggia di Caserta, ed. Tiziana Maffei, Alberta Campitelli, and Alessandro Cremona, Caserta (Reggia) 2022

Exh. cat. Chemnitz 2014
Pieter Bruegel d.Ä. und das Theater der Welt, ed. Ingrid Mössinger and Jürgen Müller, Chemnitz (Kunstsammlungen) 2014

Exh. cat. Crema 1999
La ragione e il metodo. Immagini della scienza nell'arte italiana dal XVI al XIX secolo, ed. Marco Bona Castellotti, Enrico Gamba, and Fernando Mazzocca, Crema (Centro Culturale Sant'Agostino) 1999

Exh. cat. Cremona 2000/01
Vicenzo Campi. Scene del quotidiano, ed. Franco Paliaga, Cremona (Museo Civico) 2000/01

Exh. cat. Cremona 2016/17
Janello Torriani. Genio del Rinascimento, ed. Cristiano Zanetti, Cremona (Museo del Violino) 2016/17

Exh. cat. Cremona and Vienna 2000/01
Dipingere la musica. Musik in der Malerei des 16. und 17. Jahrhunderts, ed. Sylvia Ferino-Pagden, Cremona (Santa Maria della Pietà) and Vienna (Kunsthistorisches Museum) 2000/01

Exh. cat. Dresden 2005
Mannes Lust & Weibes Macht. Geschlechterwahn in Renaissance und Barock, ed. Claudia Schnitzer and Cordula Bischoff, Dresden (Staatliche Kunstsammlungen, Kupferstich-Kabinett) 2005

Exh. cat. Edinburgh, London, and Vienna 1978/79
Giambologna. Ein Wendepunkt der europäischen Plastik, ed. Charles Avery, Edinburgh (Royal Scottish Museum), London (Victoria and Albert Museum), and Vienna (Kunsthistorisches Museum) 1978/79

Exh. cat. Essen 1988
Prag um 1600. Kunst und Kultur am Hofe Kaiser Rudolfs II., ed. Eliška Fuciková, Essen (Kulturstiftung Ruhr) 1988

Exh. cat. Fabriano 2006
Gentile da Fabriano e l'altro Rinascimento, ed. Laura Laureati and Lorenza Mochi Onori, Fabriano (Spedale di Santa Maria del Buon Gesù) 2006

Exh. cat. Florence 1961
Mostra di disegni di Jacopo Ligozzi (1547–1626), ed. Mina Bacci and Anna Forlani, Florence (Gabinetto Disegni e Stampe degli Uffizi) 1961

Exh. cat. Florence 2006
Giambologna. Gli dei, gli eroi. Genesi e fortuna di uno stile europeo nella scultura, ed. Beatrice Paolozzi Strozzi and Dimitrios Zikos, Florence (Museo Nazionale del Bargello) 2006

Exh. cat. Florence 2009
Il cannocchiale e il pennello. Nuova scienza e nuova arte nell'età di Galileo, ed. Lucia Tongiorgi Tomasi and Alessandro Tosi, Florence 2009

Exh. cat. Florence 2014
Jacopo Ligozzi: 'pittore universalissimo', ed. Alessandro Cecchi, Lucilla Conigliello, and Marzia Faietti, Florence (Palazzo Pitti) 2014

Exh. cat. Florence 2014a
Jacopo Ligozzi, 'altro Apelle', ed. Maria Elena De Luca and Marzia Faietti, Florence (Gabinetto Disegni e Stampe degli Uffizi) 2014

Exh. cat. Fontanellato 2024
Musca depicta. C'è una mosca nel quadro, ed. Sylvia Ferino-Pagden, Fontanellato (Labirinto della Masone) 2024

Exh. cat. Frankfurt 1985
Natur und Antike in der Renaissance, ed. Dieter Blume and Herbert Beck, Frankfurt am Main (Liebieghaus Skulpturensammlung) 1985

Exh. cat. Frankfurt and Vienna 2023/24
Renaissance im Norden. Holbein, Burgkmair und die Zeit der Fugger, ed. Guido Messling and Jochen Sander, Frankfurt am Main (Städel Museum) and Vienna (Kunsthistorisches Museum) 2023/24

Exh. cat. Ghent 1986/87
Joachim Beuckelaer. Het markt- en keukenstuk in de Nederlanden, 1550–1650, ed. Paul Verbraeken, Ghent (Museum voor Schone Kunsten) 1986/87

Exh. cat. Hamm and Mainz 2000
Gärten und Höfe der Rubenszeit im Spiegel der Malerfamilie Brueghel und der Künstler um Peter Paul Rubens, ed. Ursula Härting, Hamm (Gustav-Lübcke-Museum) and Mainz (Landesmuseum) 2000

Exh. cat. Helsinki 2024
Jacopo Bassano. Renaissance Painter of Venetian Country Life, ed. Claudia Caramanna and Kirsi Eskelinen, Helsinki (Sinebrychoffin taidemuseo) 2024

Exh. cat. Hradec Králové 2021
Rudolf II. Umění pro císaře / Art for the Emperor, ed. Eliška Fučíková, Hradec Králové (Muzeum východních Čech) 2021

Exh. cat. Innsbruck 2009
Ferdinand Karl. Ein Sonnenkönig in Tirol, ed. Sabine Haag, Innsbruck (Schloss Ambras) 2009

Exh. cat. Innsbruck 2012
Splash! Das Bad der Philippine Welser, ed. Sabine Haag, Innsbruck (Schloss Ambras) 2012

Exh. cat. Innsbruck 2015
Echt tierisch! Die Menagerie des Fürsten, ed. Sabine Haag, Innsbruck (Schloss Ambras) 2015

Exh. cat. Innsbruck 2022
One World. Die Macht der 4 Elemente, ed. Claudia Lehner-Jobst and Veronika Sandbichler, Innsbruck (Schloss Ambras) 2022

Exh. cat. Innsbruck and Vienna 2006/07
Die Entdeckung der Natur. Naturalien in den Kunstkammern des 16. und 17. Jahrhunderts, ed. Wilfried Seipel, Innsbruck (Schloss Ambras) and Vienna (Kunsthistorisches Museum) 2006/07

Exh. cat. Krems 1999
Zeit/Los. Zur Kunstgeschichte der Zeit, ed. Carl Aigner et al., Krems (Kunsthalle Krems) 1999

Exh. cat. Las Vegas 2002/03
Art through the Ages. Masterpieces of Painting from Titian to Picasso, ed. Thomas Krens, Las Vegas (Guggenheim Hermitage Museum) 2002/03

Exh. cat. Leiden 2011
Lucas van Leyden en de Renaissance, ed. Christiaan Vogelaar, Leiden (Museum De Lakenhal) 2011

Exh. cat. Lemgo and Antwerp 2002
Hans Vredeman de Vries und die Renaissance im Norden, ed. Heiner Borggrefe, Thomas Fusenig, and Barbara Uppenkamp, Lemgo (Weserrenaissance-Museum Schloß Brake) and Antwerp (Koninklijk Museum voor Schone Kunsten) 2002

Exh. cat. London 1981
Leonardo da Vinci. Nature Studies from the Royal Library at Windsor Castle, ed. Carlo Pedretti, London (Royal Academy of Arts) 1981

Exh. cat. London 2009
Palladio, ed. Guido Beltramini and Howard Burns, London (Royal Academy of Arts) 2009

Exh. cat. London and Edinburgh 2019/20
Leonardo da Vinci: A Life in Drawing, ed. Martin Clayton, London (Buckingham Palace) and Edinburgh (Palace of Holyroodhouse) 2018

Exh. cat. Lugano 1998
Rabisch, Il grottesco nell'arte del Cinquecento. L'Accademia della Val di Blenio, Lomazzo e l'ambiente milanese, ed. Giulio Bora, Manuela Kahn-Rossi, and Francesco Porzio, Lugano (Museo Cantonale d'Arte) 1998

Exh. cat. Lugano 2014/15
Bramantino. L'arte nuova del Rinascimento lombardo, ed. Mauro Natale and Edoardo Rossetti, Lugano (Museo Cantonale d'Arte) 2014/15

Exh. cat. Madrid 2002
Los Bassanos en la España del Siglo de Oro, ed. Miguel Falomir Faus, Madrid (Museo Nacional del Prado) 2002

Exh. cat. Madrid 2016
El Bosco. La exposición del V centenario, ed. Pilar Silva Maroto, Madrid (Museo Nacional del Prado) 2016

Exh. cat. Madrid 2022
El arte del trampantojo, ed. Mar Borobia and Guillermo Solana, Madrid (Museo Nacional Thyssen-Bornemisza) 2022

Exh. cat. Milan 2011
Arcimboldo. Artista milanese tra Leonardo e Caravaggio, ed. Sylvia Ferino-Pagden, Milan (Palazzo Reale) 2011

Exh. cat. Milan 2012
Tiziano e la nascita del paesaggio moderno, ed. Mauro Lucco, Milan (Palazzo Reale) 2012

Exh. cat. Milan 2014/15
Bramante a Milano. Le arti in Lombardia 1477–1499, ed. Matteo Ceriana et al., Milan (Pinacoteca di Brera) 2014/15

Exh. cat. Milan 2015
Arte lombarda dai Visconti agli Sforza, ed. Mauro Natale and Serena Romano, Milan (Palazzo Reale) 2015

Exh. cat. Mannheim 2012
Sammeln! Die Kunstkammer des Kaisers in Wien, ed. Sabine Haag and Alfried Wieczorek, Mannheim (Reiss-Engelhorn-Museen) 2012

Exh. cat. Mechelen 2024
Eeuwige Lente. Tuinen en Wandtapijten in de Renaissance, ed. Carlotta Striolo, Mechelen (Museum Hof van Busleyden) 2024

Exh. cat. Modena 1986
I secoli d'oro della medicina. 700 anni di scienza medica a Padova, ed. Margherita Azzi Visentini and Loris Premuda, Modena 1986

Exh. cat. Nara and Tokyo 1995/96
Kaiserliche Schätze aus dem Hause Habsburg – Meisterwerke des Kunsthistorischen Museums, Nara (Prefectural Museum of Art) and Tokyo (The Bunkamura Museum of Art) 1995/96

Exh. cat. New York 2008
Andrea Riccio. Renaissance Master of Bronze, ed. Denise Allen, Peta Motture, and Richard Stone, New York (The Frick Collection) 2008

Exh. cat. New York 2014
Bartholomeus Spranger. Splendor and Eroticism in Imperial Prague, ed. Nancy Grubb, New York (The Metropolitan Museum of Art) 2014

Exh. cat. New York 2023
Bellini and Giorgione in the House of Taddeo Contarini, ed. X.F. Salomon, New York (The Frick Collection) 2023

Exh. cat. New York, Tulsa, and Dayton 1983
Italian Still Life Paintings from Three Centuries, ed. John T. Spike, New York (National Academy of Design), Tulsa (Philbrook Art Center), and Dayton (Dayton Art Institute) 1983

Exh. cat. Nuremberg 1985
Wenzel Jamnitzer und die Nürnberger Goldschmiedekunst 1500–1700, ed. Gerhard Bott, Nuremberg (Germanisches Nationalmuseum) 1985

Exh. cat. Nuremberg 2002
Quasi Centrum Europae: Europa kauft in Nürnberg 1400–1800, ed. Hermann Maué and Christine Kupper, Nuremberg (Germanisches Nationalmuseum) 2002

Exh. cat. Nuremberg 2011
Die gottlosen Maler von Nürnberg. Konvention und Subversion in der Druckgrafik der Beham-Brüder, ed. Jürgen Müller and Thomas Schauerte, Nuremberg (Albrecht-Dürer-Haus) 2011

Exh. cat. Nuremberg 2022
Hans Hoffmann. Ein europäischer Künstler der Renaissance, ed. Yasmin Doosry, Nuremberg (Germanisches Nationalmuseum) 2022

Exh. cat. Padua 2013
Pietro Bembo e l'invenzione del Rinascimento, ed. Guido Beltramini, Davide Gasparotto, and Adolfo Tura, Padua (Palazzo del Monte di Pietà) 2013

Exh. cat. Paris and Vienna 2007/08
Arcimboldo 1526–1593, ed. Sylvia Ferino-Pagden, Paris (Musée du Luxembourg) and Vienna (Kunsthistorisches Museum) 2007/08

Exh. cat. Parma 2003
Parmigianino e il manierismo europeo, ed. Sylvia Ferino-Pagden and Lucia Fornari Schianchi, Parma (Galleria Nazionale) 2003

Exh. cat. Pavia 2003/04
Andrea Mantegna e l'incisione italiana del Rinascimento nelle collezioni dei Musei Civici di Pavia, ed. Saverio Lomartire, Pavia (Castello Visconteo) 2003/04

Exh. cat. Pavia and Ariccia 2000
I Piaceri della Vita in Campagna nell'Arte dal XVI al XVIII secolo, ed. Franco Moro, Pavia (Castello di Belgioioso) and Ariccia (Palazzo Chigi) 2000

Exh. cat. Pisa 1980
Livorno e Pisa: due città e un territorio nella politica dei Medici, ed. Mario Mirri, Pisa 1980

Exh. cat. Pisa 2024
Casabona, Dyckman e la Flora di Creta / Casabona, Dyckman and the Flora of Crete, ed. Giovanni Astuti, Roberta Vangelisti, and Lorenzo Peruzzi, Pisa (Orto e Museo Botanico) 2024

Exh. cat. Potsdam and Paris 2023
Sonne: die Quelle des Lichts in der Kunst, ed. Michael Philipp, Ortrud Westheider, and Daniel Zamani, Potsdam (Museum Barberini Potsdam) and Paris (Musée Marmottan Monet) 2023

Exh. cat. Prague 1997
Rudolf II and Prague. The Court and the City, ed. Eliška Fučíková, Prague (Wallenstein Riding Hall) 1997

Exh. cat. Praglia 1988
Di sana pianta. Erbari e taccuini di sanità. Le radici storiche della nuova farmacologia, ed. Rolando Bussi, Praglia (Abbazia di Praglia) 1988

Exh. cat. Rome 1999
Villa Medici. Il sogno di un Cardinale. Collezioni e artisti di Ferdinando de' Medici, ed. Michel Hochmann, Rome (Accademia di Francia) 1999

Exh. cat. Rome 2007
Dürer e l'Italia, ed. Kristina Herrmann Fiore, Rome (Scuderie del Quirinale) 2007

Exh. cat. Rome 2011
Dürer, l'Italia e l'Europa, ed. Sybille Ebert Schifferer and Kristina Herrmann Fiore, Rome (Bibliotheca Hertziana) 2011

Exh. cat. Rome 2013
Augusto, ed. Eugenio La Rocca, Rome (Scuderie del Quirinale) 2013

Exh. cat. Rome 2017/18
Arcimboldo, ed. Sylvia Ferino-Pagden, Rome (Palazzo Barberini) 2017/18

Exh. cat. Rome 2019
Leonardo e i suoi libri, ed. Carlo Vecce, Rome (Accademia Nazionale dei Lincei) 2019

Exh. cat. Rotterdam 2015
De ontdekking van het dagelijkse leven. Van Bosch tot Bruegel, ed. Peter van der Coelen and Friso Lammertse, Rotterdam (Museum Boijmans Van Beuningen) 2015

Exh. cat. 's-Hertogenbosch 2016
Hieronymus Bosch. Visions of a Genius, ed. Matthijs Ilsink and Jos Koldeweij, 's-Hertogenbosch (Het Noordbrabants Museum) 2016

Exh. cat. Salzburg 1967
Salzburgs alte Schatzkammer, ed. Johannes Neuhardt, Salzburg (Oratorien des Domes) 1967

Exh. cat. Salzburg 1987
Fürsterzbischof Wolf Dietrich von Raitenau. Gründer des barocken Salzburg, ed. Ulrike Engelsberger and Franz Wagner, 4. Salzburger Landesausstellung, Salzburg (Residenz-Neugebäude and Dommuseum zu Salzburg) 1987

Exh. cat. San Francisco, Baltimore, and London 1997/98
Masters of Light: Dutch Painters in Utrecht during the Golden Age, ed. Joaneath A. Spicer and Lynn Federle Orr, San Francisco (Museum of Fine Arts), Baltimore (Walters Art Gallery), and London (The National Gallery) 1997/98

Exh. cat. Schallaburg 1976
Italienische Kleinplastiken, Zeichnungen und Musik der Renaissance, Waffen des 16. und 17. Jahrhunderts, ed. Erich Zöllner, Schallaburg (Schloss Schallaburg) 1976

Exh. cat. Schallaburg 2011
Venedig. Seemacht, Kunst und Karneval, ed. Matthias Pfaffenbichler, Schallaburg (Schloss Schallaburg) 2011

Exh. cat. Schallaburg 2024
Schallaburg Betriebs GmbH, *Renaissance einst, jetzt & hier*, Schallaburg 2024

Exh. cat. St Florian and Linz 1965
Die Kunst der Donauschule. 1490–1540, ed. Otto Wutzel, St Florian (Stift) and Linz (Schloßmuseum) 1965

Exh. cat. St Gallen 2023
Jost Bürgli (1552–1632). Schlüssel zum Kosmos, ed. Peter Fux et al., St Gallen (Kulturmuseum) 2023

Exh. cat. Stuttgart 1980
Zeichnung in Deutschland. Deutsche Zeichner 1540–1640, ed. Heinrich Geissler, 2 vols., Stuttgart (Staatsgalerie) 1980

Exh. cat. Stuttgart 1982/83
Vom Manierismus zum Barock. Italienische Gemälde des sechzehnten und siebzehnten Jahrhunderts aus dem Besitz der Staatsgalerie Stuttgart, ed. Gerhard Ewald and Monika Kopplin, Stuttgart (Staatsgalerie) 1982/83

Exh. cat. Tokyo 2017
Arcimboldo. Nature into Art, ed. Sylvia Ferino-Pagden, Tokyo (The National Museum of Western Art) 2017

Exh. cat. Tokyo and Kobe 2004
Meisterwerke der holländischen und flämischen Malerei aus der Gemäldegalerie des Kunsthistorischen Museums Wien, ed. Karl Schütz and Gerlinde Gruber, Tokyo (Metropolitan Art Museum) and Kobe (Kobe City Museum) 2004

Exh. cat. Tokyo, Sendai, and Nagoya 2008/09
Stillleben aus der Gemäldegalerie des Kunsthistorischen Museums Wien, Tokyo (The National Art Center), Sendai (The Miyagi Museum of Art), and Nagoya (Hyogo Prefectural Museum of Art) 2008/09

Exh. cat. Trento 1999
La bellissima maniera. Alessandro Vittoria e la scultura veneta del Cinquecento, ed. Andrea Bacchi, Trento (Castello del Buonconsiglio) 1999

Exh. cat. Trento 2008
Rinascimento e passione per l'antico. Andrea Riccio e il suo tempo, ed. Andrea Bacchi, Trento (Castello del Buonconsiglio) 2008

Exh. cat. Trento 2018
Il San Sebastiano di Andrea Riccio, ed. Giancarlo Gentilini, Trento (Castello del Buonconsiglio) 2018

Exh. cat. Treviso 2019/20
Natura in Posa. Capolavori dal Kunsthistorisches Museum di Vienna in Dialogo con la Fotografia Contemporanea, ed. Francesca Del Torre Scheuch, Treviso (Museo Santa Caterina) 2019/20

Exh. cat. Turin 1990
Da Biduino ad Algardi. Pittura e scultura a confronto, ed. Giovanni Romano, Turin (Galleria Antichi Maestri Pittori) 1990

Exh. cat. Venaria 2023/24
Sovrani a tavola. Pranzi imbanditi nelle corti italiane, ed. Andrea Merlotti, Silvia Ghisotti, and Clara Goria, Venaria (Reggia di Venaria) 2023/24

Exh. cat. Venice 1987
The Arcimboldo Effect. Transformations of the Face from the 16th to the 20th Century, ed. Pontus Hulten et al., Venice (Palazzo Grassi) 1987

Exh. cat. Venice 1990
Le cortigiane di Venezia dal Trecento al Settecento: il gioco dell'amore, ed. Filippo Pedrocco, Venice (Casinò municipale) 1990

Exh. cat. Venice 1992
Leonardo & Venezia, Venice (Palazzo Grassi) 1992

Exh. cat. Venice 1998
Il Rinascimento a Venezia e la pittura del Nord ai tempi di Bellini, Dürer, Tiziano, ed. Bernard Aikema and Beverly Louise Brown, Venice (Palazzo Grassi) 1998

Exh. cat. Venice 1999
Renaissance Venice and the North. Crosscurrents in the Time of Bellini, Dürer, and Titian, ed. Bernard Aikema and Beverly Louise Brown, Venice (Palazzo Grassi) 1999

Exh. cat. Vicenza 2021
La Fabbrica del Rinascimento a Vicenza, ed. Guido Beltramini, Davide Gasparotto, and Mattia Vinco, Vicenza (Basilica Palladiana) 2021

Exh. cat. Washington 1976/77
Titian and Venetian Woodcut, ed. David Rosand and Michelangelo Muraro, Washington (National Gallery of Art) 1976/77

Exh. cat. Washington and Venice 2022/23
Vittore Carpaccio. Dipinti e disegni, ed. Peter Humfrey, Washington (National Gallery of Art) and Venice (Palazzo Ducale) 2022/23

Exh. cat. Vienna 1966
Die Kunst der Graphik III. Renaissance in Italien. 16. Jahrhundert. Werke aus dem Besitz der Albertina, ed. Konrad Oberhuber, Vienna (Graphische Sammlung Albertina) 1966

Exh. cat. Vienna 1973
Das Werden eines neuen astronomischen Weltbildes im Spiegel alter Handschriften und Druckwerke. Ausstellung zum 500. Geburtsjahr des Nicolaus Copernicus, ed. Günter Hamann and Konradin Ferrari d'Occhieppo, Vienna (Österreichische Nationalbibliothek) 1973

Exh. cat. Vienna 1978
Curiositäten und Inventionen aus Kunst- und Rüstkammer, ed. Christian Beaufort-Spontin, Vienna (Kunsthistorisches Museum) 1978

Exh. cat. Vienna 1985
Albrecht Dürer und die Tier- und Pflanzenstudien der Renaissance, ed. Fritz Koreny, Vienna (Albertina) 1985

Exh. cat. Vienna 1987
Zauber der Medusa: Europäische Manierismen, ed. Werner Hofmann, Vienna (Künstlerhaus) 1987

Exh. cat. Vienna 2002/03
Die Kunst des Steinschnitts. Prunkgefäße, Kameen und Commessi aus der Kunstkammer, ed. Wilfried Seipel, Vienna (Kunsthistorisches Museum) 2002/03

Exh. cat. Vienna 2003
Kaiser Ferdinand I. 1503–1564. Das Werden der Habsburgermonarchie, ed. Wilfried Seipel, Vienna (Kunsthistorisches Museum) 2003

Exh. cat. Vienna 2003a
Albrecht Dürer, ed. Klaus Albrecht Schröder and Maria Luise Sternath, Vienna (Albertina) 2003

Exh. cat. Vienna 2004
Giorgione. Mythos und Enigma, ed. Sylvia Ferino-Pagden and Giovanna Nepi Scirè, Vienna (Kunsthistorisches Museum) 2004

Exh. cat. Vienna 2006
Giambologna. Triumph des Körpers, ed. Wilfried Seipel, Vienna (Kunsthistorisches Museum) 2006

Exh. cat. Vienna 2011/12
Von Fischen, Vögeln und Reptilien. Meisterwerke aus den kaiserlichen Sammlungen, ed. Christina Weiler, Vienna (Österreichische Nationalbibliothek) 2011/12

Exh. cat. Vienna 2014
Väter Europas. Augustus und Karl der Große, ed. Sabine Haag, Vienna (Kunsthistorisches Museum) 2014

Exh. cat. Vienna 2015
Fäden der Macht. Tapisserien des 16. Jahrhunderts aus dem Kunsthistorischen Museum, ed. Katja Schmitz-von Ledebur, Vienna (Kunsthistorisches Museum) 2015

Exh. cat. Vienna 2016
Feste feiern. 125 Jahre Jubiläumsausstellung, ed. Sabine Haag and Gudrun Swoboda, Vienna (Kunsthistorisches Museum) 2016

Exh. cat. Vienna 2017
Pieter Bruegel. Das Zeichnen der Welt, ed. Eva Michel, Vienna (Albertina) 2017

Exh. cat. Vienna 2018/19
Bruegel. Die Hand des Meisters, ed. Sabine Haag, Vienna (Kunsthistorisches Museum) 2018/19

Exh. cat. Vienna 2019
Albrecht Dürer, ed. Christof Metzger, Vienna (Albertina) 2019

Exh. cat. Vienna 1988/89
Prag um 1600. Kunst und Kultur am Hofe Kaiser Rudolfs II., ed. Eliška Fuciková, Vienna (Kunsthistorisches Museum) 1988/99

Exh. cat. Vienna and Essen 2002/03
Das Flämische Stillleben 1550–1680, Vienna (Kunsthistorisches Museum) and Essen (Kulturstiftung Ruhr) 2002/03

Exh. cat. Vienna and Milan 2018/19
Spitzmaus Mummy in a Coffin and other Treasures, Wes Anderson & Juman Malouf, ed. Sabine Haag and Jasper Sharp, Vienna (Kunsthistorisches Museum) and Milan (Fondazione Prada) 2018/19

Exh. cat. Vienna and Zurich 2011/12
Wintermärchen. Winter-Darstellungen in der europäischen Kunst von Bruegel bis Beuys, ed. Christoph Becker, Sabine Haag, and Ronald de Leeuw, Vienna (Kunsthistorisches Museum) and Zurich (Kunsthaus Zürich) 2011/12

MUSEUM CATALOGUES

Mus. cat. Baltimore 1967
Philippe Verdier, *The Walters Art Gallery. Catalogue of the Painted Enamels of the Renaissance.* Baltimore 1967

Mus. cat. Berlin 1999
Susanne Netzer, *Maleremails aus Limoges. Der Bestand des Berliner Kunstgewerbe-museums* (Bestandskatalog XXII des Kunstgewerbemuseums Staatliche Museen zu Berlin), Berlin 1999

Mus. cat. Budapest 1991
Vilmos Tátrai (ed.), *Museum of Fine Arts Budapest. Old Masters' Gallery. A Summary Catalogue of Italian, French, Spanish and Greek Paintings*, Budapest and London 1991

Mus. cat. Budapest 2020
Szilvia Bodnár (comp.), *German Drawings of the Fifteenth and Sixteenth Centuries in the Museum of Fine Arts Budapest*, Budapest 2020

Mus. cat. Budapest 2024
Vilmos Tátrai et al. (eds.) *A Summary Catalogue of Italian Paintings 1250–1800. Museum of Fine Arts Budapest,* Budapest 2024

Mus. cat. Florence 1967
Cristina Piacenti Aschengreen (ed.), *Il Museo degli Argenti a Firenze*, Florence 1967

Mus. cat. Milan 1915
Carlo Vicenzi, *Milano. Castello Sforzesco. Le pitture e le migliori opere descritte e illustrate con 52 tavole*, Milan 1915

Mus. cat. Milan 1987
Maria Teresa Fiorio and Mercedes Garberi, *La Pinacoteca del Castello Sforzesco*, Milan 1987

Mus. cat. Milan 1998
Maria Grazia Balzarini, Carlo Pirovano, and Maria Teresa Fiorio (eds.), *Museo Archeologico ed Artistico nel Castello Sforzesco. Pinacoteca*, vol. ii, Milan 1998

Mus. cat. New York 1984
John P. O'Neill (ed.), *The Jack and Belle Linsky Collections in the Metropolitan Museum of Art*, New York 1984

Mus. cat. New York 2022
Denise Allen et al. (eds.), *Italian Renaissance and Baroque Bronzes in the Metropolitan Museum of Art*, New York 2022

Mus. cat. Salzburg 1962
Ernst H. Buschbeck, *Residenzgalerie Salzburg mit Sammlung Czernin und Sammlung Schönborn-Buchheim*, Salzburg 1962

Mus. cat. Stuttgart 1907
Konrad Lange (comp.), *Verzeichnis der Gemälde-sammlung im Kgl. Museum der bildenden Künste zu Stuttgart*, Stuttgart 1907

Mus. cat. Venice 1982
Maria Agnese Chiari Moretto Wiel, *Incisioni da Tiziano. Catalogo del fondo grafico a stampa del Museo Correr*, Venice 1982

Mus. cat. Vicenza 2003
Maria Elisa Avagnina, Margaret Binotto, and Giovanni Carlo Federico Villa (eds.), *Pinacoteca Civica di Vicenza. Dipinti dal XIV al XVI secolo. Catalogo scientifico delle collezioni*, Vicenza 2003

Mus. cat. Vienna 1933
Hans Tietze, Erica Tietze-Conrat, Otto Benesch, and Karl Garzarolli-Thurnlackh, *Die Zeichnungen der Deutschen Schulen bis zum Beginn des Klassizismus* (Beschreibender Katalog der Handzeichnungen in der Graphischen Sammlung Albertina 4/5), Vienna 1933

Mus. cat. Vienna 1938
Ludwig Baldass et al., *Katalog der Gemäldegalerie*, Vienna 1938

Mus. cat. Vienna 1954
Günther Heinz and Ernst H. Buschbeck, *Kunsthistorisches Museum. Gemälde-Galerie. Die italienischen, spanischen, französischen und englischen Malerschulen* (Führer durch das Kunsthistorische Museum 3), Vienna 1954

Mus. cat. Vienna 1971
Walter Koschatzky and Alice Strobl, *Die Dürerzeichnungen der Albertina*, Salzburg 1971

Mus. cat. Vienna 1981
Klaus Demus (ed.), *Flämische Malerei von Jan van Eyck bis Pieter Bruegel d.Ä.* (Führer durch das Kunsthistorische Museum 31), Vienna 1981

Mus. cat. Vienna 1991
Sylvia Ferino-Pagden, Wolfgang Prohaska, and Karl Schütz, *Die Gemäldegalerie des Kunsthistorischen Museums in Wien. Verzeichnis der Gemälde*, Vienna 1991

Mus. cat. Vienna 1997
Wilfried Seipel (ed.), *Pieter Bruegel d.Ä. im Kunsthistorischen Museum*, Vienna 1997

Mus. cat. Vienna 2009
Meisterwerke der Antikensammlung (Kurzführer durch das Kunsthistorische Museum 4), ed. Sabine Haag, Vienna 2009

Mus. cat. Vienna 2010
Meisterwerke der Kunstkammer (Kurzführer durch das Kunsthistorische Museum 12), ed. Sabine Haag, Vienna 2010

Mus. cat. Vienna 2012
Sabine Haag and Franz Kirchweger (eds.), *Die Kunstkammer. Die Schätze der Habsburger*, Vienna 2012

Mus. cat. Vienna 2013
Meisterwerke aus der Kunstkammer Wien (Kurzführer durch das Kunsthistorische Museum 12), ed. Sabine Haag, Vienna 2013 (reprint)

Mus. cat. Vienna 2022
Christof Metzger (ed.), *The Print*, Vienna (Albertina) 2022

SECONDARY LITERATURE

Agnoli 2002
Nadia Agnoli, *Museo archeologico nazionale di Palestrina. Le sculture*, Rome 2002

Aikema 1996
Bernard Aikema, *Jacopo Bassano and his Public: Moralizing Pictures in an Age of Reform, ca. 1535–1600*, Princeton 1996

Aikema 2011
Bernard Aikema, *Bassano, i fiamminghi e l'Europa*, in Hochmann 2011, 101–38

Alberti 1550
Leandro Alberti, *Descrittione di tutta Italia*, Bologna 1550

Alberton Vinco da Sesso 1986
Livia Alberton Vinco Da Sesso, s.v. 'Bassano Francesco', 'Bassano Leandro', in DBI 32, 1986, 173–77, 188–92

Albonico and Moro 2020
Simone Albonico and Simone Moro (eds.), *Gaspare Ambrogio Visconti e la Milano di fine Quattrocento. Politica, arti e lettere,* Rome 2020

Alciato 1542
Clarissimi viri D. Andreae Alciati Emblematum libellus, uigilanter recognitus, & iam recens per Wolphgangum Hungerum Bauarum, rhythmis Germanicis uersus, Paris (Christian Wechel) 1542, URL: https://www.emblems.arts.gla.ac.uk/alciato/books.php?id=A42b (last accessed: 13 Aug. 2024)

Alciato 1602
Omnia Andreae Alciati V. C. emblemata cum commentariis, quibus emblematum detecta origine, dubia omnia, et obscura illustrantur, ed. Claude Mignault, Paris 1602, URL: https://www.digitale-sammlungen.de/de/details/bsb11400471 (last accessed: 13 Aug. 2024)

Aldrovandi 1600
Ulisse Aldrovandi, *Ornithologiae Tomus alter,* Bologna 1600

Allers 1944
Rudolf Allers, 'Microcosmus. From Anaximandros to Paracelsus', *Traditio,* 2 (1944), 319–407

Alpago-Novello 1937
Luigi Alpago-Novello, 'Agostino Alpago botanico bellunese del Cinquecento', *Archivio storico di Belluno Feltre e Cadore,* 9 (1937), 841–49

Alpago-Novello 1940
Luigi Alpago-Novello, 'Ancora di Agostino Alpago botanico bellunese del Cinquecento', *Archivio storico di Belluno Feltre e Cadore,* 12 (1940), 1229–31

Alpini 1591
Prospero Alpini, *De Medicina Ægyptiorum libri quatuor,* Venice 1591

Alpini 1656
Prospero Alpini, *De plantis exoticis Libri Duo,* Venice 1656

Alpini 1719
Prospero Alpini, *De medicina methodica libri tredecim,* 2nd printing, Leiden 1719

Ambrosoli 1992
Mauro Ambrosoli, *Scienziati, contadini e proprietari. Botanica e agricoltura nell'Europa occidentale,* Turin 1992

Ames-Lewis 1997
Francis Ames-Lewis, 'Leonardo's Botanical Drawings', *Achademia Leonardi Vinci,* X, 1997, 117–24

Angelini 1999
Annarita Angelini, *Sapienza prudenza eroica virtù. Il mediomondo di Daniele Barbaro,* Florence 1999

Anguillara 1561
Luigi Squalermo, detto Anguillara, *Semplici dell'eccellente M. Lvigi Angvillara Liquali in più Pareri à diversi nobili huomini scritti appaiono, Et Nuovamente da M. Giovanni Marinello mandati in luce,* Venice 1561

Apianus 1484
Johannes Apianus [Johannes Bennewitz], *Joannis Apiani Tractatus de archangelis eorumque plantis, sicut ex antiquissimis hebraeorum sapientium scriptis compertum est, Abraha Löw adiuuante diligenter in Latinum sermonem uersus et nunc primum editus,* Strasbourg (Heinrich Knoblitzer) 1484

Aretini 1998
Paola Aretini, A destra e a sinistra. *L'orientamento nel mondo classico,* Pisa, 1998

Aristoteles 1912
William David Ross and John Alexander Smith, *The Works of Aristotle Translated into English,* Oxford 1912, URL: https://archive.org/details/worksofaristotle512aris/mode/2up (last accessed: 20 Aug. 2024)

Aristoteles 2007
Aristoteles, Über die Teile der Lebewesen, trans. with commentary by Wolfgang Kullmann, Berlin 2007

Armstrong 2003
Lilian Armstrong, *The Pico Master: A Venetian Miniaturist of the Late Quattrocento,* in Dies., *Studies of Renaissance Miniaturists in Venice,* i, London 2003, 233–338

Arslan 1936
Edoardo Arslan, 'Bassanesca', *Studi trentini,* 17 (1936), II, 100–15

Arslan 1960
Edoardo Arslan, *I Bassano,* 2 vols., Milan 1960

Arslan 1966
Michele Arslan, *Sull'amicizia fra Galileo Galilei e Fabrizio d'Acquapendente,* in *Scritti e discorsi nel IV centenario della nascita di Galileo Galilei,* Padua 1966, 123–8

Avagnina 1992
Maria Elisa Avagnina, 'The Pictorial Technique of Jacopo Bassano as Discussed in the Early Sources', in exh. cat. Bassano and Fort Worth 1992, 233–44

Avery 1987
Charles Avery, *Giambologna. The Complete Sculpture,* Oxford 1987

Azzi Visentini 1984
Margherita Azzi Visentini, *L'orto botanico di Padova e il giardino del Rinascimento,* Milan 1984

Azzi Visentini 1986
Margherita Azzi Visentini, 'Il giardino dei semplici', in exh. cat. Modena 1986, 19–25

Azzi Visentini 1988
Margherita Azzi Visentini (ed.), *Il giardino veneto. Storia e conservazione,* Milan 1988

Bachtin 1965
Mikhail M. Bachtin, *Rabelais and His World* (trans. Helene Iswolsky), Bloomington, Indiana, 1965

Bachtin 1987
Mikhail M. Bachtin, *Rabelais und seine Welt. Volkskultur als Gegenkultur,* Frankfurt am Main 1987

Baffioni 1981
Carmela Baffioni, *Il IV libro dei 'Meteorologica' di Aristotele,* Naples 1981

Baldacchini 2011
Lorenzo Baldacchini, *Alle origini dell'editoria in volgare. Niccolò Zoppino da Ferrara a Venezia. Annali (1503–1544),* Manziana 2011

Baldacci and Saccardo 1900
Antonio Baldacci and Pier Andrea Saccardo, 'Onorio Belli e Prospero Alpino e la Flora dell'isola di Creta', *Malpighia,* 14 (1900), 140–63

Baldass 1923
Ludwig Baldass, 'Sittenbild und Stilleben im Rahmen des niederländischen Romanismus', *Jahrbuch der kunsthistorischen Sammlungen in Wien,* 36 (1923), 15–46

Baldass 1936
Ludwig Baldass, 'Laux Furtenagels Bildnis des Ehepaars Burgkmair', *Pantheon,* 17 (1936), 143–7

Baldass 1949
Ludwig Baldass, 'Some Remarks on Francesco Bassano and His Historical Function', *Art Quarterly,* 12 (1949), 198–219

Baldass 1955
Ludwig Baldass, 'Les tableaux champêtres des Bassano et la peinture réaliste des Pays-Bas au XVI siècle', *Gazette des Beaux-Arts,* 45 (1955), 143–60

Ballarin 1966
Alessandro Ballarin, 'Chirurgia bassanesca I', *Arte Veneta,* 20 (1966), 112–136

Ballarin 1967
Alessandro Ballarin, 'Jacopo Bassano e lo studio di Raffaello de dei Salviati', *Arte Veneta,* 21 (1967), 77–101

Ballarin 1968
Alessandro Ballarin, 'Pittura veneziana nei musei di Budapest, Dresda, Praga e Varsavia', *Arte Veneta*, 22 (1968), 237–55

Ballarin 1995
Alessandro Ballarin, 'L'orto del Bassano. A proposito di alcuni quadri e disegni inediti singolari', in Ballarin 1995b, i, 3–26

Ballarin 1995a
Alessandro Ballarin, 'Jacopo Bassano. Ritratto di Levriero', in Ballarin 1995b, ii, 377–408

Ballarin 1995b
Alessandro Ballarin, *Jacopo Bassano. Scritti 1964–1995*, ed. Vittoria Romani, Cittadella (PD) 1995

Ballarin 1995c
Alessandro Ballarin, 'La bottega di Jacopo Bassano negli anni settanta: un tentativo di bilancio con qualche esempio', in Ballarin 1995b, ii, 335–61

Ballarin 2004
Alessandro Ballarin, 'Jacopo Bassano, Francesco Bassano, Inverno', in Altomani 2004, 71–104, URL: https://books.google.at/books?id=spbsDwAAQBAJ&printsec=frontcover&hl=de&source=gbs_ge_summary_r&cad=0#v=onepage&q&f=false (last accessed: 2 Jan. 2025)

Ballarin 2007
Alessandro Ballarin, 'L'"Annunzio ad Abramo della partenza per Canaan" Giusti del Giardino', *Artibus et Historiae*, 28/56 (2007), 33–48

Ballarin 2010
Alessandro Ballarin, *Jacopo Bassano 1545-1555*, in exh. cat. Bassano del Grappa 2010, 41–55

Ballarin 2010
Alessandro Ballarin, Jacopo Bassano 1545-1555, in exh. cat. Bassano del Grappa 2010, 41–55

Barbaro 1534
Ermolao Barbaro, *In C. Plinii Naturalis Historiae Libros Castigationes*, Basel 1534

Baroni Vannucci 1997
Alessandra Baroni Vannucci, *Jan van der Straet detto Giovanni Stradano: flandrus pictor et inventor*, Milan 1997

Baroni Vannucci 2017
Alessandra Baroni Vannucci, 'L'autore delle incisioni del comento e la controversa figura di Baccio Baldini', in Lorenz Böninger and Paolo Procaccioli (eds.), *Per Cristoforo Landino lettore di Dante. Il contesto civile e culturale, la storia tipografica e la fortuna del Comento sopra la Comedia*, Florence 2017, 153–69

Bastelaer 1908
René van Bastelaer, *Les estampes de Peter Bruegel l'Ancien*, Brussels 1908

Battilotti et al. 2016
Donata Battilotti, Guido Beltramini, Edoardo Demo, and Walter Panciera (eds.), *Storia dell'architettura nel Veneto. Il Cinquecento*, Venice 2016

Bauer 2000
Rotraud Bauer, 'Gartenlandschaften mit Tieren. Zur Tapisserienserie der sogenannten Granvellagärten in Wien', in exh. cat. Hamm and Mainz 2000, 151–4

Bava 1995
Anna Maria Bava, 'La collezione di pittura e i grandi progetti decorativi', in Giovanni Romano (ed.), *Le collezioni di Carlo Emanuele I di Savoia*, Turin 1995, 212–21

Bava 2016
Anna Maria Bava, 'Il collezionismo di Carlo Emanuele I di Savoia', in Ericani, Caramanna, and Millozzi 2014, ii, 505–17

Beazley 1963
John D. Beazley, *Attic Red-figure Vase-painters*, 2nd printing, Oxford 1963

Beitl 1995
Klaus Beitl, '"Ruhender Holzfäller" ist ein rastender Mäher. Ethnographisch-realienkundlicher Befund zu einer Terracotta von Andrea Riccio [*recte* Andrea Broscio] in der Kunstkammer des Kunsthistorischen Museums Wien', *Osterreichische Zeitschrift fur Volkskunde*, new series XLIX, 1995, 98, 57–71

Belfiore 2015
Valentina Belfiore, 'Grenz- und Torgottheiten im Mittelmeerraum', *Thetis. Mannheimer Beiträge zur Klassischen Archäologie und Geschichte Griechenlands und Zyperns*, 22 (2015), 150–63

Belli 2000
Onorio Belli, *Scritti di antiquaria e botanica (1586–1602)*, introduction, critical edition, and commentary by L. Beschi, Rome 2000

Beltramini and Demo 2022
Guido Beltramini and Edoardo Demo, *Palladio. Architettura e impresa nella Vicenza del Rinascimento*, Venice 2022

Beltramini, Gasparotto, and Vinco 2021
Guido Beltramini, Davide Gasparotto, and Mattia Vinco, *La fabbrica del Rinascimento. Processi creativi, mercato e produzione a Vicenza*, Venice 2021

Benedetti 1571
Rocco Benedetti, *Ragguaglio delle Allegrezze, Solennità, e feste, fatte in Venetia per la felice Vittoria, al Clariss. Sig. Girolamo Diedo, digniss. Consigliere di Corfù*, Venice 1571

Benveniste 1971
Émile Benveniste, *Problemi di linguistica generale*, Milan 1971

Benzoni 1998
Gino Benzoni, s.v. 'Gallo, Agostino', in DBI 51, 1998, 693–97

Berdini 1997
Paolo Berdini, *The Religious Art of Jacopo Bassano: Painting as Visual Exegesis*, Cambridge 1997

Berengo 1975
Marino Berengo, 'Introduzione', in Camillo Tarello, *Ricordo di agricoltura*, Turin 1975, VII–XLVIII

Berenson 1932
Bernard Berenson, *Italian Pictures of the Renaissance. A List of the Principal Artists and their Works with an Index of Places*, Oxford 1932

Berra 1988
Giacomo Berra, 'Allegoria e mitologia nella pittura dell'Arcimboldi: la "Flora" e il "Vertunno" nei versi di un libretto sconosciuto di rime', *Acme*, XLI, II (1988), 11–39, URL: http://archiv.ub.uni-heidelberg.de/artdok/volltexte/2008/606/ (last accessed: 2 Jan. 2025)

Berra 1996
Giacomo Berra, 'Arcimboldi e Caravaggio: "diligenza" e "patienza" nella natura morta arcaica', *Paragone*, XLVII, 8-9-10 (1996), 108–61

Berra 2011
Giacomo Berra, 'Frutti e fiori dell'Arcimboldo "cavati dal naturale": l' influsso sulla nascente natura morta lombarda e sul giovane Caravaggio', in exh. cat. Milan 2011, 315–47

Berra 2017
Giacomo Berra, 'Le teste "composte" e "reversibili" dell'Arcimboldo e la nascita della natura morta', in exh. cat. Rome 2017/18, 120–7

Berra 2020
Claudia Berra, 'I "doi philosophi": un tema ficiniano dall'affresco di casa Visconti al poemetto di Antonio Fregoso', in Albonico and Moro 2020, 173–99

Berra 2021
Giacomo Berra, 'Le teste "composte" e "reversibili" dell'Arcimboldo e la nascita della natura morta', in Heidelberg, arthistoricum.net 2021, URL: https://archiv.ub.uni-heidelberg.de/artdok/7200/1/Berra_Le_teste_composte_e_reversibili_dell%27Arcimboldo_e_la_nascita_della_natura_morta_2017.pdf (last accessed: 2 Jan. 2025)

Berti 1986
Enrico Berti, 'Il ruolo storico dell'aristotelismo nello Studio di Padova', in exh. cat. Modena 1986, 19–25

Bertoldini 2006
Marisa Bertoldini (ed.), *Esprit sphérique: dalla collezione Legler*, exh. cat. Galleria Gottardo Lugano, 27 September to 23 December 2006, Milan 2006

Berveglieri 1995
Roberto Berveglieri, *Inventori stranieri a Venezia (1474–1788). Importazione di tecnologia e circolazione di tecnici artigiani inventori. Repertorio*, Venice 1995

Beutler 1973
Corinne Beutler, 'Un chapitre de la sensibilité collective: la littérature agricole en Europe continentale au XVIe siècle', *Annales. Economies, sociétés, civilisations,* 5 (1973), 1280–1301

Beyer 2008
Andreas Beyer, '"...il gran pittore Giuseppe Arcimboldi" Zur Konstruktion von Arcimboldos Ruhm', in exh. cat. Paris and Vienna 2007/08, 25–31

Beyer 2012
Andreas Beyer, 'Ruhmesblätter. Giuseppe Arcimboldos Selbstporträt von 1587 als memoria cartacea', in Sebastian Egenhofer et al. (eds.), *Was ist ein Bild? Antworten in Bildern*, Munich 2012, 287–89

Beyer 2017
Andreas Beyer, 'L'arte delle configurazioni molteplici: le teste composte di Giuseppe Arcimboldi e la pratica delle immagini a doppio senso', in exh. cat. Rome 2017/18, [140]–45

Bezza 1995
Giuseppe Bezza (ed.), *Arcana mundi : antologia del pensiero astrologico antico*, ii vols., Milan 1995

Bianchi 1998
Eugenia Bianchi, 'Jacopo da Ponte detto Jacopo Bassano', in mus. cat. Milan 1998, ii, 38–44

Bird and Clayton 2017
Rufus Bird and Martin Clayton (eds.), *Charles II – Art and Power*, London 2017

Birnfeld 2009
Nicole Birnfeld, *Der Künstler und seine Frau. Studien zu Doppelbildnissen des 15.–17. Jahrhunderts*, Weimar 2009

Blume 2000
Dieter Blume, *Regenten des Himmels. Astrologische Bilder in Mittelalter und Renaissance* (Studien aus dem Warburg-Haus 3), Berlin 2000

Blunt and Raphael 1990
Wilfrid Blunt and Sandra Raphael, *Gli Erbari*, Turin 1990

Bode 1980
Wilhelm von Bode, *The Italian Bronze Statuettes of the Renaissance*, New York 1980

Boeheim 1889
Wendelin Boeheim (ed.), 'Urkunden und Regesten aus der k.k. Hofbibliothek (Fortsetzung)', *Jahrbuch der kunsthistorischen Sammlungen des Allerhöchsten Kaiserhauses,* 10 (1889), I–XIX

Bollati 2003
Milvia Bollati, 'Il Libro d'ore di Gian Galeazzo Visconti: Giovannino, Salomone de Grassi e il Maestro del Libro d'Ore di Modena', in Milvia Bollati (ed.), *Il Libro d'ore Visconti. Commentario al codice,* Modena 2003, 259–346

Bollati 2004
Milvia Bollati, 'Grassi, Giovannino de', in Milvia Bollati (ed.), *Dizionario biografico dei miniatori italiani. Secoli IX-XVI,* Milan 2004, 318–21

Bonorand and Haffter 1983
Conradin Bonorand and Heinz Haffter (eds.), *Die Dedikationsepisteln von und an Vadian. Personenkommentar II zum Vadianischen Briefwerk von Conradin Bonorand* (Vadian Studien, Untersuchungen und Texte 2), St Gallen 1983

Borchert 2019
Till-Holger Borchert, *Pieter Bruegel the Elder and Flemish Book Illumination, in: Alice Hoppe-Harnoncourt et al. (eds.), Bruegel. The Hand of the Master. Essays in Context*, Vienna 2019, 96–108

Bordignon Favero 1994
Elia Bordignon Favero, *Giovanni Battista Volpato critico e pittore*, Treviso 1994

Borea 2009
Evelina Borea, *Lo specchio dell'arte italiana. Stampe in cinque secoli*, 4 vols., Pisa 2009

Borghini 1584
Raffaello Borghini, *Il riposo, in cui della pittura, e della scultura si favella, de' piu illustri pittori, e scultori, a delle piu famose opere loro si fa mentione, e le cose principali appartenenti a dette arti s'insegnano,* Florence 1584

Bortolami 2009/10
Erica Bortolami, 'Precisazioni iconografiche sugli affreschi di casa Dal Corno', in Ericani, Caramanna, and Millozzi 2014, i, 171–80

Bortolotti 1999
Luca Bortolotti, 'Prolegomeni alla riflessione sul significato della "scena di genere" nella produzione di Jacopo Bassano', *Venezia Cinquecento,* IX/18 (1999), 137–71

Boschini 1660 (1960)
Marco Boschini, *La carta del navegar pitoresco,* Venice 1660, ed. Anna Pallucchini, Venice and Rome 1960

Boschung 2013
Dietrich Boschung, 'Tempora anni: Personfikationen der Jahreszeiten in der römischen Antike', in Thierry Greub (ed.), *Das Bild der Jahreszeiten im Wandel der Kulturen und Zeiten*, Munich 2013, 179–200

Bottari and Ticozzi 1822
Stefano Bottari and Giovanni Ticozzi, *Raccolta di lettere sulla pittura, scultura ed architettura,* Milan 1822

Bouché-Leclercq 1882
Auguste Bouché-Leclercq, *Histoire de la divination dans l'Antiquité*, 4 vols., Paris 1882

Bovey 2005
Alixe Bovey, *An Early Renaissance Guide to Health*, London 2005

Braida and Infelise 2010
Lodovica Braida and Mario Infelise (eds.), *Libri per tutti. Generi editoriali di larga circolazione tra antico regime ed età contemporanea,* Turin 2010

BRCP 2016
Bosch Research and Conservation Project (BRCP): Matthijs Ilsink et al. (eds.), *Hieronymus Bosch, Painter and Draughtsman / Jheronimus Bosch. Maler und Zeichner*, Brussels 2016, URL: http://boschproject.org/#/artworks/Christ_Carrying_the_Cross_KHM (last accessed: 13 Dec. 2024)

Brown 2021
Beverly Louise Brown, 'Who Let the Dogs Out: Jacopo Bassano, Naturalism and Prints', *Artibus et historiae*, XLII/83 (2021), 111–45

Brücher 2019
Günther Brücher, *Geschichte der venezianischen Malerei*, vi: *Paolo Veronese und Jacopo Bassano*, Vienna, Cologne, and Weimar 2019, 309–431

Buchanan 1990
Ian Buchanan, 'The Collections of Niclaes Jongelinck: II. The "Months" by Pieter Bruegel the Elder', *The Burlington Magazine,* 132 (August 1990), 541–50

Buganza 2020
Stefania Buganza, 'Tra città e campagna. Gaspare Ambrogio Visconti committente d'arte', in Albonico and Moro 2020, 79–108

Buonanno 1890
Gennaro Buonanno, *I due rarissimi globi di Mercatore nella Biblioteca governativa di Cremona. Notizia*, Cremona 1890

Burgess 2012
Richard W. Burgess, 'The Chronograph of 354. Its Manuscripts, Contents and History', *Journal of Late Antiquity*, 5 (2012), 345–96

Burgess 2017
Richard W. Burgess, 'The New Edition of the Chronograph of 354: A Detailed Critique', *Zeitschrift für antikes Christentum*, 21 (2017), 383–415

Busbecq 2005
Ogier Ghislain de Busbecq, *The Turkish Letters of Ogier Ghiselin de Busbecq, Imperial Ambassador at Constantinople, 1554–1562*, Baton Rouge 2005

Buscaroli 1935
Rezio Buscaroli, *La pittura di paesaggio in Italia*, Bologna 1935

Bussadori 1988
Paola Bussadori, 'Gli orti privati padovani', in exh. cat. Praglia 1988, 47–54

Bussato 1592
Marco Bussato, *Giardino di agricoltura… Nel quale… s'insegna… la vera maniera di piantare & incalmare arbori e viti di tutte le sorti… Si mostra il modo di lavorar le terre, di mietere e battere i grani & acconciar le viti e far i vini… Aggiontoui nel fine vna visita, che far si deue ogni mese alla campagna, con alcuni vtilissimi ricordi*, Venice (Giouanni Fiorina) 1592, URL: https://books.google.at/books?vid=IBNR:CR000053425&redir_esc=y (last accessed: 2 Jan. 2025)

Cadei 1970
Antonio Cadei, 'Giovannino de Grassi nel Taccuino di Bergamo', *Critica d'arte,* XVI/109 (1970), 17–36

Cafà 2005
Valeria Cafà, cat. 20 in *Andrea Palladio e la villa veneta. Da Petrarca a Carlo Scarpa*, ed. Guido Beltramini and Howard Burns, Venice 2005, 212–13

Calapà 2022
Annalisa Calapà, *Sacra civitatium Etruriae: Untersuchungen zur Religionsgeschichte des römischen Etrurien*, Stuttgart 2022

Calzolari 1566
Francesco Calzolari, *Il viaggio di Monte Baldo, della magnifica città di Verona,* Venice 1566

Campori 1870
Giuseppe Campori, *Raccolta di cataloghi ed inventari inediti di quadri, statue, disegni, bronzi, dorerie, smalti, medaglie, avori ess. dal secolo XV al secolo XIX*, Modena 1870

Cantalupus 1571
Onofrius Cantalupus, *Iter creticum*, Venice (Hieronymus Scotus) 1571

Caracausi 2004
Andrea Caracausi, *Nastri, nastrini, cordelle. L'industria serica nel Padovano secc. XVII–XIX,* Padua 2004

Caracausi 2008
Andrea Caracausi, *Dentro la bottega. Culture del lavoro in una città d'età moderna*, Venice 2008

Caracausi 2014
Andrea Caracausi, 'Textiles Manufacturing, Product Innovations and Transfer of Technology in Padua and Venice between the Sixteenth and Eighteenth Centuries', in Davids Karel and Bert De Munck (eds.), *Innovation and Creativity in Late Medieval and Early Modern European Cities,* Farnham 2014, 131–60

Caracausi, Grosso, and Romani 2019
Andrea Caracausi, Marsel Grosso, and Vittoria Romani (eds.), *Il paesaggio veneto nel Rinascimento europeo. Linguaggi, rappresentazioni, scambi*, Milan 2019

Caramanna 2004
Claudia Caramanna, 'La fortuna delle opere di Jacopo Bassano nelle raccolte antiche: novità sulle presenze bassanesche nella collezione Ludovisi', *Bolletino del Museo Civico di Bassano,* 25 (2004), 173–87

Caramanna 2013
Claudia Caramanna, 'La precoce diffusione delle opere dei Bassano in Francia', *Studiolo,* 10 (2013), 228–41

Caramanna 2024
Claudia Caramanna, 'From the Venetian Countryside to the European Courts – the Success of Jacopo Bassano and his Workshop', in exh. cat. Helsinki 2024, 35–50

Carlino 1994
Andrea Carlino, *La fabbrica del corpo. Libri e dissezione nel Rinascimento,* Turin 1994

Carlino 2004
Andrea Carlino, 'Vesalio e la cultura visiva delle anatomie a stampa del Rinascimento', in exh. cat. Bologna 2004, 75–91

Cecchi 1999
Alessandro Cecchi, 'La collezione di quadri di Villa Medici', in exh. cat. Rome 1999, 59–65

Cennini 2004
Cennino Cennini, *Il Libro dell'arte della pittura: il manoscritto della Biblioteca nazionale centrale di Firenze, con integrazioni dal Codice riccardiano*, ed. Antonio P. Torresi, Ferrara 2004

Ceradini 1889–1891
Giulio Ceradini, 'Memorie originali. Due globi mercatoriani della Biblioteca di Cremona', *Il politecnico. Giornale dell'ingegnere architetto civile ed industriale*, 1889, 721–39; 1890, 390–437, 497–512, 605–17; 1891, 61–84, 194–240, 368–400, 743–65

Cerasuolo 2016
Angela Cerasuolo, 'Sulle tecniche di riproduzione seriale e l'impiego del lucido: ipotesi per la bottega dei Bassano', in Ericani, Caramanna, and Millozzi 2014, iii, 787–801

Cermenati 1908
Mario Cermenati, 'Francesco Calzolari da Verona e sue lettere ad Ulisse Aldrovandi', *Annali di Botanica*, 7 (1908), 83–138

Cermenati 1912
Mario Cermenati, 'Un diplomatico naturalista del Rinascimento. Andrea Navagero', *Nuovo Archivio Veneto*, new series, 12 (1912), 164–205

Cerri 1998
Giovanni Cerri, 'L'ideologia dei quattro elementi da Omero ai Presocratici', *Annali di archeologia e storia antica / Università degli studi di Napoli 'L'Orientale', Dipartimento di Asia Africa e Mediterraneo,* 20 (1998), 5–58

Ceruti and Chiocco 1622
Benedetto Ceruti and Andrea Chiocco, *Musaeum Franc. Calceolari Iun. Veronensis,* Verona 1622

Cessi 1965
Francesco Cessi, *Andrea Briosco, detto il Riccio: Scultore (1470–1532),* Trento 1965

Chatzidakis, Haug, Roemer, and Rombach 2021
Michail Chatzidakis, Henrike Haug, Lisa Marie Roemer, and Ursula Rombach (eds.), *Con bella maniera. Festgabe für Peter Seiler zum 65. Geburtstag*, Heidelberg 2021

Chew 1962
Samuel C. Chew, *The Pilgrimage of Life*, New Haven and London 1962

Ciancio 2015
Luca Ciancio, '"Per questa via s'ascende a magior seggio". Pietro Andrea Mattioli e le scienze mediche e naturali alla corte di Bernardo Cles', *Studi Trentini di Scienze Storiche*, 94 (2015), 159–84

Cioni 1975
Alfredo Cioni, under the entry 'Capcasa, Matteo', in DBI 18, 1975, 401–3

Ciriacono 2019
Salvatore Ciriacono, under the entry 'Tarello, Camillo', in DBI 95, 2019, 16–20

Classen 2017
Albrecht Classen, 'Everyday Life and Culture in the Late Middle Ages: the Evidence of the Tacuinum Sanitatis: Historical-medical and Social-cultural Aspects', *Mediaevistik*, 30 (2017), 225–40

Clayton 2010
Martin Clayton, *Leonardo. Il genio nei disegni*, Milan 2019

Cogliati Arano 1976
Luisa Cogliati Arano, *The Medieval Health Handbook: Tacuinum Sanitatis*, New York 1976

Coletti 1925/26
Luigi Coletti, Paesi di Paolo Veronese, *Dedalo*, VI/2 (1925/26), 377–410

Colonna 1499
Francesco Colonna, *Hypnerotomachia Poliphili*, Venice (Aldus Manutius) 1499

Colonna 1964 (1980)
Francesco Colonna, *Hypnerotomachia Poliphili*, critical edition with commentary, ed. Giovanni Pozzi and Lucia A. Ciapponi, Padua 1964 (new printing 1980)

Colonna 1999
Francesco Colonna, *Hypnerotomachia Poliphili*, with translation and commentary, ed. Marco Ariani and Mino Gabriele, Milan 1999 (2nd printing)

Comanini 1591 (1962)
Gregorio Comanini, 'Il Figino. Overo del fine della pittura [1591]', in Paola Barocchi, *Trattati d'arte del Cinquecento fra Manierismo e Controriforma*, iii, Bari 1962, 237–379

Comanini 2001
Gregorio Comanini, *The Figino, or On the purpose of Painting: Art Theory in the Late Renaissance*, Toronto 2001

Conger 1922
George Perrigo Conger, *Theories of Macrocosms and Microcosms: in the History of Philosophy*, New York 1922

Conigliello 1991
Lucilla Conigliello, 'Pesci, crostacei e un'iguana per l'imperatore Rodolfo II', *Paragone*, 42 (1991), 22–9

Conigliello 1992
Lucilla Conigliello, 'L'altra faccia di Arcimboldo', *Paragone. Arte*, 43 (1992), 509/511 (new series, 34/35, 44–50)

Conigliello 2014
Lucilla Conigliello, 'Jacopo Ligozzi. La vita e le opere', in exh. cat. Florence 2014, 13–18

Corsato 2010
Carlo Corsato, 'Production and Reproduction in the Workshop of Jacopo Bassano: Four Matrices for the Four Seasons in the Kunsthistorisches Museum in Vienna', *Jahrbuch des Kunsthistorischen Museums Wien*, 12 (2010), 40–53

Cottrell 2009
Philip Cottrell, 'Painters in Practice: Tintoretto, Bassano and the Studio of Bonifacio de' Pitati', in Falomir 2009, 50–7

Cottrell and Humfrey 2021
Philip Cottrell and Peter Humfrey, *Bonifacio de' Pitati*, Treviso 2021

Crescenzi 1505
Pietro Crescenzi, *De agricultura. Istoriato*, Venice 1504, URL: http://id.sbn.it/bid/VIAE011111 (last accessed: 2 Jan. 2025)

Crescenzi 1561
Pietro Crescentio bolognese tradotto nuovamente per Francesco Sansovino. Nel quale si trattano gli ordini di tutte le cose che si appartengono a' commodi & a gli utili della villa. Con le figure delle herbe & de gli animali poste a' suoi luoghi. Con un ampio vocabolario delle voci difficili che sono in questa opera, et con i disegni de gli stromenti co' quali si cultiva & si lavora la terra, Venice (Francesco Sansovino) 1561, URL: http://id.sbn.it/bid/MILE000829 (last accessed: 2 Jan. 2025)

Cuillandre 1943
Joseph Cuillandre, *La Droite et la gauche dans les poemes homeriques en concordance avec la doctrine pythagoricienne et avec la tradition celtique*, Rennes 1943

Cunningham 2006
Andrew Cunningham, 'Fabrici and Harvey', in Giuseppe Ongaro, Maurizio Rippa Bonati, and Gaetano Thiene (eds.), *Harvey a Padova, Atti del convegno celebrativo*, Treviso 2006, 129–49

Curletto 1990
Giuseppe Silvio Curletto, *La norma e il suo rovescio: coppie di opposti nel mondo religioso antico*, Genoa 1990

CVA Österreich 1959
Fritz Eichler, *Corpus Vasorum Antiquorum, Österreich, Wien, Kunsthistorisches Museum*, ii: *Rotfigurige attische Vorratsgefäße*, Vienna 1959

DaCosta Kaufmann 1976
Thomas DaCosta Kaufmann, 'Arcimboldo's Imperial Allegories: G.B. Fonteo and the Interpretation of Arcimboldo's Painting', *Zeitschrift für Kunstgeschichte*, 39 (1976), 275–96

DaCosta Kaufmann 1978
Thomas DaCosta Kaufmann, *Variations on the Imperial Theme in the Age of Maximilian II and Rudolf II*, New York and London 1978

DaCosta Kaufmann 1982
Thomas DaCosta Kaufmann, 'The Eloquent Artist. Towards an Understanding of the Stylistics of Painting at the Court of Rudolf II', *Leids Kunsthistorisch Jaarboeck*, 1982, 119–48

DaCosta Kaufmann 1985
Thomas DaCosta Kaufmann, *L'école de Prague. La peinture à la cour de Rodolphe II*, Paris 1985

DaCosta Kaufmann 1987
Thomas DaCosta Kaufmann, 'The Allegories and Their Meaning', in exh. cat. Venice 1987, 89–109

DaCosta Kaufmann 1993
Thomas DaCosta Kaufmann, *The Mastery of Nature. Aspects of Art, Science, and Humanism in the Renaissance*, Princeton 1993

DaCosta Kaufmann 2008
Thomas DaCosta Kaufmann, 'Arcimboldos Kompositköpfe. Ursprünge und Invention', in exh. cat. Paris and Vienna 2007/08, 97–101

DaCosta Kaufmann 2008a
Thomas DaCosta Kaufmann, 'Giuseppe Arcimboldo: Humanismus, Literatur und Kunst', in exh. cat. Paris and Vienna 2007/08, 273–80

DaCosta Kaufmann 2009
Thomas DaCosta Kaufmann, *Arcimboldo. Visual Jokes, Natural History, and Still-Life Painting*, Chicago and London 2009

DaCosta Kaufmann 2018
Thomas DaCosta Kaufmann, 'Interpreting Arcimboldo: Grotesque Parodies or Serious Jokes?', *The Burlington Magazine*, 160/1382 (May 2018), 368–75

Dal Pozzo 1718
Bartolomeo Dal Pozzo, *Le vite de' pittori degli scultori et architetti veronesi,* Verona 1718

De Grummond 2006
Nancy Thomson de Grummond, *Etruscan Myth, Sacred History, and Legend*, Philadelphia 2006

Deiters 2019
Wencke Deiters, cat. 9 in exh. cat. Treviso 2019/20, 50–1

Della Pergola 1959
Paola Della Pergola, Galleria Borghese. I dipinti, vol. i, Rome 1959

Del Torre Scheuch 2019
Francesca Del Torre, 'Francesco Bassano', in exh. cat. Treviso 2019/20, 38–40

Del Torre Scheuch 2009
Francesca Del Torre Scheuch, 'Dalla laguna fino agli Asburgo: i tanti viaggi di un ciclo di 12 Bassano (ma uno è sparito) / From Venice to the Habsburgs: the Many Voyages of a Cycle of 12 Bassanos (but One is Missing)', *VeneziAltrove*, 8 (2009), 111–31

Del Torre Scheuch 2021
Francesca Del Torre Scheuch, 'Il genio di Jacopo Bassano: invenzione e imprenditorialità', in exh. cat. Vicenza 2021, 159–69

Demo 2001
Edoardo Demo, *L'«anima della città». L'industria tessile a Verona e Vicenza (1400–1550),* Milan 2001

Demo 2003
Edoardo Demo, 'L'impresa nel Veneto tra Medioevo ed Età Moderna', *Annali di storia dell'impresa*, 14 (2003), 251–262

Demo 2004
Edoardo Demo, *Le manifatture tra Medioevo e Età moderna, in L'industria vicentina dal Medioevo ad oggi*, Padua 2004

Demo 2005
Edoardo Demo, '"Da Bressa se traze panni fini e altre sorte de panni de manco precio". L'esportazione dei prodotti tessili bresciani nel '400', *Annali Queriniani*, 6 (2005), 101–30

Demo 2006
Edoardo Demo, Wool and Silk: The Textile Urban Industry of the Venetian Mainland (XV-XVII Centuries), At the Centre (2006), 217–43

Demo 2008
Edoardo Demo, 'Le attività economiche dei committenti vicentini di Palladio. Nuove suggestioni sulla base dei recenti ritrovamenti archivistici', in *Palladio 1508-2008. Il simposio del Cinquecentenario*, Venice 2008, 22–5

Demo 2012
Edoardo Demo, *Mercanti di Terraferma. Uomini, merci e capitali nell'Europa del Cinquecento,* Milan 2012

Demo 2013
Edoardo Demo, 'Industry and Production in the Venetian Terraferma (15th–18th Centuries)', in Erich Dursteler (ed.), *A Companion to Venetian History, 1400–1797,* Leiden and Boston 2013, 291–318

Demo 2013a
Edoardo Demo, 'Manifattura vs agricoltura: la difficile gestione delle acque nella Pedemontana veneta della prima età moderna', in Luca Mocarelli (ed.), *Quando manca il pane. Origini e cause della scarsità delle risorse alimentari in età moderna e contemporanea,* Bologna 2013, 19–33

Demo 2014
Edoardo Demo, 'Manifatture, merci e uomini d'affari bresciani in Europa e nel Vicino Oriente nei secoli XV–XVI', in Maurizio Pegrari (ed.), *Moneta, credito e finanza a Brescia dal Medioevo all'Età Moderna,* Brescia 2014, 115–48

Demo 2021
Edoardo Demo, 'Vicenza nel Cinquecento: l'economia', in Guido Beltramini, Davide Gasparotto, and Mattia Vinco (eds.), *La fabbrica del Rinascimento. Processi creativi, mercato e produzione a Vicenza,* Venice 2021, 83–93

Demo 2021a
Edoardo Demo, 'I libri di conto degli artisti: il caso del libro secondo di Francesco e Jacopo Bassano', in Guido Beltramini, Davide Gasparotto, and Mattia Vinco (eds.), *La fabbrica del Rinascimento. Processi creativi, mercato e produzione a Vicenza,* Venice 2021, 266–71

Demo 2023
Edoardo Demo, 'Bianca Nievo, Laura Thiene e le altre. Le donne e la mercatura a Vicenza nel Rinascimento', in Adriana Chemello and Maria Avagnina (eds.), *Maddalena Campiglia nel suo tempo,* Vicenza 2023, 89–97

Demo and Vianello 2011
Edoardo Demo and Francesco Vianello, 'Manifatture e commerci nella Terraferma veneta in età moderna', *Archivio Veneto*, 142 (2011), 27–50

De Rock and Limberger 2018
Jelle de Rock and Michael Limberger, 'Die städtische Elite und das ländliche Brabant im 16. Jahrhundert', in Meganck and Sprang 2018, 151–67

Derosas 2006
Renzo Derosas, 'Introduzione', in Renzo Derosas (ed.), *Villa. Siti e contesti*, Treviso 2006

Des Places 1964
Édouard des Places, *Syngeneia. La parenté de l'homme avec dieu d'Homère à la Patristique*, Paris 1964

De Toni 1908
Giovan Battista De Toni, *Contributo alla conoscenza delle relazioni del patrizio veneziano Pietro Antonio Michiel con Ulisse Aldrovandi* (Memorie della R. Accademia di Scienze, Lettere ed Arti in Modena IX), Modena 1908

De Toni 1922
Giambattista De Toni, *Le piante e gli animali in Leonardo da Vinci*, Bologna 1922

De Toni 1940
Pietro Antonio Michiel, I cinque libri di piante. Codice Marciano, partial transcription and commentary by Ettore De Toni, Venice 1940

De Visiani 1840
Roberto De Visiani, *Illustrazione delle piante nuove o rare dell'orto di Padova* (Memoria I), Padua 1840

Dhanens 1956
Elisabeth Dhanens, *Jean Boulogne. Giovanni Bologna Fiammingo. Douai 1529 – Florence 1608*, Brussels 1956

Diodorus 1508
Diodorus Siculus, trans. Giovanni Francesco Poggio Bracciolini, Paris (Jehan Petit) 1508

Dioskurides 1544
Pietro Andrea Mattioli, *Di Pedacio Dioscoride Anazarbeo libri cinque della historia, & materia medicinale*, Venice 1544

Di Schino 2019
June di Schino, 'Iconografia della cucina e coreografia del banchetto in Opera di Bartolomeo Scappi', in Myriam Chiabò (ed.), *A tavola nella Roma dei papi nel Rinascimento*, Rome 2019, 21–55

Distelberger 2002
Rudolf Distelberger, *Die Kunst des Steinschnitts: Prunkgefäße, Kameen und Commessi aus der Kunstkammer*, Milan 2002

Distelberger 2002/03
Rudolf Distelberger, 'Die Steinschneidekunst der Neuzeit in Italien', in exh. cat. Vienna 2002/03, 75–99

Divjak and Wischmeyer 2014
Johannes Divjak and Wolfgang Wischmeyer (eds.), *Das Kalenderhandbuch von 354. Der Chronograph des Filocalus*, i: *Der Bildteil des Chronographen*, Vienna 2014

Donattini 1980
Massimo Donattini, 'Giovanni Battista Ramusio e le sue "Navigationi". Appunti per una biografia', *Critica storica*, 17 (1980), 55–100

Donattini 2019
Massimo Donattini, 'Da Gonzalo Fernández de Oviedo a Fernão Alfonso: l'umanesimo mercantile di Giovanni Battista Ramusio', in Wietse de Boer, Vincenzo Lavenia, and Giuseppe Marcocci (eds.), *La ghianda e la quercia. Saggi per Adriano Prosperi*, Rome 2019

Dondi 1960
Raffaele Flaminio Dondi, 'Di Leone Bonzio incisor pubblico di anatomia a Venezia e del suo ritratto dipinto da Leandro da Ponte detto il Cavalier Bassano', *Rivista di Storia della Medicina*, 4 (1960), 205–16

Doosry 2022
Yasmin Doosry, 'Zwischen Imitation und Autonomie. Hans Hoffmann als europäischer Künstler der Renaissance', in exh. cat. Nuremberg 2022, 10–30

Dragonzino 1981
Gian Battista Dragonzino, *Nobiltà di Vicenza*, Vicenza 1981

Draper and Zappo 1998
James David Draper and Agostino Zappo, 'Chronos', in Joan Holt (ed.), *Recent Acquisitions. A Selection 1997–1998* (The Metropolitan Museum of Art Bulletin, Fall 1998, LVI/2), New York 1998

Düring 1944
Ingemar Düring, *Aristotle's Chemical Treatise, Meteorologica, Book IV*, Göteborg 1944

Eastwood 2007
Bruce S. Eastwood, *Ordering the Heavens. Roman Astronomy and Cosmology in the Carolingian Renaissance*, Leiden and Boston 2007

Eckhardt 1976
Wolfgang Eckhardt, 'Erasmus Habermel: Zur Biographie des Instrumentenmachers Kaiser Rudolfs II.', *Jahrbuch der Hamburger Kunstsammlungen*, 21 (1976), 55–92

Eckhardt 1977
Wolfgang Eckhardt, 'Erasmus und Josua Habermel: Kunstgeschichtliche Anmerkungen zu den Werken der beiden Instrumentenmacher', *Jahrbuch der Hamburger Kunstsammlungen*, 22 (1977), 13–74

Egmond 2013
Florike Egmond, 'A Collection within a Collection. Rediscovered Animal Drawings from the Collections of Conrad Gessner and Felix Platter', *Journal of the History of Collections*, 25/2 (2013), 149–70

Egmond and Kusukawa 2016
Florike Egmond and Sachiko Kusukawa, 'Circulation of Images and Graphic Practices in Renaissance Natural History: the Example of Conrad Gessner', *Gesnerus, Swiss Journal of the History of Medicine and Science*, 73/1 (2016), 29–72

Emboden 1987
William Emboden, *Leonardo da Vinci on Plants and Gardens*, London 1987

Emmens 1973
Jan A. Emmens, '"Eins aber ist nötig". Zu Inhalt und Bedeutung von Markt- und Küchenstücken des 16. Jahrhunderts', in *Album Amicorum J.G. van Gelder*, The Hague 1973, 93–101

Ericani 2011/12
Giuliana Ericani, 'Per la ritrattistica di Leandro Bassano. Considerazioni e aggiunte', in Ericani, Caramanna, and Millozzi 2014, ii, 475–87

Ericani, Caramanna, and Millozzi 2014
Giuliana Ericani, Claudia Caramanna, and Federica Millozzi (eds.), *Jacopo Bassano, i figli, la scuola, l'eredità, Atti del Convegno Internazionale di* Studio, *Bollettino del Museo civico di Bassano* 30/31 (2009/10), 32/33 (2011/12), 34 (2013), 3 vols., Bassano del Grappa 2014

Eskelinen 2024
Kirsi Eskelinen, 'Contextualising the Iconography of Jacopo Bassano's Four Seasons', in exh. cat. Helsinki 2024, 97–109

Fabbri 2022
Federica Fabbri, 'Teaching the History of Art: My Primary Responsibility. In Memoriam: Lilian Armstrong (1936–2021)', *Teca*, 12 (June 2022), 131–8

Fabrici d'Acquapendente 2021
Girolamo Fabrici d'Acquapendente, *Le valvole delle vene*, with an introduction by M. Rippa Bonati and a note by R. Schievenin, Cittadella (PD) 2021

Fahy 1993
Conor Fahy, *Printing a Book at Verona in 1622. The Account Book of Francesco Calzolari Junior*, Paris 1993

Falcone 1597
Giuseppe Falcone, *La nuoua, vaga, et diletteuole villa, del molto r.p.m. Giuseppe Falcone carmelitano. Opera d'agricoltura, più che necessaria, per chi desidera d'accrescere l'entrate, de suoi poderi, utile a tutti quelli che fanno professione d'agricoltura per piantare, alleuare, incalmare arbori, coltiuar giardini, seminar campi, secondo la qualità de terreni & paesi, edificar palaggi, case, & edifitij pertinenti alla villa. Estratto da tutti gli autori greci, latini, & italiani, che sin' hora hanno scritto di tal materia*, Pavia (Andrea Viano) 1597, URL: http://id.sbn.it/bid/CERE016609 (last accessed: 2 Jan. 2025)

Falk 1968
Tilman Falk, *Hans Burgkmair. Studien zu Leben und Werk des Augsburger Malers* (Bruckmanns Beiträge zur Kunstwissenschaft), Munich 1968

Falkenburg 1989
Reinderd Falkenburg, '"Alter Einoutus." Over de aard en herkomst van Pieter Aertsens stilleven conceptie', *Nederlands Kunsthistorisch Jaarboek*, 40 (1989), 41–66

Falomir 2001
Miguel Falomir, *Los Bassanos en la España nel siglo de oro*, exh. cat. Madrid (Museo Nacional del Prado) 2001

Falomir 2009
Miguel Falomir (ed.), *Jacopo Tintoretto, Actas del Congreso internacional Jacopo Tintoretto*, Madrid 2009

Faßbinder 1971
Brigitte Faßbinder, *Paolo Veronese. Susanna und die beiden Alten*, n.p. 1971 (typescript)

Favaro 1890–1907
Antonio Favaro (ed.), *Le opere di Galileo Galilei*, iv, Florence 1890–1907

Federici Vescovini 2008
Graziella Federici Vescovini, 'Pietro d'Abano. Il Conciliatore tra magia e scienza', *Medicina nei secoli*, 20/2 (2008), 607–40

Federici Vescovini 2020
Graziella Federici Vescovini, *Pietro d'Abano tra storia e leggenda*, Lugano 2020

Feichtinger 1502
Livianus Feichtinger O.S.B., 'De summorum caelitus nuntiorum plantis sacris, nempe de Gabrielis lilio, de Michaelis urtica, de Raphaelis allio', in idem, *Opera omnia*, Basel (Johannes de Amerbach) 1502, 77r–89v

Ferino-Pagden 2008
Sylvia Ferino-Pagden, 'Arcimboldo als "conterfeter" der Natur', in exh. cat. Paris and Vienna 2007/08, 103–11

Ferino-Pagden 2010
Sylvia Ferino-Pagden, *Arcimboldo 1526–1593 Nature and Fantasy,* Washington 2010

Ferino-Pagden 2011
Sylvia Ferino-Pagden, '"...e massime con le invenzioni e capricci, ne' quali egli è unico al mondo". Il rebus Arcimboldo', in exh. cat. Milan 2011, 153–219

Ferino-Pagden 2015
Sylvia Ferino-Pagden, 'Le arti a Milano nel Cinquecento', in *Made in Milano*, Fontanellato (Parma) 2015, 39–76

Ferino-Pagden 2017/18
Sylvia Ferino-Pagden, 'Arcimboldo: un Proteo alla corte degli Asburgo', in exh. cat. Rome 2017/18, [48]–55

Ferino-Pagden 2017/18a
Sylvia Ferino-Pagden, 'I mestieri e gli esordi della caricatura', in exh. cat. Rome 2017/18, 157–69

Ferino-Pagden 2023
Sylvia Ferino-Pagden, 'Opere e artisti. Giuseppe Arcimboldo e l'imperatore Ferdinando I', *Finestre sull'arte,* 17 (2023), 80–95

Ferrari 1996
Giovanna Ferrari, *L'esperienza del passato. Alessandro Benedetti filologo e medico umanista,* Florence 1996

Ferri 1997
Sara Ferri (ed.), *Pietro Andrea Mattioli (Siena 1501 – Trento 1578). La vita e le opere con l'identificazione delle piante,* Ponte San Giovanni 1997

Ferri 2001
Sara Ferri, 'Il "Dioscoride", I "discorsi", I "Commentarii": gli amici e i nemici', in Sara Ferri (ed.), *Pietro Andrea Mattioli (Siena 1501 – Trento 1578). La vita – le opere. Con l'identificazione delle piante*, Perugia 2001, 15–48

Ferri Piccaluga 1988
Gabriella Ferri Piccaluga, 'Gli affreschi di casa Panigarola e la cultura milanese tra Quattro e Cinquecento', *Arte Lombarda*, 86/87 (1988), 14–25

Findlen 2002
Paula Findlen, 'Inventing Nature. Commerce, Art, and Science in the Early Modern Cabinet of Curiosities', in Pamela H. Smith and Paula Findlen (eds.), *Merchants & Marvels. Commerce, Science, and Art in Early Modern Europe,* New York and London 2002, 297–323

Findlen 2005
Paula Findlen, 'The Market and the World: Science, Culture, and Collecting in the Venetian Republic', in Bernard Aikema, Rosella Lauber, and Max Seidel (eds.), *Il collezionismo a Venezia e nel Veneto ai tempi della Serenissima,* Venice 2005, 55–68

Fiocco 1928
Giuseppe Fiocco, *Paolo Veronese 1528–1588*, Bologna 1928

Fiocco 1955
Giuseppe Fiocco, 'La Mostra di Fra Galgario e l'Accademia Carrara', *Arte Veneta,* IX (1955), 269–72

Fischel 2009
Angela Fischel, *Natur im Bild. Zeichnung und Naturerkenntnis bei Conrad Gessner und Ulisse Aldrovandi* (Humboldt-Schriften zur Kunst- und Bildgeschichte 9), Berlin 2009

Fischer 2013
Stefan Fischer, *Hieronymus Bosch: Complete Works*, Cologne 2013

Fontana 1997
Giovanni Luigi Fontana, *Le vie dell'industrializzazione europea: sistemi a confronto*, Bologna 1997

Fontana 2003
Giovanni Luigi Fontana (ed.), *L'industria vicentina dal medioevo a oggi,* Padua 2004

Fontana 2004
Giovanni Luigi Fontana, 'Industria e impresa nel Nord Est d'Italia', in Carlos Barciela Lopez, Giovanni Luigi Fontana, and Antonio Di Vittorio, *Storiografia d'industria e d'impresa in Italia e Spagna in età moderna e contemporanea,* Padua 2004, 161–218

Fontana and Gayot 2004
Giovanni Luigi Fontana and Gerard Gayot (eds.), *Wool: Products and Markets (13th–20th Century),* Padua 2004

Fontana and Sandal 1997
Giovanni Luigi Fontana and Ennio Sandal (eds.) *Cartai e stampatori in Veneto,* Brescia 1997

Franchini et al. 1979
Dario A. Franchini et al., *La scienza a corte. Collezionismo eclettico natura e immagine a Mantova fra Rinascimento e Manierismo*, Rome 1979

Fregoso 1506
Antonio Fregoso, *Riso de Democrito,* Milan (Pietro Martire Mantegazza) 1506

Fregoso 1976
Antonio Fileremo Fregoso, *Opere*, ed. Giorgio Dilemmi, Bologna 1976

Frizzoni 1897
Gustavo Frizzoni, *Le Gallerie dell'Accademia Carrara in Bergamo con alcune digressioni nelle raccolte private*, in *L'arte in Bergamo e l'Accademia Carrara. Pubblicazione fatta a cura del circolo artistico di Bergamo col concorso dell'Accademia nel I° centenario della sua fondazione*, Bergamo, Istituto Italiano d'Arti Grafiche editore, 1897, 17–95

Fuchs 1976
Agnes Fuchs, 'Dürers Erzengel Michael mit der Brennessel und die Engelspflanzen in den Schriften von Apian und Feichtinger', in Felix Wiesner (ed.), *Heilkräuter in der Renaissancekunst*, Munich 1976, 43–60

Fuchs 1987
Agnes Fuchs, 'Die Renaissance des Unkrauts. Brennessel, Phoinix und Palingenese im 16. Jahrhundert', *Mitteilungen der Münchner Gesellschaft für Geschichte und Gegenwart,* 29 (1987), 70–83

Fučíková 2002
Eliška Fučíková (ed.), *Praga Magica 1600: l' art à Prague au temps de Rodolphe II.,* Dijon *et al.* 2002

Gabrieli 1989
Gabrieli Giuseppe, *Il carteggio Linceo,* Rome 1989

Gallo 1569
Agostino Gallo, *Le vinti giornate dell'agricoltura et de' piaceri della villa ...] con le figure de gli istrumenti pertinenti, & con due tauole; una della dichiaratione di molti uocaboli, & l'altra delle cose notabili,* Venice (Gratioso Percaccino) 1569, URL: http://id.sbn.it/bid/VIAE000772 (last accessed: 2 Jan. 2025)

Gamba 1984
Antonio Gamba, 'Prospero Alpini: il suo migliore autentico ritratto', in *Prospero Alpini nella sua città e nel suo tempo* (Tagungsakten Marostica, 16 Oct. 1983), Padua 1984

Garin 1983
Eugenio Garin, 'Aristotelismo veneto e scienza moderna', in Luigi Olivieri (ed.), *Aristotelismo veneto e scienza moderna, Atti del 25 Anno Accademico del Centro per la storia della tradizione aristotelica nel Veneto*, i, Padua 1983, 3–33

Gasparotto 2013
Davide Gasparotto, 'Il mito della collezione', in exh. cat. Padua 2013, 48–65

Gatti Perer and Rossi 1989
Maria Luisa Gatti Perer and Marco Rossi, in *Codici e incunaboli miniati della Biblioteca Civica di Bergamo,* Bergamo 1989

Gaulin 2007
Jean-Louis Gaulin, 'Trattati di agronomia e innovazione agricola', in Philippe Braunstein and Luca Molà (eds.), *Il Rinascimento Italiano e l'Europa*, III. *Produzione e tecniche*, Treviso 2007, 145–63

Gehring 2020
Rudolf Gehring, 'Pietra Paesina: Fantastische Steinwelten', *Lapis. Monatsmagazin für Liebhaber & Sammler von Mineralien & Edelsteinen*, 45/1 (2020), 44–8

Geiger 1954
Benno Geiger, *I dipinti ghiribizzosi di Giuseppe Arcimboldi, pittore illusionista del Cinquecento (1527–1593)*, Florence 1954

Geiger 1960
Benno Geiger, *Die skurrillen Gemälde des Giuseppe Arcimboldi (1527–1593)*, Wiesbaden 1960

Gettings 1981
Fred Gettings, *Dictionary of Occult, Hermetic and Alchemical Sigils*, London 1981

Gijzen 1986
Agatha Gijzen, 'De Vismarkt van Joachim Beuckelaer', in exh. cat. Ghent 1986/87, 67–70

Gizzi 1974
Corrado Gizzi, *L'astronomia nel poema sacro*, 2 vols., Naples 1974

Goldberg 1996
Edward L. Goldberg, 'Artistic Relations between the Medici and the Spanish Courts, 1587–1621: Part II', *The Burlington Magazine*, 138 (1996), 529–40

Gottarelli 2013
Antonio Gottarelli, *Contemplatio. Templum solare e culti di fondazione*, Bologna 2013

Grant 1994
Edward Grant, *Planets, Stars, and Orbs. The Medieval Cosmos, 1200–1687*, Cambridge 1994

Gray 2012
Emily Rosanna Gray, *Early Florentine Engravings and the Devotional Print: Origins and Transformations, c. 1460–85*, 2 vols., Ph.D. thesis, London University, 2012

Gruber 2011
Gerlinde Gruber, Cat. 29 on Saive, 'Fleischmarkt (November / Dezember)', in exh. cat. Vienna and Zurich 2011/12, 157

Guderzo 1996/97
Mario Guderzo (ed.), *Jacopo Bassano (1510 c.–1592). Tre lezioni del XXXIV Corso Internazionale di Alta Cultura tenutosi alla Fondazione Giorgio Cini di Venezia nel 1992 dal titolo 'Civiltà di Terraferma e Venezia nell'Età dei Bassano'*, Bassano del Grappa 1996/97

Gundel 1992
Hans Georg Gundel, *Zodiakos. Tierkreisbilder im Altertum. Kosmische Bezüge und Jenseitsvorstellungen im antiken Alltagsleben*, Mainz am Rhein 1992

Haag, Kirchweger, and Rainer 2015
Sabine Haag, Franz Kirchweger, and Paulus Rainer (eds.), *Spielarten begehrenswerter Dinge, Die Sammlung als Text*, Vienna 2015

Hallonquist 2010
Sven-Göran Hallonquist, *The Runic Calendar Project*, 2010, URL: https://www.khm.uio.no/english/research/publications/7th-symposium-preprints/documents/runic-calendar.pdf (last accessed: 18 Sept. 2024)

Halsema-Kubes 1989
Willy Halsema-Kubes, 'Johan Gregor van der Schardt, Sol (Zon), ca. 1580', *Bulletin van het Rijksmuseum*, 37, 1989, 182–4

Hammer-Tugendhat 2001
Daniela Hammer-Tugendhat, 'Disturbances in the Art of the Early Modern Netherlands and the Formation of the Subject in Pieter Aertsen's Christ at the House of Martha and Mary', *American Imago*, 57/4 (2000), 387–402

Hankins 1991
James Hankins, 'The Myth of the Platonic Academy of Florence', *Renaissance Quarterly*, 44/3 (1991), 429–75

Hassmann 2024
Elisabeth Hassmann, 'Jacopo Strada als Berater Ferdinands II. von Tirol. Wenzel Jamnitzers Silberkredenz, der Spanische Saal, das Kaiserzimmer und das Antiquarium von Schloss Ambras', *Jahrbuch des Kunsthistorischen Museums Wien*, 23 (2024), 35–105

Hauber 1916
Anton Hauber, *Planetenkinderbilder und Sternbilder*, Strasbourg 1916

Hauschke 2002
Sven Hauschke, 'Messingguss und Eisenschnitt aus Nürnberg', in exh. cat. Nuremberg 2002, 241–70

Hausmann 1972
Ulrich Hausmann, 'Oidipus und die Sphinx', *Jahrbuch der Staatlichen Kunstsammlungen in Baden-Württemberg*, 9 (1972), 7–36

Heidel 1906
William Arthur Heidel, 'Qualitative Change in Pre-Socratic Philosophy', *Archiv für Geschichte der Philosophie*, 19 (1906), 333–79

Hendrix 1997
Lee Hendrix, 'Natural History Illustration at the Court of Rudolf II', in exh. cat. Prague 1997, 157–71

Heninger 1977
Simeon K. Heninger, *The Cosmographical Glass, Renaissance Diagrams of the Universe*, San Marino (CA) 1977

Herrera 1513
Gabriel Alonso de Herrera, *Obra de agricultura copilada de diuersos auctores por de mandado del muy illustre y reuerendissimo Señor el Cardenal de España Arcobispo de Toledo*, Alcala de Henares (Arnao Guilleme de Brocar) 1513

Herrera 1557
Gabriel Alonso de Herrera, *Libro di agricoltura utilissimo, tratto da diversi auttori, novamente venuto a luce, dalla spagnuola nell'italiana lingua traportato*, Venice (Michel Tramezzino) 1557, URL: http://id.sbn.it/bid/BVEE004064 (last accessed: 4 Jan. 2025)

Herrmann Fiore 2006
Kristina Herrmann Fiore, *Roma scopre un tesoro dalla pinacoteca ai depositi un museo che non ha piú segreti*, Sesto Ulteriano 2006

Hind 1910
Arthur M. Hind, *Early Italian Engraving. A Critical Catalogue with Complete Reproduction of All the Prints Described*, i: *Florentine Engravings and Anonymous Prints of Other School*, London 1910

Hinz 1974
Berthold Hinz, 'Studien zur Geschichte des Ehepaarbildnisses', *Marburger Jahrbuch für Kunstwissenschaft*, 19 (1974), 139–218

Hochedlinger 1979
Jacobus Hochedlinger SJ, 'Lilium. Urtica. Allium. Vom Duft der Erzengel', in *Cherubim atque Seraphim Dominum benedicite in aeternum. Almanach der Pfarre Unserer Lieben Frau zu den Schotten*, Vienna 1979, 14–21

Hochmann 1997
Michel Hochmann, 'La collection de Giacomo Contarini', *Mélanges de l'Ecole française de Rome. Moyen-Age, Temps modernes*, 99/1 (1997), 447–89

Hochmann 2010
Michel Hochmann, *Plinio Scarpelli, pittore di Daniele Barbaro e dei Grimani di Santa Maria Formosa*, in Arte Veneta 67, 2010, 42–53

Hochmann 2011
Michel Hochmann (ed.), *Venise et Paris 1500–1700. La peinture vénitienne de la Renaissance et sa réception en France* (Actes des colloques de Bordeaux et de Caen, 24–25 February 2006, 6 May 2006), Geneva 2011

Hoeninger 2006
Cathleen Hoeninger, 'The Illuminated Tacuinum Sanitatis Manuscripts from Northern Italy, ca. 1380–1400: Sources, Patrons, and the Creation of a New Pictorial Genre', in Jean Ann Givens, Karen M. Reeds, and Alain Touwaide (eds.), *Visualizing Medieval Medicine and Natural History, 1200–1550*, London and New York 2006, 51–81

Hollstein 1996
Hollstein's Dutch & Flemish etchings, engravings and woodcuts 1430–1700, xliv (Maarten de Vos), compiled by Christiaan Schuckman, ed. Dieuwke de Hoop Scheffer, Rotterdam and Amsterdam 1996

Hollstein, Veldman, and Luijten 2006
Friedrich W.H. Hollstein, Ilja M. Veldman, and Ger Luijten (eds.), *The New Hollstein. Dutch & Flemish etchings, engravings and woodcuts, 1450–1700*, xxvii (Bruegel), Rotterdam 2006

Honig 1998
Elizabeth Alice Honig, *Painting and the Market in Early Modern Antwerp*, New Haven and London 1998

Honnens de Lichtenberg 1991
Hanne Honnens de Lichtenberg, *Johan Gregor van der Schardt, Bildhauer bei Kaiser Maximilian II., am dänischen Hof und bei Tycho Brahe*, Copenhagen 1991

Howard 2021
Deborah Howard, *Proto-industrial Architecture of the Veneto in the Age of Palladio*, Rome 2021

Hugelshofer 1939
Walter Hugelshofer, 'Wolf Huber als Bildnismaler', *Pantheon*, 24 (1939), 230–36

Hyde 2013
Elizabeth Hyde (ed.), *A Cultural History of Gardens in the Renaissance*, London 2013

Ilg 1884
Albert Ilg, 'Die Limousiner-Grisaillen in den Kaiserlichen Haussammlungen', *Jahrbuch der Kunsthistorischen Sammlungen des allerhöchsten Kaiserhauses*, 2 (Vienna, 1884), 111–28

Infelise 2018
Mario Infelise, s.v. 'Scottoni, Giovanni', in DBI 91, 2018, 670–2

Jansen 2019
Dirk Jacob Jansen, *Jacopo Strada and Cultural Patronage at the Imperial Court: Antiquity as Innovation*, 2 vols., Boston and Leiden 2019

Jiménez Díaz 2001
Pablo Jiménez Díaz, *El coleccionismo maniersta de los Austrias entre Felipe II y Rodolfo II*, Madrid 2001

Juffinger and Plasser 2007
Roswitha Juffinger and Gerhard Plasser, *Salzburger Landessammlungen 1939–1955*, Salzburg 2007

Kaschek 2012
Bertram Kaschek, *Weltzeit und Endzeit. Die 'Monatsbilder' Pieter Bruegels d.Ä.*, Munich 2012

Katritzky 2006
M.A. Katritzky, *The Art of Commedia: A Study in the Commedia Dell'Arte 1560–1620 with Special Reference to the Visual Records*, Amsterdam and New York 2006

Kavaler 1986
Ethan Matt Kavaler, 'Erotische elementen in de markttaferelen van Beuckelaer, Aertsen en hun tijdgenoten', in exh. cat. Ghent 1986/87, 18–26

Kemp 2000
Martin Kemp, '"Il mio bell'ingegno". L'anatomia visiva del Theatrum totius animalis fabricae di Fabrici', in Maurizio Rippa Bonati and José Pardo Tomás (eds.), *Il teatro dei corpi. Le pitture colorate d'anatomia di Girolamo Fabrici d'Acquapendente*, Milan 2000, 83–107

Kiang 1992
Dawson Kiang, 'The "Mappamondo" in Bramante's Heraclitus and Democritus', *Achademia Leonardi Vinci*, 5 (1992), 128–35

Klerck 2000/01
Bram de Klerck, 'Scene del quotidiano? Interpretando la pittura di genere di Vincenzo Campi', in exh. cat. Cremona 2000/01, 39–49

Klibansky, Panofsky, and Saxl 1964
Raymond Klibansky, Erwin Panofsky, and Fritz Saxl, *Saturn and Melancholy. Studies in the History of Natural Philosophy, Religion and Art*, London 1964

Klibansky, Panofsky, and Saxl 1990
Raymond Klibansky, Erwin Panofsky, and Fritz Saxl, *Saturn und Melancholie: Studien zur Geschichte der Naturphilosophie und Medizin, der Religion und der Kunst*, Frankfurt am Main 1990

Knedlik 2005
Manfred Knedlik, s.v. 'Fröschl, Daniel', in *Allgemeines Künstler-Lexikon. Die Bildenden Künstler aller Zeiten und Völker*, xxxxv, Munich and Leipzig 2005

Koreny 1985
Fritz Koreny, *Albrecht Dürer und die Tier- und Pflanzenstudien der Renaissance*, Munich 1985

Koreny 2012
Fritz Koreny, *Hieronymus Bosch: die Zeichnungen. Werkstatt und Nachfolge bis zum Ende des 16. Jahrhunderts: catalogue raisonné*, Turnhout 2012

Koreny and Segal 1989/90
Fritz Koreny and Sam Segal, 'Hans Hoffmann – Entdeckungen und Zuschreibungen', *Jahrbuch der kunsthistorischen Sammlungen in Wien*, 49/50 (1989/90), 57–65

Krahn 1988
Volker Krahn, 'Eine "Schalkhaftigkeit" von Christian Daniel Rauch – Metamorphosen eines antiken Käuzchens', *Zeitschrift des Deutschen Vereins für Kunstwissenschaft*, 42.2 (1988), 82–92

Kraus 1978
Hans Peter Kraus, *A Rare Book Saga: the Autobiography of H.P. Kraus*, London 1978

Kraus 1978a
Hans Peter Kraus, *In Retrospect: A Catalogue of 100 Outstanding Manuscripts Sold in the Last Four Decades by H.P. Kraus*, London 1978

Krauskopf 1997
Ingrid Krauskopf, 'Influences grecques et orientales sur les répresentations de dieux étrusques', in Françoise Gaultier and Dominique Briquel (eds.), *Les Étrusques. Les plus religieux des hommes, État de la recherche sur la religion étrusque, Actes du Colloque international (Paris 1992)*, Paris 1997, 25–36

Kriegeskorte 1986
Werner Kriegeskorte, *Giuseppe Arcimboldo*, Cologne 1986

Kris 1926
Ernst Kris, 'Der Stil "Rustique". Die Verwendung des Naturabgusses bei Wenzel Jamnitzer und Bernard Palissy', *Jahrbuch der Kunsthistorischen Sammlungen in Wien*, new series 1 (1926), 137–208

Krohn 2008/09
Deborah L. Krohn, 'Picturing the Kitchen. Renaissance Treatise and Period Room', *Studies in the Decorative Arts*, 16/1 /(2008/09), 20–34

Kryza-Gersch 2015
Claudia Kryza-Gersch, 'Giambologna's Astronomy – or rather Astrology – in Vienna Reconsidered', in Caroline Miner (ed.), *The Eternal Baroque. Studies in Honour of Jennifer Montagu*, Milan 2015, 67–80

Kusukawa 2010
Sachiko Kusukawa, 'The Sources of Gessner's Pictures for the Historia animalium', *Annals of Science,* 67 (2010), 303–28

Kusukawa 2012
Sachiko Kusukawa, *Picturing the Book of Nature. Image, Text, and Argument in Sixteenth-Century Human Anatomy and Medical Botany*, Chicago 2012

Lanaro 2003
Paola Lanaro (ed.), *La pratica dello scambio. Sistemi di fiere, mercanti e città in Europa (1400–1700),* Venice 2003

Lanaro 2006
Paola Lanaro (ed.), *At the Centre of the Old World: Trade and Manufacturing in Venice and the Venetian Mainland (1400–1800),* Toronto 2006

Lanciani 1900
Rodolfo Lanciani, 'Iter Italicum di A. von Buchell', *Archivio della Società Romana di Storia Patria,* XXIII, 1–2 (1900), 5–66

Lannier 2011
Hélène Lannier, *La publication des Libri de re rustica à la Renaissance: étude d'une production. Les Libri de re rustica chez Sébastien Gryphe, à Lyon* (HAL Open Science: Histoire, 2011), URL: https://dumas.ccsd.cnrs.fr/dumas-00707532 (last accessed: 4 Jan. 2025)

Lanteri 1560
Giacomo Lanteri, *Della economica, trattato di M. Giacomo Lanteri gentilhuomo bresciano nel quale si dimostrano le qualità, che all'huomo et alla donna separatamente conuengono pel gouerno della casa*, Venice (Vincenzo Valgrisi) 1560, URL: http://id.sbn.it/bid/BVEE004758 (last accessed: 4 Jan. 2025)

***La vita* 1907**
La vita d'Ulisse Aldrovandi cominciando dalla sua natività sin'a l'età di 64 anni vivendo ancora, in *Intorno alla vita e alle opere di Ulisse Aldrovandi,* Bologna 1907, 1–27

Le Boeuffle 1987
André Le Boeuffle, *Astronomie, astrologie – Lexique latin*, Paris 1987

Legers 1906
Paul Legers, 'Kardinal Matthäus Lang. Ein Staatsmann im Dienste Kaiser Maximilians I. Auf urkundlicher Grundlage dargestellt', *Mitteilungen der Gesellschaft für Salzburger Landeskunde,* 46 (1906), 437–517

Leithe-Jasper 1963
Manfred Leithe-Jasper, *Alessandro Vittoria. Beiträge zu einer Analyse seiner figürlichen Plastiken unter Berücksichtigung der Beziehungen zur gleichzeitigen Malerei in Venedig*, Diss., University of Vienna, 1963

Lemerle et al. 2017
Frédérique Lemerle et al. (eds.), *Daniele Barbaro 1514–1570. Vénitien, patricien, humaniste,* Turnhout 2017

Lemnius 1566
Levinus Lemnius, *Herbarum atque arborum quae in Bibliis passim obviae sunt, & ex quibus sacri vates similitudines desumunt, ac collationes rebus accommodant, dilucida explicatio*, Antwerp (Gulielmum Simonem) 1566

Lergier and Börner 2001
William Lergier and Klaus Börner, 'Landschaften in Stein Pietra paesina – Marmor aus Italien', *Lapis. Monatsmagazin für Liebhaber & Sammler von Mineralien & Edelsteinen,* 26/10 (2001), 13–20

Levi 1941
Doro Levi, 'The Allegories of the Months in Classical Art', *The Art Bulletin,* 23/4 (1941), 251–91

Lichner 2001
Magdolna Lichner, 'Additional Material to Establishing the Subject of Jacopo Bassano's Sleeping Shepherd', *Bulletin du Musée Hongrois des Beaux-Arts*, 95 (2001), 91–114

Lietzmann 1987
Hilda Lietzmann, *Das Neugebäude in Wien: Sultan Süleymans Zelt – Kaiser Maximilians II. Lustschloß; ein Beitrag zur Kunst- und Kulturgeschichte der zweiten Hälfte des sechzehnten Jahrhunderts*, Munich 1987

Lietzmann 2003
Hilda Lietzmann, 'Ferdinands I. Verdienste um die Gartenkunst', in exh. cat. Vienna 2003, 259–63

Lietzmann 2007
Hilda Lietzmann, *Irdische Paradiese: Beispiele höfischer Gartenkunst der 1. Hälfte des 16. Jahrhunderts* (Kunstwissenschaftliche Studien 141), Munich 2007

Lippmann 1895
Friedrich Lippmann, *Die sieben Planeten*, publication of the Internationale Chalkographische Gesellschaft, Berlin 1895

Lobeck 1829
Christian August Lobeck, *Aglaophamus sive de Theologiae Mysticae graecorum causis*, 2 vols., Königsberg 1829

Lobeck 1961
Christian August Lobeck, *Aglaophamus: 3 Bücher über die Grundlagen der Mysterienreligion der Griechen. Mit einer Sammlung der Fragmente der orphischen Dichter*, photomechanical reprint of the first printing (Königsberg 1829), Darmstadt 1961

Löcher 1965
Kurt Löcher, 'St. Florian. Die Kunst der Donauschule (Malerei)', *Pantheon*, 23 (1965), 346

Lomazzo 1584 (1973/74)
Giovan Paolo Lomazzo, 'Trattato dell'arte della Pittura, scultura ed architettura (1584)', in Roberto Paolo Ciardi (ed.), *Scritti sulle arti*, 2 vols., Florence 1973/74

Lomazzo 1590 (1973/74)
Gian Paolo Lomazzo, 'Idea del Tempio della pittura [1590]', in Roberto Paolo Ciardi (ed.), *Scritti sulle arti*, 2 vols., Florence 1973/74

Lowry 1979
Martin Lowry, *The World of Aldus Manutius: Business and Scholarship in Renaissance Venice*, Oxford 1979

Lowry 1991
Martin Lowry, *Nicholas Jenson and the Rise of Venetian Publishing in Renaissance Europe*, Oxford 1991

Lucchichenti and Di Schino 2007
Furio Lucchichenti and June di Schino (eds.), *Il cuoco segreto dei papi. Bartolomeo Scappi e la Confraternita dei cuochi e dei pasticcieri*, Rome 2007

Lugato 1994
Elisabetta Lugato, 'Catalogo, con il contributo di G. Mazzucco e M.G. Negri', in Susy Marcon and Marino Zorzi (eds.), *Aldo Manuzio e l'ambiente veneziano, 1494–1515*, Venice 1994, 205–48

Lüdemann 2016
Peter Lüdemann, *Tiziano. Le botteghe e la grafica*, Florence 2016

Maccaneo 1490
Domenico della Bella detto Maccaneo, *Chorographia Verbani Lacus,* Milan (Ulrich Scinzenzeler) 1490

Macrobius 1969
Macrobius, *The Saturnalia*, trans. Percival Vaughan Davies, New York 1969, URL: https://archive.org/details/macrobius-saturnalia-book-01-english-1969/mode/2up (last accessed: 20 Aug. 2024)

Macrobius 2008
Ambrosius Theodosius Macrobius, *Tischgespräche am Saturnalienfest*, with introduction, translation and notes by Otto und Eva Schönberger, Würzburg 2008

Malaspina di Sannazzaro 1824
Marchese Luigi Malaspina di Sannazzaro, *Catalogo di una Raccolta di Stampe Antiche*, Milan 1824

Manutius 1975
Aldus Manutius, *Aldo Manuzio editore. Dediche, prefazioni, note ai testi*, with introduction by Carlo Dionisotti, translation and notes by Giovanni Orlandi, Milan 1975

Marcon and Moretti 2015
Susy Marcon and Laura Moretti (eds.), *Daniele Barbaro 1514–1570. Letteratura, scienze e arti nella Venezia del Rinascimento,* Crocetta del Montello (TV) 2015

Mariani Canova 1988
Giordana Mariani Canova, 'La tradizione europea degli erbari miniati e la scuola veneta', in exh. cat. Praglia 1988, 21–8

Marini 1992
Paola Marini, 'Jacopo Bassano Seen Anew', in exh. cat. Bassano del Grappa and Fort Worth 1992, 13–44

Marini 1994
Paola Marini, 'Considerazioni sui Bassano di Praga', in exh. cat. Belluno 1994, 25–31

Marshall 2024
Richard Marshall, 'New Light on the History of the Codex Arcerianus and the Fate of Varro's De geometria and De arithmetica', *Revue d'histoire des textes,* 19 (2024), 187–232

Marsili 1840
Giovanni Marsili, *Notizie inedite,* Padua 1840

Marucini 1577
Lorenzo Marucini, *Il Bassano*, Venice 1577

Mason 1999
Stefania Mason, 'Lowlife and Landscape: minor pictura in the Late Sixteenth-Century Venice', in exh. cat. Venice 1999, 558–67

Mason 2009
Stefania Mason, L'inventario di Gerolamo Bassano e l'eredità della bottega, *Notiziario dell'Associazione degli amici dei musei e dei monumenti di Bassano del Grappa*, nos. 16–17 (December 2009), 7–94

Mason and Pardo Tomás 2020
Peter Mason and José Pardo Tomás, 'Bringing it Back from Mexico. Eleven Paintings of Trees in "I cinque libri delle piante" of Pier'Antonio Michiel (1510–1576)', *Journal of the History of Collections*, 32/2 (2020), 225–37

Mattioli 1549
Pietro Andrea Mattioli, *Il Dioscoride dell'eccellente dottor medico M.P. Andrea Matthioli da Siena, co i suoi discorsi da esso la seconda uolta illustrati, & diligentemente ampliati. Con la giunta del Sesto libro de i rimedi di tutti i veleni... Con la giunta di tutte le figure delle piante, delle herbe, delle pietre, et de gli animali, tratte dal vero & istesso naturale, & non più stampate*, Mantua (Iacomo Roffinello) 1549, URL: http://id.sbn.it/bid/BVEE059081 (last accessed: 5 Jan. 2025)

Mattioli 1568
Pietro Andrea Mattioli, *I Discorsi di M. Pietro Matthioli Sanese, Medico Cesareo, et del Serenissimo Principe Ferdinando Archiduca d'austria &c., Nelli sei libri Di Pedacio Dioscoride Anazarbeo della materia Medicinale*, Venice 1568

Mazzucco 2022
Melania G. Mazzucco, *I Bassano. Storia di una famiglia di pittori,* Bassano del Grappa 2022

McGinty 1998
Alice B. McGinty, *Stradanus (Jan van der Straet): His Role in the Visual Communication of Renaissance Discoveries, Technologies, and Values*, Ph.D. thesis, Tufts University 1974, Ann Arbor 1998

McTighe 2004
Sheila McTighe, 'Foods and the Body in Italian Genre Paintings, about 1580: Campi, Passarotti, Carracci', *The Art Bulletin*, 86/2 (2004), 301–23

Meder 1932
Joseph Meder, *Dürer-Katalog. Ein Handbuch über Albrecht Dürers Stiche, Radierungen, Holzschnitte, deren Zustände, Ausgaben und Wasserzeichen*, Vienna 1932

Meganck and Sprang 2018
Tine Luk Meganck and Sabine van Sprang, *Bruegels Winterlandschaften. Historiker und Kunsthistoriker im Dialog*, Berlin 2018

Menegazzi 1957
Luigi Menegazzi, 'Ludovico Toeput (il Pozzoserrato)', *Saggi e memorie di storia dell'arte,* I (1957), 167–223

Mensi 1899
Luigi Mensi, *Dizionario biografico piacentino,* Piacenza 1899

Mentzel 2011
Jan-David Mentzel, 'Taufe im Sündenbad. Sebald Behams "Jungbrunnen" von 1531', in exh. cat. Nuremberg 2011, 98–114

Michel 2017
Eva Michel, 'Zwischen Feldarbeit und Kirmes', in exh. cat. Vienna 2017, 67–71

Michiel 1800
Marcantonio Michiel, *Notizia d'opere di disegno nella prima metà del secolo XVI, esistenti in Padova, Cremona, Milano, Pavia, Bergamo, Crema e Venezia. Pubblicata e illustrata da D. Jacopo Morelli*, Bassano 1800

Michiel 1896
Der Anonimo Morelliano (Marcanton Michiel's 'Notizia d'opere del disegno'), text with a translation by Dr Theodor Frimmel, Vienna 1896

Michiel 1940
Pietro Antonio Michiel, *I cinque libri di piante. Codice Marciano*, transcription and commentary by Ettore De Toni, Venice 1940

Michiel 2000
Marcantonio Michiel, *Notizia d'opere del disegno. Edizione critica a cura di Theodor Frimmel, Vienna 1896*, Florence 2000

Minelli 1995
Alessandro Minelli (ed.), *L'orto botanico di Padova 1545–1995*, Padua 1995

Minelli 2010
Alessandro Minelli, s.v. 'Michiel, Pietro Antonio', in DBI 74, 2010, 325–26

Minuzzi 2016
Sabrina Minuzzi, *Sul filo dei segreti. Farmacopea, libri e pratiche terapeutiche a Venezia in età moderna,* Milan 2016

Minuzzi 2017
Sabrina Minuzzi, *The Invention of the Author. The Privilegio di Stampa in Renaissance Venice*, Venice 2017

Minuzzi 2021
Sabrina Minuzzi, '15th Century Practical Medicine in Print: Beyond the Profession, towards the miscere utile dulci', *Nuncius. Journal of the Material and Visual History of Science*, 2 (2021), 199–263, URL: http://doi.org/10.1163/18253911-03602016 (last accessed: 5 Jan. 2025)

Molà 2000
Luca Molà, *The Silk Industry of Renaissance Venice,* Baltimore and London 2000

Molà, Mueller, and Zanier 2000
Luca Molà, Reinhold C. Mueller, and Claudio Zanier (eds.), *La seta in Italia dal Medioevo al Seicento. Dal baco al drappo,* Venice 2000

Moldovan 2021
Anca-Delia Moldovan, 'From Carnival to Pious Cities: Scenes of Urban Life in Leandro Bassano's The Months', *Renaissance and Reformation,* 44.2 (Spring 2021), 113–46

Moly Mariotti 1993
Florence Moly Mariotti, 'Contribution à la connaissance des Tacuina sanitatis lombards', *Arte Lombarda,* 104 (1993), 32–9

Mommsen 1850
Theodor Mommsen, *'Über den Chronographen vom J. 354', Abhandlungen der philologisch-historischen Klasse der königlich sächsischen Gesellschaft der Wissenschaft,* 1 (1850), 549–634

Montanari 1994
Tomaso Montanari, 'Cristina di Svezia, il cardinale Azzolino e il mercato veronese', *Ricerche di Storia dell'Arte,* 54 (November 1994), 25–52

Moosleitner 2017
Fritz Moosleitner, *Albrecht Altdorfer in Salzburg. Salzburger Landschaft und Architektur in den Werken des Regensburger Malers,* Salzburg 2017

Morassi 1963
Antonio Morassi, *Il tesoro dei Medici. Oreficerie – argenterie – pietre dure,* Florence 1963

Morel 2008
Philippe Morel, 'Giuseppe Arcimboldo: Die Kultivierung und Verarbeitung von Seide', in exh. cat. Paris and Vienna 2007/08, 233–6

Moret 1984
Jean-Marc Moret, *Oedipe, la Sphinx et les Thébains. Essai de Mythologie Iconographique,* 2 vols., Geneva 1984

Morgagni 1763
Giovanni Battista Morgagni, *De Prospero Alpino epistolae duae,* in *Opusculorum miscellaneorum, pars altera,* Venice 1763, 7–8

Morigia 1592
Paolo Morigia, *Historia dell'antichità di Milano, divisa in quattro libri,* Venice 1592

Mosco and Casazza 2003
Marilena Mosco and Ornella Casazza (eds.), *Il Museo degli Argenti. Collezioni e collezionisti,* Florence 2003

Moxey 1976
Keith P.F. Moxey, 'The Humanist Market Scenes of Joachim Beuckelaer: Moralizing Example or "Slices of Life"?', *Jaarboek van het Koninklijk Museum voor Schone Kunsten Antwerpen,* 1976, 109–89

Moxey 1977
Keith P.F. Moxey, *Pieter Aertsen, Joachim Beuckelaer, and the Rise of Secular Painting in the Context of the Reformation,* London 1977

Müllenmeister 1988
Kurt J. Müllenmeister, *Roelant Savery: Die Gemälde mit kritischem Oeuvrekatalog,* Freren 1988

Müller 2007
Jürgen Müller, 'Italienverehrung als Italienverachtung. Hans Sebald Behams Jungbrunnen von 1536 und die italienische Kunst der Renaissance', in Philine Helas et al. (eds.), *Bild-Geschichte: Festschrift für Horst Bredekamp,* Berlin 2007, 309–18

Müller 2011
Mathias F. Müller, 'Das Bildnis des Fürst-Erzbischofs von Salzburg, Matthäus Kardinal Lang von Wellenburg. Ein Porträtgemälde von Albrecht Altdorfer um 1528', *Verhandlungen des Historischen Vereins für Oberpfalz und Regensburg,* 151 (2011), 109–19

Muraro 1992
Michelangelo Muraro, *Il libro secondo di Francesco e Jacopo Bassano,* Bassano del Grappa 1992

Muraro and Rosand 1976
Michelangelo Muraro and David Rosand, *Tiziano e la silografia veneziana del Cinquecento,* Vicenza 1976

Nalezyty 2017
Susan Nalezyty, *Pietro Bembo and the Intellectual Pleasures of a Renaissance Writer and Art Collector,* New Haven and London 2017

Nardelli 2014
Rosalie Anne Nardelli, *Giuseppe Arcimboldo's Composite Portraits and the Alchemical Universe of the Early Modern Habsburg Court (1546–1612),* Master's thesis, Kingston University, Ontario, 2014

Neumann 1966
Jaromir Neumann, *Die Gemäldegalerie der Prager Burg,* Prague 1966

New Hollstein S. Beham
The New Hollstein. German Engravings, Etchings and Woodcuts 1400–1700, Sebald Beham Part IV, Ouderkerk aan den Ijssel (in preparation)

Nichols 2018
Tom Nichols, *Jacopo Bassano, regionalism, and rural painting.* The Oxford art journal 41/2 (2018), 147–70

Nichols 2023
Tom Nichols, *Local and non-local in Jacopo Bassano's depictions of peasants,* Artibus et historiae 44/87 (2023), 75–101

Nielsen 1945
Karl Nielsen, 'Remarques sur les noms grecs et latins des vents et des régions du ciel', *Classica et Medievalia,* 7 (1945), 1–113

Novotny 1948
Fritz Novotny, *Die Monatsbilder Pieter Bruegels d.Ä.,* Vienna 1948

Obrist 1997
Barbara Obrist, 'Wind Diagrams and Medieval Cosmology', *Speculum,* 72 (1997), 33–84

Obrist 2004
Barbara Obrist, *La cosmologie médiévale. Textes et images I. Les fondements antiques,* Florence 2004

Occhi 2006
Katia Occhi, *Boschi e mercanti. Traffici di legname tra la contea di Tirolo e la Repubblica di Venezia (secoli XVI–XVII),* Bologna 2006

Olmi 1991
Giuseppe Olmi, '"Molti amici in varij luoghi": studio della natura e rapporti epistolari nel secolo XVI', *Nuncius,* 6 (1991), 3–31

Olmi 1992
Giuseppe Olmi, *L'inventario del mondo. Catalogazione della natura e luoghi del sapere nella prima età moderna,* Bologna 1992

Olmi 2007
Giuseppe Olmi, 'Per la storia dei rapporti scientifici fra Italia e Germania: le lettere di Francesco Calzolari a Joachim Camerarius II', in Gian Paolo Brizzi and Giuseppe Olmi (eds.), *Dai cantieri della storia. Liber amicorum per Paolo Prodi,* Bologna 2007, 343–61

Olmi 2009
Giuseppe Olmi, 'Sfogliare le pagine del codex naturae: il viaggio scientifico nella prima età moderna', *Antologia Vieusseux,* new series, 15/45 (2009), 5–32

Olmi 2010
Giuseppe Olmi, 'Bologna nel secolo XVI: una capitale europea della ricerca naturalistica', in Sabine Frommel (ed.), *Crocevia e capitale della migrazione artistica: forestieri a Bologna e bolognesi nel mondo (XV–XVI secolo),* Bologna 2010, 61–80

Olmi 2015
Giuseppe Olmi, '"Things of Nature" from the New World in Early Modern Bologna', in Alessandra Russo, Gerhard Wolf, and Diana Fane (eds.), *Images Take Flight: Feather Art in Mexico and Europe 1400–1700*, Munich 2015, 229–39

Olmi 2015a
Giuseppe Olmi, *Ulisse Aldrovandi e la natura del Nuovo Mondo*, in Giorgio Antei (ed.), *Tesoro Mexicano. Visioni della natura fra Vecchio e Nuovo Mondo,* Fontanellato (Parma) 2015, 179–203

Olmi 2015b
Giuseppe Olmi, 'Un "simplicista" fiammingo alla corte dei Medici: note su Giuseppe Casabona "servitore de virtuosi"', in Massimiano Bucchi, Luca Ciancio, and Arianna Dröscher (eds.), *L'esperimento della storia. Saggi in onore di Renato G. Mazzolini,* Trento 2015, 13–26

Olmi and Tongiorgi Tomasi 1993
Giuseppe Olmi and Lucia Tongiorgi Tomasi, *De piscibus. La bottega artistica di Ulisse Aldrovandi e l'immagine naturalistica,* Rome 1993

Olmi and Tongiorgi Tomasi 2011
Giuseppe Olmi and Lucia Tongiorgi Tomasi, 'Raffigurazione della natura e collezionismo enciclopedico nel secondo Cinquecento tra Milano e l'Europa', in exh. cat. Milan 2011, 113–52

Olmi and Tongiorgi Tomasi 2017/18
Giuseppe Olmi and Lucia Tongiorgi Tomasi, 'Giuseppe Arcimboldo tra natura, arte e artificio', in exh. cat. Rome 2017/18, [80]–7

Olmi and Tongiorgi Tomasi 2024
Giuseppe Olmi and Lucia Tongiorgi Tomasi, 'In Chartis musca. Immagini della mosca tra arte e scienza', in exh. cat. Fontanellato 2024, 93–108

Omodeo 2001
Pietro Omodeo, 'La zoologia dei "Commentarii" nel Quadro dell'editoria del Cinquecento', in Ferri 2001, 315–29

Ongaro 1961/62–1962/63
Giuseppe Ongaro, 'Contributi alla biografia di Prospero Alpini', *Acta Medicae Historiae Patavina*, 8–9, 1961/62–1962/63, 81–168

Ongaro 1976–1986
Giuseppe Ongaro, 'La medicina nello Studio di Padova e nel Veneto', in Girolamo Arnaldi and Manlio Pastore Stocchi (eds.), *Storia della cultura veneta,* vol. 3/III, Vicenza 1976–1986, 76–134

Ongaro 2008
Giuseppe Ongaro, 'Pietro d'Abano e l'anatomia', *Medicina nei secoli*, 20 (2008), 567–90

Ongaro 2011
Giuseppe Ongaro, 'I rapporti tra Gaspard Bauhin e Prospero Alpini (con quattordici lettere di Prospero Alpini a Gaspard Bauhin)', *Alpiniana. Studi e testi,* 1 (2011), 333–44

Ongaro 2016
Giuseppe Ongaro, 'I rapporti tra il medico e botanico tedesco Joachim Camerarius II e Prospero Alpini (con venticinque lettere di Prospero Alpini)', *Alpiniana. Studi e testi,* 2 (2016), 365–91

Ongaro and Gamba 1994/95
Giuseppe Ongaro and Antonio Gamba, 'Contributo all'iconografia di Prospero Alpini', *Atti e Memorie dell'Accademia Patavina di Scienze, Lettere ed Arti,* 107 (1994/95), part II: 'Memorie della Classe di Scienze Matematiche e Naturali', 177–87

Ovid 1955
The Metamorphoses of Ovid, trans. Mary M. Innes, London 1955, URL: https://archive.org/details/innes-ovid-metamorphoses/mode/2up (last accessed: 20 Aug. 2024)

Ovid 1990
Publius Ovidius Naso, *Metamorphosen*, rendered in German hexameters by Erich Rösch, with an introduction by Niklas Holzberg, Munich and Zurich 1990

Ovid 2015
Ovidio, *Metamorfosi. Vol. VI Libri XIII–XV*, ed. Ph. Hardie, trans. G. Chiarini, Milan 2015

Oy-Marra 2008
Elisabeth Oy-Marra, 'Mimesis und "phantasia": Arcimboldo und die Beurteilung der Imaginatio in der italienischen Kunstliteratur des 16. Jahrhunderts', in Martin Zenck, Tim Becker, and Raphael Woebs (eds.), *Signatur und Phantastik in den schönen Künsten und in den Kulturwissenschaften der frühen Neuzeit*, Munich 2008, 99–122

Pächt 1950
Otto Pächt, 'Early Italian Nature Studies and Early Calendar Landscape', *Journal of the Warburg and Courtauld Institutes,* 13 (1950), 13–47

Pächt 2011
Otto Pächt, *La scoperta della natura. I primi studi italiani*, Turin 2011

Pagliara 2001
Pier Nicola Pagliara, s.v. 'Giovanni Giocondo da Verona', in DBI 56, 2001, 326–38

Paliaga 1997
Franco Paliaga, *Vincenzo Campi,* Cremona 1997

Paliaga 2000/01
Franco Paliaga, 'Vincenzo Campi tra realismo grottesco e natura morta: la nascita di un genere e l'eredità della pittura cremonese', in exh. cat. Cremona 2000/01, 21–37

Paliaga 2000/01a
Franco Paliaga, 'Vincenzo Campi e la pittura di genre fiamminga', in exh. cat. Cremona 2000/01, 51–9

Palladius 1526
Rutilius Taurus Palladius, *Palladio dignissimo et antiquo scrittore Della agricultura tradotto uolgare,* Siena (Simione di Nicolo libraio) 1526), URL: http://id.sbn.it/bid/RLZE016357 (last accessed: 6 Jan. 2025)

Palladius 1538
Rutilius Taurus Palladius, *Palladio dignissimo & antiquo scrittore della agricultura, tradutto volgare, acciò quelli che non sanno latino, frutto & gran diletto, per li suoi breui & ordinati precetti acquistino, con el suo repertorio alphabetario,* Venice (Bernardino de Viano de Lexona Vercellese) 1538, URL: http://id.sbn.it/bid/MODE010682 (last accessed: 6 Jan. 2025)

Palladius 1560
Rutilius Taurus Palladius, *La villa di Palladio Rutilio Tauro Emiliano tradotta nuouamente per Francesco Sansovino, nella quale si contiene il modo di cultiuar la terra di mese in mese, di inserir gli arbori, di gouernar gli horti, & i giardini, con la proprieta de frutti, delle herbe, & de gli animali, con molte altre cose utili a prò del contado*, Venice (Francesco Sansovino) 1560, URL: http://id.sbn.it/bid/BVEE003155 (last accessed: 6 Jan. 2025)

Pallecchi 2012
Nicola Pallecchi, 'The Making of the Book Market in Siena (XVI–XVII): Production, Circulation, Belonging | La costruzione del mercato del libro a Siena (secoli xvi–xvii): produzione, circolazione, possesso', *Bibliothecae.it*, 1 (2012), 121–56

Panciera 1996
Walter Panciera, *L'arte matrice. I lanifici della Repubblica di Venezia nei secoli XVII e XVIII,* Treviso 1996

Panciera 2005
Walter Panciera, *Il governo delle artiglierie. Tecnologia bellica e istituzioni veneziane nel secondo Cinquecento,* Milan 2005

Panofsky 1943
Erwin Panofsky, *The Life and Art of Albrecht Dürer*, Princeton 1943

Panofsky 1967
Erwin Panofsky, *La vita di Albrecht Dürer,* Milan 1967

Panofsky 1995
Erwin Panofsky, *Das Leben und die Kunst Albrecht Dürers,* Hamburg 1995

Pardo Tomás 2006
José Pardo Tomás, 'Tra "oppinioni" e "dispareri": la flora americana nell'erbario di Pier'Antonio Michiel (1510–1576)', in Giuseppe Olmi and Giuseppe Papagno (eds.), *La natura e il corpo. Studi in memoria di Attilio Zanca,* Florence 2006, 73–100

Paruzzo 2021
Valeria Paruzzo, 'Die Wiedergeburt der Allegorien der Jahreszeiten in der italienischen Renaissance: Antikenrezeption und neue Ikonographien', in Chatzidakis, Haug, Roemer, and Rombach 2021, 79–94

Pauli 1901
Gustav Pauli, *Hans Sebald Beham: Ein Kritisches Verzeichniss seiner Kupferstiche Radirungen und Holzschnitte* (Studien zur deutschen Kunstgeschichte 33), Strasbourg 1901

Pautasso 1994
Antonella Pautasso, *Il deposito votivo presso la porta nord a Vulci,* Rome 1994

Pavesi 2017
Mauro Pavesi, *Giovanni Ambrogio Figino pittore,* Canterano 2017

Pederson 2020
Jill Pederson, *Leonardo, Bramante, and the Academia: Art and Friendship in Fifteenth-Century Milan,* London and Turnhout 2020

Pedretti 1982
Carlo Pedretti, *The Drawings and Miscellaneous Papers of Leonardo da Vinci in the Collection of Her Majesty The Queen at Windsor Castle* (Landscapes, Plants and Water Studies I), London and New York 1982

Pedretti and Vecce 1995
Carlo Pedretti and Carlo Vecce (eds.), *Libro di Pittura. Codice urbinate lat. 1270 nella Biblioteca Apostolica Vaticana,* Florence 1995

Pedrocco 1990
Filippo Pedrocco, cat. 8 in exh. cat. Venice 1990, 115

Pegrari 1988
Maurizio Pegrari (ed.), 'Agostino Gallo nella cultura del Cinquecento', *Atti del convegno Brescia, 23–24 ottobre 1987* (Annali 1), Brescia 1988

Peltzer 1924
Rudolf Arthur Peltzer, 'Niederländisch-venezianische Landschaftsmalerei: Pauwels Franck genannt Ludovico Pozzoserrato', *Münchner Jahrbuch,* I/1 (1924), 126–53

Peltzer 1933
Rudolf Arthur Peltzer, 'Lod. Toeput (Pozzoserrato) und die Landschaftsfresken der Villa Maser', *Münchner Jahrbuch,* X/1 (1933), 270–9

Pennuto 2007
Concetta Pennuto, 'La diffusione manoscritta e a stampa degli Scriptores rei rusticae nel Quattrocento', *Schede umanistiche,* 21/1 (2007), 91–106

Pénot and Oberthaler 2018/19
Sabine Pénot and Elke Oberthaler, 'Zyklus der Jahreszeiten', in exh. cat. Vienna 2018/19, 214–41

Pesenti 1992
Tiziana Pesenti, s.v. 'Dondi dall'Orologio, Giovanni', in DBI 41, Rome 1992, 96–104

Pesenti 1985
Tiziana Pesenti, *Il 'Dioscoride' di Pier Andrea Mattioli e l'editoria botanica,* in *Trattati di prospettiva, architettura militare, idraulica e altre discipline,* Vicenza 1985, 61–103

Pettazzoni 1956
Raffaele Pettazzoni, 'Per l'iconografia di Giano', *Studi Etruschi,* 24 (1956), 79–90

Pezzuto 2015
Luca Pezzuto, 'I "pianeti finiguerra". Il recupero della "fortuna" di un modello iconografico noto tra la fine del quattrocento e gli inizi del cinquecento', *Iconographica. Rivista di iconografia medievale e moderna,* 14 (2015), 141–52

Pfiffig 1975
Ambros Josef Pfiffig, *Religio Etrusca,* Graz 1975

Pignatti 1976
Terisio Pignatti, *Veronese,* 2 vols., Venice 1976

Pignatti 2017
Franco Pignatti, s.v. 'Ruffinelli, Venturino', in DBI 89, 2017, 97–102

Pilz 1962
Kurt Pilz, 'Hans Hoffmann. Ein Nürnberger Dürer-Nachahmer aus der 2. Hälfte des 16. Jahrhunderts', *Mitteilungen des Vereins für Geschichte der Stadt Nürnberg,* 51 (1962), 236–72

Piquard 1950
Maurice Piquard, 'Le Cardinal de Granvelle, Amateur de Tapisseries', *Revue belge d'archéologie et d'histoire de l'art,* 1950, 111–26

Pitacco 2002
Francesca Pitacco, 'Un prestito mai refuso: le vicende del Liber de Simplicibus di Benedetto Rinio', in Linda Borean and Stefania Mason (eds.), *Figure di collezionisti a Venezia tra Cinque e Seicento,* Udine 2002, 11–23

Pitteri 2006
Mauro Pitteri, 'Indizi di ville nelle campagne trevigiane del XVI secolo', *Derosas,* 2006, 63–91

Planiscig 1924
Leo Planiscig, *Die Bronzeplastiken, Statuetten, Reliefs, Geräte und Plaketten,* Vienna 1924

Planiscig 1927
Leo Planiscig, *Andrea Riccio,* Vienna 1927

Pomian 1989
Krzysztof Pomian, 'Le collezioni venete nell'epoca della curiosità', in idem (ed.), *Collezionisti, Amatori e curiosi. Parigi–Venezia XVI–XVIII secolo,* Milan 1989, 83–162

Pomian 2004
Krzysztof Pomian, 'Collezioni pubbliche e private a Venezia dal XIII al XVIII secolo', in idem (ed.), *Dalle sacre reliquie all'arte moderna. Venezia–Chicago dal XIII al XX secolo,* Milan 2004, 21–123

Pona 1601
Giovanni Pona, *Index multarum rerum quae in repositorio Ioannis Ponae Pharmacopœi Veron. asservantur,* Verona 1601

Pona 1608
Giovanni Pona, *Plantae sev simplicia vt vocant, qvae in Baldo Monte, et in via ab Verona ad Badum reperivntvr: Cum Iconibus, & nominibus aliarum quamplurimarum, quae a nullo ante sunt observatae,* Basel 1608

Poni 1970
Carlo Poni, 'Un privilegio d'agricoltura. Camillo Tarello e il Senato di Venezia', *Rivista Storica Italiana,* 82 (1970), 592–610

Porzio 1979
Francesco Porzio, *L' universo illusorio di Arcimboldi,* Milan 1979

Porzio 1987
Francesco Porzio, *L' universo illusorio di Arcimboldi,* Milan 1987

Porzio 1993
Francesco Porzio, 'Fonti carnevalesche del naturalismo nel Cinquecento milanese: alcune ipotesi su Giuseppe Arcimboldi', *Arte Lombarda,* new series, 105/107, 2/4 (1993), 37–42

Porzio 2011
Francesco Porzio, 'Arcimboldo. Le Stagioni "milanesi" e l'origine dell'invenzione', in exh. cat. Milan 2011, 221–53

Porzio and Kahn Rossi 1998
Francesco Porzio and Manuela Kahn Rossi, *Rabisch: il grottesco nell'arte del Cinquecento. L'Accademia della Val di Blenio, Lomazzo e l'ambiente milanese*, Milan 1998

Pregari 1988
Maurizio Pegrari (ed.), *Agostino Gallo nella cultura del Cinquecento*, Brescia 1988

Premuda 1957
Loris Premuda, *Storia dell'iconografia anatomica*, Milan 1957

Preti 2008
Cesare Preti, under the entry 'Mattioli, Pietro Andrea', in DBI 72, 2008, 308–12

Primisser 1819
Alois Primisser, *Die kaiserlich-königliche Ambraser-Sammlung*, Vienna 1819

Pugliano 2011
Valentina Pugliano, 'Botanici e artigiani a Venezia: i (pochi) amici di Carolus Clusio', *Jahrbuch für europäische Wissenschaftkultur / Yearbook for European Culture of Science*, 6 (2011), 1–25

Pugliano 2023
Valentina Pugliano, 'Fake Specimens in the Renaissance', in Marjoljin Bol and Emma C. Spary (eds.), *The Matter of Mimesis. Studies of Mimesis and Materials in Nature, Art and Science*, Leiden and Boston 2023, 381–416

Radke 1965
Gerhard Radke, *Die Götter Altitaliens*, Münster 1965

Rainer 2015
Paulus Rainer, 'Wissen. Schafft. Kunst: Tycho Brahe, Johannes Kepler und das Kunstkammer-objekt als Erkenntnisträger', in Sabine Haag, Franz Kirchweger, and Paulus Rainer (eds.), *Das Haus Habsburg und die Welt der fürstlichen Kunstkammern im 16. und 17. Jahrhundert* (Schriften des Kunst-historischen Museums 15), Vienna 2015, 79–105

Rainer 2016
Paulus Rainer, 'Die gleichsam ins Kleine gebrachte Herrlichkeit der Natur. Oder eine kurze aber wahre Geschichte der Steinschneidekunst', in Wilhelm Lindemann, Paulus Rainer, and Regina Prange (eds.), *Edelstein / Kunst. Renaissance bis heute*, Stuttgart 2016, 11–59

Rallo 2022
Giuseppe Rallo, cat. 54 in exh. cat. Caserta 2022, 272

Ramharter 2011
Johannes Ramharter, 'Die Fürsterzbischöfliche Silberkammer', in Roswitha Juffinger (ed.), *Zentrum der Macht*, ii: *Die Kunstsammlungen der Salzburger Fürsterzbischöfe. Gemälde, Graphik, Kunstgewerbe*, Salzburg 2011, 337, V.1

Rapp 1976
Anna Rapp, *Der Jungbrunnen in Literatur und bildender Kunst des Mittelalters*, Zurich 1976

Raugei 2018
Anna Maria Raugei, *Gian Vincenzo Pinelli e la sua biblioteca*, Geneva 2018

Rearick 1989
William Roger Rearick, *Jacobus a Ponte Bassanensis*, Bassano del Grappa 1989

Rearick 1992/93
William Roger Rearick, 'The Life and Works of Jacopo Dal Ponte, called Bassano, c. 1510–1592', in exh. cat. Bassano and Fort Worth 1992/93, 45–171

Rearick 1996/97
William Roger Rearick, 'I clienti veneziani di Jacopo Bassano', *Guderzo*, 1996/97, 53–82

Recanati 1998
Maria Grazia Recanati, *Il taccuino di disegni della Biblioteca Civica di Bergamo. Giovannino de Gerassi e la sua eredità*, in *Commentario al Codice di disegni di Giovannino de Grassi*, Bergamo 1998, 17–43

Reitzenstein 1975
Alexander von Reitzenstein, 'Zum Burgkmairschen Doppelbildnis von 1529', *Pantheon*, 35 (1975), 106–10

Renouard 1834
Antoine Augustin Renouard, *Annales de l'Imprimerie des Alde, ou Histoire des trois Manuce et de leurs éditions*, 3rd printing, Paris 1834

Ridolfi 1648
Carlo Ridolfi, *Le maraviglie dell'arte, Overo Le vite de gl'illustri pittori veneti, e dello Stato*, part 1, Venice 1648

Ridolfi 1648 (1914/24)
Carlo Ridolfi, *Le Maraviglie dell'arte*, Venice 1648, ed. Detlev von Hadeln, Berlin 1914/24

Rigon 1983
Fernando Rigon, *Gli animali di Jacopo Bassano*, Bassano 1983

Rigon Forte 2021
Fernando Rigon Forte, *Qualche inverno prima. Iconografia delle Stagioni*, Milan 2021

Rippa Bonati and Pardo Tomás 2004
Maurizio Rippa Bonati and José Pardo Tomás (eds.), *Il teatro dei corpi. Le pitture colorate d'anatomia di Girolamo Fabrici d'Acquapendente*, Milan 2000

Roeck 1999
Bernd Roeck, 'Venice and Germany. Commercial Contacts and Intellectual Inspirations', in exh. cat. Venice 1999, 44–55

Romanini 2007
Fabio Romanini, *'Se fussero più ordinate, e meglio scritte …'. Giovanni Battista Ramusio correttore ed editore delle 'Navigationi et viaggi'*, Rome 2007

Rossacher 1966
Kurt Rossacher, *Der Schatz des Erzstiftes Salzburg. Ein Jahrtausend deutscher Goldschmiedekunst*, Salzburg 1966

Rossetti 2012
Edoardo Rossetti, 'Ritratti di baroni in città e vedute urbane in campagna. Un inedito inventario di Gaspare Ambrogio Visconti (1499)', in idem (ed.), *Squarci di interni. Inventari milanesi per il Rinascimento*, Milan 2012, 70–101

Rossetti 2020
Edoardo Rossetti, '"Tactus veneno viperae tuae". Istantanee, riflessi e distorsioni: la società milanese nelle opere di Gaspare Ambrogio Visconti', in Albonico and Moro 2020, 291–333

Rossetti 2021
Edoardo Rossetti, 'Libri e uomini in viaggio. "Imprenditori culturali" tra Milano e nord Europa nel Rinascimento, alcuni appunti', in Gabriele Baldassarri et al. (eds.), *Rinascimenti in transito a Milano. 1450–1525*, Milan 2021

Rossetti forthcoming
Edoardo Rossetti, 'Abitare tra continuità e fratture: antiche aristocrazie e nuove nobiltà in un tessuto urbano in perenne metamorfosi', in Rosa Cafiero et al., *Dimore e gusto. Architettura, arti e moda nelle residenze dell'aristocrazia lombarda fra Sei e Settecento*, monograph volume of *Arte Lombarda*, forthcoming

Rossi 2002
Marco Rossi, s.v. 'Grassi, Giovannino de', in DBI 58, Rome 2002, 640–47

Rossi 1995
Marco Rossi, *Giovannino de Grassi. La corte e la cattedrale*, Milan 1995

Rossi 1997
Francesca Rossi, '"Il porto e la scala di Alemagna": artisti del Nord a Verona', in Caterina Limentani Virdis (ed.), *La pittura fiamminga nel Veneto e nell'Emilia*, Verona 1997, 167–201

Rossi 2000
Francesco Rossi, in exh. cat. Pavia and Ariccia 2000, 48–9

Rossi 2001
Francesca Rossi, *'Mill'altre maraviglie ristrette in angustissimo spacio'. Un repertorio dell'arte fiamminga e olandese a Verona tra Cinque e Seicento*, Venice 2001

Rossi, Peretti, and Rossetti 2020
Francesca Rossi, Gianni Peretti, and Edoardo Rossetti (eds.), *Caroto. Giovan Francesco Caroto (1480 circa–1555)*, Cinisello Balsamo (MI) 2020

Roth 1912
Friedrich Roth, 'Der Augsburger Jurist Hieronymus Fröschel und seine Hauschronik 1528–1600', *Zeitschrift des Historischen Vereins für Schwaben und Neuburg*, 38 (1912), 1–82

Roveda 2012
Enrico Roveda, *Uomini, terre e acque: studi sull'agricoltura della Bassa lombarda tra XV e XVII secolo*, Milan 2012

Rudolf 1995
Karl Rudolf, 'Die Kunstbestrebungen Kaiser Maximilians II. im Spannungsfeld zwischen Madrid und Wien: Untersuchungen zu den Sammlungen der Österreichischen und spanischen Habsburger im 16. Jahrhundert', *Jahrbuch der Kunsthistorischen Sammlungen in Wien*, 91 (1995 (1996), 165–256

Rudolf 2015
Karl Rudolf, 'Arcimboldo im kulinarischen Wissensraum. Die Kunstkammer Kaiser Ferdinands I. (1503–1564)', in Sabine Haag, Franz Kirchweger, and Paulus Rainer (eds.), *Das Haus Habsburg und die Welt der fürstlichen Kunstkammern im 16. und 17. Jahrhundert* (Schriften des Kunsthistorischen Museums 15), Vienna 2015, 133–65

Rüpke 2015
Jörg Rüpke, 'Geteilte und umstrittene Geschichten: Der Chronograph von 354 und die Katakombe an der Via Latina', in Hartmut Leppin (ed.) *Antike Mythologie in christlichen Kontexten der Spätantike* (Millennium-Studien zu Kultur und Geschichte des ersten Jahrtausends n.Chr. 54), Berlin and Boston 2015, 221–38

Sallaberger 1997
Johann Sallaberger, *Kardinal Matthäus Lang von Wellenburg (1468–1540): Staatsmann und Kirchenfürst im Zeitalter von Renaissance, Reformation und Bauernkriegen*, Salzburg *et al.* 1997

Salzmann 1990
Michelle Renee Salzmann, *On Roman Time. The Codex-Calendar of 354 and the Rhythms of Urban Life in Late Antiquity* (The Transformation of the Classical Heritage 17), Berkeley, Los Angeles, and Oxford 1990

Samson 2012
Alexander Samson (ed.), *Locus Amoenus: Gardens and Horticulture in the Renaissance*, Malden (MA) 2012

Sangl 2004
Sigrid Sangl, *Rundgang durch die Kunst und Wunderkammer Burg Trausnitz*, Munich 2004

Sansovino 1561
Francesco Sansovino, *Orationi volgarmente scritte da molti huomini illustri de tempi nostri*, Venice 1561

Sansovino 1561a
Francesco Sansovino (ed.), *Della materia medicinale libri quattro. Nel primo & secondo de quali si contengono i semplici medicamenti con le figure delle herbe … nel terzo s'insegna il modo di preparare & comporre i medicamenti secondo l'uso de i Medici approvati … nel quarto … son poste le malattie che vengono al corpo humano*, Venice (Gio. Andrea Valvassori detto Guadagnino) 1561, URL: http://id.sbn.it/bid/RMLE0c6306 (last accessed: 6 Jan. 2025)

Sansovino 1663
Francesco Sansovino, *Venetia città nobilissima et singolare, Descritta in XIIII. Libri*, Venice 1663

Santamaría and Salvador Palomo 1996
María Teresa Santamaria and Pedro José Salvador Palomo, 'Valencia y los agrios: del jardin de los cinco sentidos al huerto productivo-burgués', in Alessandro Tagliolini and Margherita Azzi Visentini (eds.), *Il giardino delle Esperidi. Gli agrumi nella storia, nella letteratura e nell'arte. Atti del V Colloquio Internazionale Cetro Studi Giardini Storici e Contemporanei Pietrasanta 13–14 ottobre 1995*, Florence 1996, 141

Saraina 1540
Torello Saraina, *De origine et amplitudine civitatis Veronae*, Verona 1540

Savio 2018
Andrea Savio, 'Rilatione di Vicenza di Mons PG', in Francesco Bianchi and Walter Panciera (eds.), *'Bellissimo per le doti della natura e per l'industria umana'. Immagini e descrizione del territorio vicentino tra medioevo ed età moderna*, Rome 2018, 151–55

Savio and De Leeuw 1977
Michele Savio and Flora de Leeuw, 'Uccelli rapaci e piante meravigliose nell' "Iter creticum" di Onofrio Cantalupo', in Eduard Behr (ed.), *Die Renaissance-Natur. Festschrift für Felix Wiesner*, Munich 1977, 45–59

Saxl 1985
Fritz Saxl, *La fede negli astri. Dall'antichità al Rinascimento*, Turin 1985

Scheicher 1973
Elisabeth Scheicher, 'Die Groteskenmonate. Eine Tapisserienserie des Kunsthistorischen Museums in Wien', *Jahrbuch der kunsthistorischen Sammlungen in Wien*, LXIX (1973), 55–84

Scheller 1995
Robert W. Scheller, *Exemplum, Model-Book Drawings and the Practice of Artistic Trasmission (ca. 900–ca.1470)*, Amsterdam 1995

Schilling 1960
Robert Schilling, 'Janus, le dieu introducteur, le dieu des passages', *Mélanges de l'école française de Rome (MEFRA)*, 72 (1960), 89–131

Schindler 1964
Rudolf Schindler, 'Ein Mandl-Kalender aus Elfenbein in Schloss Ambras', in *Tiroler Heimatblätter*, 39/40 (1964), 5–8

Schlegel 2022
Konrad Schlegel, 'Aus der Wiener Kunstkammer. Fragmente zur Rolle der Kleinplastik bei Julius von Schlosser', *Wiener Jahrbuch für Kunstgeschichte*, LXVI (2022), 9–28

Schleier 1981
Reinhart Schleier, *Neue Zeichnungen alter Meister. Entdeckungen aus einer Barocksammlung*, Münster 1981

Schmitz-von Ledebur 2011/12
Katja Schmitz-von Ledebur, 'Der Lauf der Zeit – Zur Darstellung des Winters in Tapisserien', in exh. cat. Vienna and Zurich 2011/12, 67–81

Schmitz-von Ledebur 2024
Katja Schmitz-von Ledebur, *Si hortum in bibliotheca habes, deerit nihil – Tapisserien mit Gartenlandschaften für Kardinal Antoine Perrenot de Granvelle*, in exh. cat. Mechelen 2024, 74–85

Schoch, Mende, and Scherbaum 2002
Rainer Schoch, Matthias Mende, and Anna Scherbaum, *Albrecht Dürer. Das druckgraphische Werk*, ii: *Holzschnitte und Holzschnittfolgen*, Munich *et al.* 2002

Schofield 1995
Richard V. Schofield, 'Gaspare Visconti, mecenate di Bramante', in Arnold Esch and Christoph Luitpold Frommel (eds.), *Arte, committenza ed economia a Roma e nelle corti del Rinascimento. 1420–1530*, Turin 1995, 297–330

Schofield 2013
Richard V. Schofield, 'Bramante dopo Malaguzzi Valeri', *Arte Lombarda*, 167 (2013), 5–51

Scholten 2013
Frits Scholten, 'Johan Gregor van der Schardt in Nuremberg', in Peta Motture, Emma Jones, and Dimitrios Zikos (eds.), *Carvings, Casts & Collectors. The Art of Renaissance Sculpture*, London 2013, 134–47

Scholten 2015
Frits Scholten (ed.), *Rijksmuseum: 1100–1600*, Amsterdam 2015

Scholten, Van Langh, and Verber 2005
Frits Scholten, Robert van Langh, and Monique Verber, *From Vulcan's Forge. Bronzes from the Rijksmuseum, Amsterdam 1450–1800*, London 2005

Schöner 1964
Erich Schöner, *Das Viererschema in der antiken Humoralpathologie* (Sudhoffs Archiv, Beiheft 4), Wiesbaden 1964

Schreiber 1888
Theodor Schreiber, *Die Wiener Brunnenreliefs aus Palazzo Grimani: eine Studie über das hellenistische Reliefbild mit Untersuchungen über die bildende Kunst in Alexandrien,* Leipzig 1888

Schürer 1986
Ralf Schürer, 'Wenzel Jamnitzers Brunnen für Maximilian II. Überlegungen zu Ikonographie und Zweck', *Anzeiger des Germanischen Nationalmuseums,* 1986, 55–9

Schütz 2008
Karl Schütz, 'Kunst und Kultur am Hof Kaiser Maximilians II.', in exh. cat. Paris and Vienna 2007/08, 73–9

Schütz 2008a
Karl Schütz, 'Giuseppe Arcimboldo als "der Rom: Kay: Mt: conterfeter"' in exh. cat. Paris and Vienna 2007/08, 81–4

Sclosa 2009/10
Meri Sclosa, 'Per la ritrattistica di Leandro Bassano e Domenico Tintoretto', in Ericani, Caramanna, and Millozzi 2014, i, 131–40

Scully 2008
Terence Scully, *The Opera of Bartolomeo Scappi (1570). The Art and Craft of a Master Cook*, Toronto 2008

Scuro 2021
Rachele Scuro, 'Bassano del Grappa', in Deborah Howard (ed.), *Proto-industrial Architecture of the Veneto in the Age of Palladio,* Rome 2021

Sears 1986
Elizabeth Sears, *The Ages of Man. Medieval Interpretations of the Life Cycle*, Princeton 1986

Sellink (2007) 2011
Manfred Sellink, *Bruegel. The Complete Paintings, Drawings and Prints*, Ghent (2007) 2011

Seneca 1974
L. Annaeus Seneca, *Oedipus*, Latin/German, ed. and trans. Konrad Heldmann, Stuttgart 1974

Seneca 1995
Seneca, *The Tragedies*, ii, ed. David R. Slavitt, The Johns Hopkins University Press, Baltimore Maryland 1995, URL: https://archive.org/details/senecaoosene_o/mode/2up (last accessed: 20 Aug. 2024)

Sickel 2016
Lothar Sickel, 'Die römische Antikensammlung des Kanonikers Mario Conti. Wie die Wiener Grimani-Reliefs und die Ara Grimani nach Venedig gelangten', *Jahrbuch des Kunsthistorischen Museums Wien*, 17/18 (2016), 9–25

Silver 2006
Larry Silver, *Hieronymus Bosch*, New York and London 2006

Simon 1986
Erika Simon, *Augustus. Kunst und Leben in Rom um die Zeitenwende,* Munich 1986

Simon 1990
Erika Simon, *Die Götter der Römer*, Munich 1990

Simon 1990a
Erika Simon, s.v. 'Ianus', in *Lexicon Iconographicum Mythologiae Classicae,* v (1990), 618–23

Simonsfeld 1887
Henry Simonsfeld, *Der Fondaco dei Tedeschi in Venedig und die deutsch-venetianischen Handelsbeziehungen,* 2 vols., Stuttgart 1887

Sorbelli 1933
Albino Sorbelli, 'Bibliografia delle edizioni', in *Pier de' Crescenzi. Studi e documenti,* Bologna 1933, 307–69

Sotheby's London 1991
Sale cat. Sotheby's London, 'Western Manuscripts and Miniatures' (17 December 1991)

Sotheby's New York 1981
Sale cat. Sotheby's New York, 'Carleton R. Richmond sale' (30 October 1981)

Spike and Zucker 1993
John T. Spike and Mark J. Zucker (eds.), *The Illustrated Bartsch*, xxiv: *Early Italian masters*, New York 1993

Stampart and Prenner 1735
Franz Stampart and Anton Prenner, *Prodromus, Oder Vor-Licht Des eröffneten Schau- und Wunder-Prachtes Aller deren An dem Kaiserl. Hof In Allerhöchst Seiner Kaiserl. Königl., und Cathol. Majestät unsers glorwürdigst Regierenden Monarchens Carl des Sechsten Haupt- und Residentz-Stadt Wienn sich befindlichen Kunst-Schätzen, und Kostbarkeiten: Sonderheitlichen Deren alldarinnen häuffig aufbehaltenen Bewunderungs-würdigen Schildereyen, Gemählden, Statuen, Bild-Saulen und anderen von denen allervornehmsten Meistern verfertigten Gemächtnüssen,* Vienna 1735

Staudinger 2008
Manfred Staudinger, 'Arcimboldo und Ulisse Aldrovandi', in exh. cat. Paris and Vienna 2007/08, 113–17

Stern 1953
Henri Stern, *Le calendrier de 354. Étude sur son texte et ses illustrations*, Paris 1953

Stewart 1989
Alison G. Stewart, 'Sebald Beham's Fountain of Youth-Bathhouse Woodcut: Popular Entertainment and Large Prints by the Little Masters', *Register of the Spencer Art Museum*, 6/6 (1989), 64–88

Stockbauer 1874
Jacob Stockbauer, *Die Kunstbestrebungen am Bayerischen Hofe unter Herzog Albrecht V. und Wilhelm V.*, Vienna 1874

Strauss 1974
Walter L. Strauss, *The Complete Drawings of Albrecht Dürer*, 6 vols., New York 1974 (with two supplementary volumes, 1977 and 1982)

Strocka 1965
Volker Michael Strocka, 'Die Brunnenreliefs Grimani', *Antike Plastik*, 4 (1965), 87–102

Strzygowski 1888
Josef Strzygowski, 'Die Calenderbilder des Chronographen vom Jahre 354', *Jahrbuch des Deutschen Archäologischen Instituts*, supplement, 1 (1888), 21–95

Stüwe 1998
Rainer Stüwe, *Dürer in der Kopie. Die Gemälde und Graphiken der Nürnberger Dürer-Kopisten des 16. und 17. Jahrhunderts zwischen altdeutscher Manier und barockem Stil*, 3 vols., Diss., Heidelberg University, 1998

Sullivan 2014
Margaret A. Sullivan, 'Peter Brueghel the Elder's "Two Monkeys": a New Interpretation', *The Art Bulletin*, 63/1 (2014), 114–26

Svalduz 2019
Elena Svalduz, 'Architettura e paesaggio: la villa veneta nel Rinascimento', in Caracausi, Grosso, and Romani 2019, 133–50, 280–87

Swoboda 2004/05
Gudrun Swoboda, 'Das Ambraser Bilderinventar von 1663. Addenda zu Provenienzen der Gemäldegalerie des Kunsthistorischen Museums', *Jahrbuch des Kunsthistorischen Museums Wien*, 6/7 (2004/2005), 263–307

***Tabula Cebetis* 1497**
Censorinus de die natali. Tabula Cebetis. Dialogus Luciani. Enchiridion Epicteti. Basilius. Plutarchus de Inuidia & Odio, trans. Ludovicus Odaxius, Bologna (Benedictus Hectoris) 1497

***Taccuino* 1997**
'Il Taccuino di Giovannino de' Grassi della Biblioteca Civica di Bergamo: tecnica di esecuzione e restauro', *OPD Restauro. Rivista dell'Opificio delle Pietre Dure e Laboratori di Restauro*, 9 (1997), 15–37

***Taccuino* 1998**
Giulio Orazio Bravi, Maria Grazia Recanati, Maria Grazia Vaccari, Letizia Montalbano, and Chiara Rossi Scarzanella, *Taccuino di disegni di Giovannino de' Grassi. Commentario al codice*, facsimile edition, Modena 1998

***Taccuino* 2005**
Giulio Orazio Bravi and Maria Grazia Recanati, *Il Taccuino di disegni di Giovannino de' Grassi*, Bergamo 2005

Tafuri 1985
Manfredo Tafuri, *Venezia e il Rinascimento. Religione, scienza, architettura*, Turin 1985

Taglialagamba 2010
Sara Taglialagamba, *Leonardo & Nature*, Poggio a Caiano 2010

Tait 1988
Hugh Tait, *Catalogue of the Waddesdon Bequest in the British Museum II. The Silver Plate*, London 1988

Tanzi 2004
Marco Tanzi, *I Campi* (Gallerie delle Arti 1), Milan 2004

Tarabochia Canavero 2021
Alessandra Tarabochia Canavero, 'Virtù e pianeti: compagni della vita attiva e della vita contemplativa, in Otium e negotium nel Rinascimento', *Atti del XXXI Convegno internazionale Chianciano Terme-Montepulciano, 18–20 luglio 2019*, Florence 2021, 279–86

Tarello 1567
Camillo Tarello, *Ricordo d'agricoltura*, Venice (Francesco Rampazetto) 1567, URL: http://id.sbn.it/bid/TO0E030955 (last accessed: 6 Jan. 2025)

Tartaglini 1551
Leone Tartaglini, *Opera nuoua nella quale se contiene la natura dil sonno cioe come lhuomo debbe dormire per mantenersi sano con alchuni bellissimi & vtilissimi secreti medicinali*, Venice 1551

Tartaglini 1996
Leone Tartaglini, *Opera Nuova ... Con il testamento inedito*, ed. Marcello Brusegan, Fermo (AP) 1996

Tassi 1793
Francesco Maria Tassi, *Vite de' pittori, scultori e architetti bergamaschi*, Bergamo 1793

Tátrai, Dobos, and Béres 2024
Vilmos Tátrai, Zsuzsanna Dobos, and Csenge Júlia Béres, *A Summary Catalogue of Italian Paintings 1250–1800. Museum of Fine Arts Budapest*, ed. Nikoletta Koruhely, Budapest 2024

Tatti 1560
Giovanni Tatti [i.e. Francesco Sansovino], *Della agricoltura ... libri cinque. Ne quali si contengono tutte le cose appartenenti al bisogno della villa, tratte da gli antichi & da moderni scrittori. Con le figure delle biaue, delle piante, de gli animali et delle herbe cosi medicinali, come comuni et da mangiare*, Venice (F. Sansovino et compagni) 1560, URL: http://id.sbn.it/bid/CFIE000071 (last accessed: 6 Jan. 2025)

Tenenti 1988
Alberto Tenenti, 'La fortuna di Agostino Gallo in Francia', in Pegrari 1988, 9–21

Tergolina Gislanzoni Brasco 1934
Umberto Tergolina Gislanzoni Brasco, 'Francesco Calzolari Speziale Veronese', special imprint in *Bollettino Storico Italiano dell'Arte Sanitaria, allegato alla Rassegna di Clinica, Terapia e Scienze Affini*, 33/6 (November/December 1934)

Testa 2019
Simone Testa, under the entry 'Tatti, Francesco (detto Sansovino)', in DBI 95, 2019, URL: https://www.treccani.it/enciclopedia/francesco-tatti_(Dizionario-Biografico)/(last accessed: 4. Jan. 2024)

Thieme-Becker 1935
Ulrich Thieme and Felix Becker, *Das Allgemeine Lexikon der Bildenden Künstler*, xxix, 1935

Tholen 1987
Sybille Tholen, *Moraltheologische und moralpädagogische Allegorien (Pieter Aertsen und Joachim Beuckelaer) mit einem vorläufigen Oeuvre-Verzeichnis*, Diss., Cologne University, 1987

Toesca 1905
Pietro Toesca, 'Michelino da Besozzo e Giovannino de' Grassi. Ricerche sull'antica pittura lombarda', *L'Arte*, VIII (1905), 321–39

Tongiorgi Tomasi 1980
Lucia Tongiorgi Tomasi, 'Il Giardino dei Semplici dello Studio pisano. Collezionismo, scienza e immagine tra Cinque e Seicento', in exh. cat. Pisa 1980, 514–98

Tongiorgi Tomasi 1984
Lucia Tongiorgi Tomasi, 'L'isola dei semplici', *Kos*, 1/5 (1984), 61–84

Tongiorgi Tomasi 1988
Lucia Tongiorgi Tomasi, 'Daniel Froeschl before Prague: His Artistic Activity in Tuscany at the Medici Court', in exh. cat. Vienna and Essen 1988/89, 289–98

Tongiorgi Tomasi 1993
Lucia Tongiorgi Tomasi, *I ritratti di piante di Jacopo Ligozzi*, Pisa 1993

Tongiorgi Tomasi 2000
Lucia Tongiorgi Tomasi, 'L'immagine naturalistica: tecnica e invenzione', in Giuseppe Olmi, Lucia Tongiorgi Tomasi, and Attilio Zanca (eds.), *Natura–Cultura. L'interpretazione del mondo fisico nei testi e nelle immagini*, Florence 2000, 133–52

Tongiorgi Tomasi 2001
Lucia Tongiorgi Tomasi, 'Il problema delle immagini nei "Commentarii"', in Ferri 2001, 369–76

Tongiorgi Tomasi 2009
Lucia Tongiorgi Tomasi, 'Galileo, le arti, gli artisti', in exh. cat. Florence 2009, 21–43

Tongiorgi Tomasi 2014
Lucia Tongiorgi Tomasi, '"Tutte le pitture dipinte al vivo dal signor Jacomo Ligozzi a' quali non mancha se non il spirito"', in exh. cat. Florence 2014, 29–37

Tongiorgi Tomasi 2019
Lucia Tongiorgi Tomasi, 'Leonardo, le erbe e i libri', in exh. cat. Rome 2019, 49–79

Tongiorgi Tomasi 2024
Lucia Tongiorgi Tomasi, *Animali in un serraglio pisano tra Cinque e Seicento*, Pisa 2024

Tongiorgi Tomasi and Garbari 1995
Lucia Tongiorgi Tomasi and Fabio Garbari, *Il Giardiniere del Granduca. Storia e immagini del Codice Casabona*, Pisa 1995

Tongiorgi Tomasi, Garbari, and Tosi 1991
Lucia Tongiorgi Tomasi, Fabio Garbari, and Alessandro Tosi, *Giardino dei Semplici*, Pisa 1991

Tongiorgi Tomasi and Willis 2009
Lucia Tongiorgi Tomasi and Tony Willis, *An Oak Spring Herbaria. Herbs and Herbals from the Fourteenth to the Nineteenth Centuries*, Upperville 2009

Tosi 1989
Alessandro Tosi (ed.), *Ulisse Aldrovandi e la Toscana. Carteggio e testi documentari*, Florence 1989

Tosi 2001
Alessandro Tosi, 'In Matthioli effigiem', in Ferri 2001, 377–89

Toubert 1984
Pierre Toubert, s.v. 'Crescenzi, Pietro de' (Pier, Petrus de Crescentiis)', in DBI 30, 1984, 649–56

Trentini 2016
Angela Trentini, 'Una fonte per la storia dell'alimentazione e della medicina: il Tacuinum Sanitatis del vescovo Georg von Liechtenstein', *Studi Trentini. Storia*, 95 (2016/1), 141–70

Tschetschik-Hammerl 2023
Ksenija Tschetschik-Hammerl, *Nach Dürer. Kunst begegnet Natur bei Hans Hoffmann und Daniel Fröschl*, Petersberg 2023

Tucci 1972
Ugo Tucci, s.v. 'Bussatti (Busatti, Bussato), Marco', in DBI 15, 1972, 553–4

Unterkircher 1959
Franz Unterkircher, *Inventar der illuminierten Handschriften, Inkunabeln und Frühdrucke der Österreichischen Nationalbibliothek*, Vienna 1959

Valerini 1586
Adriano Valerini, *Le bellezze di Verona, Nuovo ragionamento*, Verona 1586

Valles 1588
Francisco Valles, *Francisco Vallesii, de iis quae scripta sunt physice in libris sacris, siue de Sacra Philosophia. Liber singularis. Cui, propter argumenti similitudinem, adiuncti sunt duo alij. Nempe Levini Lemnii de plantis sacris: Et Francisci Ruei de Gemmis, ante quidem editi, sed nunc emendatius expressi*, Lyon (Franciscus Le Fevre) 1588

Valseriati 2018
Enrico Valseriati, 'Descrizioni, cronache, diari di viaggio: le testimonianze scritte', in Francesco Bianchi and Walter Panciera (eds.), *'Bellissimo per le doti della natura e per l'industria umana'. Immagini e descrizioni del territorio vicentino tra medioevo ed età moderna*, Rome 2018, 51–103

Van der Coelen and Lammertse 2019
Peter van der Coelen and Friso Lammertse, 'Bosch to Bruegel: Uncovering Everyday Life', *Journal of Historians of Netherlandish Art*, 11/1 (2019), URL: https://jhna.org/articles/bosch-to-bruegel-uncovering-everyday-life/ (last accessed: 5 Nov. 2024)

Van Mander 1604
Karel van Mander, *Het schilder-boeck waerin voor eerst de leerlustighe lueght den grondt der edel vry schilderconst in vercheyden deelen wort voorghedraghen ...*, Haarlem 1604

Van Ommen 2016
Kasper van Ommen, 'What does an Oriental Scholar look like? Some Portraits of Joseph Scaliger and Other Sixteenth-century Oriental Scholars: A Selection', in Ann Blair and Anja Silvia Goeing (eds.), *For the Sake of Learning. Essays in Honor of Anthony Grafton*, 2 vols., Leiden 2016, i, 73–90

Van Suchtelen 2024
Ariane van Suchtelen, 'Roelant Savery's Wondrous World', *Mauritshuis Magazine*, 1 (2024), 6–12

Van Winter 1986
Johanna Maria van Winter, 'Voedselverbruik in de Nederlanden in de vijftiende en zestiende eeuw', in exh. cat. Ghent 1986/87, 63–6

Vasari 1568 (1880)
Giorgio Vasari, *Le Vite de' più eccellenti pittori, scultori e architettori* [1568], ed. Gaetano Milanesi, Florence 1880

Vecce 2017
Carlo Vecce, *La biblioteca perduta: i libri di Leonardo*, Rome 2017

Vecce 2024
Carlo Vecce, *Leonardo, la vita*, Florence 2024

Venturi 2010
Gianni Venturi (ed.), *De Sphaera. Commentario all'edizione in facsimile del codice miniato a.x.2.14 = lat. 209 della Biblioteca Estense Universitaria di Modena*, Modena 2010

Verci 1775
Giambatista Verci, *Notizie intorno alla vita de' pittori scultori ed intagliatori della città di Bassano*, Venice 1775

Vergani 2003
Raffaello Vergani, *Miniere e società nella montagna del passato. Alpi venete, secoli XIII–XIX*, Verona 2003

Vianello 2004
Francesco Vianello, *Seta fine e panni grossi. Manifatture e commerci nel Vicentino 1570–1700*, Milan 2004

Vianello 2004a
Francesco Vianello, 'Mercanti, imprese e commerci nel Cinque e Seicento', in Giovanni Luigi Fontana (ed.), *L'industria vicentina dal Medioevo a oggi*, Padua 2004, 187–229

Vianello 2013
Francesco Vianello, 'Economia e popolazione in età moderna', in Paolo Preto (ed.), *Storia di Bassano*, II, *L'età moderna*, Bassano 2013, 13–75

Vinco 2021
Mattia Vinco, *Pittori di Terraferma a Vicenza e dintorni*, in exh. cat. Vicenza 2021, 42–61

Weber 1970
Ingrid Weber, 'Bildvorlagen für Silberreliefs an Arbeiten von Paul Hübner und Kornelius Erb, heute im Palazzo Pitti und im Britischen Museum. Eine Studie zur Arbeitsweise in nachmittelalterlichen Goldschmiedewerkstätten', *Mitteilungen des Kunsthistorischen Institutes in Florenz*, 14/3 (June 1970), 323–86

Weihrauch 1967
Hans R. Weihrauch, *Europäische Bronzestatuetten*, Braunschweig 1967

Wharf 1999
Alan Wharf, 'The Bassano Family. Renaissance Painters with an Eye for Tools and Trades', *Journal of the Tools and Trades History Society*, 11 (1999), 4–35

White and Crawley 1994
Christopher White and Charlotte Crawley, *The Dutch and Flemish Drawings at Windsor Castle*, Cambridge 1994

Wied 1990
Alexander Wied, *Lucas und Marten van Valckenborch (1535–1597 und 1534–1612). Das Gesamtwerk mit kritischem Oeuvrekatalog*, Freren 1990

Wied 1997
Sotheby's London, sale 3 July 1997, lots 17 and 18 (information supplied by Alexander Wied)

Wied 2002
Alexander Wied, cat. 57 in exh. cat. Vienna and Essen 2002/03, 180–81

Wied 2008
Alexander Wied, cats. IV.3 and IV.18 in exh. cat. Paris and Vienna 2007/08, 127–28, 148

Wied 2008/09
Alexander Wied, cat. 2 in exh. cat. Tokyo, Sendai, and Nagoya 2008/09, 40–1

Wied 2010
Alexander Wied, 'Erzherzog Ernst von Österreich (1553–1595), Statthalter der spanischen Niederlande. Das Kassabuch der Jahre 1589 bis 1595', *Jahrbuch des Kunsthistorischen Museums Wien*, 12 (2010), 153–275

Wiesner 1971
Felix Wiesner, 'Adler nach Kreta und Eulen nach Athen. Cantalupos Iter creticum (1571) als Paradigma der Reise zwischen Mythos und Realität', *Mitteilungen der Münchner Gesellschaft für Geschichte und Gegenwart*, 14 (1971), 77–98

Wiesner 1975
Felix Wiesner, 'Lilie, Brennessel und Knoblauch. Engelskräuter der Kabbalah in den Werken Dürers, Altdorfers, Becks und Cranachs d.J.', in Georg Bißmeyer (ed.), *Kunst und Kabale. Cyriak Kernstock herzlich zugeeignet*, Munich 1975, 98–114

Wilding 2014
Nick Wilding, *Galileo's Idol. Gianfrancesco Sagredo and the Politics of Knowledge*, Chicago and London 2014

Wind 1975
Barry Wind, 'Genre as Season: Dosso, Campi, Caravaggio', *Arte Lombarda*, 42/43 (1975), 70–3

Winkler 1936–1939
Friedrich Winkler, *Die Zeichnungen Albrecht Dürers*, 4 vols., Berlin 1936–1939

Wirtz 2006
Carolin Wirtz, *Köln und Venedig. Wirtschaftliche und kulturelle Beziehungen im 15. und 16. Jahrhundert*, Cologne, Weimar, and Vienna 2006

Wolf-Heidegger and Cetto 1967
Gerhard Wolf-Heidegger and Anna Maria Cetto, *Die anatomische Sektion in bildlicher Darstellung*, Basel and New York 1967

Woltmann 1877
Alfred Woltmann, 'Die Gemäldesammlung in der kaiserlichen Burg zu Prag', *Mitteilungen der K.K. Central-Commission zur Erforschung und Erhaltung der Kunst- und historischen Denkmale*, III (1877), 25–50

Wörz 2007
Adèle Lorraine Wörz, *The Visualization of Perspective Systems and Iconology in Dürer's Cartographic Works: An In-Depth Analysis Using Multiple Methodological Approaches*, Ph.D. thesis, Oregon State University, 2007, URL: https://ir.library.oregonstate.edu/concern/graduate_thesis_or_dissertations/2j62s789w (last accessed: 6 Jan. 2025)

Yasui 2016
Ayumi Yasui, 'Where Has Paris Gone? Sebald Beham's *Fountain of Youth* Reconsidered', in Kayo Hirakawa (ed.), *Sacred and Profane in Early Modern Art* (Kyoto Studies in Art History 1), Kyoto 2016, 19–35

Zaccariotto 2024
Giulia Zaccariotto, *Vivitur ingenio. Giorgione, Taddeo Contarini e i Tre filosofi*, Rome 2024

Zanker 1987
Paul Zanker, *Augustus und die Macht der Bilder*, Munich 1987

Zanotto 1850
Pinacothèque Barbini-Breganze placée dans le Palais Zaguri S.nt Maurice n. 2632, décrite et illustrée, avec des notes par François Zanotto membre de l'Athénée de Venise et de plusieurs autres académies, deuxième édition tirée de l'original italien-français imprimée en 1847, Venice 1850

Zeleny 2008
Karin Zeleny, 'Giorgiones drei Philosophen: eine philologische Identifizierung', in Sylvia Ferino-Pagden (ed.), *Giorgione entmythisiert*, Turnhout 2008, 191–98

Zeleny 2008a
Karin Zeleny, 'Drei Philosophen und drei Humanisten', *Wiener Humanistische Blätter*, 49/2007 (2008), 40–69

Zimmermann 1889
Heinrich Zimmermann, Inventare, Acten und Regesten aus der Schatzkammer des Allerhöchsten Kaiserhauses, *Jahrbuch der Kunsthistorischen Sammlungen des Allerhöchsten Kaiserhauses*, 10 (1889), 201–324

Zinner 1967
Ernst Zinner, *Deutsche und niederländische astronomische Instrumente des 11. bis 18. Jahrhunderts*, 2nd printing, Munich 1967

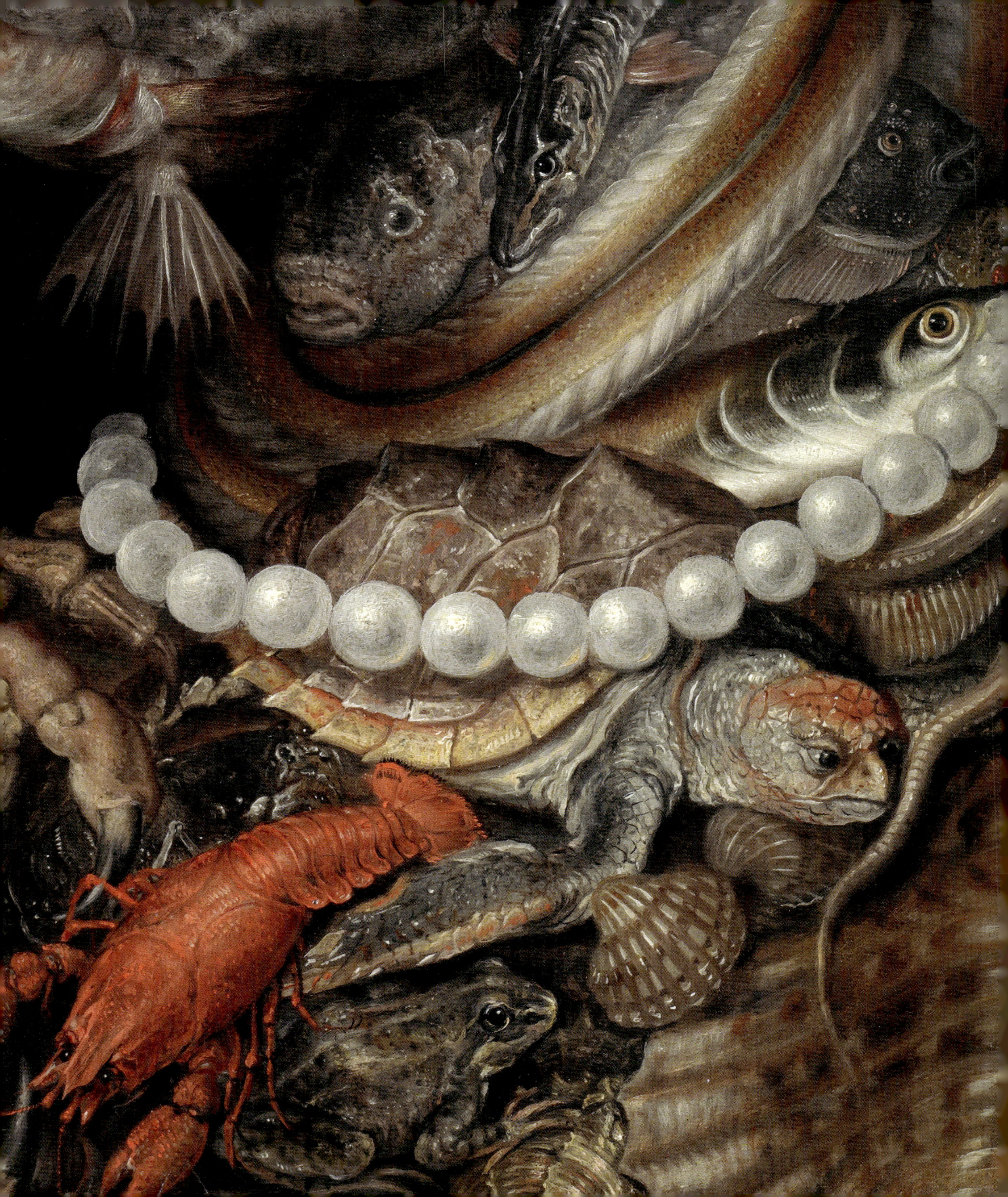

Acknowledgments

Marion Ackermann
Laura Aldovini
Denise Allen
Lászlo Baán
Martina Bagnoli
Raffaella Barbierato
Vincenzo Bellelli
Guido Beltramini
Luigi de Benedetto
Claudia Benvestito
Szilvia Bodnar
Stefania Buganza
Guido Caneto
Daniele Cianchi
Francesco Citti
Martin Clayton
Valentina Conticelli
Angelo Crespi
Elisabetta Dal Carlo
Francesca Debolini
Taco Dibbits
Laura Donati
Kaywin Feldman
Federico Fischetti
Christine Follmann
Eliška Fučikova
Francesca Giupponi
Ralph Gleis
Maria Paola Guidobaldi
Jörn Günther
Annette Hoier
Lilli Hollein
Max Hollein
Ingrid Hopfner
Michael Hering
Christian Herrmann
Cristiana Iommi
Eszter Kardos
Katharina Kaska
Monika Kiegler-Griensteidl
Tim Knox
Stefan Koja
Dagmar Korbacher
Nikoletta Koruhely
Olga Kotkova
Claudia Kryza-Gersch
Christiane Lange
Daria Lovrek
Franca Lugato
Bernhard Maaz
Mark MacDonnell
Mailena Mallach
Sofia Magnaguagno
Prefetto Don Mauro Mantovani
Francesca Manzari
Mario Marubbi
Christof Metzger
Luca Mizzan
Alessandra Necci
Valentino Nizzo
Nicola Novarini
Sara Öberg Strådal
Adalgisa Ottaviani
S. E. Card. Pietro Parolin
Barbora Patočkova
Hans Petschar
Paolo Plebani
Lauren Porter
Cristina Quattrini
Johanna Rachinger
Paulus Rainer
Achim Riether
Sandra Rossi
Flaminia Rukavina-Vidovgrad
Rupert Schaab
Konrad Schlegel
Claudia Schnitzer
Frits Scholten
Klaus Albrecht Schröder
Andreas Schumacher
Cecilia Seilern
Friedrich Simader
Vladimír Sonntag
Eve Straussman-Pflanzer
Christine Surtmann
Helena Szepe
Francesca Tasso
Julia Tatrai
Luca Tosi
Stefano Trovato
Federica Toniolo
Luana Toniolo
Maria Pia Torricelli
Ute Tüchler
Claudia Valeri
Simone Verde
Raffaella Vincenti
Iris Yvonne Wagner

AD MVNDVM VIVVM
Chloridis carmen supplex

iam nihil aeterni nihil immutabile nobis
  tempora naturae sub ioue fine carent
nox lucem sequitur tenebras lux mox peritura
  et latet in pulchris spina dolenda rosis
uer florens aestas feruens autumne feraxque
  et tu bruma rigens auscultate preces
obsecro terra parens uosque aer ignis aquaeque
  praesidia infirmae fortia ferte mihi
exsiccate malum date cornua pellite curas
  inter uos uigiles fit mihi certa salus

TO THE LIVING WORLD
a poem of supplication by Chloris

Nothing eternal is left to us, nothing immutable:
In this world, nature's times have no end.
Night follows light, and light, soon to fade, darkness,
And roses fair conceal a painful thorn.
Flowering spring, burning summer, fruitful autumn,
And you too, harsh winter, hear my prayers.
I beseech you, Mother Earth, and you, air, fire, water,
Give me, weak as I am, powerful protection.
Exsiccate evil, grant strength, drive away cares:
With you as my guardians, I will surely be safe.

Translation: John Nicholson & Karin Zeleny

Image Credits

All images © KHM-Museumsverband, Kunsthistorisches Museum, if not stated otherwise

Cover: cat. 29.1

Image pages: pp. 6–7 (cat. 15.2); p. 10 (cat. 67.8); pp. 16–17 (cat. 67.6); pp. 114–15 (cat. 67.5); pp. 304–5 (cat. 60); p. 332 (cat. 30.2, detail)

© ALBERTINA, Vienna: pp. 73, 121, 122 (top), 180 (right), 224, 225, 283

© Ashmolean Museum/Bridgeman Images: p. 85

© Bayerische Staatsbibliothek: p. 43

© Biblioteca Angelica Rom: pp. 102, 105

© Bibliotheca Apostolica Vaticana, Città del Vaticano: p. 203

© Biblioteca Civica Angelo Mai e Archivi storici: p. 119

© Biblioteca Nazionale MARCIANA: pp. 18, 58, 65, 68 (top), 75, 92, 94, 95, 98, 99, 148 (bottom), 206, 275, 276 (top)

© Biblioteca Statale Cremona / Roberto Caccialanza: p. 134

© Biblioteca Universitaria di Bologna, Ms. Aldrovandi, Tavole di animali: p. 173

© Biblioteca Universitaria di Pisa su concessione del Ministero della Cultura: pp. 82, 261 (left), 286, 287

© bpk/Bayerische Staatsgemäldesammlungen: pp. 165–7

© bpk/Kupferstichkabinett, SMB/Dietmar Katz: p. 228

© bpk/Kupferstichkabinett, SMB/Jörg P. Anders: p. 45

© bpk/Staatliche Kunstsammlungen Dresden: pp. 196–7

© Bridgman Images: p. 42

© Castello del Buonconsiglio, Trento – Italy: p. 57

© Comune di Bassano del Grappa: pp. 110–11

© Comune di Milano/Anelli 1997: p. 274

© Cristoforo di Bindoccio and Meo di Pero, Hall of the Seasons, Museo Palazzo Corboli, C.so G. Matteotti 122 ASCIANO (Siena): p. 30

© Dorotheum Vienna: p. 232

© Fondazione Accademia Carrara, Bergamo: p. 218

© Fondazione Luigi Einaudi in Turin, Italy: p. 97

© Gabinetto fotografico Museo Biblioteca Archivio – Bassano del Grappa: p. 52

© Gallerie degli Uffizi, Gabinetto dei disegni: p. 282

© Gallerie degli Uffizi, Gabinetto Fotografico: p. 108

© Gallerie degli Uffizi, Gabinetto Fotografico – Foto Roberto Palermo: p. 106, 208

© Ghigo Roli/Bridgeman Images: p. 56

© GrandPalaisRmn (musée du Louvre)/Gérard Blot: p. 71

© GrandPalaisRmn (musée du Louvre)/Jean-Gilles Berizzi: p. 68 (bottom)

© GrandPalaisRmn (musée du Louvre)/Stéphane Maréchalle: p. 50

Guidolotti guidolotti@gmail.com/ BRIDGEMAN: p. 107

© LIECHTENSTEIN,The Princely Collections, Vaduz – Vienna/SCALA, Florence: pp. 34, 172

© The Lobkowicz Collections, Palais Lobkowicz: pp. 38, 40

Photo: © MAK/Vladimir Narbutt-Lieven: p. 152

© Metropolitan Museum of Art, New York: pp. 41, 193

© Musée archéologique, El Jem, Tunisia: p. 28

© Museo Nacional Thyssen-Bornemisza, Madrid/Bridgeman Images: p. 72

© Museo Nazionale Etrusco di Villa Giulia. Archivio fotografico. Foto Mauro Benedetti: p. 202

Courtesy National Gallery of Art, Washington: pp. 26, 301

© Österreichische Nationalbibliothek, Wien: pp. 23 (bottom), 35, 74, 78, 91, 145, 148 (top), 149, 214–15, 261 (right), 273 (bottom), 276 (bottom), 284–5

© Pavia, Musei Civici del Castello Visconteo: pp. 23 (top), 204–5

© Pinacoteca di Brera, Milano – MiC: pp. 131, 240

© Prague Castle Administration, Photo: Jan Gloc: pp. 257–8

© Rijksmuseum, Amsterdam: pp. 164, 176

© Royal Collection Enterprises Limited 2024/Royal Collection Trust: pp. 54–5, 120, 262

Royal Collection Trust/© His Majesty King Charles III, 2024 / Bridgeman Images: p. 70

© Skoklosters slott/SHM: p. 175

© The Spier Collection: p. 60

© Staatliche Graphische Sammlung München: p. 132

Staatliche Museen zu Berlin, Gemäldegalerie/Christoph Schmidt; Public Domain Mark 1.0: p. 80

© Staatliches Museum Schwerin SSGK (lost in 1945): p. 84

© Staatsgalerie Stuttgart: p. 273 (top)

© Su concessione del Ministero della Cultura – Archivio fotografico delle Gallerie Estensi – Foto Carlo Vannini: p. 238

© Szépművészeti Múzeum/Museum of Fine Arts, Budapest, 2024: pp. 122 (bottom), 226–7

© Tiroler Landesmuseen/Grafische Sammlung: p. 32

© Württembergische Landesbibliothek: pp. 29, 88

List of Lenders

ALBERTINA, Vienna

Bayerische Staatsgemäldesammlungen, Munich

Biblioteca Civica 'Angelo Mai' e Archivi Storici, Bergamo

Biblioteca Nazionale Marciana, Venice

Biblioteca Statale di Cremona

Biblioteca Universitaria di Bologna

Biblioteca Universitaria di Pisa

Città del Vaticano, Biblioteca Apostolica Vaticana

Fondazione Accademia Carrara, Bergamo

Gallerie degli Uffizi

Dr. Jörn Günther, Rare Books, Basel

Kupferstich-Kabinett, Staatliche Kunstsammlungen Dresden

LIECHTENSTEIN. The Princely Collections, Vaduz – Vienna

MAK – Museum for Applied Arts, Vienna

The Metropolitan Museum of Art, Edith Perry Chapman Fund, 1997 (1997.512)

Ministry for Cultural Heritage, Activities and Tourism/Modena, Gallerie Estensi

Musei Civici del Castello Visconteo, Pavia

Museo Nazionale Etrusco di Villa Giulia, Rome

National Gallery of Art, Washington, Paul Mellon Fund, 2010.77.1

Österreichische Nationalbibliothek, Vienna

Pinacoteca del Castello Sforzesco, Mailand

Pinacoteca di Brera, Milan

Prague Castle Collections, Czech Republic

Rijksmuseum, Amsterdam

The Royal Collection / HM King Charles III

Staatliche Graphische Sammlung München

Staatliche Museen zu Berlin, Kupferstichkabinett

Staatsgalerie Stuttgart

Szépmüvészeti Múzeum, Budapest

Württembergische Landesbibliothek Stuttgart

Colophon

This book accompanies
the exhibition
*Arcimboldo – Bassano – Bruegel.
Nature's Time.*

Kunsthistorisches Museum
www.khm.at
11 March to 29 June 2025

Director General
Jonathan Fine

EXHIBITION

Curator
Francesca Del Torre Scheuch

Curatorial assistance
Alexandra Sattler

Exhibition management
Julia Neudorfer

Exhibition design
Gerhard Veigel

Partner
UNIQA

We thank William S. Barrett
and Katherina Minardo Macht
for their generous support of the
digital exhibition presentation in
our web journal.

PUBLICATION

Media owner
KHM-Museumsverband, Vienna

Edited by
Francesca Del Torre Scheuch

Editorial assistance
Alexandra Sattler

Editorial coordination
Sara Colson (Hannibal Books)
Rafael Kopper (KHM)

Copy editor
Cath Phillips

Translations
Gerald Brennan
David Graham
Jacqueline Todd

Graphic design
Tim Bisschop

Image rights and coordination
Séverine Lacante

Image editing
Michael Eder
Jakob Gsöllpointner
Thomas Ritter
Daniel Sostaric

Printed by
Printer Trento, Trento

Paper
Gardapat 11 High White 150 g/m2

English edition & distribution
Hannibal Books, Veurne
www.hannibalbooks.be
Gautier Platteau

HANNIBAL
BOOKS

*Bibliographic information published by
the Deutsche Nationalbibliothek*
The Deutsche Nationalbibliothek
lists this publication in the Deutsche
Nationalbibliografie; detailed
bibliographic data is available online
at http://dnb.d-nb.de.

ISBN 978 94 6494 191 3
D/2025/11922/17
NUR 654